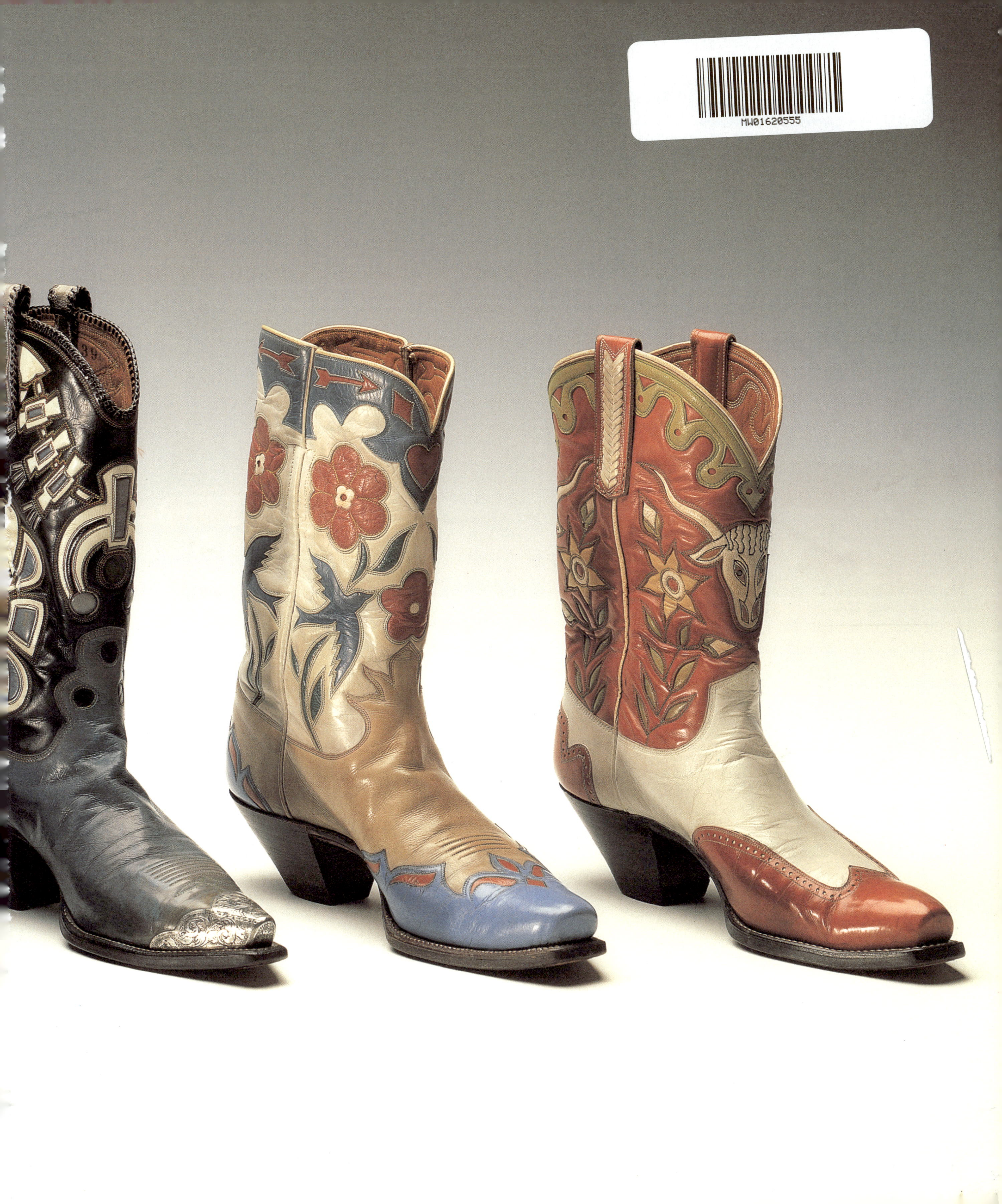

MW01620555

Fine Art of the West

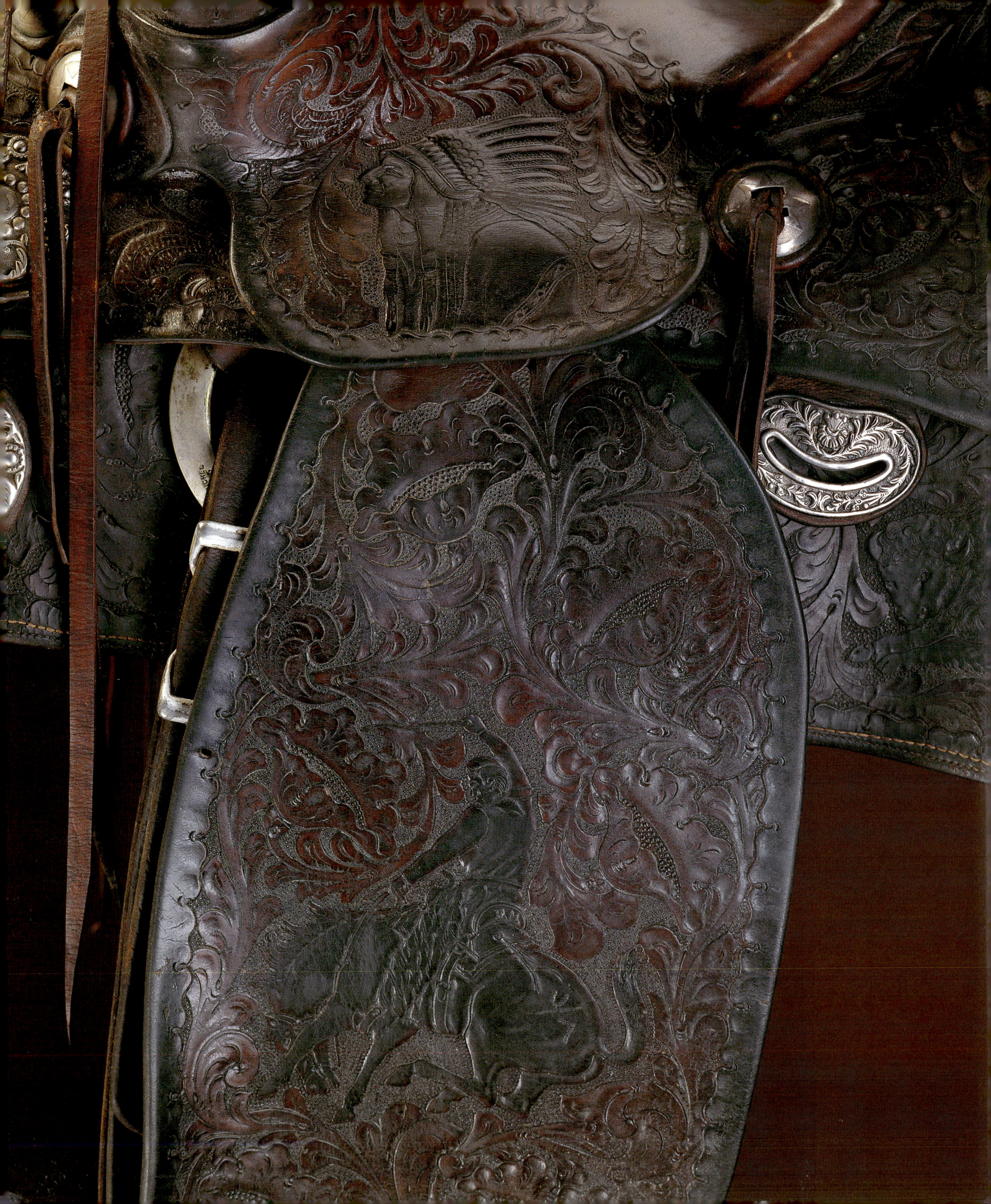

FINE ART OF THE WEST

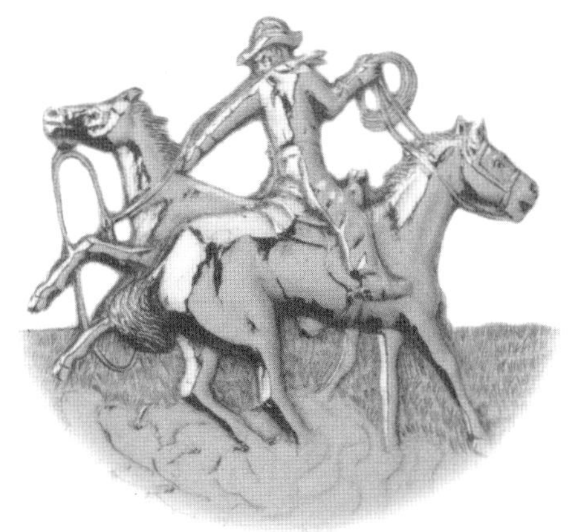

B. BYRON PRICE

ABBEVILLE PRESS PUBLISHERS
NEW YORK LONDON

For John and Saralynn Geraghty

Abbeville Press gratefully acknowledges the generous and enthusiastic support of Mort and Donna Fleischer.

EDITOR: Christopher Lyon
DESIGN: Celia Fuller
PRODUCTION MANAGER: Louise Kurtz

FRONT COVER: *Frank H. Coenen, Alhambra, California. "San Fernando" saddle, c. 1947,* FLEISCHER COLLECTION, SCOTTSDALE
BACK COVER: *Buscadero-pattern gun belt with twin holsters and dyed vine-and-leaf-pattern stamping,* FLEISCHER COLLECTION, SCOTTSDALE
FRONTISPIECE: *Frank Mueller, Denver. Saddle, detail*
FLEISCHER COLLECTION, SCOTTSDALE
THIS PAGE: *Frank H. Coenen, Alhambra, California. "San Fernando" saddle, c. 1947, detail of breast collar*
FLEISCHER COLLECTION, SCOTTSDALE

Library of Congress Cataloguing-in-Publication Data
Price, B. Byron.
Fine art of the West / B. Byron Price.– 1st ed.
p. cm.
Includes bibliographical references and index.
ISBN 0-7892-0659-5 (alk. paper)
1. Western saddles–Design and construction. I. Title.
TS1032.P73 2004
658'.1-dc22 2004047745
Printed in South Korea

 The text of this book was set in New Baskerville.

FIRST EDITION

10 9 8 7 6 5 4 3 2 1

Contents

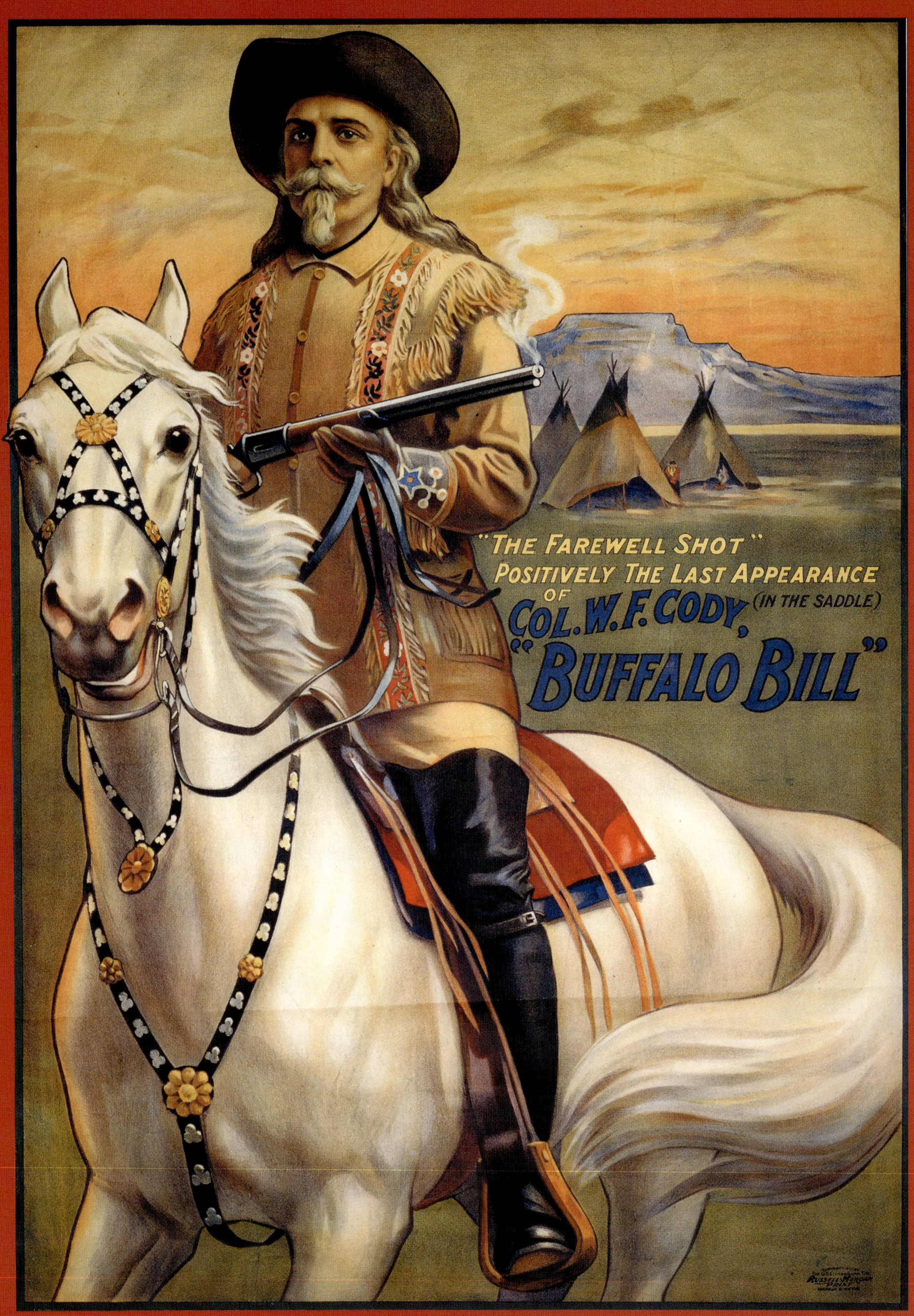
"THE FAREWELL SHOT"
POSITIVELY THE LAST APPEARANCE
OF
COL. W. F. CODY, (IN THE SADDLE)
"BUFFALO BILL"

Introduction

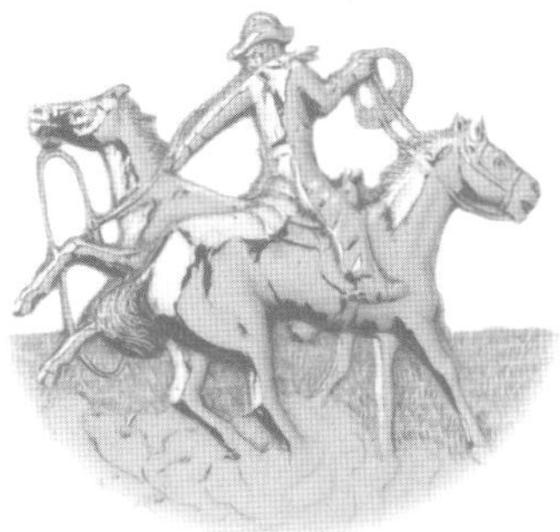

The cowboys of the American West have always depended upon a variety of specialized gear—hats and boots, bits and spurs, ropes and quirts, chaps and gloves, firearms and gun leather, saddles and other tack—to do a difficult, dirty, and sometimes dangerous job. Many of these objects possess aesthetic as well as utilitarian qualities and contribute importantly to the cowboy's individual, occupational, and mythical identities. They are frequently the products of fine craftsmen inspired by prevailing aesthetic and cultural conventions as well as their own creativity.

American herders were not, of course, the first equestrians to festoon themselves and their mounts with durable yet decorative regalia. Their characteristic garb and accoutrements evolved over many centuries from Eurasian, North African, European, and Latin American ancestry. The demands of the environment, the availability of materials and artisans, ethnic and religious traditions, individual taste, and economic circumstance all exerted an influence.

Cowboys first gained prominence in the United States during the brief but colorful boom in open range cattle ranching during the last quarter of the nineteenth century. The picturesque look and pastoral occupation of these hired

Opposite. *U.S. Lithograph Co., Russell-Morgan Print*
The Farewell Shot, Positively the Last Appearance (in the Saddle) of Col. W. F. Cody, "Buffalo Bill," *c. 1910*
40.5 x 28 in.
Buffalo Bill Historical Center, Cody, Wyoming

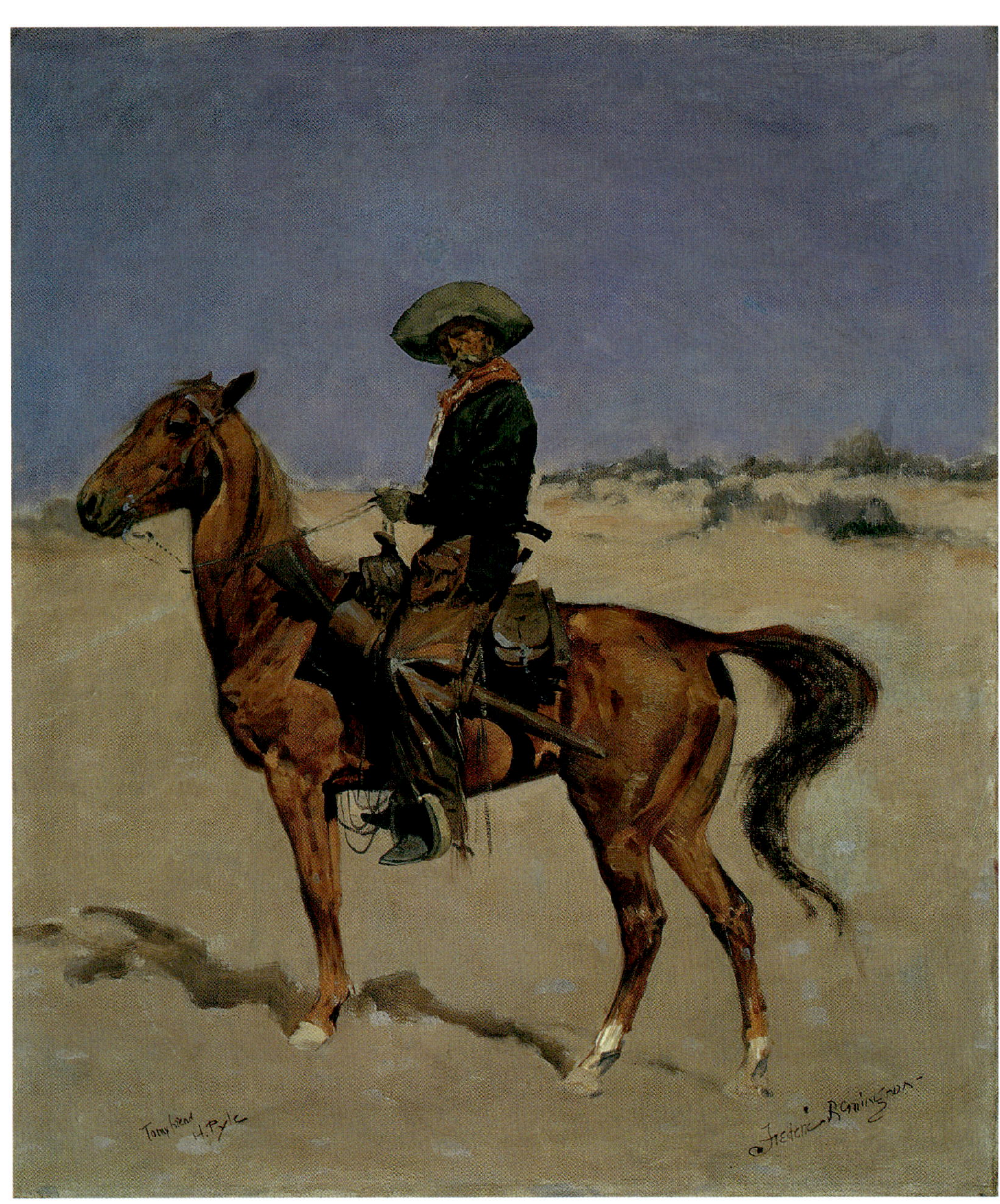

Frederic Remington (1861–1909)
The Puncher, *1895*
Oil on canvas, 24 x 20 1/8 in.
Sid Richardson Collection of Western Art, Fort Worth

men on horseback captivated several influential writers and artists, including Theodore Roosevelt, Owen Wister, Frederic Remington, and Charles M. Russell, who, along with showman William F. "Buffalo Bill" Cody, helped transform them into heroic icons who could be easily identified by the cut of their clothes and the tools of their trade. Romantic literary, artistic, and theatrical depictions of cowboy life, however, invariably exaggerated and distorted reality and, with the help of motion pictures, the sport of rodeo, enterprising entrepreneurs, and shrewd advertisers, defined a powerful, if illusory, cowboy image that the public and even some working cowboys eagerly embraced.

Owen Wister sketched the broad outlines of this new breed of horseback hero in his essay, "The Evolution of the Cow Puncher," illustrated by Frederic Remington and published in *Harper's New Monthly Magazine* in 1895. The cowboys who inhabited this influential Philadelphia writer's imagination were the crossbred descendants of lowly Mexican vaqueros, who bequeathed them the tools, methods, and language of their trade, and the bold and chivalrous knights of Camelot. Clad in leather armor to fend off thorny brush and flinty hoof, these modern knights of the prairie rode forth to tame the wild and perilous West.

Wister's cowpunchers took "barbaric pleasure in finery" and donned "tribal dress" that reflected individual pride, aesthetic awareness, and sex appeal. Their costume and accoutrement not only identified and united men from diverse backgrounds in a common economic pursuit, but also served an important social function. "Come to town for his holiday," Wister observed,

> he wore his careful finery, and from his wide hat-brim to his jingling heels made something of a figure—as self-conscious and deliberate a show as any painted buck in council or bull-elk among his aspiring cows; and out of town in the mountains, as wild and lean and dangerous as buck or bull knows how to be.

Owen Wister's description of cowboy equipment and dress echoed that of fellow author Julian Ralph, another eastern "swell." In 1893 Ralph wrote of

Charles Christian Nahl (1818–1878)
"Mr. Gringo's Experience as a Ranchero," illustrated letter sheet (San Francisco: Anthony B. Baker, c. 1855)
Museum of the American West, Los Angeles

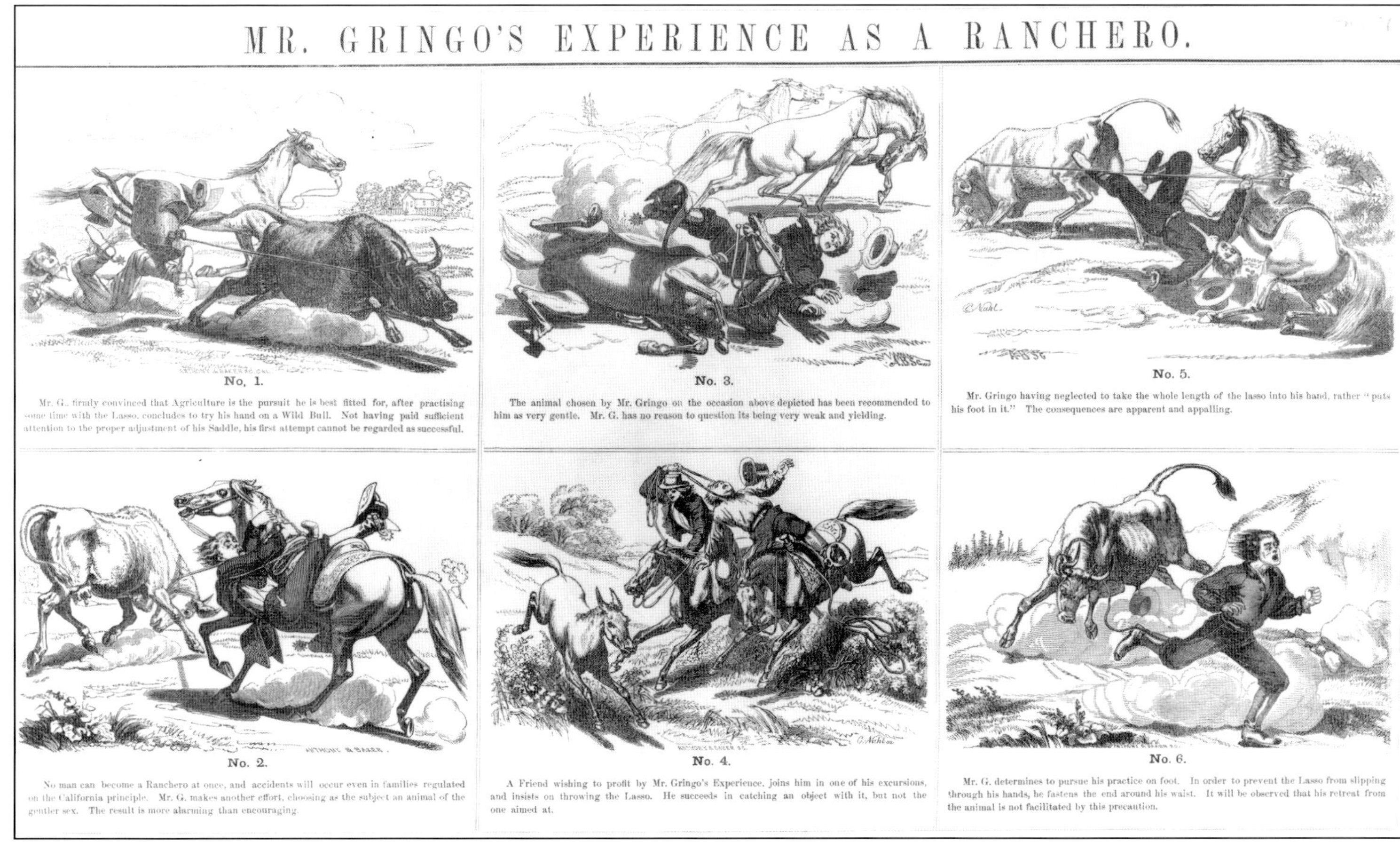

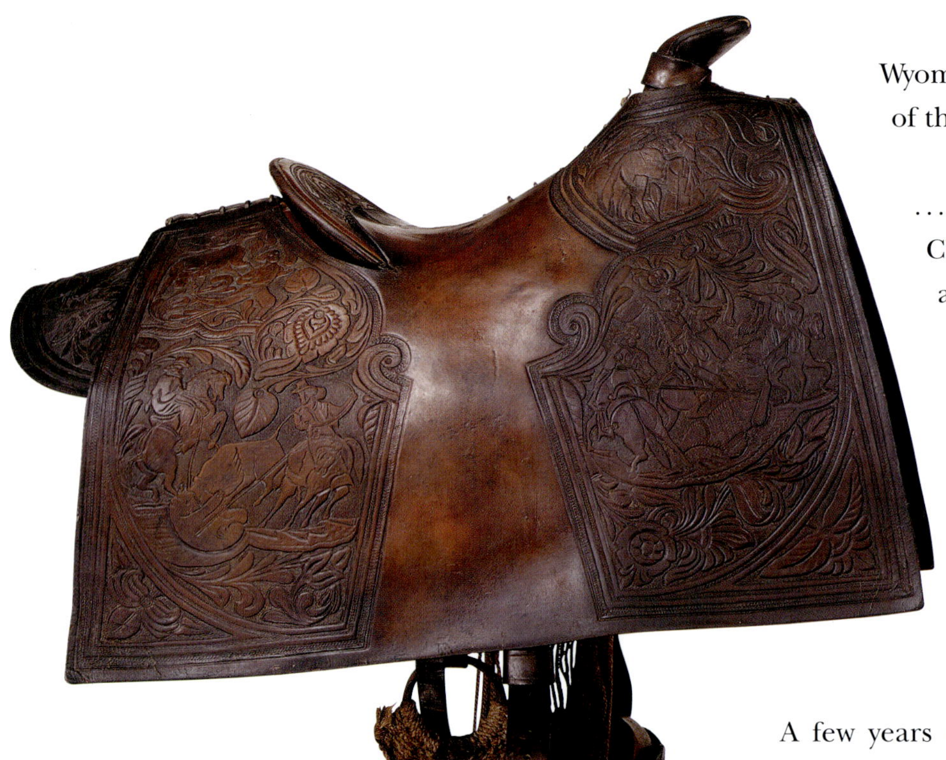

Wyoming cowboys of the 1880s, who at the "the zenith of their romantic glory,"

> ...rode good horses....bought hand-stamped Cheyenne saddles and California bits that were as ornate as jewelry, and stuck their feet in grand tapaderos, or hooded stirrups, richly ornamented, padded with lamb's wool, and each as big as a fire-hat. Their spurs were fit for grandees, their "ropes," or lariats, were selected with more care than a circus tight-rope, and their big broad felt sombreros cost more than the Prince of Wales ever paid for a pot-hat.

A few years earlier a Cheyenne, Wyoming, newspaper had declared the broad brimmed headgear, large roweled spurs, and leather leggings worn by cowboys "as decorous a dress as the silk hat and patent leathers and kerseymeres" worn in fashionable Saratoga, New York.

Although pervasive in popular culture and imagination from the 1880s onward, the image of cowboys as colorful "dandies" did not always square with reality. As one British visitor to a western cattle ranch wrote in 1884:

"Mr. Gringo" saddle, c. 1855 California-style, center-fire rigged saddle with two-piece carved mochila *and* anquerita
MUSEUM OF THE AMERICAN WEST, LOS ANGELES

> Every member of his class is pictured as a kind of Buffalo Bill, as a long-haired ruffian who, decked out in gaudy colors and tawdry ornaments, booted like a cavalier, and chivalrous as a Paladin, his belt stuck full of knives and pistols, makes the world to resound with bluster and braggadocio. From this character the cowboy of fact is entirely distinct.

Thirty years earlier, artist Christian Nahl published a humorous broadside recounting the misadventures of "Mr. Gringo," an aspiring American *ranchero* just learning his trade. Inspired by Nahl's satirical portrayal, a creative craftsman of the period rendered scenes from the broadside on saddle leather. Later, action-packed western paintings by such illustrious artists as Charles M. Russell and N.C. Wyeth inspired the tableau-style embellishment of saddles, spurs, belt buckles, and other cowboy gear.

Ranchers and investors anxious to distance themselves from the "wild and wooly" reputation of their employees portrayed the cattle industry as a mature, businesslike enterprise and its workers as disciplined and reliable. "During the last ten or twelve years," James Cox remarked in his 1894 tome *Historical and Biographical Record of the Cattle Industry and the Cattlemen of Texas and the Adjacent Territory*, "exaggeration has been largely abandoned, and although the cowboy's dress is still attractive and a little peculiar, it is not a little conspicuous or gaudy, whatever may be said to the contrary."

The research of modern scholars, however, suggests that cowboys dressed one way on the range and another in town or when photographers were present. Fashion historian Laurel Wilson, for example, has demonstrated that posed photographs of Montana cowboys taken in town for the benefit of friends and relatives were more likely to include such stereotypical elements of cowboy garb as leather leggings and especially firearms, which were symbols of power and manhood, than pictures snapped in the field.

Texas cowboy Charles Siringo once observed that a cowboy's outfit, like that of a Boston dude, could "be bought for a small or a large amount of money." The ability of cowboys to indulge their material impulses depended of course on the size of their pocketbooks. Cowboy wages were meager; during the heyday of the open range in the 1870s and 1880s, they earned only $25 to $30 per month on average, with top hands receiving as much as $45 or $50. A serviceable rig, consisting of a saddle and bridle, hat, boots, spurs, side arms, and bedding, typically cost three months wages, fancier outfits proportionally more. Siringo estimated that a set of utilitarian gear fetched $82, horse included, in the 1870s. Within a

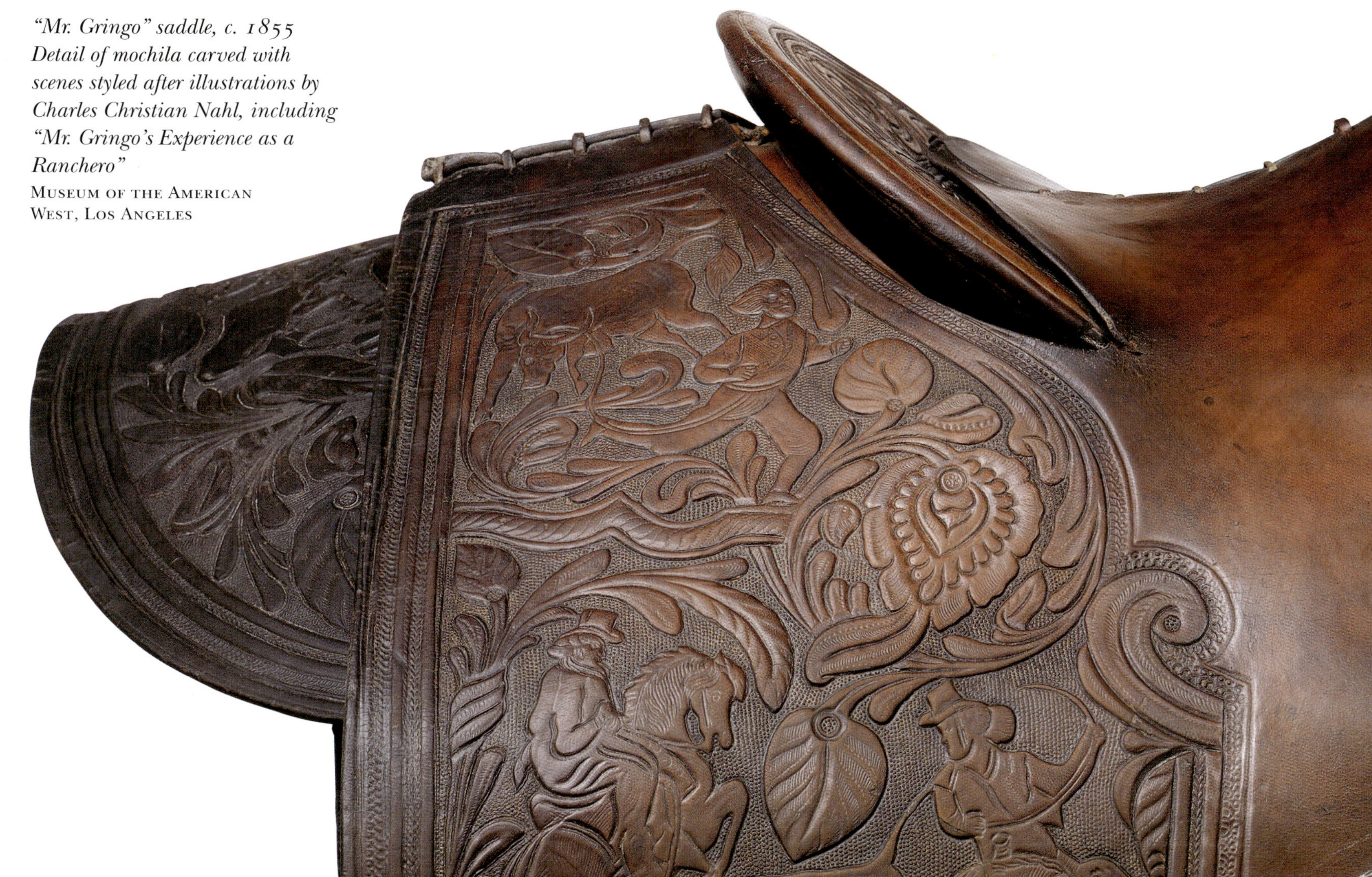

"Mr. Gringo" saddle, c. 1855
Detail of mochila carved with scenes styled after illustrations by Charles Christian Nahl, including "Mr. Gringo's Experience as a Ranchero"
Museum of the American West, Los Angeles

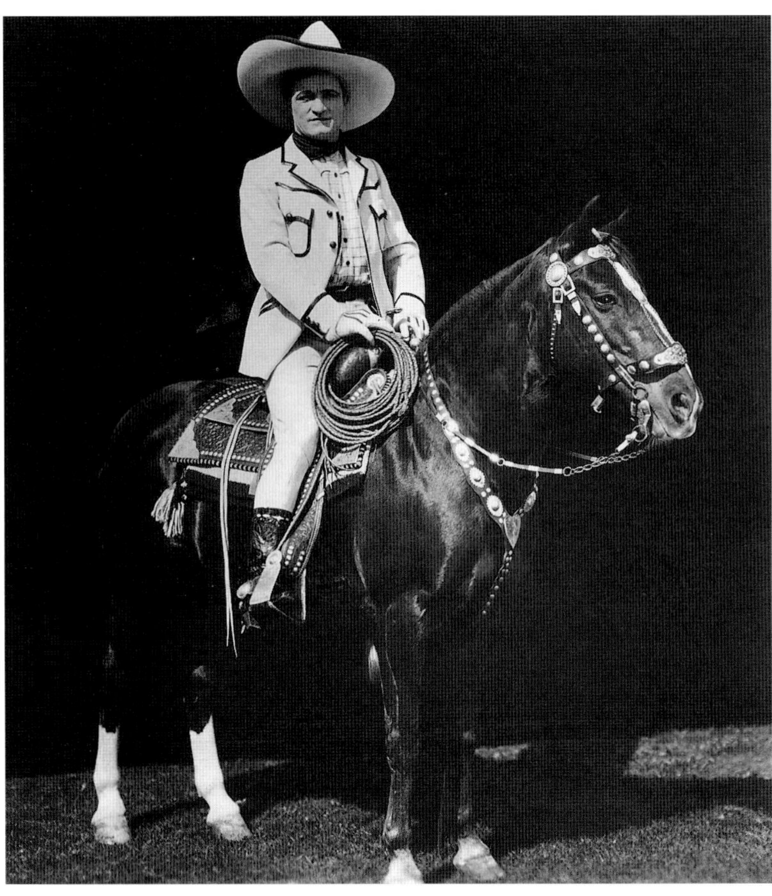

Tom Mix on his horse Tony Jr., c. 1933

decade the price of a typical outfit had risen to between $125 and $200. More elaborate equipage, for those few with the means to acquire it, might fetch $500 or more.

Despite the expense, cowboys often borrowed against their wages to buy proper clothing and equipment. Recalled one neophyte: "After several days riding around and getting broken in . . . I was a sure-enough cowboy. . . . I was put on a salary of twenty-five dollars per month, and was in debt one hundred and fifty dollars," all of it spent for gear.

Cowpunchers obtained the tools of their trade from a variety of sources. At least a few talented and enterprising herdsmen had always produced serviceable homemade gear including horsehair and rawhide ropes, hackamores and bridles, leather chaps, and even saddles. Much of the riding equipment used in the American West before the Civil War was imported from makers on the East Coast or in Mexico. With a few notable exceptions, however, the influence of eastern artisans and shops waned during the late nineteenth century as more craftsmen immigrated to the West and transportation, communication, and sources of capital improved. Large-scale enterprises located in St. Louis, San Francisco, Denver, Dallas, Omaha, Cheyenne, and San Antonio eventually eclipsed old-line New York, Hartford, and Philadelphia firms in the manufacture of saddles and other riding goods for the western market. Makers in several smaller trans-Mississippi communities, including Cheyenne, Wyoming, Pueblo, Colorado, Miles City, Montana, Elko, Nevada, and Visalia, California, became synonymous with superior handmade cowboy gear.

Although many such shops increasingly employed machinery and assembly line methods in the manufacture and embellishment of their goods, top hands continued to demand durable, handcrafted equipment. On the cattle ranges of the West the poorly accoutered were sometimes scorned as "Montgomery Ward Cowboys" or "Sears and Roebuck hands."

By the mid-1880s, however, the coming of barbed wire and the end of the open range brought about changes in working methods on western ranches and a subsequent decline in the number of full-time cowhands needed to tend the region's herds. The demand for high-quality tack and the number of suppliers declined as well, trends further exacerbated by the advent of automobiles in the early twentieth century.

While the world of working cowboys was shrinking, artists, actors, writers, and athletes were busy cultivating the cowboy of myth, a horseback hero whose stylized dress and manner resonated powerfully with the public. In his book *The Cowboy Hero*, historian William Savage argues persuasively that the accessibility and inclusivity of the cowboy myth are the keys to its power and that by donning cowboy style clothing, riding horses equipped with western tack, and exercising the imagination anyone can take part. Many did and still do.

The makers and purveyors of cowboy clothing and equipment quickly exploited this phenomenon and began to offer expanded lines of merchandise aimed at a "dude" market largely populated by tourists and recreational horsemen and, later, so-called "urban cowboys." Craftsmen designed many such goods with women in mind. Some objects were highly embellished, not only with the traditional motifs long fashionable with real cowboys but also with new and sometimes outlandish styles made popular by Wild West show performers, rodeo riders, and film makers. Motion pictures exerted an especially profound influence on the cowboy image as the utilitarian and pedestrian garb worn by actors in early western films gave way in the 1920s and 1930s to ever-fancier and fanciful regalia. Many western horsemen, including at least a few working cowboys, apparently liked what they saw on the silver screen, and obliging gear makers responded to their customers' demands for goods of similar styling. As writer Kevin Brownlow observed in his history of early American film, *The War, the West and the Wilderness*, "a fragment of fiction had splintered into fact." Movie cowboys, along with timely advances in communication, clever advertising, and the popularity of the spectator sport of rodeo, also helped to eliminate regional differences in western style and further homogenize the cowboy look.

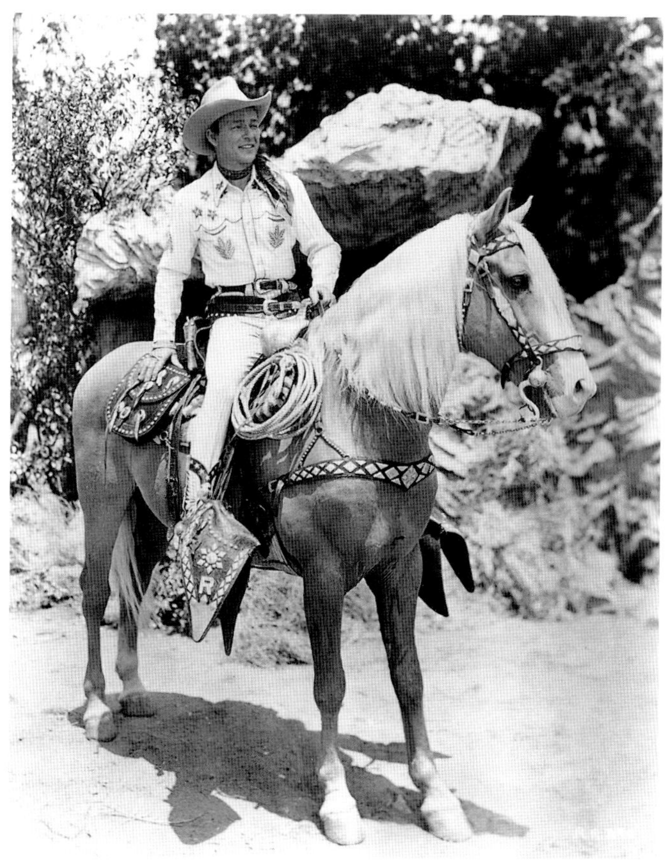

Roy Rogers on Trigger, c.1945

Despite the opening of new markets and periodic flurries of national interest, the number of fine craftsmen who produced high-quality, shop-made cowboy goods using traditional methods continued to decline throughout the twentieth century, especially after World War II. Fierce competition, the continual inroads of machines and mass production, and higher paying jobs elsewhere all exacted a toll. Nevertheless, a precious few artisans and apprentices kept the flame of craftsmanship flickering and on the eve of the twenty-first century, with the help of a growing cadre of collectors, dealers, scholars, and museums, precipitated a revival of interest in the fine arts of the West that continues to today.

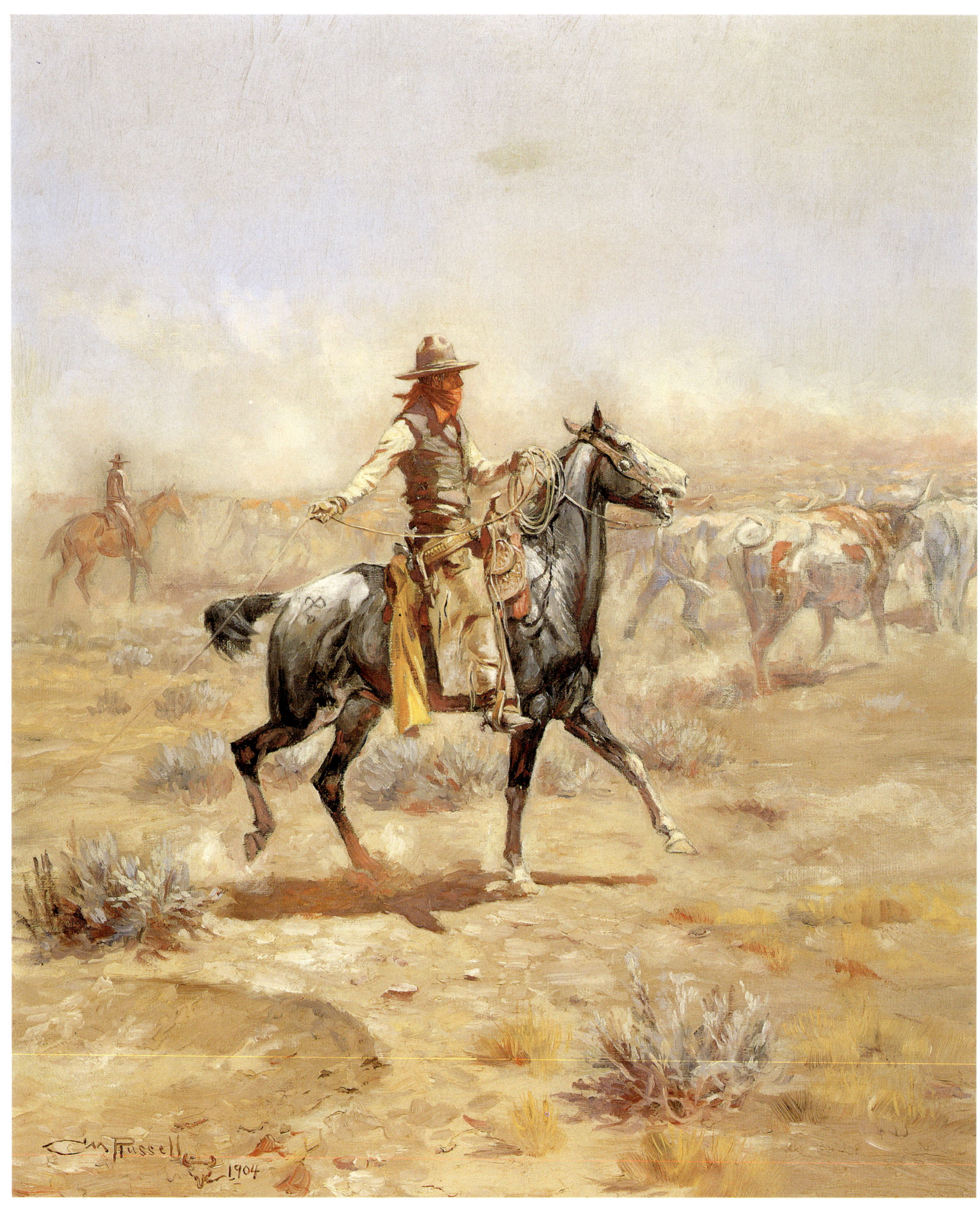
CM Russell
1904

• 1 •

Stock Saddles and Gun Leather

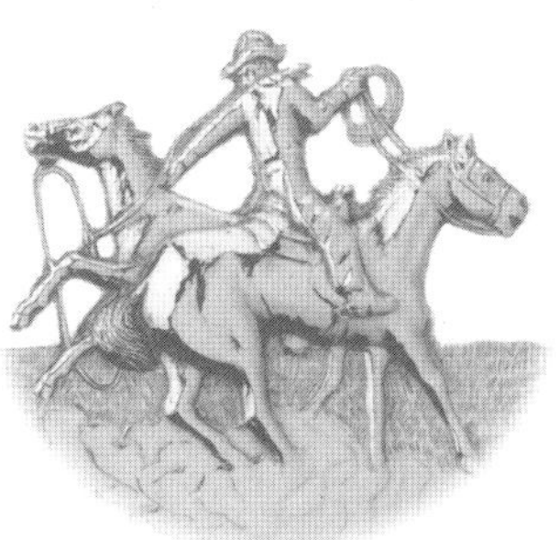

When a newspaperman once referred to saddle maker Houston Schweitzer as "the Michelangelo of the handmade saddle industry in northwest Texas,"[1] he was not merely engaging in hyperbole. For more than three decades, from the mid-1920s to the mid-1950s, cowboys near and far had clamored for Schweitzer's custom-crafted creations, delivered one a week from a modest shop in a remote cow town called Matador. His patrons were as opinionated and fussy as Pope Julius II, and most had their own ideas about saddle design and construction. Schweitzer understood his customers' needs and desires well, for he had once been a cowboy himself. He was something of an anomaly in that regard, as not many in the saddle trade had ever thrown a leg over a saddle.

Yet, every saddle maker in the American West knew well that eye-appealing tack, made stout as a bull, marked both its creator and its owner as "top hands." These craftsmen were often called upon to instill beauty as well as utility and strength into their work. Curiously, perhaps, they decorated their finest and most costly saddles with flowers, carefully carved and stamped in patterns that resembled three-dimensional wallpaper. A seemingly incongruous choice of motif given the masculine environment and rude conditions in which stock saddles were typically used, floral carving was firmly rooted in equestrian tradition.

Opposite. *Charles M. Russell (1864–1926)*
Through the Alkali, *Oil on canvas, 22 x 18 in.*
Gilcrease Museum, Tulsa

The architecture and embellishment of the stock saddles ridden by American cowboys over the last 150 years evolved over nearly two millennia from styles originated by nomadic horse cultures in the Middle East and North Africa. Moorish horsemen introduced lightweight riding saddles of Turkish design to the Iberian Peninsula in the eighth century CE. Built on wooden trees with elevated pommels and low cantles, these saddles were often the elegant products of talented Moroccan artisans who excelled in painted, embossed, and carved leatherwork. Well before the Moorish invasion of Europe, the Saharan town of Ghadames, in present-day Libya, had emerged as a leatherworking hub where accomplished craftsmen turned out beautiful tack adorned with delicately painted floral and geometric patterns, multicolored goatskin mosaics, silk and hemp thread embroidery, and gold, silver, and stone mountings.

Saddle making and other leather trades flourished in Spain under the Moors, and by the eleventh century the city of Córdoba in Andalusia had become famous for a wide variety of fine leather goods including furniture, wall hangings, and saddlery. By this time Iberian *guadamacileros* (leatherworkers) were experts at painting and gilding leather, using beaten egg whites to adhere the gold leaf. Talented *talabateros* (saddle makers) embellished their finest work with raised figures made by adhering wetted thongs of gummed leather to the surface of a tanned hide. After achieving the desired thickness and design, the artisan covered the figures with thin pigskin and secured them with silk stitching. Spaniards also excelled at carving and stamping leather in Moorish-style foliate patterns taken from nature. One noted authority has observed that Iberian craftsmen were never heavyhanded in embellishment, but always "subordinated their decorations to the leather itself."[2]

In the late fifteenth century, knights, riding heavy, armor-plated war saddles produced in northern Europe, drove the Moors from Spain. In contrast to the short stirrup leathers and bent-limb (*a la jineta*) riding style of Arab light cavalry, European knights rode with straight legs (*a la estradiota* or *a la brida*) and used long stirrup leathers. Although built to withstand the shock of combat, some of these saddles were also ornately engraved and appointed.

Within a few years Spanish conquistadors introduced both *a la jineta* and *a la brida* saddles to the Americas, and by 1549 a small cadre of professional saddle makers from Spain had formed a guild of *talabateros* in Mexico City. Members set standards for quality and workmanship, filled the saddlery needs of the upper class, and trained neophytes in the trade. While regional saddle centers eventually developed in such towns as Puebla and Michoacán, Spanish settlements extended so rapidly in every direction that the market for horse gear expanded faster than trained saddle makers could produce it. The shortage of professionally finished tack forced many riders to fashion their own crude saddles with whatever tools and materials were available.

Opposite
Pedro Una and Son,
Puebla, Mexico
Mexican saddle and saddle bags trimmed with padded flower design in combination with floral stamping; silver inlaid rigging rings and stirrup trim
Fleischer Collection, Scottsdale

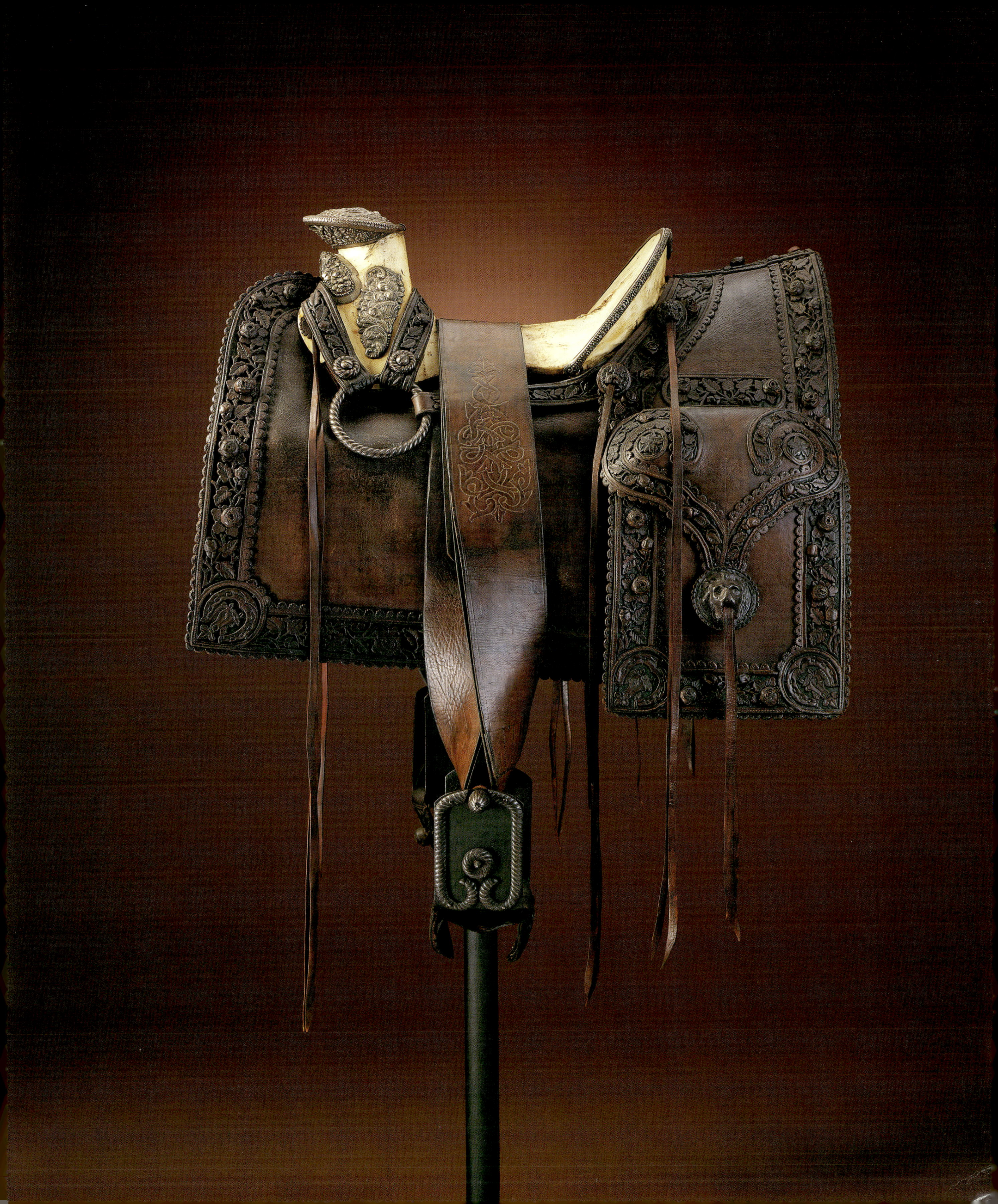

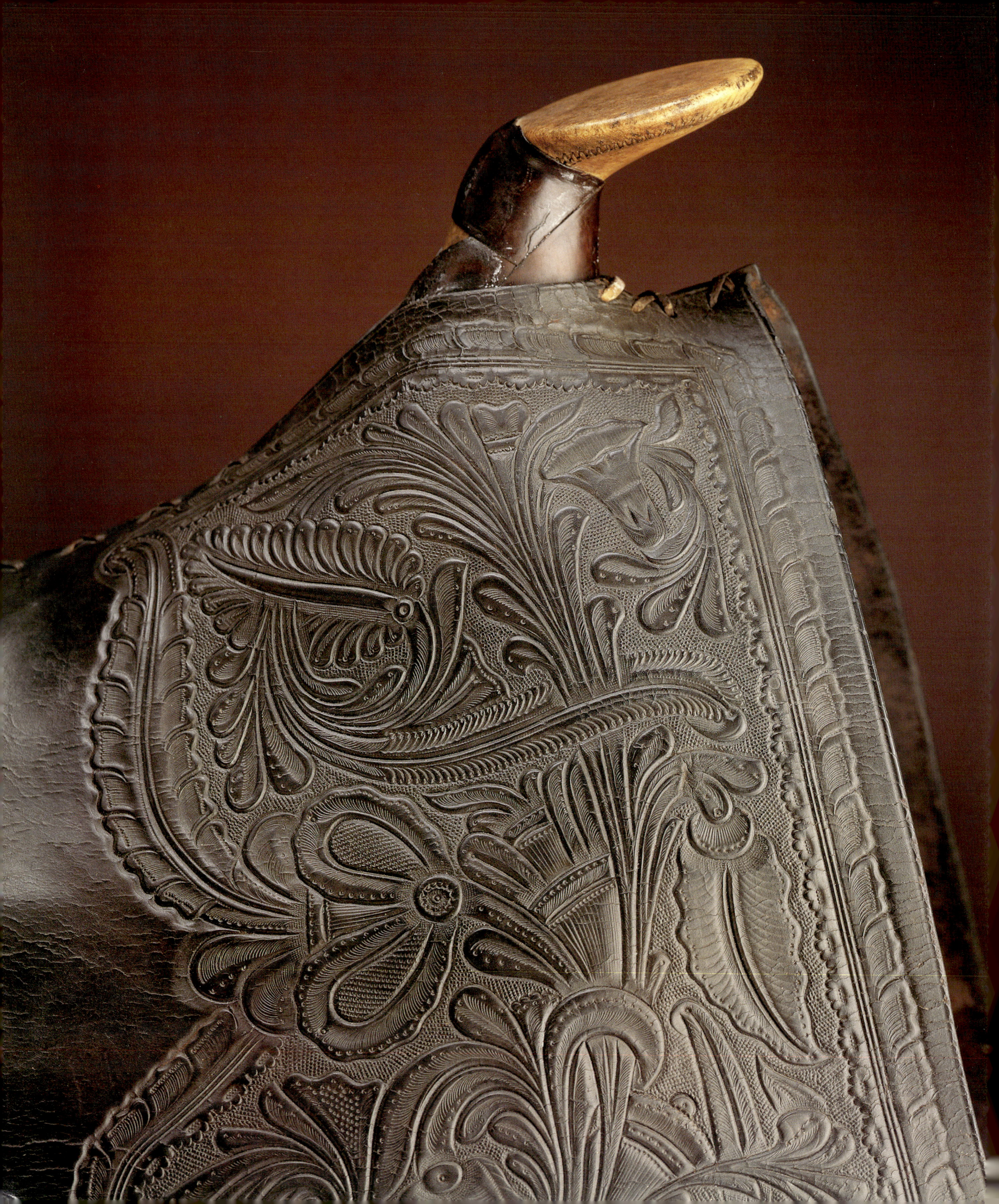

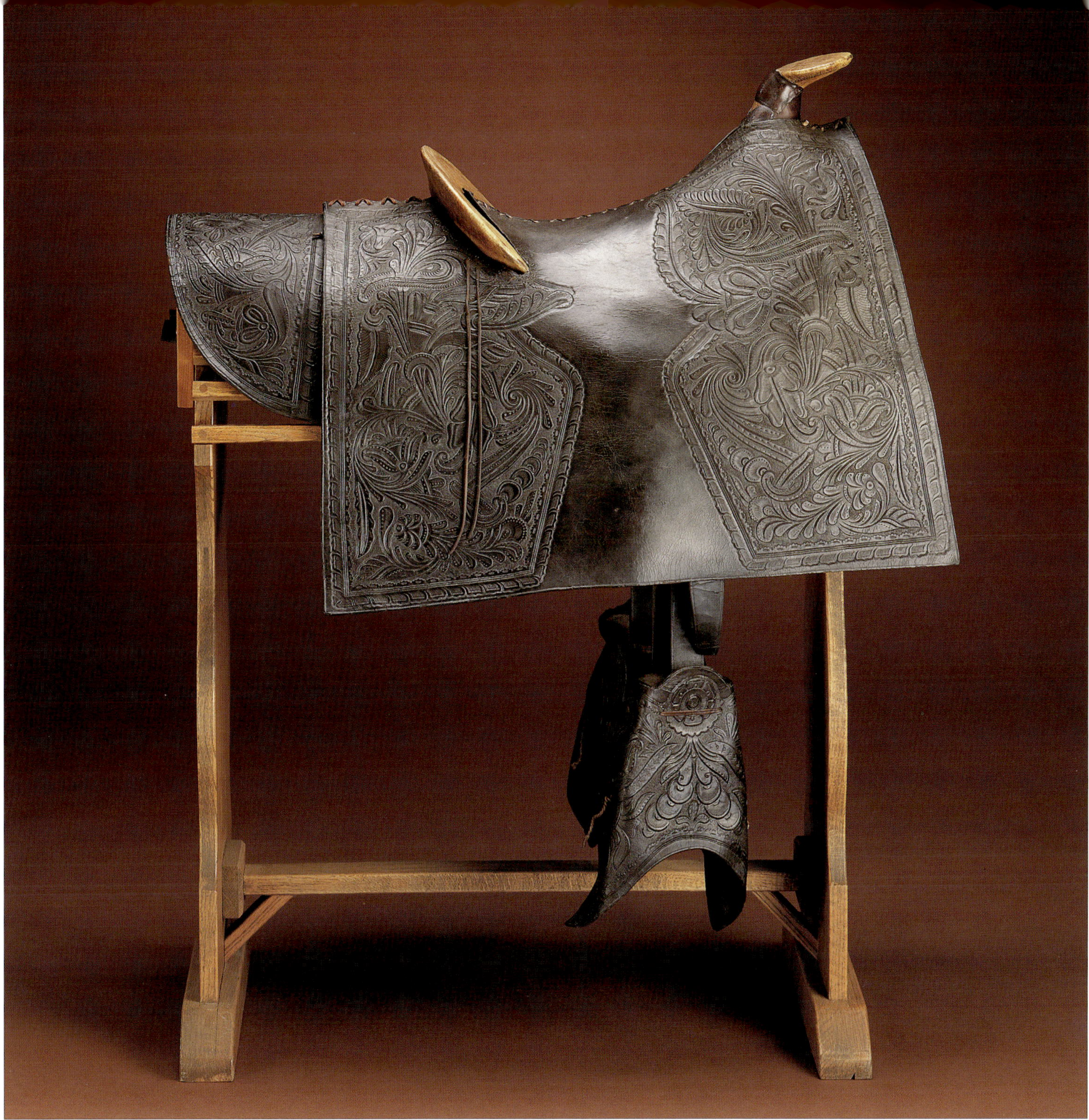

California-style saddle, Gold Rush period (c. 1850), above, with detail (opposite) of front panel of the mochila
Fleischer Collection, Scottsdale

Widespread experimentation led to new, lighter-weight and more comfortable saddle styles, suitable for pleasure riding, long-distance travel, and herding livestock. The profile and structure of the *silla de campo* (range saddle) adopted by Spanish and Indian vaqueros before the end of the sixteenth century resembled its military ancestors, although by now leather trim had replaced metal armor. Rudimentary saddle horns had developed by this time as well, but the sturdy types suited to roping cattle from horseback did not evolve until the mid-eighteenth century.

To protect the saddletree and rigging and to provide a more comfortable ride, Spanish colonial *talabateros* introduced a removable leather housing called a

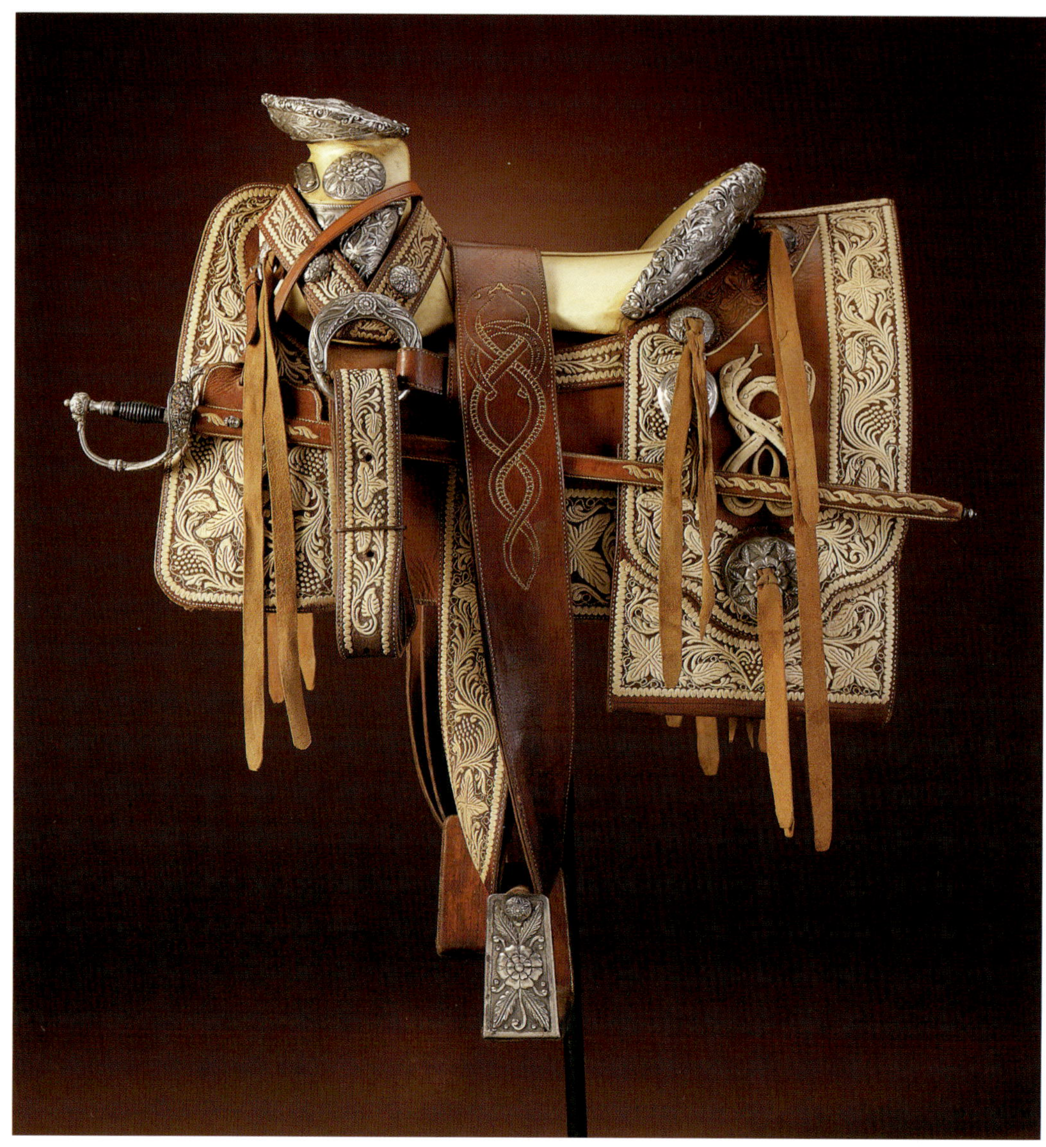

mochila. Made of two rectangular pieces of leather laced together and fitted with slots to accommodate the cantle and horn of the tree, many such devices were plain and utilitarian. Some, however, bore geometric and floral carved corners and borders and open fretwork lined with colored silk. On festive or formal occasions, well-to-do riders added a fancy carved, embroidered, and often silver-encrusted covering known as a *coraza* over the *mochila.*

Many early Spanish saddles also featured a protective rump cover or *anquera,* made of segmented leather panels that extended halfway to the ground and were held in place by melodic iron or silver bells or jinglers (*cosejos*). Remnants of medieval horse armor, these bulky appendages grew smaller and sleeker as time passed but remained fashionable in Mexico in one form or another for more than three centuries. By the early nineteenth century some makers had introduced a popular style of *anquera* known as a "duck tail" (*cola de pato*), made from long tufts of horsehair tied in a fan behind the saddle cantle.

Charro*-style saddle made in Guadalajara, Mexico, c. 1900 (above), with detail of pommel (opposite) showing fiber and silver work*
Fleischer Collection, Scottsdale

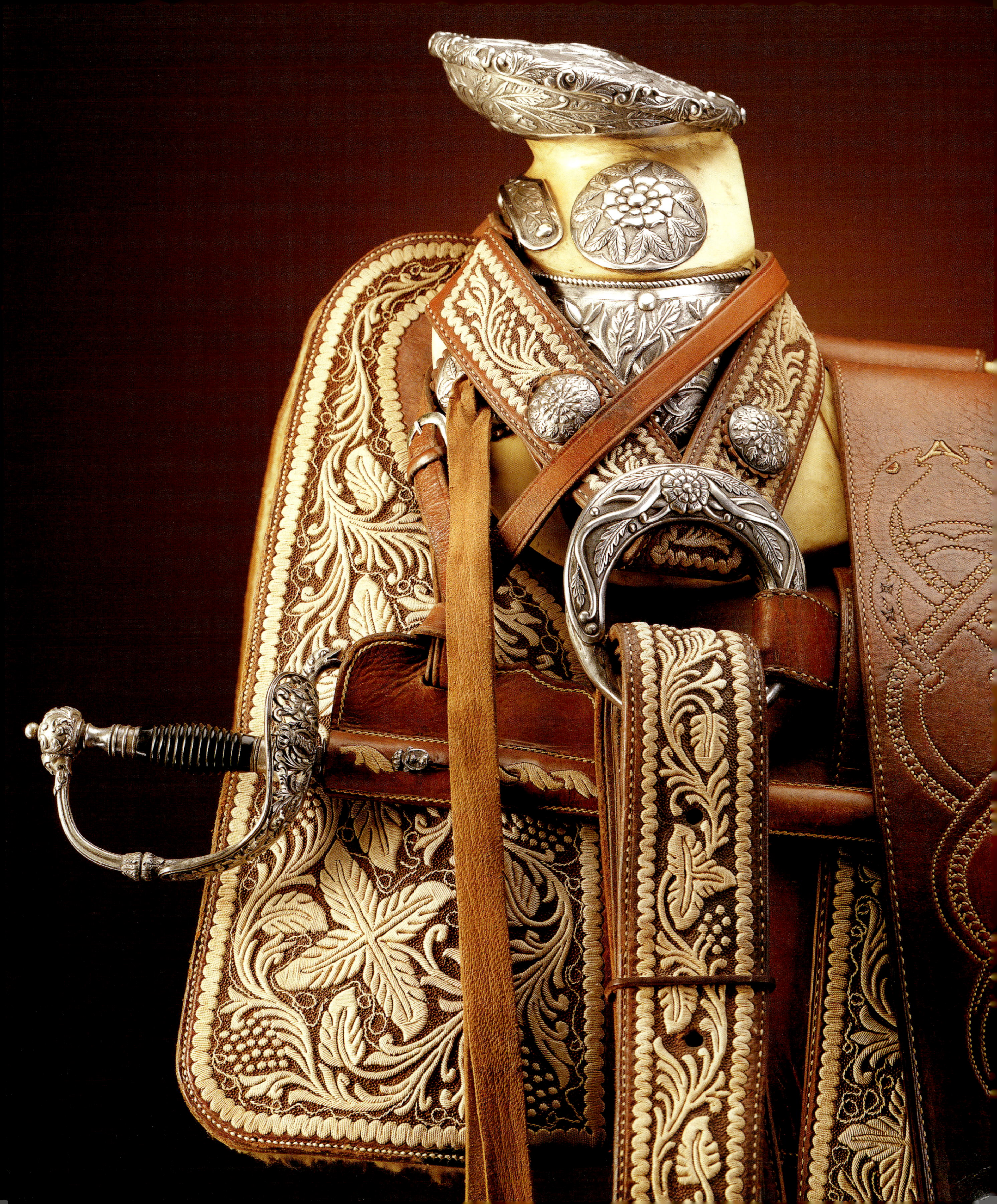

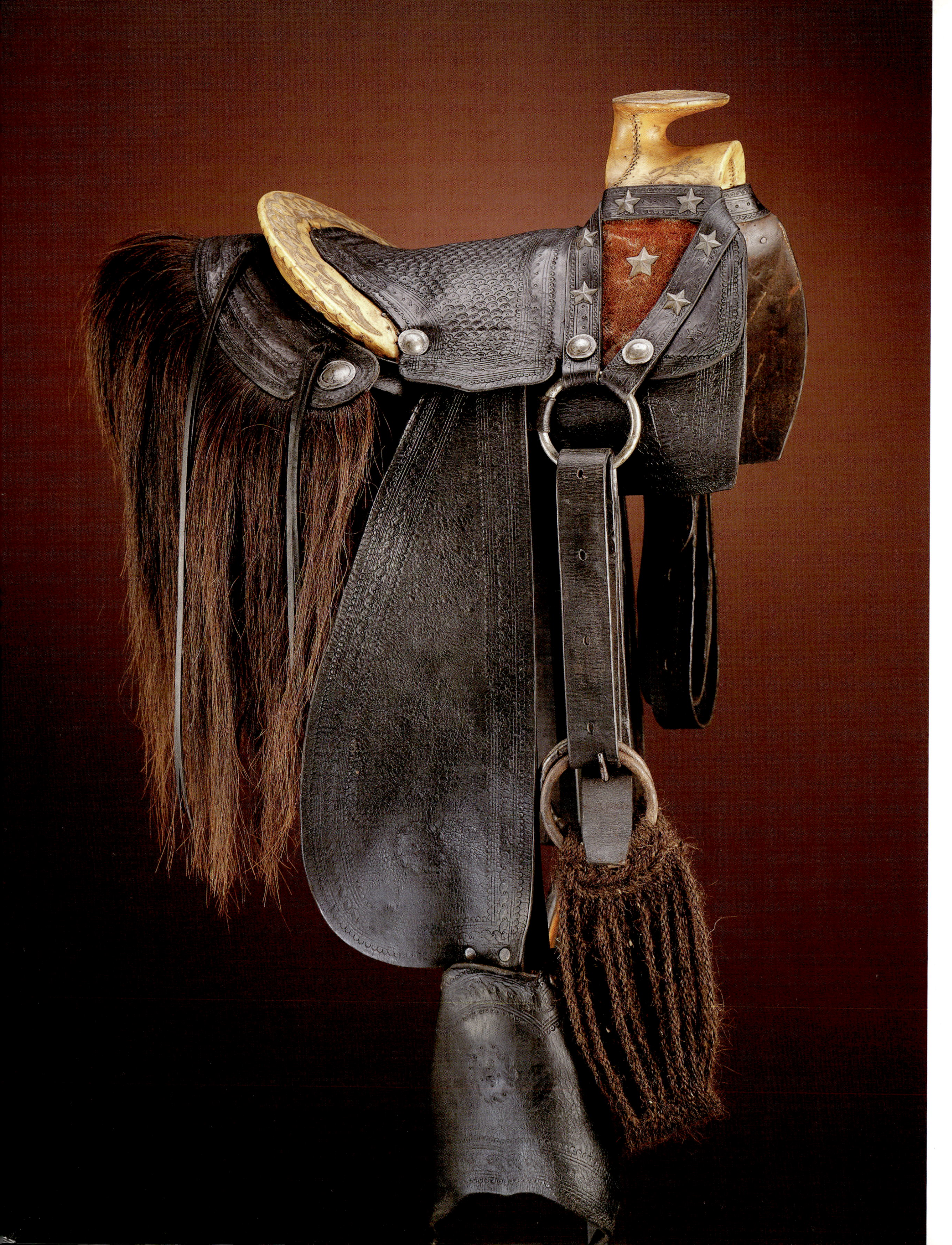

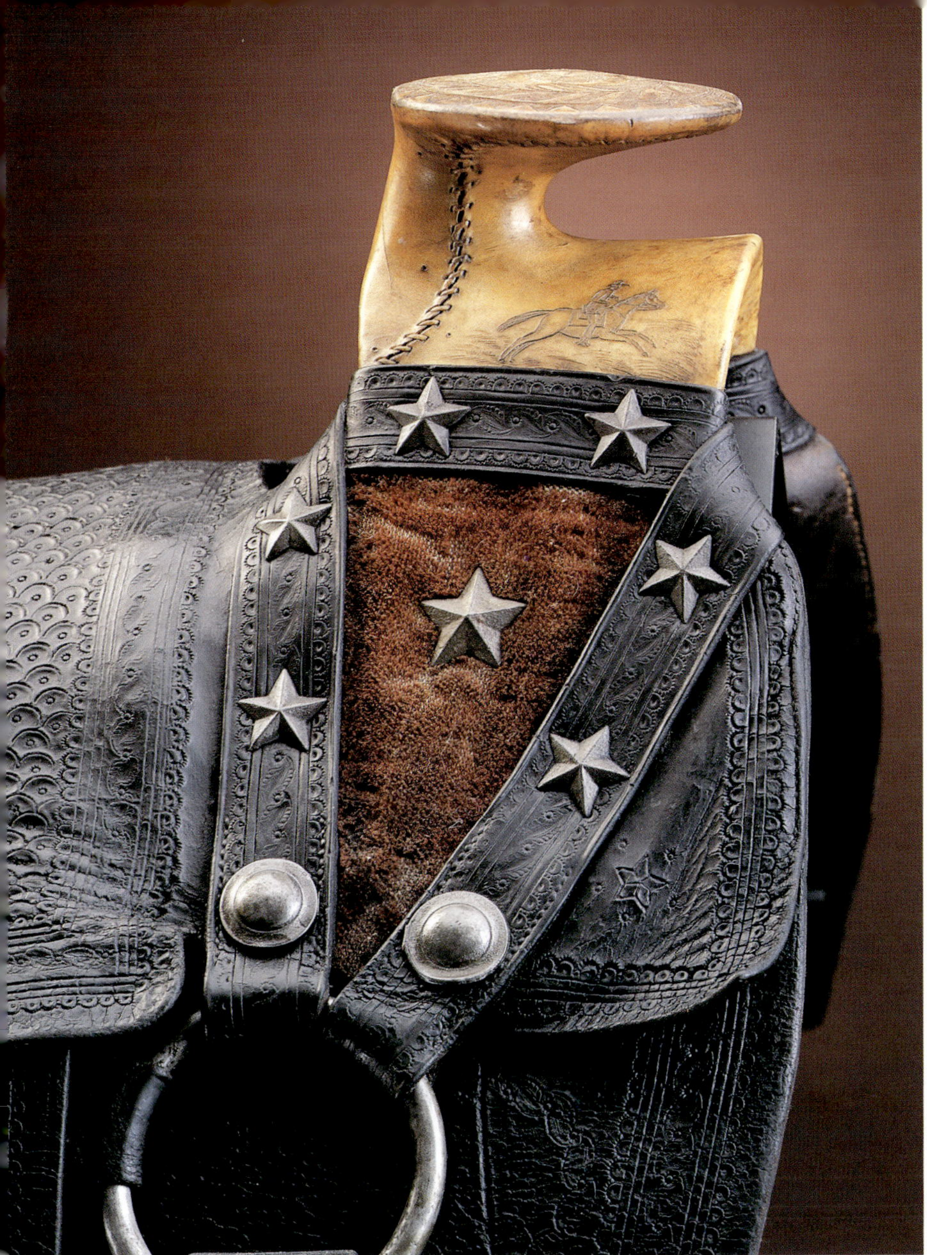

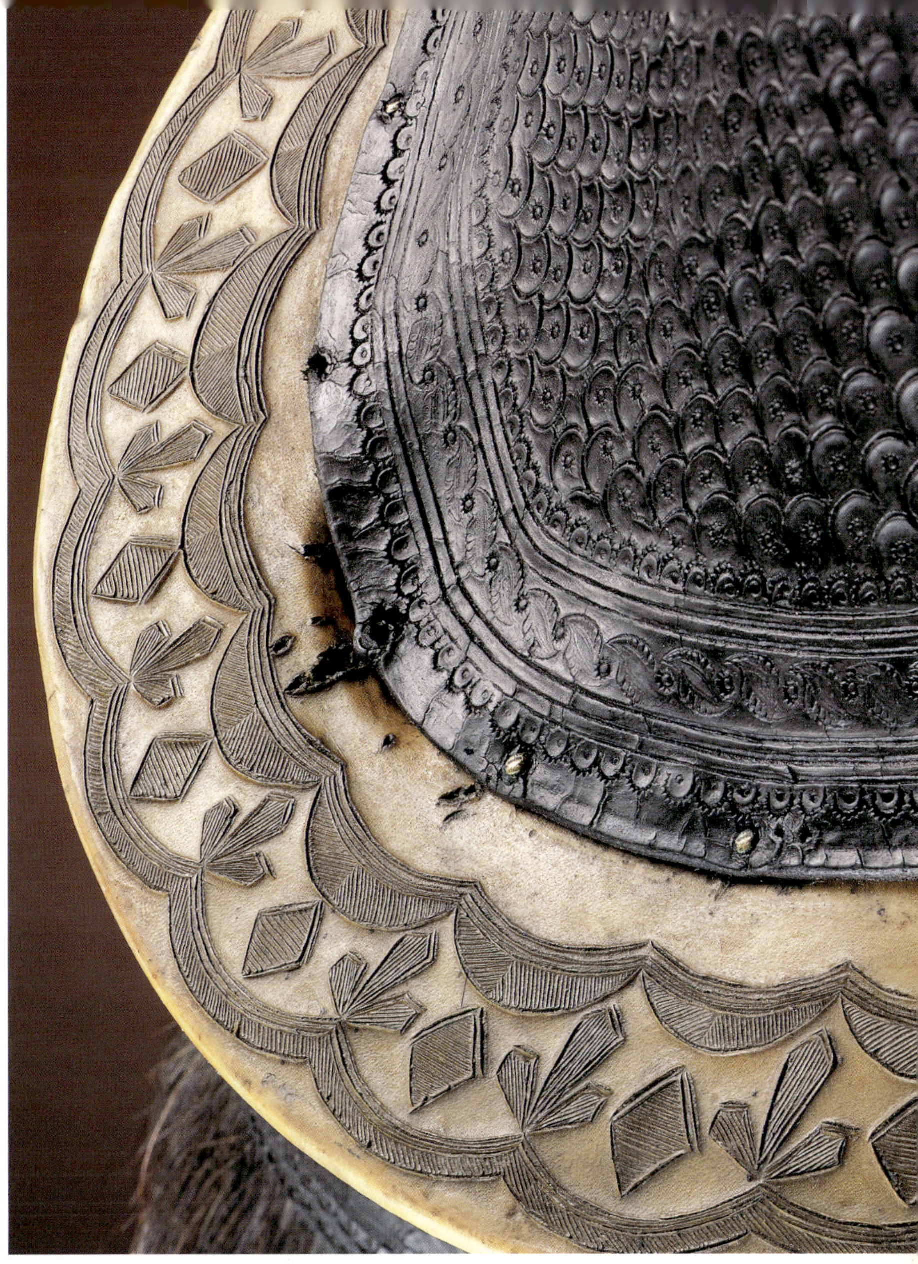

Texas-style stock saddle, c. 1840–60 (opposite), with horsehair anquera *behind exposed rawhide cantle; and details of pommel (above left) and cantle (above right)*
Fleischer Collection, Scottsdale

While the leather arts flourished in central Mexico, the same could not be said for the Spanish borderlands where fine materials and workmanship were scarce. In 1804 one Spanish government official called the tack used by Spanish soldier-herdsmen "*despreciable mueble*" (contemptible furniture).[3] Nevertheless, at least a few Indian converts at far-flung Spanish missions learned not only how to carve and rig saddletrees but also how to dye and appliqué leather. In regions where the maguey plant flourished, they also began to embellish saddle skirting and other tanned leather goods with decorative cactus fiber (*pita*) embroidery. The preparation of *pita* involved a laborious process of stripping, combing, and drying the stout plant fibers and rolling them, a few strands at a time, into thread. Hand rubbing the *pita* with a cow's tail imparted a smooth waxy finish that not only pleased the eye but also facilitated the stitching process.

The celestial and figurative forms that characterized Indian and mixed-blood *pitado*, leather carving, and silver work reflected each craftsman's cultural background and personal experience. Imaginative renderings of moons, stars, snakes, birds, flowers, and the like added variety, originality, and a folk art quality

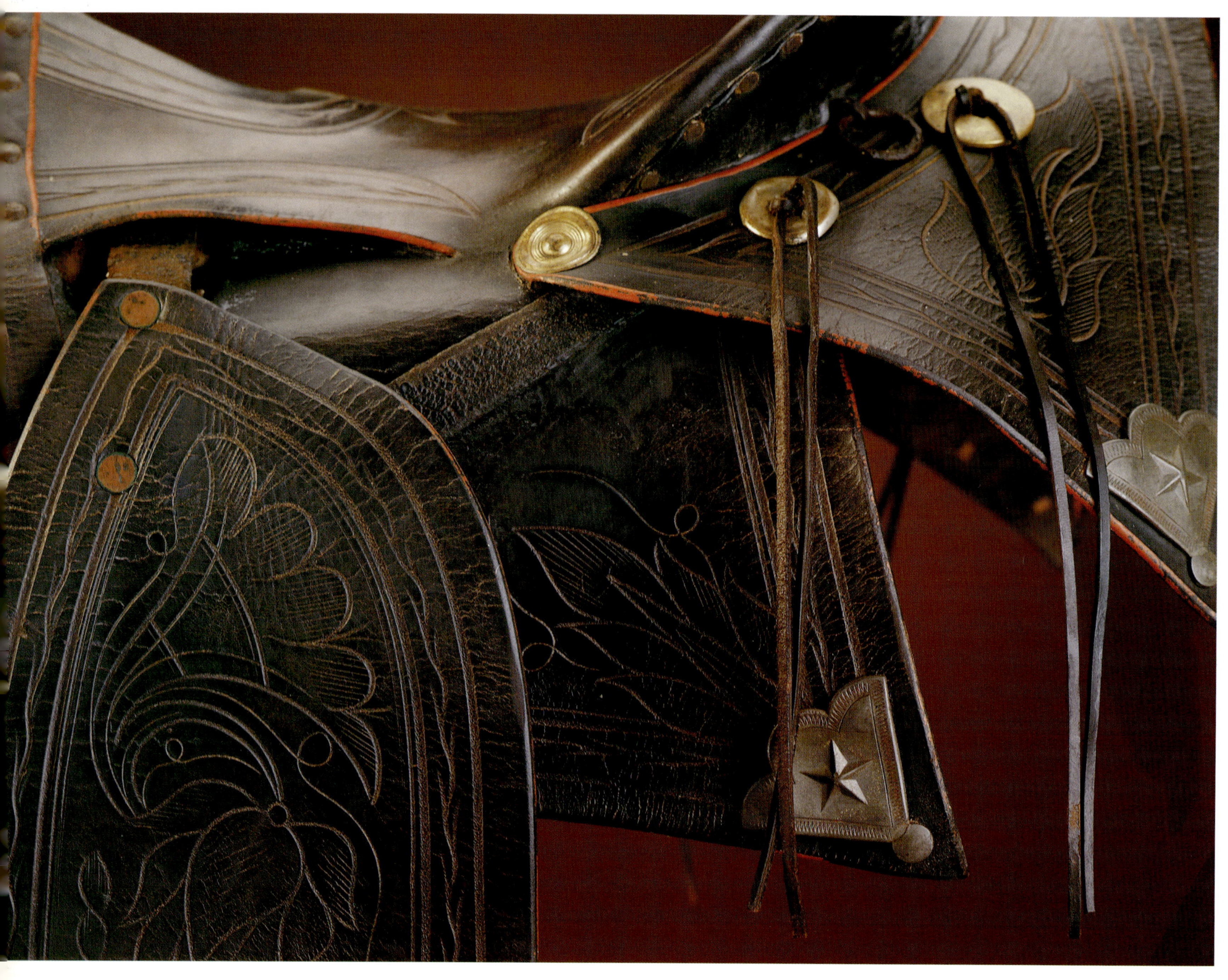

Civil War–period saddle with military-style tapederos (opposite); and detail of fender (above)
FLEISCHER COLLECTION, SCOTTSDALE

to many Mexican saddles. Such characteristics were certainly evident when talented woodcarvers shaped the horns of saddletrees into caricatures of human heads and faces.

Until the 1840s fine stock saddles ridden by horsemen in Texas, New Mexico, Arizona, and California were almost always imported from Mexico City or interior provinces such as Tamaulipas, Sonora, and Jalisco. Surviving equipment requisitions for the presidio at Santa Barbara, California, between 1779 and 1810, for example, often mention saddles imported from the town of Agualulco, Sonora. *Anqueras* and embroidered tack were also cited. On a visit to

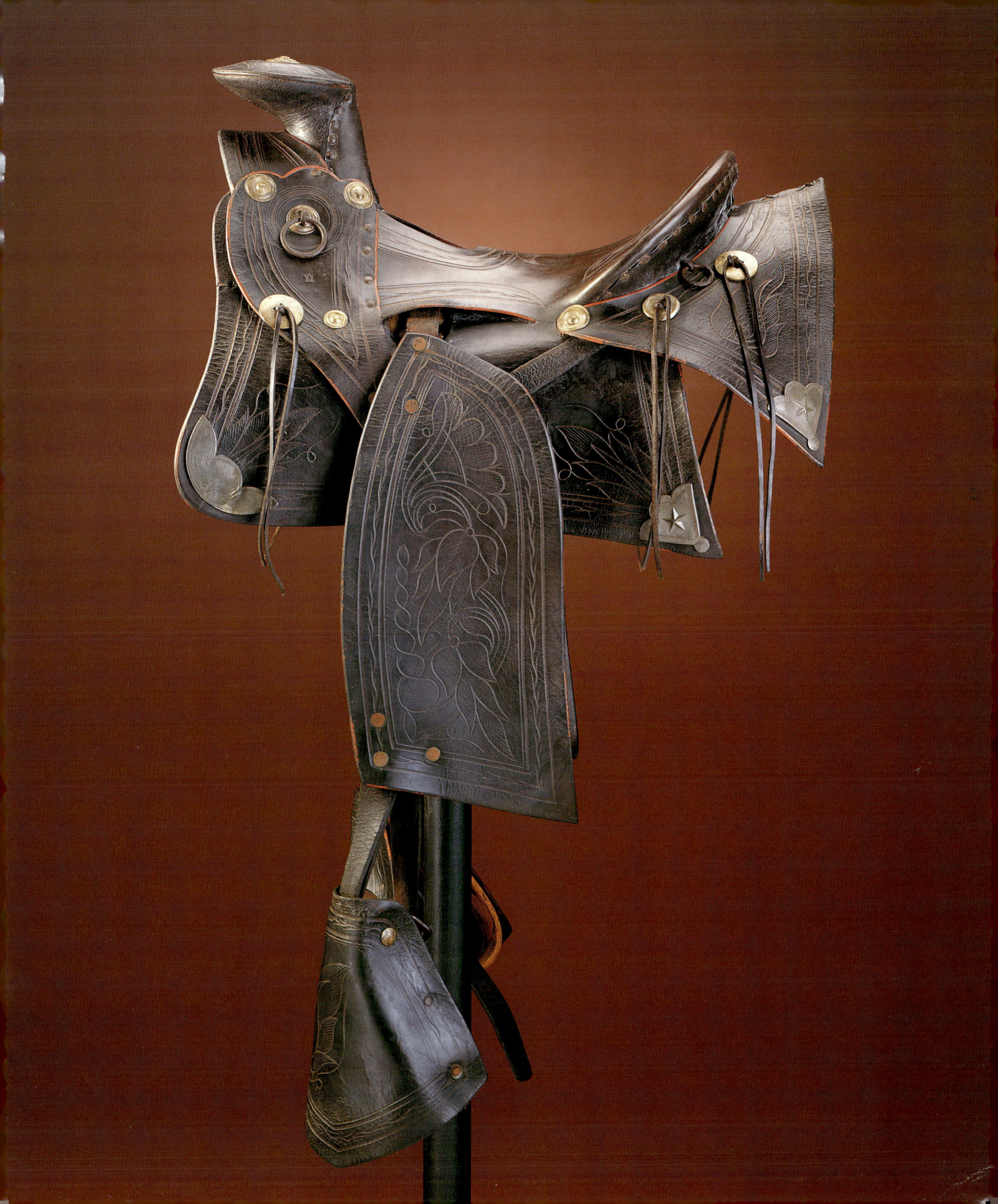

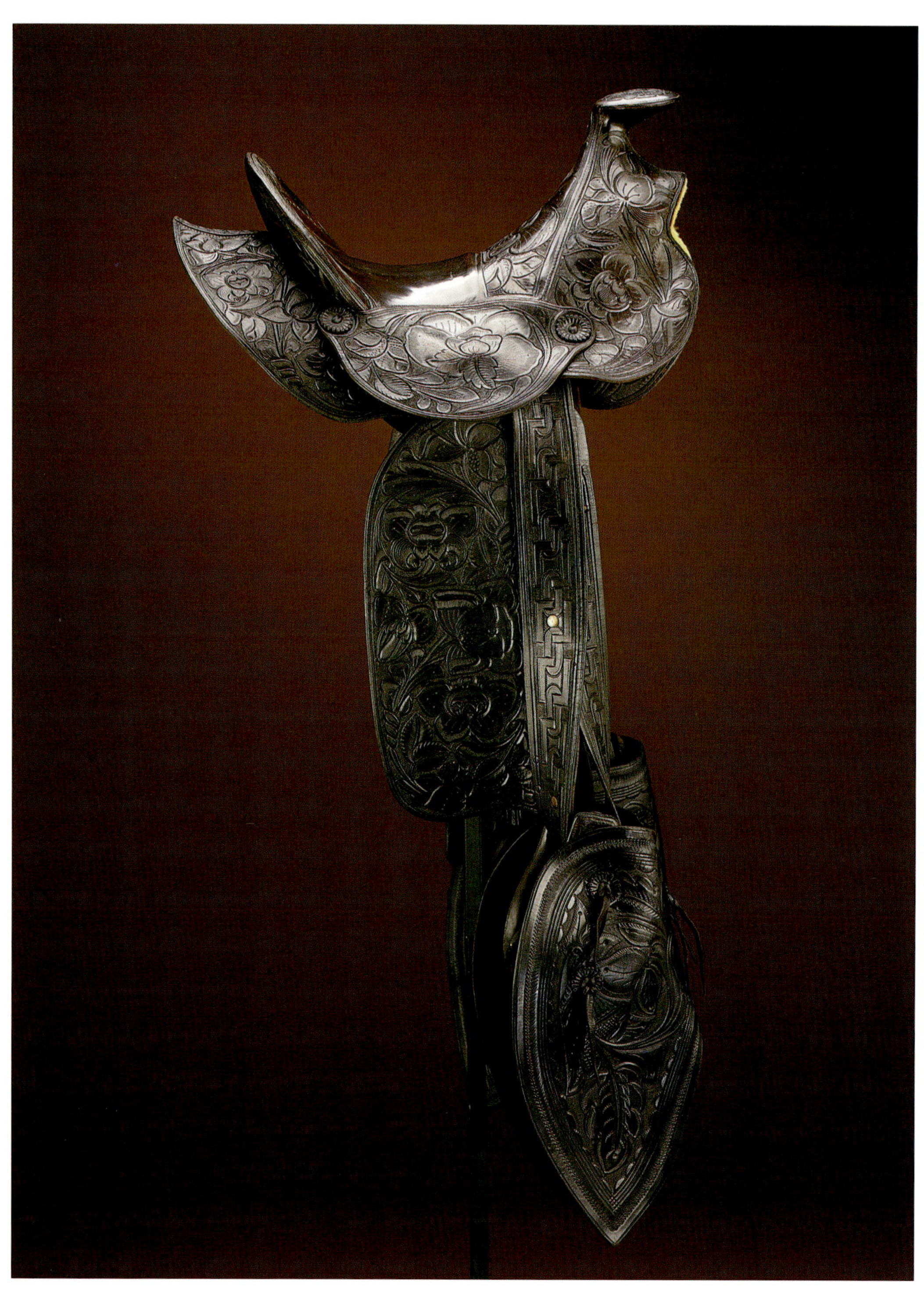

J. N. Jaquish, Reno
Saddle with large tapaderos *and handholds in cantle, 1870s; with detail (opposite) of floral carving on fender*
FLEISCHER COLLECTION, SCOTTSDALE

Santa Barbara in 1893, travel writer M. C. Frederick encountered elaborate Spanish-colonial-era *mochilas*

> literally covered with rich embroideries in gold and silver, and silks of the brightest hues, with spaces filled with stamping. . . . In time both the *mochilla* [sic] and the embroidery disappeared, and the stamping was used exclusively, with sometimes silver ornaments for embellishment.[4]

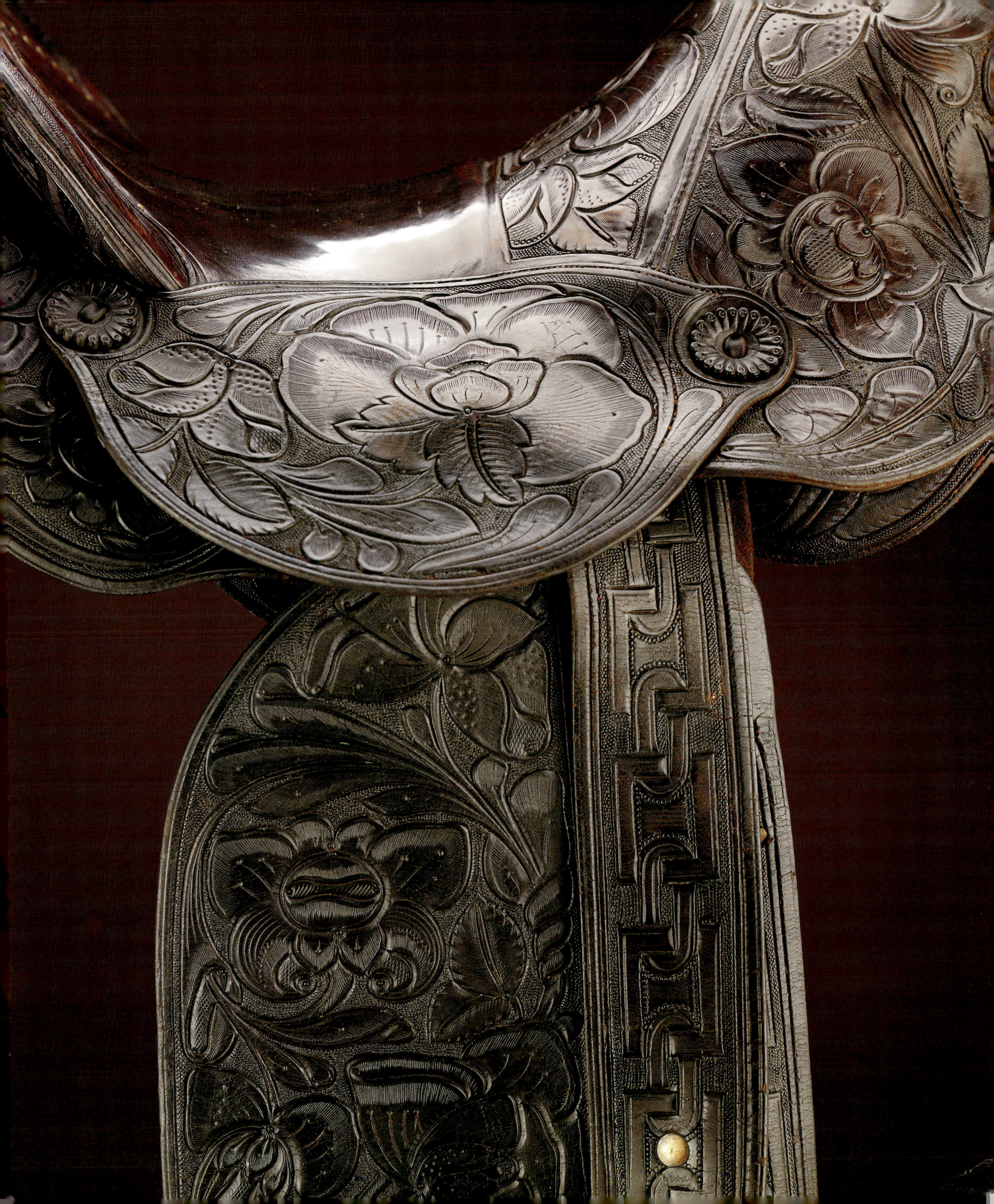

Another traveler, visiting Santa Fe, New Mexico, in 1840, remarked upon the approach of a rider who, "with saddle and other gear gorgeously decorated with silver, and little bells and ornaments jingling as he approached, rode up, dismounted, and came into the house."[5]

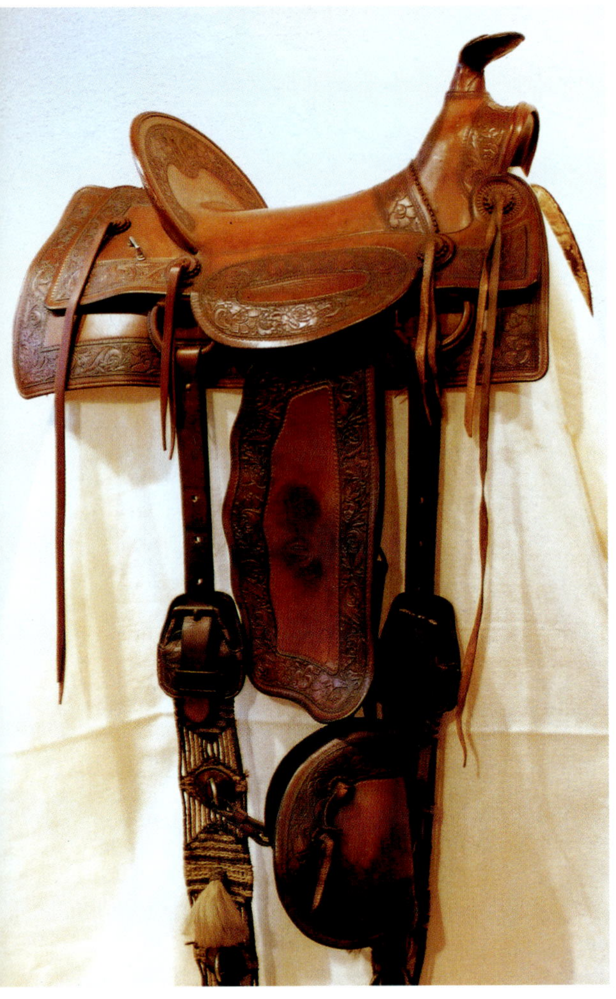

Main and Winchester, San Francisco
Double-rigged saddle with half seat and floral carving, 1870s
King Land Investments

Many American horsemen admired the utility and beauty of the Spanish- and Mexican-style stock saddles they began to encounter in the South and West during the early nineteenth century. In the 1820s East Coast makers began producing lightweight "half-Spanish" saddles that combined horned saddletrees and *mochila*-like covers with English-style rigging and embellishment that included colored, painted, and gilded leathers, japanning, decorative stitching and embossing, but little carving.

Eastern makers endowed the most expensive saddles with quilted seats made of tough but pliable hog skin or more costly buckskin, held in place with stitching, often applied in decorative patterns. To achieve the desired effect the craftsman usually sketched out the design and punched it into paper with a needle or awl. After outlining the drawing on the leather with chalk dust and using a marking wheel to locate the stitch path, the artisan sewed the seat into place by hand.

The demand for western and Mexican-style saddles, built on horned trees, accelerated following the Mexican-American War (1846–1848) and the California Gold Rush of 1849. Saddle shops in Connecticut, New York, and Pennsylvania began to copy a wide variety of popular regional styles and ship them in substantial numbers to waiting customers west of the Mississippi. Although nascent saddle-making centers eventually developed in Texas, California, and Missouri, the relative scarcity of quality tanned leather, saddle hardware, and skilled leatherworkers insured that eastern and Mexican makers would dominate the trade until after the Civil War.

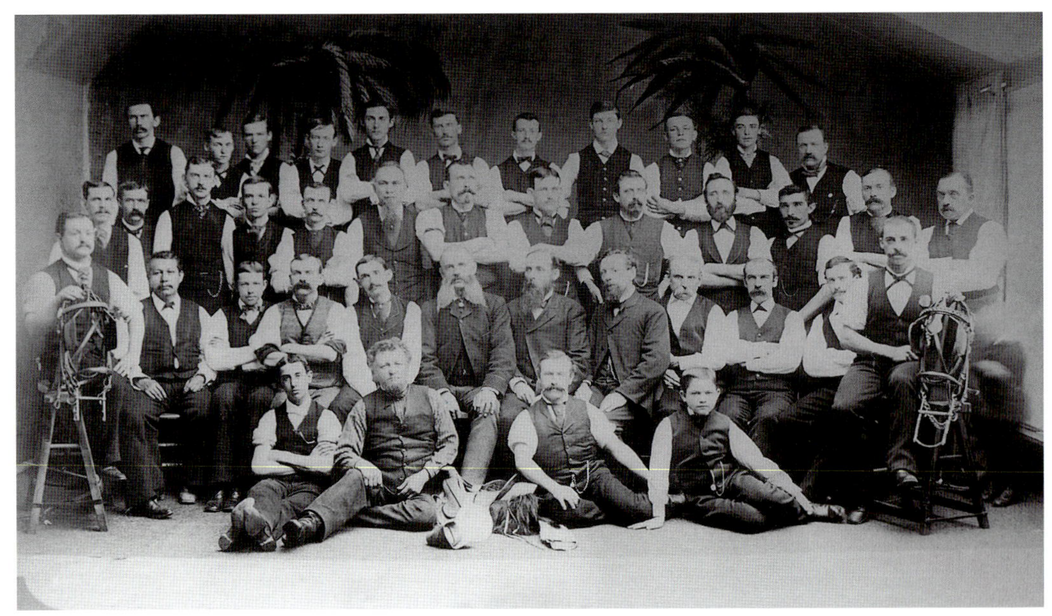

Saint Louis Art Studio
"Saddle and harness makers at Main and Winchester, San Francisco, Sept. 2d, 1883" (center, seated: Charles Main, E. H. Winchester, Thos. R. Haynes, surrounded by their workers)
California Historical Society, San Francisco

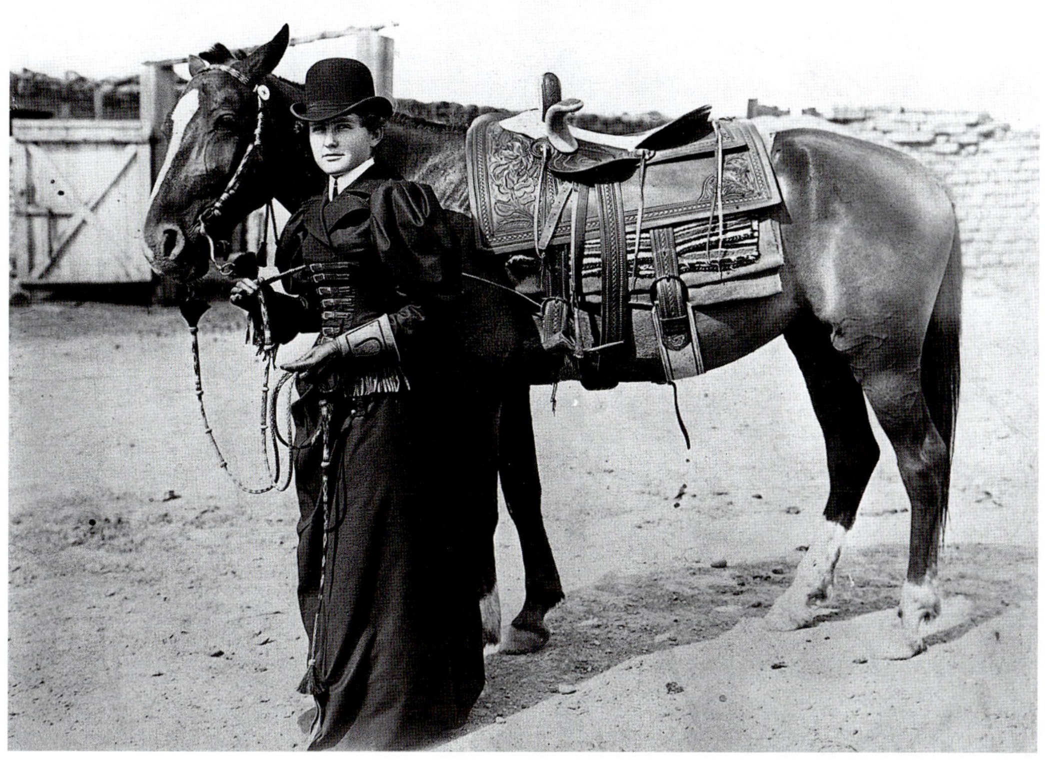

Equestrienne in bowler hat, stylish gauntlets, and with horsehair quirt, stands beside her horse, which has a horsehair bridle and cowgirl-style, double-rigged, heavily carved sidesaddle, c. 1900
PANHANDLE PLAINS HISTORICAL MUSEUM, CANYON, TEXAS

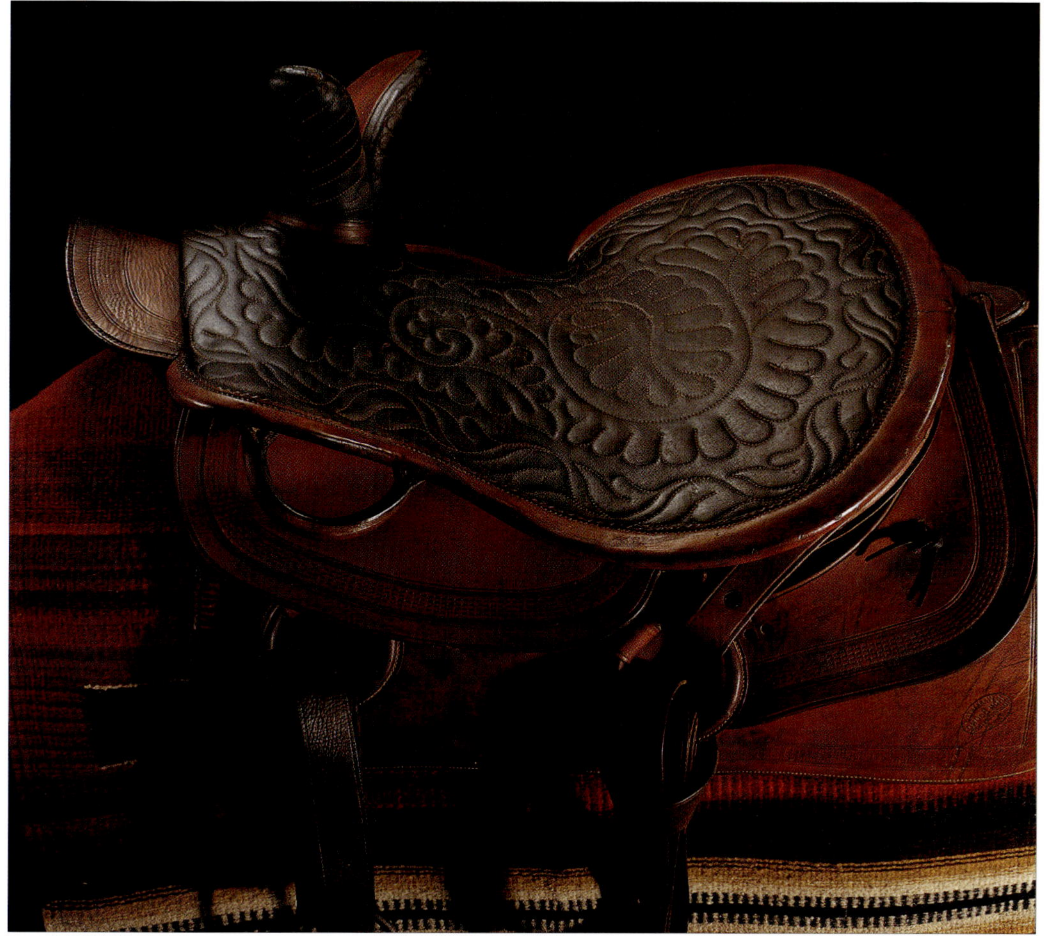

Double-rigged sidesaddle with quilted seat, marked "Warranted Iron Bound Rawhide Covered Tree" and "Warranted Genuine Buckskin" (center jockey)
SANTA BARBARA CARRIAGE AND WESTERN ART MUSEUM

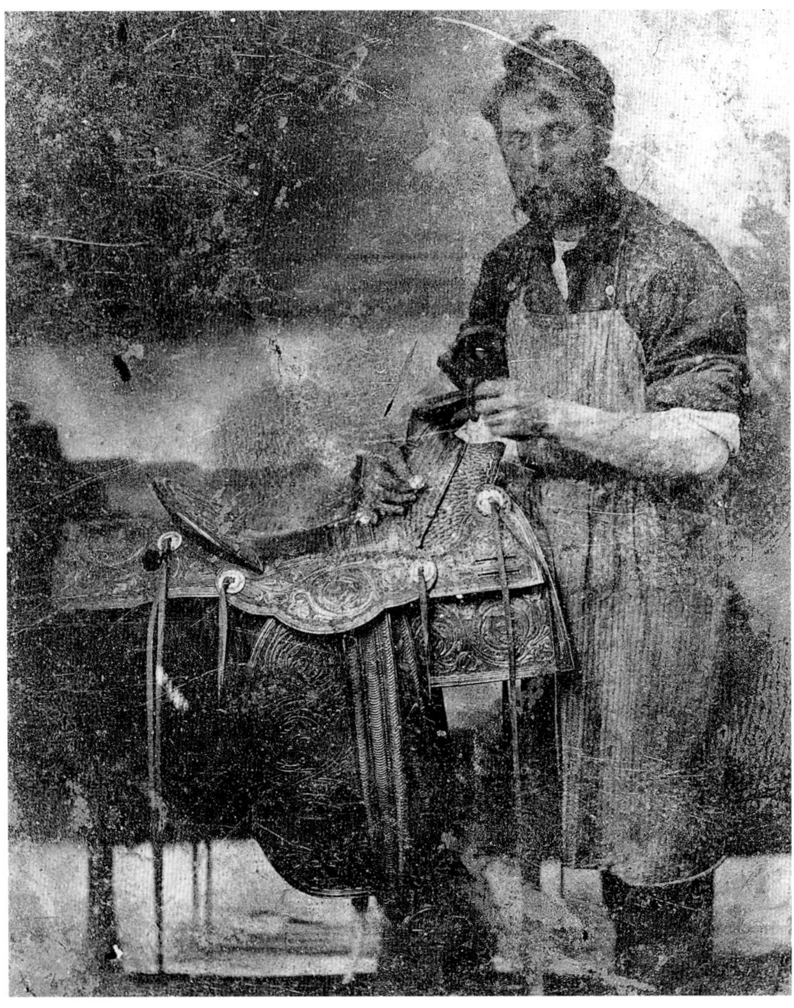

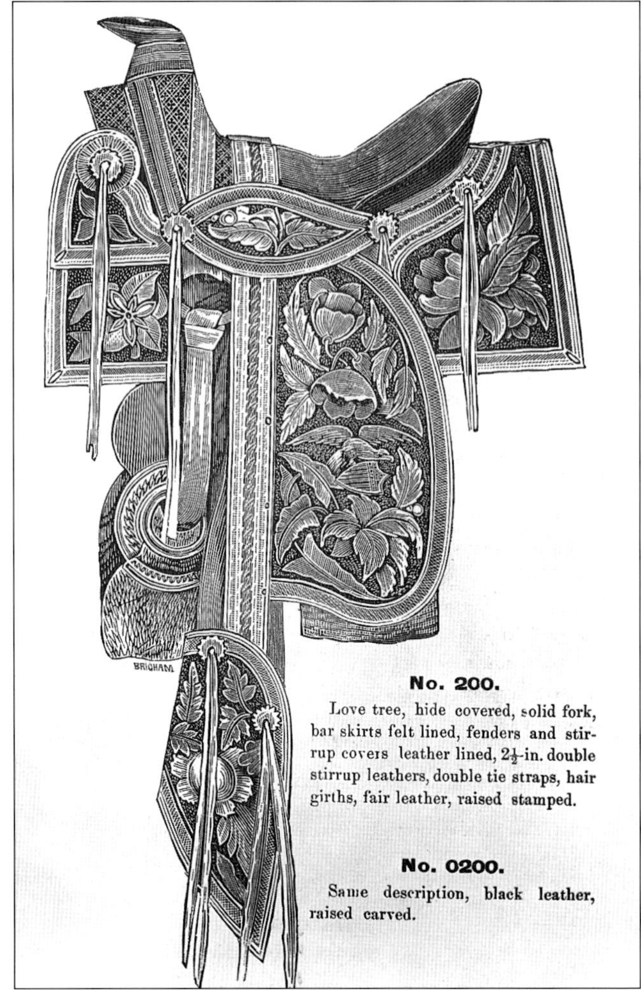

Above, left
Unknown apron-clad saddle maker, hammer in hand, poses beside one of his creations, possibly in Ford County, Kansas, late 19th century
Kansas State Historical Society, Topeka

Above, right
Risser and Reitz, Chicago. Saddle, model no. 200, engraving from Illustrated and Descriptive Catalogue of Risser and Reitz Manufacturers of Saddlery, Harness, Collars, Etc., and Dealers in Saddlery Hardware, Horse Clothing, Fly Nets, Leather and Whips, *No. 105 Lake Street, Chicago, 1879*
Panhandle Plains Historical Museum, Canyon, Texas

The rising economic importance of the western range cattle industry and the steady flow of farmers into the post–Civil War West stimulated an unprecedented demand for quality saddlery and harness. The development of a railroad network and tanning facilities and the availability of a greater number of skilled craftsmen, many of them Mexican and European immigrants or eastern transplants, also hastened the growth of the saddle-making industry in the trans-Mississippi West. Lower labor, leather, and saddletree costs played crucial roles and enabled western saddle makers in such centers as St. Louis, Omaha, Denver, Cheyenne, and San Francisco to wrest the saddlery market away from their East Coast competitors by 1875.

Craftsmen in these and other communities began to supply cowboys with heavy-duty stock saddles weighing as much as forty pounds and designed to withstand the rigors of life on the open range. In the 1870s saddle architecture evolved rapidly from the simple *mochila* housings and single-cinch styles of the past into heavier and more elaborate double-rigged creations bearing two *cinchas* and separate skirts, jockeys, and fenders. Trendsetters also tinkered with the size, shape, and configuration of saddletrees, and by the latter part of the decade, inventors in Texas

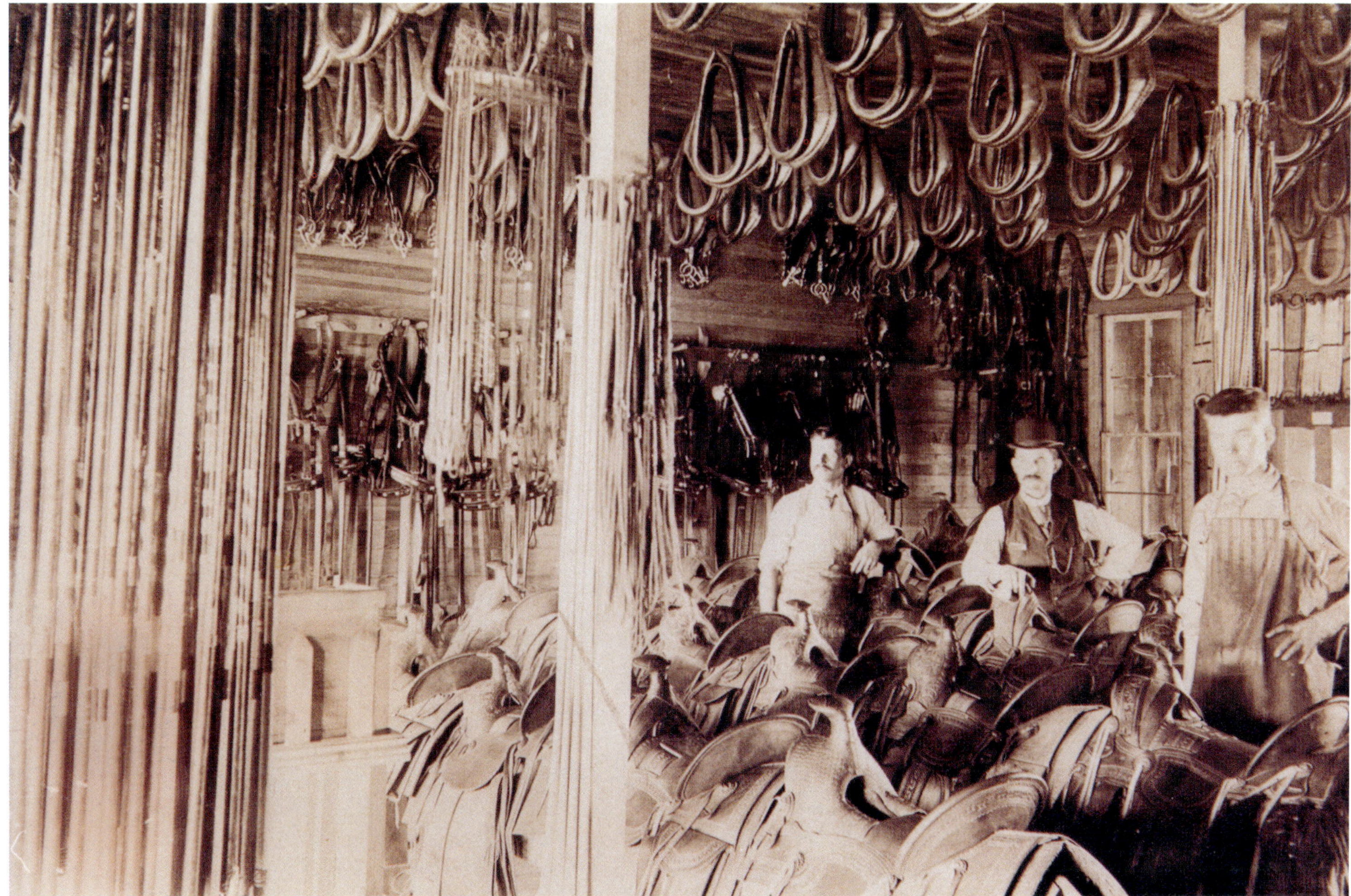

C. D. Jackson Saddle Shop, Amarillo, Texas, 1893
Pictured (left to right): Charlie Williamson, harness maker; C. D. Jackson, owner; John Addison, apprentice
PANHANDLE PLAINS HISTORICAL MUSEUM COLLECTION, CANYON, TEXAS

and Colorado had strengthened some types with metal horns and forks. During the 1880s distinctive regional styles, based primarily on structure and rigging rather than ornamentation, developed in California and Texas and on the Great Plains.

Cowboys usually furnished their own saddles and valued them for their strength, durability, and utility above all else. Although many punchers settled for plain, utilitarian rigs, others favored a more aesthetic look. All bought the best saddle that they could afford on wages that rarely exceeded $40 a month in the late nineteenth century. The price of a saddle depended upon the cost of materials, the quality of workmanship, and the type and application of embellishment. Serviceable rigs with minimal decoration typically cost a cowboy the equivalent of a month or two of pay, ornate models often much more.

Because they were made of thick skirting and subject to hard use, stock rigs did not lend themselves to the decorative leather fringe, cloth braid and embroidery, and decorative stitching prevalent on the soft leather saddles of the late nineteenth century. And while a few cowboys rode "kaks"[6] made of black leather, there was never much demand among range riders for saddles with dyed skirting, which tended to fade when exposed to the sun and prolonged wear.

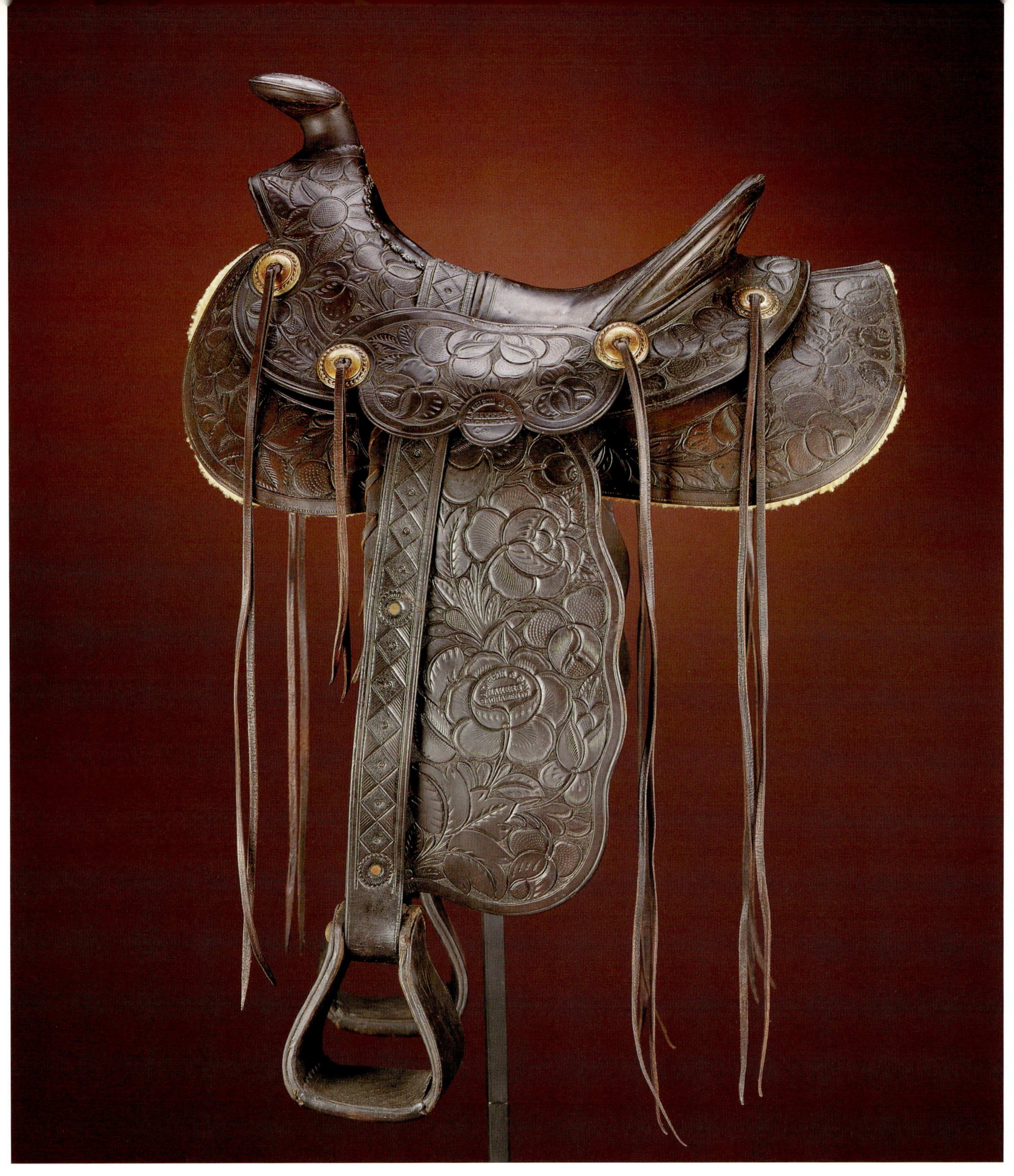

A. T. Nelson and Son, Sacramento Saddle with scalloped fenders and side jockeys, rounded skirts, center-fire rigging, and floral stamping, c. 1880 (above); with detail of fender (opposite)
FLEISCHER COLLECTION, SCOTTSDALE

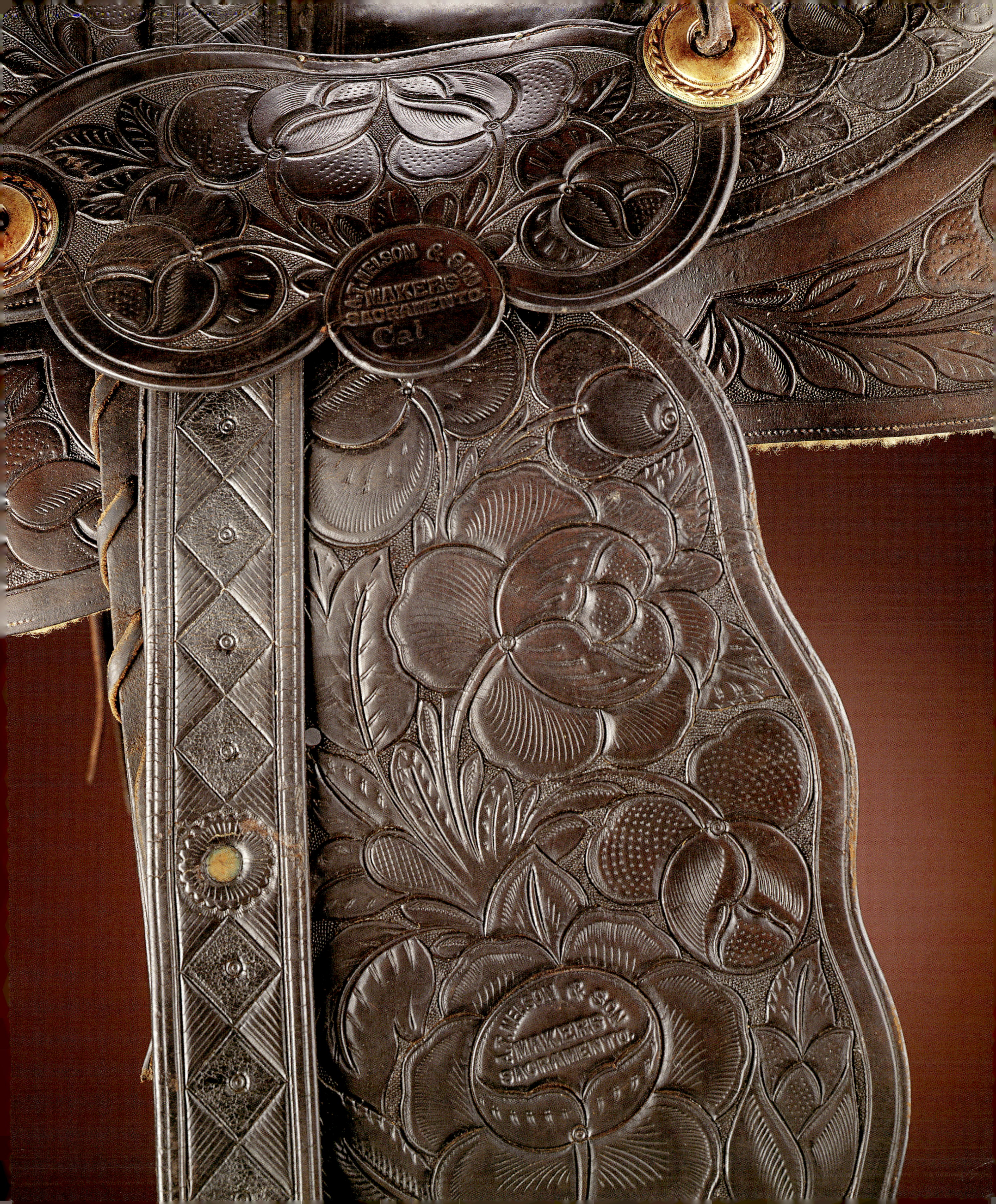
NELSON & SON
MAKERS
SACRAMENTO
Cal
NELSON & SON
MAKERS
SACRAMENTO

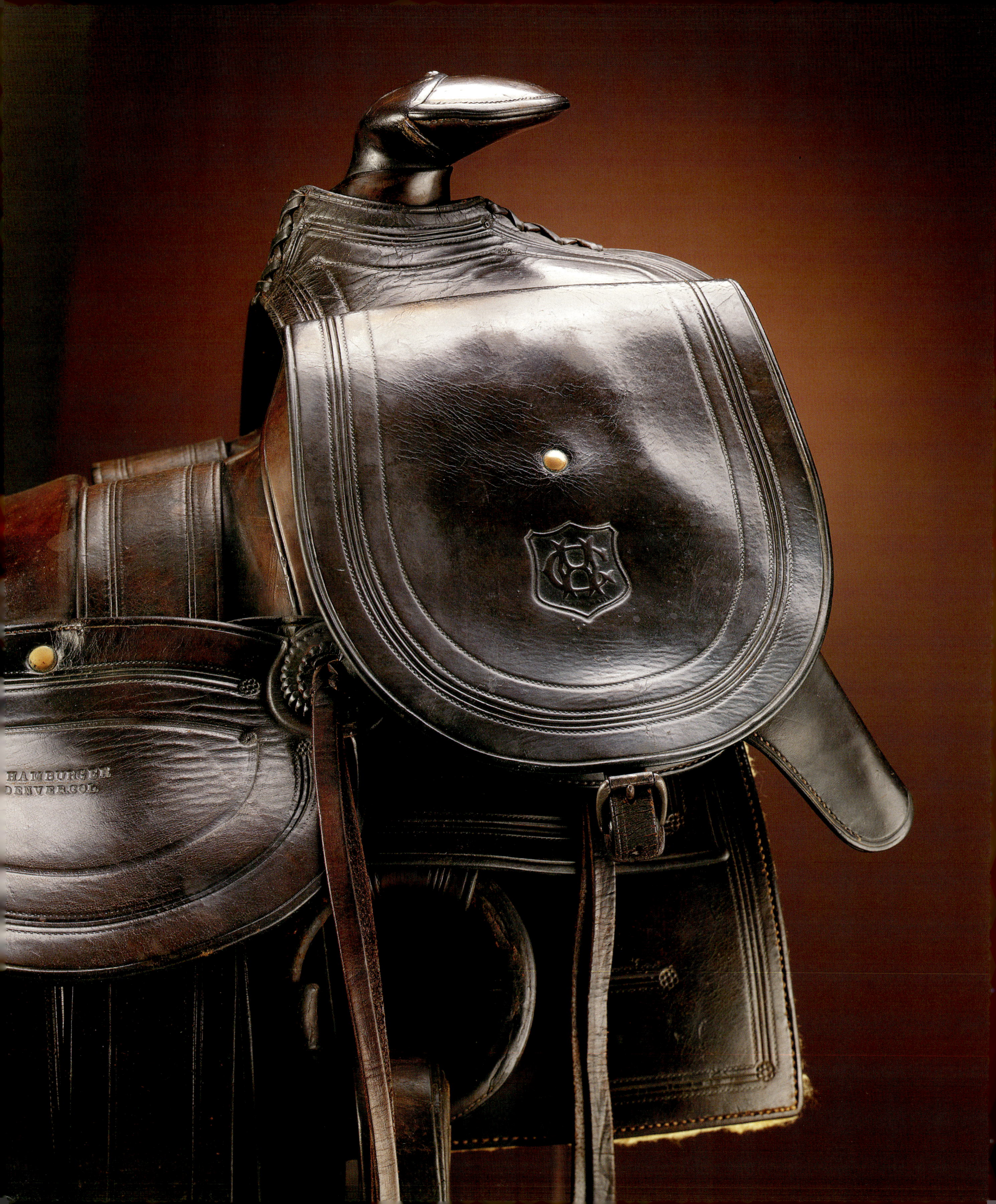
HAMBURGER
DENVER.COL.

Cowboys with an artistic bent sometimes added their own decorative touches to their rigs, forming simple designs with brass nails and tacks or trimming skirts and cantles with rattlesnake skin or bearskin. Most, however, preferred the look and feel of saddle leather that had been hand-carved and stamped. Besides lending a decorative effect, stamping, also known as "sharking" or "tooling," tended to compress the fibers of saddle skirting, thereby adding to its durability. Some makers believed that stamped and carved saddles wore as much as 50 percent longer than plain ones. One old-timer claimed to have stamped leather so deeply that it "could be used for a door mat without wearing out."[7] Stamp work also shed water more easily than slick skirting.

Malleable when dampened, tanned cowhide with a soft, fine grain lent itself to carving, stamping, and embossing in high relief. The quality of such embellishment, however, depended on the type and preparation of the leather as well as upon the skill of the artisan. In the last quarter of the nineteenth century, California tanneries began to produce commercial quantities of a superior oak-tanned skirting favored by stock saddle makers throughout the West. Possessing a white, velvety grain, California leather wore better than other varieties and was especially conducive to stamping and carving. Successful saddle stamping, wrote one observer in *Harness* magazine in 1889,

> depends upon having leather in the condition to hold the creases made by the tool, and not to draw out lines already made. There is something in the skirting leather tanned on the Pacific coast which specially fits it for embossing.... the grain is so flexible that when once creased, the line cannot be removed.[8]

Before the embellishment process commenced, however, makers cut out the various parts of the saddle from a side of leather, avoiding material that was marred by brands or "flanky," meaning thin, weak, or wrinkled. After scouring the flesh side of the pieces with a stiff brush, pumice, and water, the craftsman left them to dry in the shade or covered them with burlap, so they would not darken in the sun.

Properly "sammied" (moistened) leather was soft and pliant and, if well tanned, retained moisture uniformly over the entire surface. Because no two pieces of skirting responded in the same way to scouring, experience was paramount in determining the correct conditions for embossing and carving. The stamper began to shark the grain side of the leather when it was nearly dry, moistening the surface lightly with a soft sponge when it became too parched to hold the impression of the stamping tools. Care was taken, however, not to discolor the leather by applying too much water.

Leatherworkers pursued their craft with a sturdy set of specialized hand tools, many of ancient origin and some adapted from implements used in the

Opposite
George Hamburger, Denver
Pommel bag and holster, 1880s
Fleischer Collection, Scottsdale

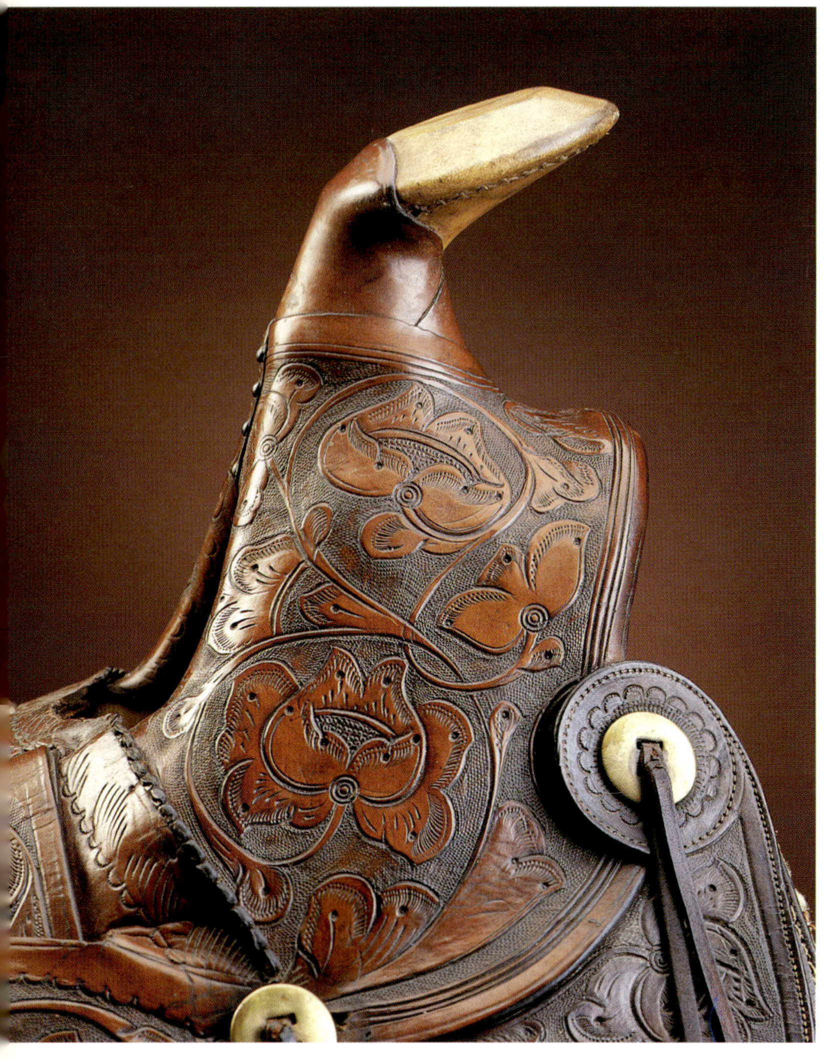
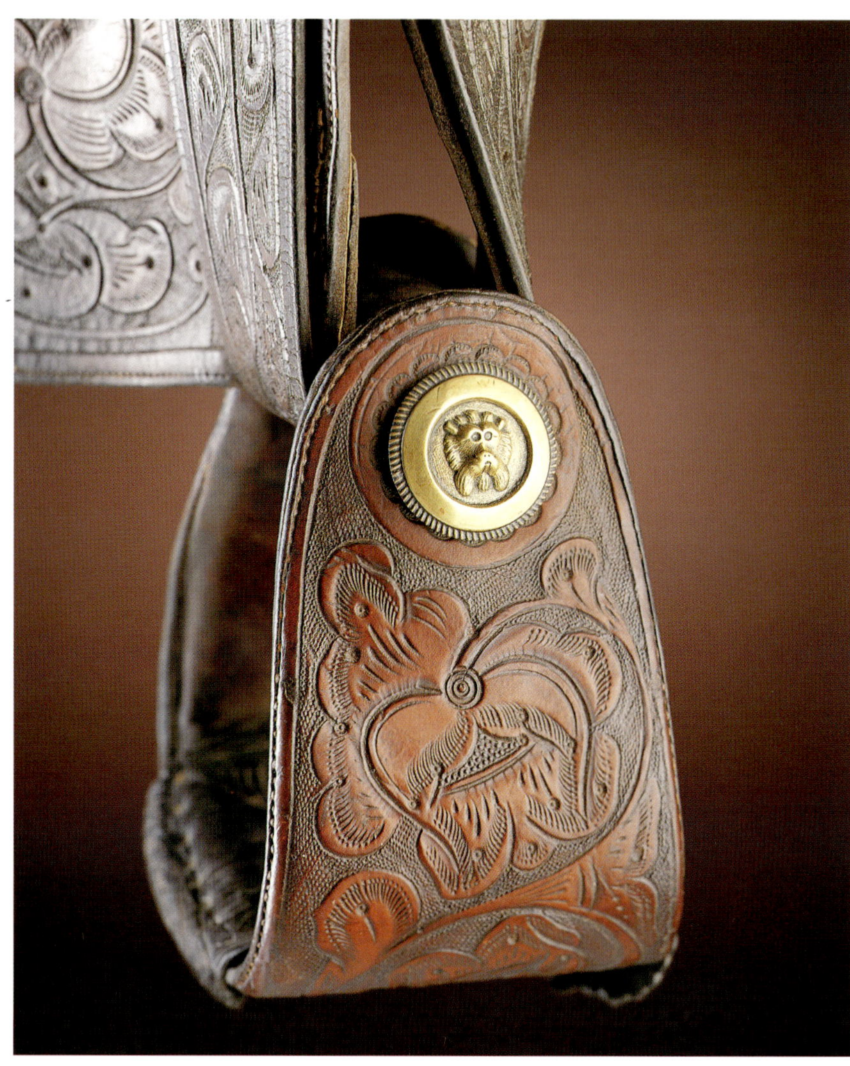

Above, left and right:
Frank A. Meanea, Cheyenne, Wyoming
Saddle with loop seat, exposed rawhide cantle and horn, c. 1885; details of pommel and stirrup
FLEISCHER COLLECTION, SCOTTSDALE

Opposite:
Frank A. Meanea, Cheyenne, Wyoming
Saddle with full seat, exposed rawhide cantle and horn, c. 1890
FLEISCHER COLLECTION, SCOTTSDALE

wood- and metalworking trades. British companies dominated the American market for leatherworking equipment until the Civil War when a group of Newark, New Jersey, foundries, led by C. S. Osborne & Co., became serious competitors in the field. Tool makers created a wide array of products including blades, gauges, and creasers of various shapes and sizes used to cut, split, skive, and carve leather; awls and punches to make holes for thread and tie strings; hammers to drive nails and tacks; and rawhide-covered mallets, mauls, and "stamping sticks" to tap ornamental embossing dies.

In 1890 only about 10 percent of American saddle shops reported using any sort of machinery in the production process. To lower labor costs and turn out mass-market merchandise more quickly and uniformly, however, many large-scale saddleries, including some in the West, turned increasingly to assembly-line methods and machinery. Despite the fact that pinking machines, screw presses, and mechanical creasing and embossing wheels could produce an almost limitless assortment of decorative motifs with speed and precision, their output inevitably lacked the texture, character, and eccentricity of handwork. To remedy

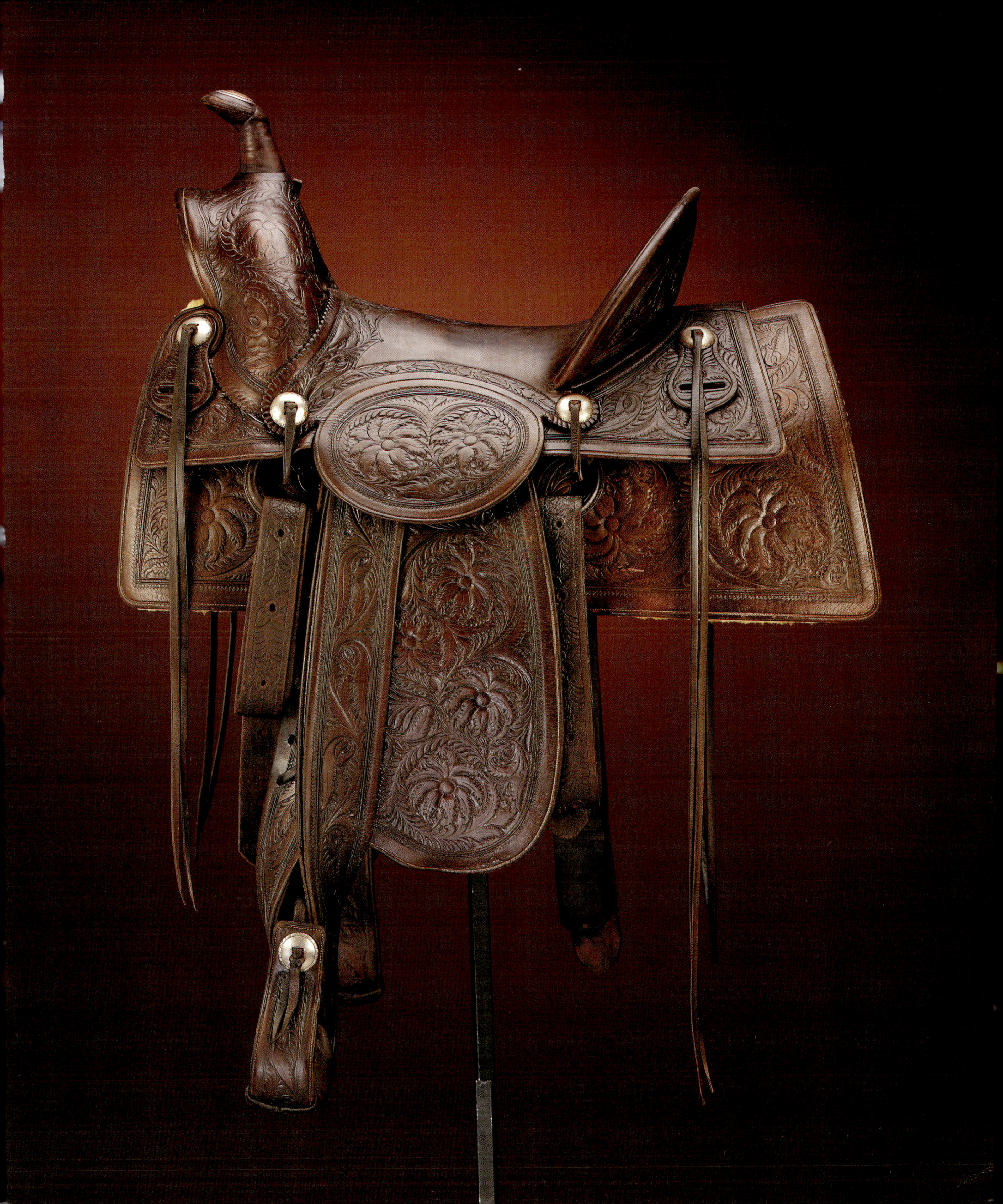

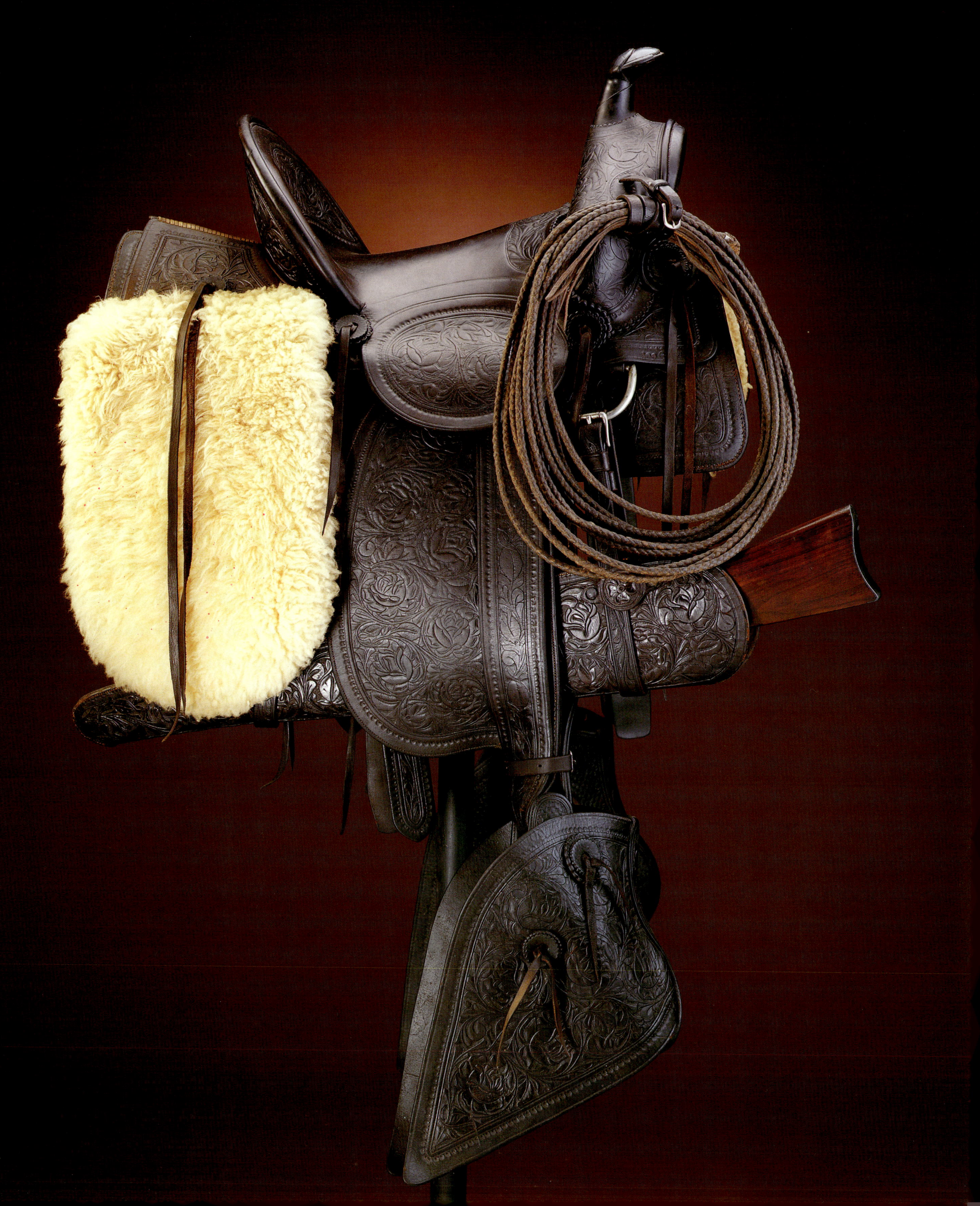

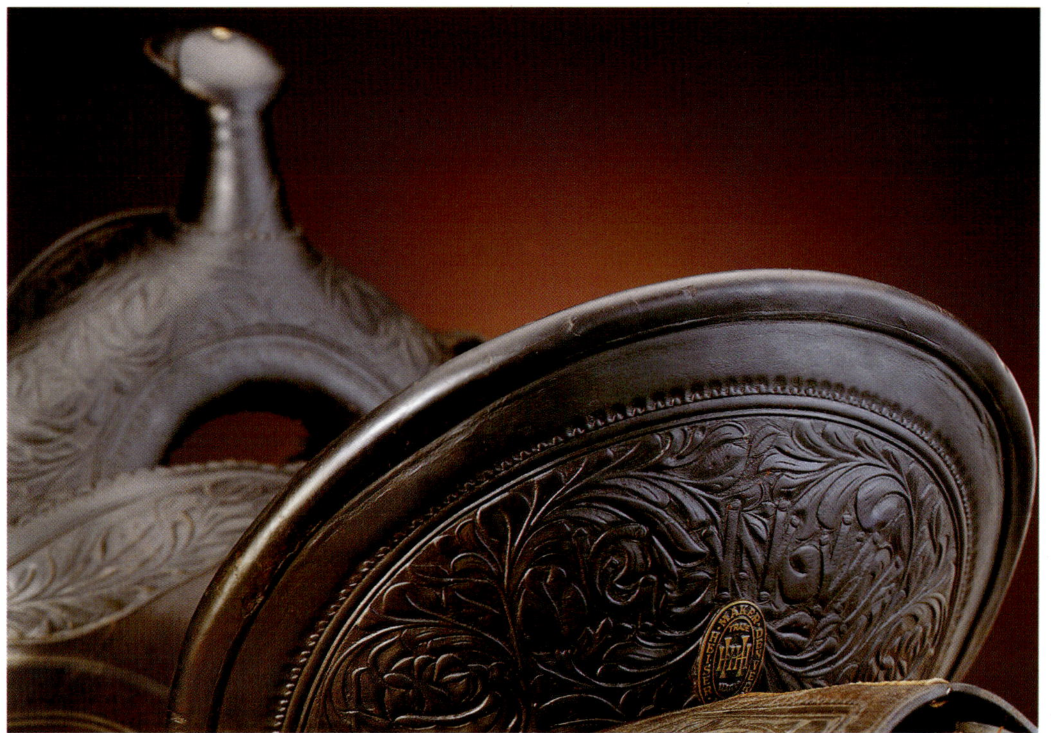

Hermann H. Heiser, Denver Model 100 saddle with matching rifle scabbard, c. 1910 (opposite), with detail of cantle (left) and headstall and bit detail (below) showing engraved initial of owner; ensemble also includes sheepskin-lined saddle bags and plaited rawhide reata
FLEISCHER COLLECTION, SCOTTSDALE

these shortcomings, saddle makers who employed such equipment, and even some who did not, often retained the services of talented specialists, known as "stamp hands," to embellish their finest products on a piecework basis.

Despite individual examples of creativity and innovation, much of the western saddlery produced in the late nineteenth and early twentieth centuries was run-of-the-mill and abounding with repetitive designs and discordant patterns. Critics blamed such ills on the saddle and harness industry for failing to reward creativity or encourage the development of artistic skills such as freehand drawing. Articles appearing in leatherworking trade publications often bemoaned the dearth of theoretical and practical knowledge of design among the industry's journeymen and the stagnation and distortion of nature it produced. "A business that is represented by fifteen thousand employers and a hundred thousand operatives," wrote one detractor in 1881, "ought not to be in such a condition, and it is time the leaders get out of the rut, and by starting in a new direction give an impetus to the trade that will lift it from its present inertness."[9]

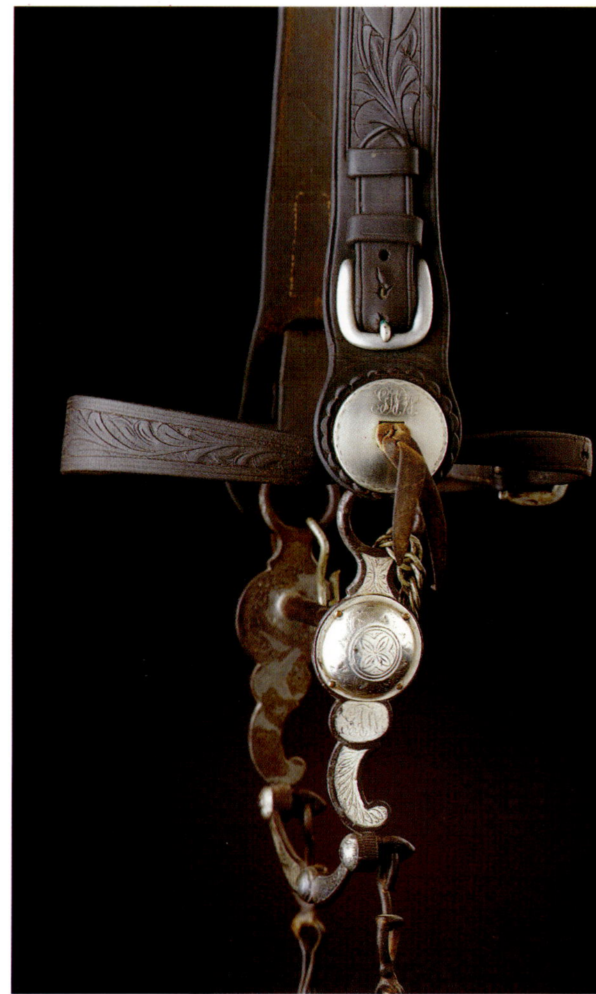

Advocates for change urged leather craftsmen to strive for greater variety in designs and to produce more restrained, tasteful, and congruent compositions with a closer fidelity to nature. "Nature is prolific," declared one authority, "and the artist needs only to copy from what he sees around him, selecting his forms from such leaves or flowers as best harmonize with the form of surface to be covered."[10] Some experts believed that training in design and draftsmanship would help apprentice saddle makers to distinguish between crudity and refinement and thus create more pleasing motifs in their work.

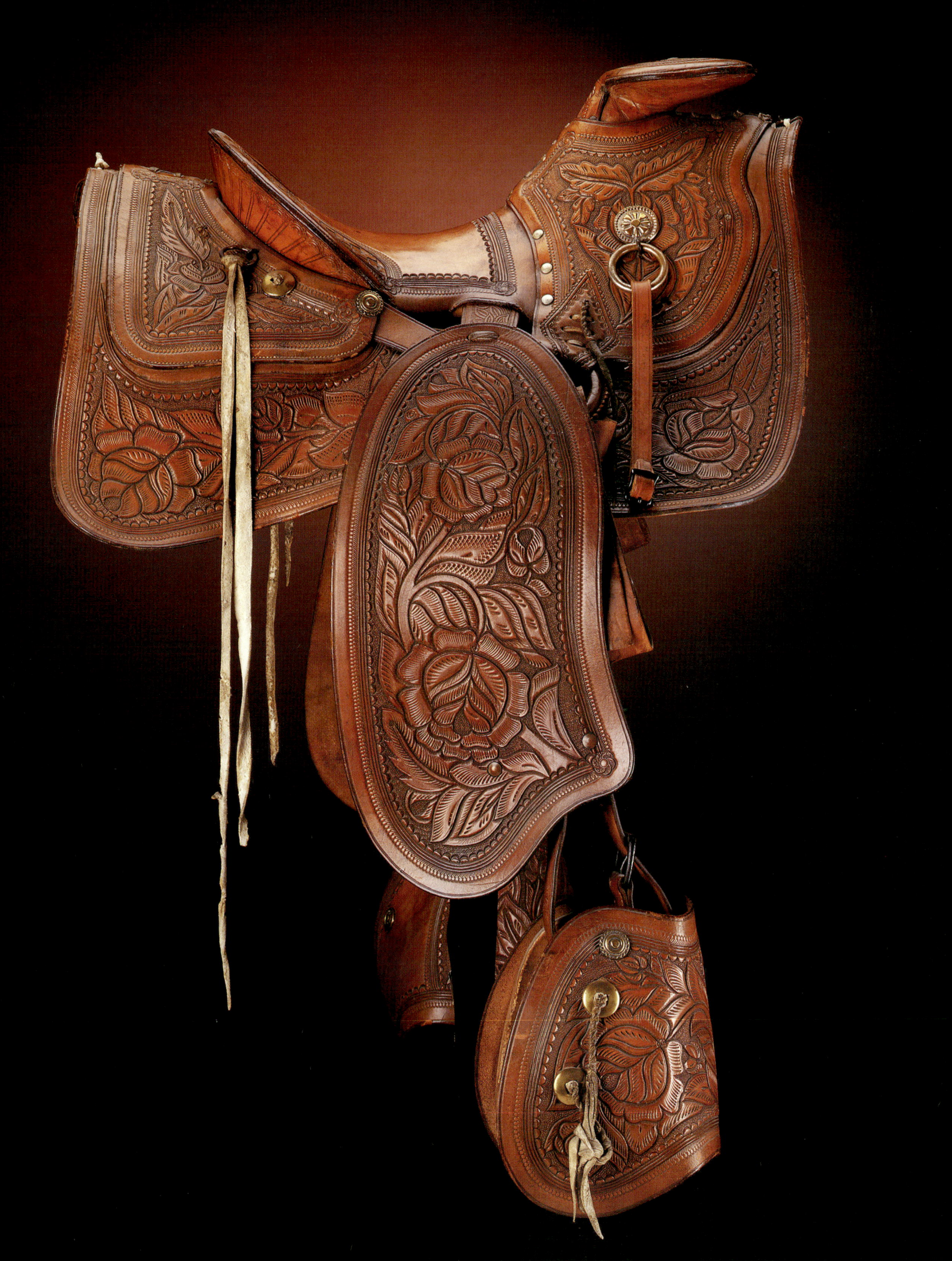

During the debate over the state of craftsmanship and design in western-style saddlery, commentators both praised and belittled the work of Hispanic saddle makers. In 1878, for example, one writer called Mexican craftsmen "wonderfully skillful in designing and ornamenting saddles ... doing their work more rapidly and in a better manner than the most expert American."[11] A few years later, however, another author excoriated Mexican saddles as inferior and a "degenerated imitation"[12] of their finely stamped Moorish-Spanish ancestors. "Embossing leather is one of the old arts," he ranted, "and one in which the present generation is far behind generations of the past."[13] The writer of another article during the same period called Hispanic artisans "skillful" in making stock saddles, "but without taste as designers."[14] Mexican "indolence," he averred with more than a little prejudice, "showed itself in the want of character"[15] of their designs. Incomprehensibly,

Opposite
California-style saddle heavily carved with floral pattern, three-quarter rig, and military-style tapaderos, *used by Frederic Remington as a studio prop for paintings and illustrations, c. 1890*
BUFFALO BILL HISTORICAL CENTER, CODY, WYOMING

Below
Saddle, c. 1895, detail of cantle showing checkerboard stamp pattern on border
FLEISCHER COLLECTION, SCOTTSDALE

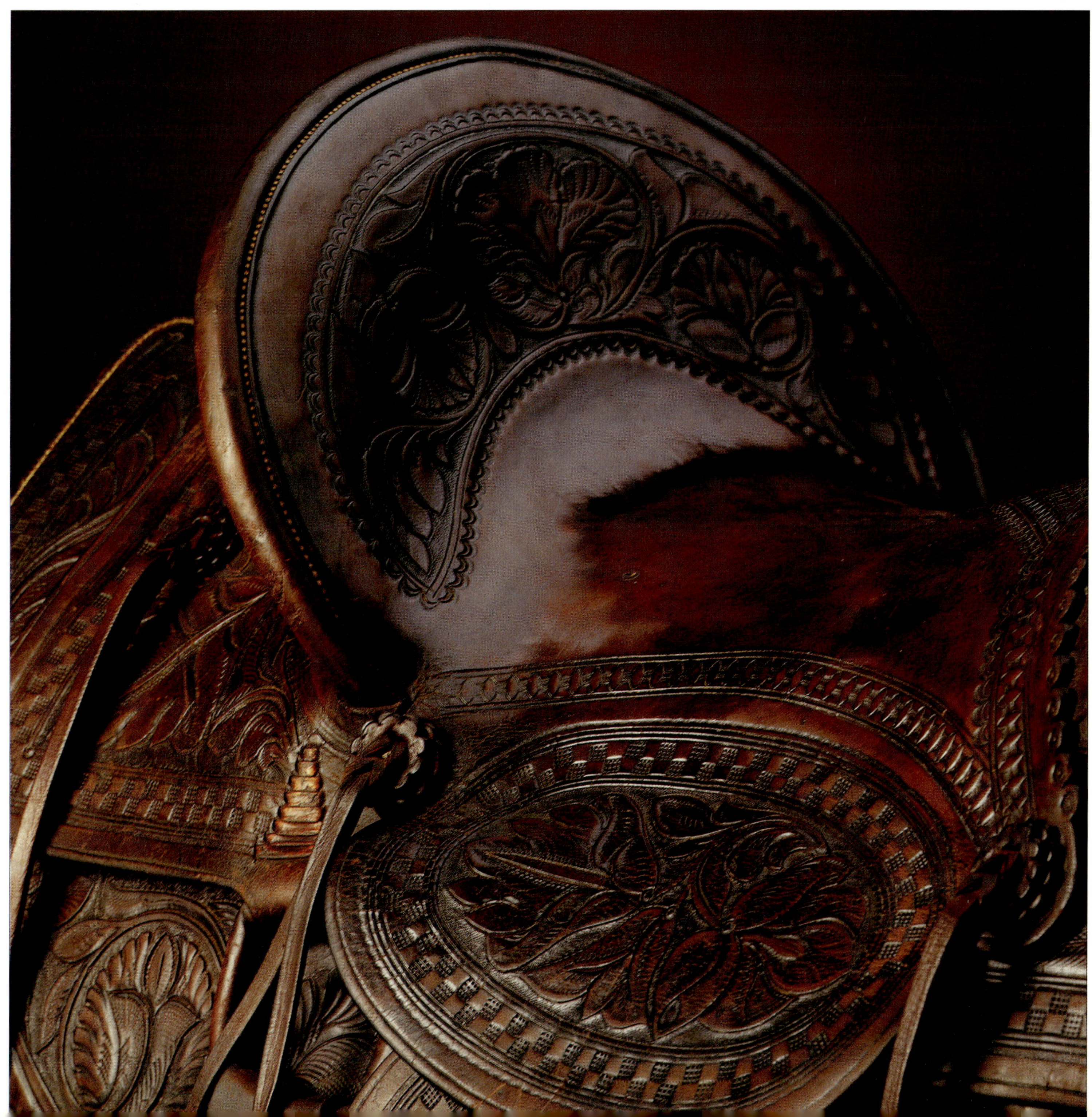

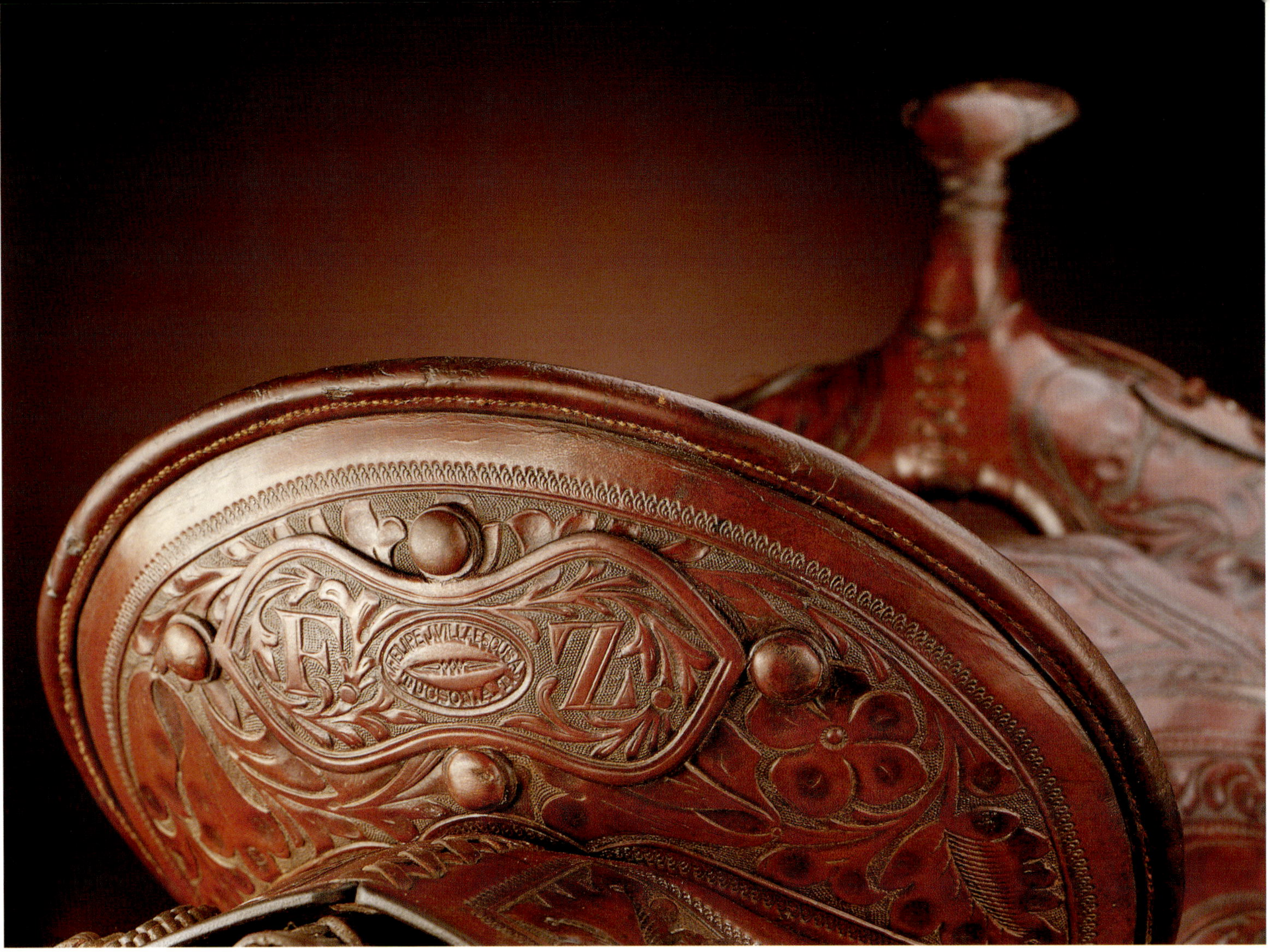

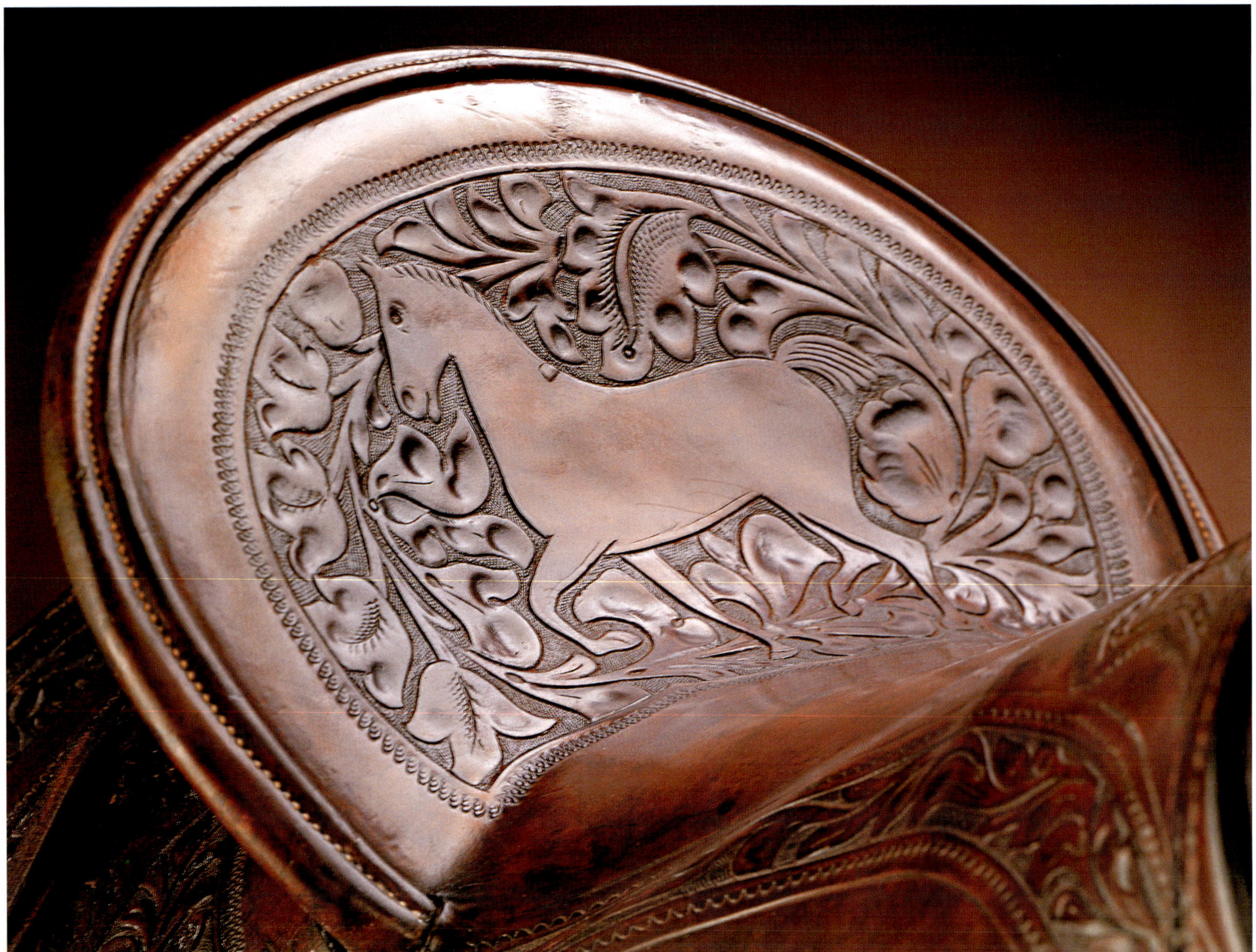

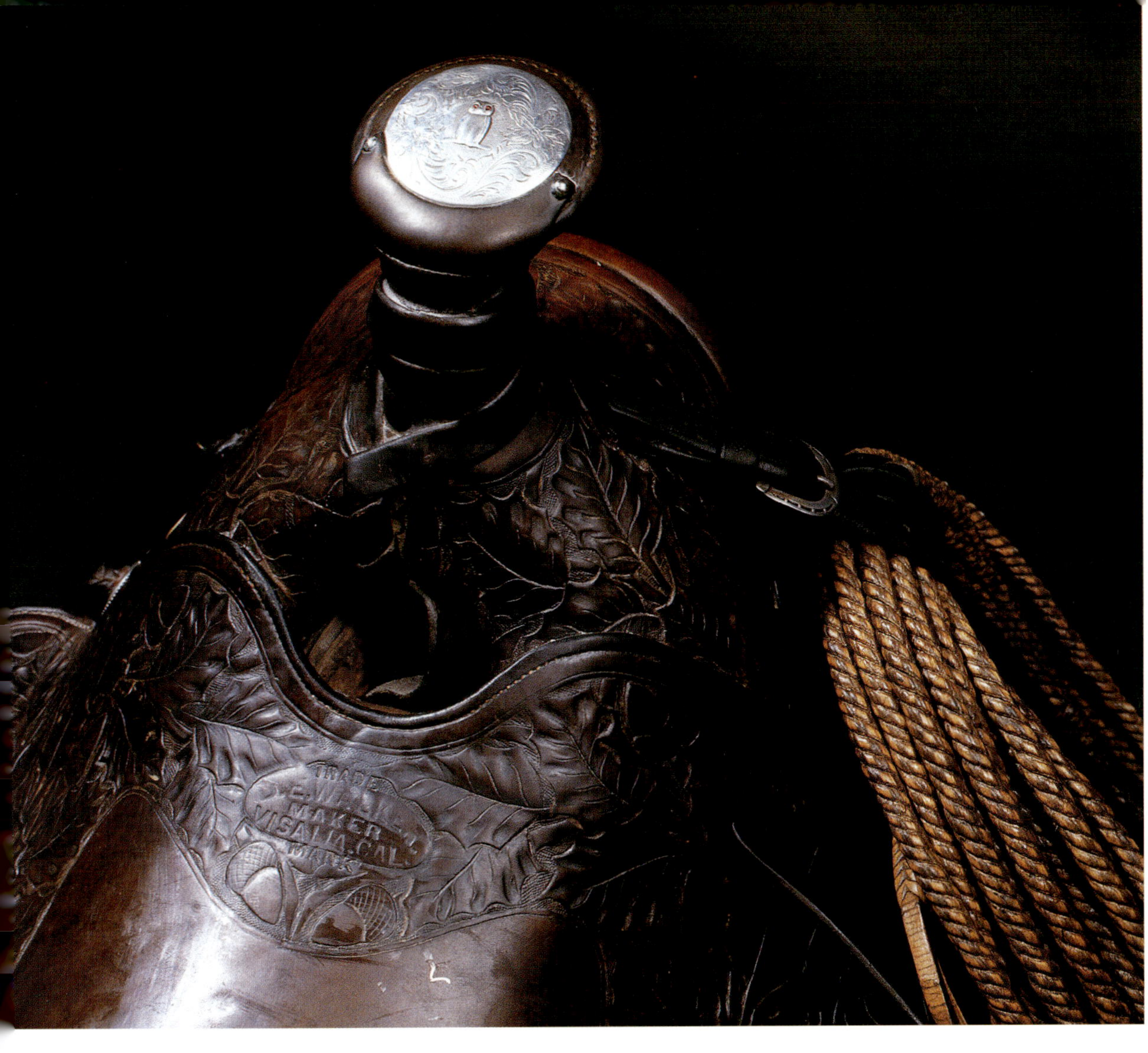

Opposite

Felipe J. Villaescusa, Tucson
Saddle, c. 1900–10, details of cantle: rear (above) with owner's initials and marker's cartouche; and seat with carving of horse (below)

FLEISCHER COLLECTION, SCOTTSDALE

Visalia Stock Saddle Co., San Francisco
Saddle made for the Tecolote Ranch, Santa Barbara County, California, with acorn stamp pattern, round skirts, and center-fire rigging (below); with detail showing horn cap featuring owl (tecolote) *with ruby eyes (left); the saddle horn is wrapped with leather to protect it when the horn is used as a snubbing post when roping cattle*

SANTA BARBARA CARRIAGE AND WESTERN ART MUSEUM

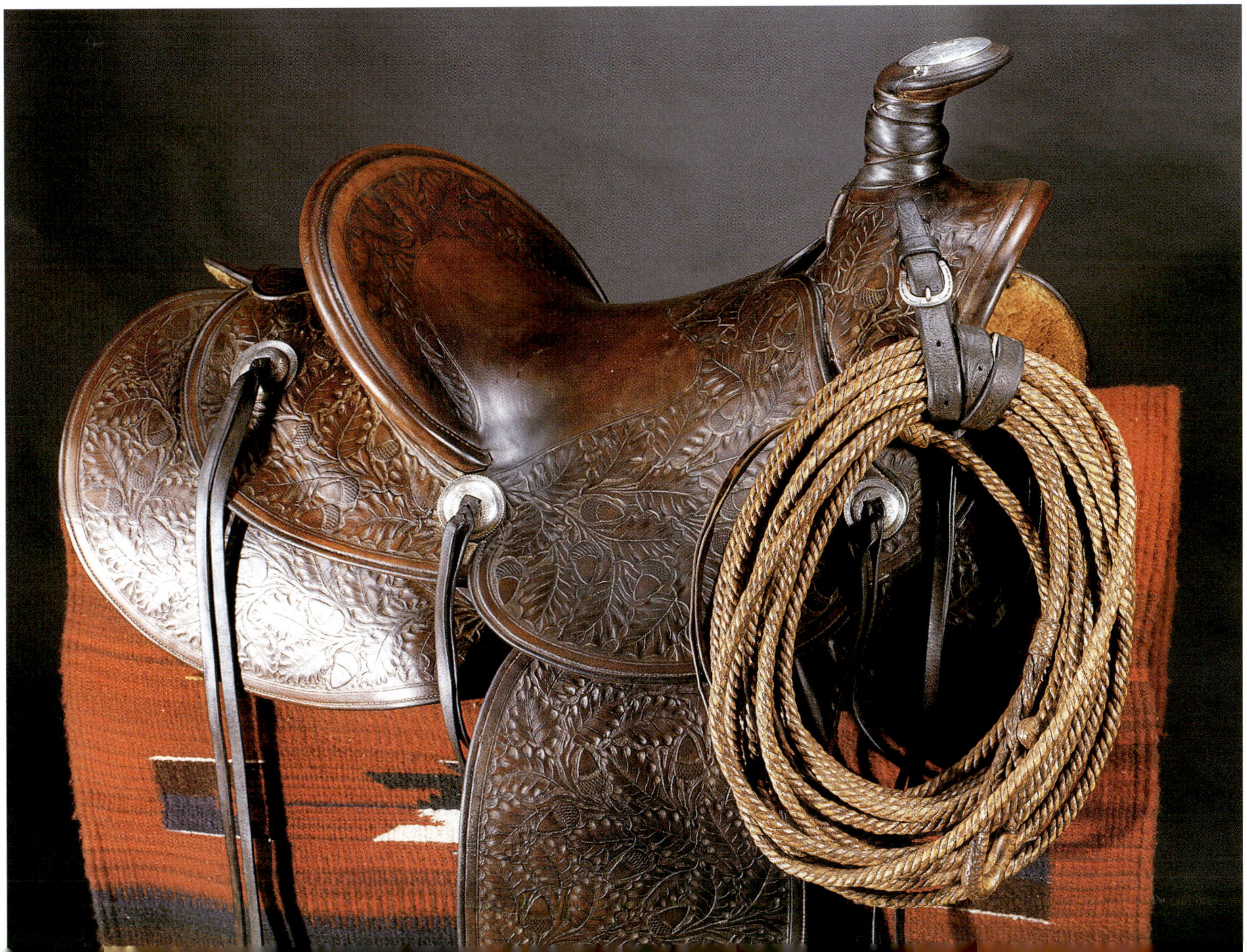

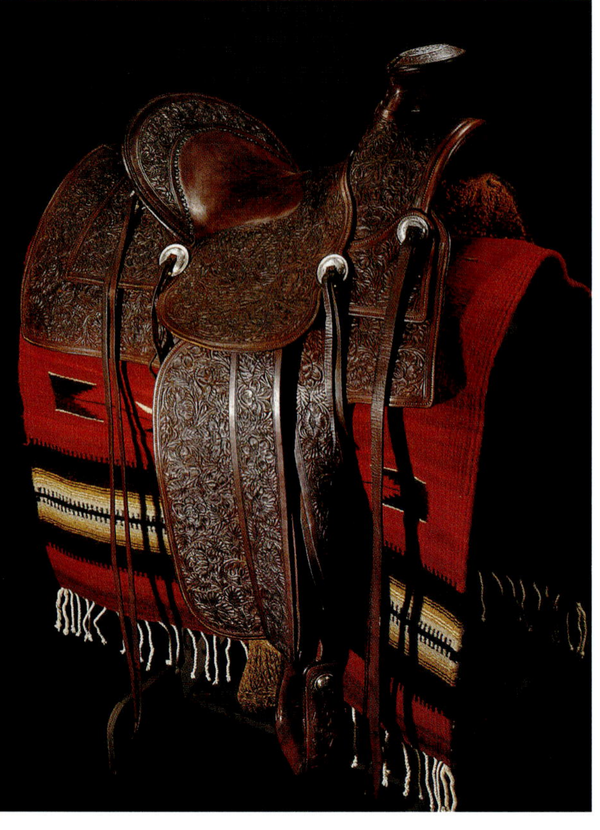

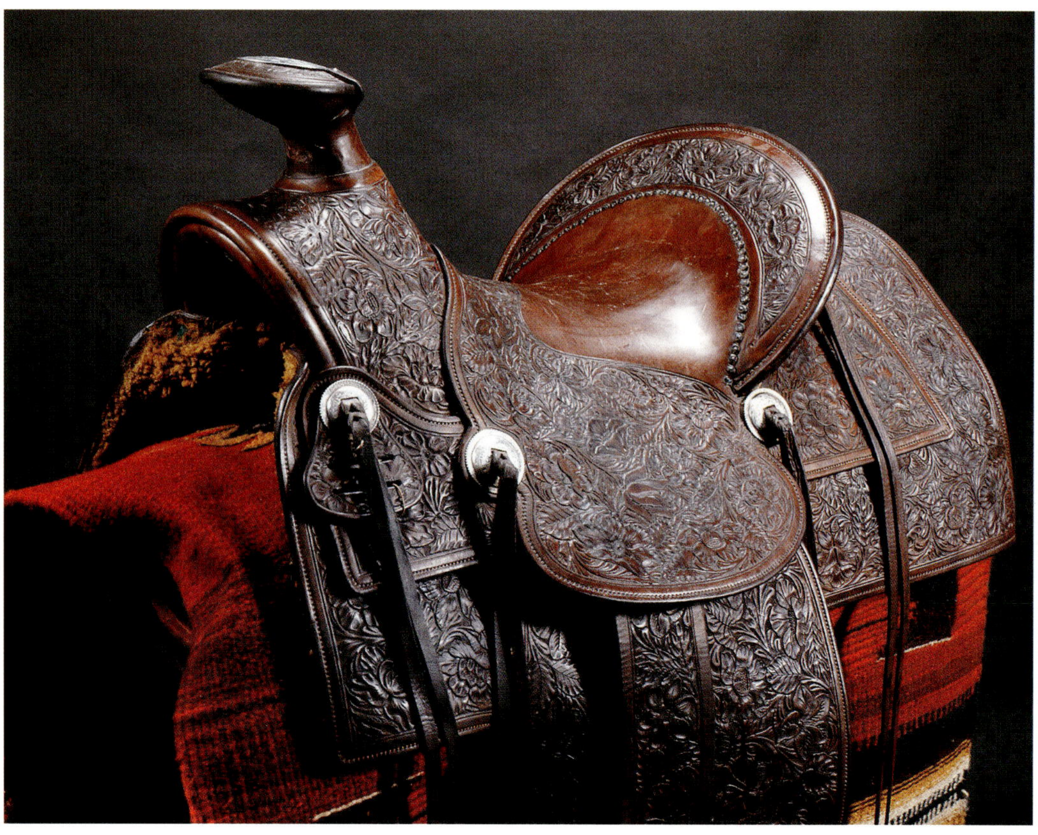

Above, left and right
Visalia Stock Saddle Co., San Francisco
Saddle, c. 1900–10, with silver horn cap, square skirts, and scalloped seat secured with decorative nails, after 1899
Santa Barbara Carriage and Western Art Museum

Opposite
W. T. Wroe and Sons, Austin
Saddle made for Chicago businessman Marshall Field II, c.1913
Fleischer Collection, Scottsdale

this same anonymous pundit praised the high-quality workmanship and ornamentation of Texas- and California-made saddles, many of which were also the products of Hispanic craftsmen.

Western stock saddle design and craftsmanship reached its zenith in California, beginning with the work of a host of talented immigrants from Mexico and Central and South America who arrived in the wake of the Gold Rush of 1849. The newcomers brought with them tools, methods, and decorative styles that differed from those of most American leatherworkers. In contrast to eastern-trained saddle makers, Hispanic carvers usually rendered the outlines of their ornamental patterns freehand instead of committing them to paper and then transferring them to the leather with an ivory point or hard lead pencil. Hispanic *talabateros* also relied on fewer tools, many times homemade from "old files or bits of steel with ends ground to the required shape."[16]

According to one knowledgeable observer, the typical California leatherworker of the 1870s developed intricate designs in high relief using only seven short implements: four creasers adjusted to cut from one to four parallel lines at a time, two three-cornered tools with bevel ends, and one wedge-shaped device for opening the leather. Each tool was gripped diagonally across the palm, steadied with the thumb and index finger, and worked with great control and precision from the wrist. In the East apprentice saddle makers were taught to manipulate their hand tools from the shoulder.

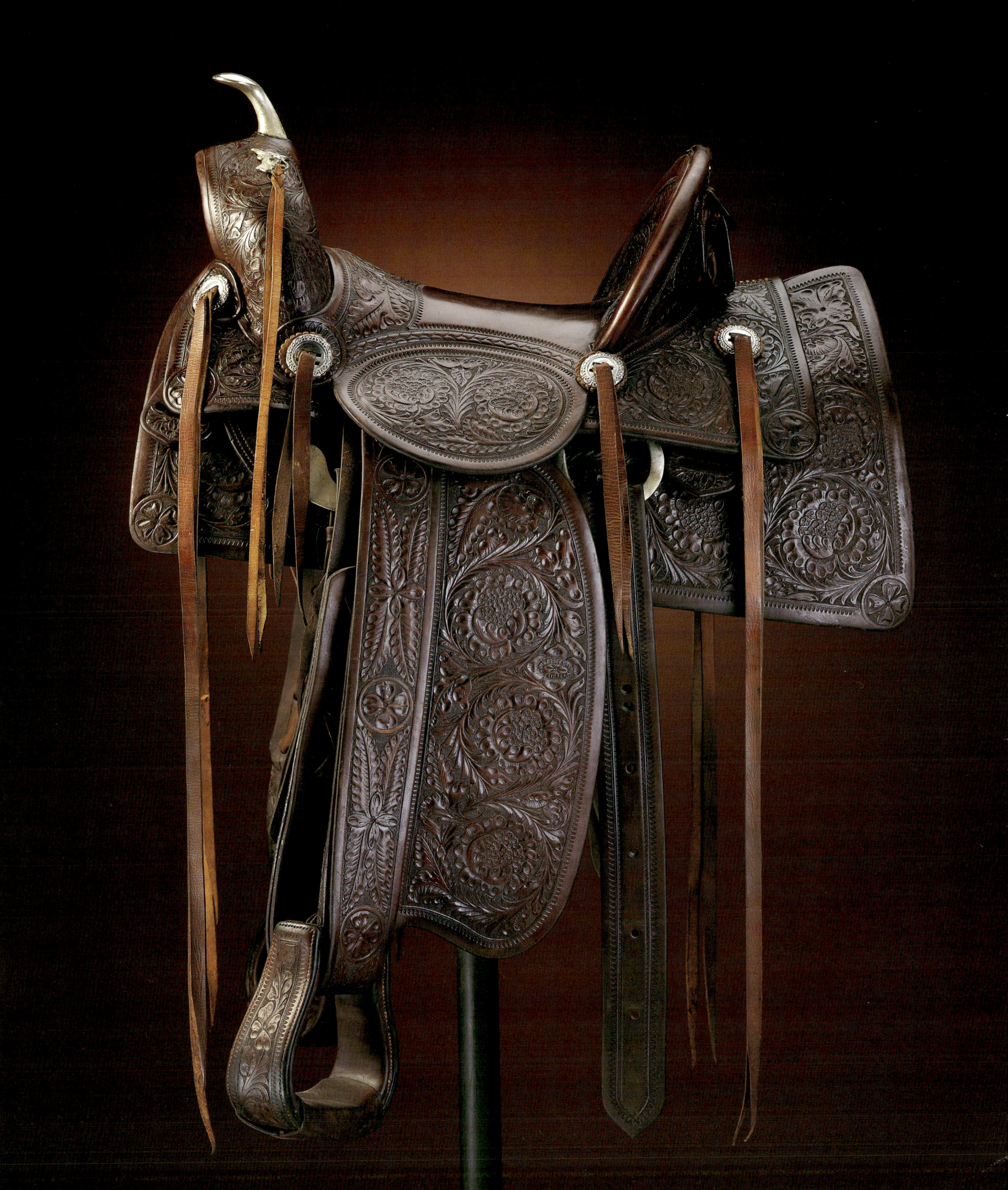

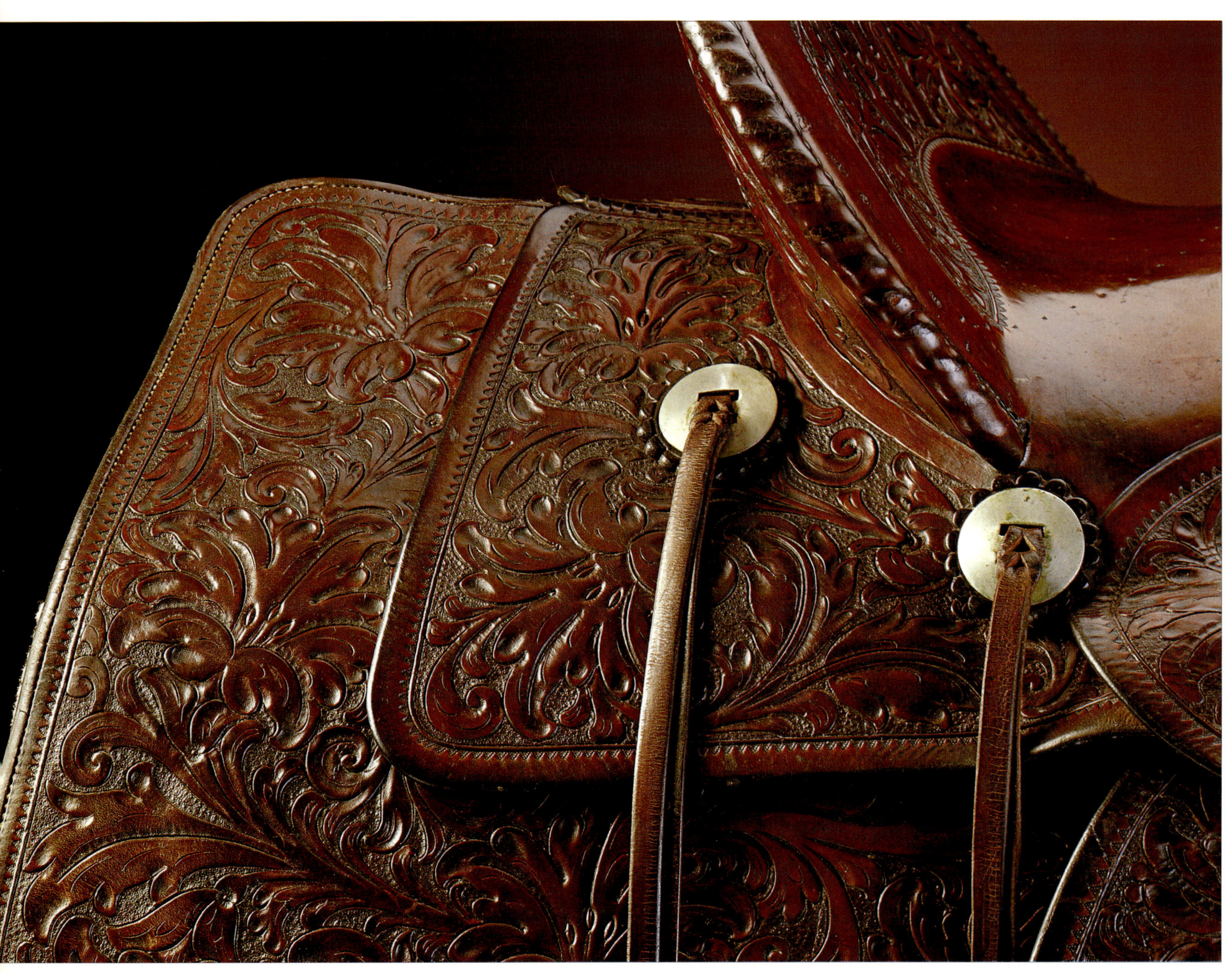

S. D. Meyers, Sweetwater, Texas Saddle, c. 1920 (opposite), with detail of rear skirt and jockey (above)
Fleischer Collection, Scottsdale

Usually used in tandem, saddle carving and stamping varied from simple, straight line and geometric borders to decorative accents on skirts, jockeys, fenders, and rigging straps to complex tableaus and floral motifs that occupied virtually the entire surface of the object. Saddle makers generally worked up border patterns first before applying interior figures. The cheapest rigs often featured a simple, stand-alone ornamental pattern on each fender rendered either in outline with an incising knife or, in the case of mass-produced work, impressed or embossed with a large die and a heavy mechanical press.

Designs on more expensive, full-stamped saddles were developed in greater detail with the help of a variety of carving and stamping tools. Checkerboard,

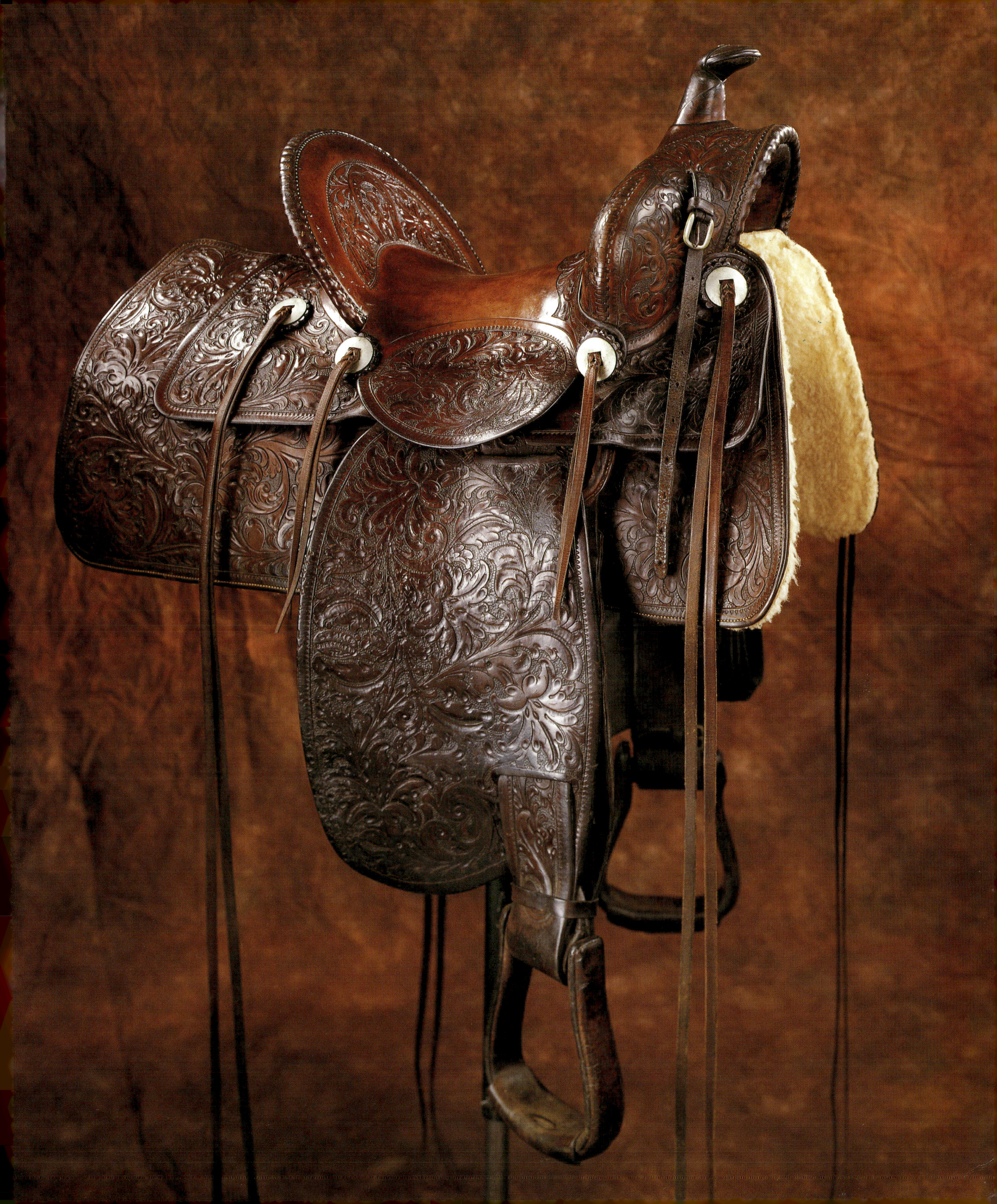

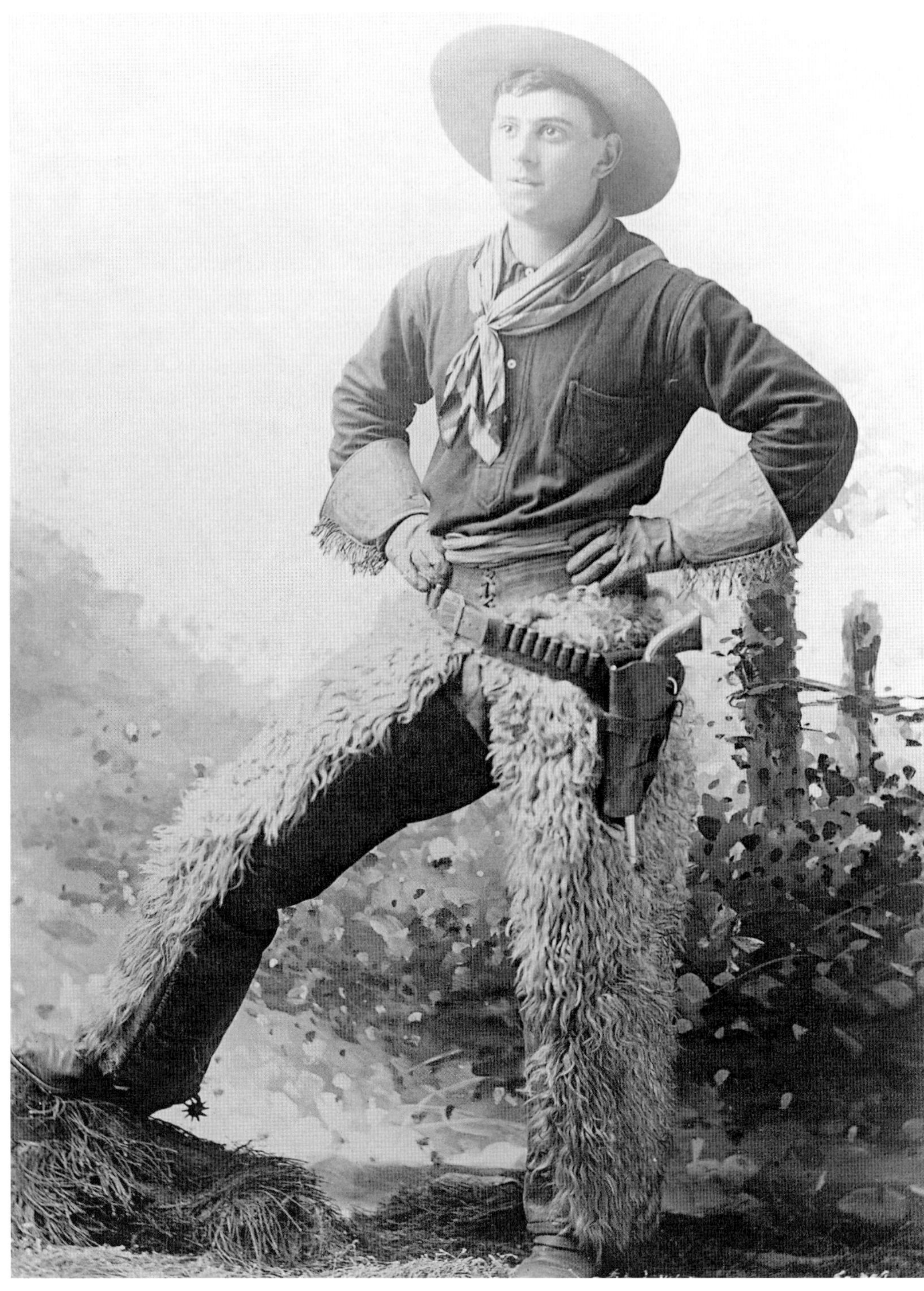

Portrait of Henry Goodman (?), sporting fringed gauntlets, wooly chaps, and a gun belt hung low on the hip, c. 1889
Cabinet photograph
5 1/2 x 3 7/8 in.
Buffalo Bill Historical Center, Cody, Wyoming, Finley A. Goodman Collection

Opposite
Mexican cartridge belt and loop holster decorated with cactus fiber embroidery
Fleischer Collection, Scottsdale

basket weave, pinwheel, and other repetitive motifs set down with a mallet and small dies, either individually or in combination, required the least skill and took the least time to apply. Leather artisans called this type of work "set stamping."

More complex pictorial effects could be achieved by widening, shading, and embellishing incised designs. Craftsman added relief to carved figures with various backgrounding tools—bevellers, shaders, seeders, veiners, and so on—equipped with heads of different shapes and surfaces.

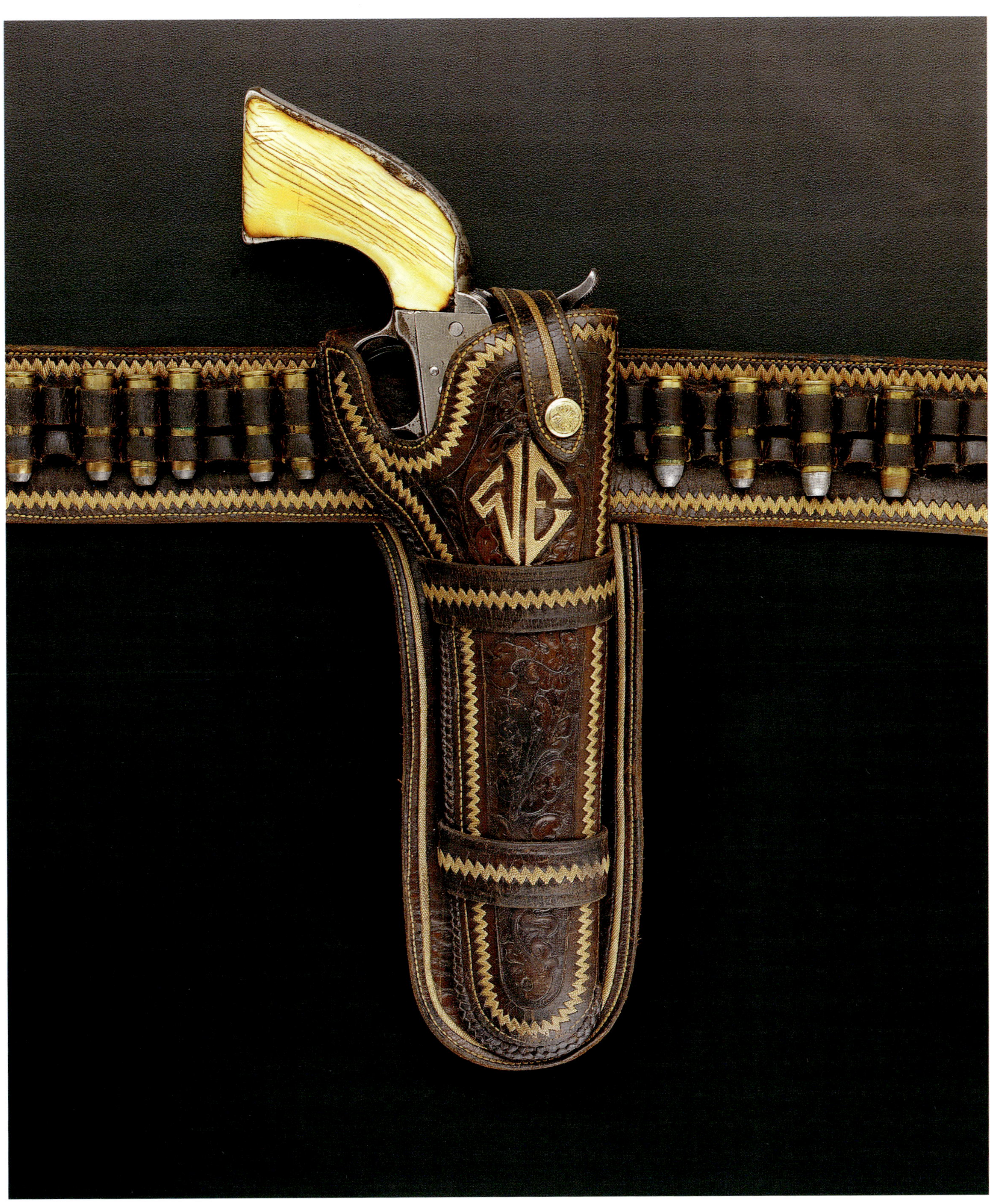

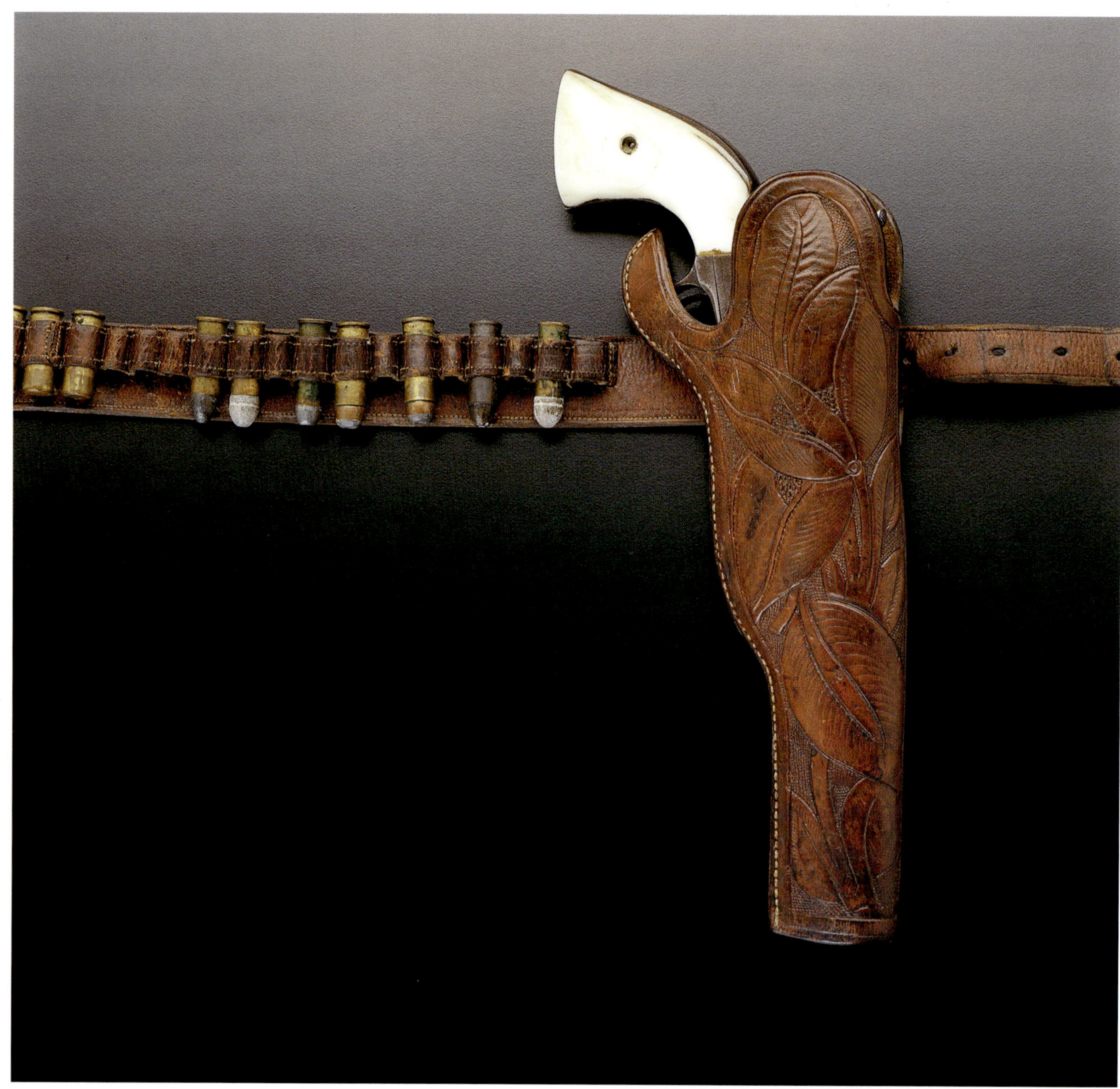

Main and Winchester,
San Francisco
California-pattern holster with contoured body, toe plug, and floral motif, 1860s
Fleischer Collection, Scottsdale

Floral carving, both drawn from nature and invented, comprised the most common style of stock saddle ornamentation. Rose patterns were the most ubiquitous. Spanish *talabateros* brought one of the oldest such designs, *la rosa de Castile* (the rose of Castile), to Mexico in the sixteenth century. Renderings of lilies, poppies, sunflowers, oak leaves, and other flora also proved popular and lent variety to designs. Late nineteenth-century trade journals sometimes carried line drawings of field and garden flowers arranged in patterns that could be transferred to leather. Popular configurations spread quickly throughout the trade.

Creative stamp hands sometimes camouflaged animals, birds, reptiles, and human figures in their floral designs. As might be expected, horses and cattle turned up most often on stock saddles. Occasionally, however, more exotic species such as lions and tigers lurked within the flora. Carvers working for the

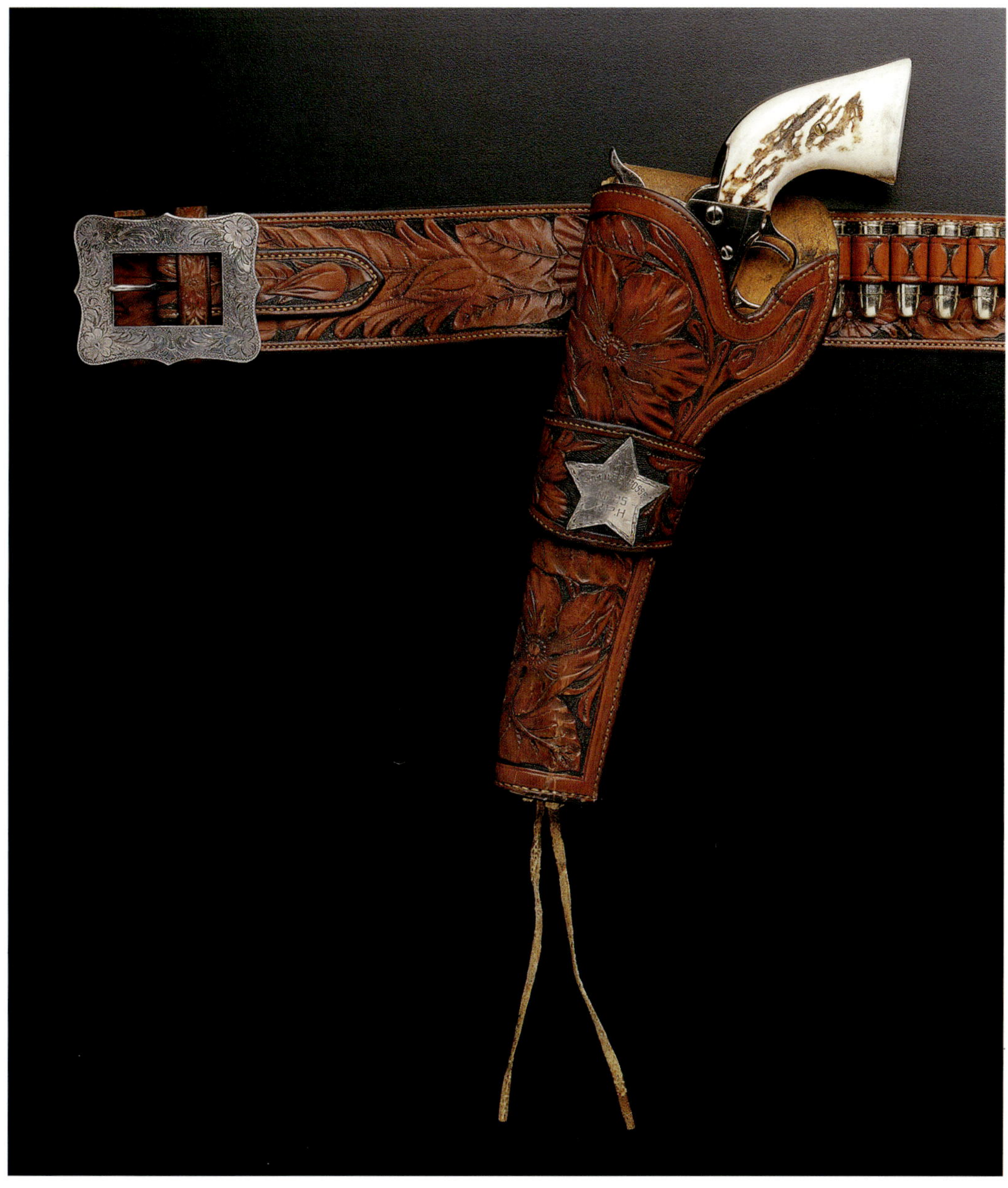

Visalia Saddle Co.,
San Francisco
Mexican loop-type holster with floral carving and metallic star
FLEISCHER COLLECTION, SCOTTSDALE

prominent San Francisco saddlery Main and Winchester even created a dapper satyr-like figure, with a bull's head on a man's suit-clad body, clutching a derby and cane in one hand.

Eagles, flags, shields, and other patriotic symbols also made their way onto saddle skirting as did portrait and full-figure carvings of women, rendered either as part of a floral montage or as stand-alone forms. The J. F. Dunn Saddlery Company, San Angelo, Texas, for example, produced a style of saddle known as the "Cattle Queen," which featured the risqué figure of a scantily clad woman in a short skirt and garters carved on the fenders. One cowboy, who had acquired such a rig, recalled his mother's scornful disapproval of the bawdy design.

The successful embellishment of saddle leather depended not only upon the skillful, creative rendering of individual elements but also the overall unity

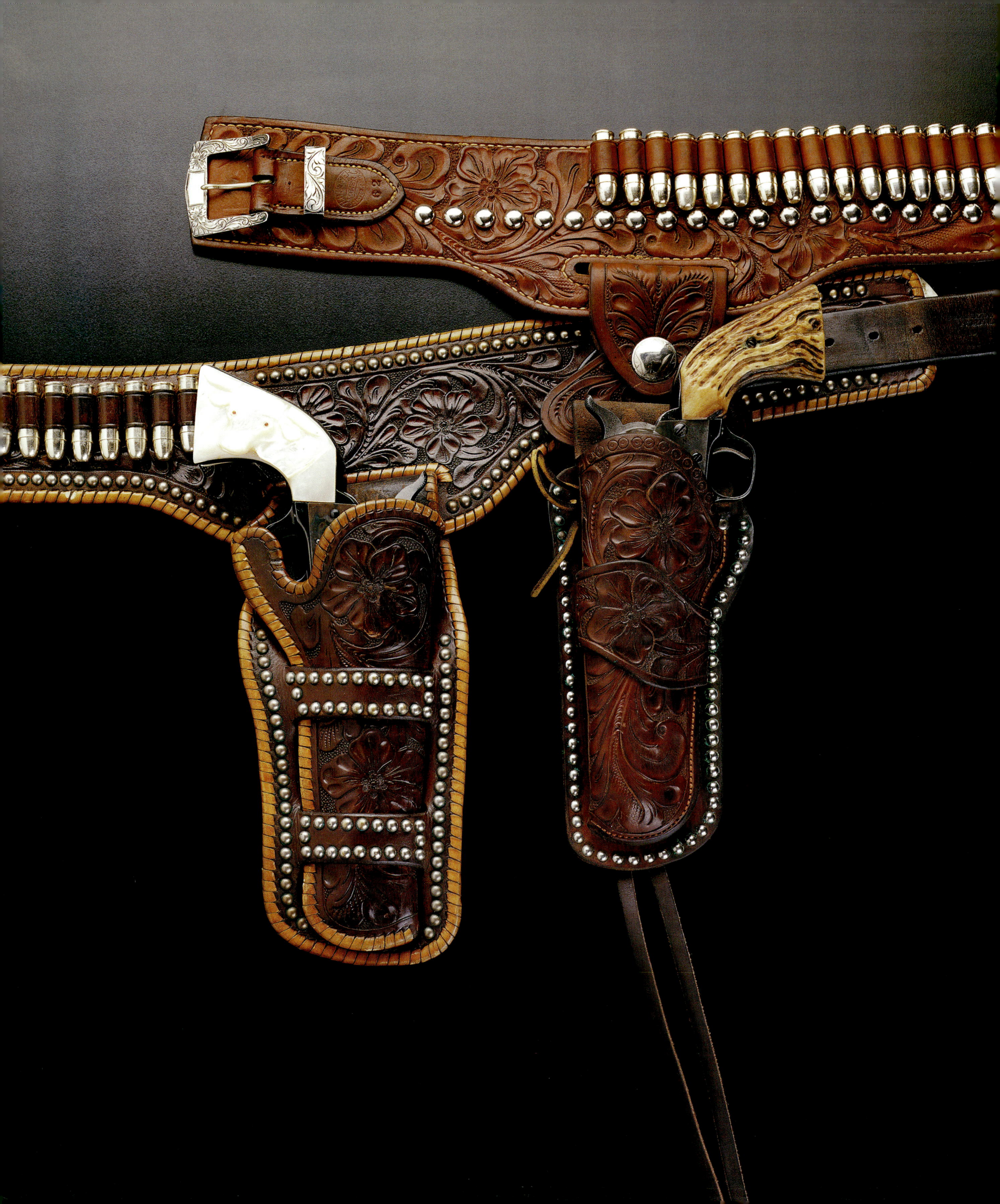

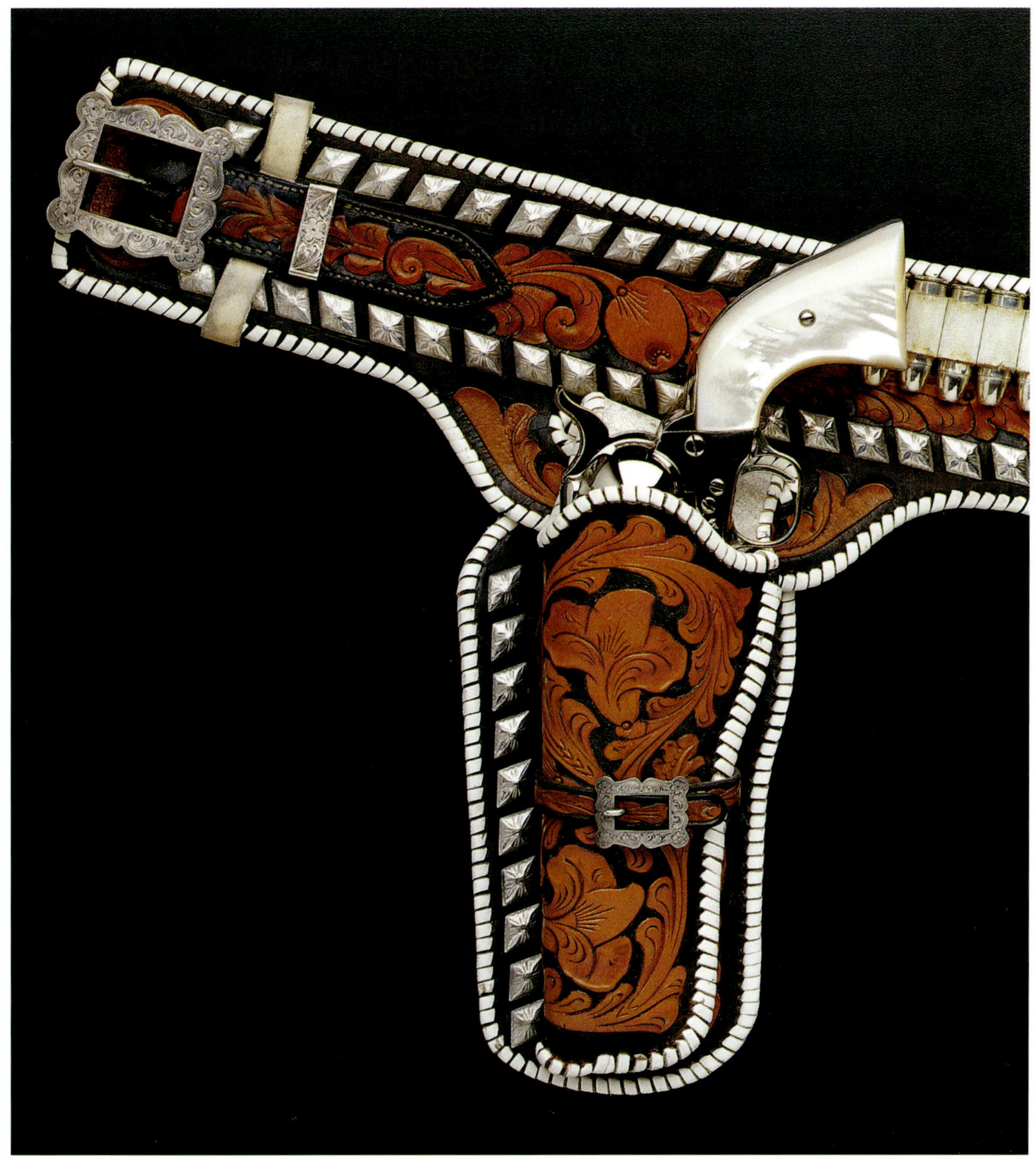

Opposite
Hermann H. Heiser, Denver
Buscadero-pattern gun belts with ranger-style buckles and Mexican loop holsters
Fleischer Collection, Scottsdale

Left
S. D. Myres, Sweetwater, Texas
Ranger-style gun belt with laced edges and floral design on belt and holsters (detail)
Fleischer Collection, Scottsdale

and symmetry of design. A primer on saddle ornamentation published in the *Harness and Carriage Journal* in 1878 counseled consistency in the choice and application of borders, rosettes, and other figures and urged stamp hands to apply motifs proportional to the size and shape of the leather surface that they covered. "If this is not done," the author cautioned, "no matter how fine the work may be, it will not be satisfactory."[17]

Although much western saddlery of the late nineteenth and early twentieth centuries was undistinguished in its design and embellishment, at least a few saddle makers became famous for beautiful and distinctive carving, stamping, and silver work. Between the 1880s and the 1930s, for example, a half-dozen shops in the coastal community of Santa Barbara, California, gained such a reputation. Wealthy Barbarenos, who spent lavishly on fine horses and tack, stimulated the creative impulses of such talented local craftsmen as Sherman Loomis, J. M.

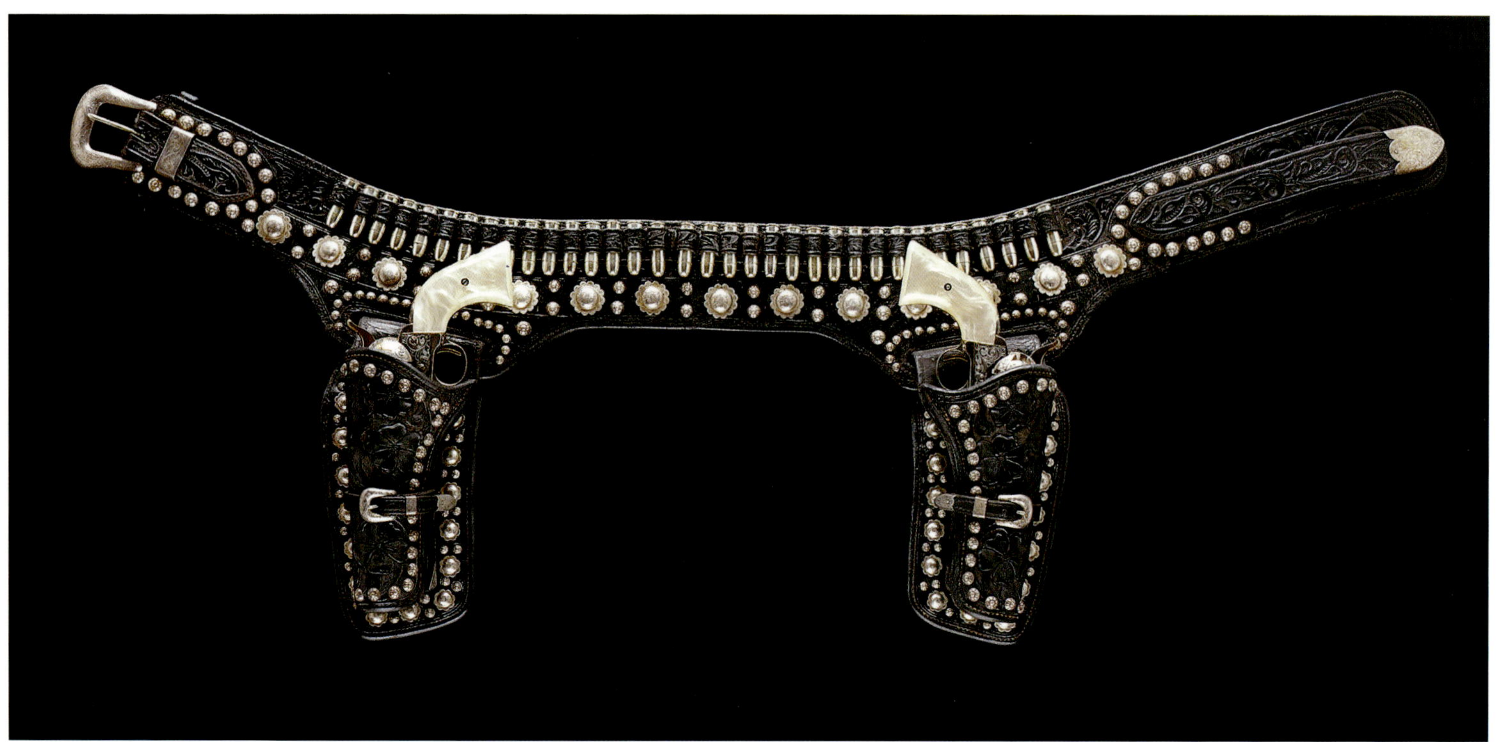

Edward H. Bohlin, Hollywood Buscadero-pattern gun belt with twin holsters, trimmed with silver conchas and secured with buckles and straps, 1930s
Fleischer Collection, Scottsdale

Forbes, and William Rafour and were rewarded with beautiful saddles replete with complex and original designs in leather and silver. "While somewhat resembling both wood carving and repoussé work," wrote one admirer of the town's leather craft in the 1890s,

> it is like neither, being wrought on the upper side, and no part of the material is cut away. No prepared patterns are used, the work being done like free-hand drawing, and the artist usually evolves his design, a fanciful and ideal mixture, as he proceeds though the same motifs are common to all. Arabesques are used almost exclusively, yet observation shows infinite variety in the free-hand floriated and foliated scrolls, and there is as much individuality as in any other art. Those familiar with the artificers can distinguish the product of each, as readily as one can distinguish paintings of different artists.[18]

The same might have been said of another influential cadre of California saddle makers who made their homes in the bustling San Joaquin Valley cow town of Visalia. Unlike Santa Barbara–made tack, which reached a relatively limited southern California market, the strong, statuesque rigs produced in the shops of D. E. Walker, Jesus Salazar, and other Visalia makers became famous all over the West. Working in relative isolation, Visalia craftsmen elevated the carving and stamping of saddle leather to a seldom-surpassed level of excellence, creating exquisite and imaginative floral and leaf patterns that influenced the entire trade for decades to come. The impact of Visalia-style saddlery, however, was due not only to its durability, comfort, and look, but also to the spread of California-bred vaqueros and cattle into the Northwest, Great Basin, and northern Great Plains in the 1870s and 1880s.

D. E. Walker, the largest and most successful of the Visalia makers, relocated his Visalia Stock Saddle Company to San Francisco in the late 1880s, in hopes of further extending the reputation of his products while enjoying the commercial advantages of a more urban locale. A major source of California saddlery since the 1850s, San Francisco already was home to several major wholesale houses including Main and Winchester, J. C. Johnson, and L. D. Stone. Besides generating mass-produced goods for the world market, each of these companies also offered a high-end line of embellished saddles, some of them crafted in the Visalia style. San Francisco's preeminence as a saddle-making center, however, lasted only into the early twentieth century before suffering irreparable damage in the earthquake and fire that destroyed much of the city in 1906.

Edward H. Bohlin, Hollywood Buscadero-pattern gun belt with single holster, with fence and bronc rider design on belt, metal spots on edges of belt and holster, and silver buckle with keeper and tip
FLEISCHER COLLECTION, SCOTTSDALE

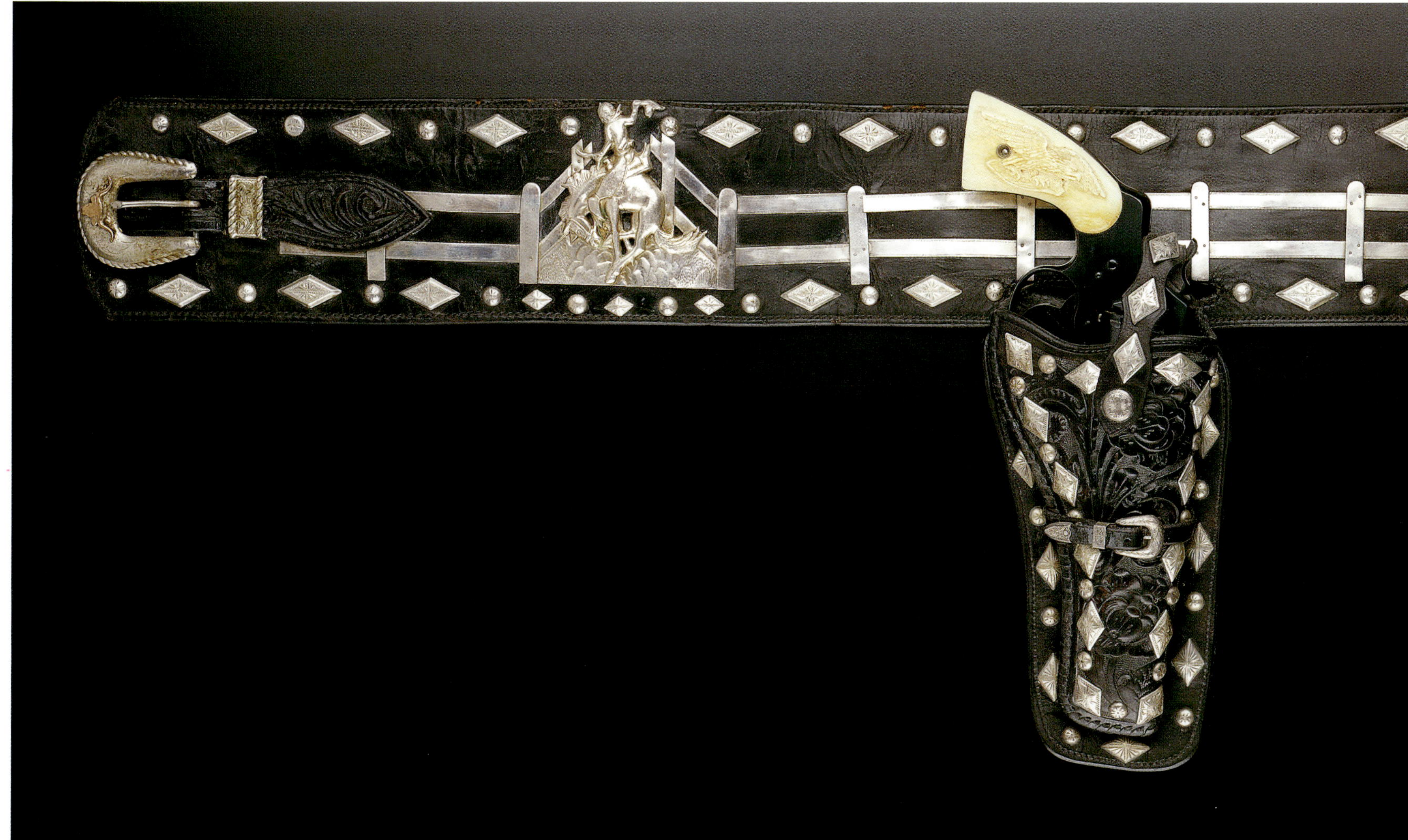

By this time several saddle houses outside of California also were beginning to gain accolades for fine leatherwork. Stamp hands in the employ of Phoenix saddler Newton Porter were among the most outstanding. Porter, who had moved to the Southwest in 1895 after pursuing his trade for two decades in Texas and Washington, found skilled carvers in relative abundance within the local Hispanic and Mexican immigrant populations. Thanks to cheap labor, a strong mail-order business, and the expansion of tourism and dude ranching in Arizona, Porter and his sons Earl and Fred resisted the prevailing trend toward mechanization. "Our saddles are all made by hand," Fred Porter proudly informed historian J. Evetts Haley in 1936, "flower carving all being free hand work and are made in the same manner by hand as the saddles made by my Father in Texas in the 70's and 80's."[19] The development around 1900 of the swivel knife, a tool that facilitated the cutting of curves in leather, expanded the range of designs available to skilled leather carvers throughout the West.

Samuel Dale Myres, another staunch advocate of handmade saddles, spent several years in apprenticeship and piecework before buying a small saddlery in Sweetwater, Texas, in 1898. In the half-century that followed, Myres, a talented designer and leather carver and even better self-promoter, became the best-known saddle maker in Texas. He often enhanced the relief of his trademark floral and oak leaf patterns by juxtaposing them against dyed backgrounds.

Some of Myres's most complex designs incorporated details from the western paintings of Charles M. Russell. Although not the only carver to translate the work of the Montana cowboy artist onto saddle leather, Myres made the best and most extensive use of Russell's famous imagery. In addition to his own substantial leatherworking skills, usually reserved for special projects, Myres employed and trained some of the finest saddle makers and stamp hands in the West.

The trend toward larger and heavier saddles during the last two decades of the nineteenth century aided S. D. Myres and his more artistic-minded colleagues in their quest to carve sometimes-elaborate scenes of western life on skirting leather. Not everyone, however, appreciated tableau-style renderings. California cowboy artist and critic Joe Mora, for example, dismissed such efforts as "just so many demonstrations and not designs. . . ."[20]

The advent of the twentieth century brought new and difficult challenges to western saddle makers. Advancing labor and material prices and the steady erosion of the saddle and harness market by automobiles forced many in the trade out of business. Most of those who remained moved more aggressively to develop other product lines.

Some turned to "art leather," and began stamping and carving belts, purses, cigar and card cases, picture frames, shopping bags, and other products out of light- and middleweight saddle skirting. Montana saddle maker A. L. Furstnow described such goods to his catalog customers as

Opposite
Edward H. Bohlin, Hollywood
Three Buscadero-pattern gun belts with extensive floral carving and stamping; holster on the left featuring an unusual open body design trimmed with contrasting lacing; holster and belt on the right featuring a filigreed floral pattern against a dyed background
FLEISCHER COLLECTION, SCOTTSDALE

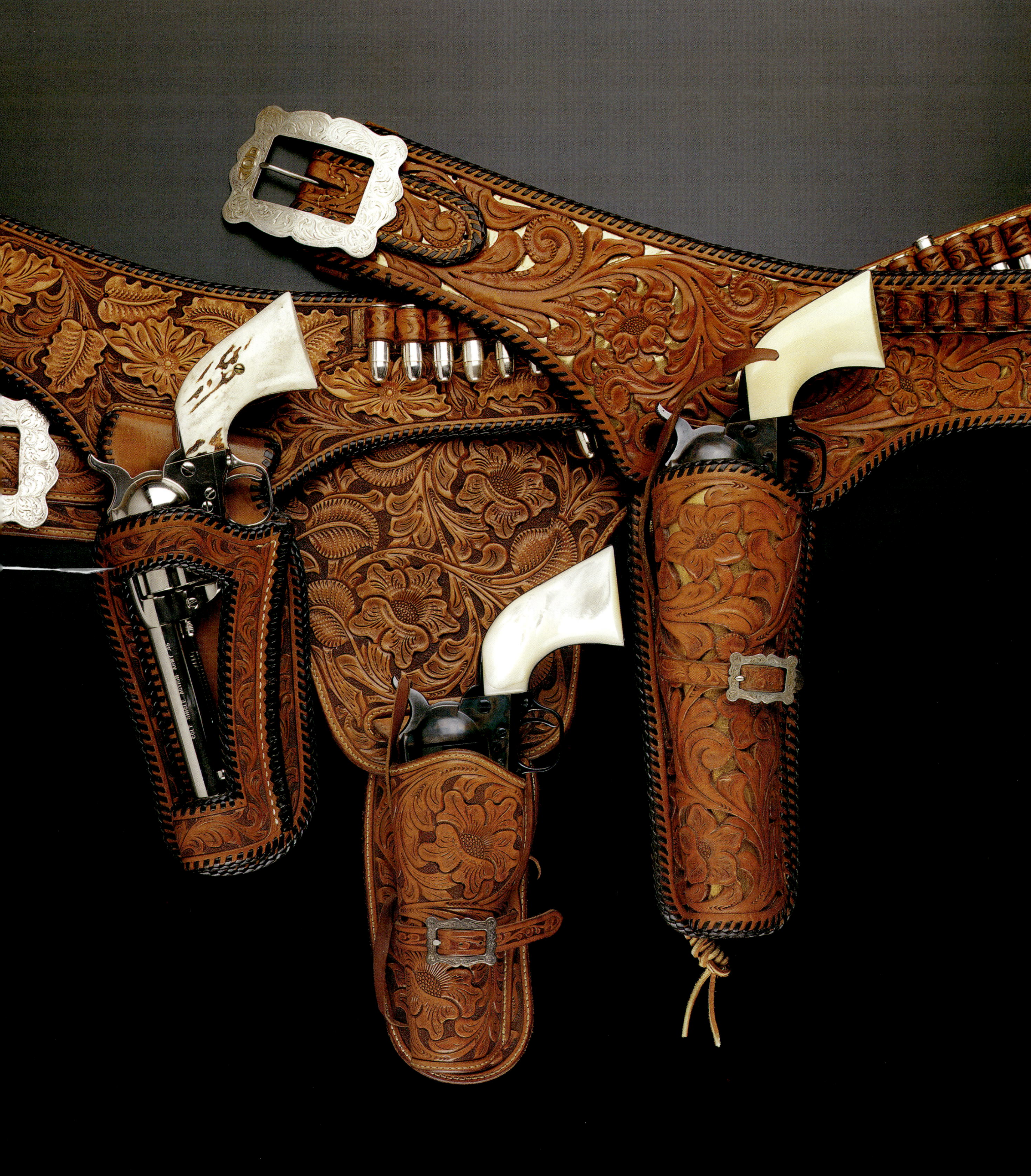
COLT SINGLE ACTION ARMY .45

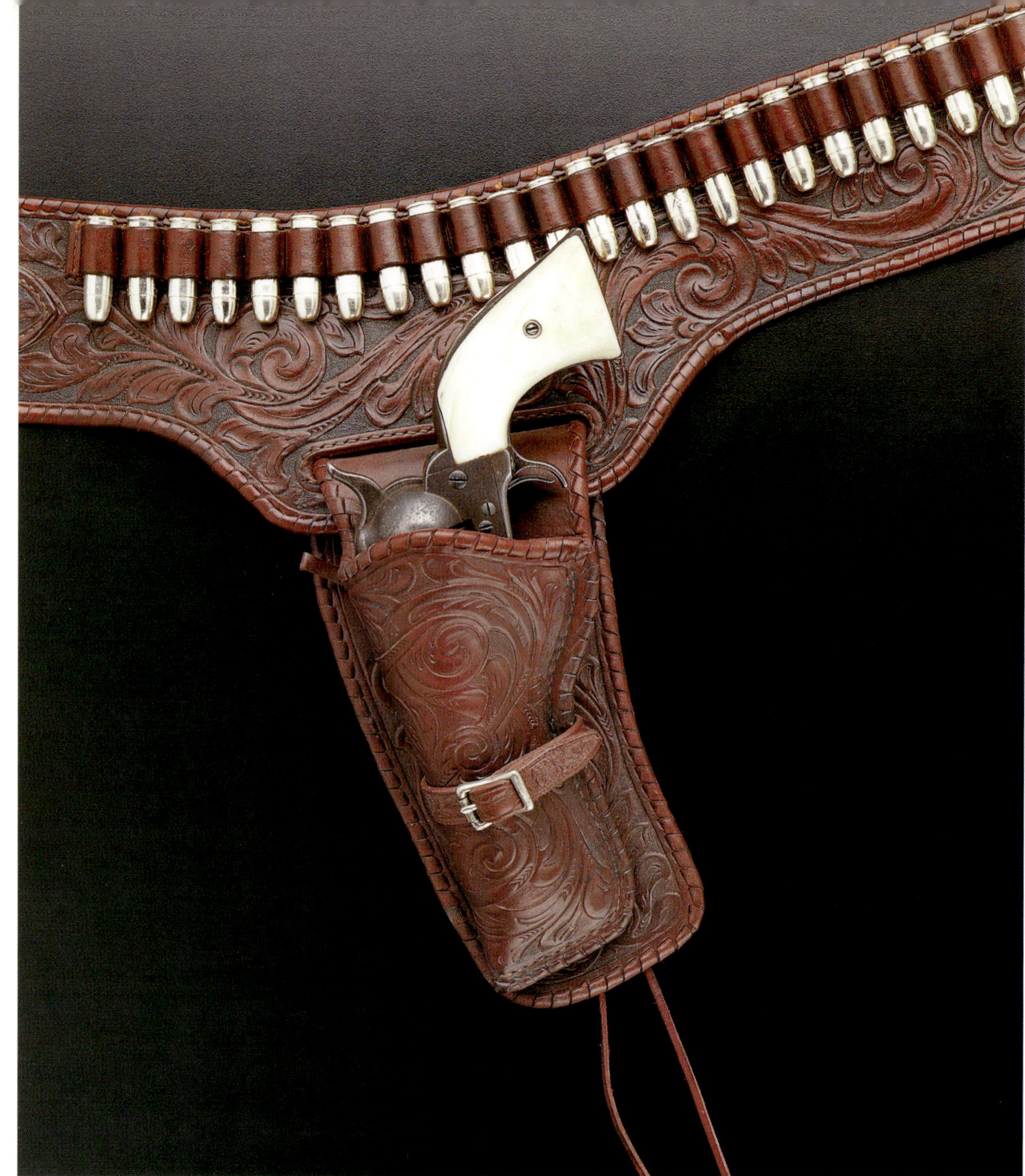

Edward H. Bohlin. Hollywood Buscadero-pattern gun belt and holster with laced edges and buckle and strap
FLEISCHER COLLECTION, SCOTTSDALE

> ...works of art in the truest sense. Although when art is spoken of we instinctly [sic] think of sculpture and painting, these, while being the highest, are by no means the only forms of art. One who has the instinct for the beautiful and the ability to bring out his ideal of beauty in any substance, produces a work of art.[21]

In California a few larger saddle houses and individual craftsmen had been offering art leather to residents and tourists at least since the early 1880s. While on a tour of the West Coast in 1883, Princess Louise of Great Britain helped popularize such handwork by commissioning some floral stamped belts and portfolios from a Santa Barbara saddle maker. By the turn of the twentieth century, the inventory of carved leather merchandise produced by San Francisco–based Main and Winchester was so extensive that it warranted a separate catalog. The market for such goods was strongest among tourists in the Southwest.

At least two saddle makers, however, found gun leather more profitable than art leather in the early decades of the twentieth century. Hermann H. Heiser of Denver and S. D. Myres, who moved his operation from Sweetwater to El Paso

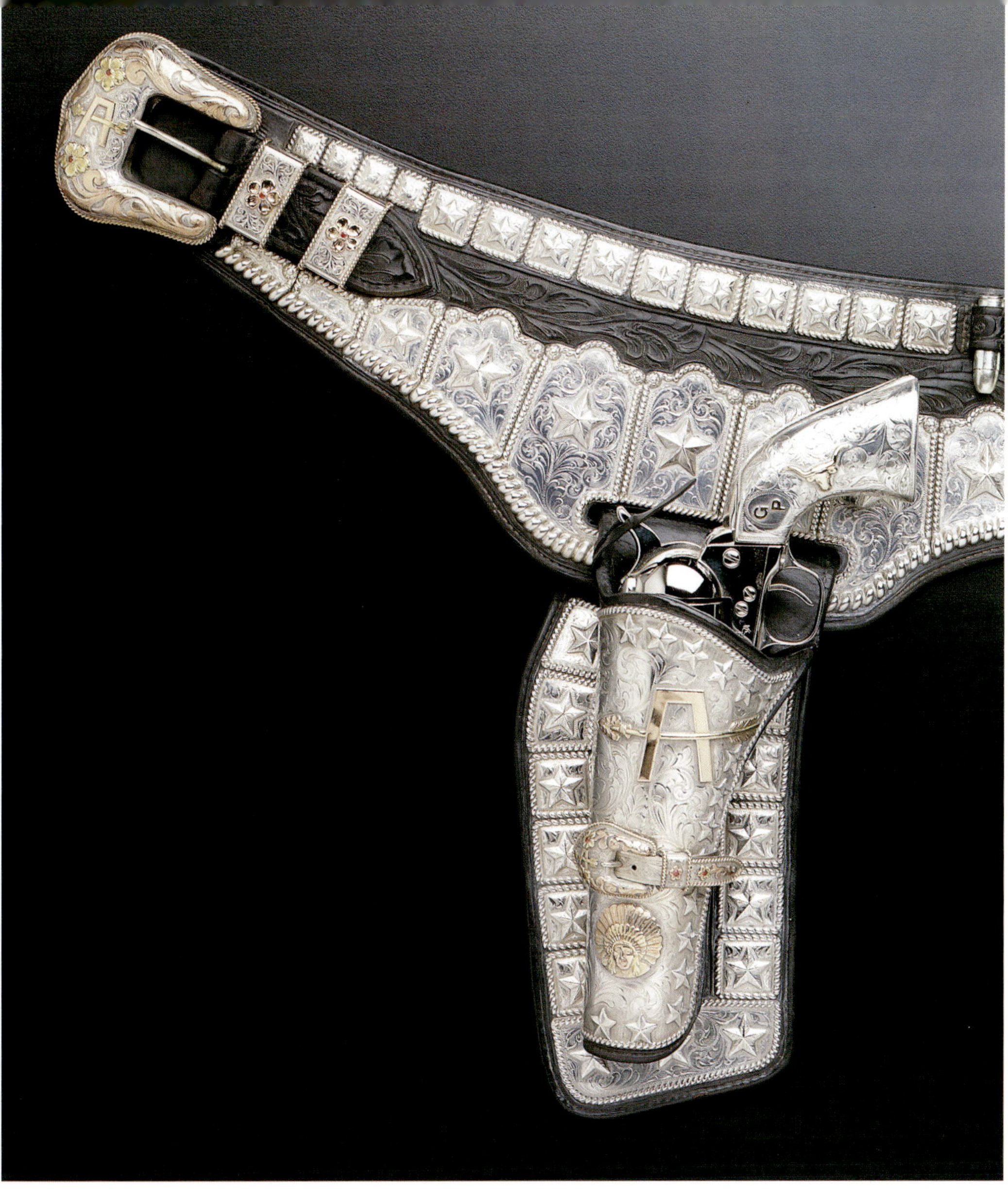

Edward H. Bohlin, Hollywood
Silver-mounted Buscadero-pattern gun belt with engraved silver- and gold-encased twin holsters, made to match the parade saddle of Leo Ahrenholtz, 1950s (detail)
FLEISCHER COLLECTION, SCOTTSDALE

in 1920 in search of cheaper labor and materials, capitalized on the steady demand for holsters and gun belts among civilians, law enforcement officers, and the military.

The crafting of pistol holsters and rifle scabbards from saddle skirting had long been a part of the repertoire of many western leatherworkers. In the 1850s, for example, West Coast saddle makers had introduced the "California pattern" holster, a style that differed significantly from the prevailing eastern and military forms. The new type consisted of a slim, formfitting holster body, recurved at the throat and looped at the back to form a narrow slot through which a belt could be inserted. A toe plug at the bottom of the holster protected the pistol barrel from dirt.

California pattern holsters exhibited the same types of embellishment as other leather goods coming from western saddleries. Dyed borders, incised or embossed floral designs rendered in outline, and more elaborate patterns created from thread and plant fiber embroidery comprised the most common motifs.

In the 1870s the "Mexican loop" holster supplanted the California pattern as the holster of choice in the West. The new design, which coincided with the advent

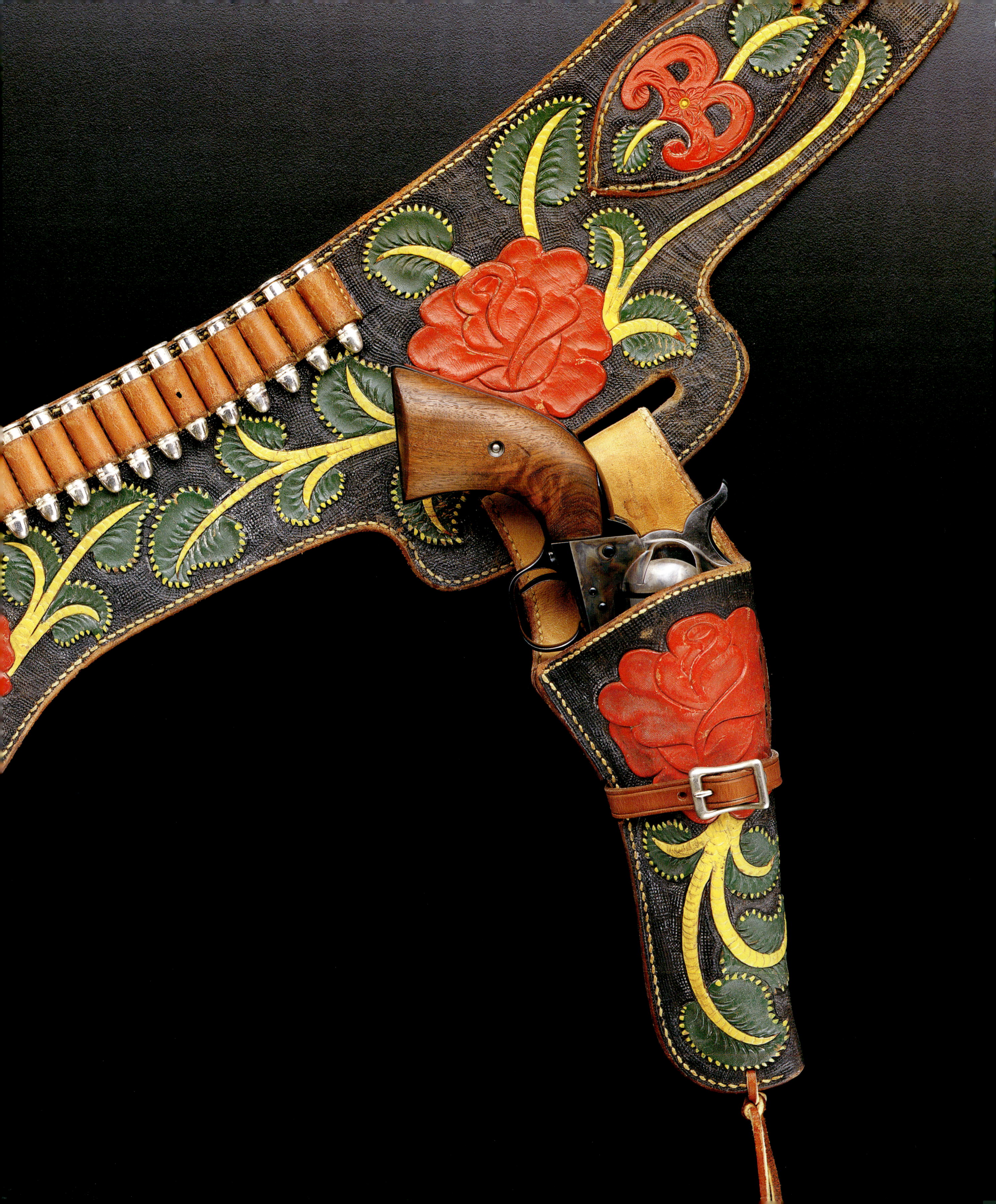

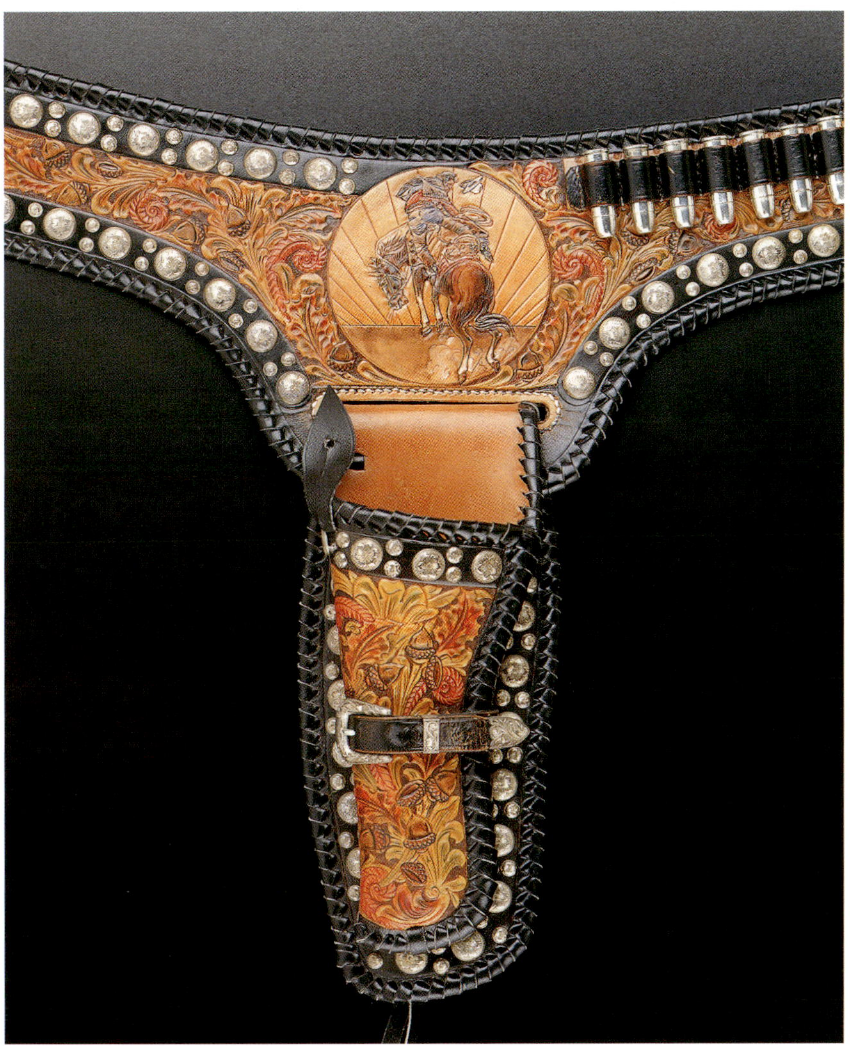

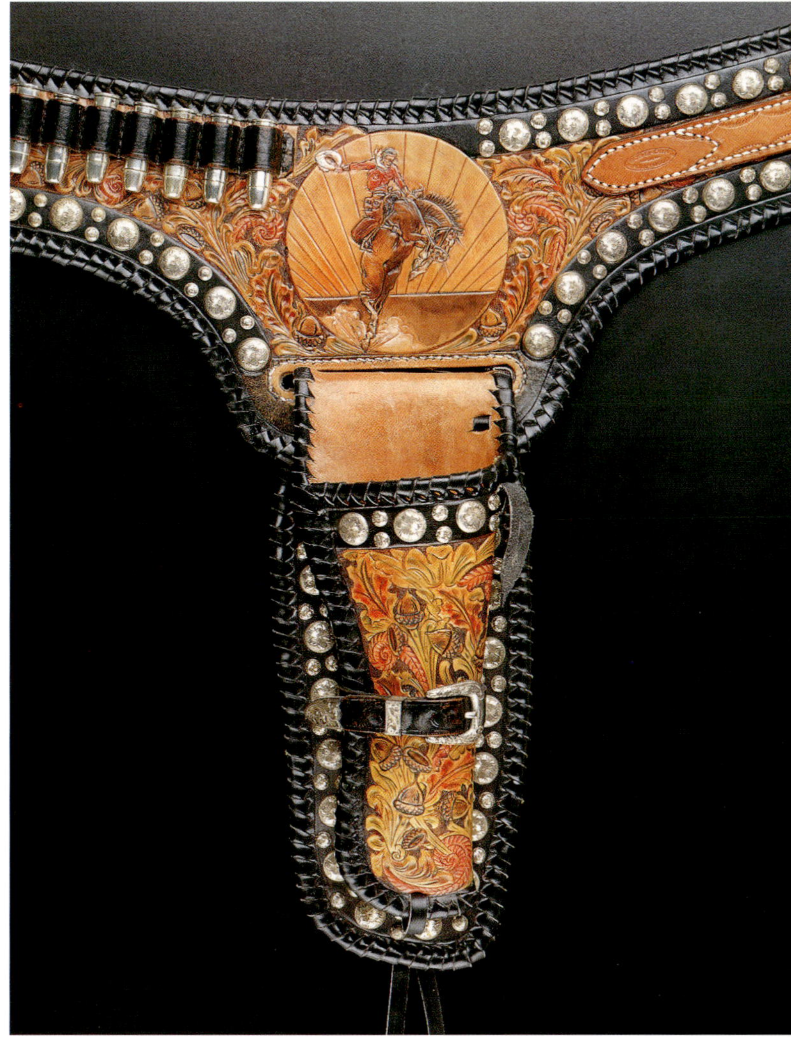

of metallic cartridge ammunition and heavy cartridge belts, consisted of a holster body secured to an integral back panel or skirt by means of one or more integral or riveted loops. The skirt of the holster appeared in several configurations: full or partial, broad or contoured. The loops often took on interesting shapes as well. Heavy carving, silver conchas, and contrasting leather lacing decorated the most ornate examples.

Two popular regional variations of the Mexican loop pattern eventually emerged, both designed to help keep the holster in place in the loop(s) when the pistol was pulled. Wyoming saddle maker Frank A. Meanea, who pioneered the Cheyenne variant, added a slight swell in the contour of the main seam of the holster body. The Texas "jockstrap" type, developed in the 1890s, featured a T-shaped loop that attached to the sides and bottom of the holster. Makers often lined their holsters with smooth materials including glove leather, felt, flannel, and chamois.

From 1880 to about 1920, prominent Denver saddle maker H. H. Heiser was the preeminent producer and wholesaler of gun leather in the West. By 1910

Above, left and right
Gun belt with twin holsters, two-tone leather with bucking bronco designs above holsters; the figure of the bronc rider on the left is taken from Charles M. Russell's watercolor Bronc to Breakfast *(1908)*
Fleischer Collection, Scottsdale

Opposite
Buscadero-pattern gun belt with twin holsters and dyed vine-and-leaf–pattern stamping
Fleischer Collection, Scottsdale

he was offering a separate catalog of such goods to a list of customers that included not only western retailers but also such eastern sporting goods dealers as Abercrombie and Fitch of New York. An innovator in gun leather design and fabrication, Heiser invented a quick draw holster and pioneered the use of wood and cast metal patterns in shaping holster leather to a specific make and model of pistol. He lavished some of his most expensive western gun leather with the same distinctive floral carved patterns seen on his saddles.

The volume production of holsters and gun belts helped rescue the economic fortunes of Myres after his Sweetwater shop burned in 1919 and he fell deeply into debt. Several law enforcement agencies, including the Texas Rangers, the FBI, and the U.S. Border Patrol and Immigration Service eventually adopted some of his designs. Myres and Texas Ranger John R. Hughes collaborated on the "buscadero" style of holster, which hung from a slot in the gun belt rather than around it and was secured to the wearer's thigh with a leather thong. The buscadero pattern was widely adopted by cowboy actors and parade participants in the 1920s and 1930s. Frequently embellished with intricate carving, engraved silver, and contrasting leather lacing and fringe, such show rigs were often part of a matching ensemble that included vests, chaps, gauntlets, and horse tack.

No one made more fancy gun leather used in Hollywood movies than Robert E. Lee "Bob" Brown, a multitalented artisan who some called the "Leonardo of Leather." During the course of a career that began in 1934 and spanned more than sixty years, Brown fashioned distinctive holsters and gun belts for such cowboy stars as John Wayne, Gary Cooper, Gregory Peck, Randolph Scott, Alan Ladd, Montgomery Clift, William Boyd, and Bill Elliott, among others. He operated a leather shop on Hollywood Boulevard, made more than fifty silver mounted saddles used in the Tournament of Roses Parade, designed silver and gold buckles for McCabe silversmiths, and served as a staff artist for famed calendar maker Brown & Bigelow. He also created many leatherworking tools that subsequently became standard in the trade. Because his skills were not always sufficiently remunerative, however, Brown also served as a Superior Court Bailiff and Deputy Sheriff in Los Angeles County from 1952 to 1970. In recognition of his many contributions as a talented designer of western gear, Brown received a special Directors' Award from the National Cowboy and Western Heritage Museum in 2001, when he was ninety.

Although the popularity of western films, rodeos, dude ranching, and pleasure riding encouraged a higher degree of saddle embellishment in the 1920s and 1930s than ever before, carved leather was often overshadowed by an abundance of elaborate hand-chased and repoussé silver mounts. The flurry of creativity that characterized the show saddle era, however, was relatively short lived. With the passing of many experienced craftsmen and with relatively few apprentices entering the trade, stylistic innovation waned during the 1940s and early 1950s. Saddle architecture, driven more by the demands of rodeo competitors and recreational

Opposite
The Bohlin Company
Saddle, 1990s
FLEISCHER COLLECTION, SCOTTSDALE

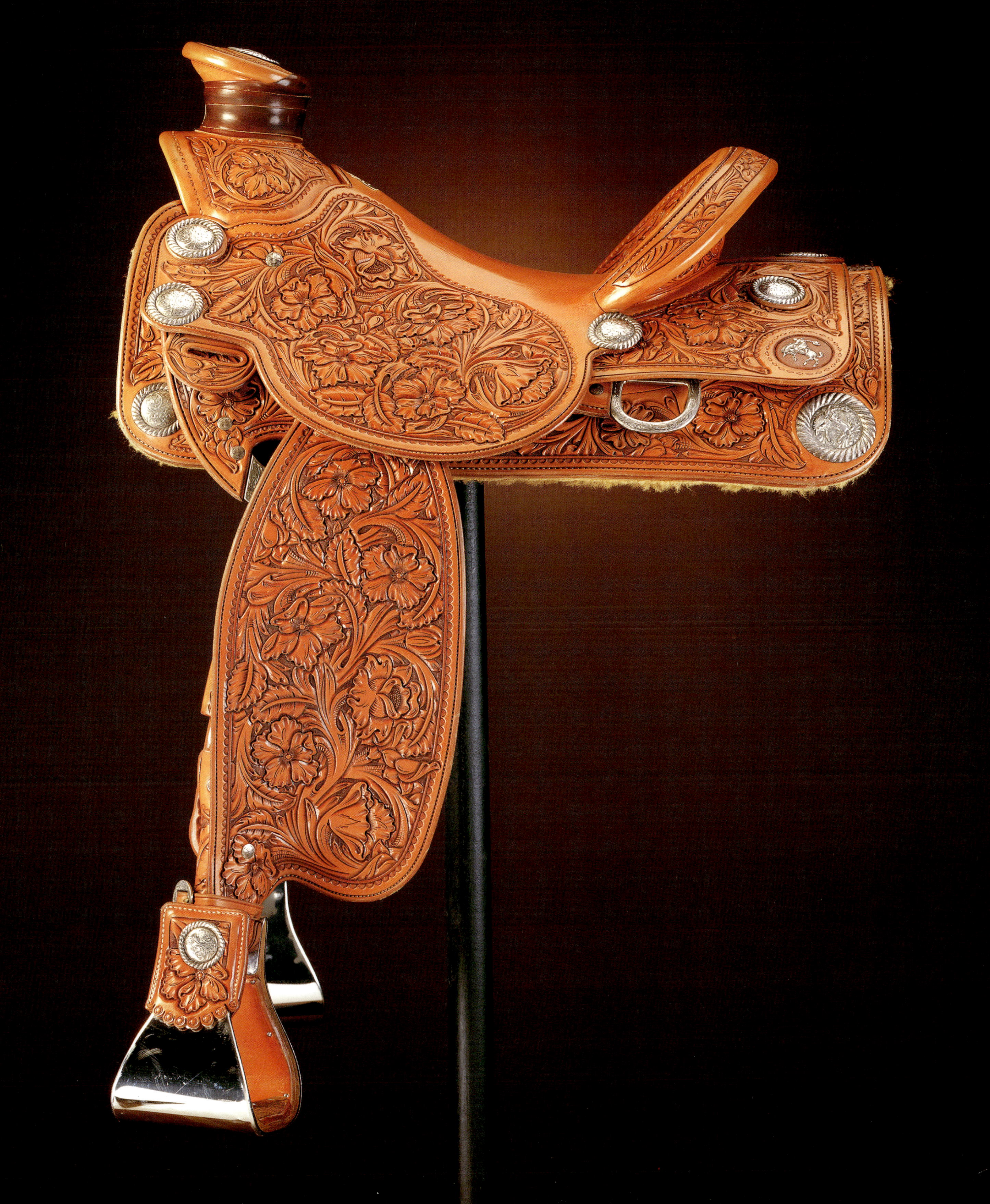

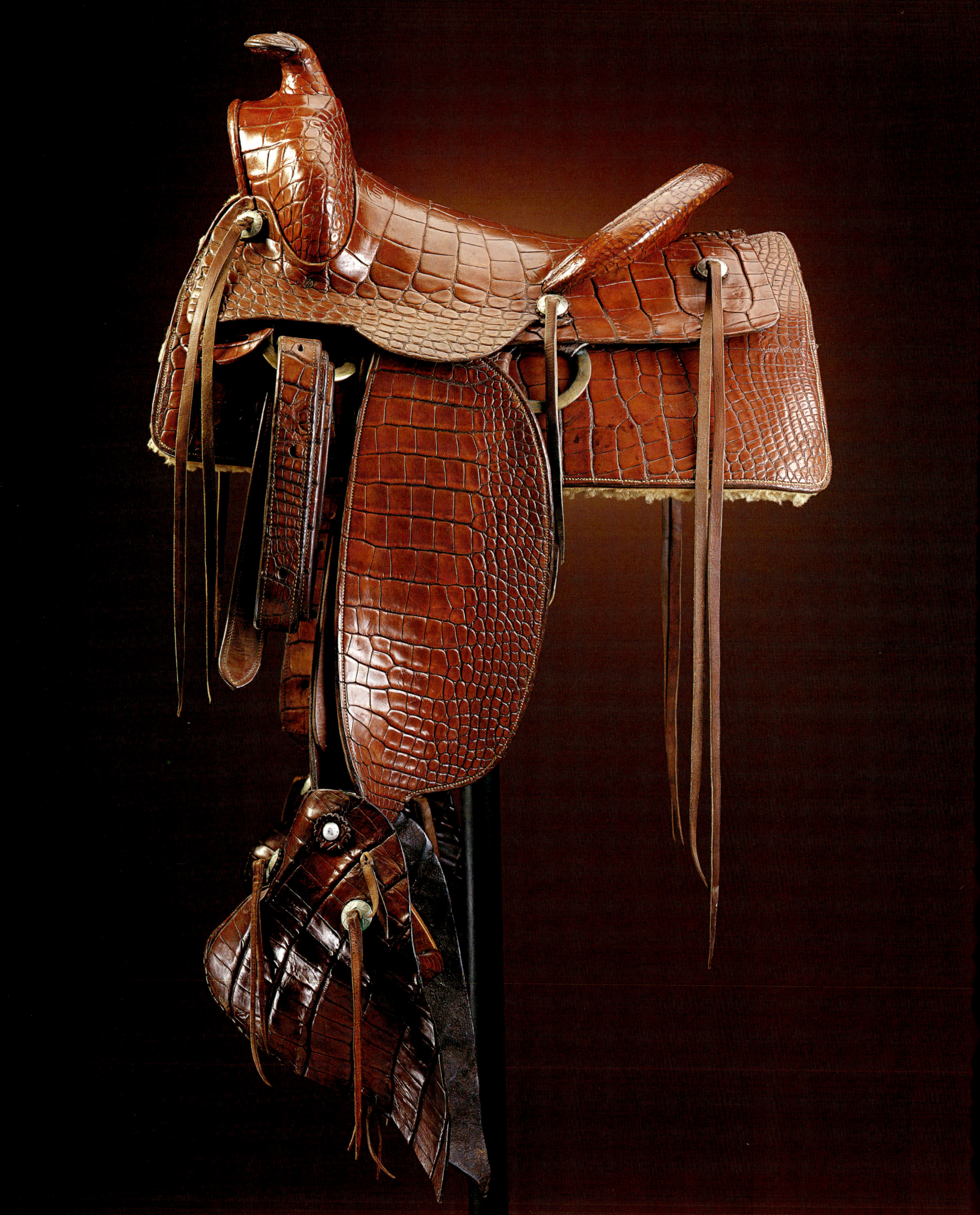

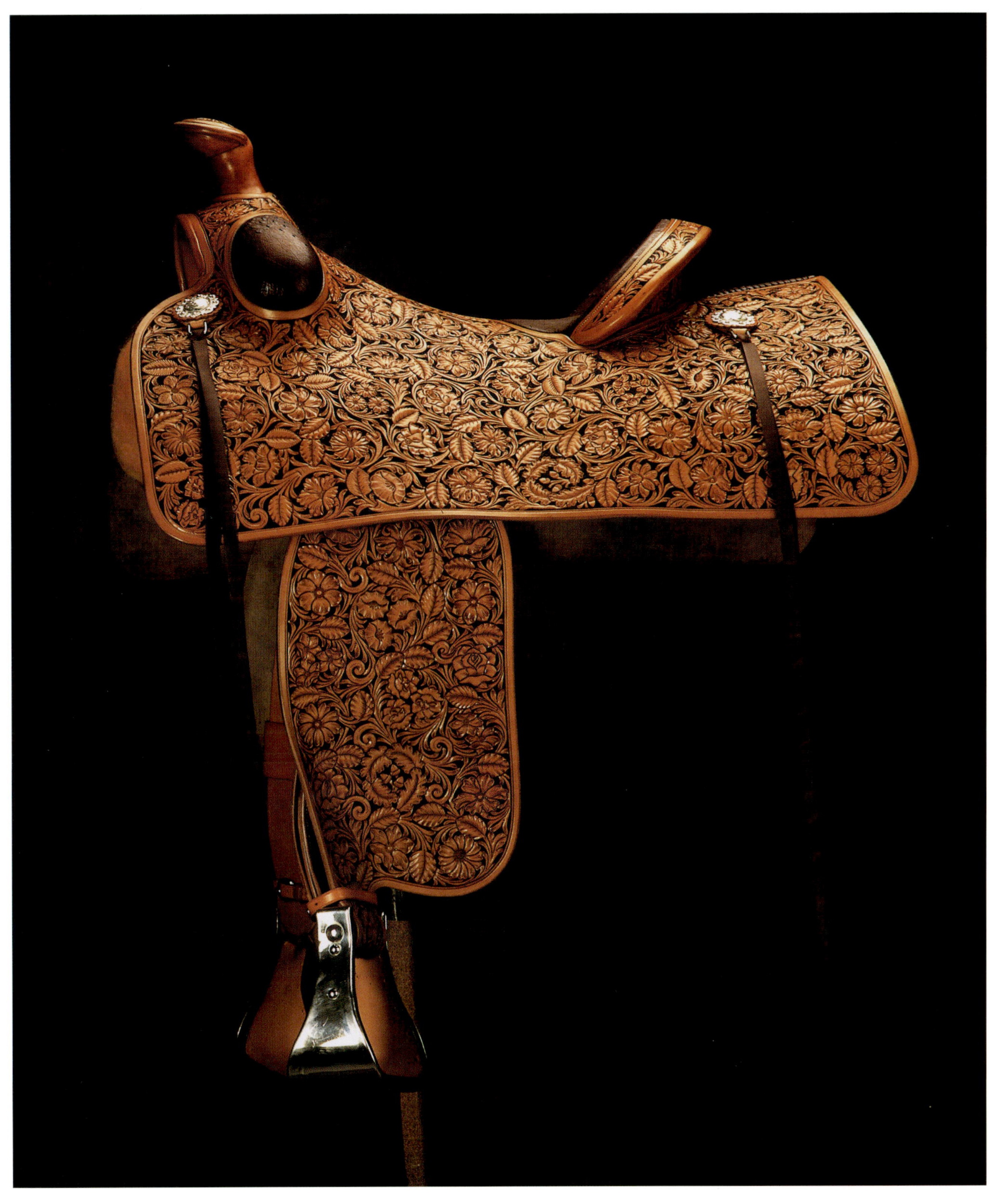

King Ranch Saddle Shop,
Kingsville, Texas
Saddle made of alligator hide, with tapaderos, *1940s*
FLEISCHER COLLECTION, SCOTTSDALE

Don King, Sheridan, Wyoming
Mother Hubbard style saddle,
2001

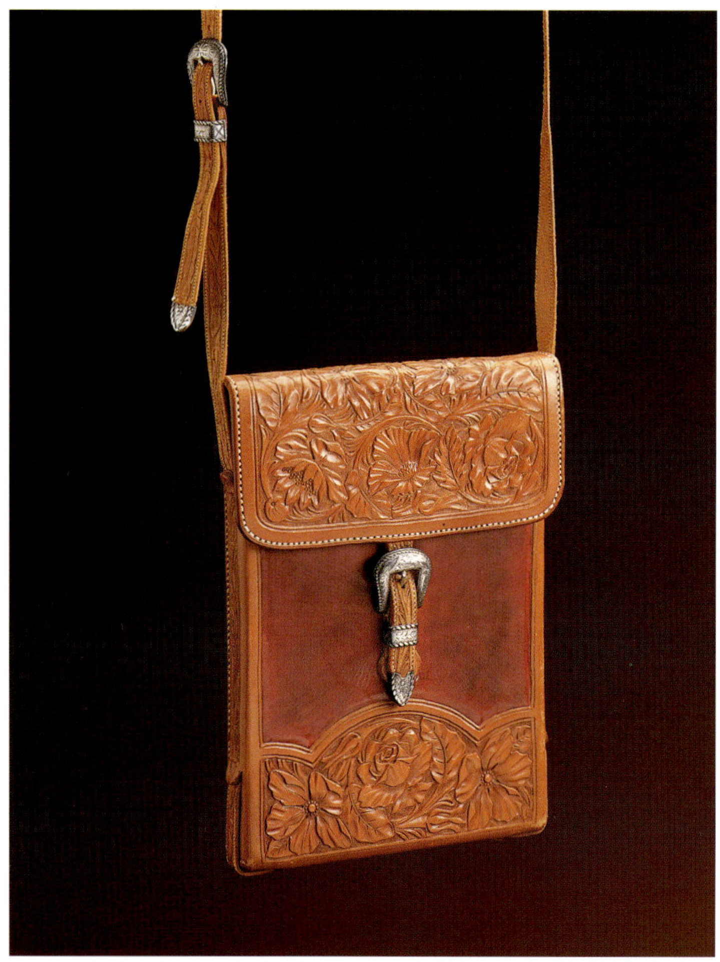

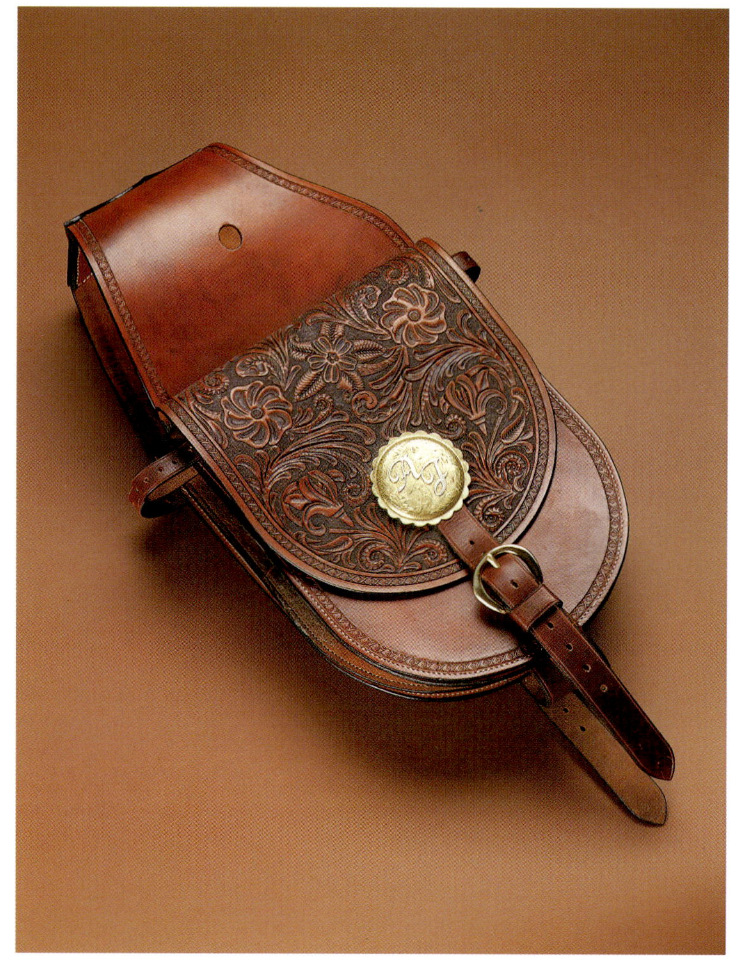

Above, left
Leather sketch book pouch belonging to artist Joe De Yong (1894–1975)
National Cowboy and Western Heritage Museum, Oklahoma City

Above, right
Verlane Desgrange, Cody, Wyoming Ladies' saddle bag

Opposite
Jim Kelly, Cody, Wyoming Stock saddle, a tribute to the working cowboy
Fleischer Collection, Scottsdale

horsemen than by cowboys and range work, became more homogenized, and regional preferences were less pronounced. Meanwhile, at saddle manufacturing plants, assembly lines quickened in the late 1940s with the introduction of "clickers," machines that cut out saddle patterns with rapidity and precision.

The decoration of saddle leather remained in the doldrums until the mid-1950s, when Wyoming saddle maker Don King introduced a new style of floral carving that would influence leather embellishment into the twenty-first century. King had become fascinated with leatherwork while traveling with his cowboy father on the dude ranch circuit through Wyoming, Arizona, and California. Such journeys afforded the youngster a unique opportunity to observe several master saddle carvers at work, but only Cliff Ketchum at Porter's in Phoenix offered to help him learn the art. King was a quick study, and by the age of fifteen he was stamping and selling belts and billfolds out of a Palm Springs, California, saddlery.

After serving in World War II, King returned to Wyoming where he learned to make saddles under the tutelage of Rudy Mudra, a respected Sheridan craftsman. For several years King combined saddle making with horse training, all the while experimenting with new patterns and methods of carving saddle leather. By the early 1960s King had opened a saddle shop in downtown Sheridan and

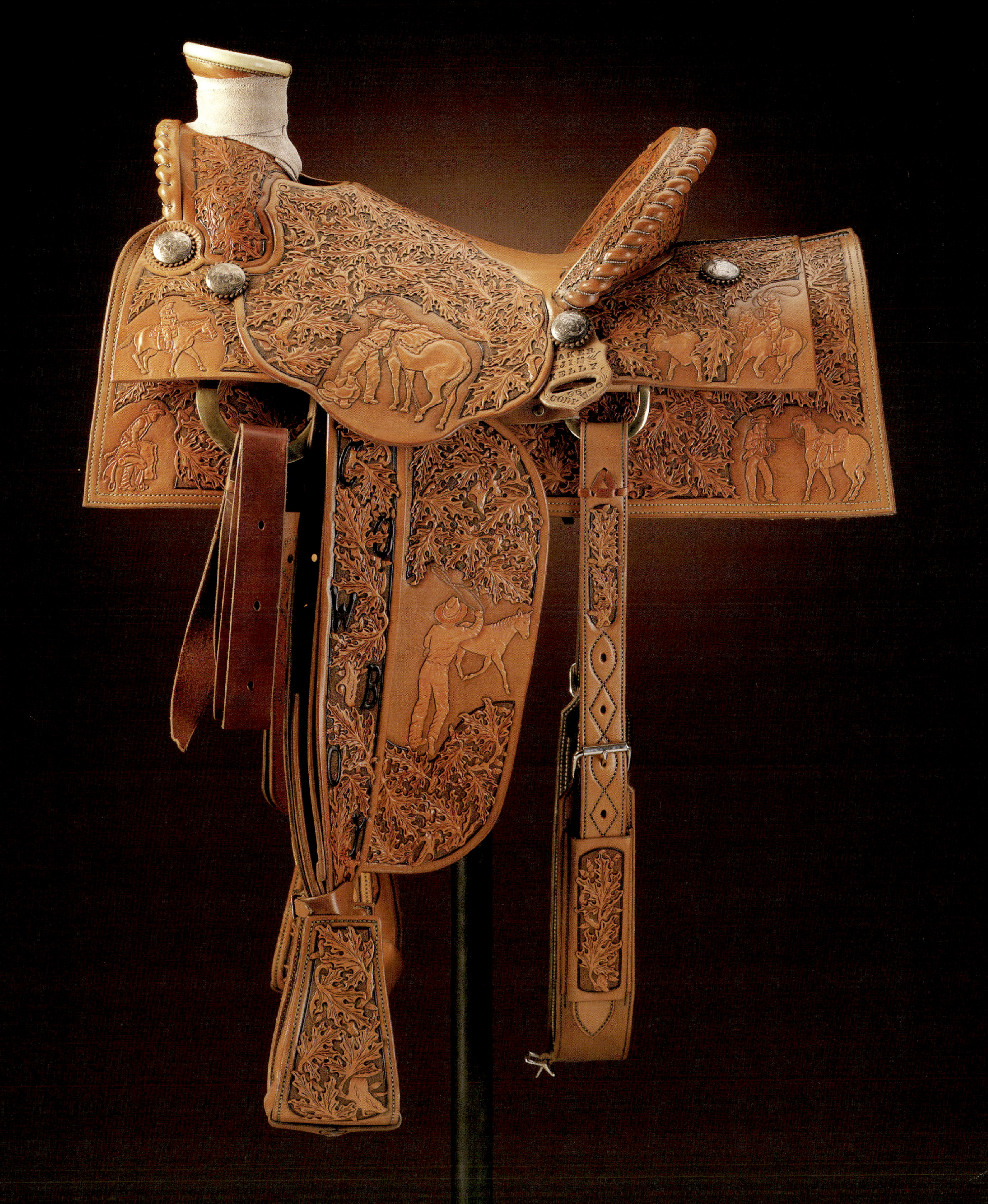
COWBOY

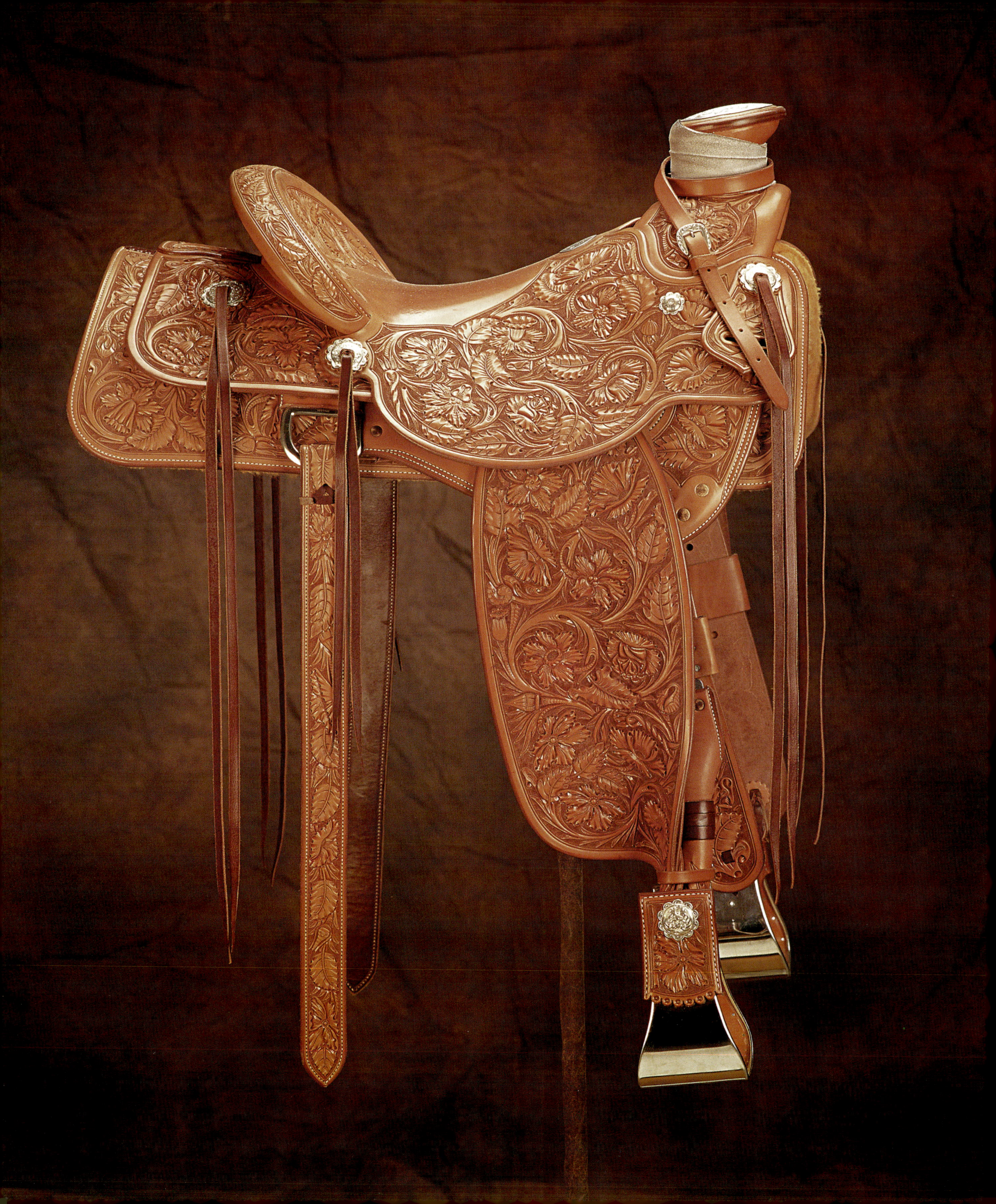

had defined a singular carving style that featured small wild roses intricately arranged in tightly woven and deeply carved sculptural patterns. King sometimes set the carvings against a contrasting background, creating a depth of relief and two-tone effect, suggestive of the work of Porter's, Visalia, and S. D. Myres in the 1930s.

King's imaginative new stamp patterns soon inspired the creativity of Bill Gardner, Chester Hape, and other members of the Sheridan saddle-making fraternity. Each of these masters not only interpreted King's original idea in his own distinctive way, but also trained several aspiring apprentices, who helped spread the "Sheridan Style" of carving throughout the West. Today, full-carved saddles by Don King and other masters are considered works of art and command top dollar from a growing number of avid collectors, who will exhibit rather than ride them. They are subjects of museum display and historical inquiry and, like their forbears of old, are still the products of skilled hands and fertile minds.

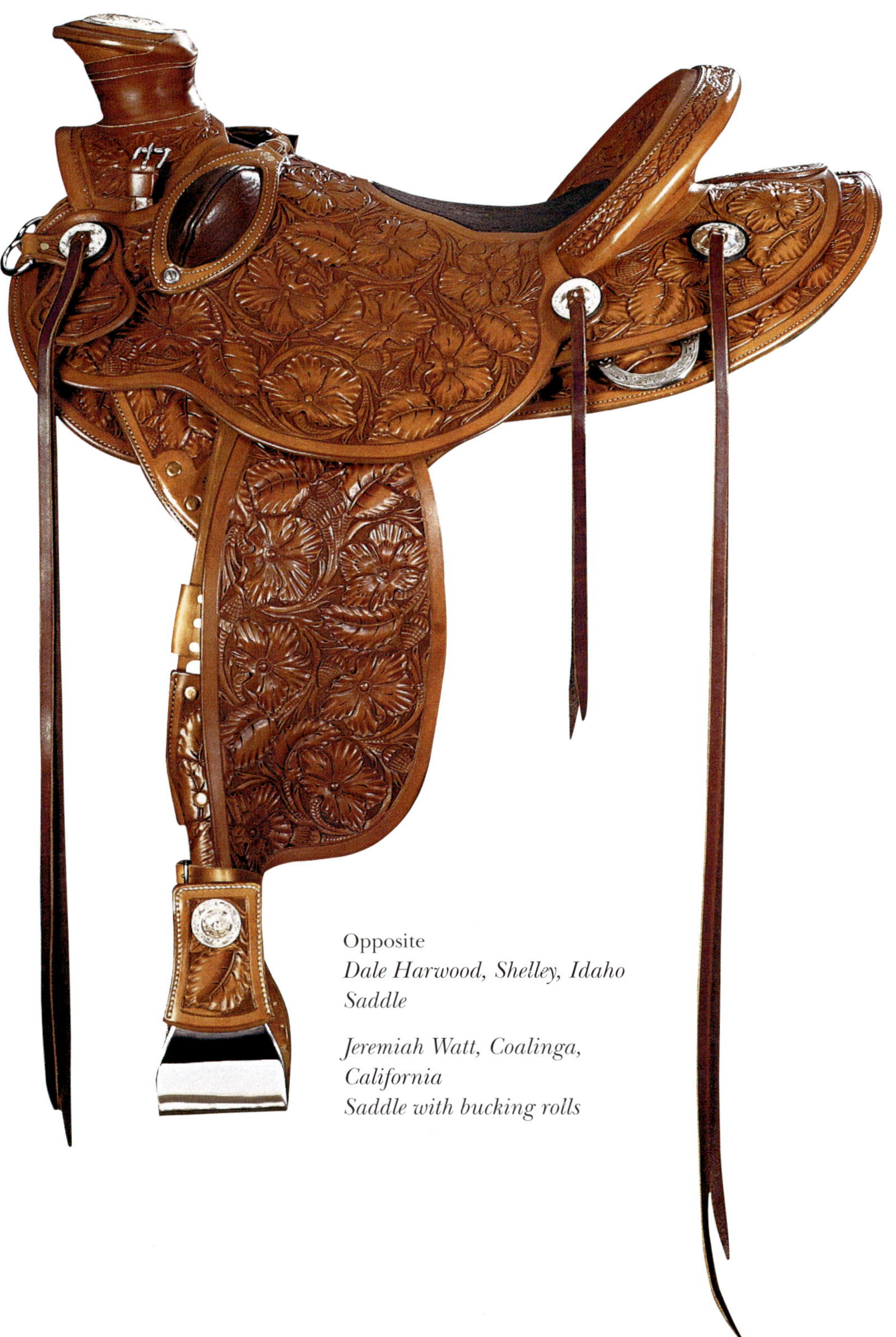

Opposite
Dale Harwood, Shelley, Idaho
Saddle

Jeremiah Watt, Coalinga, California
Saddle with bucking rolls

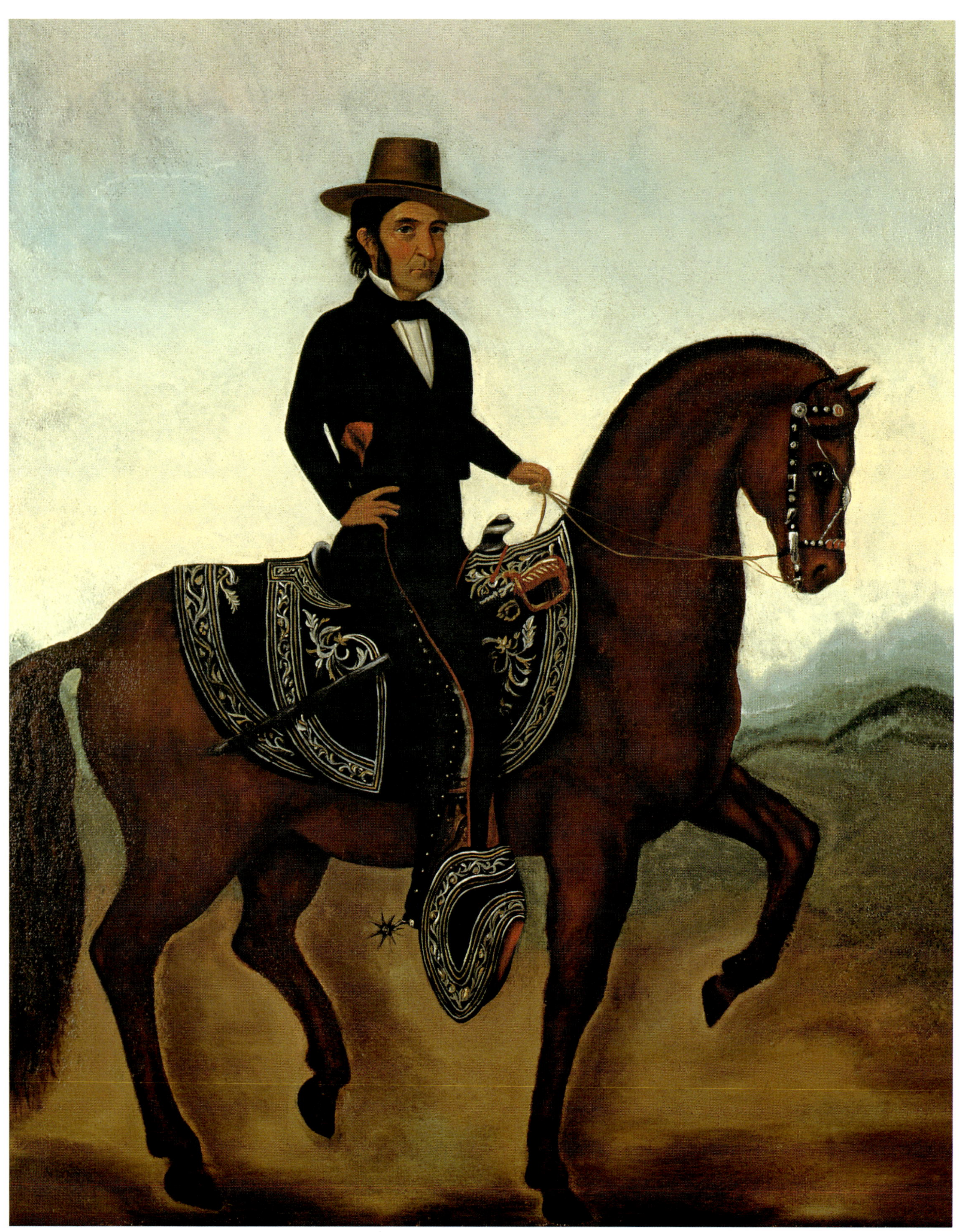

· 2 ·

Trophy, Parade, and Presentation Saddles

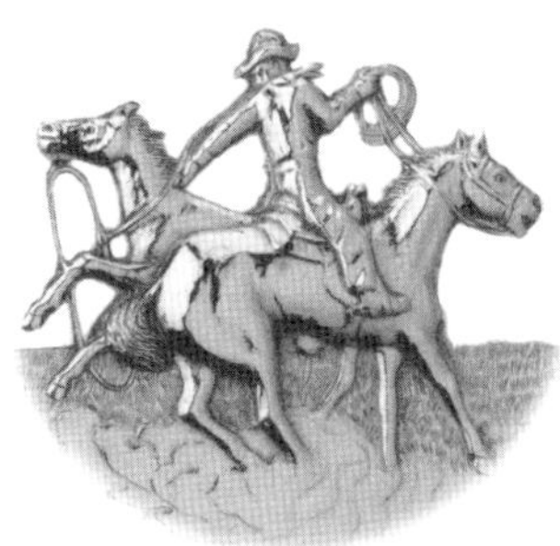

Some of the most outstanding examples of the western saddle maker's art were never intended for working the range. Wealthy horsemen in the region often commissioned ornately appointed show saddles, which they rode on special occasions as symbols of power, prosperity, and prestige. Wild West show entertainers and movie stars ordered flashy fantasy rigs designed to capture the imagination of an audience. Distinguished service earned military heroes and political dignitaries fine equestrian gear; grit and skill in the rodeo arena, beautiful trophy types. Special saddles destined for display in expositions, trade shows, and store windows represented a maker's technical ability and aesthetic sense.

More often than not fancy saddlery was a collaborative act requiring the talents of more than one artisan—leather carvers, silver- and goldsmiths, and jewelers among others. Many makers also invited their patrons to participate in the design process. Such teamwork often produced stunning motifs and exquisite workmanship. On occasion, however, the result was clumsy and garish.

Americans arriving in Mexican California in the first half of the nineteenth century observed rancheros using stylish riding gear worth thousands of dollars. "When thus mounted and fully equipped," William Heath Davis recalled,

Opposite. Henri Penelon *(1827–1885)*
Don José Andrés Sepulveda, 1856
Oil on canvas
Bowers Museum of Cultural Art, Santa Ana, California

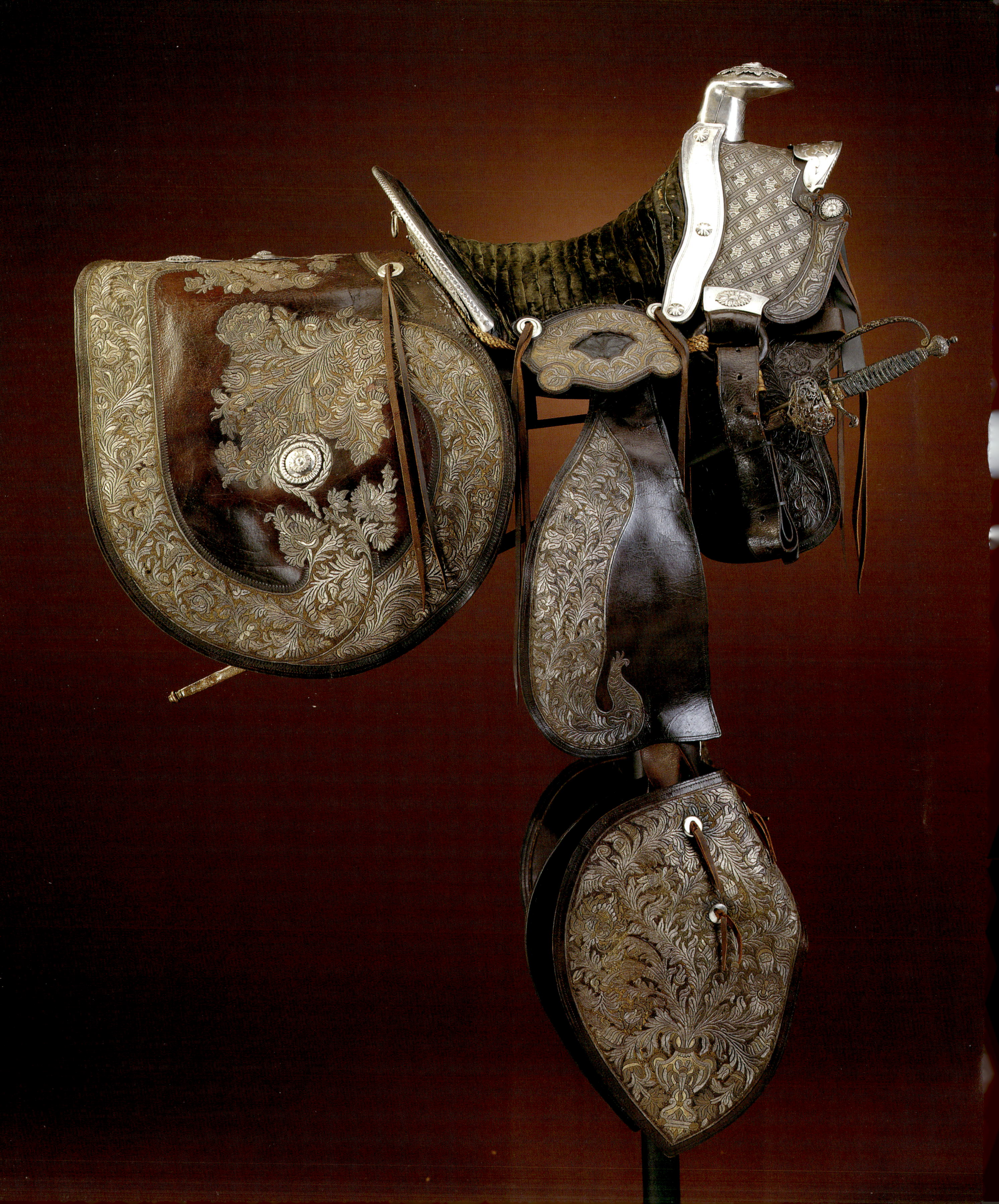

> these men presented a magnificent appearance, especially on the feast days of the Saints which were celebrated at the Missions. Then they were arrayed in their finest and most costly habiliments, and their horses in their gayest and most expensive trappings.[21]

During fiestas and holidays ranks of riders, their sumptuous saddles festooned with elaborate carving, chased, engraved, and pierced silver mounts, precious stones, wire embroidery, and plush velvet seats, pranced through the streets of California communities in self-conscious displays of wealth and vanity. Virtually all of such gear was imported from central Mexico, home to most of the nation's master *talabateros* and *plateros* (silversmiths).

Fine Mexican saddlery often embodied cosmopolitan motifs drawn from Renaissance Europe, the Far East, and indigenous American cultures. Among the ubiquitous floral and foliate patterns carved into leather or embossed into silver, for example, could be found representations of Mexican sunflowers, Spanish roses, Greek honeysuckle, and the leaves of the Mediterranean acanthus plant. Geometric designs of ancient origin, classical scrolls, and images of timeless birds and animals abounded as well.

After 1820 an increasing number of American-trained saddle makers began to make their way westward, bringing with them different traditions and training. To encourage settlement and attract skilled craftsmen of all types, agricultural and mechanical societies and civic leaders in many areas of the West began to organize fairs. Patterned on eastern models, such expositions rewarded outstanding workmanship with medals, ribbons, citations, and cash. They also offered saddle makers an opportunity to connect with an often scattered clientele and valuable exposure to new customers. In 1841 St. Louis hosted one of the first county fairs held west of the Mississippi. By 1855 several of the town's business leaders, including saddle maker Thornton Grimsley, had organized the St. Louis Agricultural and Mechanical Association to help promote the annual event.

Three years earlier, entrepreneurial Texans had sponsored a "state fair" and had awarded cash and merchandise for the best Mexican bridle and saddle, among other categories of livestock, agricultural produce, and manufactured goods. A stock saddle made by Rice and Childress, a San Antonio saddle house, won top honors at the first Western Texas Agricultural Fair, held in Bexar County in 1854. News that the winning saddle would be entered in the upcoming World's Fair in New York led *The Texas State Gazette* to remark that the Texas-made rig would do "honor to that or any other fair in the world or of the world."[23]

During the 1850s California saddle makers, too, demonstrated their prowess at an annual state fair held at Stockton and at competitions sponsored by the Mechanics' Institute of California. In 1857 and 1858, for example, Main and

Opposite
Saddle built for Emperor Maximilian of Mexico, c. 1864
Silver pommel and cantle and green padded seat, with gold and silver embroidery
FLEISCHER COLLECTION, SCOTTSDALE

Winchester, a fledgling San Francisco saddlery, garnered several prizes for fine saddles and other tack.

By the early 1860s a handful of expert saddlers had made their way to Colorado as well. During the Civil War one member of this group, Edward L. Gallatin of Denver, was called upon to create presentation saddles honoring a pair of distinguished army officers. Trained in St. Louis by renowned military saddler Thornton Grimsley, Gallatin was well equipped for the task when approached in 1862 by a group of officers and local citizens to craft a special saddle for Colonel Jesse H. Leavenworth, the popular commander of the Second Regiment of Colorado Volunteers. Built on a horned California tree, Gallatin's hybrid design included a Mexican-style *mochila* made of hemlock-tanned leather but shaped like an American military saddlecloth. An incised portrait of George Washington framed by an intricate floral and patriotic motif adorned each quadrant of the removable device, which was also trimmed with a stamped border and wire-wrapped cotton thread braid. The maker decorated the rig's fenders, skirts, cantle, and *tapaderos* with pleasing floral and foliate carving and embellished either side of the seat with the head of an eagle holding a fish in his beak.

A Denver silversmith named Frey created pierced, coin silver corner tips and regimental designations for the *mochila*, a silver rim for the cantle, silver medallions for the stirrups, and a silver horn cap embellished with the figure of an eagle, raised gold stars, and an engraved presentation inscription. The stunning outfit, which cost $350, also included a matching pair of pommel holsters; a tubular, military-style valise; a silver-mounted bit and bridle with ivory rein rings; and a martingale ornamented with a pierced shield.

Two years after he completed the Leavenworth commission, Gallatin was invited to fashion an even more elaborate saddle to honor Colonel John Chivington, commander of the First Regiment of Colorado Volunteers and architect of the important Union victory at Glorieta Pass, New Mexico, in 1863. Not long after Gallatin completed his task, Chivington led the infamous Sand Creek Massacre and fell into disgrace. His saddle, an elegant specimen for its time and said to have cost $550 new, brought a paltry $60 at auction in 1869.

At least one fine western stock saddle was presented to a Confederate officer in the eastern theater of the Civil War. In May 1862 "friends and admirers" of Colonel John Hunt Morgan presented the flamboyant Kentucky cavalryman with an ornate, Mexican-style saddle, made of black leather and decorated with silver by an accomplished artisan whose name has been lost to history. An engraved silver presentation plaque graces the arch of the pommel, which was elaborately embroidered in an imaginative floral pattern with silver wire thread. Metallic thread embroidery executed in various patterns also trimmed the fenders and the stirrup hoods, covered the latigo keepers, and formed a thin border around the skirts, pommel, and jockeys. Floral carving covered the square skirts and broad fenders; and an elegant stitch pattern, the quilted seat. The saddle also sported a silver horn and cantle rim, engraved silver tie string ornaments, and rectangular silver plates on the hoods of the stirrups.

In the post–Civil War era, western frontiersman-turned-showman William F. "Buffalo Bill" Cody began to transform western stock saddles from their role as the utilitarian tools of cattle herders into part of the exotic trappings of a mythic cowboy hero and entertainer. With the launching of Buffalo Bill's Wild West in the early 1880s, Cody began to hone his own heroic persona with the help of embellished saddlery. During the course of his long career in show business, Cody ordered several fancy show rigs from the Omaha saddlery of G. H. and J. S. Collins, who also operated branch locations in Wyoming and Montana. Cody is said to have used leather goods produced by the Collins brothers since his buffalo-hunting days with the railroad in the 1860s.

One of the first fancy rigs that the Collins produced for the showman featured a rectangular *mochila,* secured by tie strings in the "Mother Hubbard" style popular with Texas trail drivers in the 1870s and early 1880s. Tableau-style carving on the front half of the *mochila's* generous surface portrayed Cody hunting bison from horseback. The back half featured a large longhorn steer bearing the brand used by Cody and his partners Frank and Luther North on Scout's Rest Ranch, near North Platte, Nebraska, beginning in 1877. "Wm. F. Cody" carved in fancy script and surrounded by a leaf motif filled the front of the cantle. Large-scale floral carving surrounded the figures on the *mochila* and dominated the saddle's fenders and broad leather-covered stirrups. Metal ornamentation was sparse: a cheap disk with a star-shaped cutout set against a red background at the rear of the *mochila* and a plain silver concha in each corner.

In 1893, on the eve of his appearance at the World's Columbian Exposition in Chicago, Cody ordered a more elaborate saddle from Collins and Morrison, successor firm to G. H. and J. S. Collins in Omaha. The sleek sculptural architecture, California-style tree, and integral skirts and jockeys of the new model stood in marked contrast to the squat profile and bulky look of its predecessor (see p. 76).

Saddle maker Jacob Schamel, who occupied a bench at the Collins and Morrison saddlery in Omaha and who had known Cody during his days as a scout, probably made this saddle. A Civil War and Indian Wars veteran himself, the Indiana-born craftsman had apprenticed in his trade at Louisville before moving West. The saddle maker endowed the fenders of his creation with the incised portrait of a buckskin-clad Cody, taken from a photo the frontiersman had provided. A stirrup-level long Angora wool *anquera* completed the outfit.

L. J. Kass, a European-trained silversmith who worked in the shop of Omaha jeweler Albert Edholm, created sixty-five ounces of decorative silver trim for Cody's rig, a substantial amount for the time but relatively modest compared to later show saddles. In addition to silver tie-string ornaments, narrow silver pommel and cantle rims, and engraved and chased stirrup plates, each of the pommel swells boasted a large silver disk embellished with a bison rendered in repoussé. "Hon. W. F. Cody" spelled in 1 ½-inch tall silver letters formed a semicircle across the front of the cantle. A silver crescent mounted in the horn read "World's Fair, Chicago, 1893."

The saddle, along with a matching bridle and quirt, arrived in Chicago in May. In a long article about Cody's new acquisition, the *Jeweler's Circular and Horological Review* remarked:

> Buffalo Bill's friends know the fondness for handsome equipments, and can imagine him in his elegant scout's costume, mounted on his steed caparisoned with these gorgeous equipments, leading his congress of Rough Riders of the World through daring feats for the edification of World's Fair Visitors.[24]

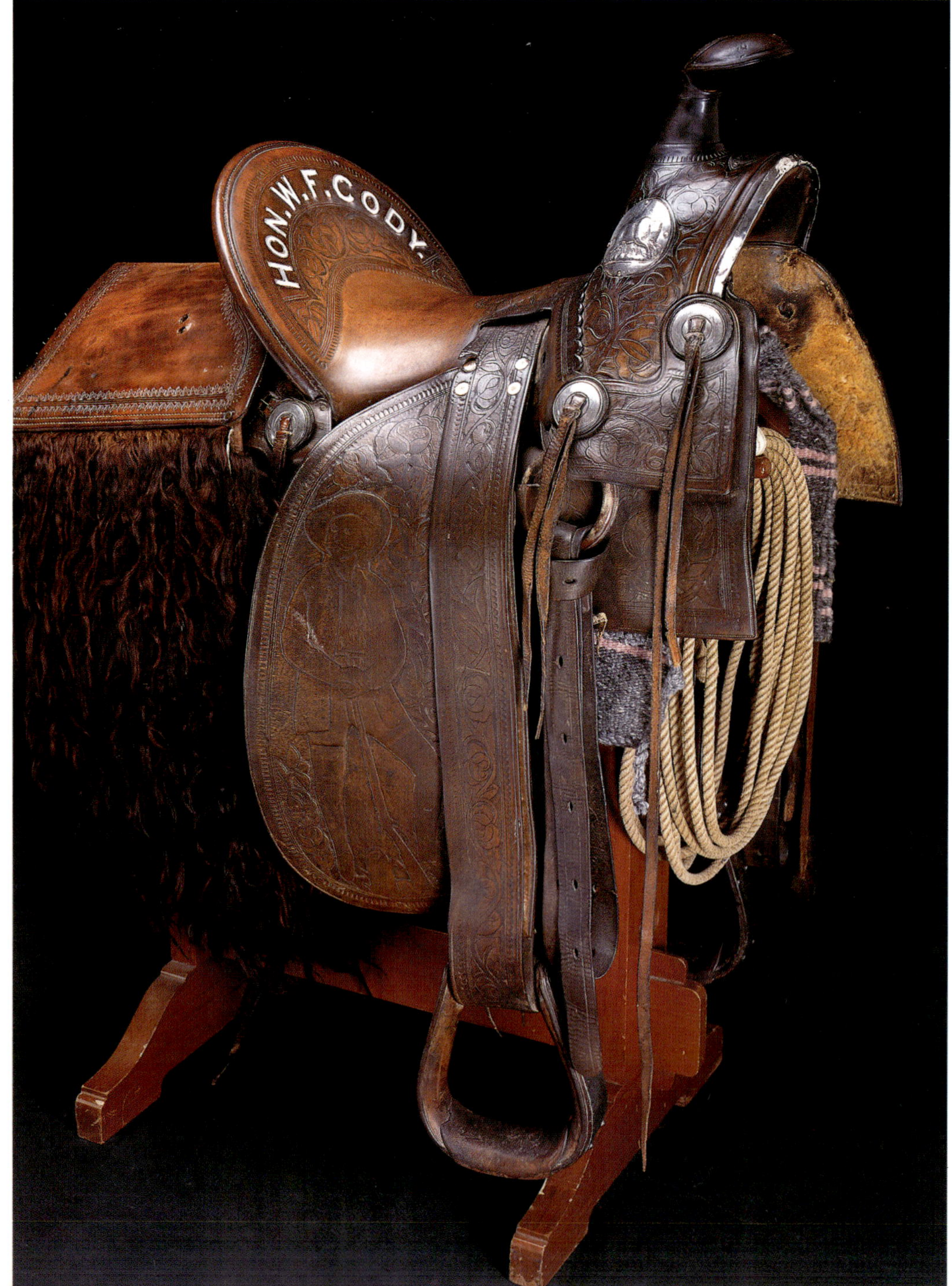

Collins and Morrison, Omaha
Saddle made for William F. "Buffalo Bill" Cody, 1893
Angora anquera *and leather with "Hon. W. F. Cody." inlaid in silver on cantle*
BUFFALO BILL HISTORICAL CENTER, CODY, WYOMING

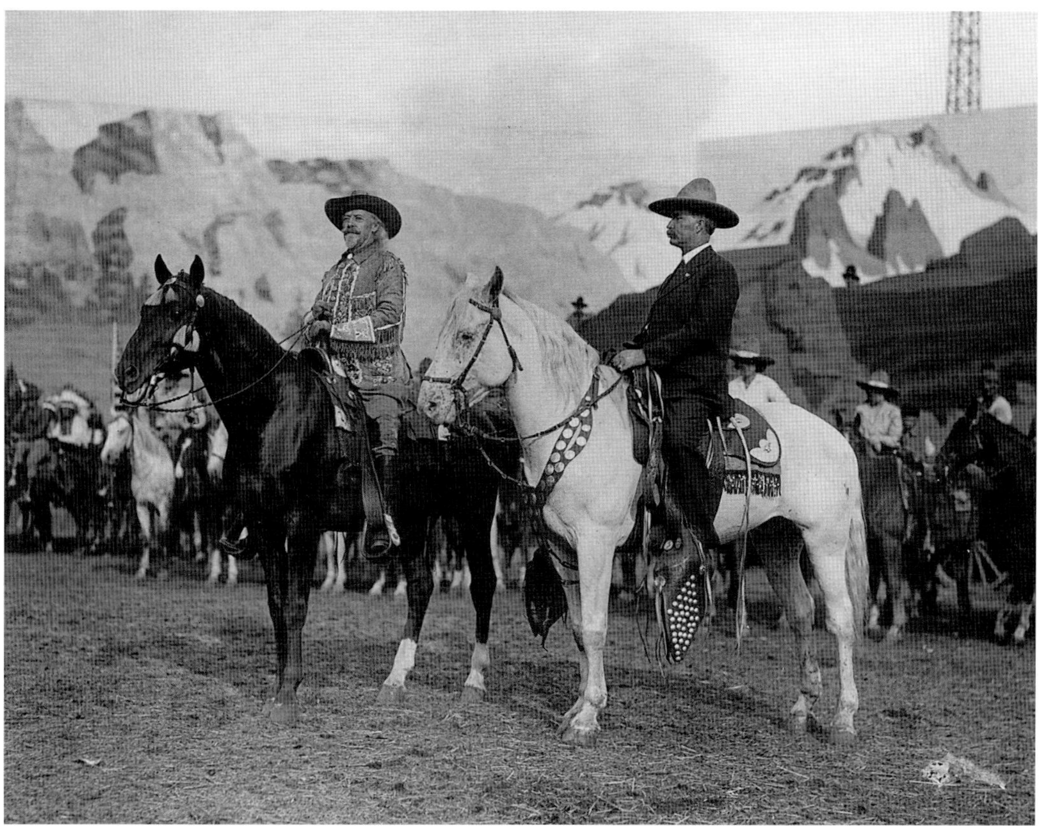

William F. Cody ("Buffalo Bill") and Colonel Zack Miller, Wild West showmen, aboard fancy silver-mounted saddles, c. 1916
BUFFALO BILL HISTORICAL CENTER, CODY, WYOMING

During his travels with the Wild West, Cody often presented dignitaries in various communities with mementos of his visit. In 1885, for example, Cody presented the mayor of Montreal with a Mexican-style, Collins-made saddle, after the community official had honored Cody and his famous troupe with a proclamation. Although run-of-the-mill and valued at a mere $50, the gift was ballyhooed in the press for its association with the famous showman.

The Collins saddleries received equipment orders from the U.S., Canada, and Europe as a result of the wide exposure of their products with Buffalo Bill's Wild West. J. S. Collins and Company, the Cheyenne branch of the Omaha firm eventually offered a saddle called "Our Wild West," which mimicked the fur *anquera* and the fender figure on Cody's personal rig. The $85 that the company charged for this saddle was $30 more than the company's next most expensive model.

Over the years several other saddle makers also provided gear for Cody's troupe or otherwise capitalized on the entertainer's incredible popularity. On the fenders of an early twentieth-century saddle created by the Denver saddlery of H. H. Heiser, for example, a bareheaded Buffalo Bill, hat in hand at his side, sits horseback amid a field of hand-raised American Beauty roses. The rose motif, accented by sterling silver tie ornaments and corner plates, continued on the skirts and jockeys of the attractive forty-five-pound rig.

The success of Buffalo Bill's Wild West spawned a host of imitators, each of whom utilized fancy tack for visual and promotional purposes. In 1913 Joe C. Miller, part owner of the famed Miller Brothers 101 Ranch Wild West Show of Oklahoma, ordered a magnificent saddle from the Wyeth Hardware and Manufacturing Co. of St. Joseph, Missouri. Encrusted with eighteen pounds of gold and filigreed silver and bejeweled with more than 210 diamonds, rubies, and sapphires furnished and mounted by New York City jeweler George F. Jordan, the entire rig outfit is said to have cost more than $5,000.

The following year, after having seen the saddle of Napoleon Bonaparte, billed as the most expensive in the world, Joe Miller approached Texas saddle maker S. D. Myres to create an even more spectacular rig. Myres turned to several trusted suppliers to provide the leather, silver, and jewels he needed to complete the job. In November 1913 the Eberhard Tanning Co. of Santa Clara, California, shipped a batch of premium California oak-tanned saddle skirting, known for its softness and finish, to Myres's Sweetwater shop. From gold and sterling silver supplied by Miller, the Chicago Art Metal Works, a prominent purveyor of saddle trimmings, fabricated mounts in the shape of stars, wreaths, and steer heads. The Wild West impresario also provided the 166 diamonds, 120 sapphires, sixteen rubies, and four garnets used to accent the mounts. A horse head–shaped broach made of seventy cut diamonds crowned the silver-inlaid horn.

One of the finest leather carvers in the West, Myres embellished the saddle skirting with his signature scroll and flower stamping, adding longhorn steer heads surrounded by butterflies and gold bugs to the fenders. According to one contemporary newspaper report, the insects were "stamped around so perfectly that one has only to draw on his imagination to see the flutter of the wings."[25]

In March of 1914 Myres brought the completed masterpiece to Oklahoma City where it was exhibited to great fanfare at a local hotel during a meeting of Oklahoma cattlemen. On April 1, Miller rode his "$10,000 saddle" at the premier performance of the 101 Ranch Wild West Show in Madison Square Garden.

With the deaths of Joe Miller in 1927 and his brother George in 1929 and the onset of the Great Depression, the 101 Ranch fell deeply into debt. By the late 1930s mounting bills forced Zack Miller to use both the S. D. Myres and the Wyeth Hardware Co. saddles, along with his own personal silver-mounted rig, as collateral for a loan from Frank Phillips, founder of the Phillips Petroleum Company. By this time, however, most of the original jewels had been removed from their mounts to pay other debts and replaced with imitation stones. In 1940 Phillips acquired the famous $10,000 saddle to help settle Miller's debt.

Meanwhile, an increasing number of western saddle makers had been exhibiting highly embellished examples of their work at world's fairs, commemorative expositions, and trade shows. Saddles made in Pueblo by S. C. Gallup & R. T. Frazier, for example, received the highest premium at the World's Columbian Exposition in Chicago in 1893. No saddle maker benefited more from the exposure at such venues, however, than G. S. Garcia of Elko, Nevada.

Born in Sonora, Mexico, in 1864, Garcia had immigrated to California as a child, learned the saddle-making trade at San Luis Obispo, and established a shop in Santa Margarita, California, in 1883. Eleven years later he relocated to northeastern Nevada, home to a burgeoning cattle trade. Garcia prospered through hard work and good luck, and he expanded his operation to include a branch location in the town of Deeth, Nevada, in 1896. In time he hired several top-notch silversmiths and engravers, who turned out saddle trimmings as well as bits and spurs.

Asked to provide silver mounts for other saddle makers planning to exhibit their wares at the Louisiana Purchase Exposition in St. Louis in 1904, Garcia determined to enter the fair himself. In late 1903 he added several more silver workers to his staff, including Susie McDonald, described by the *Elko Daily*

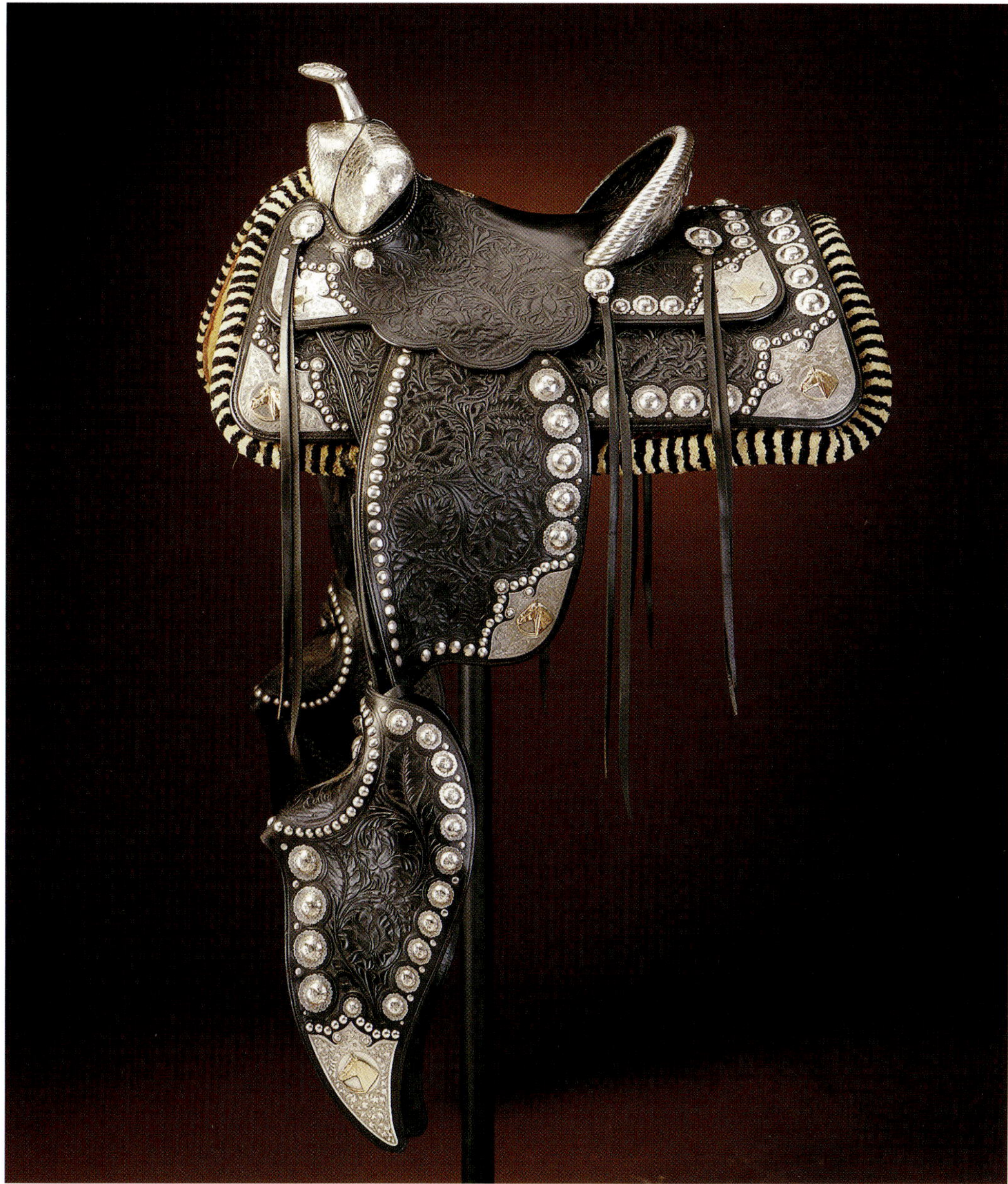

Visalia Stock Saddle Co., San Francisco
Silver-mounted saddle with horse head motif on corner plates and concha *trim, c. 1930s*
Fleischer Collection, Scottsdale

Independent as "an expert engraver."[26] With the help of these and other talents on his staff, Garcia spent eight months designing, fabricating, and embellishing the centerpiece of his display: a black leather saddle, carved with American Beauty roses and tastefully trimmed with silver mounts that not only exhibited fine workmanship but also the designer's pride in his state and nation (see p. 82).

Patriotic motifs that included eagles, flags, stars, and shields appeared in a variety of expertly chased, pierced, and engraved mounts, sometimes in creative juxtaposition with animals, cherubs, and scrolls. An elegantly tapered and filigreed silver band bearing the Nevada State Seal, flanked by a row of stars and a

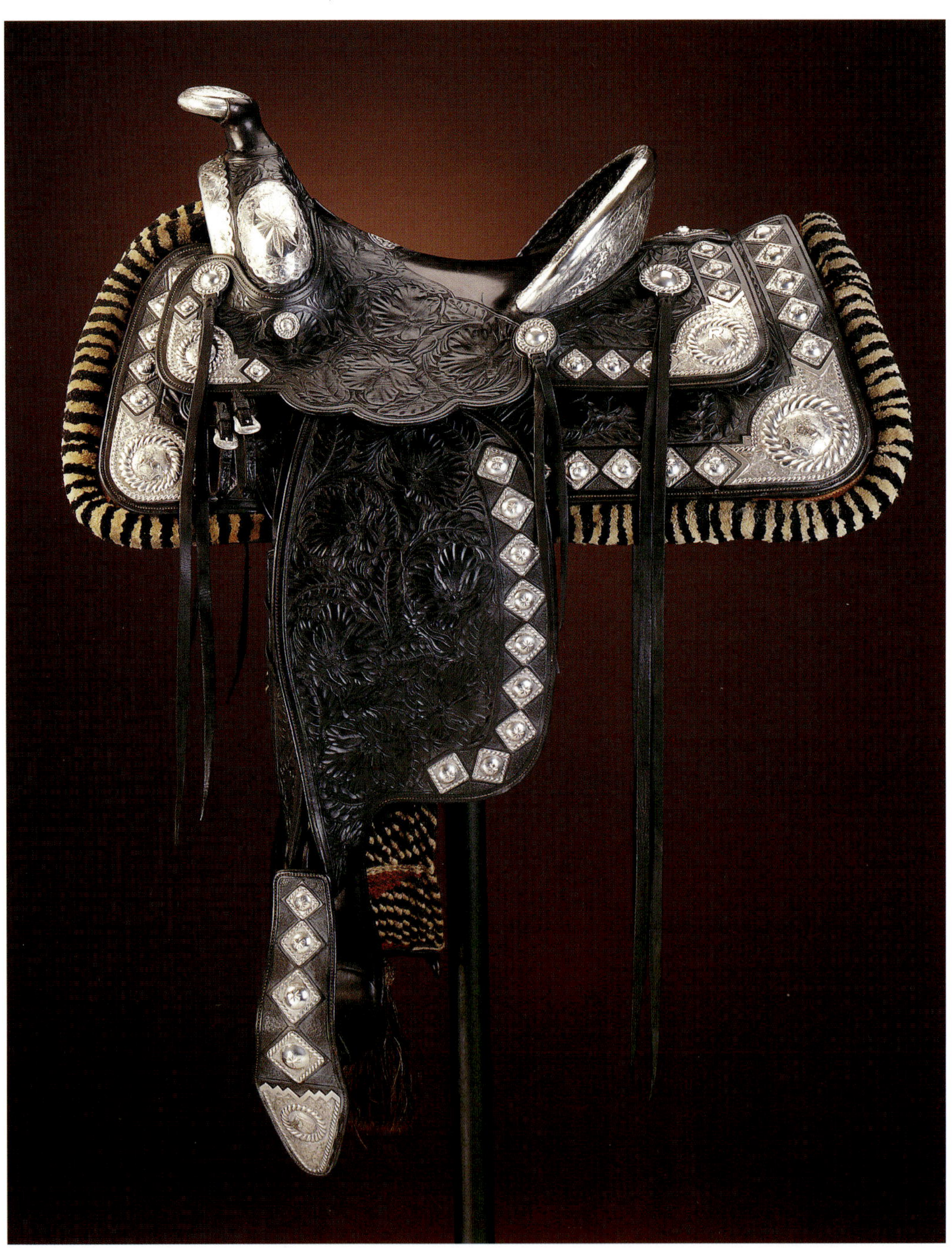

Visalia Stock Saddle Co.,
San Francisco
Rancho Visitadores saddle, 1930s, with detail (opposite)
Fleischer Collection, Scottsdale

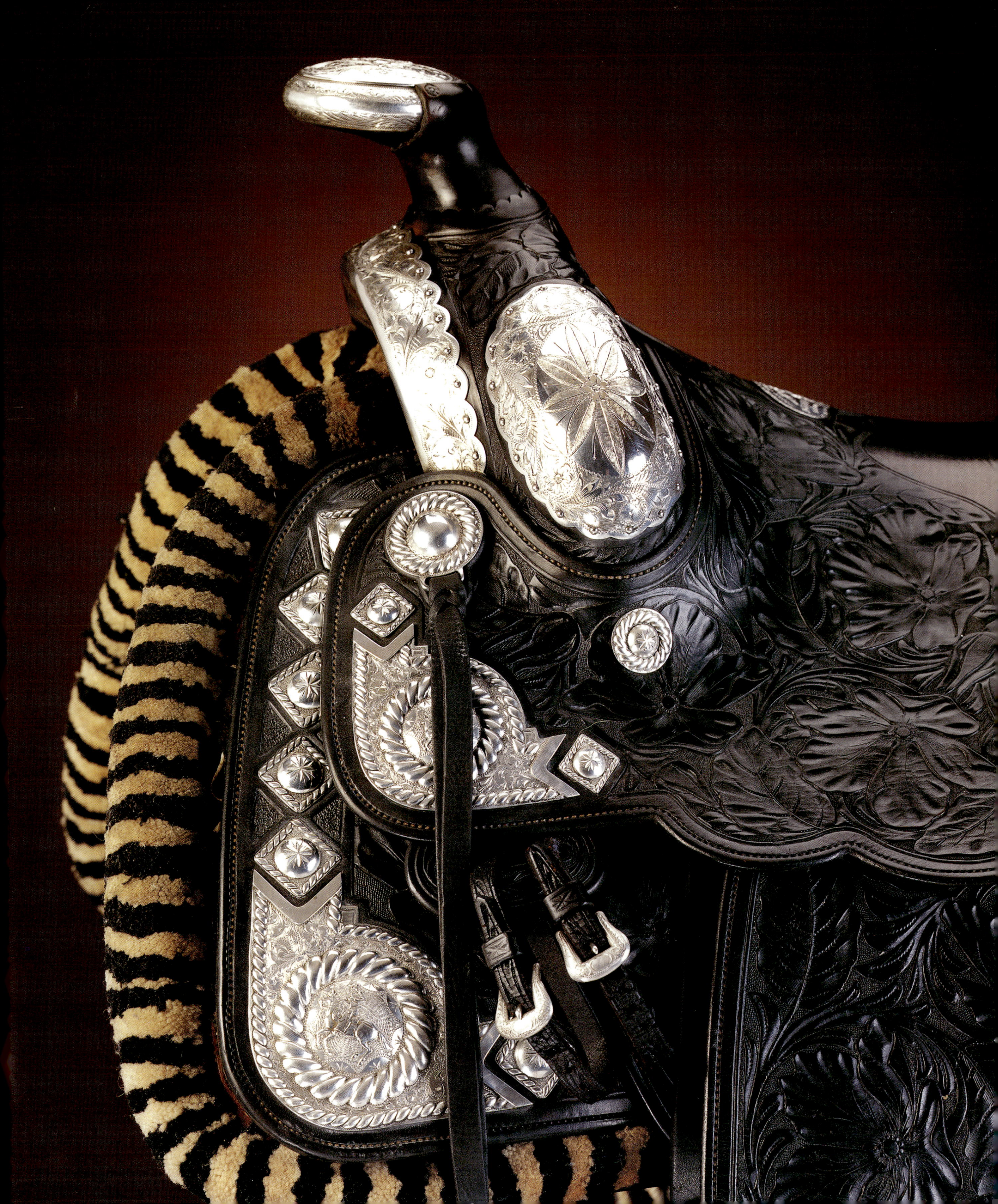

pair of delicate hummingbirds, adorned the pommel arch. Another medallion, surrounded by a wreath, formed the cap of the silver encrusted horn.

Across the front of the seat, Garcia and his colleagues carved a series of wide, silver-edged scallops where they imbedded seven engraved medallions converted from $20 gold pieces. Three contained portraits of President Theodore Roosevelt and Nevada governors John Sparks and William Nye. The others bore six-pointed stars housing the profile of Lady Liberty or the delicate images of fairy horse heads with diamond-filled eyes. Diamonds also accented star-shaped tie string ornaments. A matching martingale and a calfskin bridle, braided by Elko County rancher Domingo Aguilar, rounded out the impressive ensemble, which Garcia insured at $5,000 for its trip east.

Garcia's exhibit at St. Louis, which also included bits, spurs, and other fancy leatherwork, occupied a forty-foot front near the center of the Agriculture Building. The Elko saddle maker's work impressed not only the judges, who awarded it the gold medal in its class, but also his fellow engravers, who especially lauded the lifelike portraits of Roosevelt, Nye, and Sparks.

At the Lewis & Clark Exposition in Portland, Oregon, the following year, "The Saddle That Made Elko Famous," as the maker's ads began to call it, again

Below left
Saddlemaker G. S. Garcia stands by one of his creations in Santa Margarita, California, 1880s
Northeastern Nevada Museum, Elko

Below right
G. S. Garcia, Elko, Nevada Gold Medal Saddle, Louisiana Purchase Exposition, 1904
Northeastern Nevada Museum, Elko

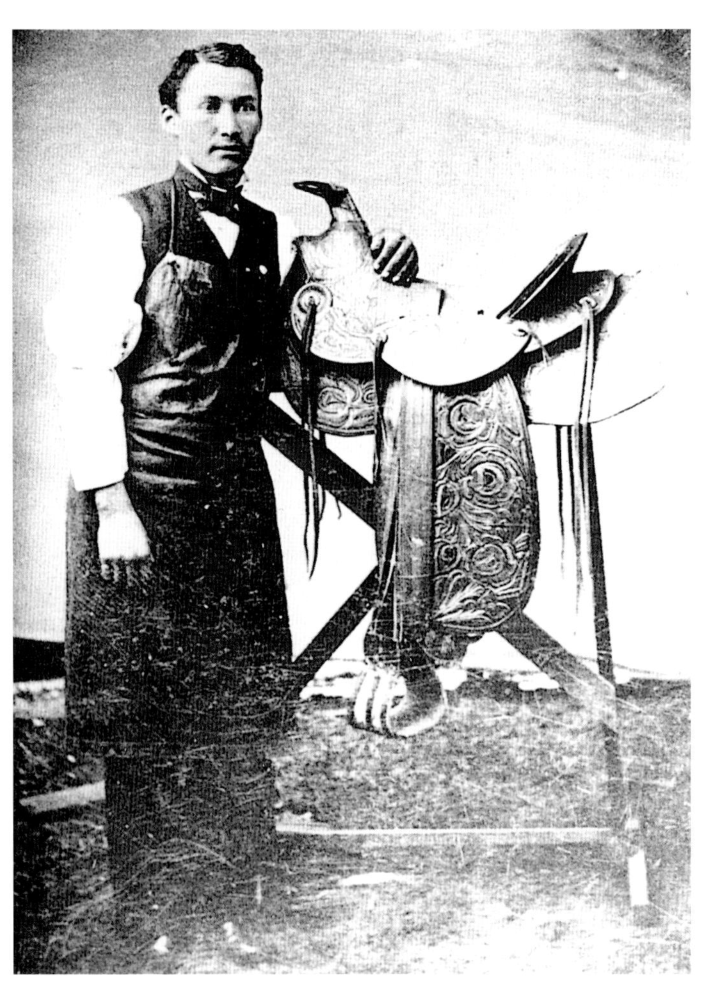

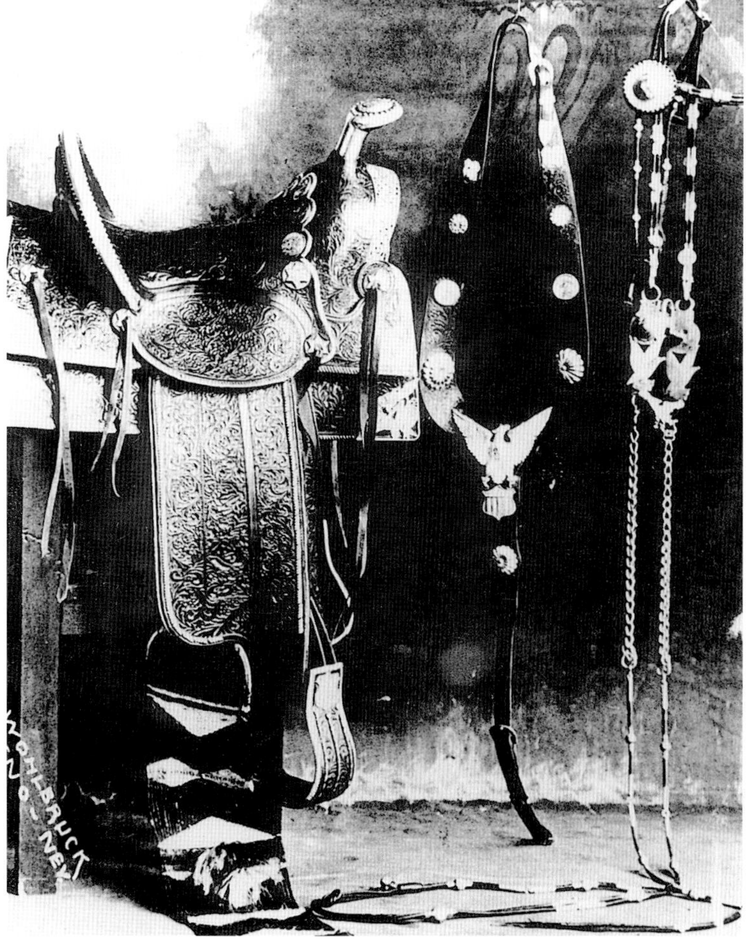

struck gold. Impressive back-to-back world's fair victories not only enhanced Garcia's reputation but also brought him a host of new customers, including a cowboy-turned-vaudevillian named Will Rogers.

When his masterpiece returned triumphant to Elko, Garcia built a special horse on which to display it in front of his shop. By this time some Nevadans were urging the saddle's purchase and presentation to President Roosevelt. Although Garcia agreed to sell and donated $500 toward the purchase price, not enough money was raised to complete the transaction, and the saddle remained in the hands of its maker.

Garcia, meanwhile, made liberal use of his award-winning saddle in trade catalogs and advertising and further capitalized on its renown by periodically taking it on tour to celebrations from coast to coast. In 1910, for example, Theodore Roosevelt rode the rig for four days while attending the Frontier Days rodeo at Cheyenne, Wyoming. In 1923 the *Elko Independent* declared with truth that Garcia's celebrated rig had "probably done more to direct attention toward this city than any other inanimate object."[27]

A master promoter, G. S. Garcia sponsored a riding tournament bearing his name at the July 4 celebration in Elko in 1912, and the following year helped establish the Elko Stampede rodeo. The saddle maker not only helped advertise the event and provided prizes for winning contestants but also erected concrete grandstands at the rodeo grounds and furnished some of the bucking stock.

Although extensive, Garcia's support of rodeo was not unusual. From the 1890s onward western saddle makers increasingly recognized the prestige and promotional opportunities that supporting the rising sport offered. Cowboys had been competing with one another in informal roping and riding contests at least as early as the late 1860s. By the 1880s promoters had begun to stage such events for the public and to offer prizes to the winners. The practice of awarding embellished trophy saddles to victorious rodeo competitors began as early as 1882, when a crowd of 10,000 at the Texas State Fair in Austin watched ten cowboys compete in a steer-roping contest for a "silver-trimmed saddle worth $300."[28]

By the turn of the twentieth century, many communities throughout the West were staging rodeos and giving away fancy saddles as prizes. Usually produced by local saddle makers, trophy rigs were typically embellished with fine stamping and modest coin silver or German silver mountings, often in the form of tie string ornaments, corner plates, and presentation plaques. Carving patterns often included action figures, usually bucking horses and riders but occasionally cattle, horses, wildlife, and even female figures. An imaginative carved image of an Indian launching an arrow skyward decorated the fenders of the silver mounted trophy saddle made by the Los Angeles Saddlery & Findings Co. and won by Arizona bronc rider Joe Isabell at the Los Angeles rodeo in 1912.

Because trophy saddles represented their best work, saddle makers often featured them in their advertising and trade catalogs, at times offering similar models to the public. On the eve of World War I, for example, H. H. Heiser of Denver advertised a "Broncho Buster's First Premium Saddle," costing a substantial $225. In addition to a full floral background, the maker carved an Indian head on the front of the cantle, bulls on the side jockeys, elk on the fenders, and bison on the rear skirts. He also added sterling silver horse and steer heads to the jockeys and large round silver ornaments to the skirt corners.

Makers sometimes donated trophy saddles to local rodeos and reaped the publicity value and good will. At other times they competed for lucrative contracts to produce fancy rodeo saddles sponsored and paid for by others. Hamley and Company of Pendleton, Oregon, and the Denver Dry Goods Company, among others, made trophy saddles awarded to champions by the Union Pacific Railway System, a prominent and longtime corporate sponsor of Cheyenne Frontier Days and the Pendleton Round-Up. The company's famous shield logo, rendered in silver, usually adorned the skirts, jockeys, and *tapaderos* of such championship rigs. The saddle given by the railroad in 1911 at the Cheyenne Frontier Days rodeo also featured the unusual carving of a cowboy riding a buffalo (see page 93).

Beginning in 1910 and continuing for more than a half-century, Hamley and Company donated at least one trophy saddle to a winning contestant at the Pendleton Round-up and made many others sponsored by various donors. These saddles and other prizes awarded to the winners decorated the company's store windows in advance of the rodeo each year. Besides making trophy saddles, Hamley and Co. also played a key role in design and production of a standard style of bronc riding saddle, used at rodeos throughout the West.

The fully carved, *tapadero*-bearing rig earned by the champion bronc rider at the Pendleton Round-up in 1914 was typical of the style and workmanship of early Hamley-made trophy saddles. An engraved silver cantle plate bearing the inscription "Red Parker 1914 rode Long Tom" commemorated the occasion. Carved lettering on the skirts, fenders, and side jockeys identified the place, date, and prize and cheered, "Let 'er buck." Contrasting white leather and rawhide braid trimmed the edges of skirts, fenders, jockeys, and conchas. Later Hamley produced a watch fob bearing the saddle's distinctive profile (see page 203).

For several years Hamley and Co. also made trophy saddles for the Madison Square Garden Rodeo, founded in New York City in 1922. Each October the prestigious Manhattan venue hosted more than forty performances. In its heyday in the late 1940s, the World Series Rodeo, as it was sometimes known, attracted as many as 150 contestants. By this time shows had also been staged in Boston, New Haven, Providence, Philadelphia, Cleveland, Pittsburgh, and Chicago.

In 1929 S. D. Myres of El Paso produced the trophy saddles for the World Series Rodeo. Upon their arrival in New York, a rodeo official wired the maker:

Opposite
Olson-Nolte, San Francisco
Saddle with ensemble including vest and chaps
FLEISCHER COLLECTION, SCOTTSDALE

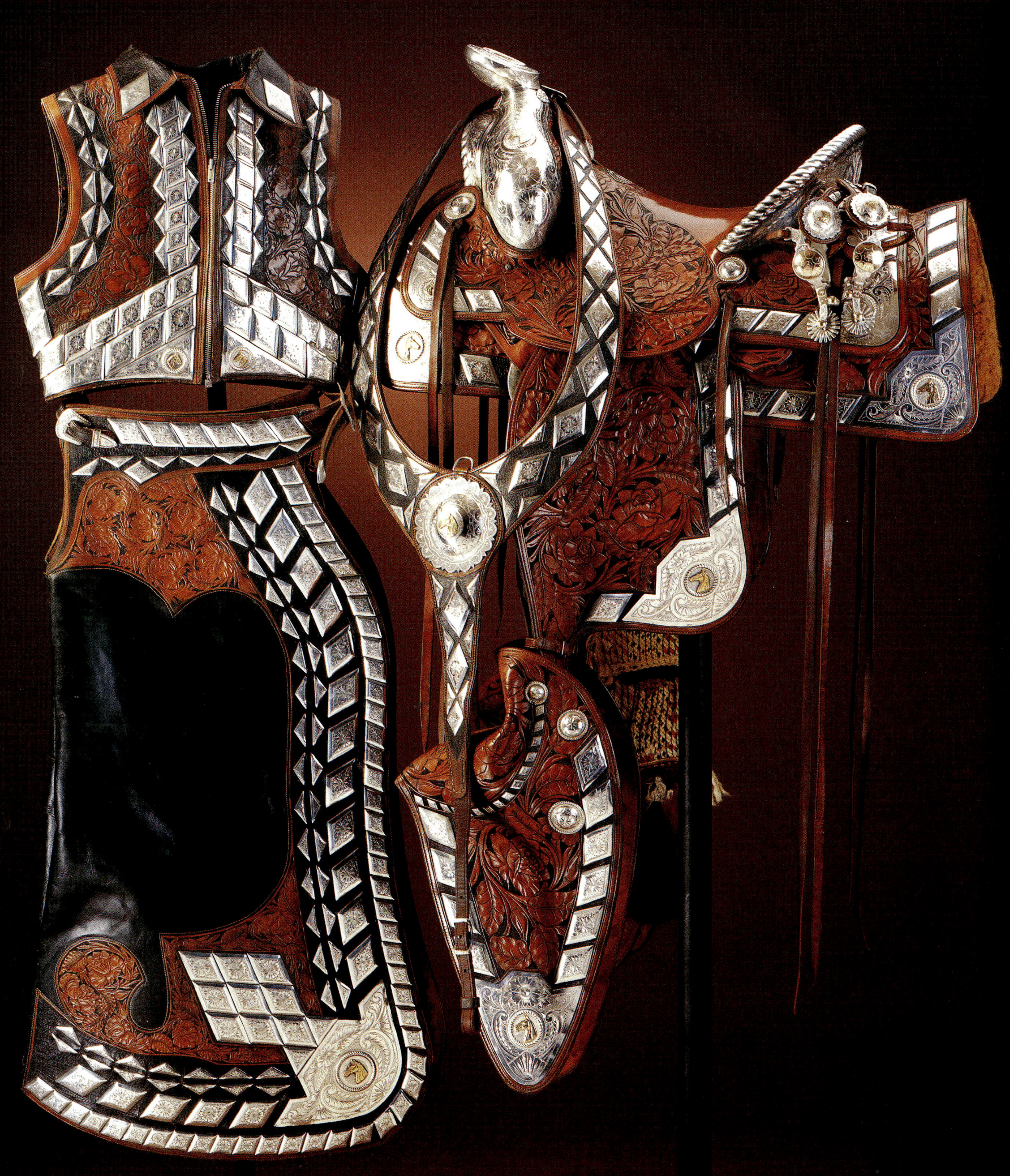

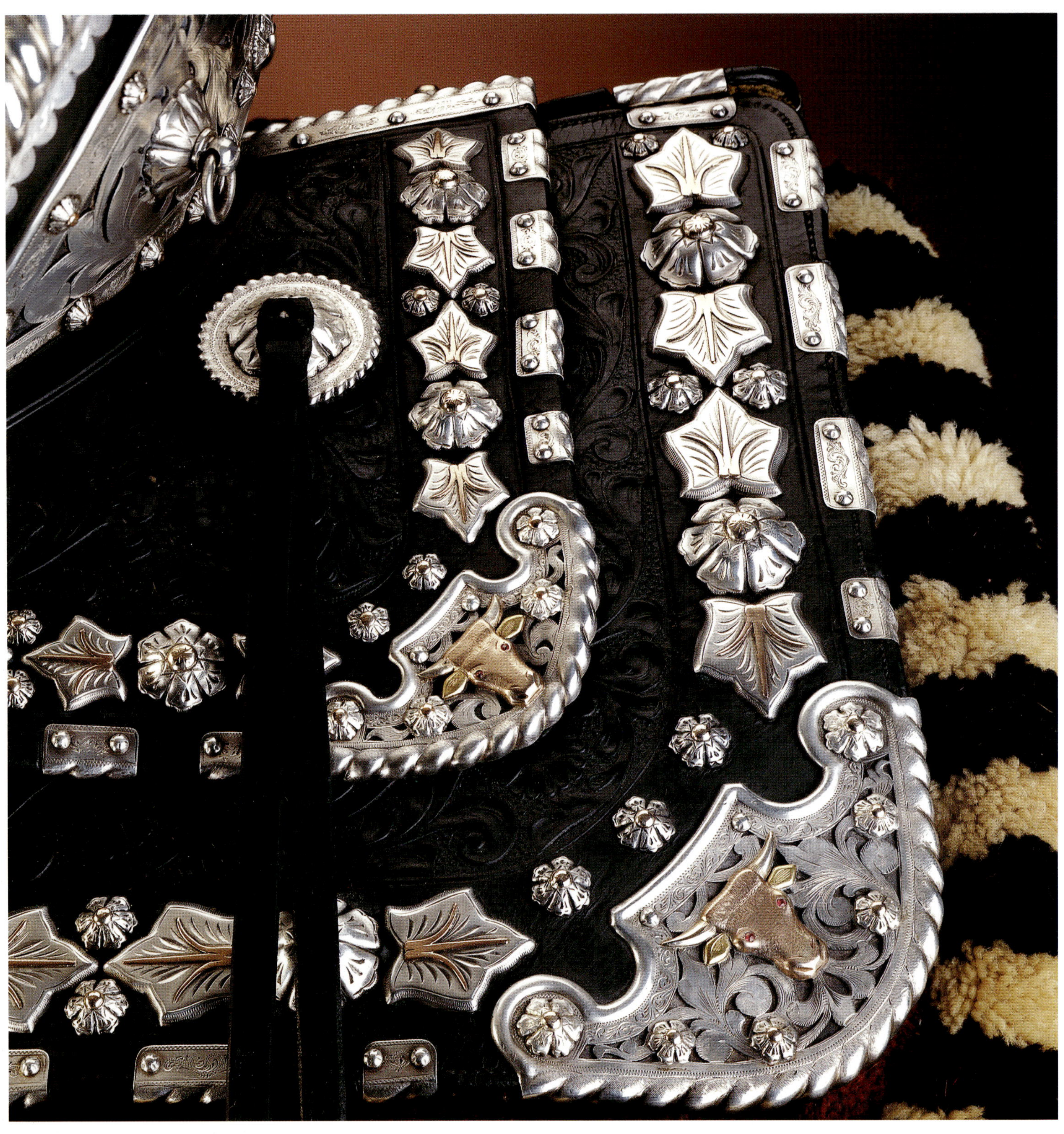

Edward H. Bohlin, Hollywood
Silver-mounted parade saddle, "Fiesta" pattern, 1920s (opposite), with detail of corner plate on rear skirt (above)
Fleischer Collection, Scottsdale

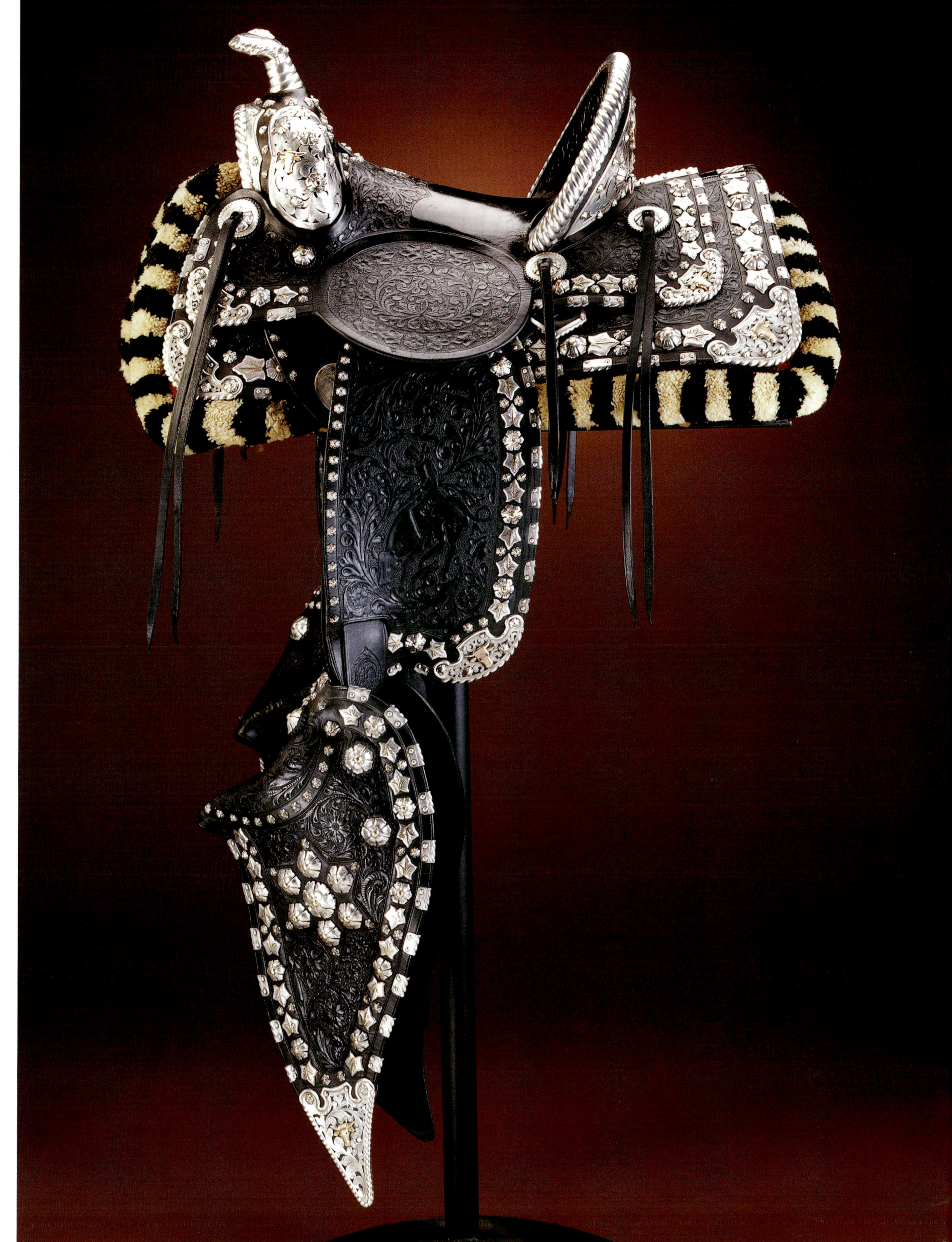

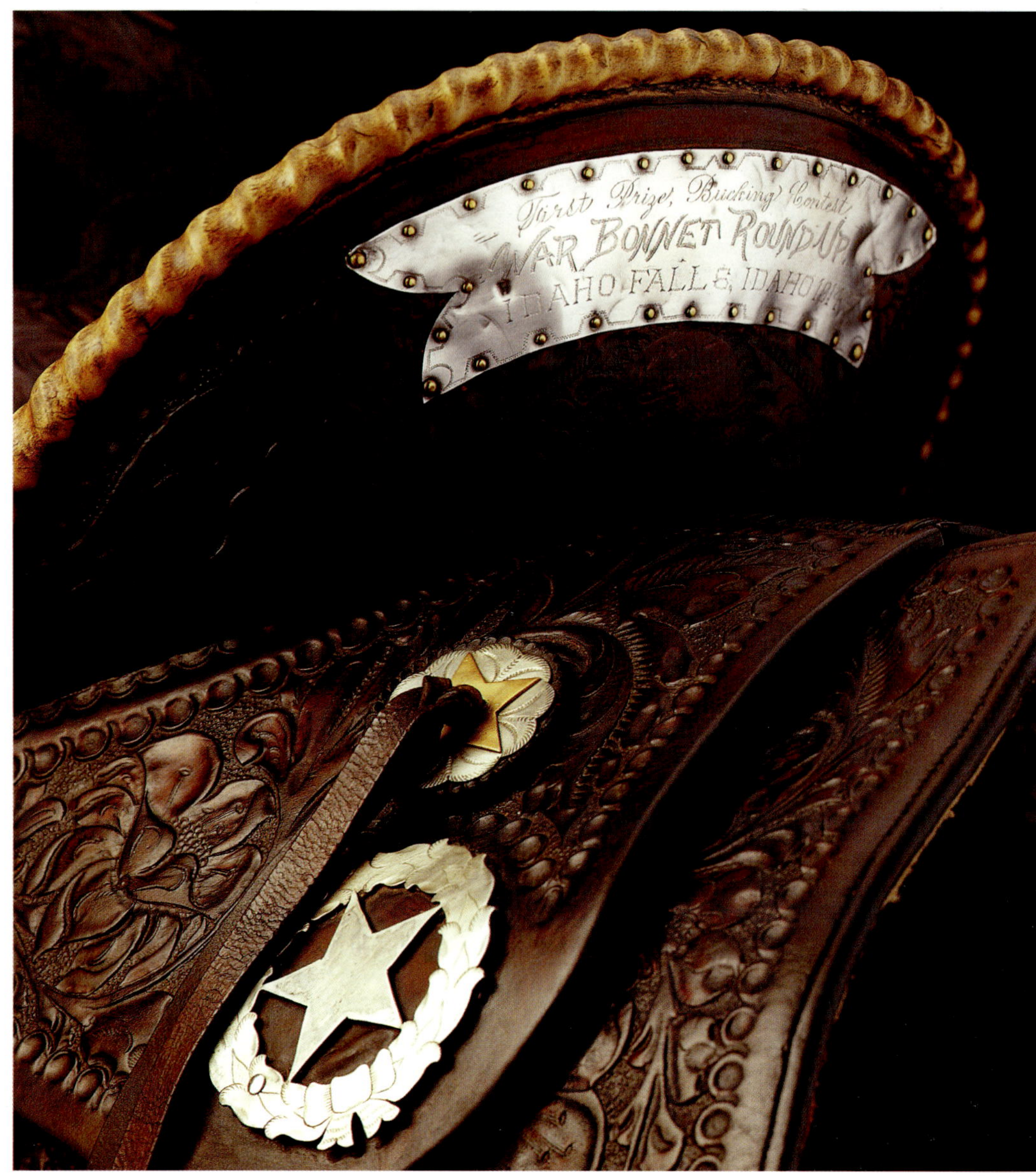

Hardware Brand Saddlery, Salt Lake City
Trophy saddle for War Bonnet Round-Up, Idaho Falls, 1914 (opposite), with detail of cantle (above)
FLEISCHER COLLECTION, SCOTTSDALE

"One hundred percent better than the best. Everybody plum wild about them. Will be exhibited in [the] best windows in New York from Times Square to Wall Street. Personally think them beautiful and proud to award them as prizes at America[']s rodeo classic."[29]

Jack Kriendler, co-founder and proprietor of the posh "21" Club in New York, was among the most enthusiastic supporters of the Madison Square Garden Rodeo. Called "Two-Trigger" Jack by some of his cronies, Kriendler enjoyed playing cowboy, decorated parts of his club with a western motif, and filled its walls with western illustrations by artist Frederic Remington. He routinely ordered western belts, buckles, billfolds, and even saddles embellished with the famous gates of the 21 Club and the Bar 21 brand from various western vendors, including Prosser Martin of Del Rio, Texas, another purveyor of Madison Square Garden trophy saddles (see p. 92). Martin acquired the silver for Kriendler's rig from famed Hollywood saddle

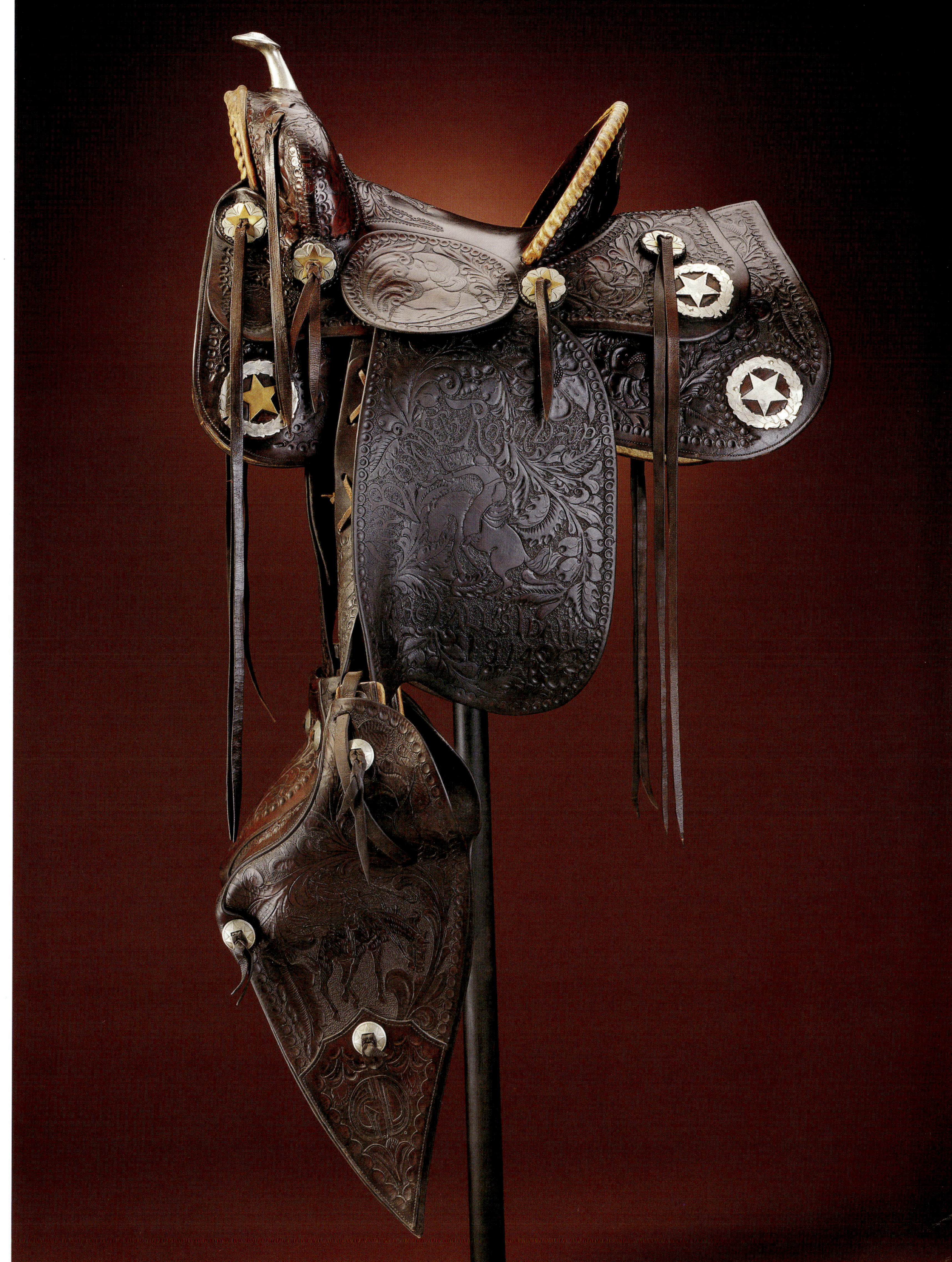

maker Edward H. Bohlin, who also produced a silver-encrusted parade saddle for the celebrated saloon keeper.

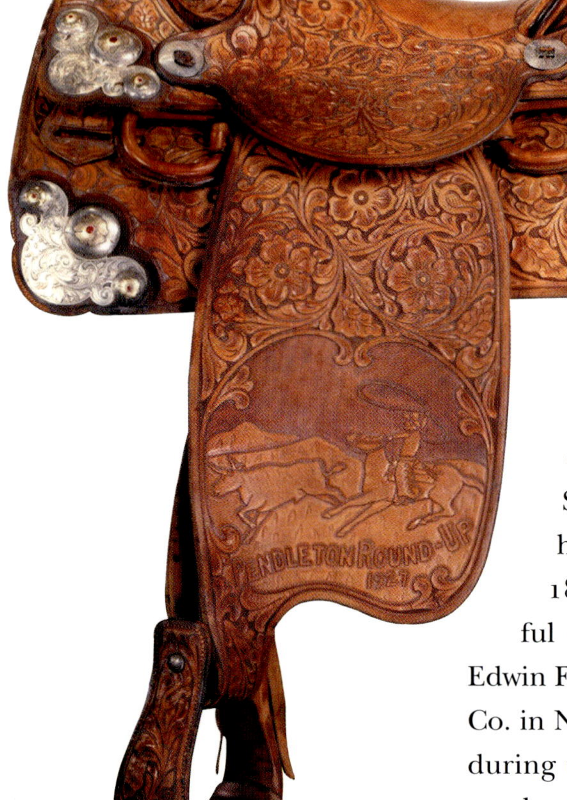

During the first half of the twentieth century, parades, horse shows, and other equestrian events held in connection with rodeos, fiestas, and fairs throughout the West fueled a demand for fancy saddlery. The phenomenon was especially pronounced in California, long accustomed to ostentatious displays of fine tack and home to some of the nation's most talented leatherworkers and silversmiths.

No region in the Bear Flag State surpassed Santa Barbara and the nearby Santa Ynez Valley for equestrian tradition, well-bred horses, and fine show saddles. Some residents considered silver-mounted saddles "almost as characteristic of Santa Barbara as Spanish architecture."[30] W. D. "Dixie" Thompson, a local rancher and hotelier, commissioned one of the town's fanciest and best-known rigs in 1889. The saddle and its matching bridle and martingale were the successful collaboration of local saddle maker Sherman Loomis and silversmith Edwin Field Sr., a Rhode Island–born jeweler and former engraver at Tiffany and Co. in New York. Field had come to California as a soldier in the American Army during the Mexican War and had returned with the Gold Rush, settling first in northern California before moving to Santa Barbara in 1870.

The silversmith patiently rolled and chased Mexican silver coins, provided a few at a time by Thompson, into delicate floral and wheat-head ornaments that were eventually affixed to the saddle leather. Some $250 worth alone went into the accompanying bridle. Valued at more than $3,000 and representing the Gold Rush era, Thompson's sumptuous outfit appeared in the California Pavilion at the Chicago World's Fair in 1894. The San Francisco *Argonaut* reported:

> This saddle and bridle, manufactured of bullion from Mexican dollars, are exquisite works of art. The saddle is of typical Mexican pattern, with a high pommel, well-hollowed seat, and the most elaborate of trappings. The leather is stamped with elegant designs, and the whole thing is a complete, costly, and elaborate equipment, of good taste and artistic design. The saddle is studded over with silver ornaments. The leather facings are set thick with buttons and rosettes; the pommel is encased in silver; the corners of the aprons are tipped with silver; the stirrups are faced and edged with silver half an inch thick, elaborately chased and carved. The saddle-tree is hung with silver rings, fore and aft, to answer all the requirements of the vaquero

Hamley and Co., Pendleton, Oregon
Saddle made for rodeo champion Bob Crosby, double rig with engraved corner plates with ruby accents on front and rear skirts and jockeys, low dished cantle, and steer-roping scene with "Pendleton Round-Up 1927" on fender
NATIONAL COWBOY AND WESTERN HERITAGE MUSEUM, OKLAHOMA CITY

Opposite
Hamley and Co., Pendleton, Oregon
Trophy saddle
FLEISCHER COLLECTION, SCOTTSDALE

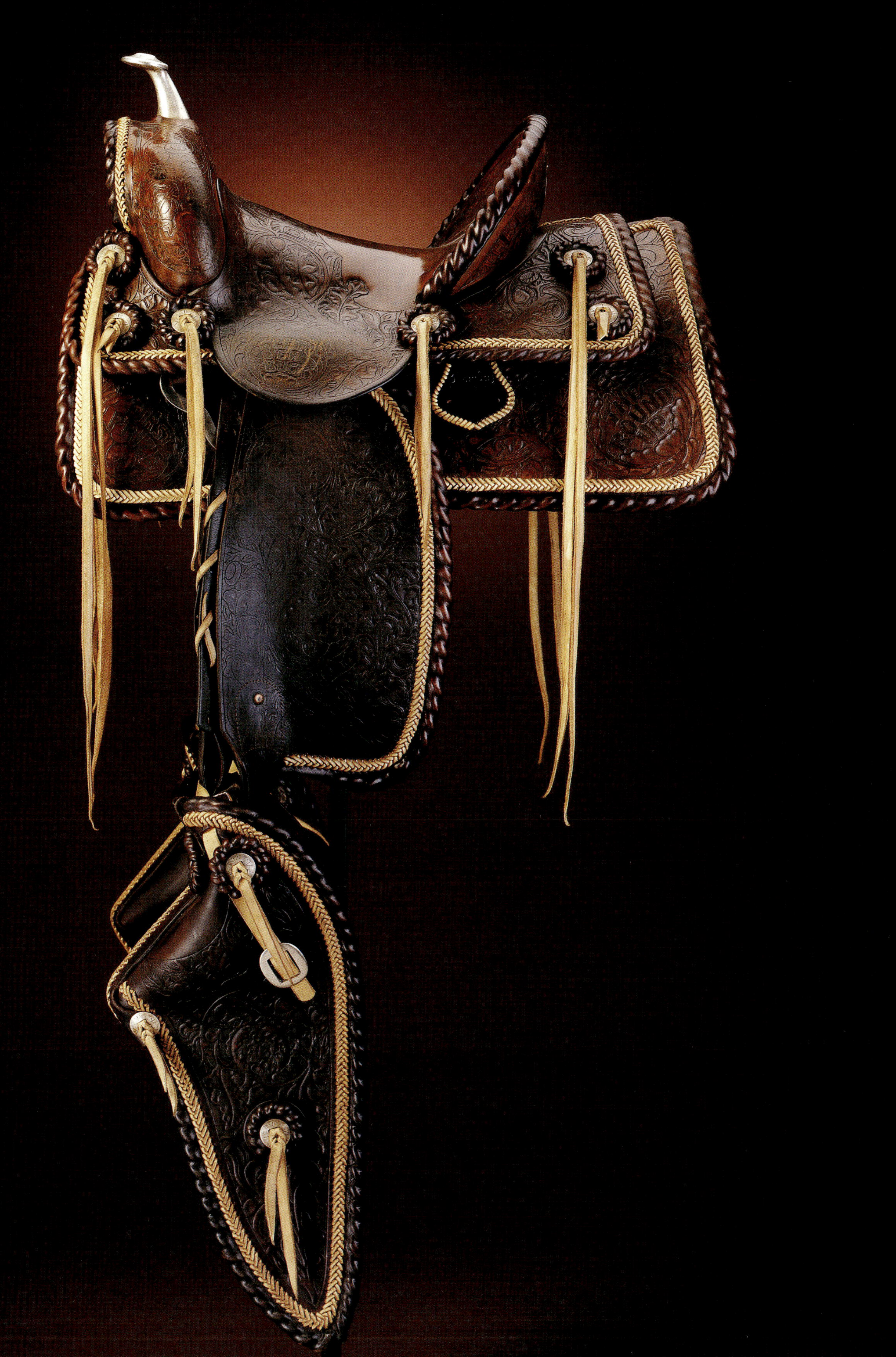

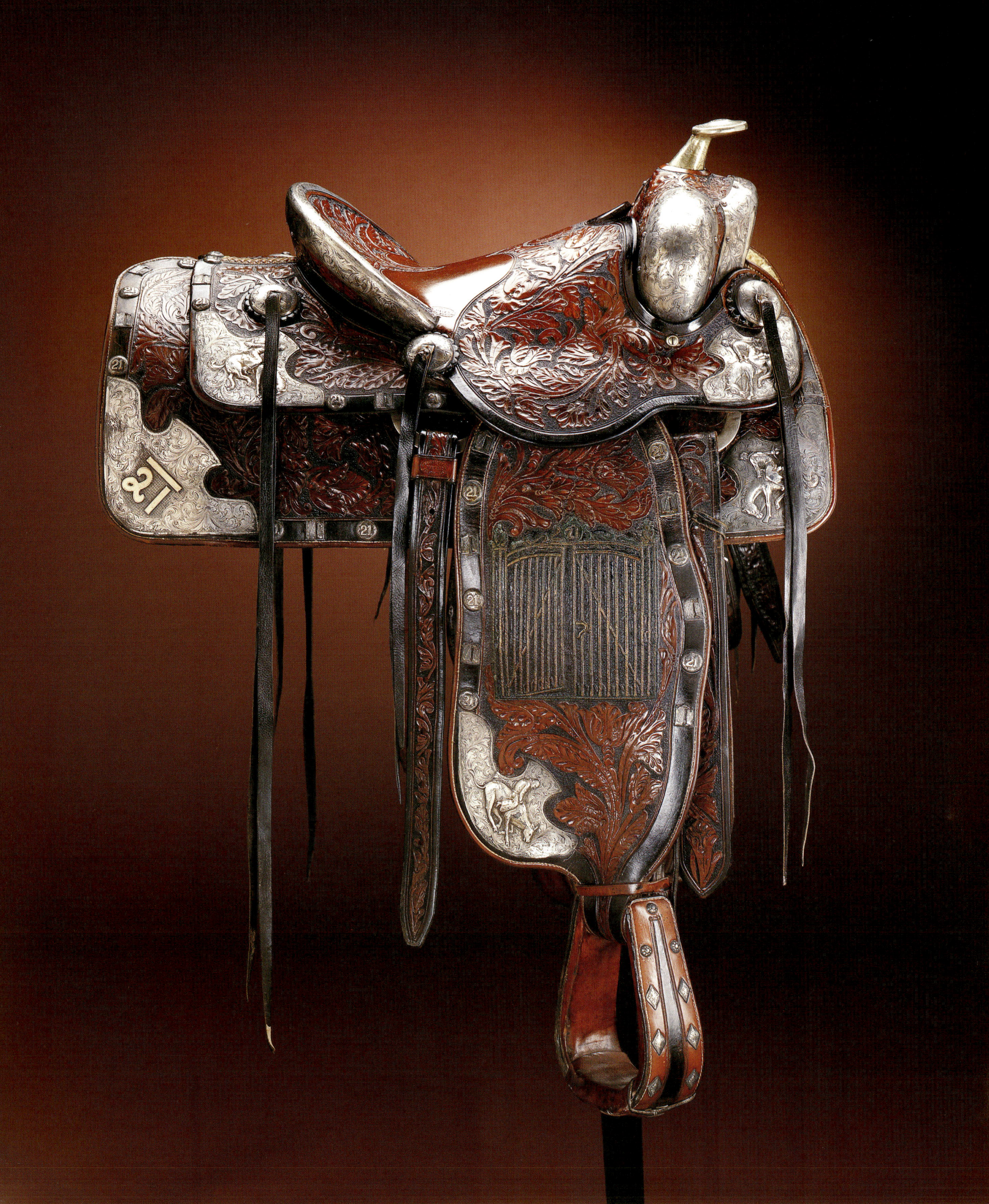
21

> in lacing up his riata. The girth, which passes under the horse's belly and cinches the saddle in place, is woven of hair from horses' manes by a native artisan, and is fully eight inches broad, with a tassel hanging at its middle. The saddle, the bridle, and all its appointments are marvels of beauty. The reins, martingale, and whip are composed of solid silver in woven strands. The headstall is covered with fluted silver, with large engraved silver rosettes at the sides, with decorations of flowers and heads of wheat, with an elaborate nose-piece with silver engraving. The side-pieces are of silver, massive and ornate, with a silver chain under the horse's jaw.[31]

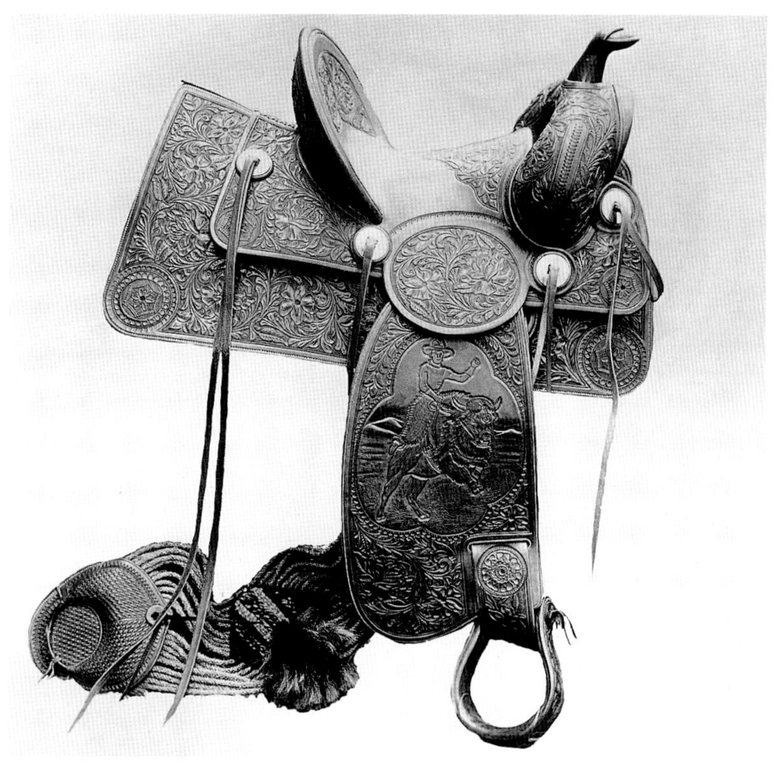

Presentation saddle commissioned by the Union Pacific Railroad, 1911, with carved image on fender of cowboy riding a buffalo
WYOMING STATE ARCHIVES, CHEYENNE

An informed observer quoted in *Harness Gazette* in 1897 called Thompson's rig the "finest and most costly saddle in America."[32] Kate Sanborn, who encountered the masterpiece of leather and silver on a visit to southern California in the early 1890s, agreed. "As his favorite mare stood before me with this magnificent saddle on . . ." she wrote later, "I never saw such a pretty sight of the kind."[33]

For many years Dixie Thompson and his famed saddle were fixtures at Santa Barbara's Floral Carnival and associated equestrian tournament, which included exhibitions of bronc riding, mustang roping, and *colgar*, the act of snatching $10 gold pieces off the ground while riding at full speed. In 1924 local civic leaders organized an even larger and more elaborate event called the Old Spanish Days Fiesta. This annual celebration of horses, horsemanship, fine tack, and the region's vaquero tradition drew thousands of spectators and hundreds of well-mounted and splendidly accoutered participants, including such celebrities as Will Rogers, William Randolph Hearst, and Charles Lindberg. Fine horseflesh and showy saddles were also in evidence at local horse shows, most of which included display classes that prized looks over performance, and during the colorful annual rides of Los Rancheros Visitadores, an elite club of affluent horsemen organized in 1930 in the Santa Ynez Valley.

Many well-heeled Barbarenos of the time rode locally made saddles, embellished with distinctive silver ornaments created by John C. Field, the son of Edwin Field. A meticulous perfectionist, the younger Field believed that traditionally engraved saddle trimmings lacked visual presence and began instead to stamp designs into the silver with steel dies in the manner of Mexican silversmiths. Some of his motifs emanated from flowers picked by his wife and mother.

Opposite
Prosser Martin, Del Rio, Texas Western stock saddle made for Jack Kriendler, owner of the "21" Club in New York, 1940s; raised reliefs on fenders depict gates to the "21" Club; skirts and jockeys feature silver corner plates with riders on bucking horses
BUFFALO BILL HISTORICAL CENTER, CODY, WYOMING

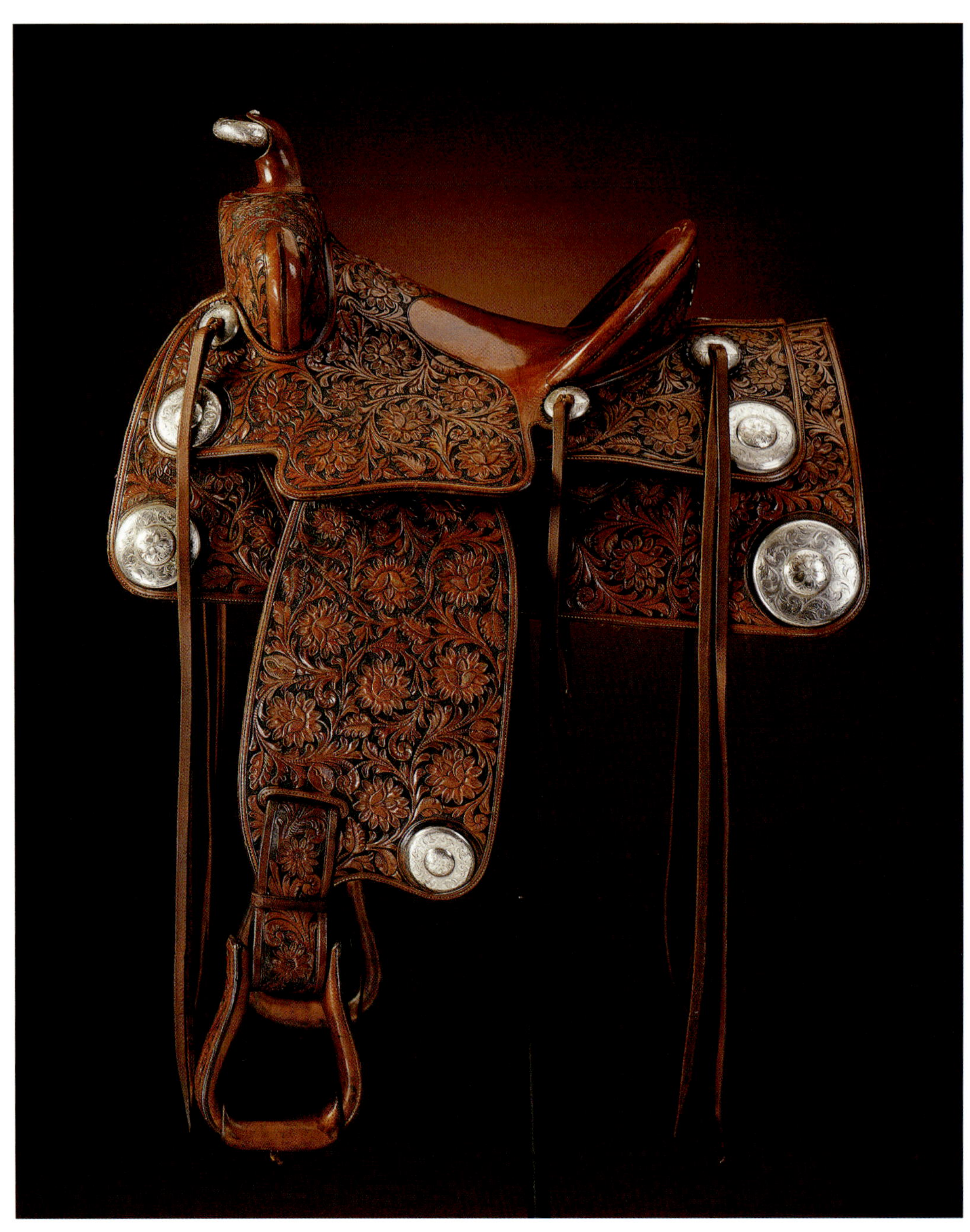

Edward H. Bohlin, Hollywood
Saddle with floral carving and large silver conchas
FLEISCHER COLLECTION, SCOTTSDALE

In 1948 the Santa Barbara Artist's Fair and Handcrafts Exhibition celebrated Field's creativity with an exhibition of his silver saddles. The same year a patron called upon the aging silversmith to trim her saddle with ornaments fashioned from the silver cups and porringer she had used as a child. John Field, who, in addition to saddle silver, designed and produced silver-inlaid bridle bits, passed his considerable silversmithing and bit-making skills on to his children. Daughter Marguerite (Rita) Field Thornburgh, for example, not only learned to stamp silver but also to design and embellish bits and spurs. Similar talents later accrued to Field's grandson Edwin and great-grandson Gary, both of whom pursued the craft part-time.

Opposite
Garcia Saddlery, Salinas, California
Leather saddle with silver filligree work
SANDRONI COLLECTION, LOS ANGELES

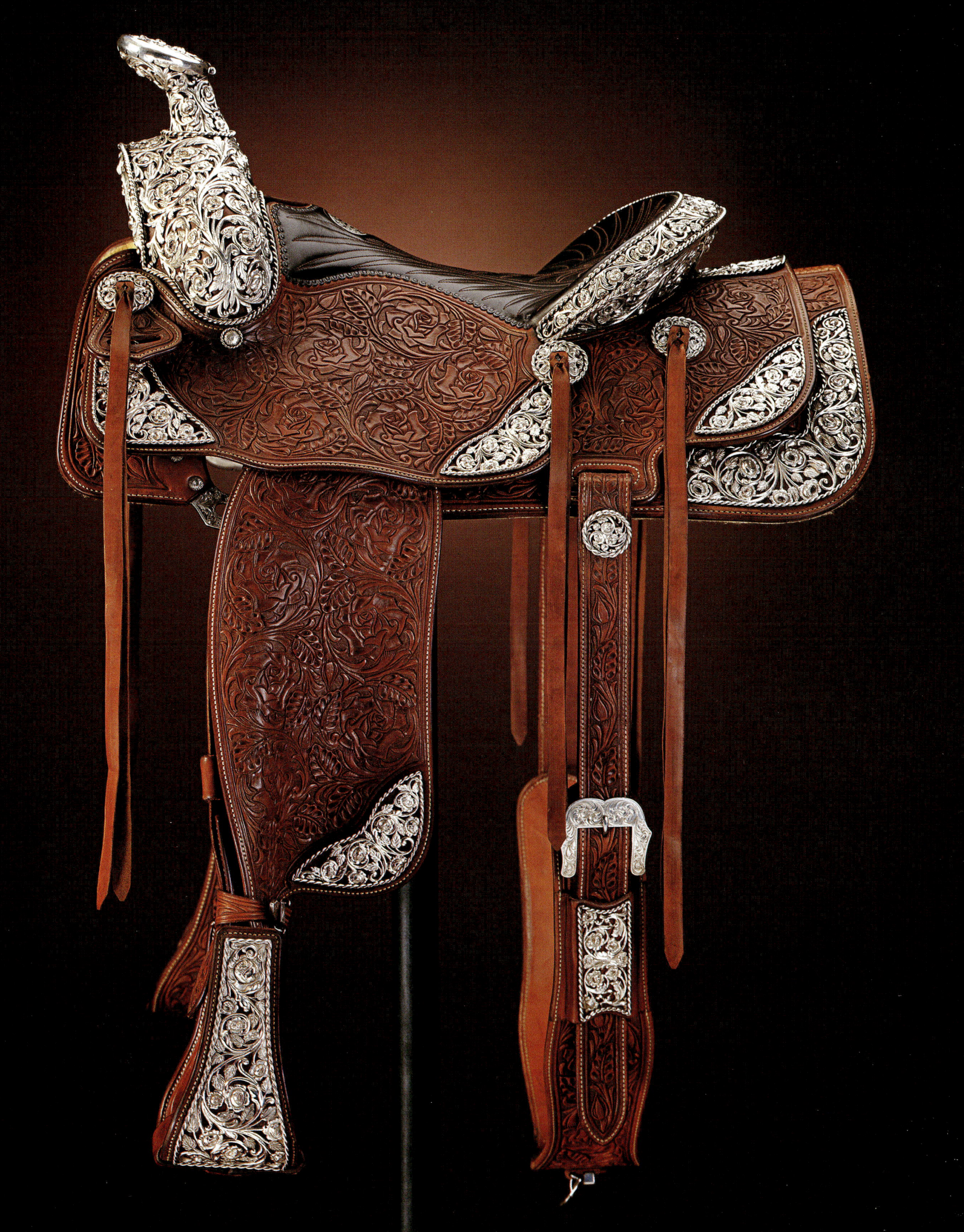

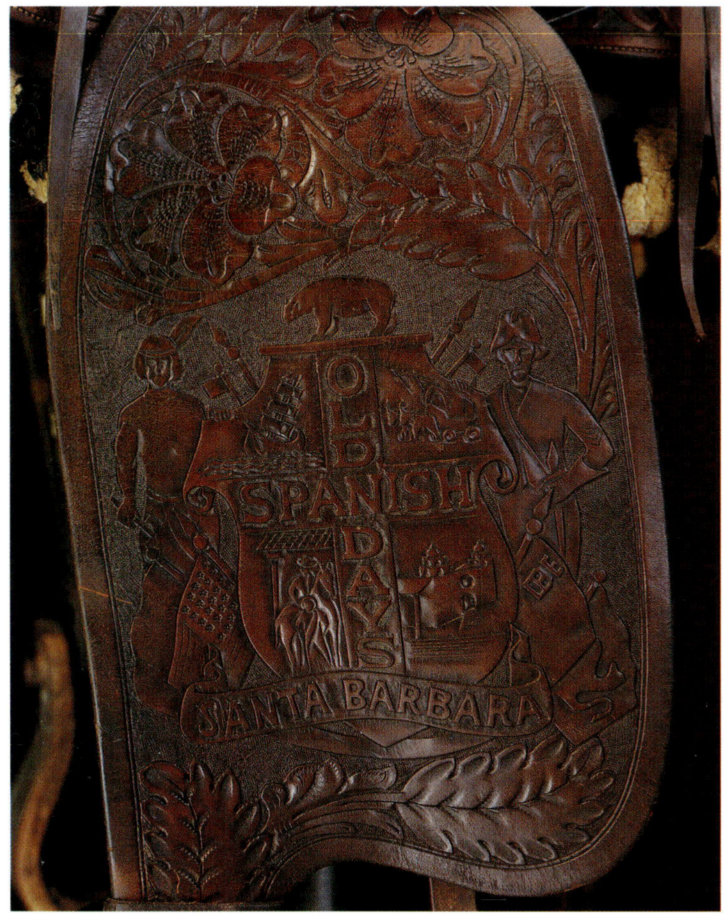

Visalia Stock Saddle Co.,
San Francisco
Saddle fender detail, commemorating the annual Old Spanish Days celebration in Santa Barbara, c. 1920s
FLEISCHER COLLECTION, SCOTTSDALE

Between the 1920s and the 1950s only Los Angeles and San Francisco surpassed Santa Barbara as centers of the show saddle production. A strong equestrian heritage, nostalgia for the Old West, and a booming motion picture industry helped sustain the saddle trade in southern California. Such prominent saddle houses as Lichtenberger-Ferguson, a large wholesaler established in the 1890s, and Brydon Brothers, founded in 1902, operated profitably even before the cameras began to roll. But as western films came into their own, such cowboy stars as Tom Mix, Buck Jones, and Hoot Gibson began to demand ever-flashier outfits and new firms entered the market.

In 1921 Edward H. Bohlin, a footloose trick roper with a traveling vaudeville company, quit the road in Los Angeles after meeting Tom Mix and landing a job as an extra in cowboy movies. The following year he opened the Hollywood Novelty Leather Shop. Born a soldier's son in Sweden in 1895, Emil Helge Bohlin had immigrated to the United States in 1912. He worked his way westward, ending up in Montana where he became a cowboy. In 1916 "Ed" Bohlin, as he was now known, moved to Cody, Wyoming, where he wrangled dudes and punched cows on nearby ranches. In his spare time he taught himself leather craft, learned to make bits and spurs, and with the help of a local jeweler, mastered basic silversmithing techniques. Bohlin opened a short-lived western shop in Cody in the fall of 1920 before show business took him to California.

Aided by a pair of investors and his own genius for promotion, Bohlin transformed his fledgling business into an upscale operation known as The Bohlin Shop in the mid-1920s. With the help of a talented staff that eventually included more than three-dozen silversmiths and leatherworkers, mainly northern Europeans and Hispanics, the entrepreneurial saddle maker began to produce silver-mounted saddles and other fancy gear for film stars and parade riders. Bohlin's well-heeled clientele would eventually include some of the most important and famous entertainers, sportsmen, businessmen, and politicos of the day. Actor Tom Mix soon dubbed his friend the "Saddlemaker for the Stars."[34]

After experiencing early success, however, Bohlin became over-extended during the Great Depression and was forced to declare bankruptcy in 1931. Although he lost dies and other precious tools in the subsequent court settlement, the undaunted saddle maker reorganized and reopened his shop at a new location in 1933. Within four years he would claim, probably with truth, to "have

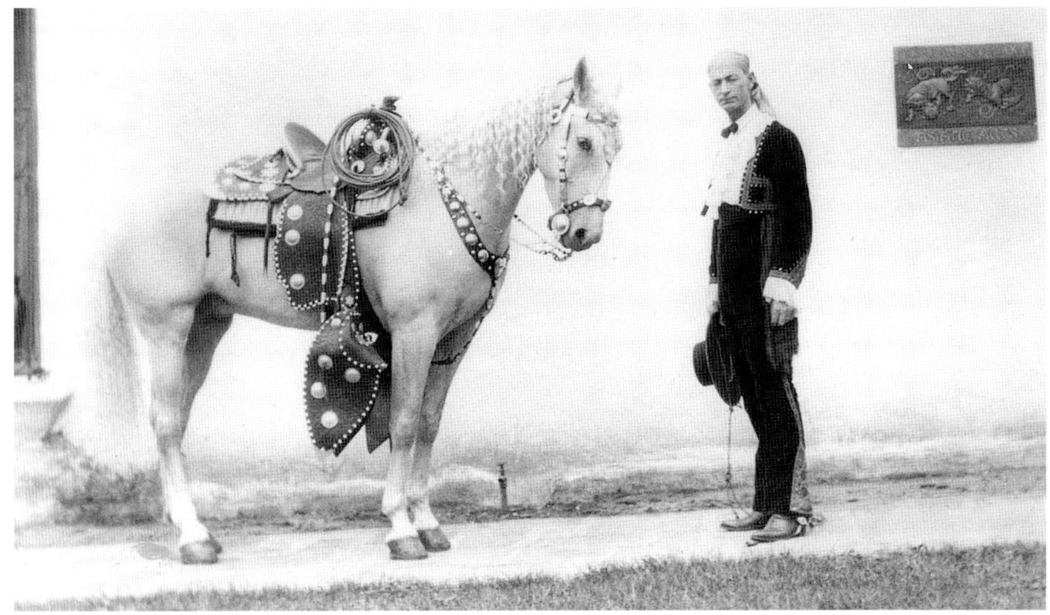

Samuel Adelstein (1861–1906)
"El Capitan, El Palomino," 1900s
California Historical Society, San Francisco

designed and made in our own shop a larger number of elaborate and artistic designs in gold and silver mounted riding equipment than any other concern in the country."[35] Between 1920 and 1974 Bohlin and the artists who worked for him produced an average of more than 225 saddles annually, most of them -silver-mounted, black leather parade saddles and accouterments customized from nearly 100 basic styles.

Ironically The Bohlin Shop sold some of its best and most expensive work, including many parade ensembles, during the financial distress of the Great Depression. Bohlin's biographer James Nottage estimated that during the 1930s and 1940s the master craftsman outfitted as many as 90 percent of the mounted contingent at the annual Tournament of Roses Parade. Bohlin-made gear also could be seen at horse shows, where appearance was always an asset, and among sheriff's posses and other riding clubs.

Bohlin drew the inspiration for his decorative designs from many quarters, including his patrons. His gold- and silverwork reflected influences that ranged from art nouveau and art deco to western American art and illustration to historical events and photography. The imagery that often appeared in tableaus owed a debt to such artists as Charles M. Russell, N. C. Wyeth, and Edward Borein. Floral leather carving and chased silver included renditions of California poppies, mariposa lilies, and several kinds of roses. The saddle Bohlin made for Chicago chewing gum magnate P. K. Wrigley included representations of all the wildflowers found on Catalina Island, home to Wrigley's ranch. Bohlin motifs and ornaments, in turn, influenced the entire field of embellished saddlery and decorated the products of many of his competitors.

Besides their visual appeal, silver cantle rims, pommel swells, and other ornaments helped protect leather at vulnerable points. On a square-skirted

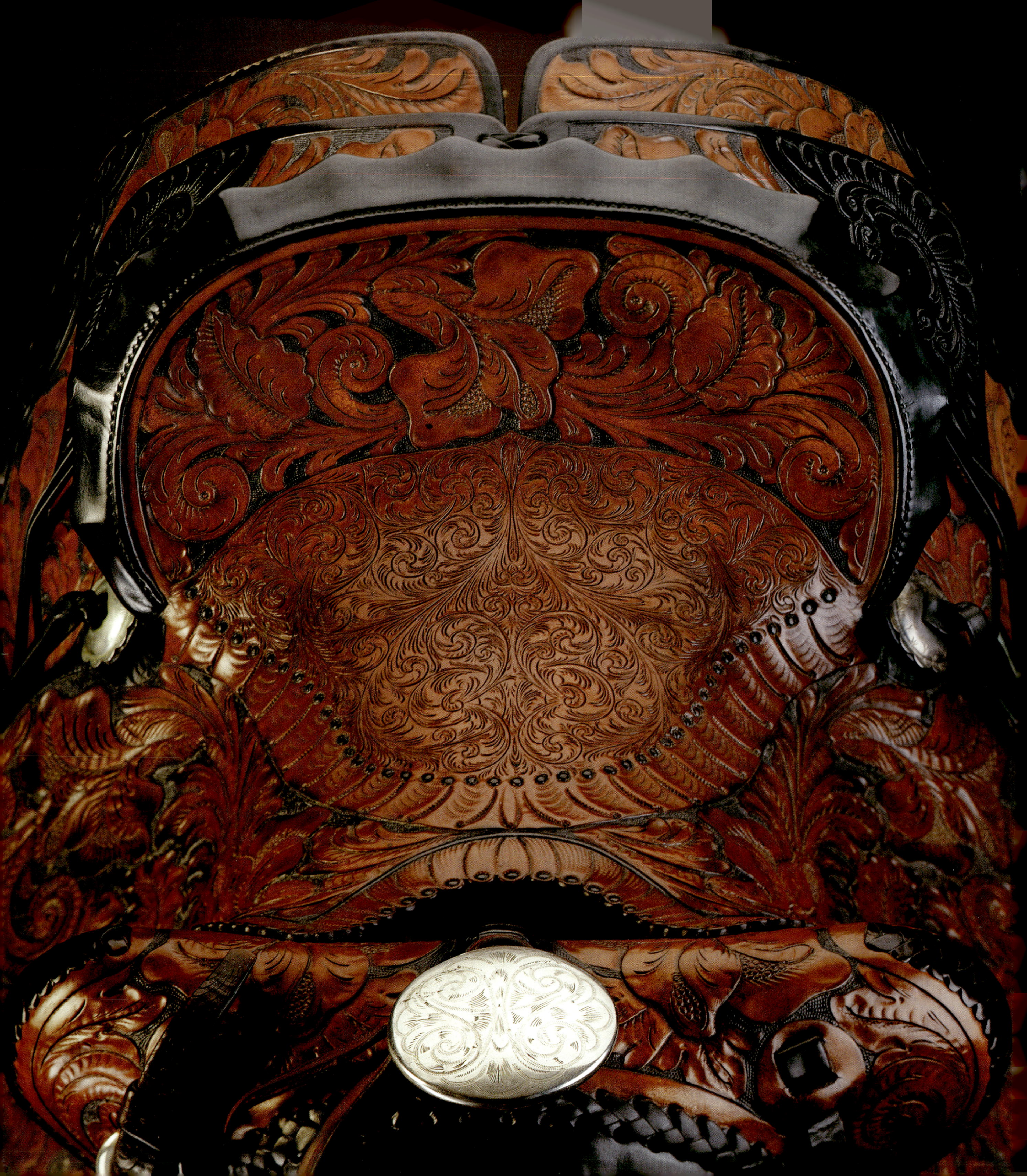

saddle, corner plates helped prevent the leather from curling into a horse's flanks. Silver conchas did not rust or promote the hardening and cracking of saddle leather, as did some other metals. Metal ornaments did, however, add weight and bulk to the saddle, as much as 150 pounds in some cases. Such a load was more than three times that of a typical heavy-duty range saddle. To aid parade riders in saddling their mounts, the maker equipped heavier models with special mechanisms that allowed some of the accoutrements to be installed separately.

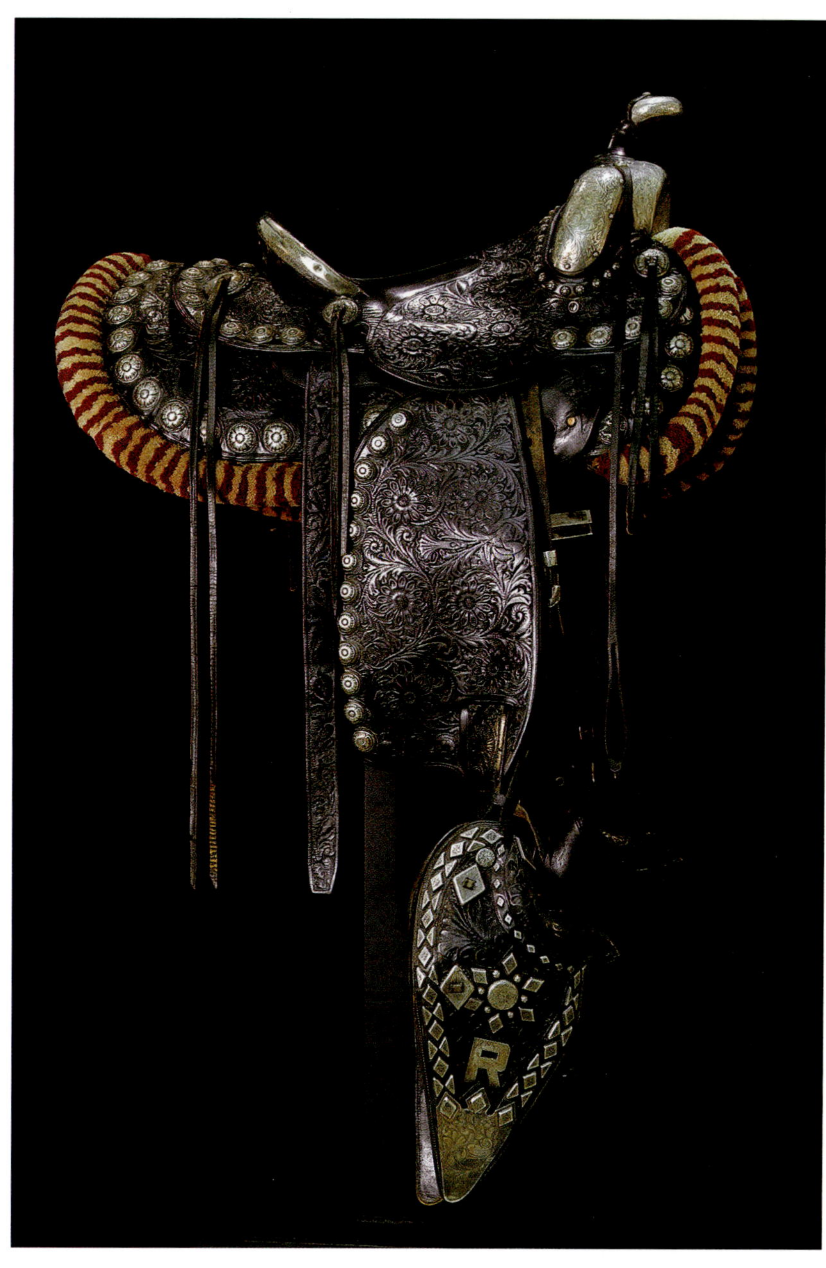

Dale Evans saddle
Previously owned by Dell Jones, Wild West show cowgirl, as a gift from her husband, Buck Jones
NATIONAL COWGIRL MUSEUM AND HALL OF FAME, FORT WORTH

One of the designer's most exquisite creations, made between about 1927 and 1930 for California businessman Marco H. Hellman, depicted twenty-one California missions and other scenes of Mexican California, hand chased and arrayed in square panels of silver around the skirts, fenders, and jockeys and on the breast collar. The horn, swell caps, pommel, cantle bindings, corner and stirrup plates were all rendered in stunning repoussé. Silver buttons outlined the front of the seat and fenders, and the owner's initials appeared in gold on the swell caps and accompanying breast collar. The maker laid rich brown leather filigreed in a floral pattern over a black patent leather background and sewed the whole with sterling silver wire. Unfortunately, Hellman went bankrupt before the $3,000 saddle was delivered, and it was eventually acquired by Jack Kriendler who exhibited it for many years at the "21" Club (see pp. 102–103).

In 1933 Bohlin began work on a personal saddle that became the benchmark of his creativity and the ultimate expression his skill as a metalsmith. Crafted from sterling silver and four colors of gold, the "Big Saddle," as it was often called, took fourteen years to produce. From the hood-ornament-appearing Indian with feather bonnet that served as the saddle horn to the tip of its long *tapaderos*, the one-of-a-kind rig was a masterpiece by any definition. Bohlin and his associates covered the saddle skirting with dozens of tableaus reflecting western scenery, wildlife, and cowboy activities. A carved bull rider adorned black-on-black filigreed leather fenders.

Opposite
N. Porter, Phoenix
Saddle, 1940s, detail of seat
FLEISCHER COLLECTION, SCOTTSDALE

Although Edward Bohlin had few peers as a designer, he was not without talented competitors. In 1923, two years after Bohlin established his first shop in Hollywood, Al L. Furstnow, a visionary Miles City saddler, who had supplied Wild West shows and visiting movie companies with saddles and other leather gear for more than a decade, opened a branch not far from Bohlin's shop. Furstnow's tenure in southern California, however, was both brief and financially disappointing, and by 1927 he had returned to the Great Plains.

The same year that Furstnow located in Hollywood, John E. McCabe founded McCabe Silversmiths in Los Angeles, a firm that produced silver saddlery, saddle trimmings, and jewelry. The company's finest creation and one of the best of the entire genre of silver saddles was a spectacular $20,000 gold- and silver-mounted outfit commissioned by a well-heeled Los Angeles horsewoman. The entire project took sixteen master artisans more than six months to complete and required some 87.5 pounds of silver, 8.5 pounds of gold, and 1,500 rubies imported from Czechoslovakia.

Los Angeles saddle maker J. P. Davis built the saddle and carved the skirting with traditional floral and figural motifs that stood out in sculptural relief. Carved bronc riders adorned the fenders. Artist Tillman Goodin, whose distinctive western imagery appeared in comic books and on tableware, ties, and billfolds, sketched the thirty-one different scenes of cowboy life that McCabe smiths expertly chased in silver and gold. Most portrayed gold figures roping and riding, often against a silver landscape that often included mountains, trees, cactus, and sage. Many drew on Western art. The tableau of a cowboy roping a wolf or coyote, for example, paid homage to Charles M. Russell, who devoted more than one painting to the same theme. Likewise, the rider whose horse bolts at the sight of a snake in another scene was a variation of a motif made famous in a bronze sculpture by artist Frederic Remington.

One authority compared McCabe's silverwork to the best Tiffany-made silver of the period and considered the saddle second only to Bohlin's personal rig in beauty and importance. Others agreed. Roy Rogers, television's "King of the Cowboys," acquired the saddle with its matching bridle, chaps, and martingale in 1950 and toured it to department stores in nearly three dozen cities in advance of personal appearances.

Bohlin's most serious rival as a designer and producer of silver saddles was Frank H. Coenen, a Dane who had entered the saddle business in 1906 at Alhambra, near Los Angeles. Although his exquisite silver-mounted show saddles never lack for buyers, including some of Bohlin's best customers, surprisingly little is known of his six decade–long career. Coenen's shop, like Bohlin's, produced entire parade outfits, including chaps, bridles, bits, spurs, and other goods. In 1939 he sent a gold medal–winning saddle valued at $20,000 to the World's Fair in

Philip "Fred" Fredholm, Los Angeles (silver work) and F. O. Baird (leather carving) Ornate hand-carved parade saddle; silver work includes shell and daisy motif edge trim, pierced plates, and rope edge on cantle, horn, and pommel
FLEISCHER COLLECTION, SCOTTSDALE

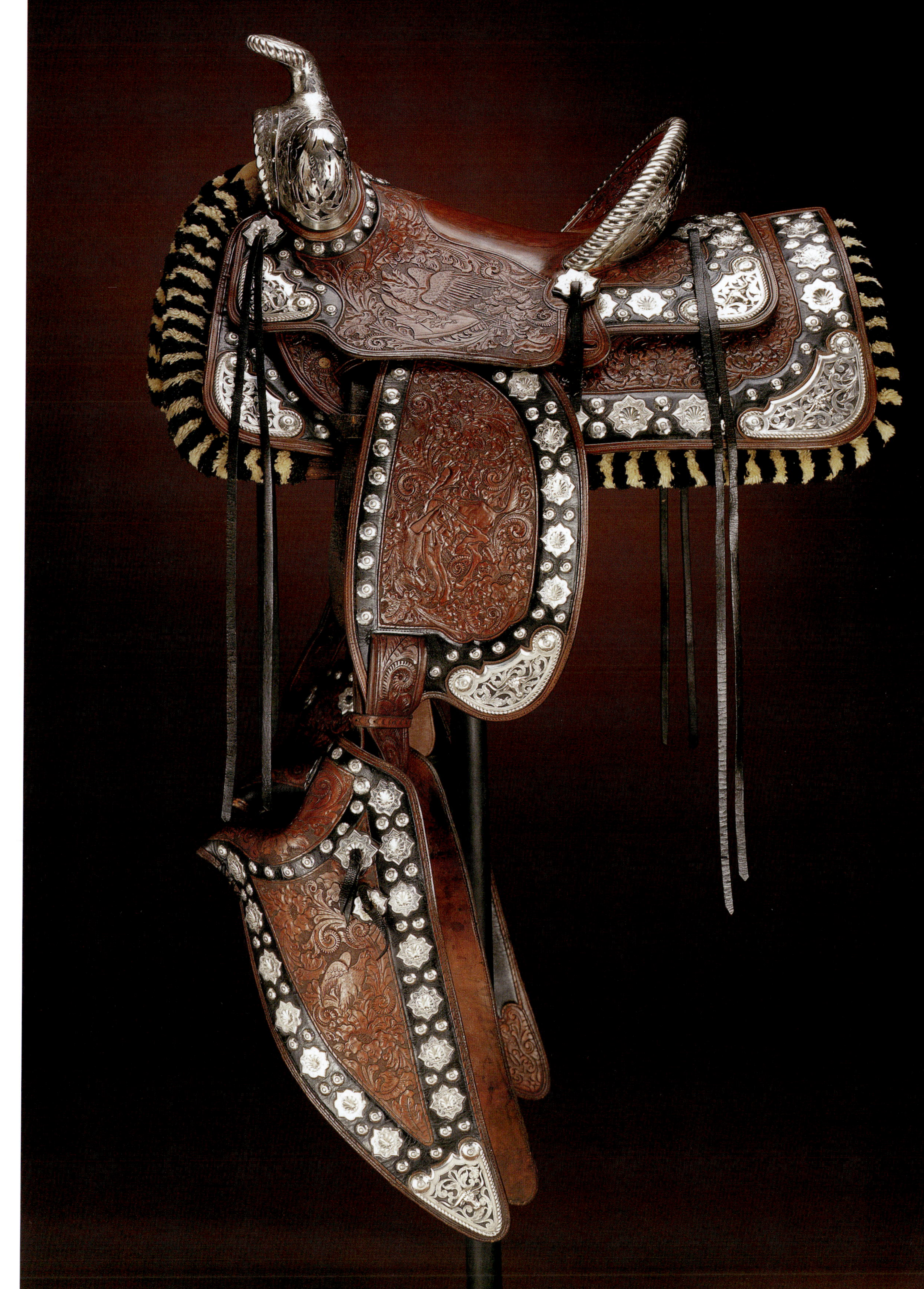

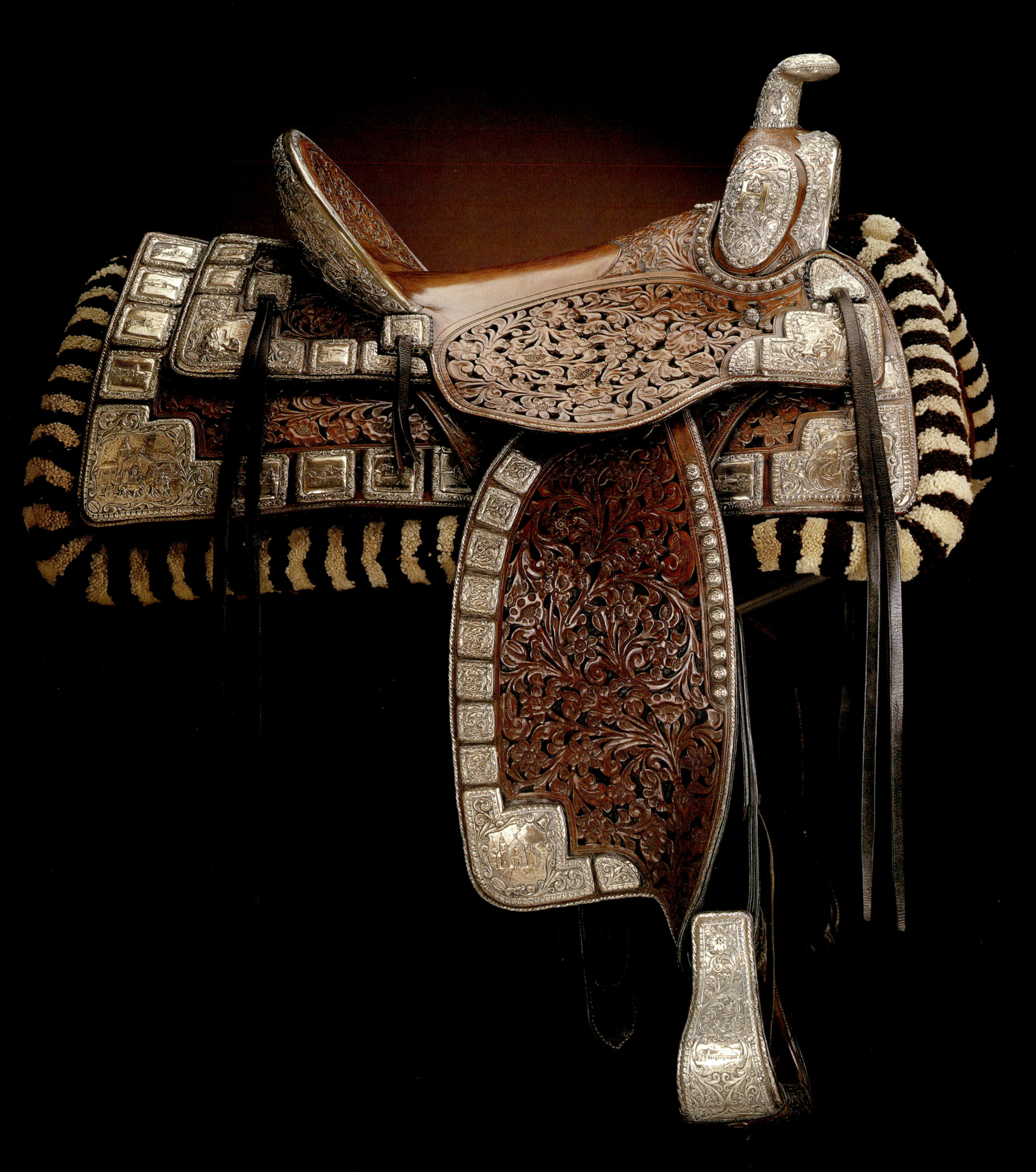

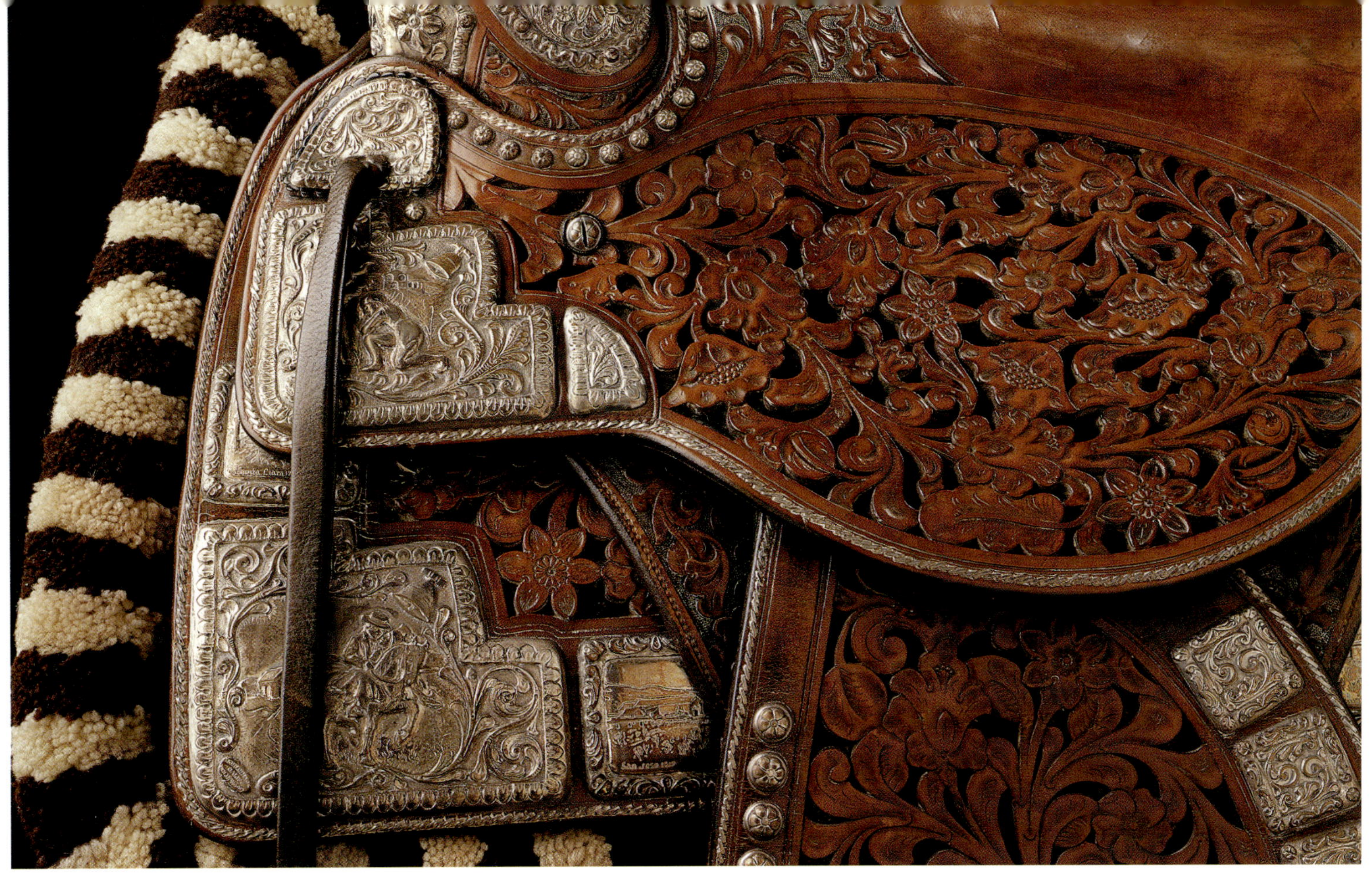

Edward H. Bohlin, Hollywood Silver-mounted "California Mission" saddle, 1930s (opposite), with details of leather filigree and pierced work (above) and rear of cantle showing California Bear motifs (below)
BUFFALO BILL HISTORICAL CENTER, CODY, WYOMING

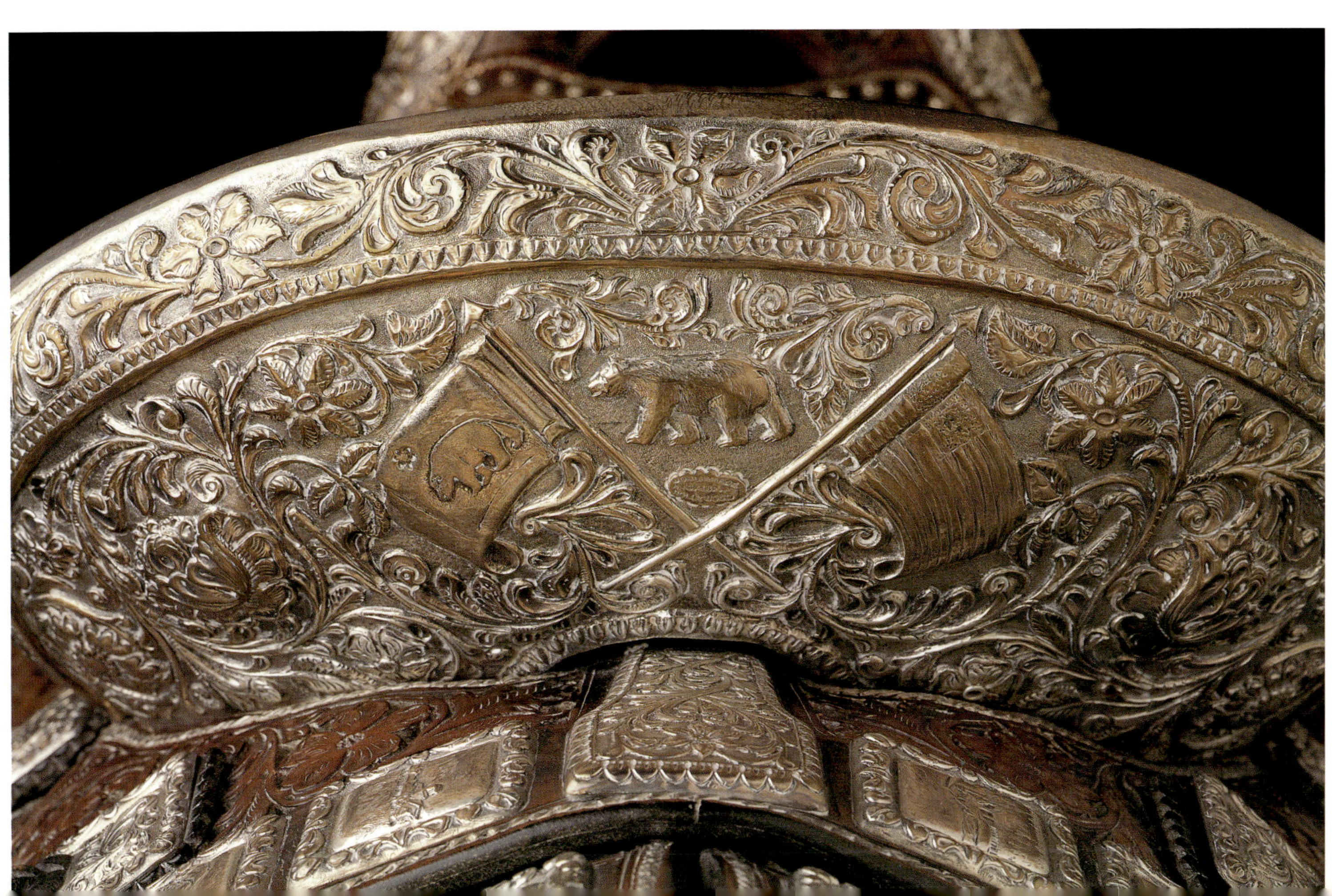

New York. The rig's expertly repoussé and engraved mounts told the story of the Santa Fe Trail and transportation in the West.

In the late 1940s, after several decades of satisfying the demands of customers, who included Will Rogers, Tom Mix, and Wallace Beery, Coenen completed his final masterpiece. Executed at the maker's own pleasure before his death in 1964, the "San Fernando Saddle," as it became known, required four years of work, included six hundred troy ounces of sterling silver and weighed 150 pounds. Coenen garnished his elegant rig with twenty-two scenes of cowboy life, rendered as silver repoussé cameos, amid an intricate floral and foliate background (see pages 106–8).

Ed Gilmore's North Hollywood saddlery and Major Monte Stone's Hollywood Saddlery also did a fair amount of business in silver-mounted goods in the 1930s. Stone absorbed Gilmore's operation after its founder was murdered in 1940. The following year Stone sold out to Lou Kosloff.

Brydon Brothers also changed hands when a partnership comprised of five saddle makers, including Carl Wilson, owner of the Coggshall Saddlery in Miles City, and Floyd O. Baird, a superb carver who had worked for both Lichtenberger-Ferguson Co. and Porter's, bought the company in 1935. Thanks to an embezzling office manager, however, the new enterprise soon failed, and fifteen men were thrown out of work.

San Francisco's saddle-making industry might have competed more successfully in the silver saddle market were it not for the lingering effects of the earthquake and fire of 1906. Only the Visalia and Olsen-Nolte saddleries emerged as large-scale producers of show saddles in the Bay Area before World War II. The latter firm opened in 1937 under the leadership of John E. Olsen and Al Nolte. Upon Nolte's death in 1942, onetime Visalia saddle maker Walt Goldsmith took over production.

At the height of the trade in fancy gear in the 1930s, Visalia operated branches in Santa Barbara and, during winters, in Palm Springs. The company also employed a designer and silversmith to assist customers with special designs and custom orders. Santa Ynez rancher and palomino breeder Dwight Murphy, one of Visalia's best customers, is said to have given one of the company's striking parade rigs to every buyer of one of his horses.

In the late 1930s California Serbs commissioned the Visalia Company to create his and hers saddles for the King and Queen of Serbia. Renowned Visalia carvers reproduced the Serbian Royal Crest on fenders of the silver-mounted presentation rig which was equipped with long *tapaderos* and matching bridles and martingales. Longtime San Francisco silversmiths R. Schaezlein & Son supplied silver saddle trimmings to Visalia, as well as several other western saddleries.

During World War II the parade saddle business entered the doldrums. News of U.S. Admiral William F. "Bull" Halsey's brash promise to ride Japanese Emperor Hirohito's white horse through Tokyo, prompted a flurry of patriotic

Opposite
Edward H. Bohlin, Hollywood
Silver-mounted parade saddle for Leo Ahrenholtz, 1950s
Fleischer Collection, Scottsdale

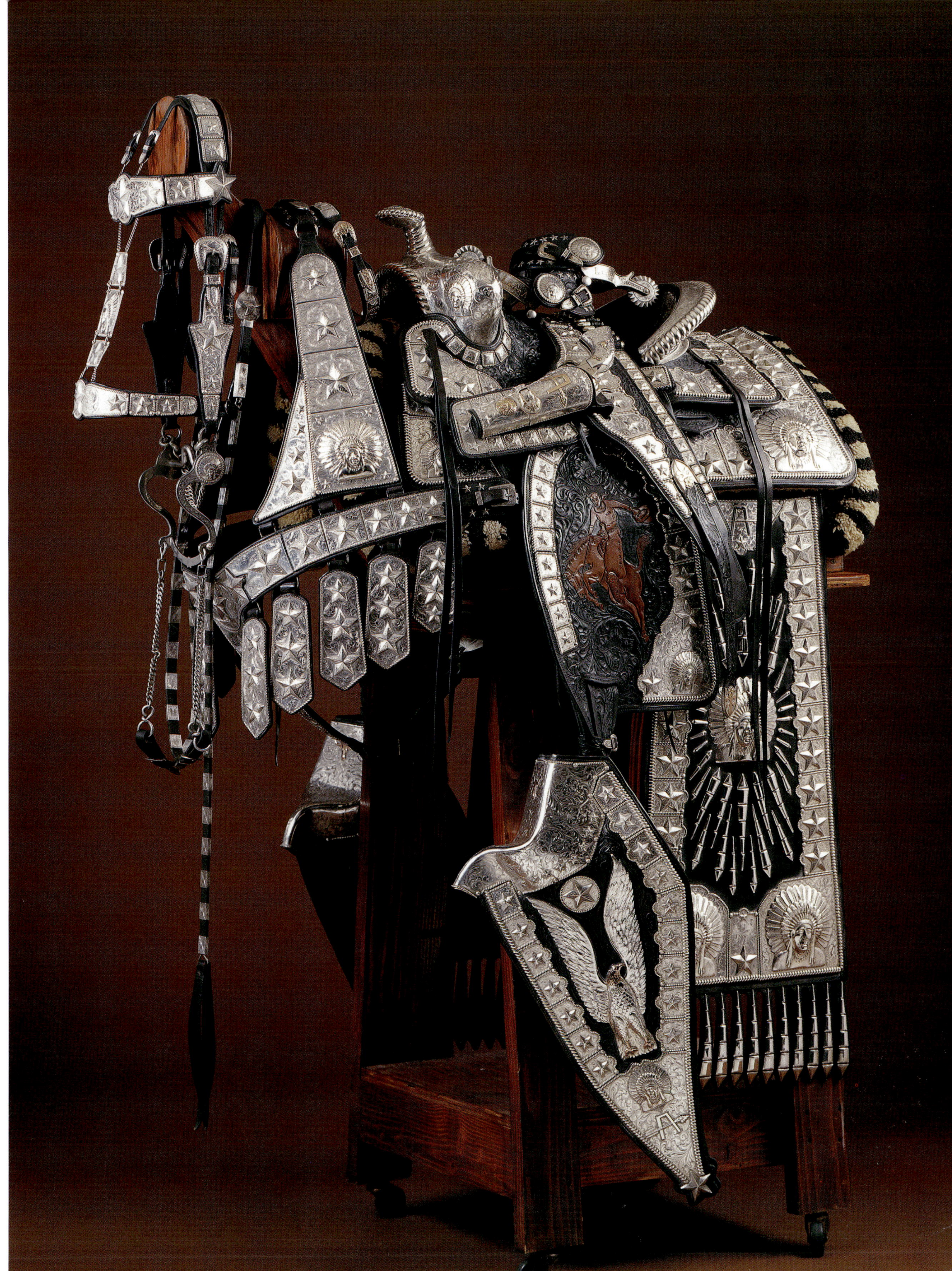

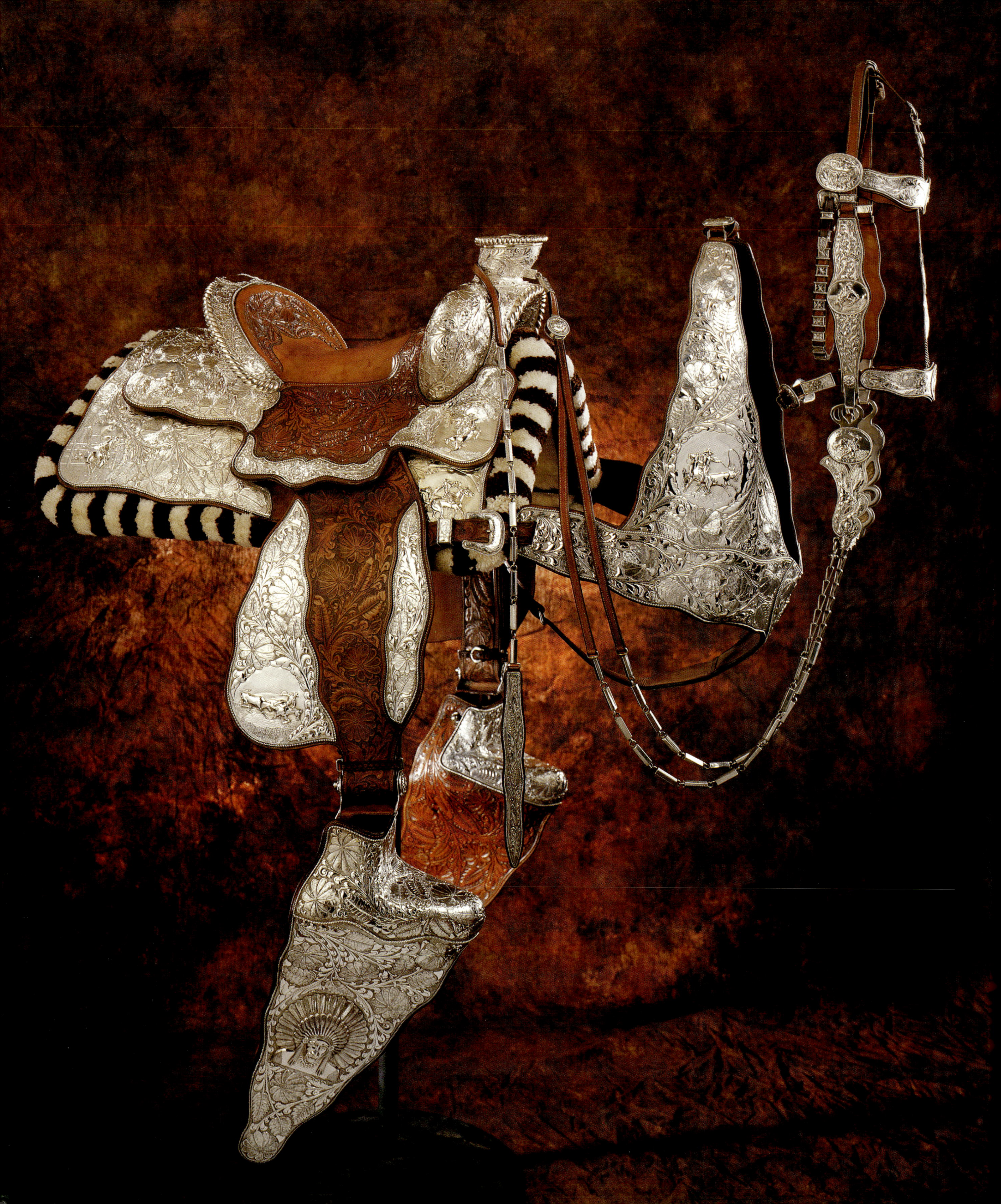

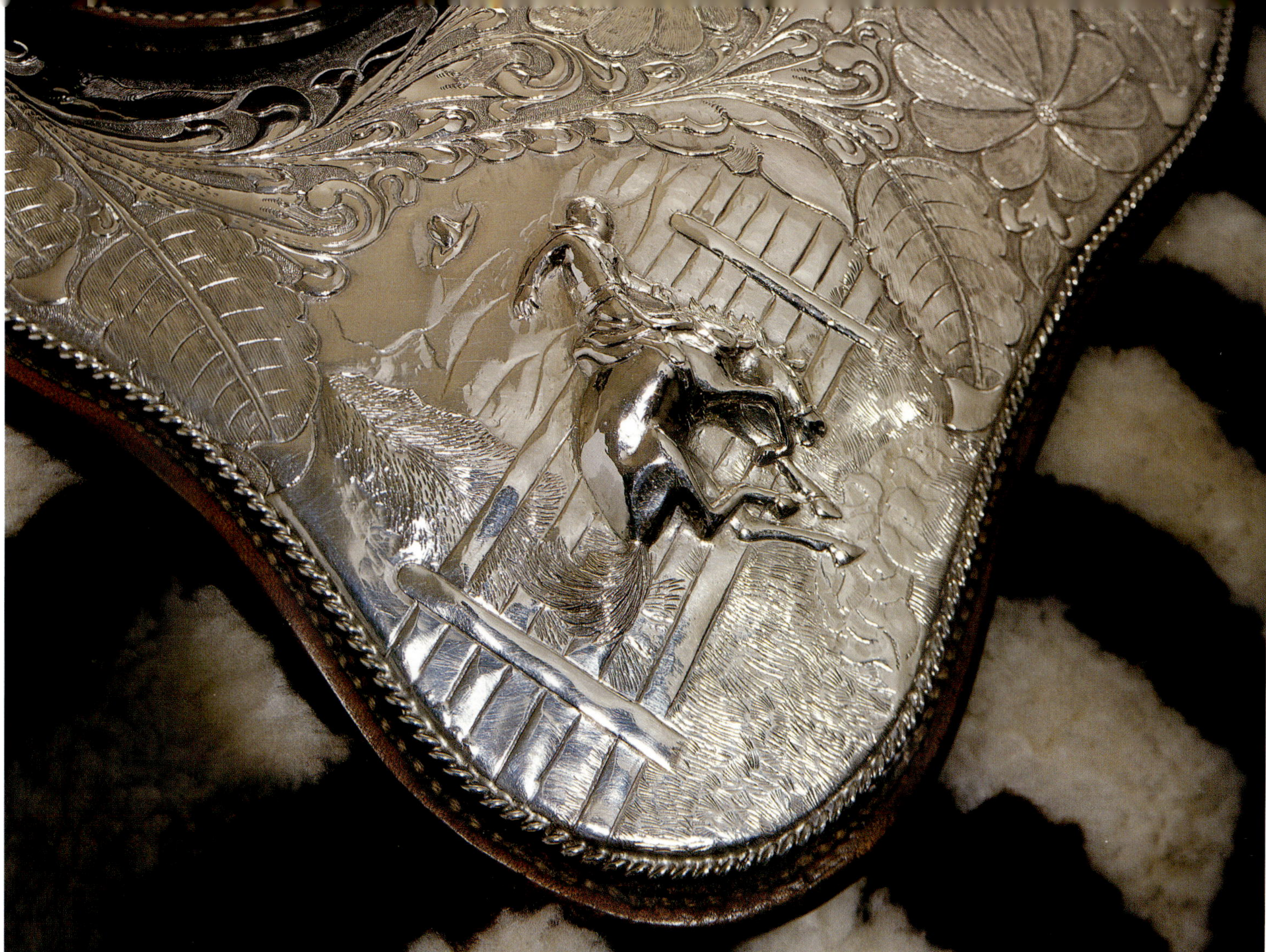

activity, however, which resulted in the creation of at least two western stock saddles to help the admiral fulfill his promise.

Frank H. Coenen, Alhambra, California
Silver-mounted "San Fernando" parade saddle, c. 1947 (opposite), with detail of repoussé silver work (above)
FLEISCHER COLLECTION, SCOTTSDALE

The Reno Chamber of Commerce sponsored the most ambitious and celebrated project, commissioning the local firm of Bools and Butler to create a silver-mounted presentation rig. Fred Lohein, a veteran artisan with more than a half-century of experience, built and carved the saddle, while M. H. Newman engraved the silver. The saddle, said to put "to shame anything Hirohito has (or had) in his royal tackroom,"[36] was accompanied to the Pacific by a matching bridle and martingale sponsored by the Reno Junior Chamber of Commerce, a nylon rope, a pair of spurs made by a Navy machinist, and a pair of gauntlets beaded by women of the Paiute tribe of Pyramid Lake. Master saddler Walter Allison of Montrose, Colorado, crafted the second Halsey rig, which was sponsored by the Lions Club of that community. Sixty-three local cattlemen paid $10 each to have their brands carved on the saddle and accompanying bridle and breast collar.

A renewed interest in recreational riding during the postwar era briefly revived the fortunes of the silver saddle business. By this time, however, critics were becoming more vocal about the lack of taste exhibited by some parade saddle makers and their customers. In his delightful 1946 volume, *Trail Dust and Saddle Leather,* California artist and vaquero Joe Mora gently chided:

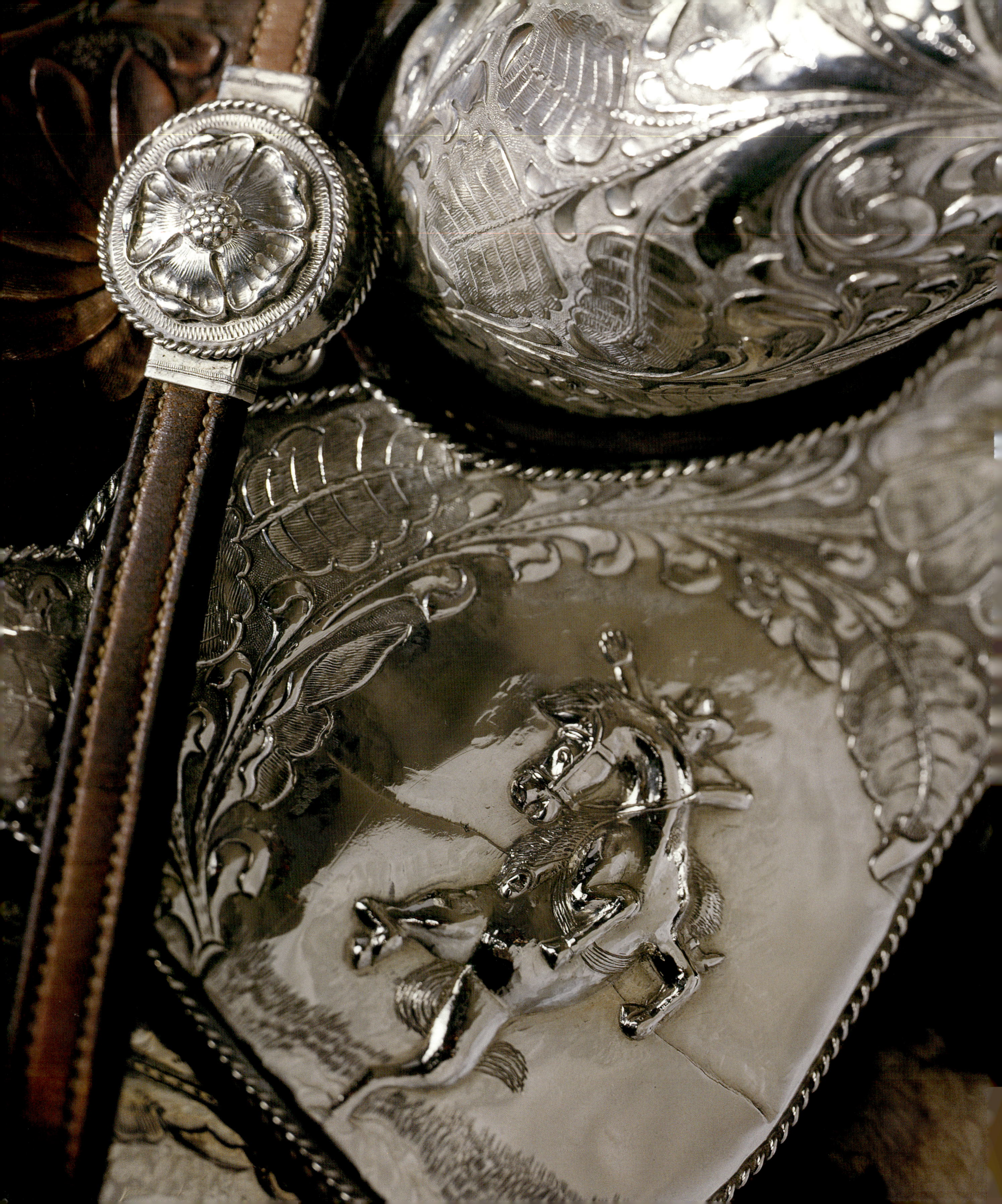

> Of late, with the rodeo shows and their parades, the popular fiestas that are getting to be annual community events, and the marked enthusiasm and boom for the Western rig and the Western way of riding, our saddle designers and craftsmen have positively run riot on the use of silver and even gold for the adornment of the saddles. You need a pair of strong specks to see the leather on some of these new creations. Horns, forks, and cantles are often completely encased in solid silver, highly embellished with motifs of cattle, lions, cowboy figures, birds, flowers, stars, what-nots, and whole family portrait groups of many figures. Such saddles are affairs, I guess, though they do lose their identity as stock saddles.[37]

Mora shunned fancy fiesta rigs in favor of a working rig with "a good dash of silver." The old vaquero always wanted to feel, as he put it, that he could "take after a runaway in the thick brush without fear of amputating Grandma's silver nose from the bas relief."[38]

By the mid-1950s the parade saddle business had virtually dried up, forcing some companies to either downsize their operations or close altogether. The market for rodeo trophy saddles and occasional presentation types, however, remained stable. In 1956, for example, the chamber of commerce of Clovis, California, known as "Rodeo City," commissioned fourteen-year-old saddle maker Ray Beaver to commemorate in leather the centennial of Fresno County. The finished product, which featured vignettes of early day gold mining, transportation, and ranching, was given to President Dwight Eisenhower, who subsequently placed it in the Eisenhower Library and Museum at Abilene, Kansas. In 1960 John Wayne gave another notable silver-trimmed saddle, this one made by Oscar Carvajal Sr. of San Antonio, to Britain's Princess Margaret at the London premier of his epic motion picture *The Alamo*. A hand-carved tableau of the historic Texas mission-fortress adorned each fender.

Meanwhile, masters of the western saddle-making fraternity were still called upon to honor rodeo champions with saddle leather. In the late 1950s and early 1960s, for example, Don King produced an early version of his famous Sheridan carving style on trophy saddles made for the Rocky Mountain Quarter Horse Association and the Rodeo Cowboys Association. Depending upon the skill of the artist and the complexity of the project, such work often required 100 hours or more to complete, twice as much as a plain saddle. Don Buetler of Sheridan estimated in the 1990s he spent as many as 160 hours to build and embellish a saddle that cost $5,000. In recent years avid collectors have encouraged Buetler and others of his ilk to experiment with new designs and more daring motifs. Meanwhile, the vintage show saddles of the 1920s and 1930s command ever higher prices from a growing number of avid collectors, one of whom hailed them as "the earthy stuff of exciting fantasies."[38]

Opposite
Frank H. Coenen, Alhambra, California
Silver-mounted "San Fernando" parade saddle, c. 1947, detail
FLEISCHER COLLECTION, SCOTTSDALE

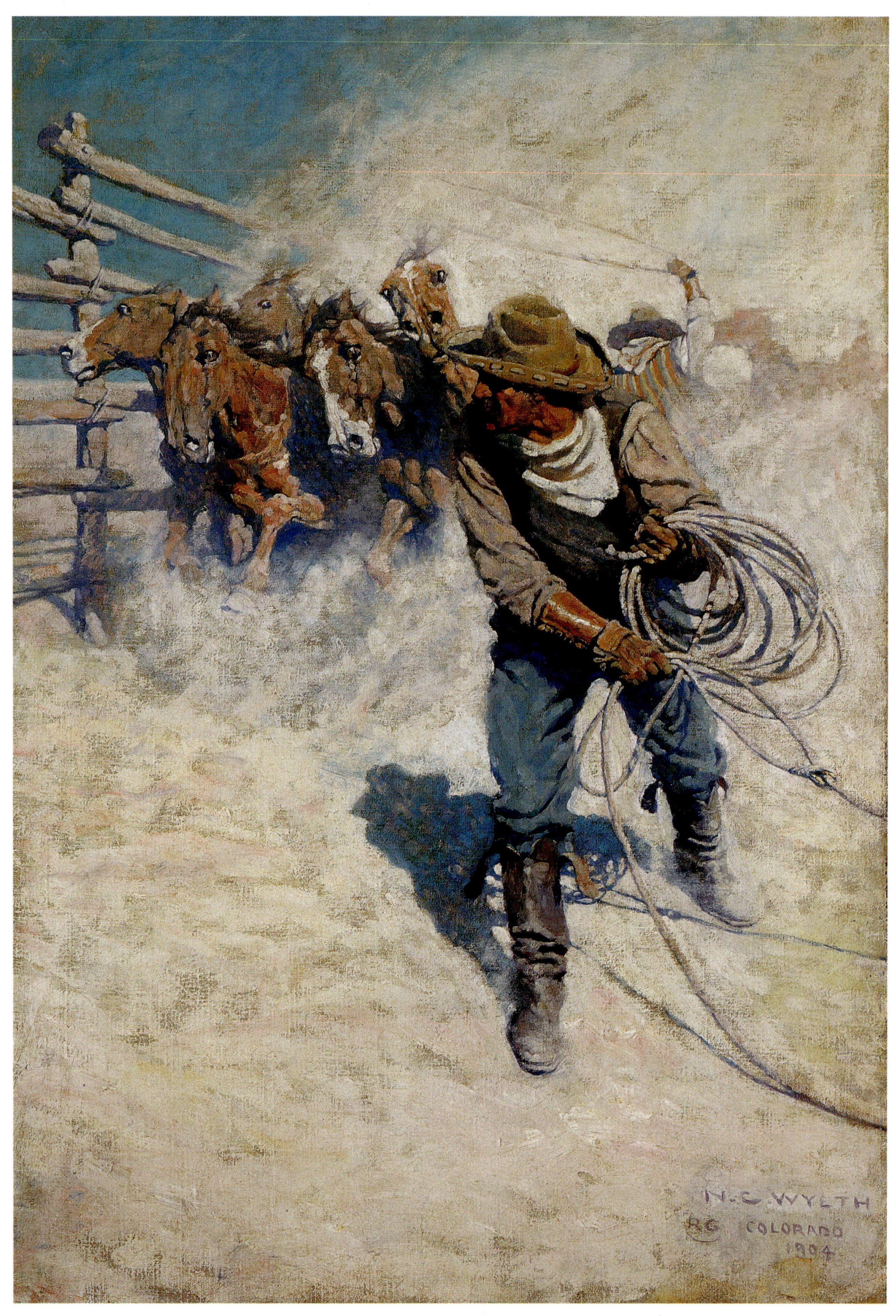
N.C. WYETH
COLORADO
1904

·3·
Artistry With Hide and Hair

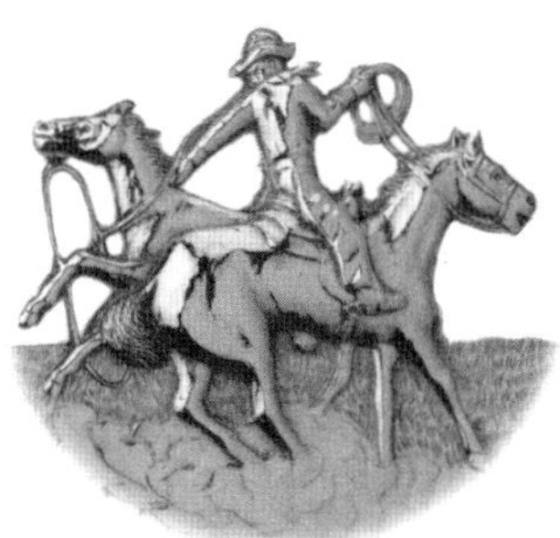

Most western saddle shops produced a wide variety of leather goods designed to meet the working cowboy's needs. As Frank Meanea, the distinguished Cheyenne saddle maker once asserted: "If it can be made in leather, we do it." [40] Besides saddles and strap work, however, large-scale cow country saddle houses either made or carried a broad selection of plain and fancy goods that ranged from protective gloves and cuffs to seatless leather breeches called chaps to accoutrements fashioned from rawhide and horsehair.

Cowboys protected their hands from rope burns, mesquite thorns, and bad weather the year round with gloves made of buckskin, horsehide, moose hide, or bearskin, depending on the season and locale. Range riders in colder climes favored gloves or mittens made of fur, wool, or wool-lined buckskin.

Many writers have suggested that at least some open range cowboys prized soft, supple hands and wore gloves more or less constantly out of vanity. "He wore gloves always, of leather or buckskin, often with gauntlets," John H. Culley, the longtime manager of the Bell Ranch in New Mexico wrote of the typical late nineteenth-century cowpuncher, "and never took them off when shaking hands or apologized for wearing them." [41]

Opposite. *N.C. Wyeth (1882–1945)*
Above the Sea of Round, Shiny Backs the Thin Loops Swirled, *1904–5*
oil on canvas, 38 x 36 in.
Buffalo Bill Historical Center, Cody, Wyoming

Many cowboys returning from the Civil War pressed military-style gauntlets into service on the cattle range. Yellow or cream colored, such gloves covered and shielded not only the hands but also the upper arms of the wearer. Moreover, the broad surface of the gauntlet cuff lent itself to fancy thread or wire stitching, embroidery, beadwork, metal spots and conchas, and simple colored inlays in the form of stars, crescents, or horseshoes. Most types were lined and stitched to stiffen and give them body.

In addition to the store-bought goods, a number of western craftsmen produced small quantities of gauntlets and gloves for the local market. Indian women on various reservations, for example, made extra money beading gauntlets with colorful floral, geometric, and figurative patterns, including popular motifs incorporating the American flag.

At the town of Medora in Dakota Territory in the 1880s, a local trapper spent brutally cold winters making buckskin gloves to sell to cowboys at the spring roundup. Rancher Theodore Roosevelt encountered a memorable female glove maker on the Dakota range and had this to say about her:

> The best buckskin maker that I ever met was, if not a typical frontiers-woman, at least a woman who could not have reached her full development save on the border. She made first-class hunting-shirts, leggins, and gauntlets. When I knew her she was living alone in her cabin on mid-prairie, having dismissed her husband six months previously in an exceedingly summary manner.[42]

About the same time on the West Texas frontier, Ella Bird Dumont was turning out small quantities of buckskin gloves, pants, and vests from deer hides tanned by her husband. Using a sewing machine capable of stitching leather as well as cloth, Dumont garnished her gauntlets with French silk thread and sometimes added beads and fringe as well. One of her neighbors recalled that the gifted seamstress made perfectly fitting gloves by sight without ever measuring her customers' hands. Dumont charged $7 a pair for her gauntlets, more than twice the price asked by some other glove makers in the region, and recalled always having "many more orders than I could fill."[43] The plucky leatherworker was eventually able to build up a small herd of cattle by trading pairs of gloves to cash-strapped cowboys in exchange for yearlings.

Although attractive and stylish, gauntlets were not without liabilities. Their cuffs were cumbersome and even dangerous when cowboys were roping. They also tended to collect dust and trash. As a result cowboys increasingly turned to wrist-length gloves, leaving gauntlets to flamboyant Wild West show performers, rodeo riders, and movie actors.

Cowboys who still wanted to protect their wrists, forearms, and shirtsleeves usually turned to stiff leather cuffs secured with metal snaps, leather lacing, or

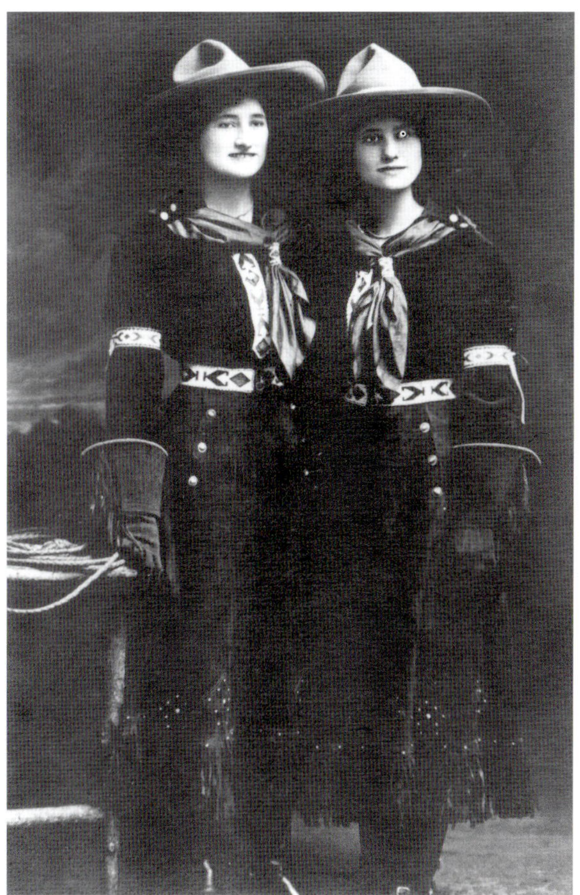

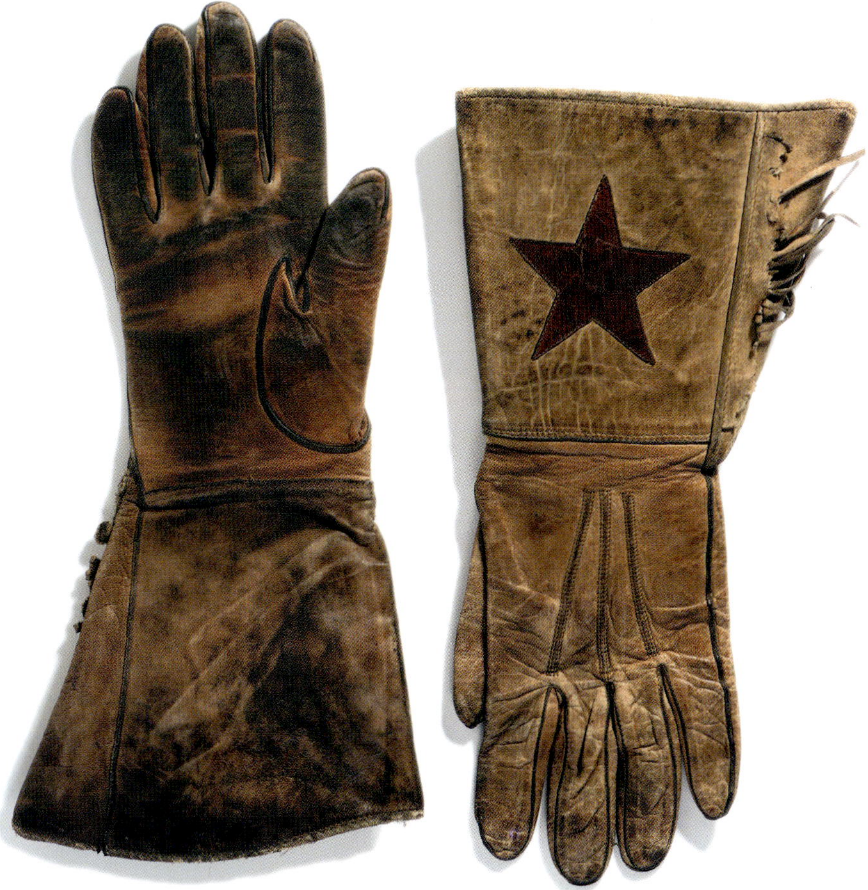

Above, left
The Parry sisters, Wild West show performers, wearing gauntlets
Buffalo Bill Historical Center, Cody, Wyoming

Above, right
Leather gauntlets with red stars sewn to the cuffs
Buffalo Bill Historical Center, Cody, Wyoming

adjustable straps and buckles. Made from brown or black saddle leather and measuring from four to more than six inches in length, cuffs of this type were subjected to considerable abuse and were often unadorned. As occurred with most cowboy gear, however, fancier types soon emerged.

Decoration ranged from modest stamp patterns to the same sort of elaborate floral carving applied to saddle leather. Conchas and spots of nickel, brass, and silver also appeared, sometimes in combination with scalloped or serrated edges, fancy lacing, and leather inlays. Purely ornamental types, used for parades or social occasions, featured Indian bead- and quillwork, decorative embroidery, and colored glass inlays.

Cowboys sometimes added their own trimmings or carved their initials or brands into the leather for identification. The following crudely scrawled message adorned the cuffs of one western bronc rider: "My name is Ernie Evenson. If I get kilt some body write and tell my Mother who lives somewhere in S[.] Dakotee [sic]."[44]

Cowboy outfitters offered cuffs and gauntlets into the 1930s, some of them created to match silver-mounted show saddles, chaps, and vests. By this time, however, they were seldom seen on the range. By the dawn of the twenty-first century, however, at least a few cowhands had revived the practice of wearing cuffs.

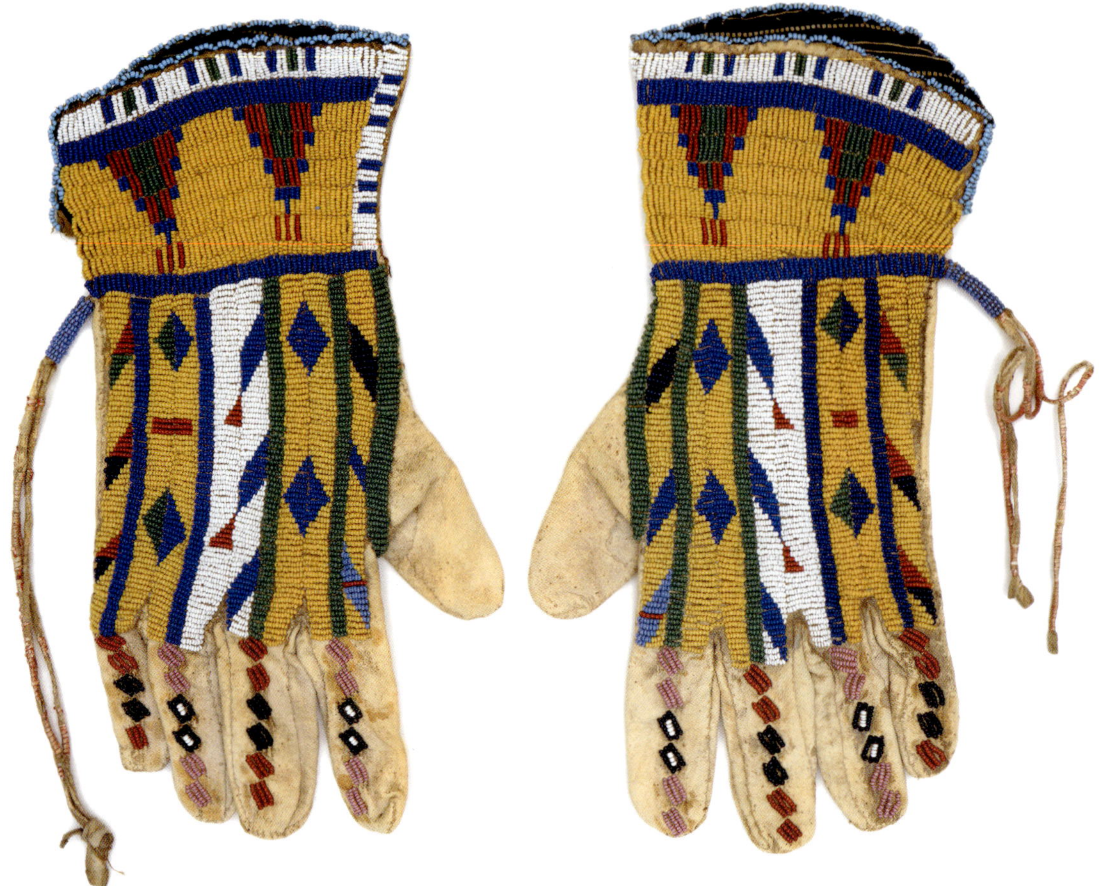

Short leather gauntlets with beaded cuffs, hands, fingers, and tassles
Buffalo Bill Historical Center, Cody, Wyoming

Leather leggings or "chaps," the latter term a contraction of the Spanish *chaparreras* or *chaparejos*, evolved in the late seventeenth or early eighteenth centuries from *armas*, cowhide and goatskin shields that the soldier-vaqueros of northern Mexico attached to their saddles for protection while riding brush-infested range. Descended from medieval horse armor, these large, oblong aprons usually hung from a leather thong on either side of the saddle horn, although in some cases saddle makers sewed or laced the protective panels onto the saddle itself. Either way, when drawn over a rider's legs and tied to his waist or to the saddle cantle, *armas* effectively repelled cactus thorns and Indian arrows alike.

Although primarily employed as a protective measure, *armas* could be beautiful as well. Their broad leather spans invited intricate stamped designs and hemp embroidery usually in floral or geometric patterns. Those made of tanned goatskins, known as *chivarras*, or the fur of grizzly bear, sheep, wolf, or mountain lion were both warm and stylish. Some *armas* were also equipped with long pockets on their undersides for carrying food, tobacco, or other goods.

Although *armas* shielded riders and their horses from branches and barbs, they were almost useless in the open country, not to mention heavy and bulky. Moreover, they did not protect vaqueros engaged in branding or other groundwork. By the early 1800s California vaqueros began to remedy these deficiencies by covering the calves of their legs with leather *botas* and their thighs with loose

Opposite
Left to right: Leather gauntlets with fringe and beaded buffalo pattern on cuffs, and beaded floral hand; Sioux gauntlets with chevron-pattern quillwork cuffs, c. 1930; leather gauntlets with deer pattern on beaded cuffs, floral beaded hand, and fringe
Buffalo Bill Historical Center, Cody, Wyoming

fitting, knee-length, deerskin or buckskin aprons known as *armitas* or *chinquederos*. Lightweight and versatile both in and out of the saddle, *armitas* and *botas* soon replaced *armas* on the western ranges of North America. Saddle-mounted shields, however, remained in use in western Mexico and may still be seen on stock saddles in this region today.

By the 1840s and probably earlier, at least some Texas "brush poppers" had traded in their *botas* and *armitas* for one-piece, snug-fitting, seatless leather overalls

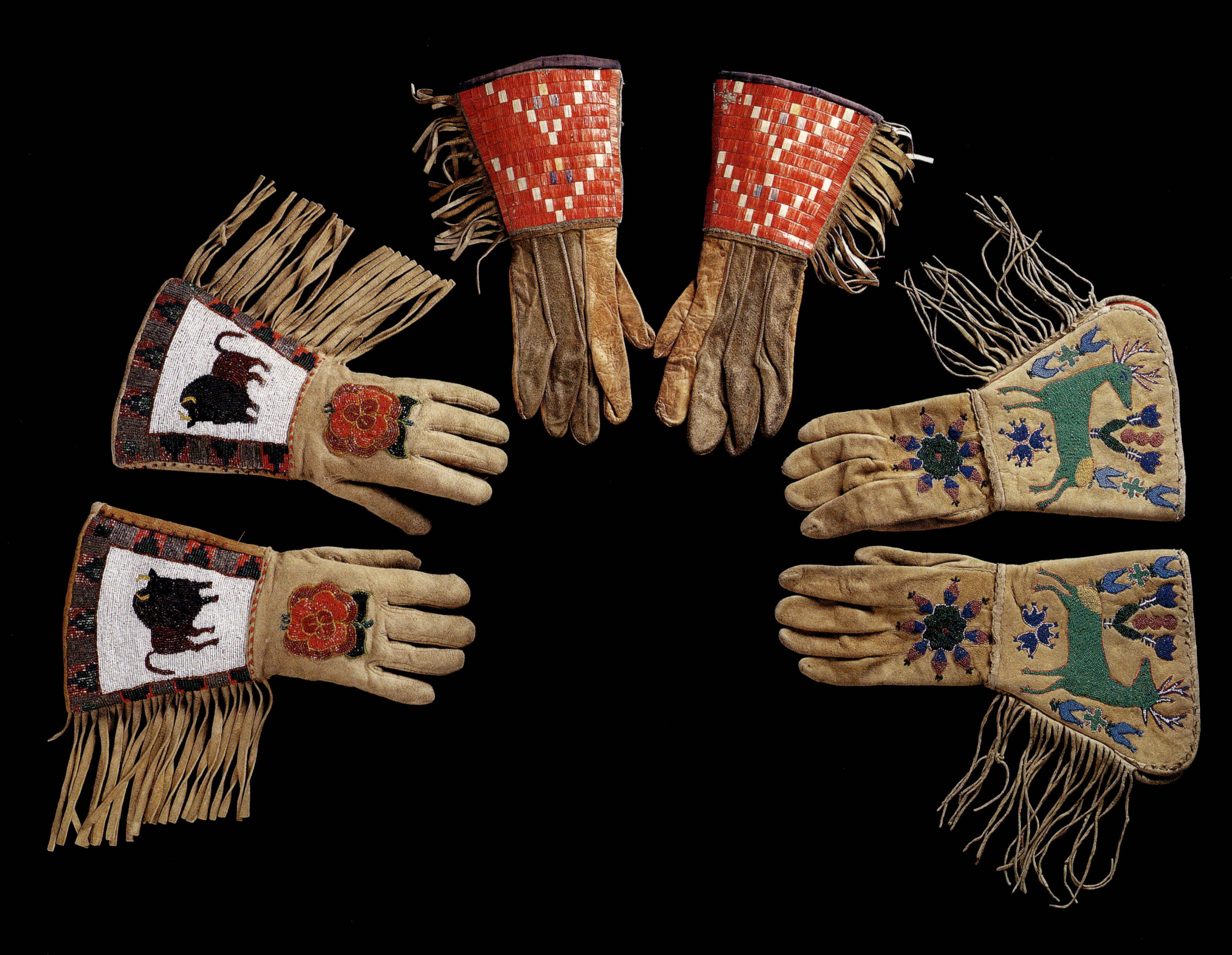

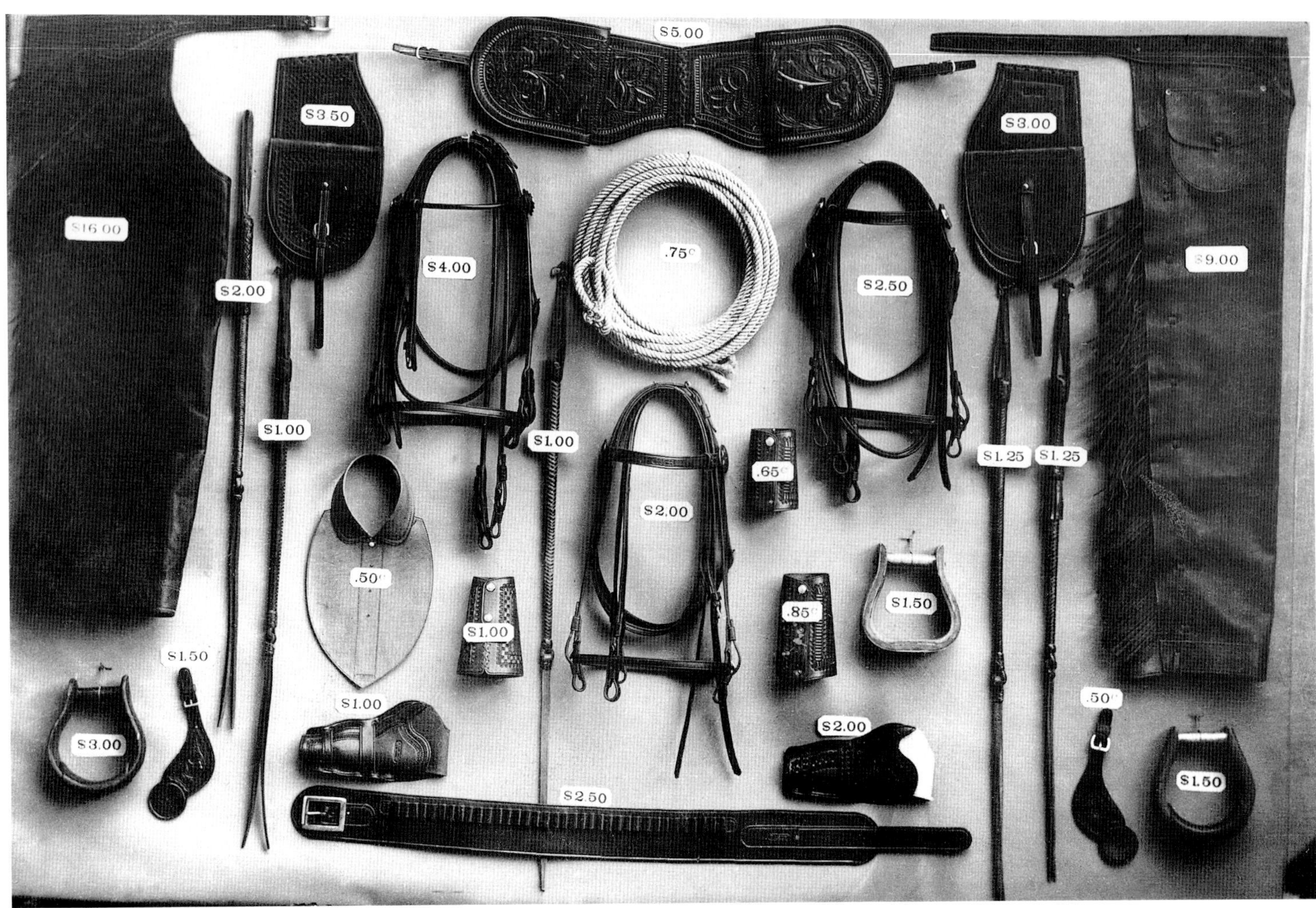

W. G. Walker, Cheyenne
Display of products of the Frank A. Meanea Saddlery, Cheyenne, c. 1900
American Heritage Center, University of Wyoming, Laramie

that resembled the buckskin leggings worn by Native Americans. A homemade rawhide-type legging predominated at first. Neophytes soon learned how to make them from relatives and obliging Mexican vaqueros, or simply cut them from a hide using another pair as a pattern.

By the late 1860s, however, shop-made chaps consisting of a supple, medium-weight, tanned steer hide began to replace the rough-hewn rawhide varieties. The typical design consisted of two close-fitting, leg-encasing leather tubes laced or sewn together at the seam and fitted with a one-piece leather belt that buckled in the back. Because the chap legs resembled shotgun barrels or stovepipes, the style became known in the 1870s as "shotgun" or "stovepipe" chaps.

Shotgun-style leggings probably originated in the brush country of South Texas, where they were part of a cowhand's protective gear that included *tapaderos*, tall-topped boots, and tight-fitting trousers and jackets made of heavy ducking. One 1880s vintage cowboy said that he and his kind wore leather chaps "not only to protect us, but to preserve our pants."[45] Another observer believed it "economy to wear the leather leggings in the mesquite underbrush, where cloth is but a poor armor."[46] Besides fending off limbs and thorns, chaps were also

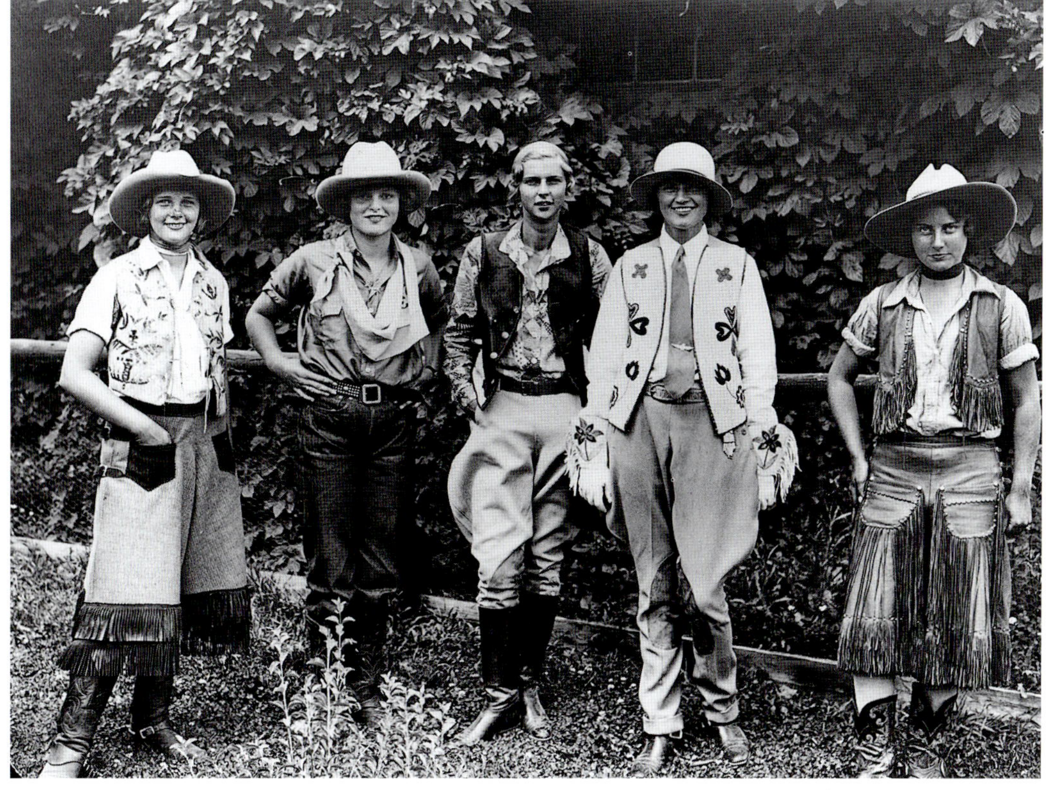

Dude cowgirls pose at a Wyoming ranch, the second one from the right wearing fancy beaded gauntlets, c. 1930
BUFFALO BILL HISTORICAL CENTER, CODY, WYOMING

pressed into service to help beat out prairie fires and to "chap" (whip) cowboys convicted of violating "range rules" by cow camp "kangaroo courts."

Savvy chap makers exposed the flesh side of cowhide to the elements because it proved tougher than the hair side. The unadorned leather leggings used in thorn-infested regions were soon rendered slick, black, and scarred by constant exposure to barbed brush, bovine blood, and campfire smoke. A serviceable pair of leggings of this sort could be bought for as little as $6 in the 1870s.

Within two decades after the Civil War, South Texas cattle drovers had exported leather leggings throughout the Great Plains. As one cowpuncher of the period recalled, "almost every Texas cowboy had a pair of chaps when he arrived in the north."[47] During the boom in the cattle industry during the 1870s and 1880s, saddle houses throughout the West began producing chaps for an expanding cowboy population.

Cowboy cuffs with stamped design, c. 1910
FLEISCHER COLLECTION, SCOTTSDALE

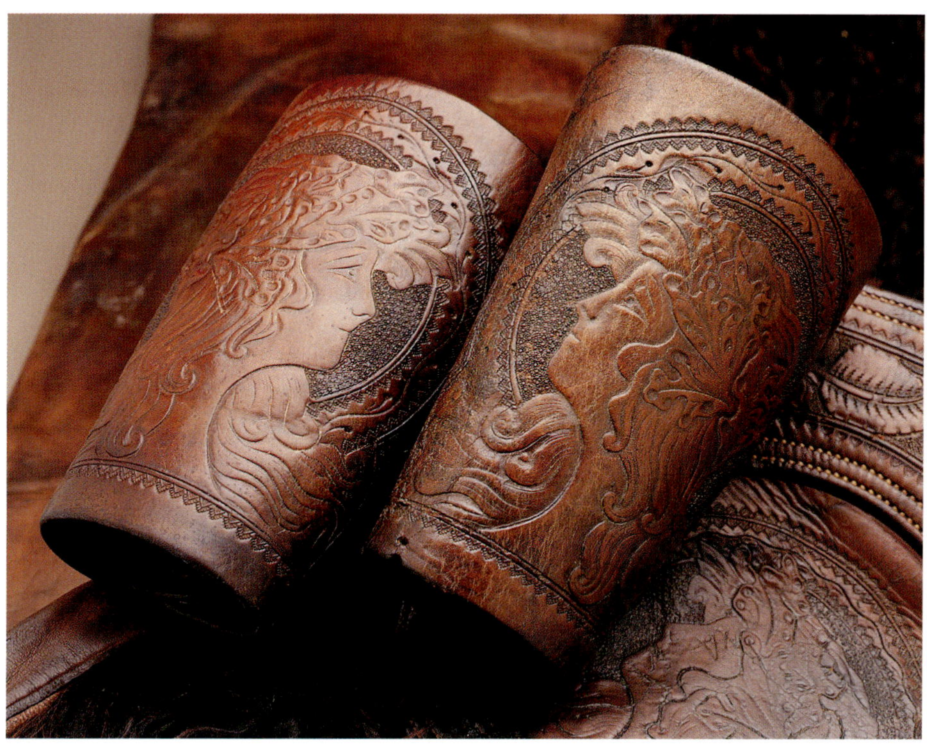

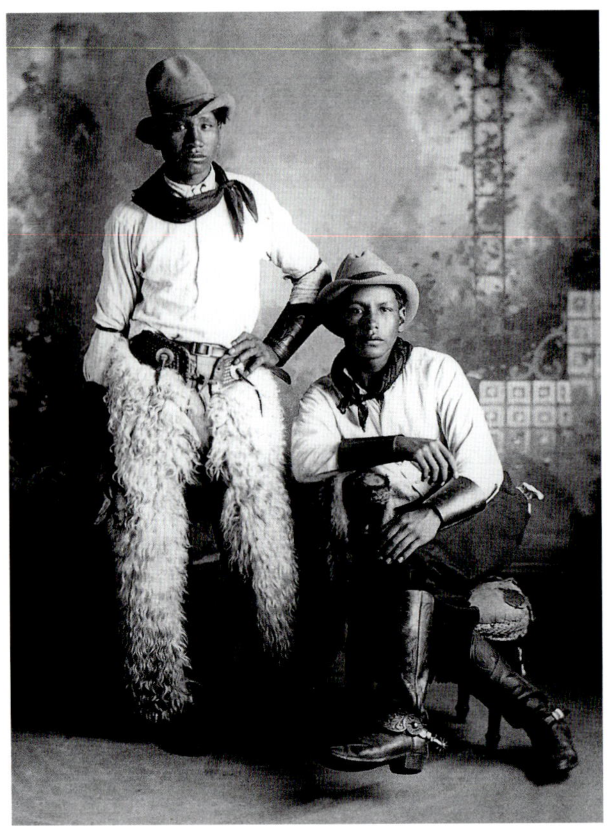

The Denver Manufacturing Co. alone offered nine variations of shotgun-style "*chapperajoes*," in its 1883 trade catalog. All were made from strong, pliable, and water-resistant oil-tanned leather. Leather lacing or hand- or machine-stitched waxed linen thread secured leg seams, and makers added extra leather to the bottoms of better quality leggings to retard fraying. Many chaps also sported one or two outside pockets where wearers carried pistols, knives, medicine, tobacco, or other articles. Makers usually laced or sewed such enclosures to the front of the leggings a few inches below the belt and equipped them with flaps held in place by buttons, snaps, or thongs. Although a few shops experimented with slotted, pants-like pockets, most horsemen found these pouches inconvenient and uncomfortable.

Saddleries usually produced leggings in stock sizes—small, medium, and large—and fitted customers based on their height, weight, and build. Most customers wanted chaps cut large enough in the leg to ease putting on and taking off.

By the 1880s chaps were viewed as fashionable as well as practical attire. Fresh from a tour of ranches on the Yellowstone

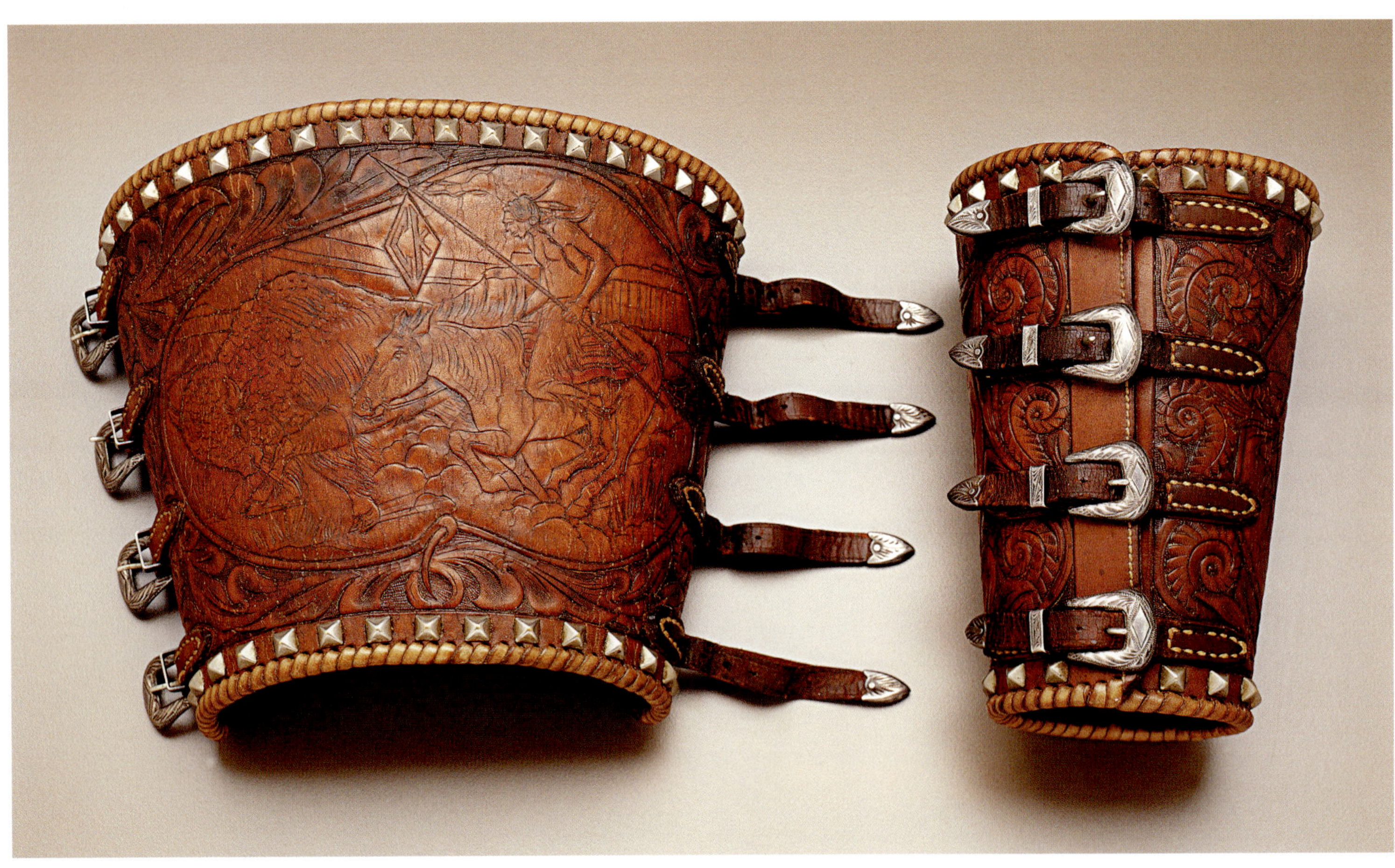

River in Montana in 1886, General George Wingate commented on the prevalence of "fancy chapareros, or overalls, made from calf skin, or stamped leather."[48] Leather fringe, made by extending and segmenting a two- or three-inch-wide strip beyond the leg seam, comprised the most common decorative element. Besides being stylish, fringe helped remove moisture from water-logged leather after rains or river crossings. Some cowboys also used the convenient strings to help repair their gear.

Opposite, top
Frank Fiske Studio, Fort Yates, North Dakota
"Indian Wranglers"
Frank Fiske Photo Collection, State Historical Society of North Dakota, Bismarck

Opposite, bottom
Leather cuffs with carved design and laced edges
Fleischer Collection, Scottsdale

Anecdotal evidence suggests that fringed chaps were ubiquitous on cattle ranges from Texas to Montana. Evan Barnard, a cowhand in the Lone Star State, recalled that every one of the more than two dozen cowboys with whom he worked on the Circle JH Ranch owned a pair. According to another eyewitness, most of the cowpunchers walking the streets of Cheyenne, Wyoming Territory, in the mid-1880s wore fringe-trimmed chaps.

In addition to fringe, makers often embellished their leggings with carved or embossed belts, pinked pockets, and metal conchas, some of the latter converted Mexican *pesos.* On shotgun chaps conchas sometimes extended the length of the leg from waist to ankle.

Cowboys themselves often added their own decorative touches and modifications. Foreman Tom Peeler of the Millett Ranch in Texas, for example, sewed cartridge loops down the legs of his chaps to accommodate ammunition for the bevy of firearms he carried.

During fall and winter range work cowboys welcomed the warmth that chaps provided. In colder climes riders favored leggings covered with various kinds of animal hair. "Hair pants" or "woolies," as they were often called, probably originated in California and were exported to the sagebrush ranges of Oregon, Nevada, and Idaho with herds and vaqueros from the Bear Flag State after the Civil War. By the early 1880s drovers from the Great Basin and Pacific Northwest had introduced hair-covered chaps to the northern

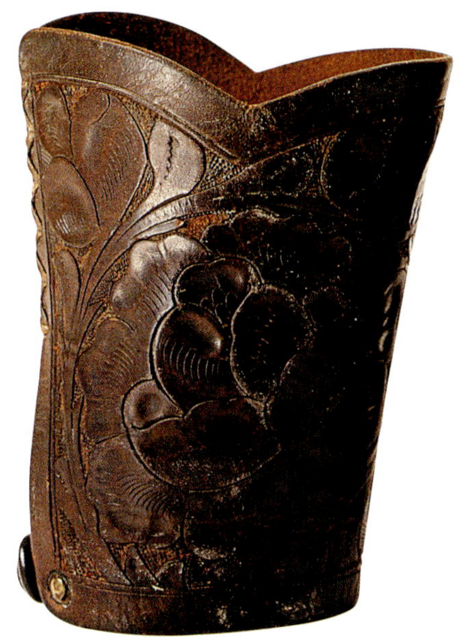

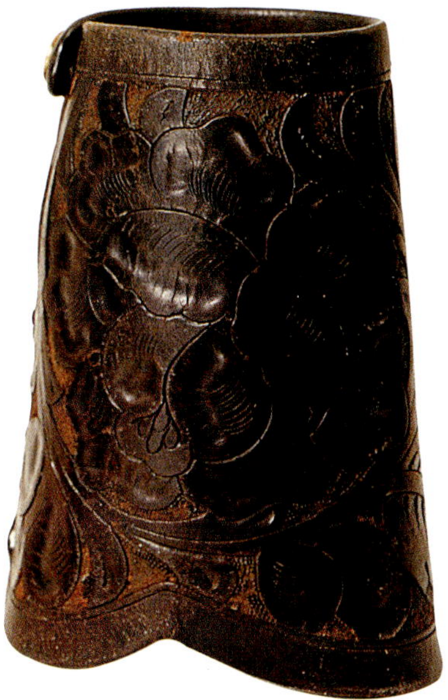

Above
Carved leather cuffs with snaps and lacing
Buffalo Bill Historical Center, Cody, Wyoming

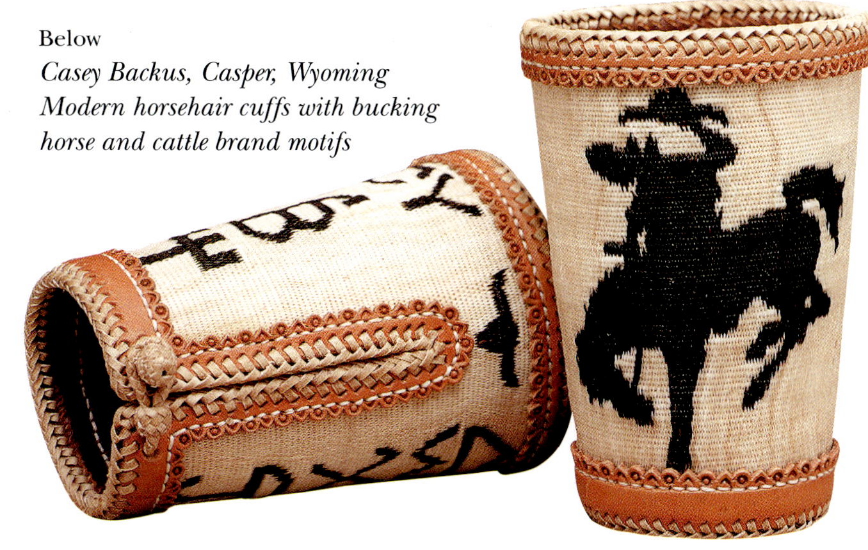

Below
Casey Backus, Casper, Wyoming
Modern horsehair cuffs with bucking horse and cattle brand motifs

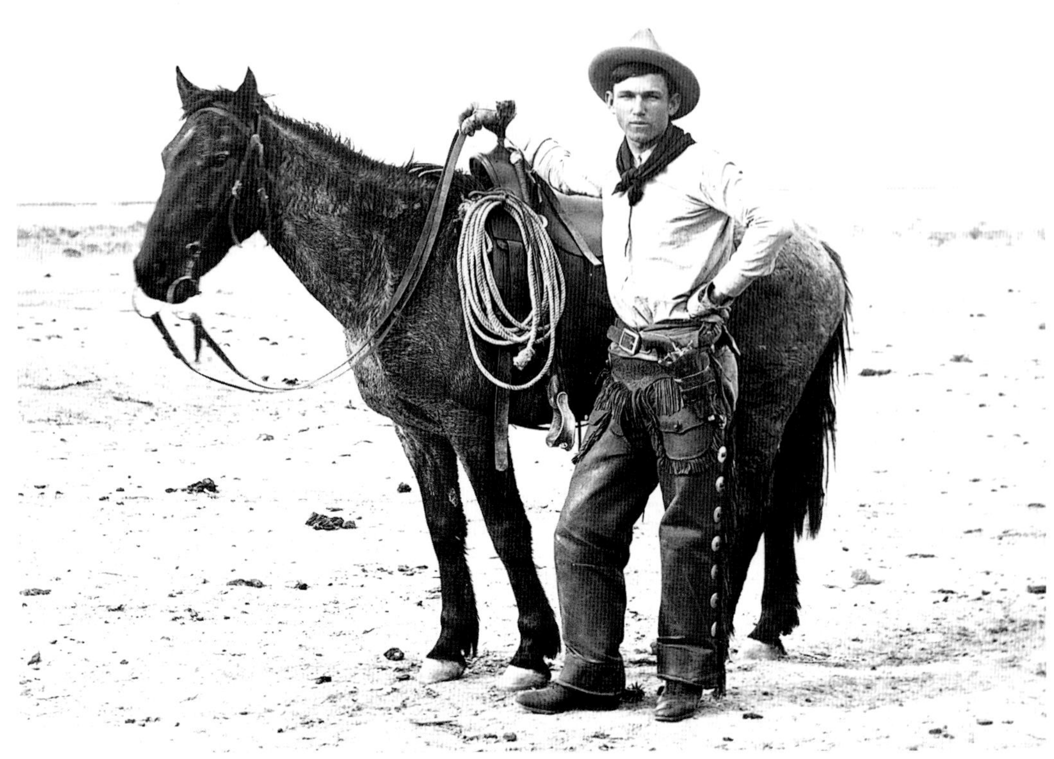

Colorado cowboy in shotgun chaps, c. 1900
PANHANDLE PLAINS HISTORICAL MUSEUM, CANYON, TEXAS

Great Plains where indigenous makers were soon producing them from the plush skins of Angora goats, domestic sheep, imported llama, sleek seal, wild bison, bear, wolf, cougar, leopard, and even Newfoundland dog. Texas outlaw King Fisher is said to have converted the skin of a Bengal tiger purloined from a traveling circus into a pair of decorative chaps whose gaudy leg seams were adorned "with gold and buckskin fringe."[49] Trail driver Jack Potter fashioned a less spectacular but no less distinctive pair of homemade leggings from the skin of a wild javelina.

Except for their hair coverings, woolies did not differ much in construction from other chaps. The closed-leg pattern prevailed. Angora goatskin, the most plentiful and popular material for hair pants, was thin and fragile and required a boot-weight calfskin leather or pliable canvas lining for support and insulation. Most makers favored durable oak-tanned goatskins over those processed with alum, which tended to rot more quickly when exposed to the elements. Whatever the tanning method, chap makers took care not to extend the skin too far inside the leg lest uncomfortable lumps of hair work their way between a rider's legs and his saddle leather.

Although woolies made fine pillows and ground covering for bedding, not everyone found them practical or appealing. Too hot for summer wear, they became easily entangled in branches and brush and, except for water-repellent sealskin, absorbed moisture, which added to their weight. At least some owners also complained of their smell when wet.

Opposite
Shotgun-pattern chaps, details of leggings trimmed with fringe; makers, left to right; R. T. Frazier, Pueblo, Colorado (1st and 5th leggings); E. L. Gallatin, Cheyenne, Wyoming; Clark Saddlery Co., Portland, Oregon; F. A. Meanea, Cheyenne, Wyoming
FLEISCHER COLLECTION, SCOTTSDALE

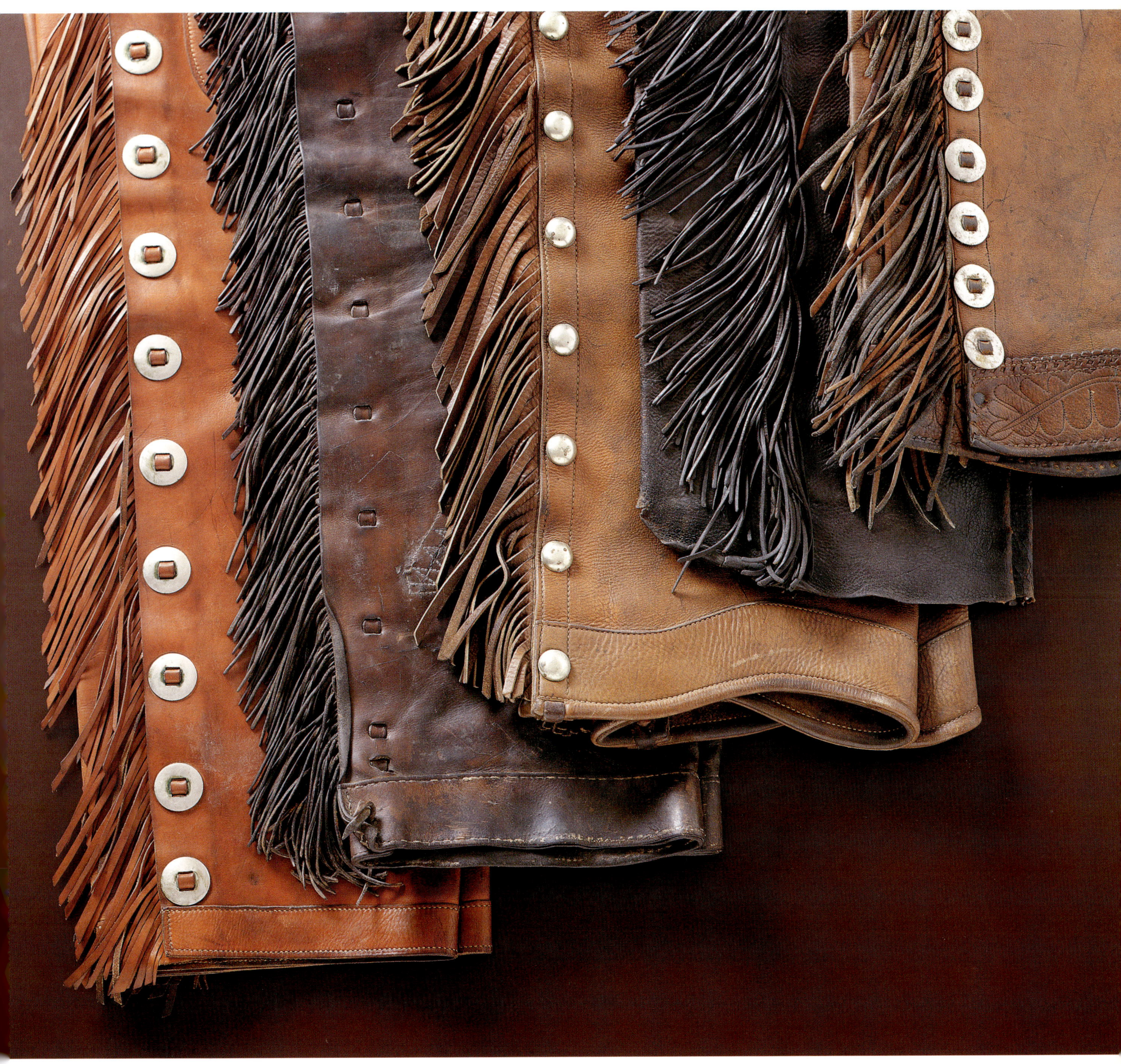

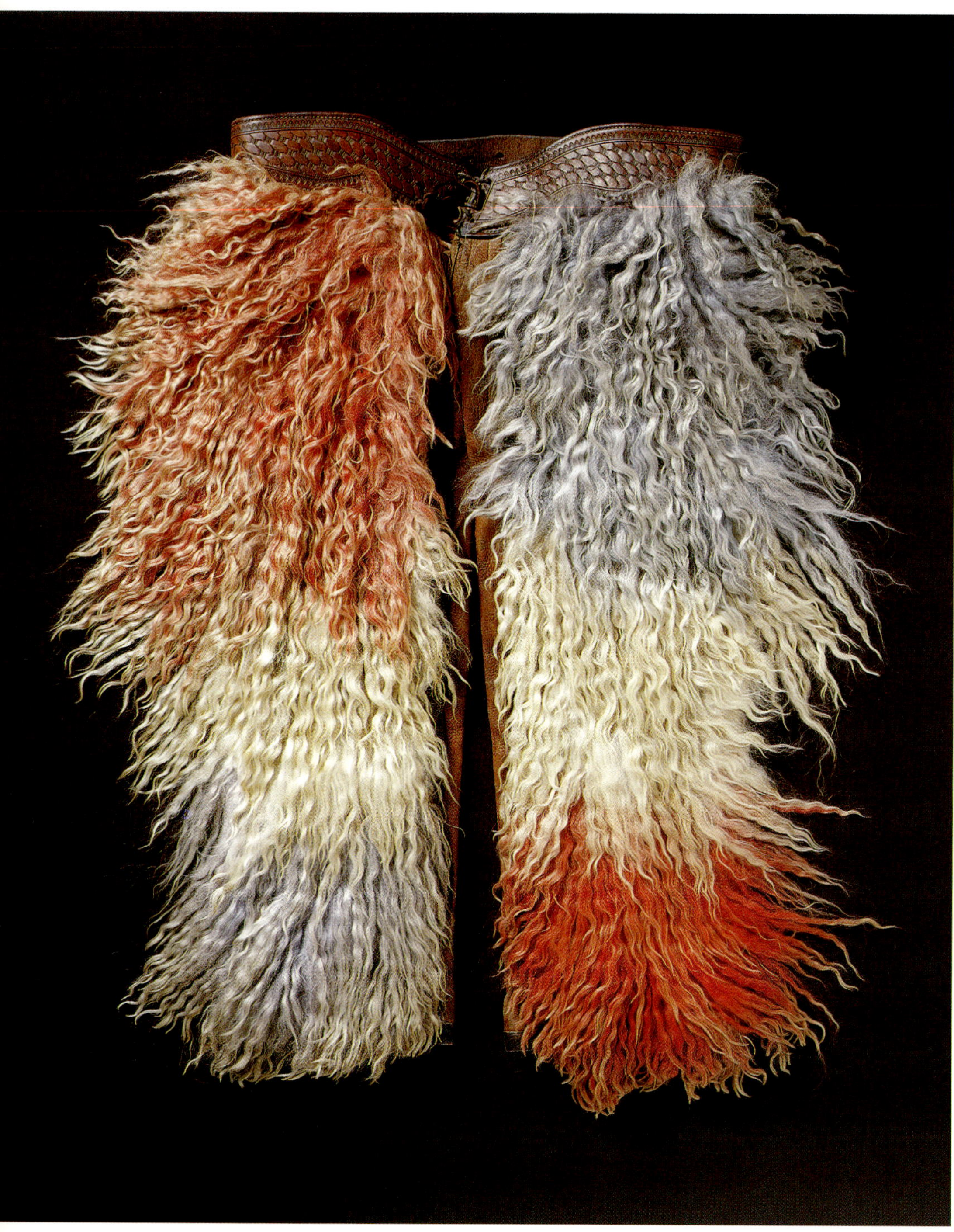

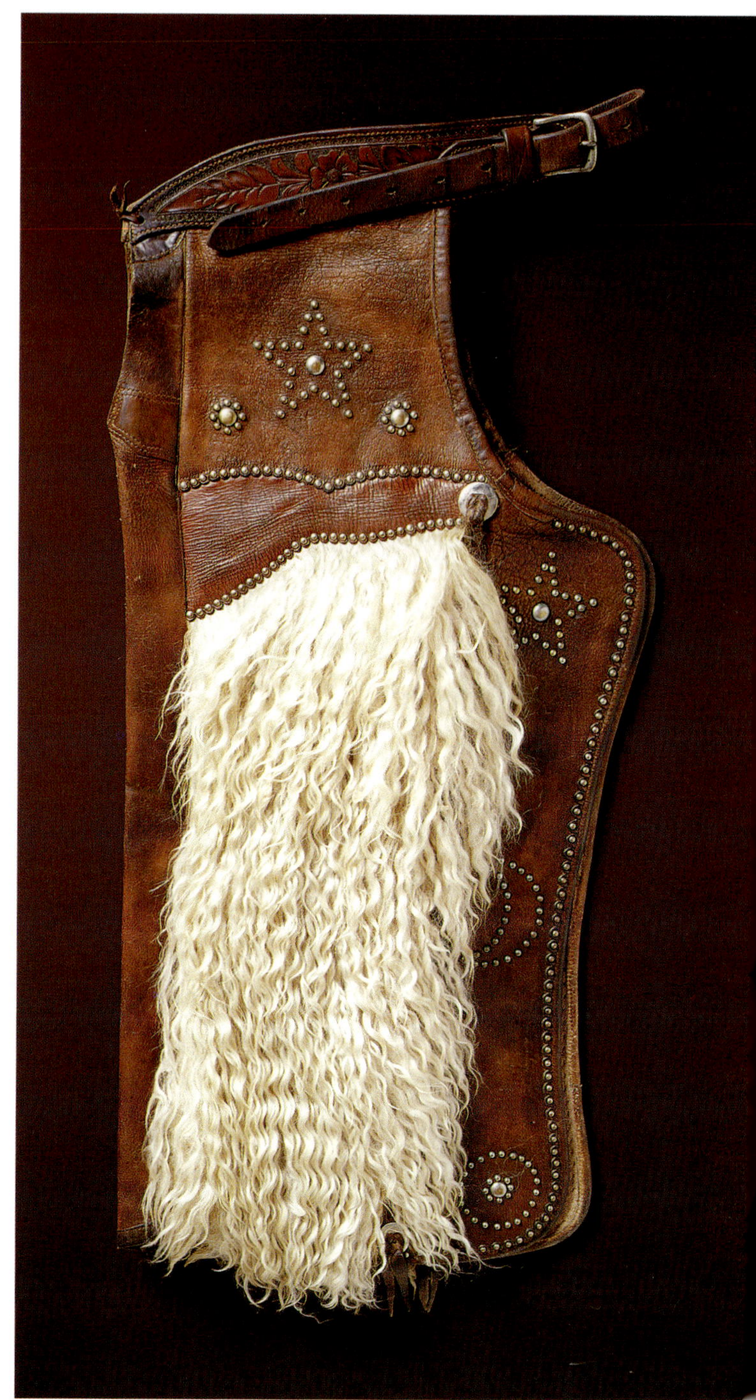

As a rule hair-covered chaps also were more expensive than basic leather types. In the 1890s, for example, San Francisco maker Main and Winchester priced plain leather chaps at from $10 to $14; those made from Angora goat at $14, French goat $16, and sealskin from $13.50 to $20. Hair pants were popular nevertheless, especially among fashion-conscious cowhands. According to photographer L. A. Huffman, a bronc buster in 1880s Montana could be identified by "his swagger, his display of artillery, his unfailing weakness for wearing heavy bearskin or llama leggings, even in the hottest weather, and his spurs."[50]

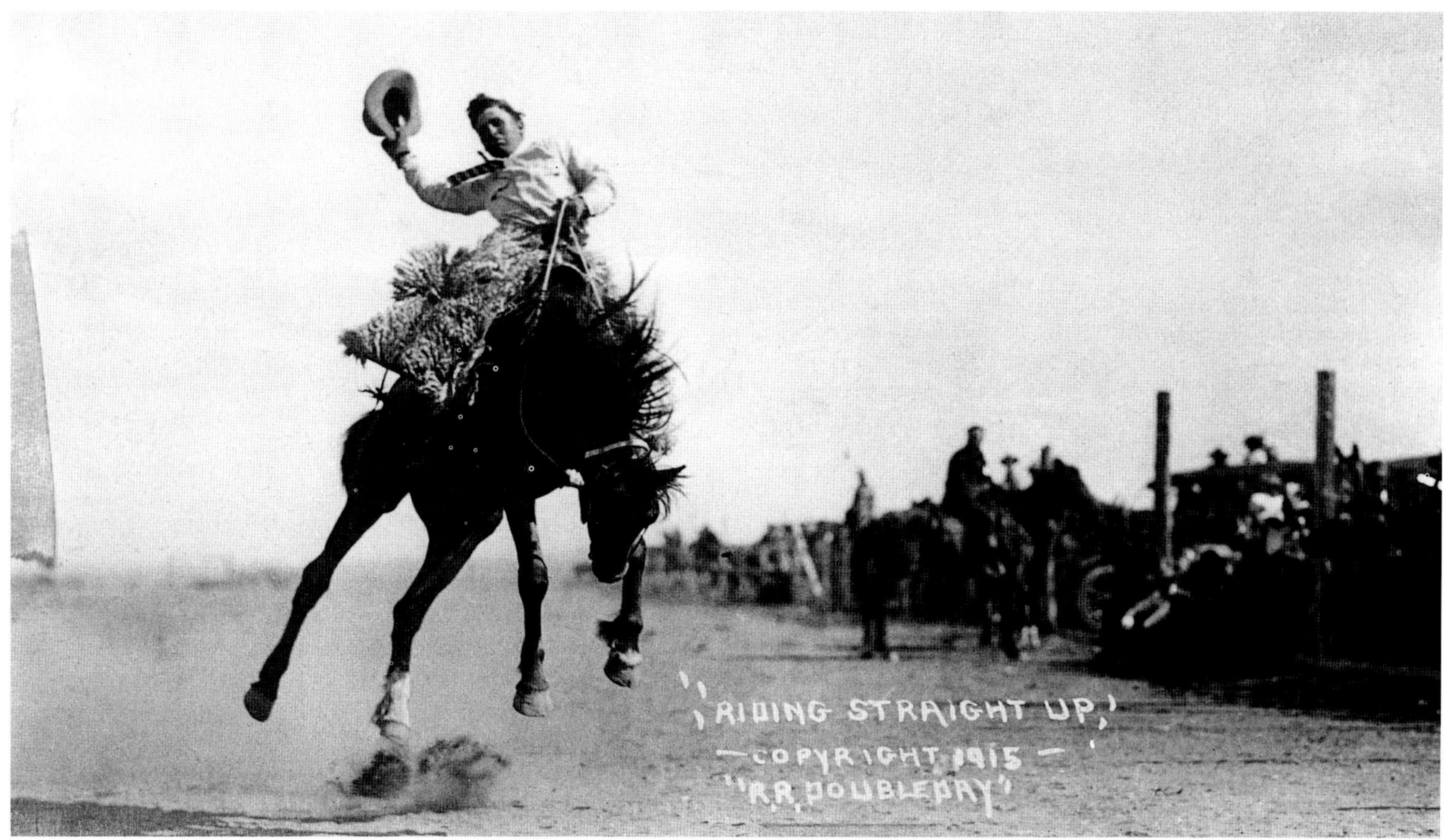

Although most cowboys appear to have owned a pair of leggings of one type or another, their use varied widely and depended upon topography, climate, and fashion. Chaps of any sort were hot, bulky, and difficult to don or remove without first taking off boots and spurs. Moreover, pulling chaps off over footwear risked smearing dirt and manure inside the leg.

Chaps also tended to impede mobility. Cowboys "do not walk well," Theodore Roosevelt wrote, "partly because they so rarely do any work out of the saddle, partly because their *chaperajos* or leather overalls hamper them when on the ground...."[51] Such a liability did not, however, dissuade the future U.S. President from purchasing his own pair of sealskin leggings from Cheyenne saddle maker J. S. Collins.

Although a necessity when working the brush-covered regions of the Southwest, chaps were seldom worn in open country during good weather. More often than not, range riders on the plains stowed their leggings inside their bedrolls in the chuck wagon. To protect their legs, many cowpunchers relied upon heavy, California-made woolen breeches with water-repellent qualities and reinforced inner thighs and crotches.

One West Texas cowhand estimated that he wore his chaps "less than a dozen times" in a two- or three-year period before selling them.[52] More than three-quarters of fifty other old-time cowboys polled in a 1951 survey reported that they seldom

Opposite, left
Miles City Saddlery, Miles City, Montana
"July Fourth" Angora chaps, c. 1910s–1920s
FLEISCHER COLLECTION, SCOTTSDALE

Opposite, right
Riley and McCormick, Ltd, Calgary, Alberta, Canada
Batwing style wooly chaps with decorative leather panel at top of leg, metal spot designs
FLEISCHER COLLECTION, SCOTTSDALE

Above
Ralph R. Doubleday (1881–1958)
"Riding Straight Up" (George Gardner, wearing wooly chaps, aboard the famous bucking horse Steamboat), 1915
AMERICAN HERITAGE CENTER, UNIVERSITY OF WYOMING, LARAMIE

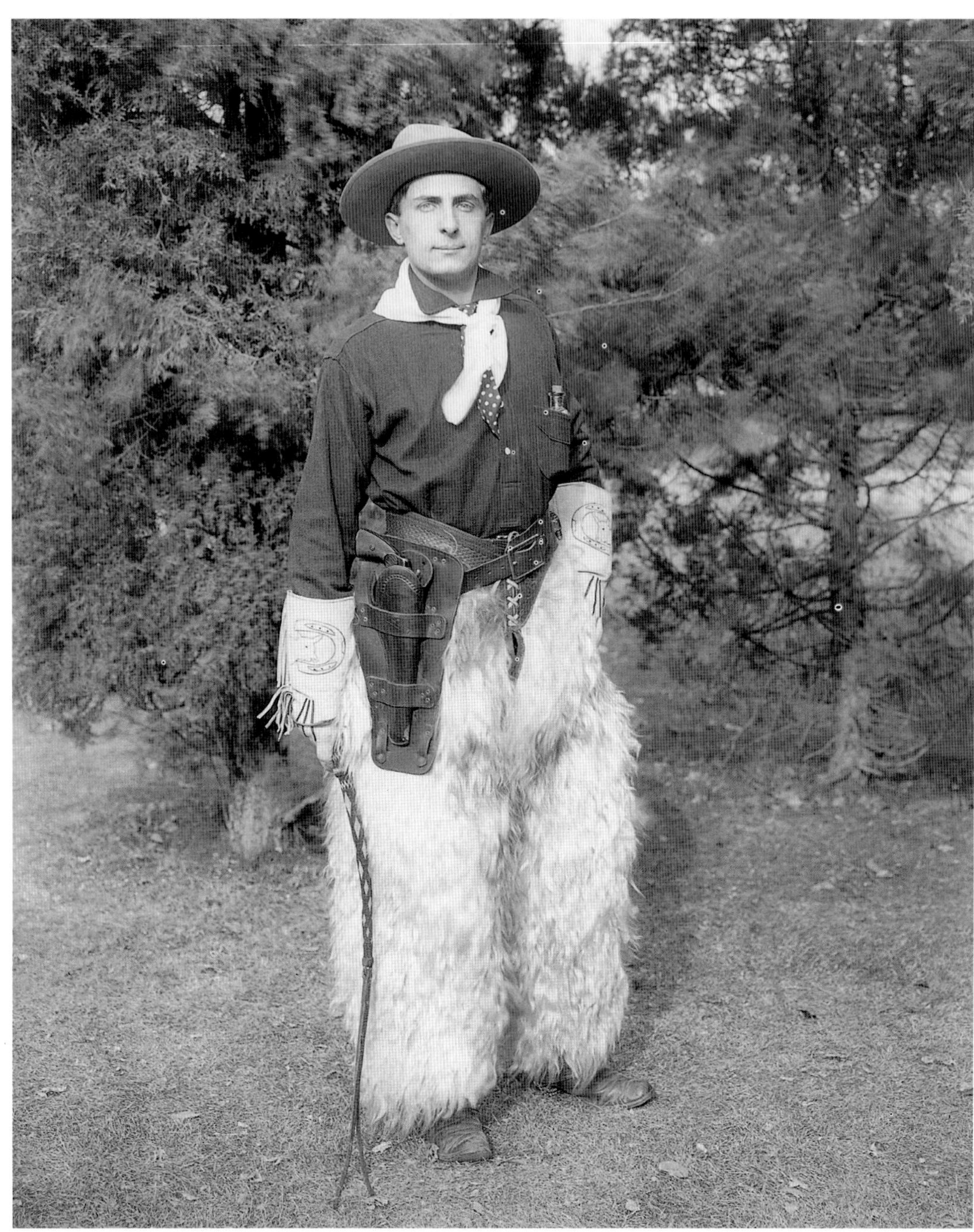

Cowboy (member of the "Birch Broncho Busters") wearing gun belt with "Mexican loop" pattern holster, wooly chaps, fringed gauntlets, and holding a horsehair quirt
COLORADO HISTORICAL SOCIETY, DENVER

or never wore chaps. These statistics square with the 1897 experience of a New York traveler, who did not see a single chap-wearing cowpuncher during a trip through the ranch districts of the southern Great Plains. Erwin E. Smith only rarely encountered them during his frequent travels to photograph cowboys in the Southwest in the first decade of the twentieth century.

Practical considerations aside, in some regions the wearing of chaps may simply have gone out of fashion from time to time. Writer Hamlin Garland, who attended an 1895 roundup near Cripple Creek in Colorado, reported that revolvers, cartridge belts, and bearskin leggings, "considered an affectation" by the cowboys, "had been discarded."[53]

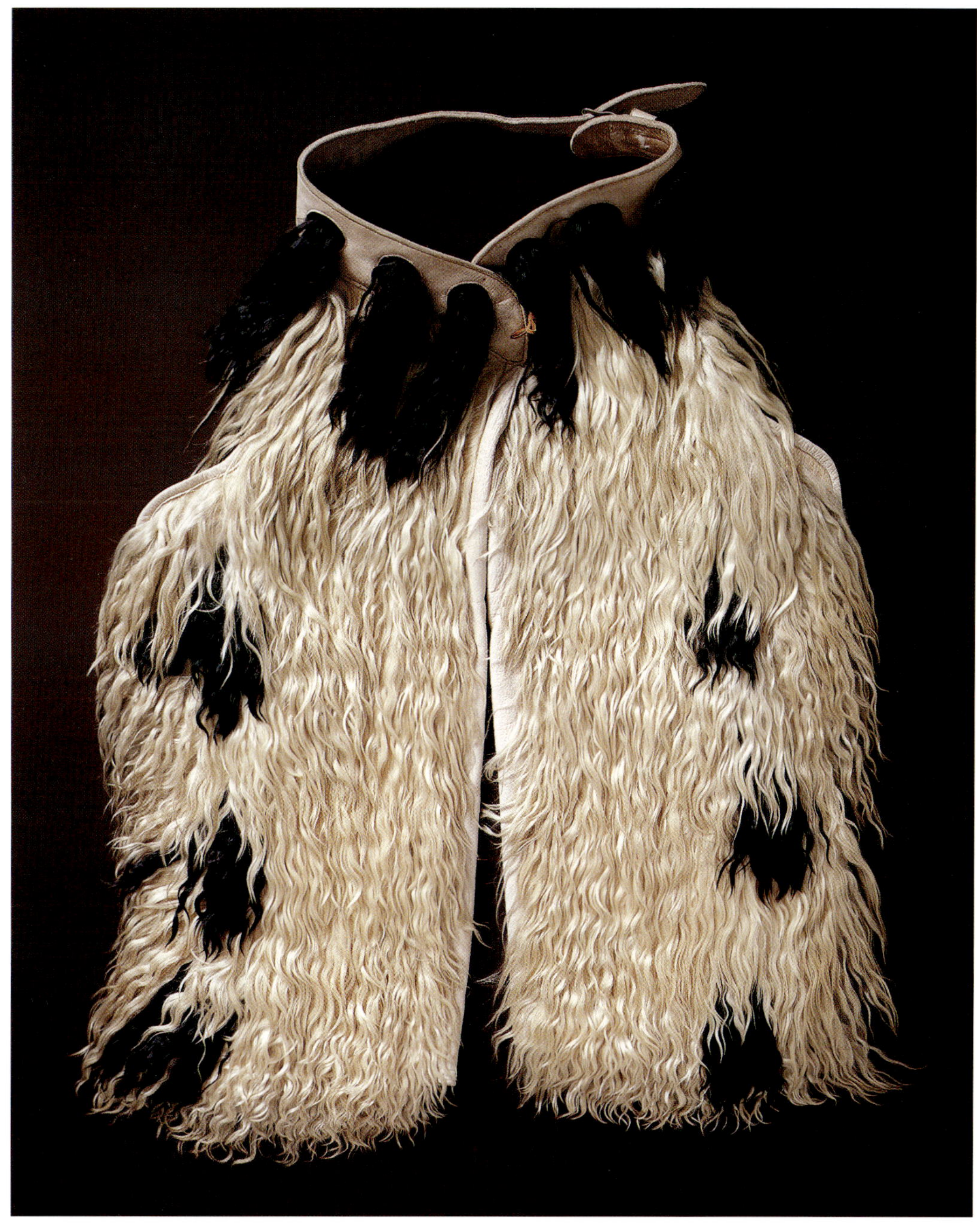

Bob Brown, North Hollywood
Black and white Angora wool chaps with black tufts extending from belt
FLEISCHER COLLECTION, SCOTTSDALE

Several recent authorities on cow country fashion have noted the prevalence of chaps in portrait photographs of cowboys compared to their appearance in images of range work. Such experts suggest that many cowboys reserved the wearing of chaps for going to town, having their photographs made for family and friends, and for other special occasions. These observations confirm that of author Philip Ashton Rollins who, in his 1936 volume *The Cowboy*, summarized the place of chaps in a working cowhand's wardrobe:

> When there was no riding to be done, no social convention to fulfill, or there were neither jealousies to excite nor hearts to conquer, the chaps,

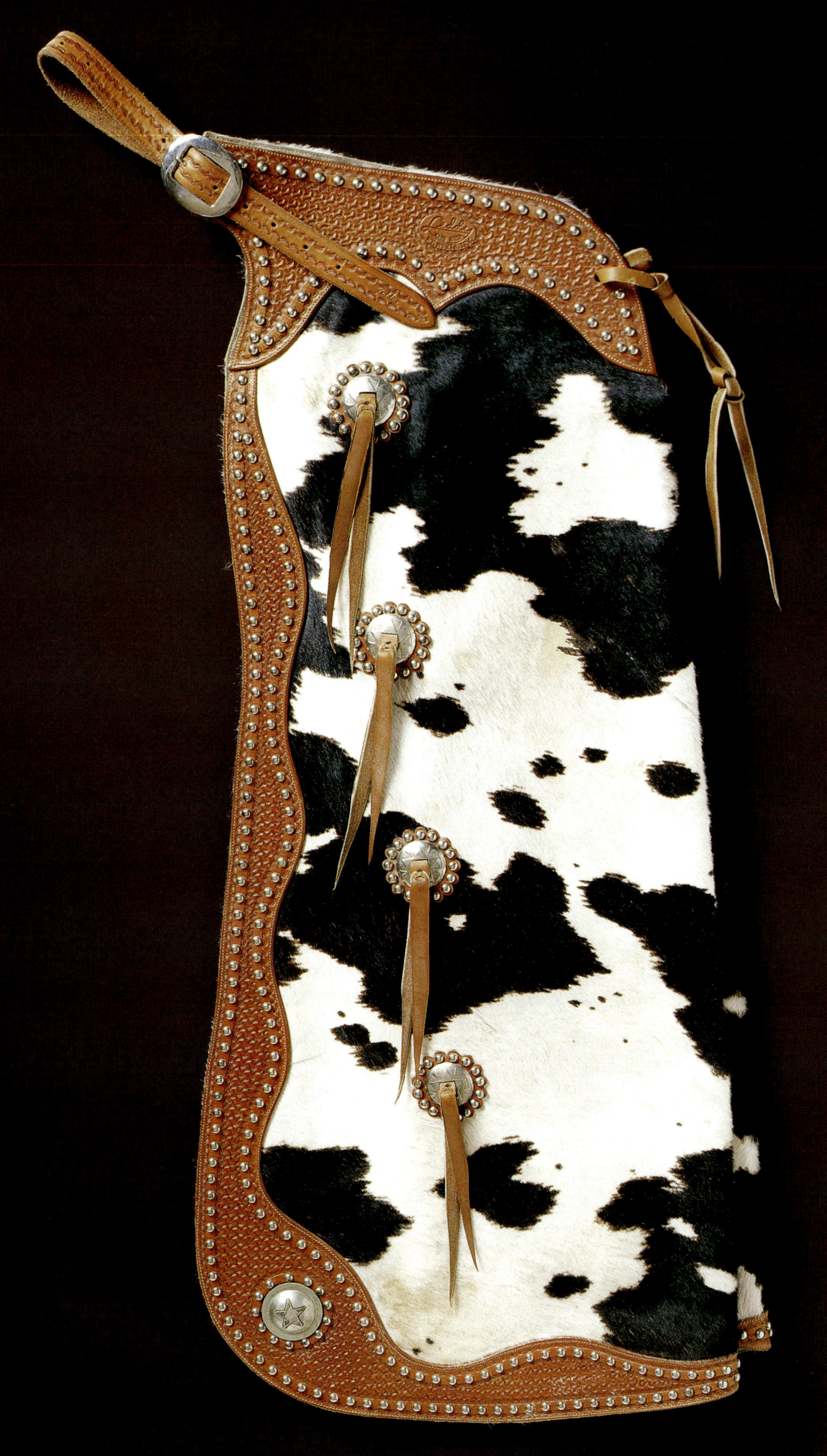

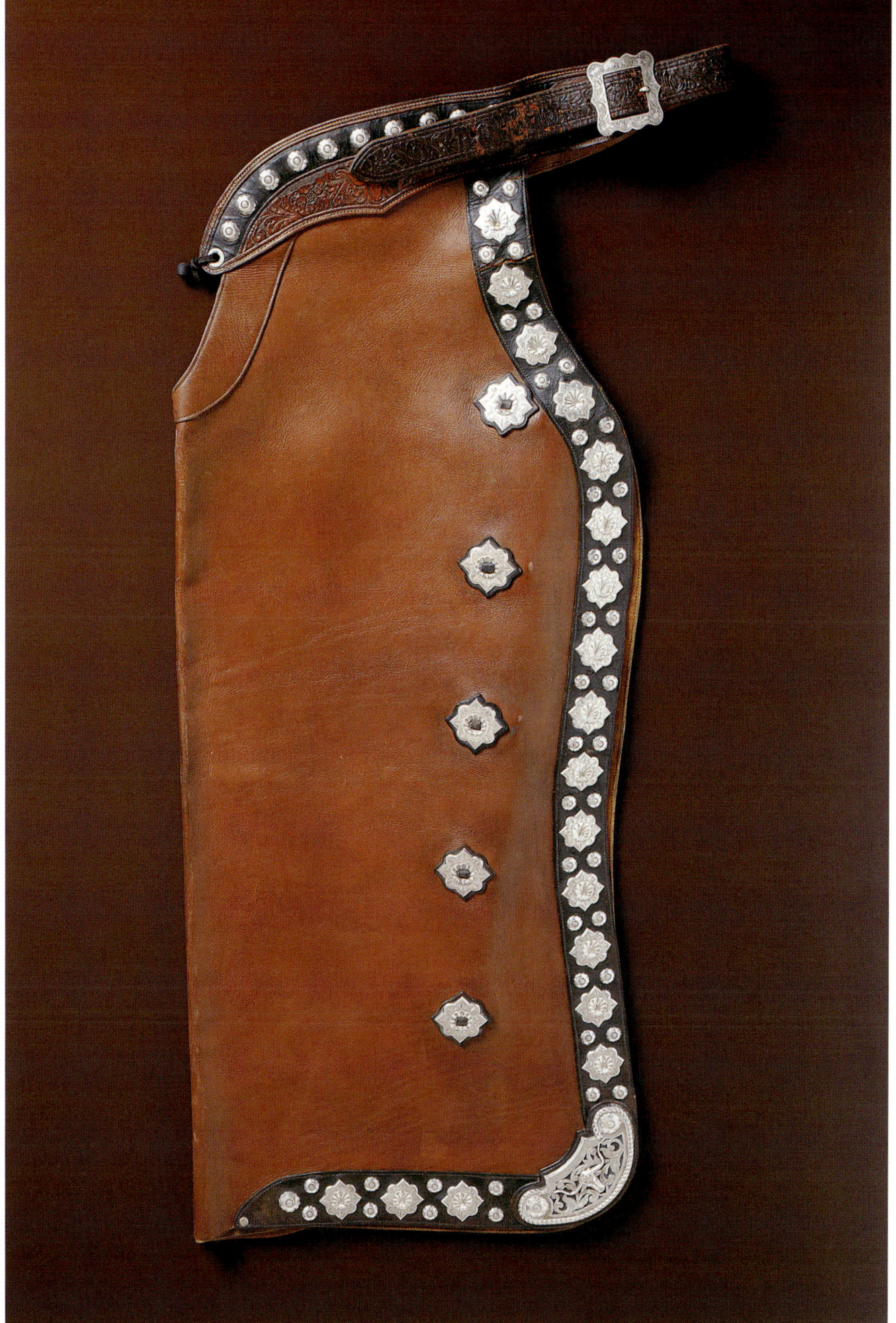

Opposite
M. L. Leddy, Fort Worth
Chaps made of unborn calfskin with silver conchas and stamped leather trim bordered with silver spots, c. 1920s
FLEISCHER COLLECTION, SCOTTSDALE

Left
Philip "Fred" Fredholm (silverwork) and F. O. Baird (leatherwork), Los Angeles
Batwing-style chaps with floral carved belt, shell and daisy pattern silver conchas, and contrasting leather trim, 1940s
FLEISCHER COLLECTION, SCOTTSDALE

> unless their owner was either a slave to habit or very vain, often hung from a nail. They were heavy and, for a pedestrian, quite uncomfortable.[54]

Whether made of smooth or fur-covered leather, closed-leg chaps remained the standard style throughout the West during late nineteenth and early twentieth centuries. From time to time, however, makers did introduce minor structural improvements. Single-piece belts, for example, eventually gave way to a safer and more comfortable two-piece variety that curved downward and laced together in the front and buckled in the rear.

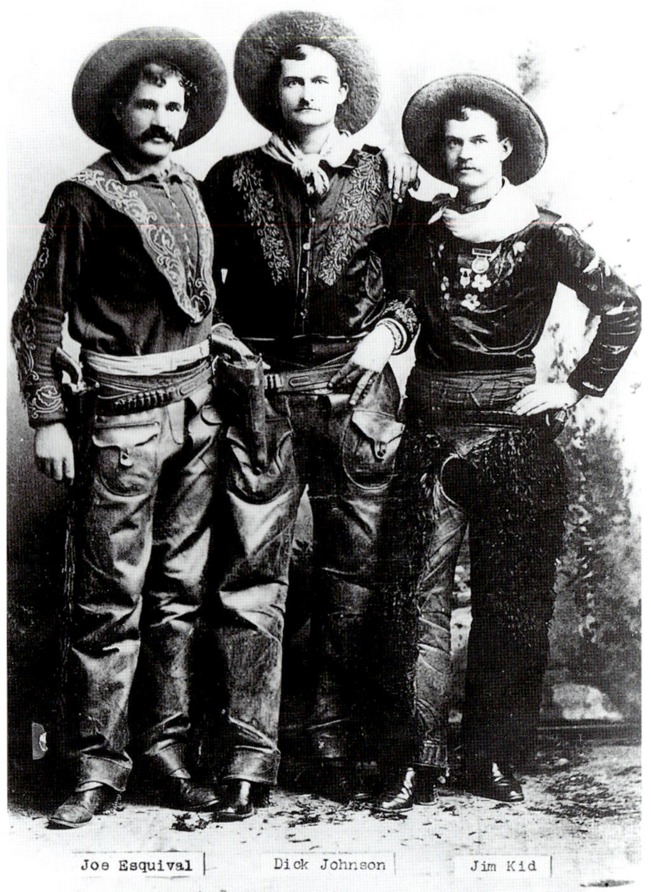

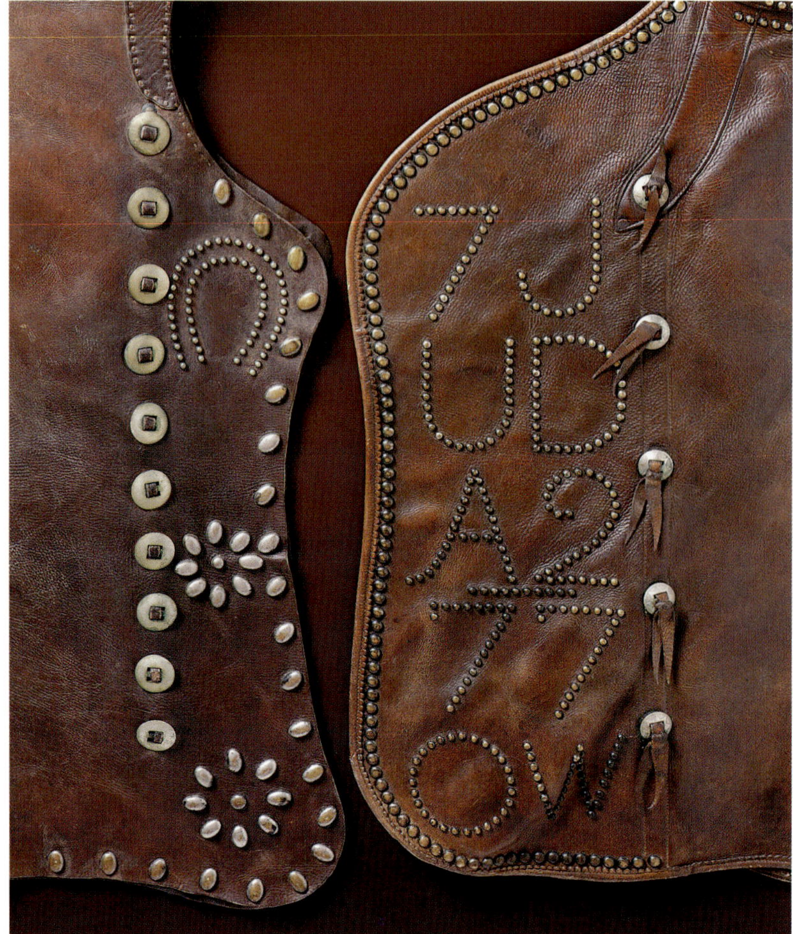

Above, left
Wild West Show performers pose in their fanciest outfits, including elaborately embroidered skirts, shotgun and wooly chaps, gun belts, and broad-rimmed hats
Buffalo Bill Historical Center, Cody, Wyoming

Above, right
Left: R. T. Frazier, Pueblo, Colorado, batwing pattern chaps with horseshoe and petal designs; right: Connolly Brothers, Butte, Montana, cattle brand decorations, c. 1910s–1920s
Fleischer Collection, Scottsdale

By 1890 some makers had introduced chaps equipped with a series of straps and buckles, which allowed the legs to be loosened or left partially open to increase ventilation on warm days. Within a few years, a snap and ring combination became the chap fastener of choice. Such hardware not only allowed chap wearers to move more freely but also to slip their leggings on and off without removing their boots and spurs.

During the first decade of the twentieth century the trim, tailored look of closed-leg chaps began to share the market with a new, more flamboyant fashion. Instead of simply cutting the outer edge of the leg straight or fringed, as before, innovative chap makers began to leave a more generous and shapely leather overlap beyond the seam. The new style, christened "batwings" or "buzzard wings" because of the propensity of the extensions to flap in the breeze, probably originated in Colorado, although at least one expert places its first appearance elsewhere in the Southwest.

Many working cowboys clung to their old shotgun-style leggings, some no doubt fearing the sudden, wind-induced flapping of winged chaps that sometimes set skittish range horses to bucking. Rodeo contestants, however, eagerly embraced winged chaps, whose flapping accentuated a bronc rider's spurring

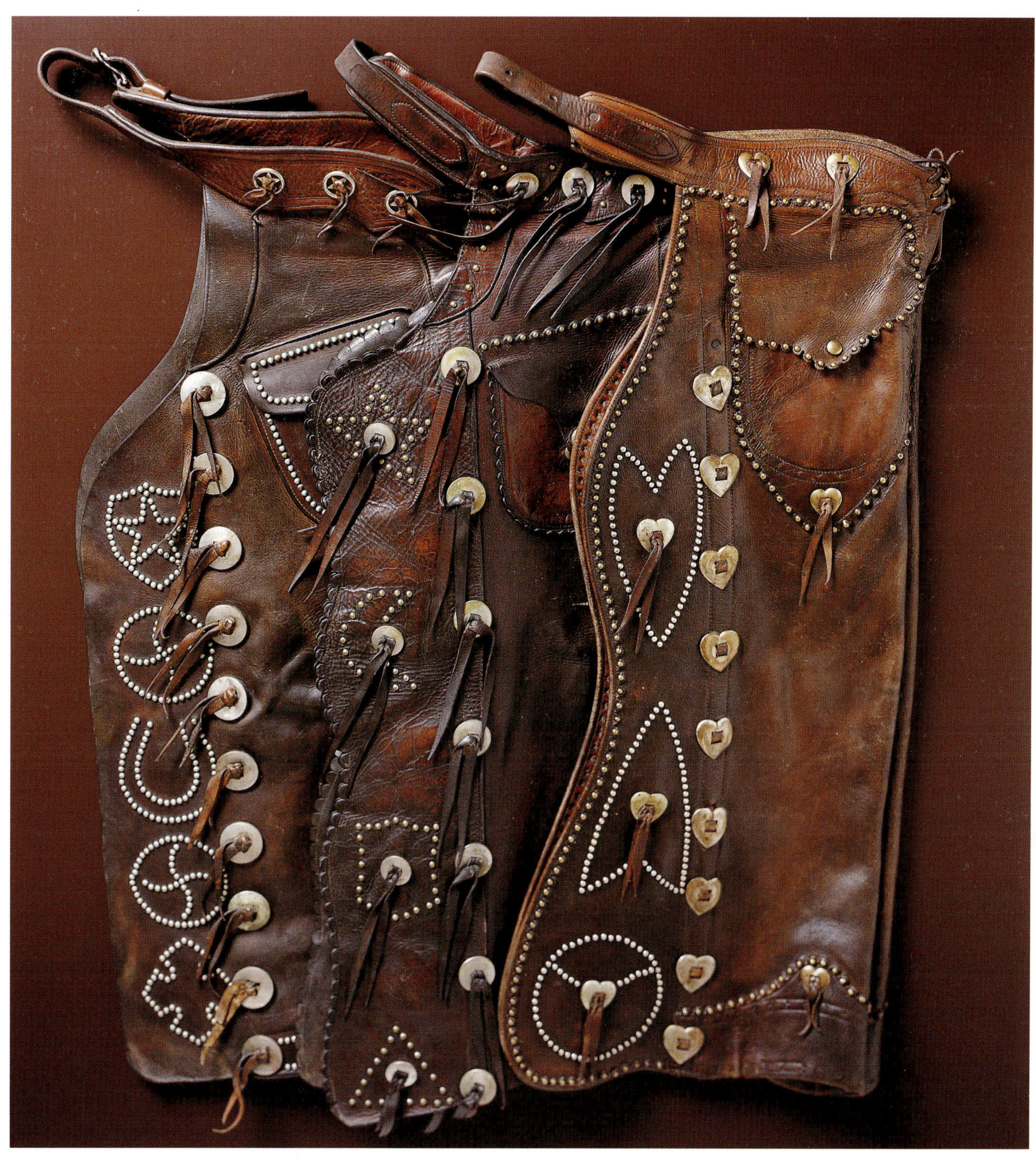

Batwing pattern chaps decorated with conchas and metal spot designs; makers, left to right: R.T. Frazier, Pueblo, Colorado; Riley and McCormick, Calgary, Alberta, Canada; and Connolly Brothers, Billings, Montana
Fleischer Collection, Scottsdale

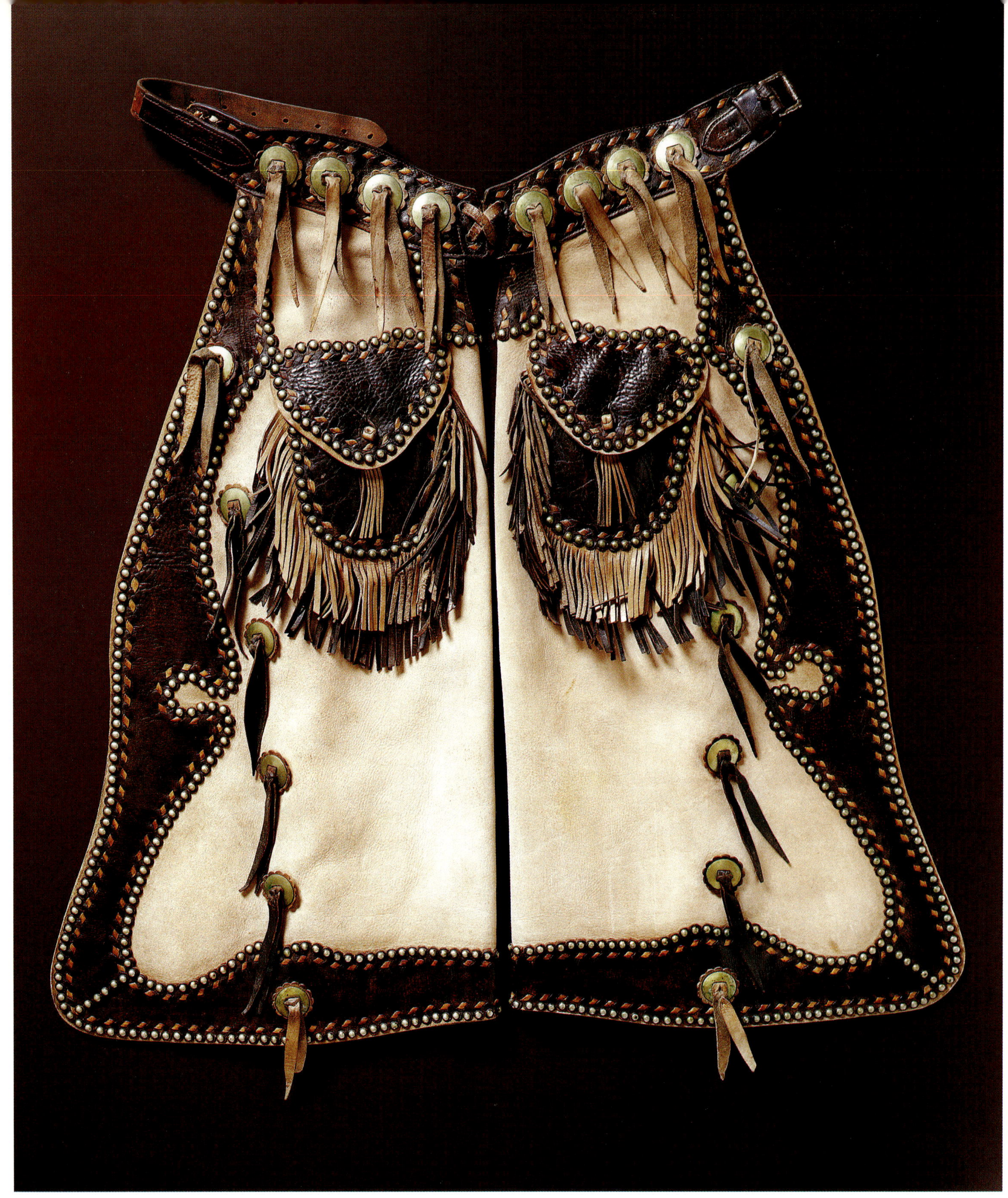

Hamley and Co., Pendleton, Oregon
Batwing pattern chaps,
contrasting leather appliqué trim
with fringed pockets
FLEISCHER COLLECTION, SCOTTSDALE

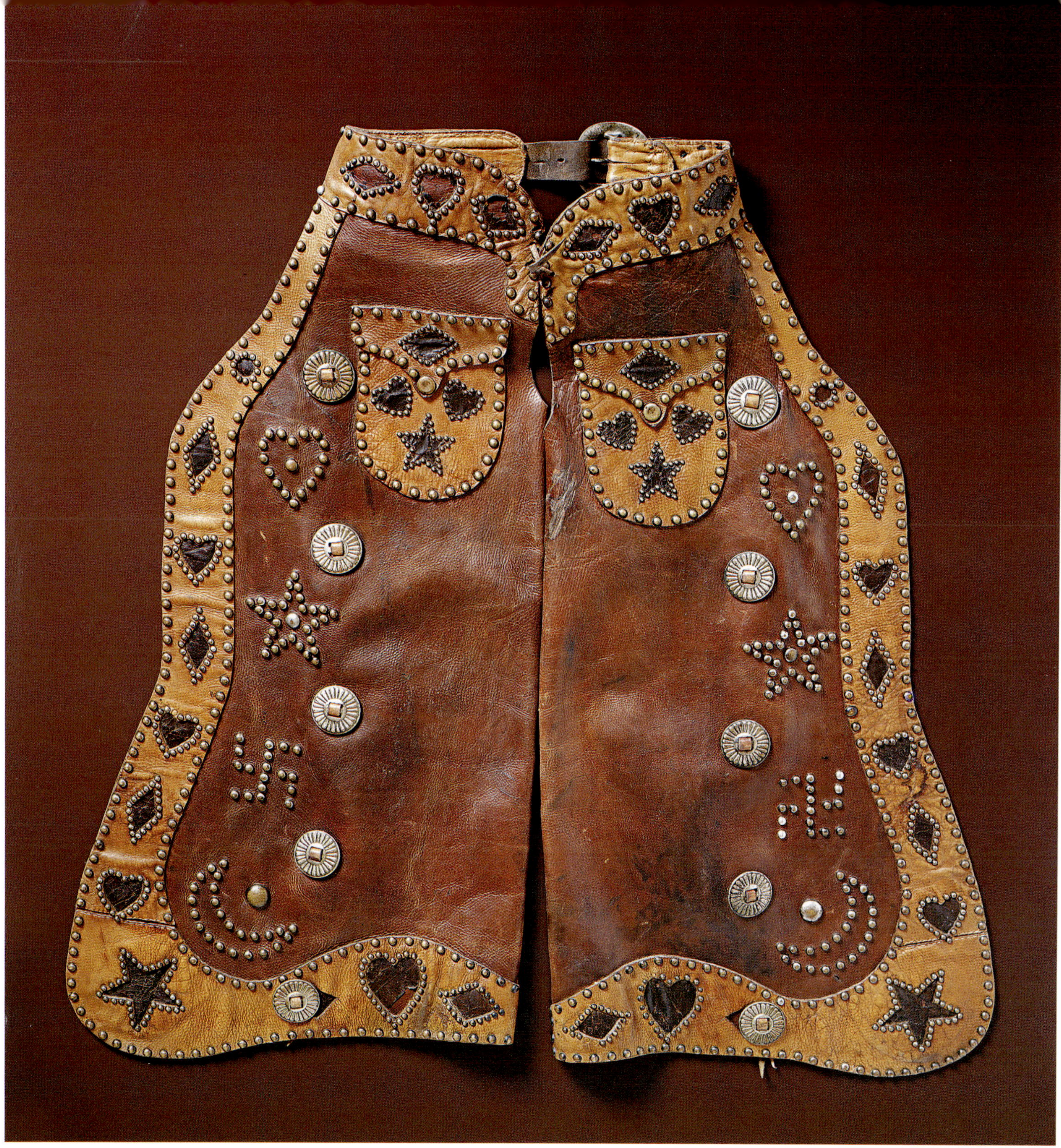

Hamley and Co., Pendleton, Oregon
Two-tone leather chaps trimmed with metal spot designs forming celestial, heart, diamond, and Native American whirling log (swastika) patterns, 1920s–1930s
Fleischer Collection, Scottsdale

action, which, in turn, drew the judges' attention, resulting in higher scores and more frequent paydays. To secure their seat in the saddle bronc riders often wetted the inside of their chap legs with water or applied neat's-foot oil, resin, soda pop, or even chewing gum to the leather to increase the friction and help them stay aboard rank horses.

As the new style gradually gained popularity among western riders, imaginative designers tinkered constantly with the size, shape, and decorative embellishment of the wings. Plain and engraved metal conchas like those used to adorn

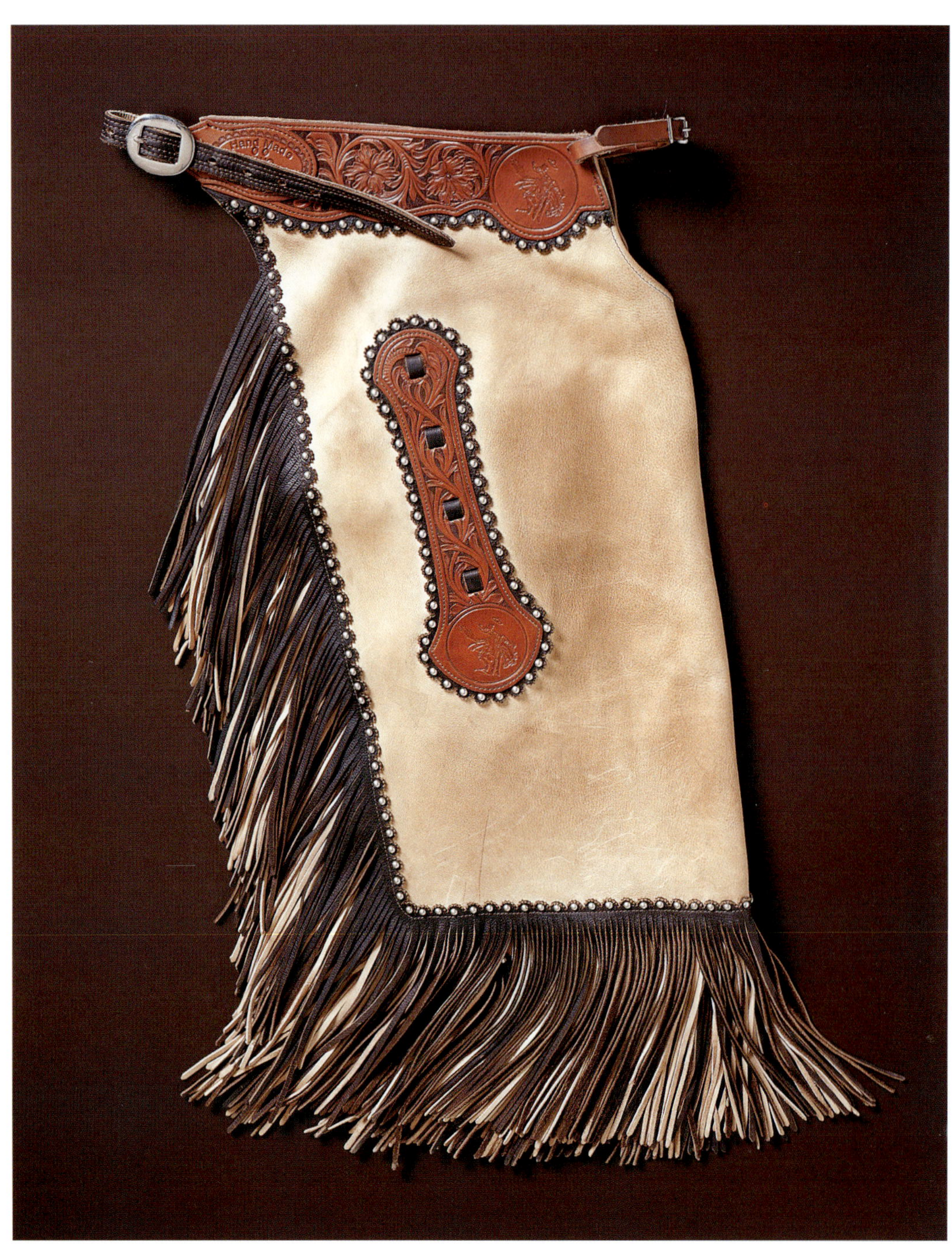

Dave Hack, Star, Idaho
Chink pattern chaps with floral stamped belt and appliqué, metal spot trim, and multi-colored fringe, contemporary
Fleischer Collection, Scottsdale

Opposite
Edward H. Bohlin, Hollywood
Batwing chaps made of two-tone, chrome-tanned leather trimmed with Californa poppy floral stamping; mountain and sunset motif on belt, trim, and pockets, c. 1930s
Fleischer Collection, Scottsdale

saddles remained popular, in part because they could be used to help reinforce snap rings. Riders who feared entangling their chaps in fences or chutes, however, sometimes covered conchas with leather.

Conchas sometimes appeared in tandem with pearl trimmings or, more often, metal spots or studs of various sizes, shapes, and materials. Makers applied such ornaments as edge trim and to form initials, brands, playing card symbols, and other simple shapes. Decorations made from coin silver adorned the finest types. On lesser quality goods many chap makers used German silver or even nickel-plated spots that tended to turn brassy when the plating wore off.

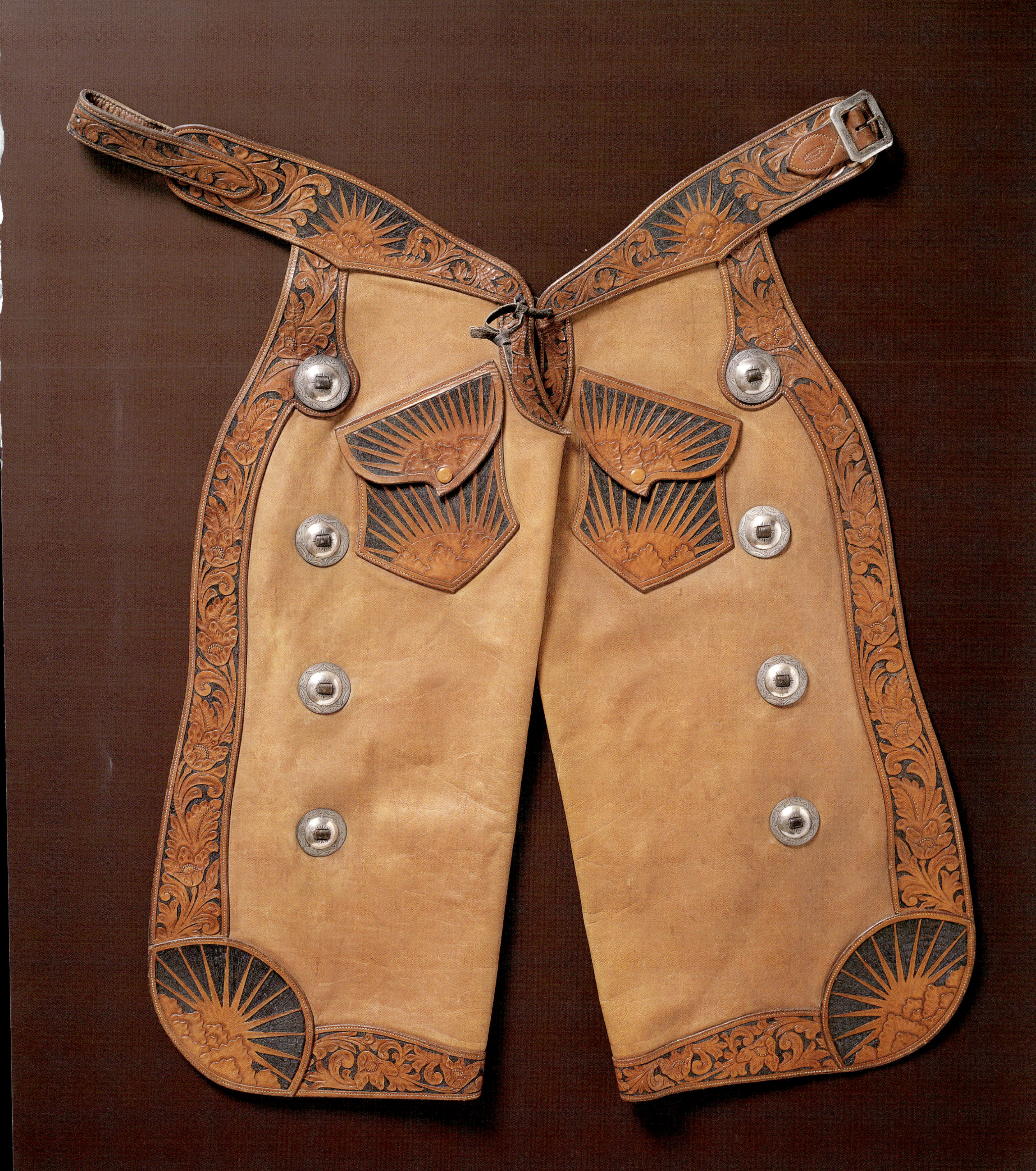

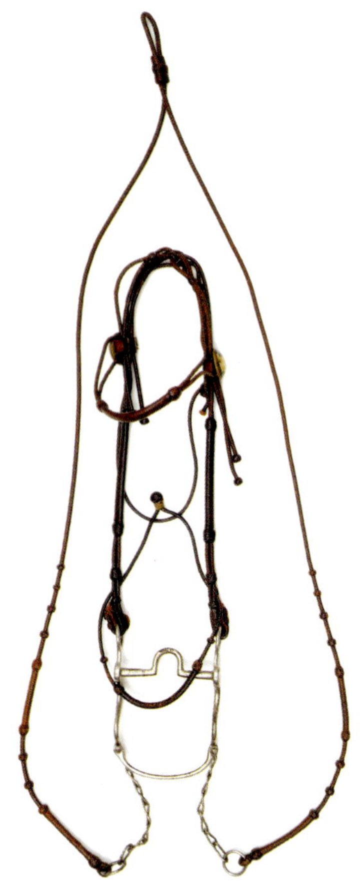

Braided leather bridle with bit
BUFFALO BILL HISTORICAL CENTER, CODY, WYOMING

Decorative patterns also were achieved with leather appliqués or inlays rendered in contrasting colors. Motifs that appeared on the wings were often repeated on chap belts and pockets, which were sometimes outlined with distinctive lacing or stitching or were stamped or carved in the manner of saddles. For variation some makers freely substituted horsehide, often called "pearl leather" in trade catalogs, and elk hide for cowhide. Customers also could specify the weight as well as type of leather desired. Most was of a medium heft but could be made lighter or heavier according to personal preference. Some recreational and show riders preferred soft, lightweight glove leather that would not do for heavy work. Besides the decorations applied by commercial makers, such famous western artists as W. H. D. Koerner and Edward Borein created one-of-a-kind works of art by painting colorful western figures on the chap wings of friends and family.

By the 1920s comfortable and colorful batwing-style chaps ruled both the cattle range and rodeo arena. Bronc riders, who preferred their chaps to fit tight around the thighs and looser below the knee to facilitate spurring, encouraged chap makers to trim and round the inner corner of the chap leg from knee to ankle. Most authorities credit Wyoming saddle maker Frank A. Meanea with this innovation shortly after the turn of the twentieth century. The Cheyenne-style leg, as it came to be known, not only reduced chap weight but also removed leather that had a tendency to double back on itself when the rider stepped into the stirrup. By the 1930s chap makers were offering chap legs cut in at least three different patterns depending upon the number of snaps and rings that affixed them to the limb. The "California cut" leg, for example, sported five snaps and rings; the Texas cut, four; and the Wyoming style, only three.

Contest riders not only advocated changes in chap legs but also in the belts that secured them to their waists. In the interest of safety, makers began to replace the heavy crisscross lacing that secured chap belts in front with a narrow leather string or a strap and buckle. The new configuration, which appeared around 1900, was stout enough to hold the chaps together under normal circumstances but would break if the thong or strap became hung on the saddle horn.

Rodeo competition and its attendant pageantry led not only to structural changes in chaps but also to more flamboyant styling. Although heavier than other type chaps, woolies attracted a considerable following among early male and female rodeo contestants, whose attire often mimicked that worn by performers in Buffalo Bill's Wild West show or one of its many imitators. Members of a Texas troupe organized in 1883 to give public roping and riding exhibitions, for example, were said to have been outfitted in "large Mexican silver hats, purchased at Laredo, leather jackets finely fringed, Angora leggins and large Mexican spurs."[55] Wild West show and rodeo performers prized the woolies' thick

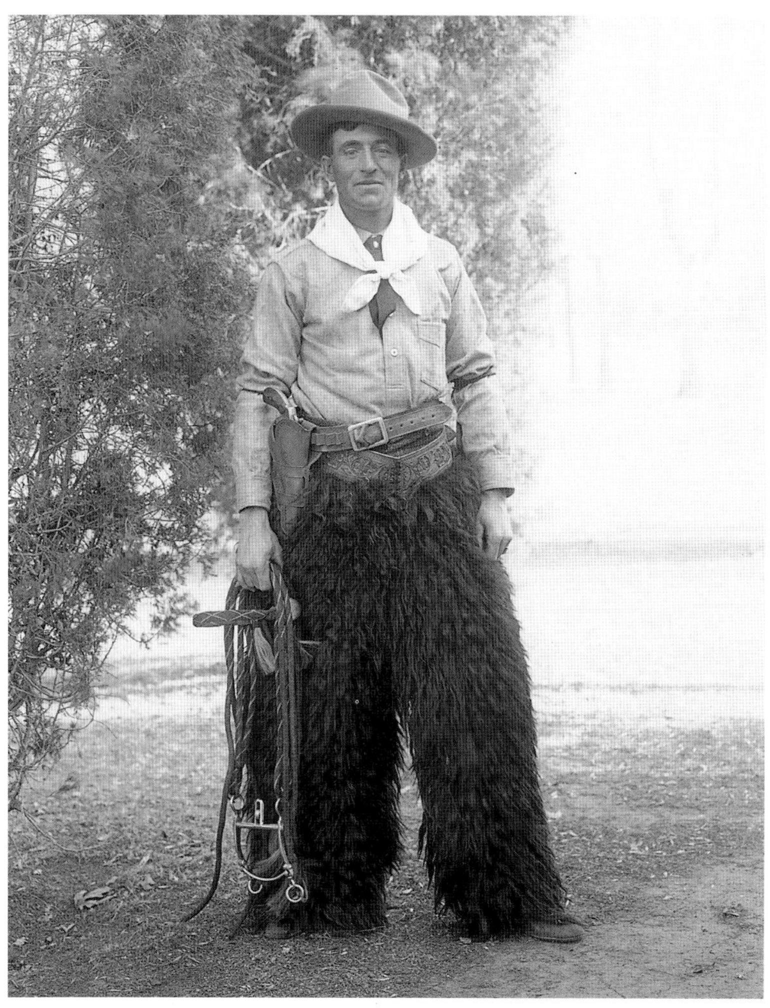

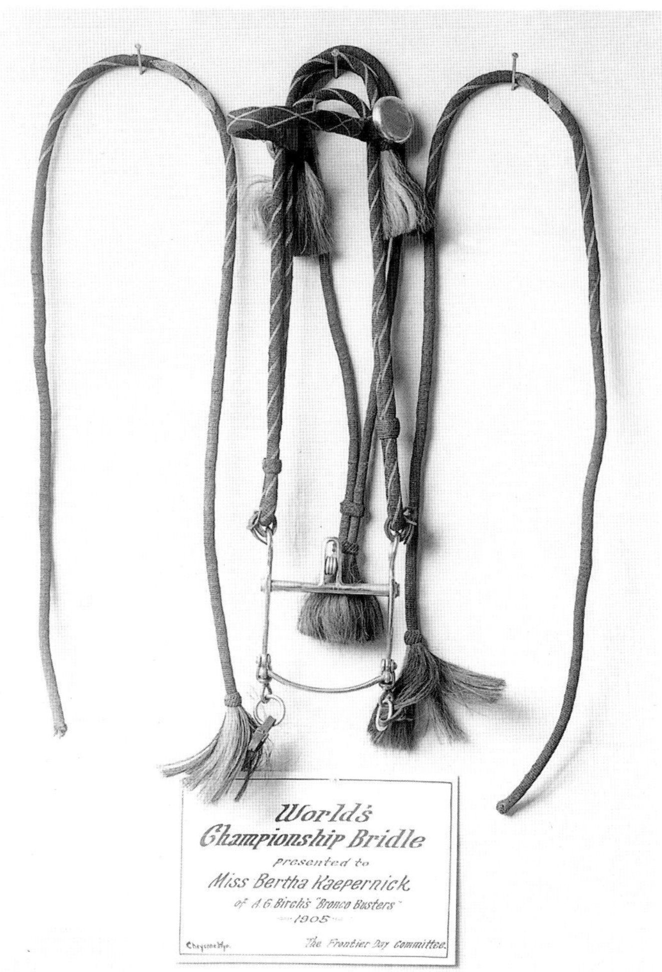

fur not only for its colorful and exotic look and texture but also for the extra padding it offered when riders collided with chutes and fences or were bucked off in the arena.

In its natural state Angora goat hair came in either white or black. For added effect creative chap makers began to dye the white skins into a variety of bright colors—gold, orange, and red ranking among the most common but also green and even pink. Multicolored varieties, including a patriotic red, white, and blue design, were not far behind. Women, who during the early years of rodeo, competed with men in rough stock events, donned some of the most flamboyant woolies.

Although outfitters large and small produced hair pants and leather leggings for the western market, too few production records survive to gauge the size of the market with any certainty. Major saddleries, which usually offered the greatest variety of designs and the most competitive prices, no doubt dominated the market. In 1912, a typical year for the trade, one such company, the R. T. Frazier Saddlery of Pueblo, is known to have produced 2,000 pairs of chaps, along with 5,000 saddles and quantities of other leather goods.

Above, left
Cowboy (member of the "Birch Broncho Busters") in wooly chaps and holding a horsehair bridle
Colorado Historical Society, Denver

Above, right
Horsehair bridle; presentation plaque reads: "World's Championship Bridle presented to Miss Bertha Kaepernick of A. G. Birch's 'Bronco Busters,' 1905, Cheyenne, Wyo., The Frontier Days Committee"
Colorado Historical Society, Denver

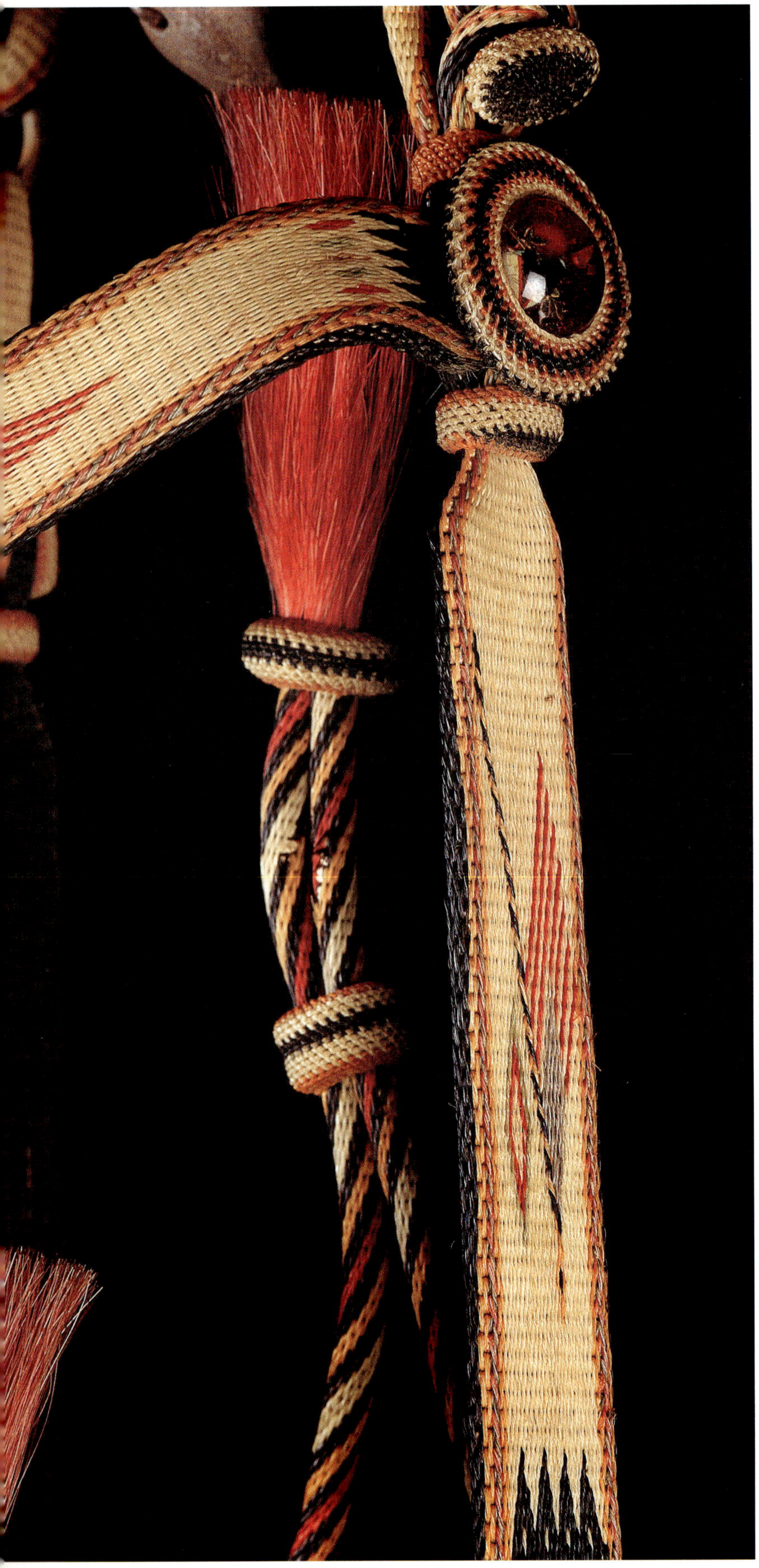

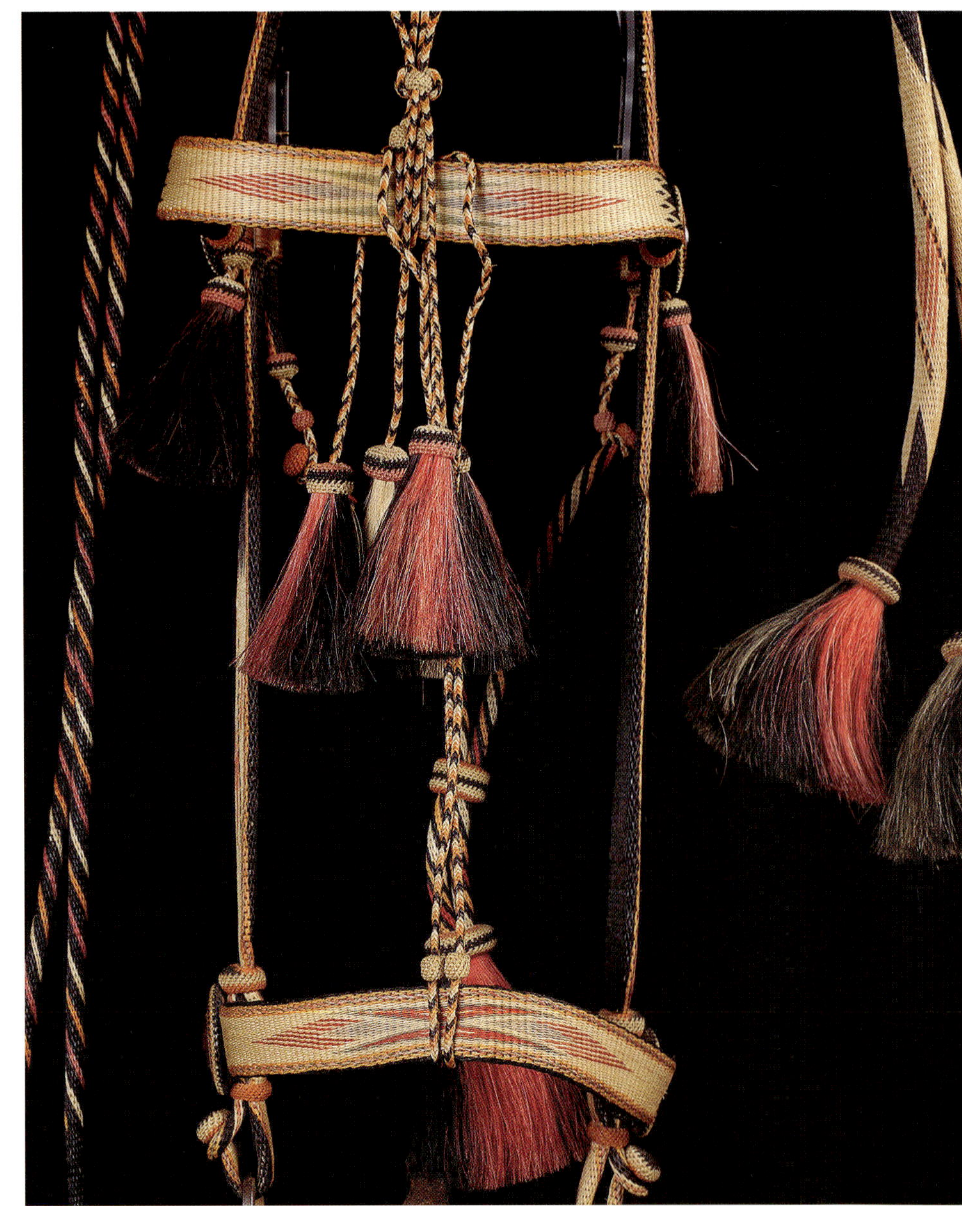

Left and above
Horsehair bridle made by an inmate of Montana State Prison, Deer Lodge, c. 1900
HIGH NOON WESTERN AMERICANA, LOS ANGELES

Opposite
Horsehair headstall, diamond pattern brow and nosebands
BUFFALO BILL HISTORICAL CENTER, CODY, WYOMING

A few firms gained special reputations as quality chap makers. The Salt Lake Hardware Company, for example, became known for its fine Angora chaps as did Hamley and Company of Pendleton. The sleek leggings produced by the latter firm gained a strong following among the rodeo contestants who, beginning in 1910, competed annually in the famous Pendleton Round-Up.

In California, few chap makers could compare with the design and workmanship of the Visalia Stock Saddle Company of San Francisco. Ed Weeks, owner of the company, is credited with introducing spotted Angora chaps in 1911. Weeks achieved the effect by sewing spots of one color against a solid background of a different hue. Spots of black or white hair sewn to a contrasting black or white background, for example, created the popular "pinto" look. In its 1938 catalog the Visalia company offered fine Angora chaps in a variety of solid colors (black, white, gold, orange, lemon, or red) and in any color combination of fronts and spots. Such decorative tufts were sometimes attached to chap belts as well.

Each hair spot added 40 cents to the cost of a pair of Angora chaps in the 1920s. Visalia priced its Angora leggings according to the length of the hair. In the late 1930s the plush longhaired variety fetched $1.50 more than those of medium length and $2.25 more than short fur. By this time, however, the popularity of Angora chaps was on the wane, the victim of changing tastes.

Much of the impetus for change in the design and embellishment of chaps had shifted from rodeo contestants to recreational horsemen, who were involved in riding clubs and parades and in breeding and showing horses. The chaps of these riders were often part of a distinctive outfit that included matching leather vests, cuffs, gauntlets, gun belts, boots and spurs, and saddles. Parade and horse show riders often acquired expensive and sometimes ostentatious accessories to compliment their tack, which in tandem with stunning horseflesh, reflected wealth, status, and tradition.

The silver-mounted leggings produced between the late 1920s and the mid-1950s by such renowned California makers as Edward H. Bohlin of Hollywood, the Visalia Company, and a few others, represent the apex of chap style and workmanship. Bohlin, for example, designed and produced

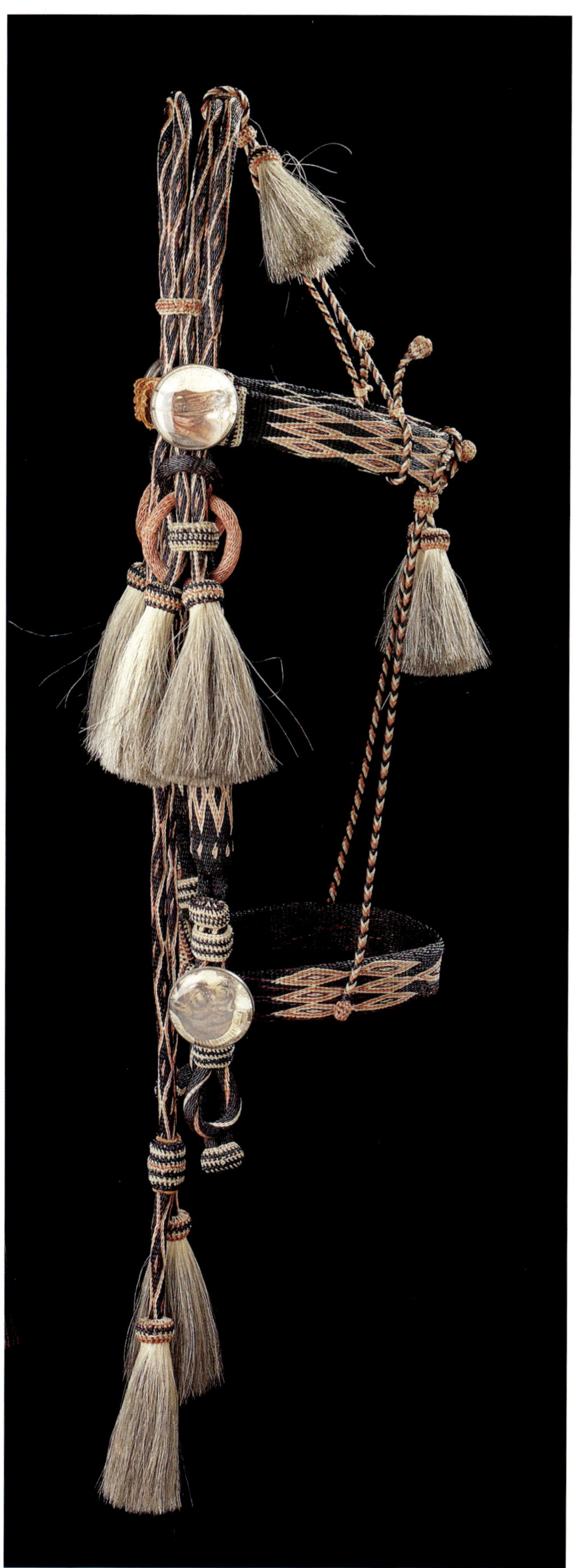

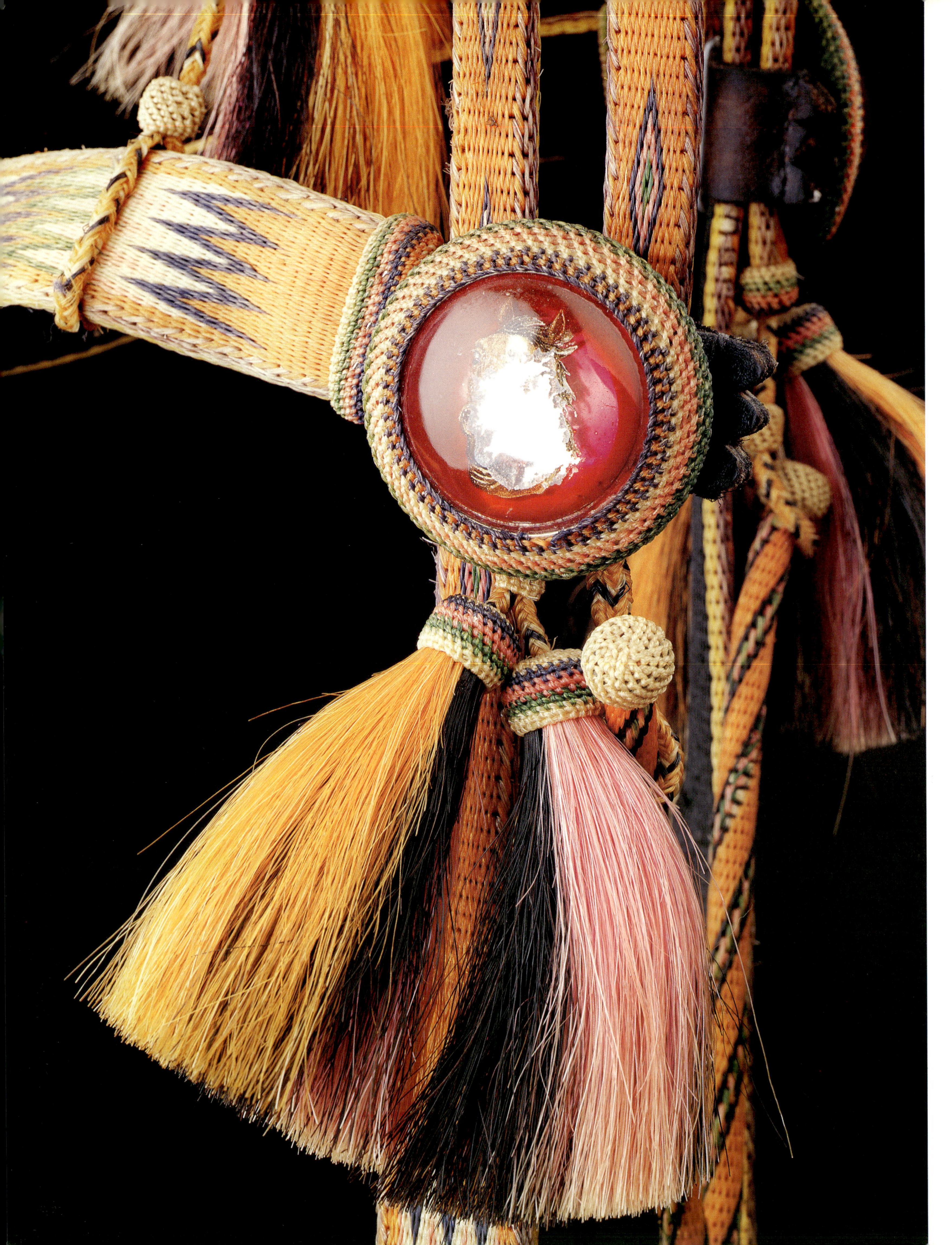

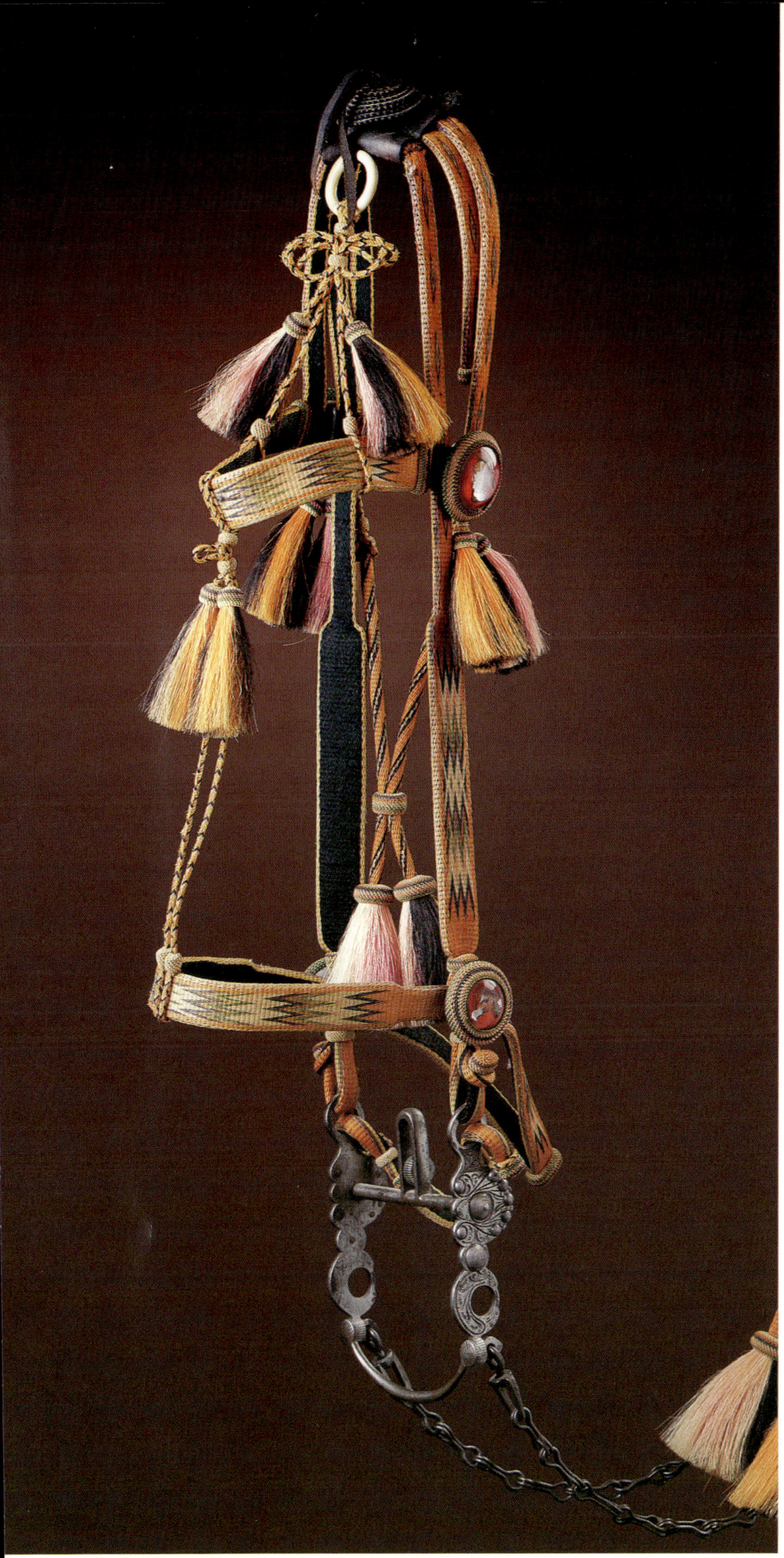

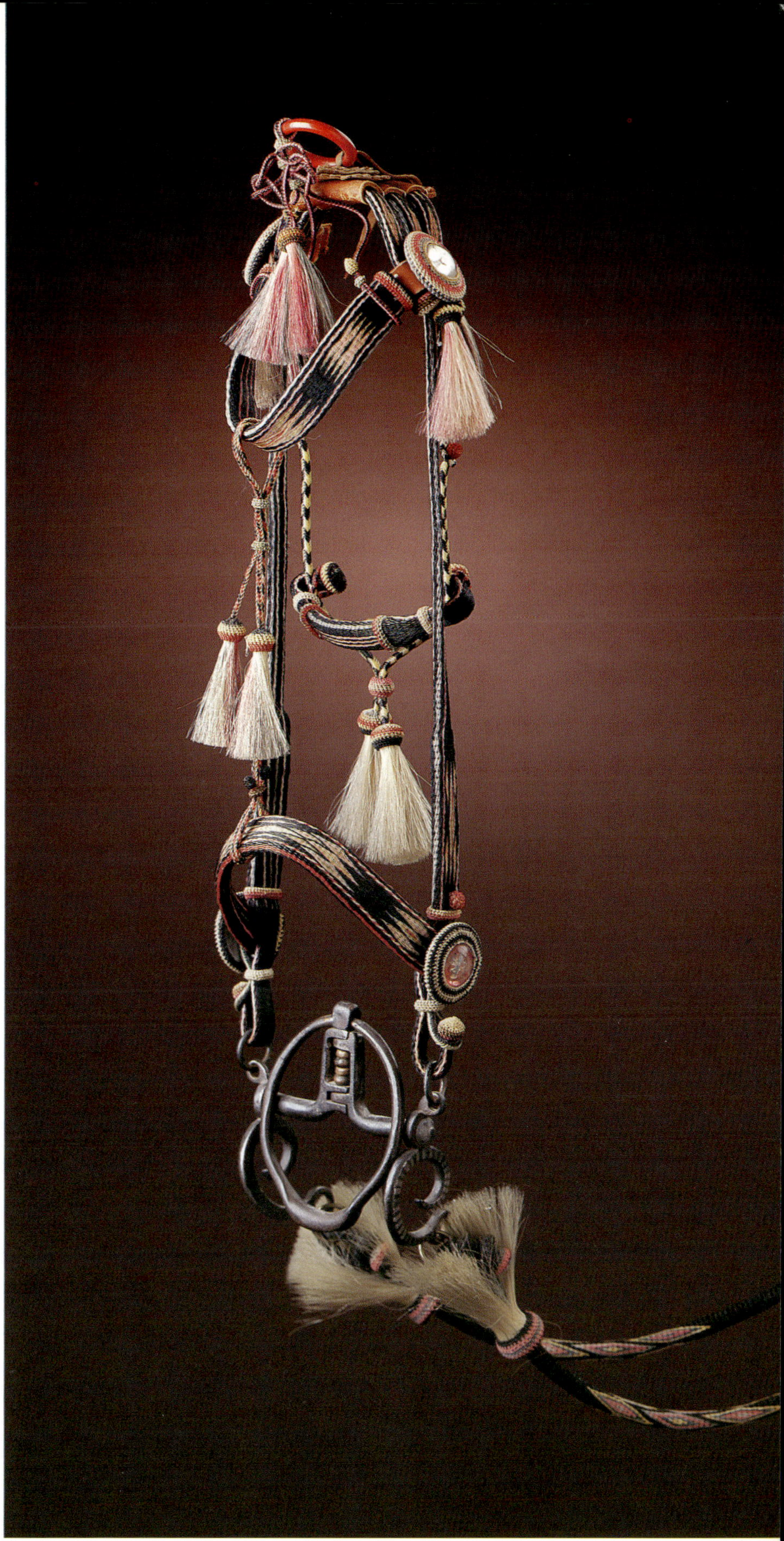

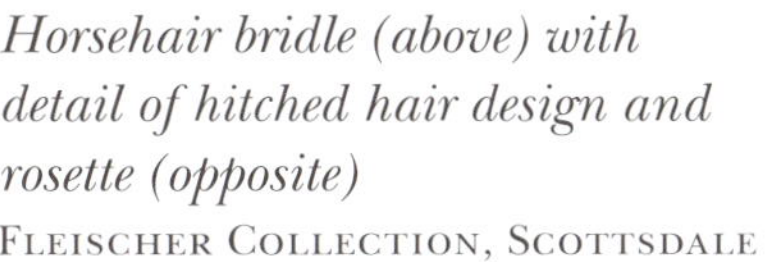

Horsehair bridle (above) with detail of hitched hair design and rosette (opposite)
Fleischer Collection, Scottsdale

Horsehair bridle with hitched design, tassles, rosettes, and ring bit
Fleischer Collection, Scottsdale

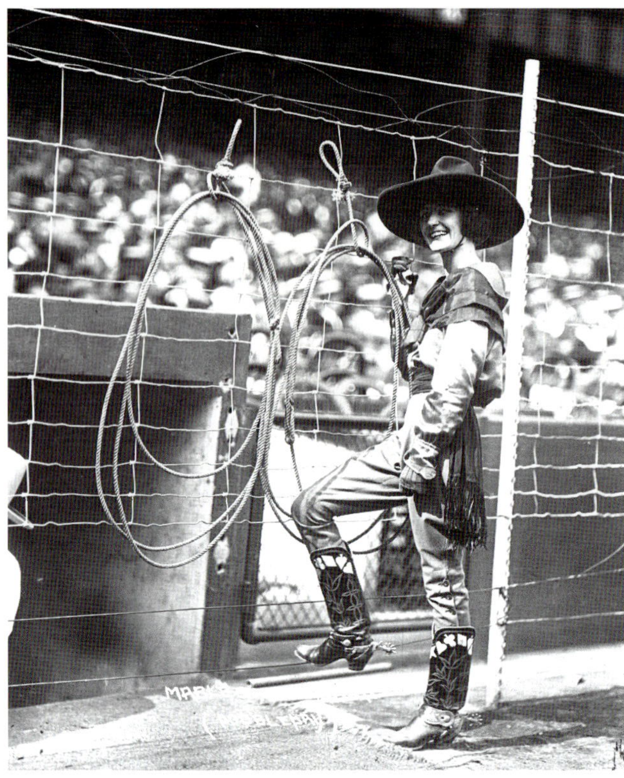

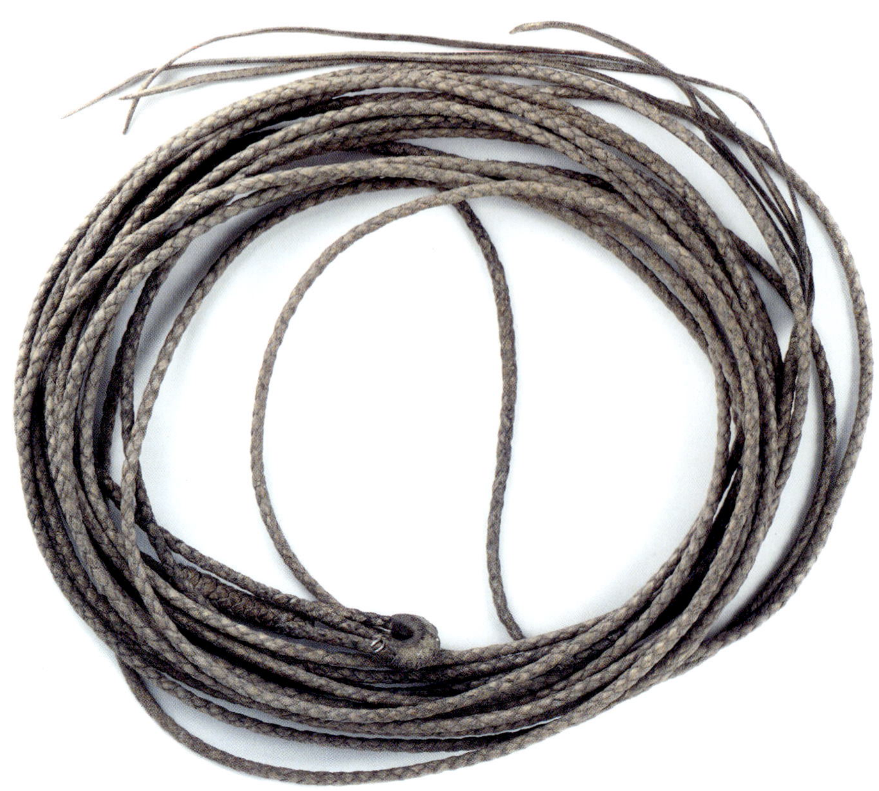

Above, left
Ralph R. Doubleday (1881–1958)
Cowgirl Mabel Strickland poses in arena beside two ropes; she wears fancy boots with playing-card symbols
National Cowboy and Western Heritage Museum, Oklahoma City

Above, right
Four-strand plaited rawhide reata with hide honda
Buffalo Bill Historical Center, Cody, Wyoming

a distinctive line of fine parade chaps made of horsehide or calfskin and heavily embellished with engraved sterling silver ornaments rendered in high relief in a variety of geometric, floral, and figural motifs. Matched against a solid background of black, tan, or dark brown leather such decorations were striking. Most were adapted for use on saddles, bridles, vests, belts, and gauntlets as well as chaps.

Some of the most exquisite designs of the era consisted of concave floral conchas and rosettes with raised buds and drooping petals, whose tips flattened out against the chap leather. Silversmiths created dies representing a variety of flowers, including California poppies, mariposa lilies, and daisies.

Another popular type of raised concha bore a rope or scalloped border and the silver- or gold-mounted image of an eagle, bison, horse head, longhorn, bronc rider, or other figure in its center in place of engraving. Edward H. Bohlin's inventory of chap ornaments also included more than a half-dozen different images of Native Americans, most of them of art deco styling and at least one inspired by the cigar store Indians of an earlier era. Still another of the elegant rosettes of the period took the shape of a Mexican sombrero with a gold flower atop the crown and delicate gold braid around the edge of the brim.

Bohlin and several imitators often combined individual geometric and floral ornaments into solid rows, as edge trim, or fashioned them into more complex mosaic designs, usually some form of star. Decorations applied in this manner were sometimes riveted to light leather strips that were then sewn to the chap wings for added strength.

Opposite
Rawhide reata, gift of Will Rogers to film director John Ford c. 1930s
National Cowboy and Western Heritage Museum, Oklahoma City

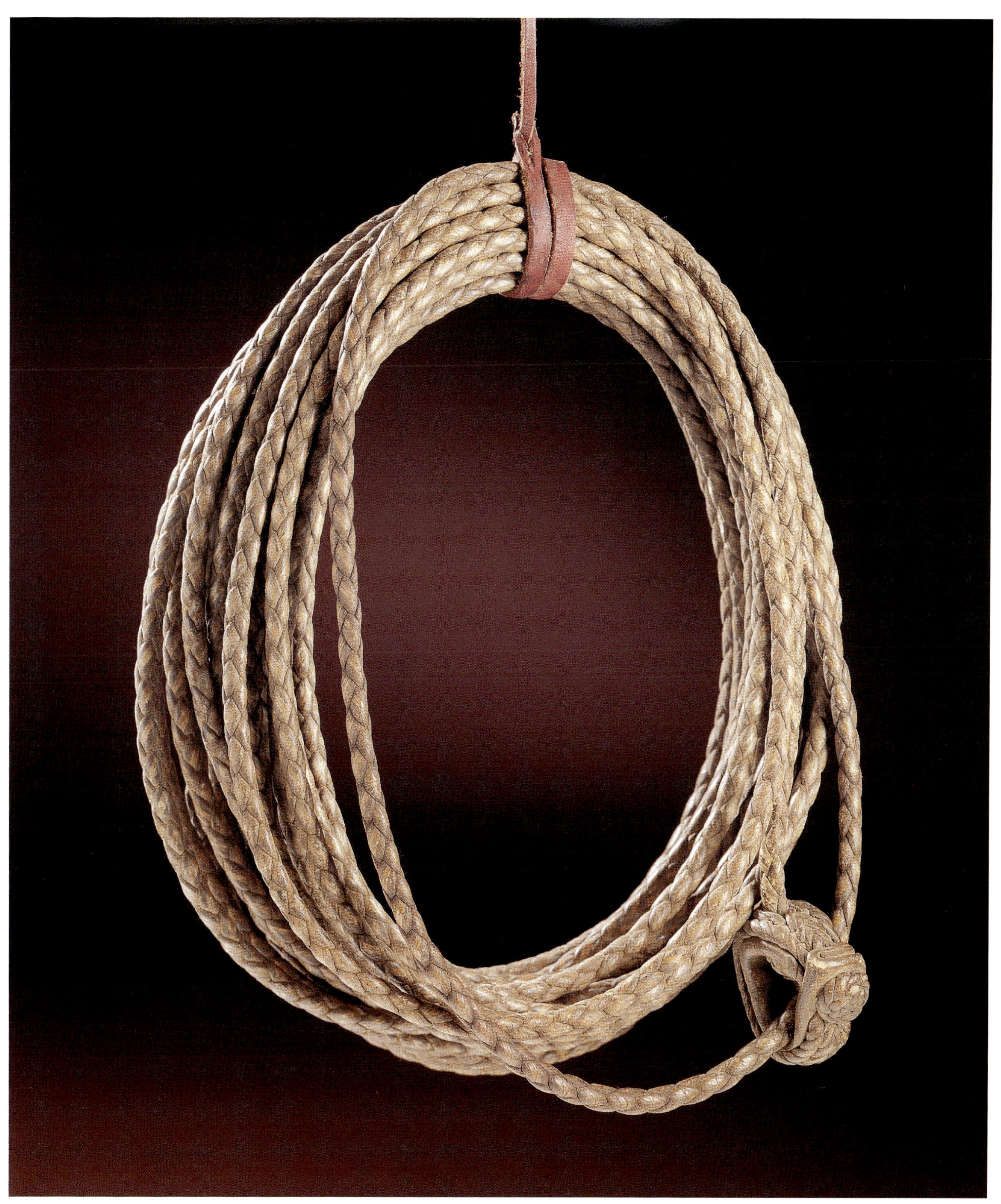

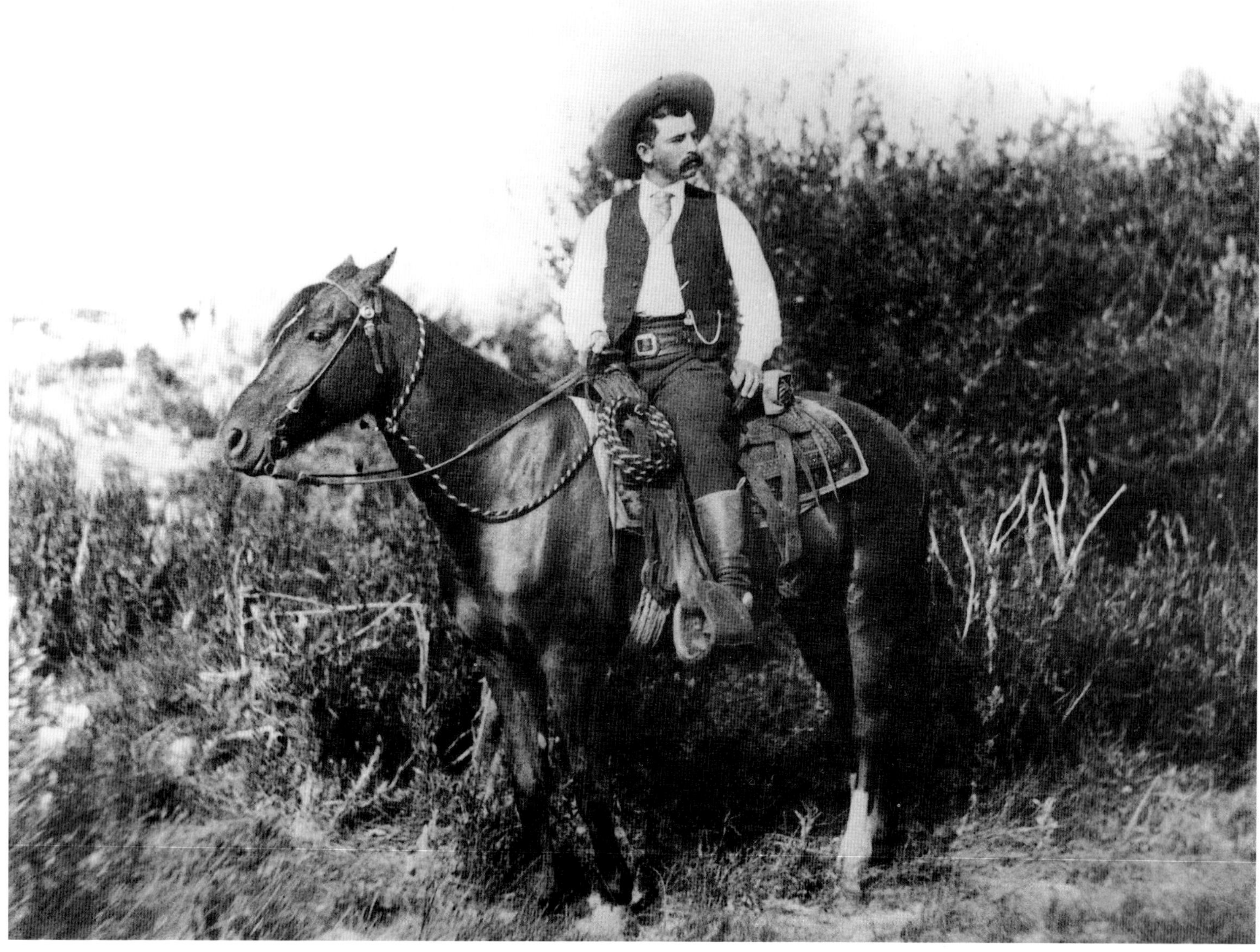

Wyoming cowboy on horseback, with two-color twisted horsehair mecate *looped around the horse's neck and coiled on the saddle, c.1890*
WYOMING STATE MUSEUM, CHEYENNE

Some top-of-the-line chap styles depended upon the creative use of leather rather than metal to achieve their aesthetic effect. Bohlin's "La Fiesta" pattern, for example, consisted of solid colored calfskin or horsehide legs, which were trimmed with contrasting white cowhide, intricately carved and filigreed in a flower and leaf pattern, to give, as the maker's 1941 trade catalog described it, "the appearance of rare old Spanish lace."[56] Pinked edges, four elegant silver conchas, and a sunset appliqué at the corners of the wings completed the design, which was priced at $125, three or four times the cost of an average pair of chaps.

Bohlin incorporated a more elaborate version of the sunset motif into the belt, pockets, and edge trim of another spectacular design that included black inlay and an elaborate floral-stamped belt and border (see page 133). The Visalia Co. also produced a version of this stunning pattern.

Opposite
Four-color horsehair rope coiled on a saddle horn
FLEISCHER COLLECTION, SCOTTSDALE

As occurred with saddlery, the use of precious metals on chaps declined drastically during World War II. Tastes changed as well, and although silver-mounted

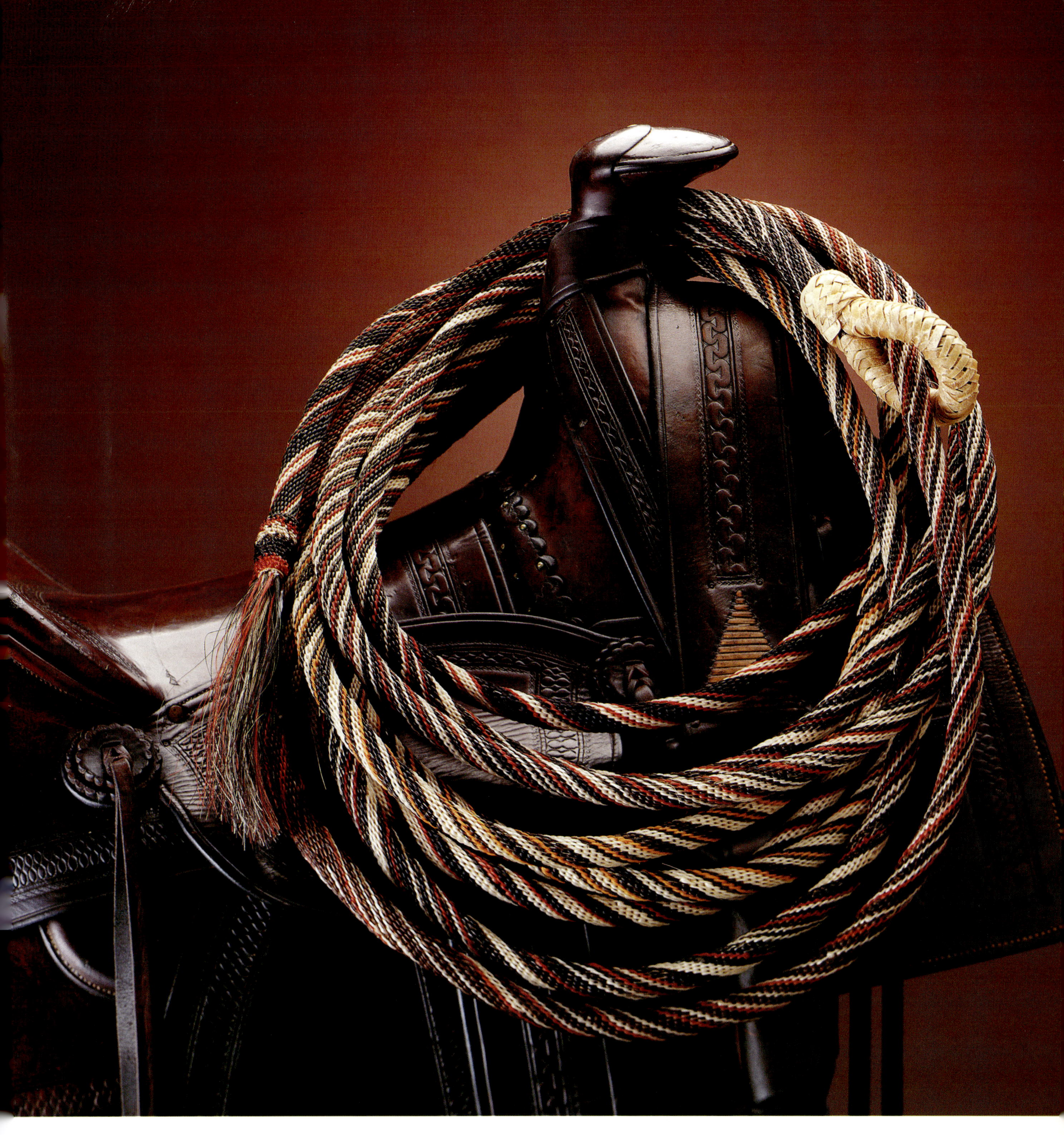

chaps still adorned singing cowboys on the silver screen and wealthy riders at festive western parades and rodeos in the post-war era, such trappings were clearly in decline by the mid-1950s. Except among the rough stock riders of rodeo and competitors in horse shows and cutting horse events, colorful batwing-style chaps eventually passed from the scene as well, eclipsed by tailored shotgun-style leggings fitted with zippers and comfortable, knee-length *armitas*, more popularly known in the late twentieth century as "chinks" (derived from the Spanish *chinquederos*).

Although colored leathers, appliqués, fringe, and engraving continued as mainstays of chap fashion among horsemen, the use of precious metals was more restrained and tasteful. Snug-fitting leggings made of lightweight suede leather, impractical for range work, became popular on the horse show circuit. In the early 1970s a single company offered suede chaps in fifteen different colors.

Besides incorporating new materials, innovative chap makers continued to experiment with new designs as well. One Wyoming craftsman, in keeping with the tenor of the times, introduced the "Aquarian Chap," which incorporated an astrological motif. Not long after, a perfume called Chaps made its national debut.

While saddle makers continued to produce chaps for the traditional cowboy market, an increasing number of companies and individuals began to specialize in custom fitted designs that attracted not only rodeo hands and show riders but also a larger audience that included bikers, rock musicians, and supermodels. By the 1990s national tastemakers had concluded that chaps worn over tight jeans exuded sex appeal. Singer Cher once called their allure, "an American thing, the bad-boy cowboy look for rebellious girls to wear."[57] On the eve of the twenty-first century it seems the world of high fashion had finally discovered what real American cowboys and cowgirls had known for more than a century.

Rawhide and Horsehair

The twisting, braiding, and hitching of horsehair and rawhide are among the oldest cowboy gear-making traditions. With finished goods often in short supply and relatively expensive in ranch country, cowpunchers converted plentiful, versatile, and easily worked hide and hair into a variety of useful products, including *cinchas*, ropes, reins, bridles, *bosales*, belts, hobbles, halters, and quirts.

Hide and hair work required few tools but was tedious and time consuming. Cowpunchers often took up braiding and hitching as an antidote to the loneliness and monotony of layoffs, inclement weather, and winter evenings ensconced in remote line camps with little to do. Others recovering from accidents or illness found such work therapeutic, and cowboys too old to ride and rope still found their gear-making skills in great demand.

The methods and techniques they employed were of ancient origin and had been perfected over centuries by many cultures. As with other horse equipment,

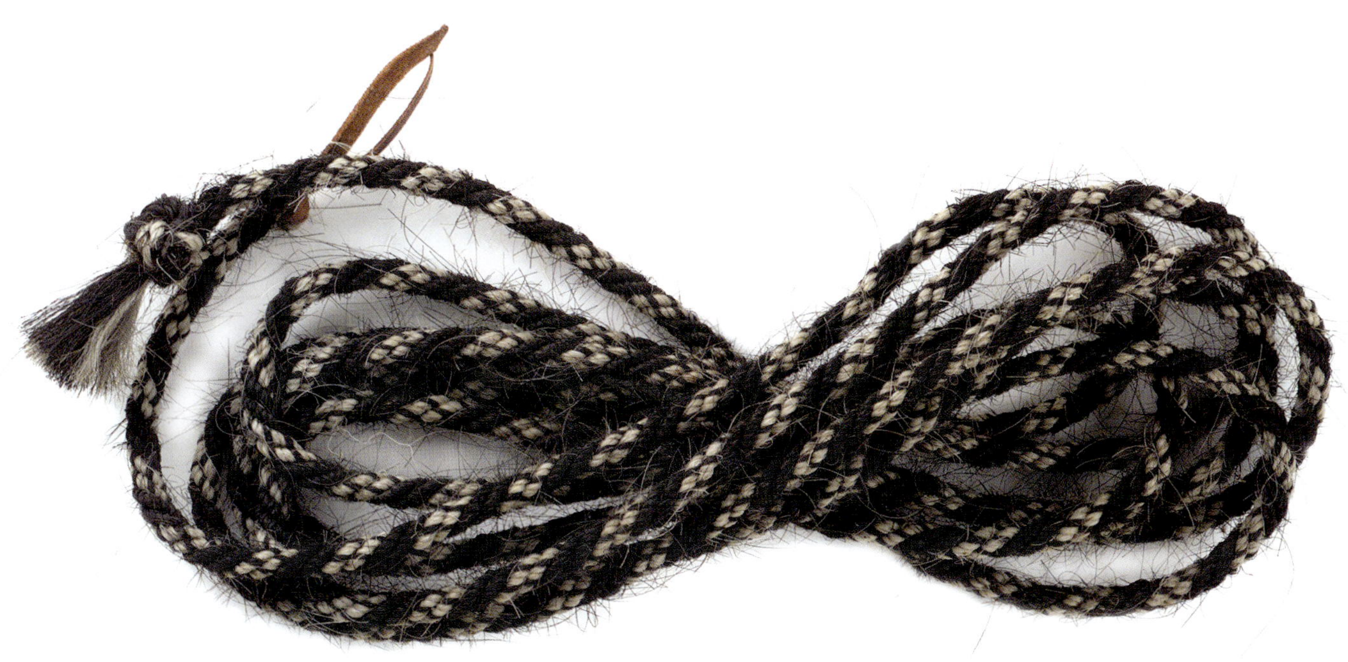

Above
Horsehair rope with latigo popper and candy stripe pattern
Buffalo Bill Historical Center, Cody, Wyoming

Below
Two-pattern horsehair rope with latigo poppers, tassel, and horsehair knot
Buffalo Bill Historical Center, Cody, Wyoming

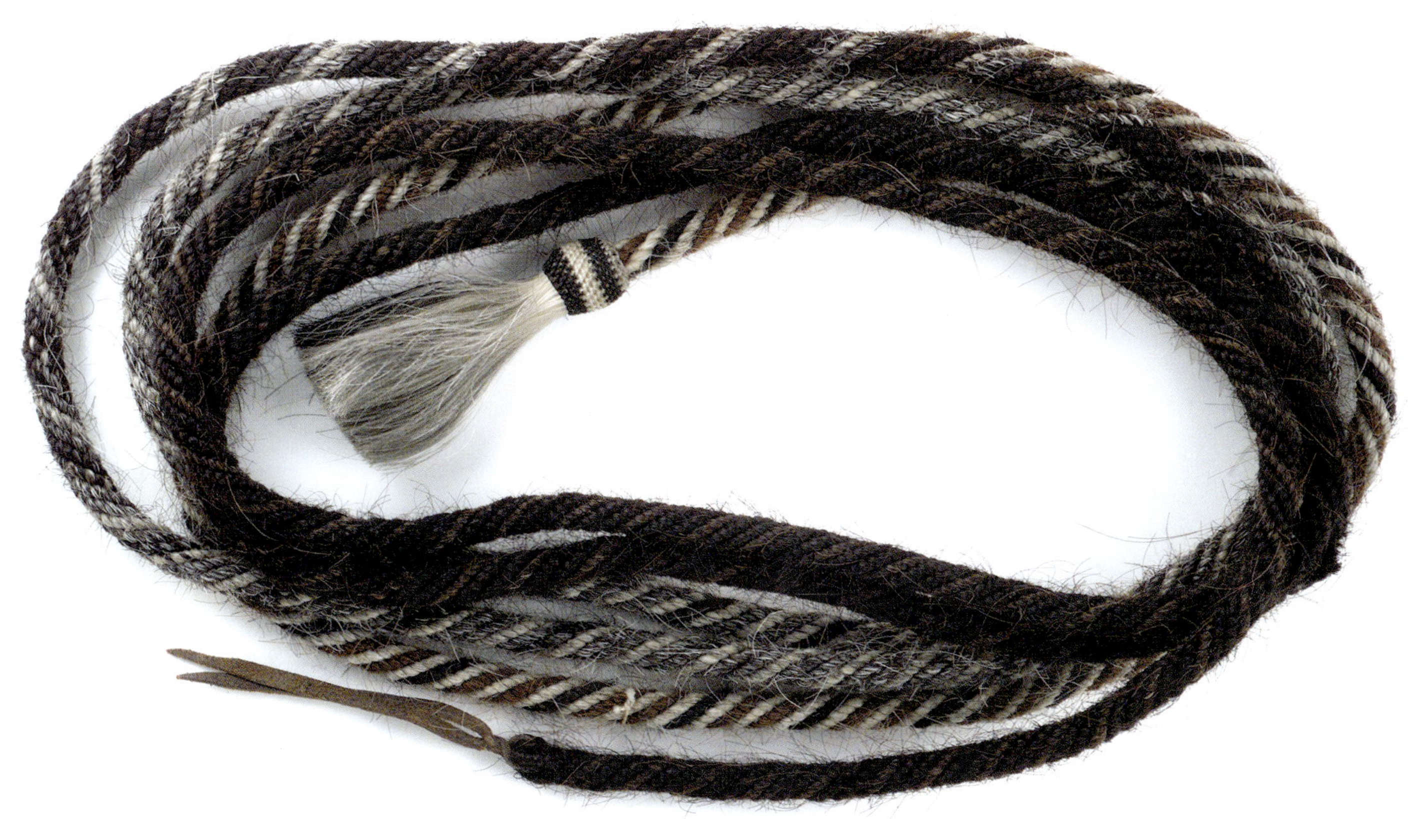

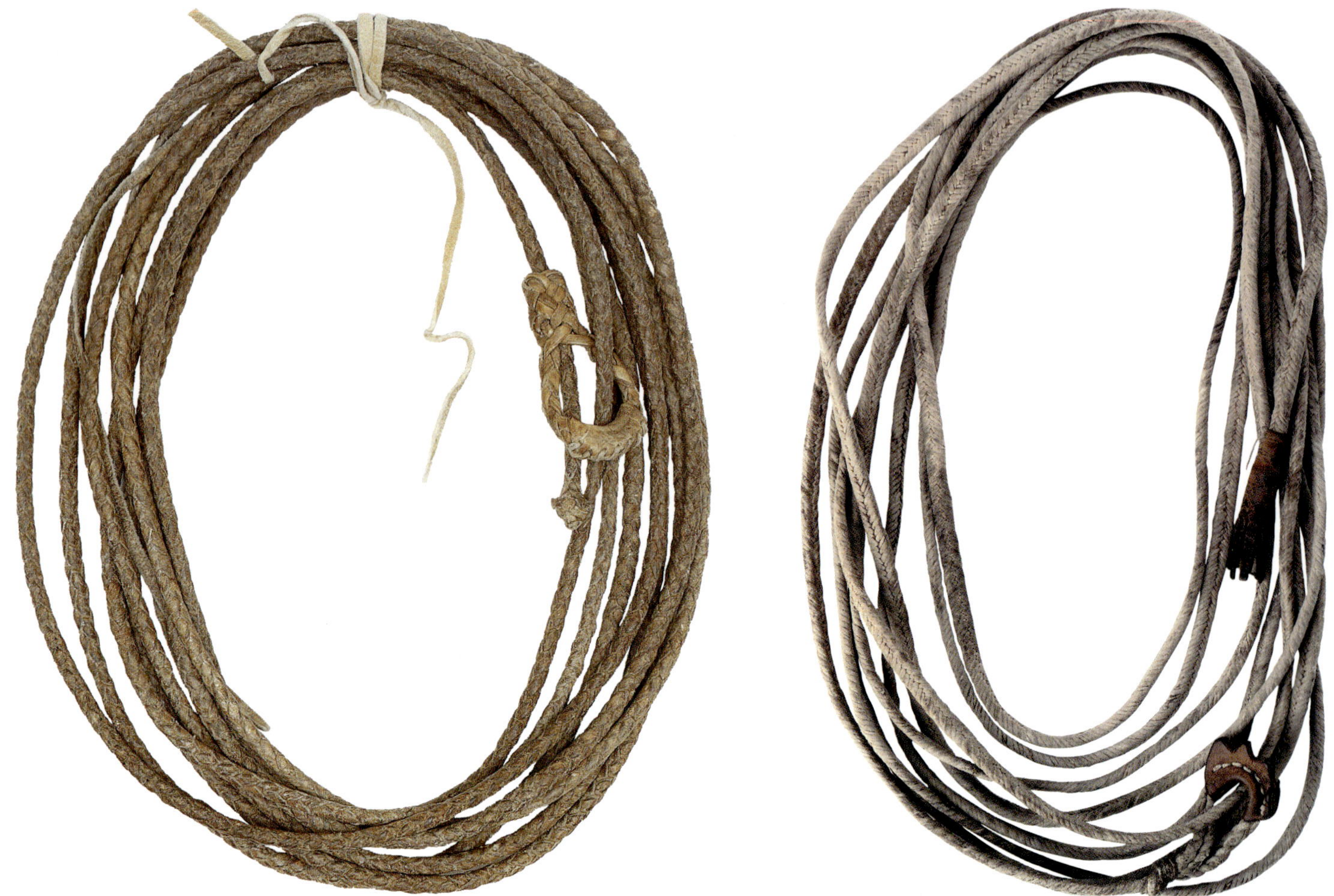

Braided reatas with hide hondas
BUFFALO BILL HISTORICAL CENTER, CODY, WYOMING

Moorish traditions, filtered through Spain and Mexico, predominated and were widely adopted by cowboys in the American Southwest. The experience of W. M. "Rawhide Bill" Shannon, who as a youngster in South Texas had learned to plait tack from a vaquero employed by his family, was typical. The region's Hispanic herdsmen had taught the same skills to Michigan-born James Cook within a few months of his arrival in the 1870s. In like manner Texas drovers passed on the secrets of braiding and hitching to comrades on the northern Plains and California vaqueros to buckaroos in the Pacific Northwest and Great Basin.

On the western range more horsehair and rawhide went to make ropes than anything else. An estimated two-thirds of the cowpunchers during the 1880s carried handmade rawhide reatas. The rest used catch ropes plaited or twisted from various plant fibers, including sea grass, maguey, yucca, and sisal.

Reateros (rope makers) took special care in the choice and preparation of the green hides from which they made heavy-duty snares. Expert plaiters favored the solid colored hides of mature steers with as few blemishes as possible. Spots, scars, and other flaws, they believed, produced weak and uneven braiding strings.

Using a sharp pocketknife and cutting a spiral path inward from the edge of the hide, a braider produced a single continuous strand of hide from a third

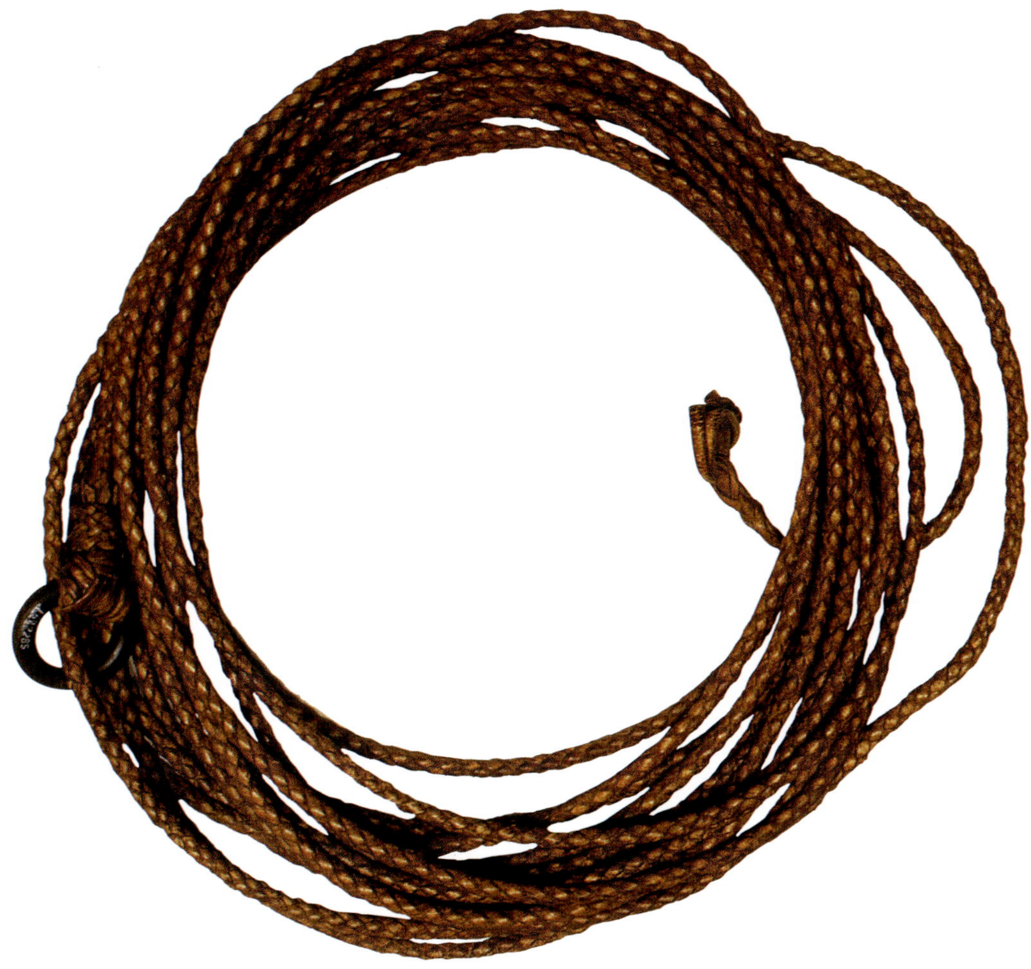

Rawhide reata with metal honda
Buffalo Bill Historical Center, Cody, Wyoming

of an inch to a half-inch in width. This thong was subsequently divided into several equal lengths, which were soaked in water, then fastened to a tree or post and the excess hair and flesh pared away. Each was rubbed with tallow or brains until soft and pliable.

Anecdotal evidence suggests that most reatas were plaited from four strings of rawhide but that types made from three, six, and even eight strands also were relatively common. The larger the number strings used in plaiting, the thinner the hide the *reatero* sought and the narrower he pared the individual elements. Accomplished braiders took pride in cutting strings of uniform width and thickness, beveling their edges for a smoother, tighter weave.

To minimize weakness and insure a smooth, symmetrical surface, experienced *reateros* used even pressure to pull each string taut around a central core made of rawhide or cotton cord. Knowing that the heft of rawhide catch ropes proved beneficial when thrown in brushy country or in high winds, makers sometimes added tiny pellets of lead shot at intervals along its length.

Because freshly braided rawhide ropes were too thick and unwieldy for effective use, makers typically pounded, rolled, stretched, and greased them with waterproofing tallow until they became round, smooth, and supple. Into one end they spliced an oval-shaped eye or *honda*, made of rawhide, horn, or metal (iron, brass, or lead). Ropers passed the opposite end through this two- or three-inch-long device to form a loop.

The lengths of hide ropes varied widely and depended upon the terrain and vegetation where they were used, the type of roping required, and the roper's skill. Adherents believed that properly made rawhide reatas could be thrown farther than other types. Californians tended to carry the longest lines, perhaps sixty feet on average. Reatas of eighty and even 100 feet were recorded among West Coast vaqueros, although some skeptics questioned their usefulness. Wrote one from New Mexico:

> What the possibilities of roping to catch are is hard to say. No doubt with a horse at full gallop down hill, the wind favorable and a good long rope, an expert may reach 100 feet, but such cases are few and far between, and most good ropers feel extremely pleased when they can reach out the full length of their forty-five foot rope and catch.[58]

On average, cowpunchers on the open ranges of the Great Plains toted ropes measuring forty to fifty feet long and seven-sixteenths of an inch in diameter. "A forty-foot lariat is the one commonly used," Theodore Roosevelt declared, "for the ordinary range at which a man can use it is only about twenty-five feet. Few men can throw forty feet; and to do this, taking into account the coil, needs a sixty-foot rope."[59] "Brush poppers" in South Texas, where dense mesquite and cactus often restricted visibility, wielded lariats a mere twenty-five or thirty feet long.

If properly plaited and cared for, a rawhide rope would last several years under typical range conditions. They were not, however, without liabilities. Rawhide tended to stretch when wet and even the best hide reatas were only as strong as the material from which they were made. Hard jerks while roping heavy cattle sometimes broke them, at times injuring the roper or his horse. Experienced vaqueros minimized such events by winding the loose end of the reata around the saddle horn and allowing it to run gradually until the captured animal could be brought the a stop. The friction often caused smoke to rise from the horn.

Lightweight lassos made of twisted horsehair lacked the body and strength to snare livestock effectively from horseback. Nevertheless, they were valuable tools in the breaking and training of young horses for range work. The mistaken belief that horsehair ropes also warded off rattlesnakes led some gullible cowhands to surround their bedrolls with such loops while on roundups or trail drives.

Cowboys gathered hair for twisting, braiding, and hitching by combing or cutting a horse's mane or tail or by jerking it out with a quick tug. Although plucking its tail hair did not harm the horse, surprised or irritated animals sometimes kicked at their tormentors and rarely stood still for a second jerk. Said one who practiced the technique: "Either you get it on the first pull, or you move on to another horse."[60] If sufficient horsehair was not available, mohair from goats and even human tresses acquired from female friends and relatives proved acceptable substitutes. One resourceful Grant County buckaroo, for example, earned $25 for a red and black hair rope fashioned from the knee-length locks of his wife and four daughters.

Some experts believed that the manes of two-year-old horses provided the best combination of strength and texture for hair work. Wealthy West Coast rancheros often reserved the silky mane hair from their remuda for their own use, leaving their vaqueros to make do with the longer, stronger, and coarser tail hair. William Davis, who arrived in Mexican California before 1830, recalled that the hair twisters of that era harvested raw material from mares only, never stallions.

Once gathered, horsehair was separated into piles by color. Before the process of spinning, hitching, or braiding began, however, the craftsman always "picked" the hair, plucking a few strands at a time from the mass and dropping them loosely on the floor in a separate pile. The picking process usually required several hours and sometimes days to complete. Fussy vaqueros made sure that the fine ends of the hair landed pointing outward in the pile and the prickly roots inward to impart a softer feel to the finished product. When sufficient hair had been gathered and sorted, the craftsman rolled the pile into a bundle ready to use.

Twisting hair into serviceable ropes required a carved wood spinning device known as a *tarabi* but also called a "whirligig," "twisting paddle," or "doll baby." Measuring more than a foot in length, *tarabies* were notched on one end. A handle set at a right angle below the notch turned the spinner on its axis.

Twisting hair with a *tarabi* was a two-person job. While the *tarabi* operator, often a child, spun the device in a continuous circular motion, the craftsman, who had attached a narrow loop of hair from the roll to the notched end, began backing slowly away, feeding out additional hair and taking care to smooth the string to minimize lumps and kinking. Depending upon the skill of the team, a forty-foot string of horsehair could be spun with a hand-cranked *tarabi*, in thirty minutes to an hour. Several such strands were twisted together to form a versatile, sixteen- to twenty-two-foot lead or tie rope called a *mecate*, a Spanish term often corrupted into "McCarty" by English-speaking cowhands.

In the hands of an expert, strings of different colored hair could be combined to form lassos endowed with stripes, checks, or other decorative patterns. Tied in an ornamental *alamar* knot, these "Sunday ropes" or "girl snares," as they were sometimes called, often adorned the necks of horses at fiestas, weddings, and other social affairs.

In addition to *mecates*, cowboys often fashioned serviceable hackamores, halters, reins, and saddle *cinchas* from twisted hair. Some of the latter measured ten inches wide and consisted of thirty or more parallel strings spliced on either end

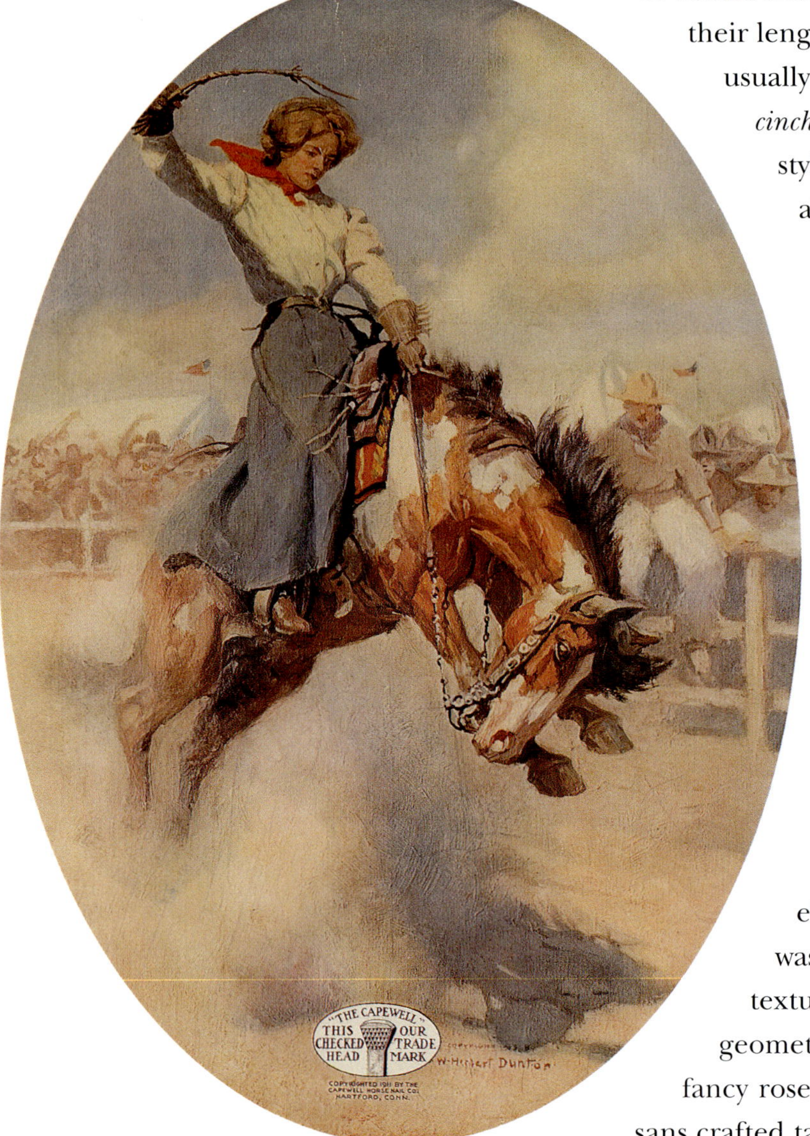

William H. Dunton, (1878–1936)
Advertisement for Capewell Horse Nails showing a female bronco rider wielding a quirt, c. 1911
BUFFALO BILL HISTORICAL CENTER, CODY, WYOMING

Opposite
Multi-colored horsehair quirt with tassels, wrist strap, and poppers
BUFFALO BILL HISTORICAL CENTER, CODY, WYOMING

to round buckles made of iron or brass and knitted together along their length with one or more cross bars. Colored or dyed hair, usually arranged in a diamond pattern in the center of the *cincha*, was often added for decorative effect as were Arab-style, spear point–shaped tassels known as *motas*, which also helped ward off flies. Unlike cotton and wool types, horsehair *cinchas* did not absorb moisture readily and were prone to chafing. Some ranches discouraged their use as a result.

Besides twisting hair with a *tarabi*, many cowboys passed the time by hand braiding a variety of simple novelties, including loop rings (slides) for bandannas, watch chains, and wrist- and hatbands. Work of this sort involved manipulating, splicing, and stitching multiple "pulls" consisting of eight to twenty hairs each to produce a herringbone pattern or other decorative design.

Horsehair hitching, the knotting of pulls over a solid core using a series of half hitches, was a more complex and time-consuming art than either braiding or twisting and was often used to fashion elaborate quirts and bridles. Unlike twisted hair that was often prickly to the touch, hitching created smooth, textured surfaces usually arranged in a myriad of colorful geometric and figural patterns and further embellished with fancy rosettes and shaving brush–like tassels. While many artisans crafted tack from natural colored hair, others used dye to create a wider and more vivid range of color. The results of these efforts varied from beautiful to bizarre.

Prison inmates, including a few Native Americans and ex-cowboys, incarcerated in Nevada, Idaho, Montana, Wyoming, Arizona, Kansas, Utah, and Washington turned out some of the finest hitched work in the West. Convict-made horsehair belts, bridles, ropes, quirts, hatbands, watch fobs, and other objects were sold in prison gift shops and by mail, a portion of the proceeds accruing to the prisoner upon his release. Rollie Burns, a onetime ranch manager in West Texas, remembered receiving an unsolicited package containing a horsehair bridle and three dozen watch chains made by an inmate at Deer Lodge Prison in Montana. Burns sold the bridle for $25 and watch chains for from $1 to $1.50 each and forwarded the money for the goods to the warden.

Inmates often passed on their knowledge of the horsehair arts to fellow prisoners and, after their release, to outsiders as well. Prison-made goods from the late nineteenth and early twentieth centuries often sported figural and patriotic motifs that included eagles and American flags. Convicts sometimes hitched such expressions as "Good Luck" into bridle headstalls as well.

Although fairly sturdy, hitched horsehair bridles were usually reserved for special occasions and were rarely used for heavy work. Their plaited rawhide counterparts, however, were far more common on the range. Nowhere was the rawhide art more beautifully expressed than in tightly plaited bridles with long, sinuous reins adorned with decorative woven knots or segmented with brass rings. Braided from four to twenty-four strings of hide and fastened to the bridle bit by small chains to avoid wetting them when the horse watered, some of the finest reins sported as many as seventy-two fancy knots that added balance as well as beauty along their length. "Turk's heads," which resembled Middle Eastern turbans, and long knots called "Japanese heads," were among the most common types. Apart from their decorative function, braided knots kept ruinous sweat away from the body of the reins and helped translate a horseman's commands to his mount.

The reins used by California horsemen and their adherents were often closed at the end and fitted with a braided *romal*, a long quirt equipped with one or two leather lashes or poppers. A shorter rawhide or horsehair quirt (*cuarta* or *quisto*) bearing ornamental knots and fringe sometimes dangled from a loop around a cowpuncher's wrist. Makers constructed many such devices around a flexible core consisting of heavy ducking filled with lead shot. Others surrounded a solid center of steel, lead, wood, twisted rawhide, or even a bull's penis. Some cowboys also carried longer braided leather stock whips, which they used to separate fighting cattle and control livestock on drives and at roundups.

Although cowboy-craftsmen supplied themselves and their comrades with much of the horsehair and rawhide gear they required, by the 1870s such goods could also be purchased locally or ordered by catalog from distant merchants. Larger saddleries, such as Main and Winchester of San Francisco, routinely stocked

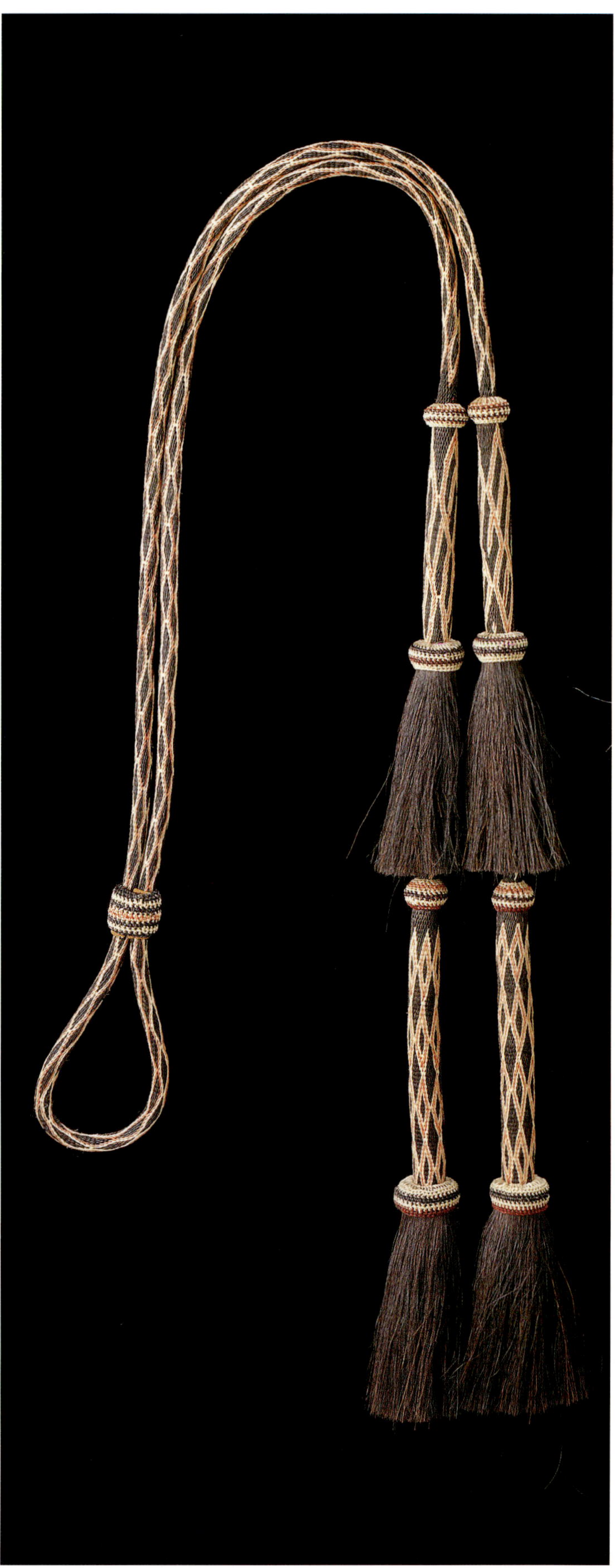

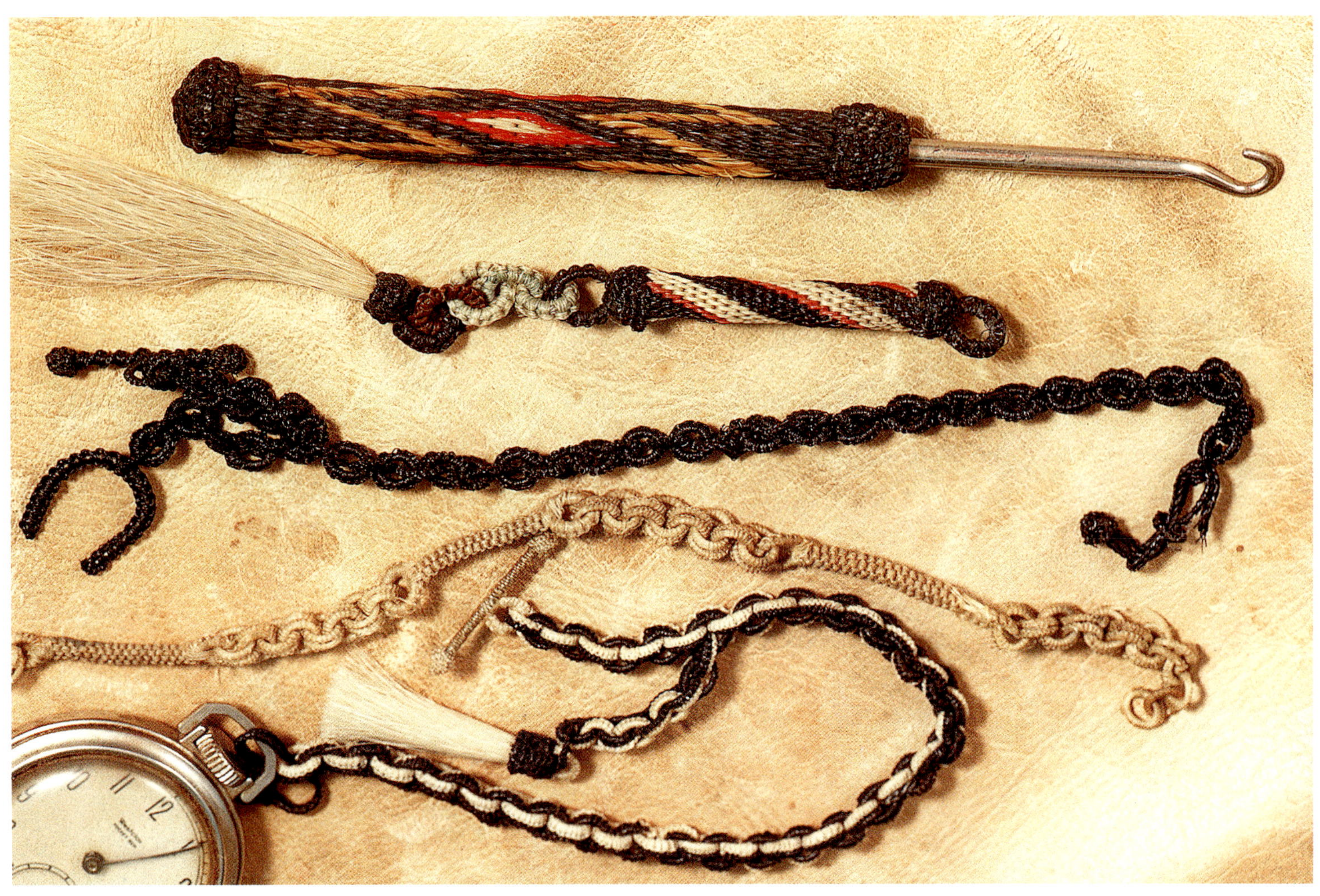

Top to bottom: prison-made horsehair button-hook, key chain or fob, and horsehair watch chains
High Noon Western Americana, Los Angeles

rawhide and horsehair ropes, quirts, bridles, and other goods made either by craftsmen in their employ or independent contractors, including a few enterprising cowboys, or imported from Mexico. In the 1880s, for example, the Neeley brothers, Texas cowboys, sold braided quirts to saddle houses in Texas, Colorado, and California for $1 to $1.50 each. In saddle shops such items typically fetched from $1.75 to $2.50. A pair of Montana punchers, however, felt cheated when two Miles City saddle makers paid them only $20 for plaited rawhide goods worth $200 retail. Dealers typically bought reatas fashioned by independent *reateros* by the *brazada*, or arm's length, but sold the same rope by the foot, thereby reaping a substantial profit. In its 1890 catalog, L. D. Stone & Co. of San Francisco offered rawhide lariats of any length, size, or plait at prices ranging from 19.5 cents per foot for four-plait types to 37.5 cents per foot for the twelve-plait variety.

By the early 1890s inexpensive, mass-produced catch ropes made of manila hemp by the Plymouth Cordage Company of Massachusetts and other eastern rope makers, were rapidly replacing rawhide reatas in many regions of the West. Cowboys east of the Rockies, whose working methods championed speed and efficiency over style, abandoned hide ropes for the new type more quickly than the buckaroos of the Great Basin and Pacific Coast, many of whom shunned hemp lines as too light-weight and lifeless to suit their taste. Writing in 1886 one advocate called rawhide ropes

> ... easier on the hands, more accurate on a cast, less affected by the wind, less wearing on the saddle horn, stronger and more durable than any other rope I know of. I'm speaking of the California style rope; one that the maker puts his conscience into; one that the best hide has been selected, and utmost pains used in the cutting, trimming, rubbing and braiding. Such a rope is flexible, elastic and immensely strong, and contains that nice weight to every foot that makes what is called a "perfectly balanced rope."[61]

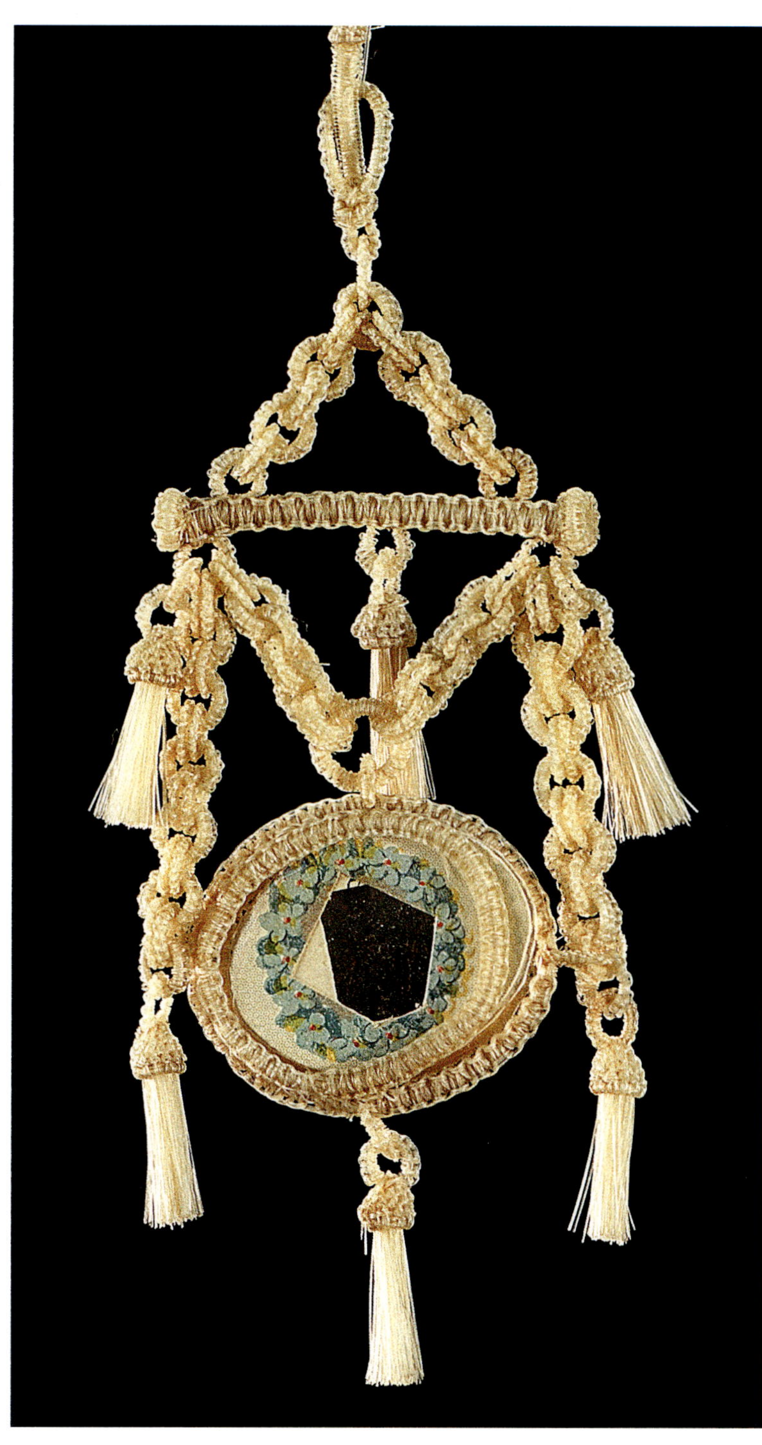

Prison-made horsehair necklace or watch fob
HIGH NOON WESTERN AMERICANA, LOS ANGELES

Despite the availability of new materials, experienced horsemen continued to value *mecates*, hackamores, bridles, reins, and other tack made of hide and hair, especially in the breaking and training of young horses. To meet the demand, at least a few saddleries continued to stock such goods, much of it imported from Mexico, throughout the twentieth century.

Although at least a few cowboy-artisans continued to pursue the hide and hair arts in the American West only one, Luis B. Ortega, gained national renown. The son of the cow boss of a large ranch on the central coast of California, Ortega began plaiting rawhide as a child under the guidance of Fernando Liberado, a Tulare Indian who had learned the art when California still belonged to Mexico. As a young man, Ortega lived the life of a vaquero on ranches from Oregon to Arizona, all the while continuing to develop his braiding skills.

In 1932, while recovering from a broken arm in Santa Barbara, Ortega was introduced to artist Edward Borein, a former vaquero who immediately recognized his talent as a rawhider. With Borein's encouragement and assistance, Ortega began working hide full time. His stellar plaiting soon attracted the attention some of the finest and most famous horsemen in the West including cowboy-author Will James and actor Leo Carrillo.

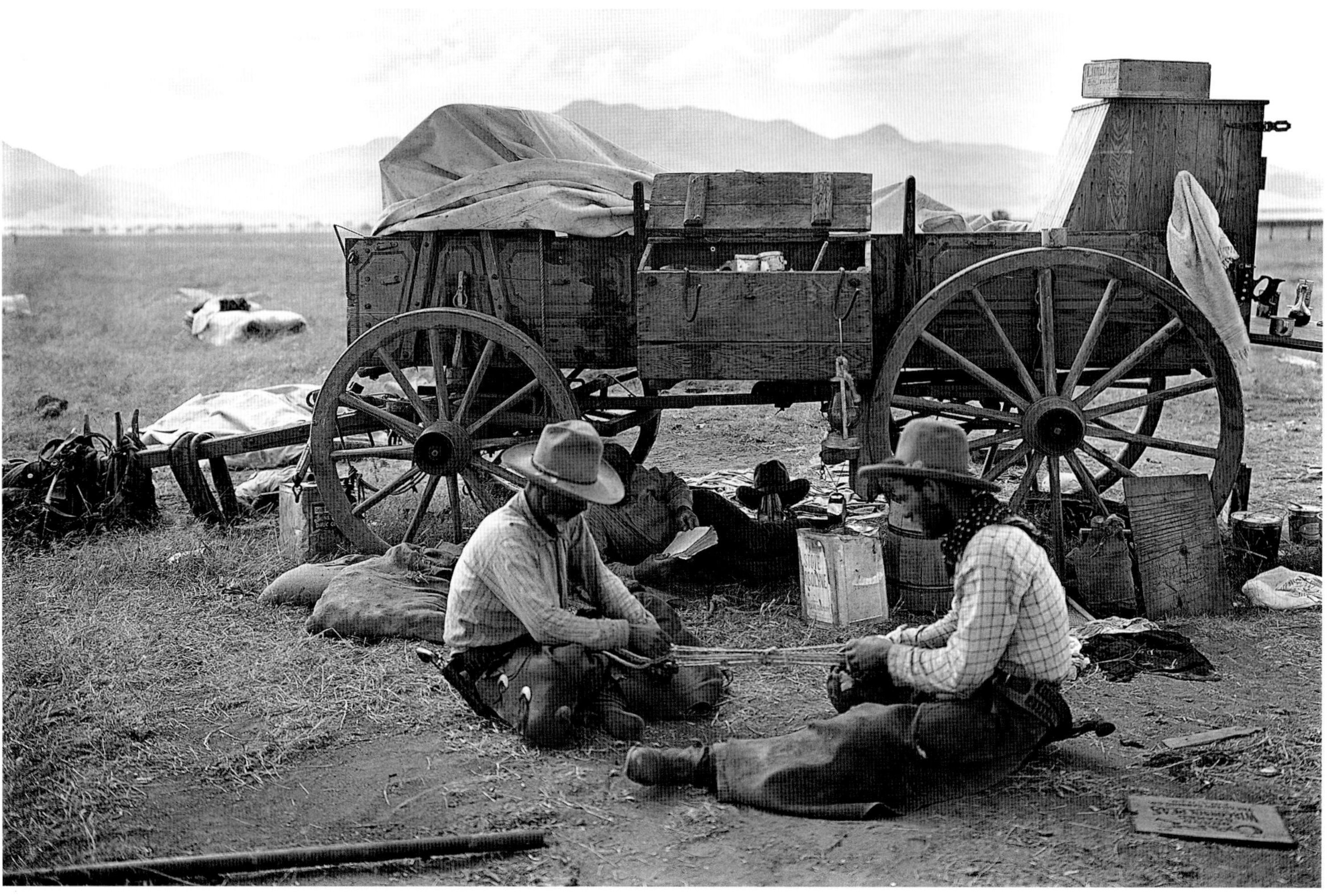

Erwin E. Smith (1886–1947) "Odd jobs in Camp," 1909; ranch cowboys Joe Gleen, "stray man" for the Sulpher Cattle Co., Gleeson, Arizona, and D.W. McFarland, "stray man" for the Wagon Rod outfit, make a horsehair or Angora hair cinch
AMON CARTER MUSEUM, FORT WORTH

Believing that fine braiding depended upon high-quality hides, Ortega selected them with care. A long reata, for example, required an eighty-five- or ninety-five-pound hide, preferably roan, brindle, or buckskin in color. Finding one with the perfect color and feel sometimes required as long as six weeks.

Ortega was just as patient with the braiding process, deftly manipulating multiple rawhide strings into functional ropes, reins, hobbles, bridles, and *bosales* endowed with what one writer in 1938 called "a sense of beauty and rhythm of line that is a heritage of his Latin blood."[62] Taciturn when it came to revealing trade secrets, Ortega experimented constantly and literally unraveled the mysteries of the rawhider's art for himself by unbraiding old gear to understand how it was made and used. Influenced early in his career by South American and Mexican braiding techniques, he began to tea-dye his rawhide and intersperse his patterns with dyed strings of brown, red, and black. As Ortega matured as an artist he began to create his own complex designs, some of which incorporated silver ferrules between knots. He cut the strings for his fanciest work so fine that he could plait a sixteen-strand rein the diameter of a pencil, and with a texture

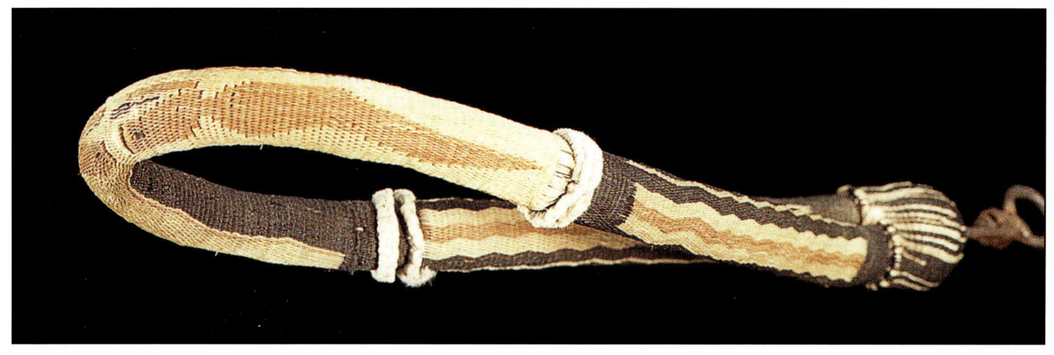

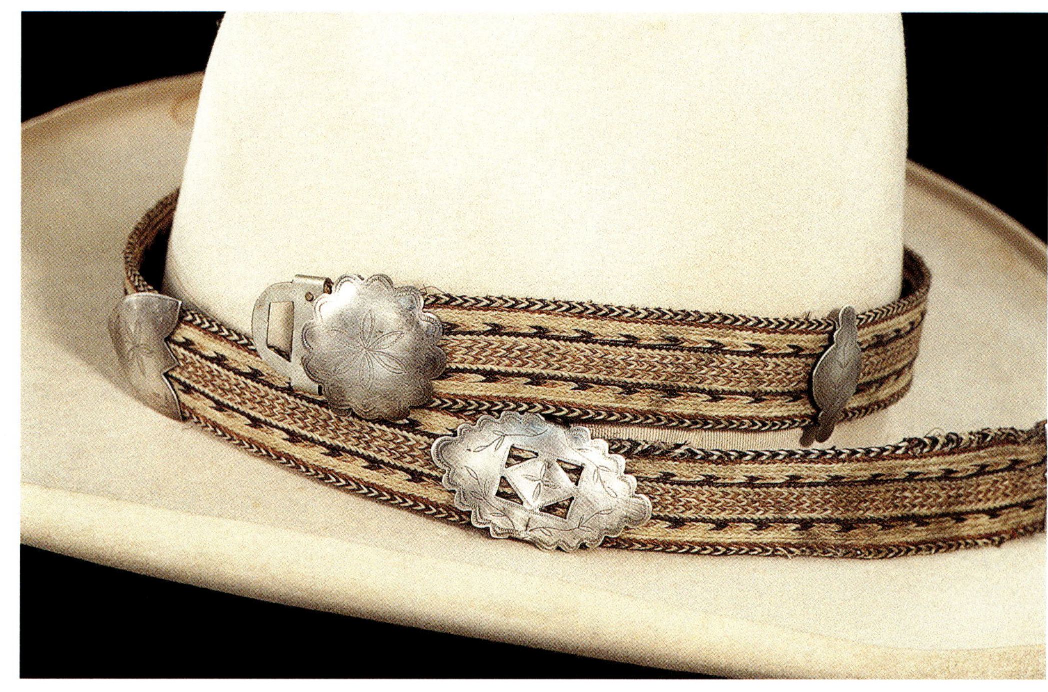

Prison-made bosal (above), flat-braided horsehair hatband with silver detials (right), and gentlemen's brush (below), 1890s
High Noon Western Americana, Los Angeles

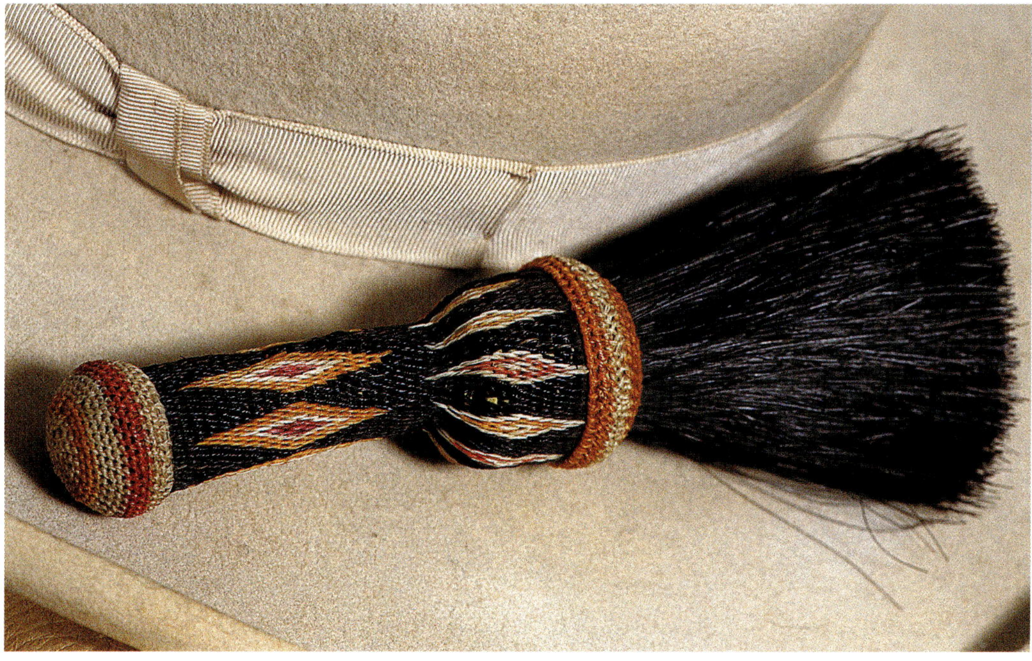

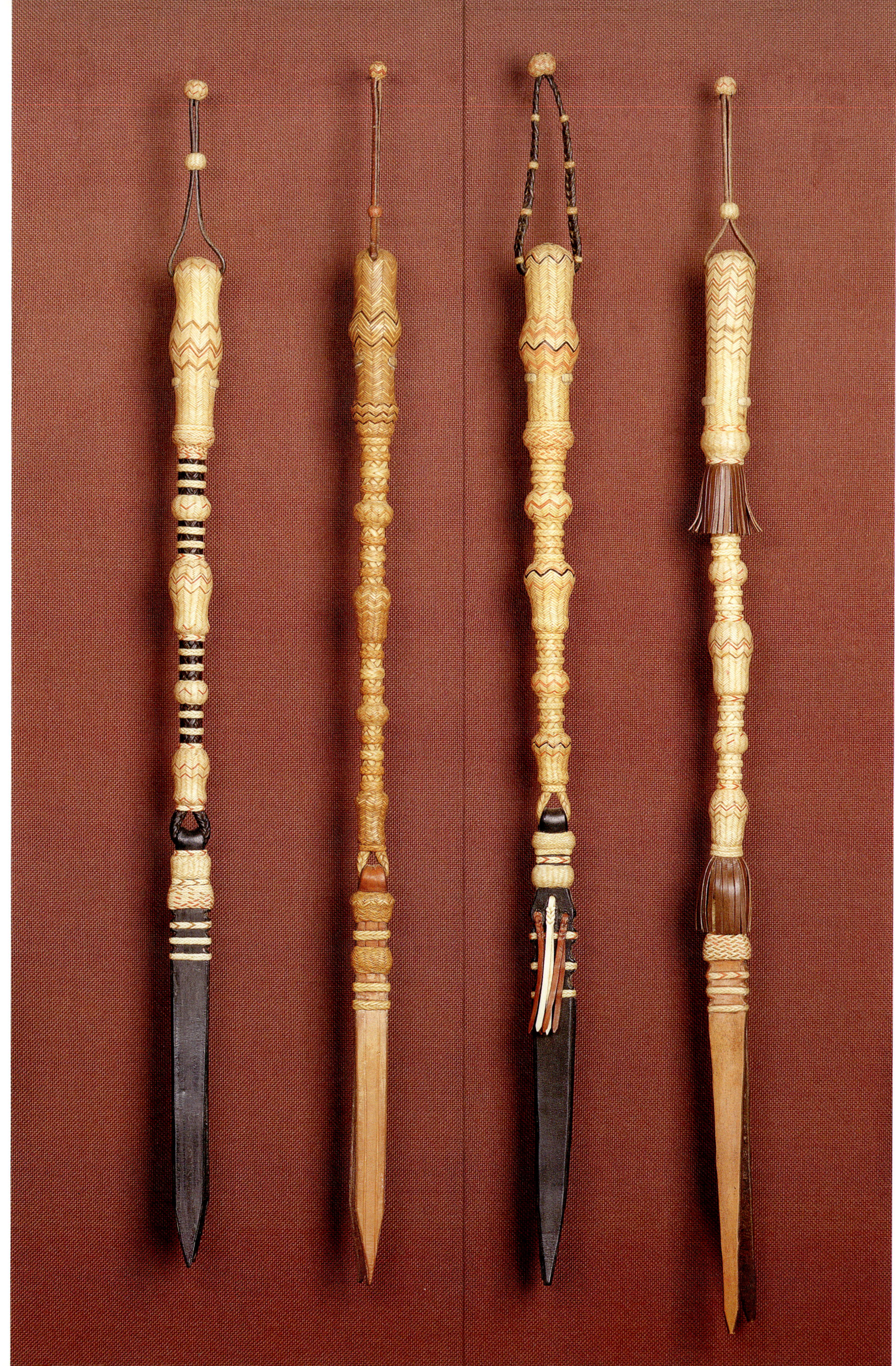

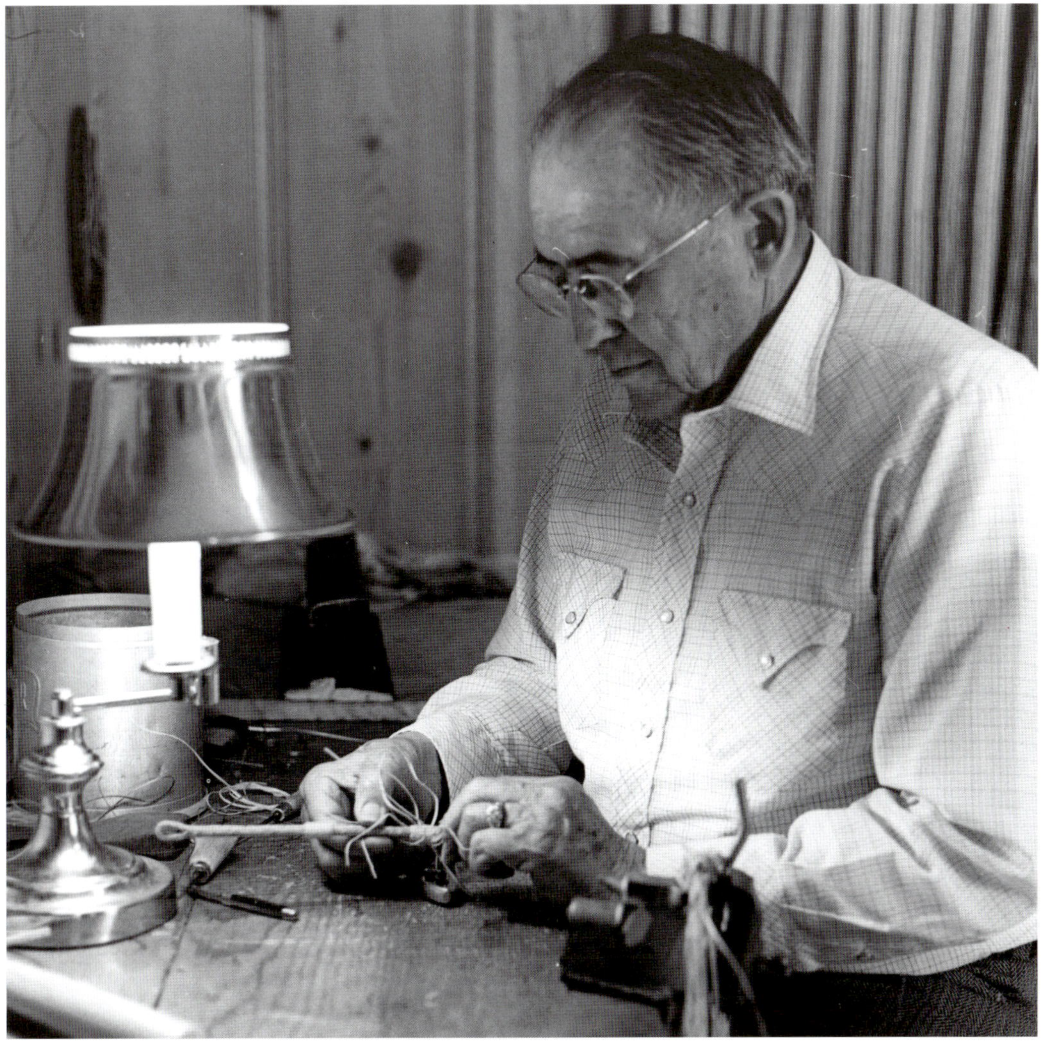

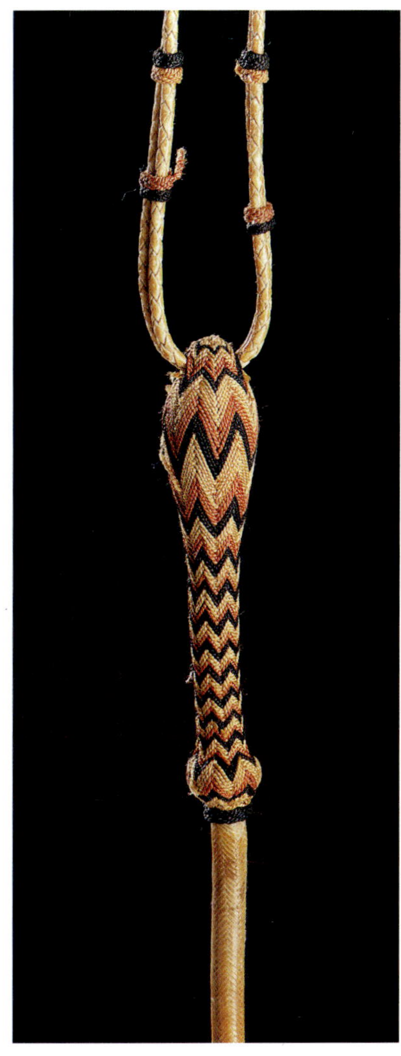

that one admirer described as "almost as silky and pliable as fabrics . . ."[63] His signature twenty-four-strand Santa Ynez–style reins were even more intricate. Partway down the length of the most elaborate examples, Ortega divided his standard twenty-four-string braid into three braids of eight strands each and then reunited them into a single twenty-four-strand braid at the other end of the rein.

Ortega's plaited goods were not only beautiful but also durable. During the early years of his career, working gear dominated his production. Braiding heavy-duty tack took its toll, however, and the artisan eventually developed painful arthritis in his hands and fingers. Fortunately, Ortega's wife, Rose, had become an expert braider and was able to assist her husband in his work. After retiring from the trade in 1974, Ortega continued to plait special gear for collectors, including several elaborate heart-shaped martingales and pieces of miniature tack.

In 1986 the National Endowment for the Arts recognized Luis Ortega as a Master Traditional Artist and presented him with a National Heritage Fellowship in Washington, D.C. By this time his peerless work was avidly sought by museums and private collectors throughout and beyond the West. Before his death on

Opposite
Luis Ortega (1897–1995)
Fancy plaited rawhide quirts
National Cowboy and Western Heritage Museum, Oklahoma City

Above, left
Luis Ortega at work at his braiding bench, c. 1970

Above, right
Braided rawhide quirt with thread decoration, owned by Joe DeYong, detail
National Cowboy and Western Heritage Museum, Oklahoma City

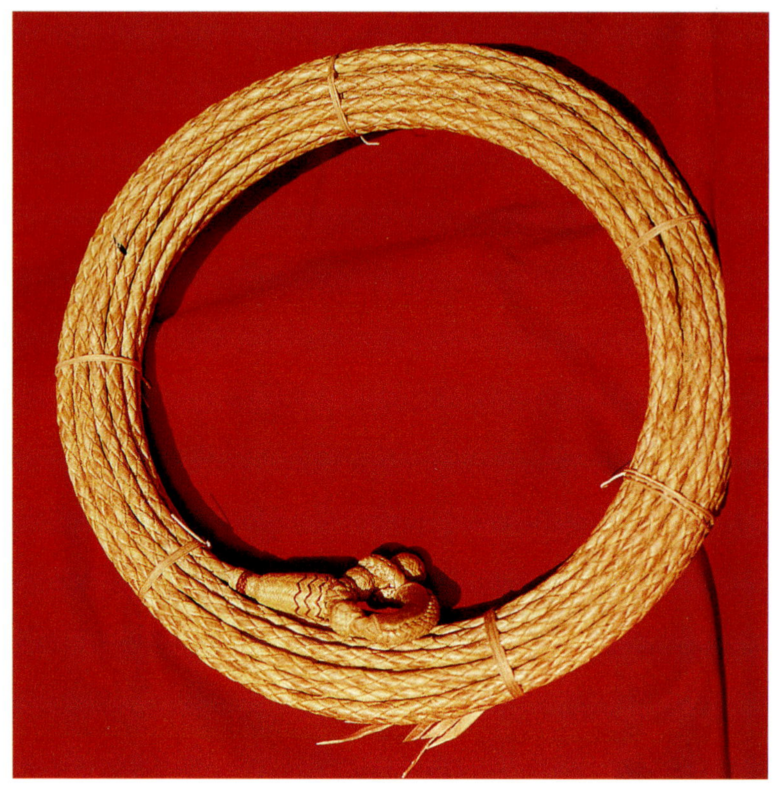

Michael Beaver, Hayden Lake, Idaho
Contemporary rawhide reata with San Juan–style honda
(detail below)

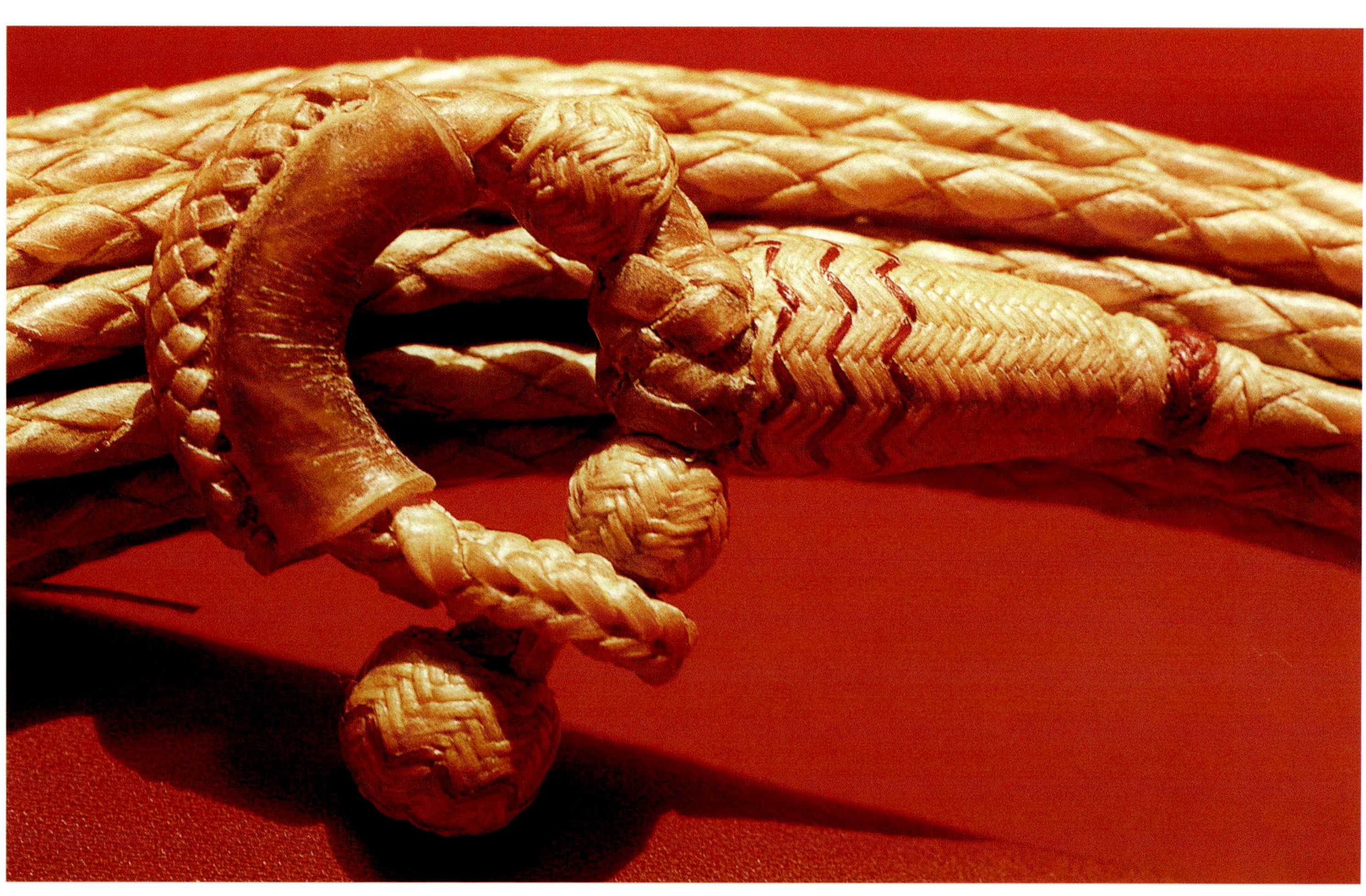

April 6, 1995, at the age of ninety-seven, Ortega donated more than two dozen pieces of his finest work to the National Cowboy and Western Heritage Museum in Oklahoma City.

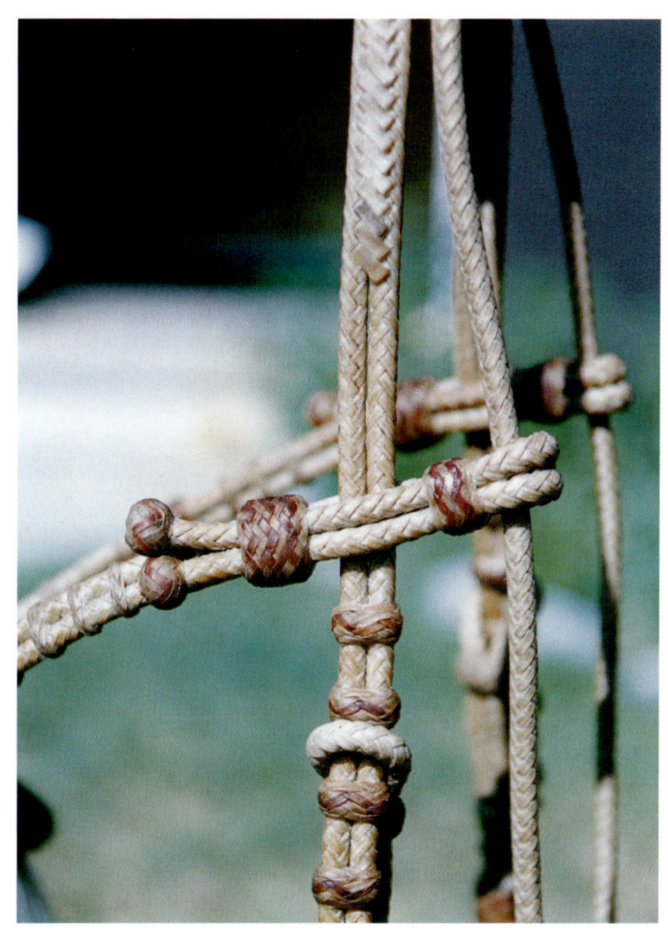

Jeff Minor, Salmon, Idaho
Contemporary rawhide headstall, detail

Thanks to the efforts of Luis Ortega and a few others of his ilk, rawhide and horsehair artistry not only survives but also flourishes in many parts of the West in the twenty-first century. Like their forebears, relatively few western rawhide braiders and horsehair hitchers work at the task full time. For most, including an increasing number of women, hide and hair work is still a leisure-time activity pursued at night, on weekends, or in retirement. Many twist, braid, and hitch for their own amusement or to supplement regular incomes. If sold in the marketplace, their work must compete with cheaper goods imported from Mexico and South America.

In the hands of modern craftsmen, the hide and hair arts continue to evolve. Techniques that were once closely guarded secrets are now taught openly in workshops and "how-to" books and videos. Goods plaited from nylon and parachute cord now share the market with those made of natural materials. Commercial fabric softeners are sometimes used to condition horsehair before it is twisted. Electricity powers remote-controlled *tarabies* operated by lone artisans.

Both historic and contemporary horsehair and rawhide gear has become highly collectible and commands increasingly high prices at auction and in a burgeoning number of cowboy gear shows. With skill and passion such contemporary masters as Mike Beaver, Nate Wald, and Alfredo Campos continue to braid tradition with creativity to produce horse gear that is both durable and beautiful

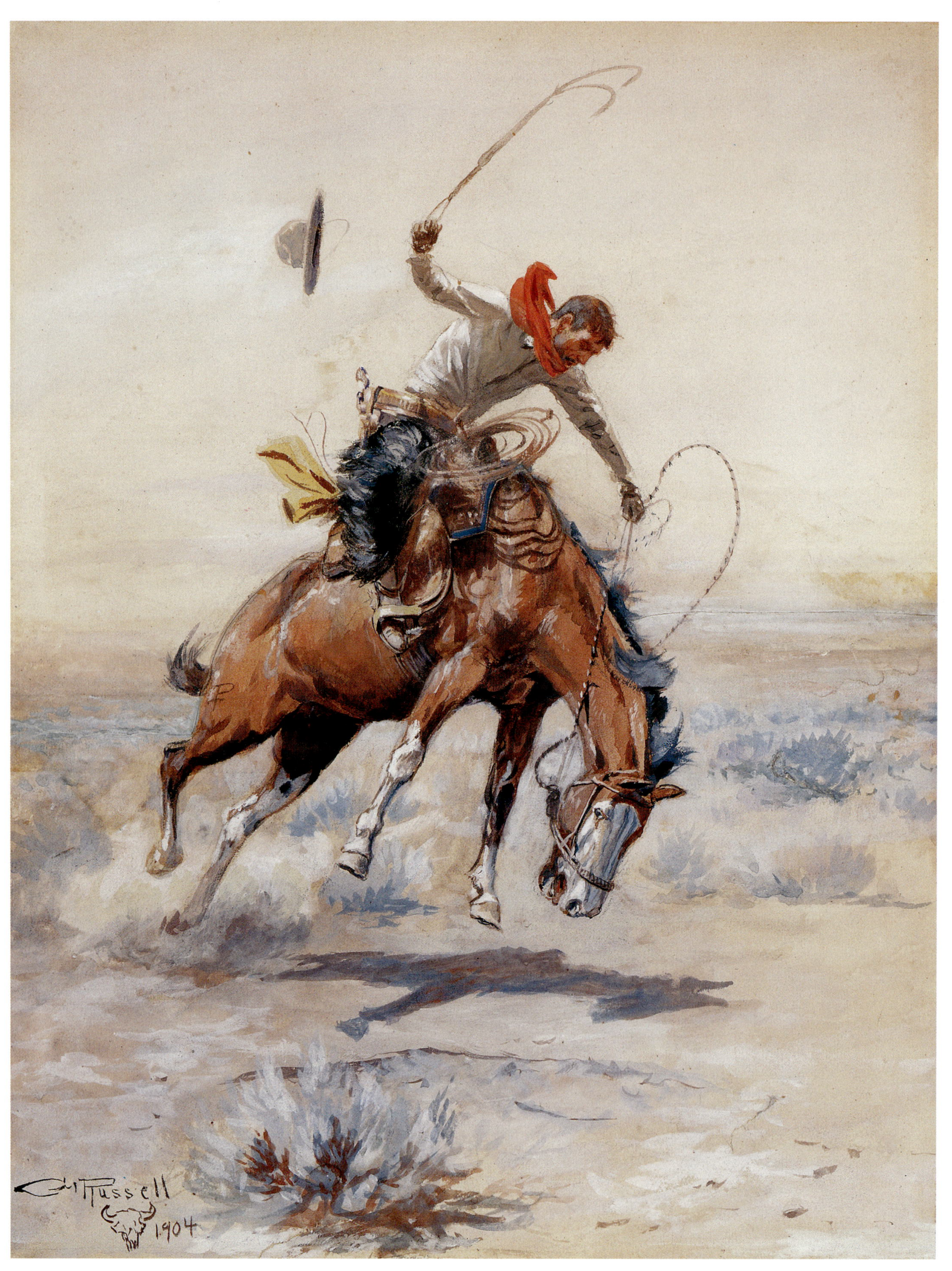
CM Russell
1904

· 4 ·

Metalwork: Bits and Spurs to Gun Engraving

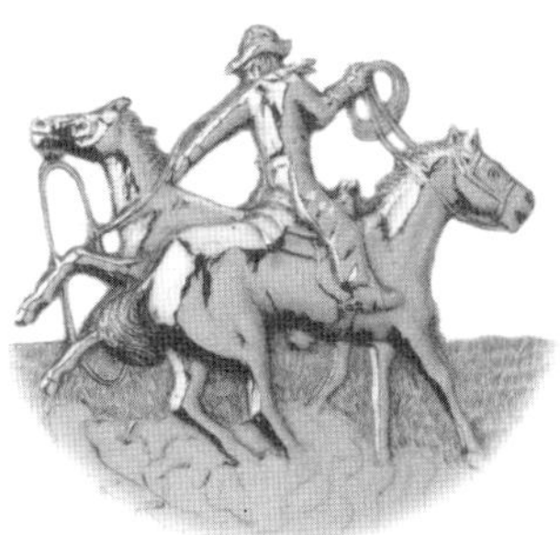

The unmistakable tattoo of a demanding hammer on an unyielding anvil echoed from blacksmith shops throughout the American West during the late nineteenth and early twentieth centuries. From hinges to horseshoes, the products of their forges were mostly prosaic and functional. When the task called for more imagination, however, master smiths were sometimes able to invest utilitarian objects with unexpected beauty and appeal. The hand-forged spurs, stirrups, and bridle bits used by the region's cowboys often reflected such qualities.

Of these quintessential tools of the cowboy's trade, none was vested with more symbolism and mystique, nor inspired more excited comment from outsiders, than his spurs. Menacing, yet melodic, practical but often decorative, these metal hooks evoked the age of chivalry and helped elevate hired men on horseback to the status of romantic heroes.

During the open range era, cowboys were seldom seen without a pair of spurs strapped to their boot heels. Once attached, spurs were rarely removed in the field and in many cases not until the footwear wore out. Texas trail driver Ab Blocker, one who continued to wear his spurs long after his riding days were done, was buried with a pair still fastened to his boots.

Opposite. *Charles M. Russell (1864–1926).* The Bucker, *1904*
Pencil, watercolor, and gouache on paper, 16¼ x 12¼ in.
Sid Richardson Collection of Western Art

On infrequent visits to town during the cowboy's heyday, young hands on the make often could be found prowling the streets on foot, their spur straps loosened to the "town notch," so that the rowels dragged noisily along the boardwalks. To writer-rancher Philip Ashton Rollins, the effect "suggested the transit of a knight in armor. This purposely created jangle fought loneliness when one was completely isolated, and was not abhorrent in public, even though it might announce the presence of a noted man."[64] Spurs with a pair of tiny chains slung underfoot or metal "jinglebobs" dangling from the rowel pins added to the chorus of noise that reminded one western pundit of the sound of "a hand-organ in full blast."[65]

Until more refined customs took hold in cow country, waddies wore their spurs to parties and other social events without protest. They eventually abandoned this practice in polite company, and the wearing of spurs indoors, where they might scratch furniture or snag rugs, was considered not only uncouth and a breach of etiquette but also an impediment to graceful movement on a crowded dance floor.

In the saddle, top hands used their spurs sparingly and with caution, usually to induce a quick burst of speed from their horses while in pursuit of cattle or to coax their mounts over rough country. Although spurs left a rider's hands free

Below
Wrought-iron Spanish colonial spurs (espuelas grandes) with pierced metal decoration c. 1650
Fleischer Collection, Scottsdale

Opposite
Spanish ring bit with multi-row pajados *(jinglebobs), 18th century*
Fleischer Collection, Scottsdale

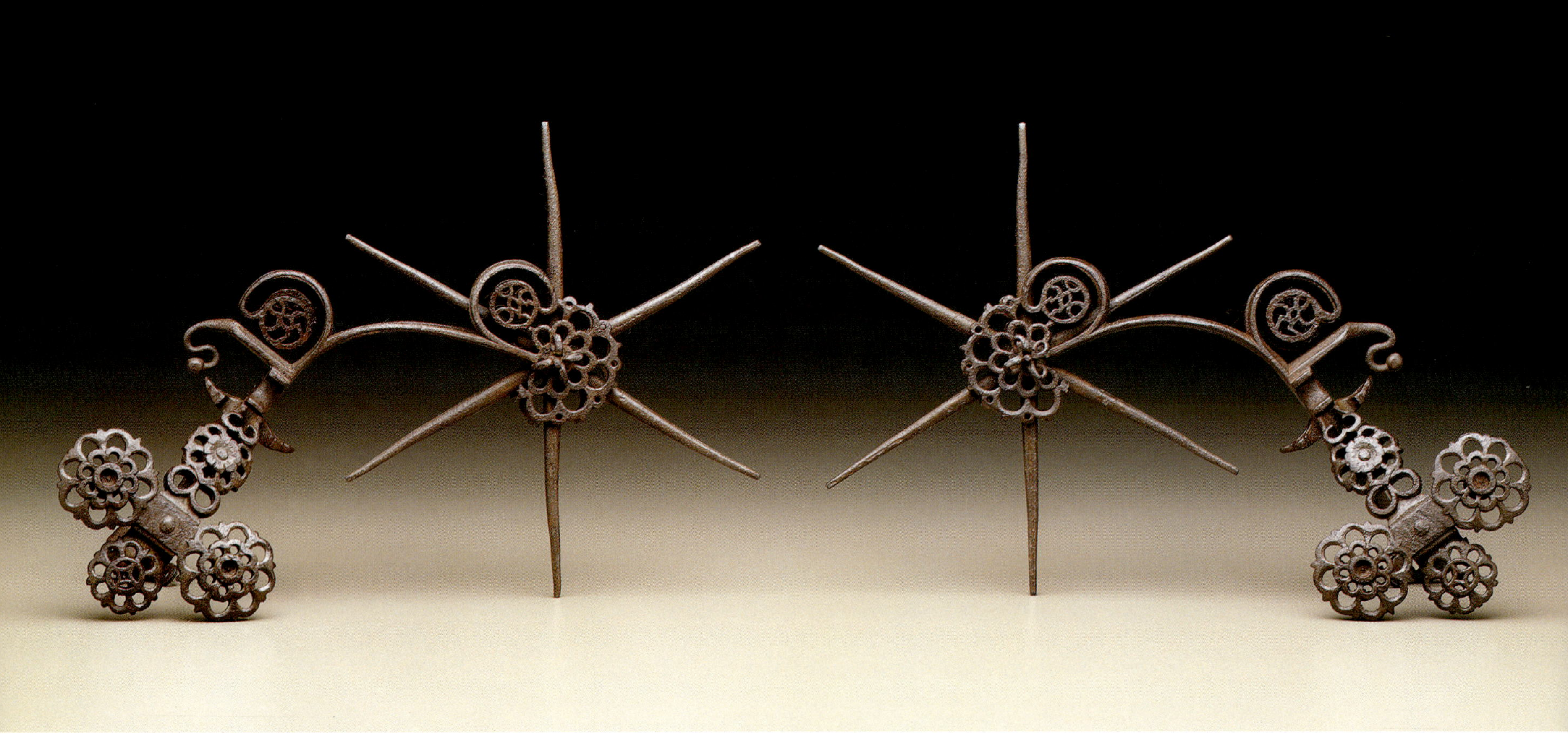

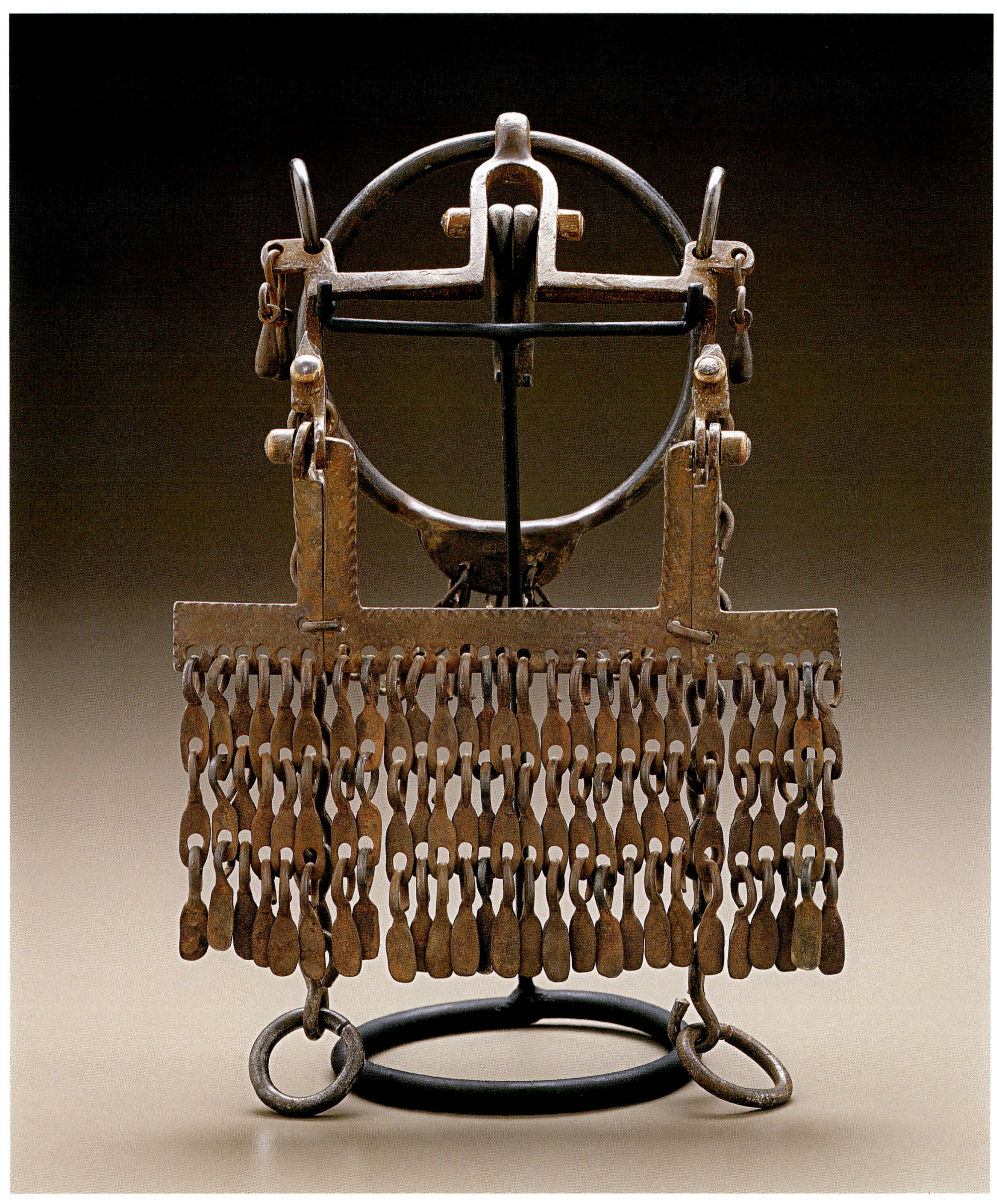

for roping, some cowboys preferred quirts, especially in brushy country where the nick of thorns and the prick of spur rowels were nearly indistinguishable.

Most outfits forbade sharp rowels and excessive spurring, and a few ranchers banned the wearing of spurs by their bronc busters, believing that they induced wild horses to buck even worse. The fact that prudent cowhands usually filed off the points of their spur rowels to prevent them from scratching company-owned horsehide did not, however, prevent them from referring to their spurs as gut-hooks, grappling irons, can openers, rib lancers, hell rousers, diggers, persuaders, and gads, among other colorful monikers.

The basic spur form, consisting of a heel band, buttons, shank, and rowel, had developed centuries before American cowboys began to ride the range. Some authorities believe that sharp-pointed goads, attached to a horseman's bare feet by means of leather straps, may have appeared as early as 700 BC. Punishing pricks of wood and bone eventually gave way to even deadlier bronze and iron spikes affixed to metal heel bands. In the mid-thirteenth century, however, loriners in northern Europe began to equip spur shanks with fixed rowels of various shapes and sizes. More than a century passed, however, before prick styles disappeared for good. By this time spur makers had introduced movable rowels, some of which took the shape of stars, roses, and various foliated patterns.

During the Middle Ages spurs became emblematic of knighthood, chivalry, and class distinctions, and their possession was governed by decree. The social importance attached to spurs, in turn, fostered a period of unprecedented creativity among European spur makers, and a host of new designs appeared, many of them embellished with gilding, engraving, inlay, repoussé, and pierced work. Medieval spur design was not only subject to the dictates of society and fashion but also to the demands of mounted armored warfare. At the end of the fifteenth century, Spanish conquistadors arrived in the Americas wearing cumbersome iron spurs with narrow heel bands, long, drooping shanks, and sharp-pointed rowels that often measured six or eight inches in diameter. The unwieldy form of the *espuela grande* (large spur) made walking while wearing a pair somewhat awkward.

Although fierce-looking and dangerous to horses if ill-used, conquistador spurs were often handsome and decorative. Some featured engraved shanks rimmed with tiny metal animals or, more often, decorative metal scrolls. Weight-saving pierced work beautified the heel bands and rowel boxes of many examples and provided aesthetically pleasing backdrops for crown- or pomegranate blossom–shaped rowel pins.

Although the construction of Spanish colonial spurs was primarily of European origin, Iberian loriners also borrowed from Arab blacksmithing traditions and iconography. The round plate located where the spur shank connected to the heel band, for example, was a Moorish innovation and, among European spurs, peculiar to Spain.

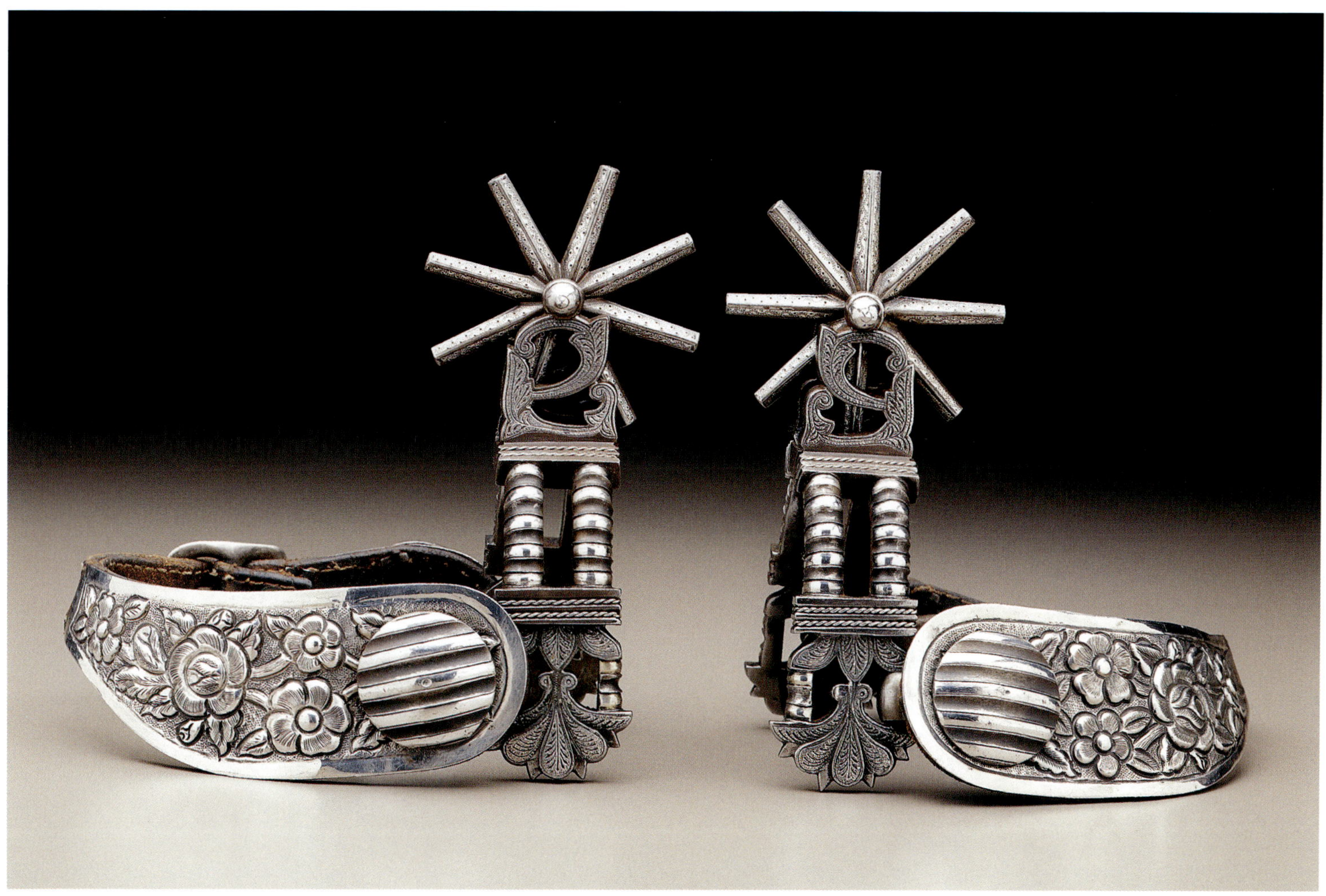

Silver-inlaid Mexican spurs with pierced work below buttons, large pierced work rowels, and floral pierced heelbands
Fleischer Collection, Scottsdale

Arab influence was more evident in the design of Spanish bridle bits. North African horsemen had long favored bits with a port-shaped mouthpiece, equipped with copper rollers and an iron ring that encircled the horse's lower jaw. This configuration gave riders tremendous leverage in reining their mounts but required a light hand to avoid hurting the animal. Like spurs, such bits were often stylish as well as practical, especially in the shape and embellishment of their hand-wrought cheek pieces and the melodic *pajados* (jinglebobs) that often hung in rows from the lip bar below the horse's mouth. Short chains connected the bits to the reins to prevent enemies from cutting them in combat.

The bit and spur patterns brought to Mexico and South America by the conquistadors persisted much longer in the isolation of the New World than they did in Europe, where metalsmiths continually introduced new designs and innovations. The *espuela grande* style, for example, was still in vogue in New Spain more than a century after it had become passé in Iberia. With the arrival of accomplished European artisans and the development of bountiful silver mines in central Mexico, however, a more compact and elegant spur form finally replaced the bulky conquistador variety in the eighteenth century. New and more streamlined rowel and shank patterns emerged and there was considerable experimentation with engraved metal inlays and overlays using geometric and floral motifs. Although most such spurs continued to be handwrought from iron or steel, makers also cast at least a few pair from solid bronze or silver.

Spanish colonial blacksmiths not only forged bits and spurs but also wrought iron saddle stirrups. From the mid-seventeenth to the early nineteenth centuries, horsemen in Mexico embraced a popular cross-shaped pattern, topped with a ring to accommodate the stirrup straps. Imaginative Hispanic blacksmiths often endowed *estribos de cruz* (cross stirrups) with intricate Rococo-style repoussé and pierced work, rendered in silver and brass. The finest examples

Silver-inlaid Mexican charro *spurs with pierced heel bands, rowels and buttons, floral and facial motifs, c. 1920s–1930s*
FLEISCHER COLLECTION, SCOTTSDALE

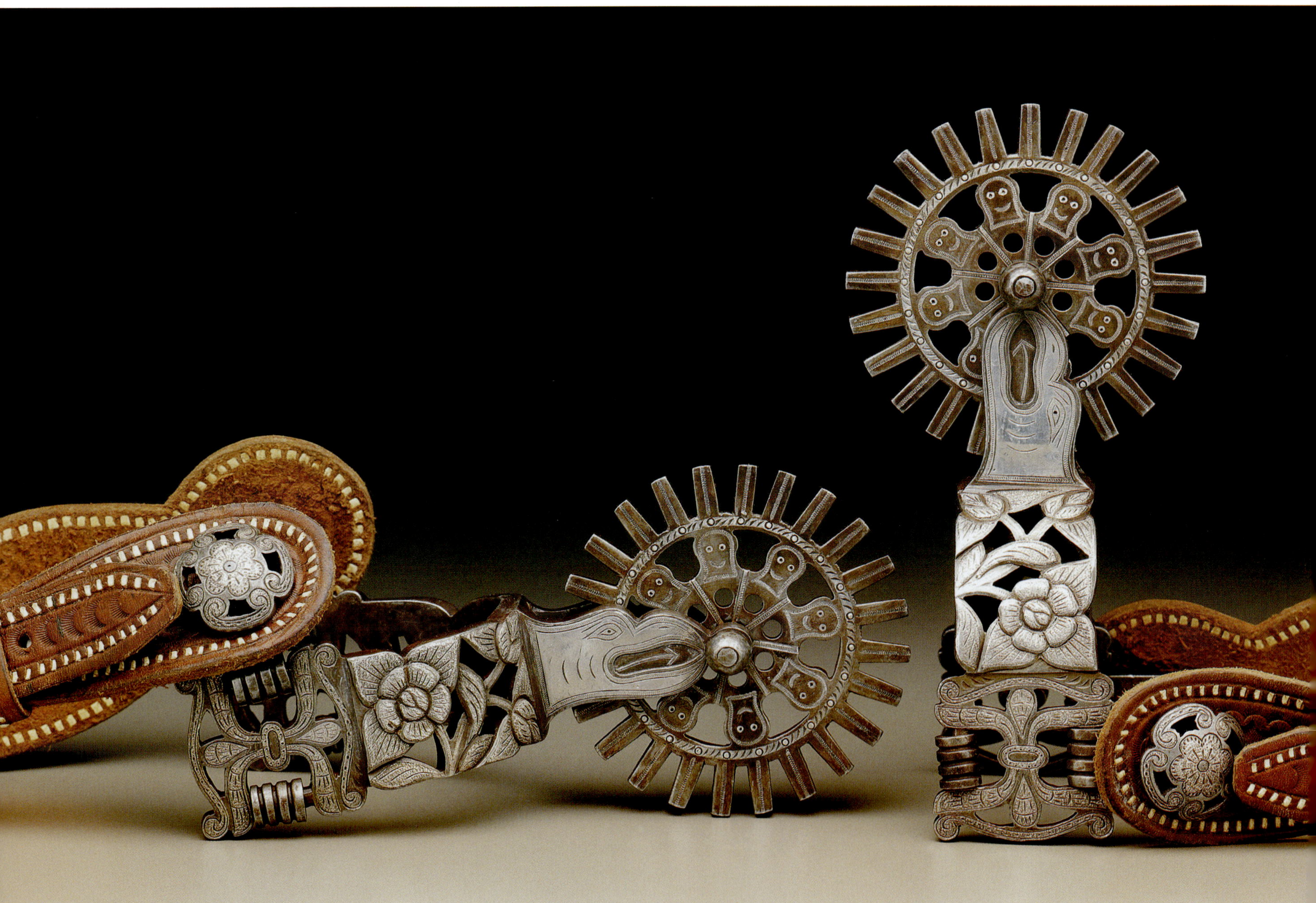

reflected European, Arab, and even Chinese floral and figurative motifs, the latter brought to Mexico by way of the Philippine Islands. The largest of these stirrups measured eighteen inches long and twelve inches wide and weighed fifteen pounds or more. In regions where iron and silver were precious, smaller, less elaborate cruciform stirrups, some with crude designs merely scratched or punched into the metal, were the norm. Despite a royal edict in 1778 declaring *estribos de cruz* a sacrilege and banning their creation and use, cross-shaped stirrups continued to adorn Spanish saddles in some parts of rural Mexico, including California, into the nineteenth century.

Highly embellished bits, spurs, and stirrups were rare on the remote Spanish borderlands frontier, whose residents experienced chronic shortages of skilled craftsmen, imported goods, and such raw materials as iron and silver. Most of the region's horsemen made do with a few rude imports from northern Mexico or locally produced horse gear fashioned from discarded plowshares, wagon wheel rims, or other scrap iron.

After about 1800 Spanish colonial spur styles gradually surrendered to new and heavier patterns with wider heel bands, shorter shanks, and smaller rowels. This evolution was well underway when Mexico ceded the American Southwest to the United States in 1848 following the Mexican War. Hispanic horsemen in northern Mexico and southern Texas during the 1840s were observed using spurs with two-inch rowels, bridles festooned with diamond-shaped pieces of silver, and ring bits laden with *pajados*. An unidentified Englishman who hunted on the Texas frontier in the 1850s described heavy Mexican spurs with "rowels often as large in circumference as five shilling pieces, generally divided into five blunt prongs shaped like a star." The hooks, he observed, "bruise a horse and hurt him excessively though they rarely puncture the skin."[66]

Despite the arrival of a few American-trained blacksmiths in the West before the Civil War, horsemen from Texas to California continued to depend upon sources in Mexico and the eastern United States to supply most of the demand for bits and spurs. During the 1850s foundries located in Newark and New Britain, Connecticut, began to dominate the American market for such goods. Alexander Barclay & Company, Joseph Baldwin & Company, and North and Judd Manufacturing Co., among others, eagerly acquired bit and spur patterns popular in the West, reproduced them in their own shops, and then aggressively marketed them to western customers. According to its advertisement in an 1860s San Francisco business directory, for example, Barnet, Stainsby & Co. of Newark produced and sold "all kinds of Mexican & California Bitts [sic] and Spurs."[67] Although the company's ad suggests that a California style, distinct from Mexican patterns, may have emerged, the type of spurs made on the Pacific Coast of the United States still had much in common with those produced in western Mexico (Sonora and Sinaloa).

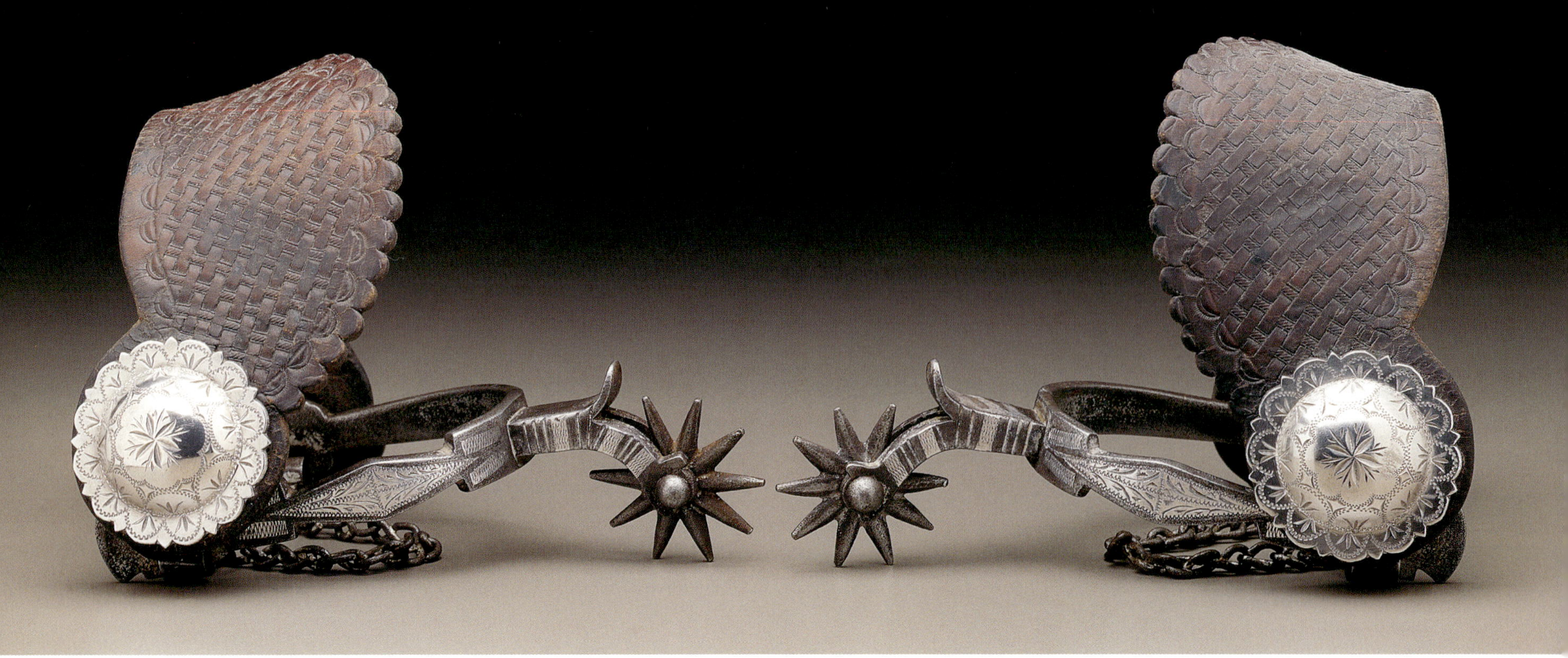

Above
California-style drop-shank spurs with chap guard, sculpted diamond-shaped heel band, heel chains, and basket-weave stamped spur leather with silver concha ornament
Fleischer Collection, Scottsdale

Below
California-style drop-shank spurs with chap guards, silver inlay in harp pattern on one side of heel band, and incised linear and geometric pattern on opposite side, c. 1890s
Fleischer Collection, Scottsdale

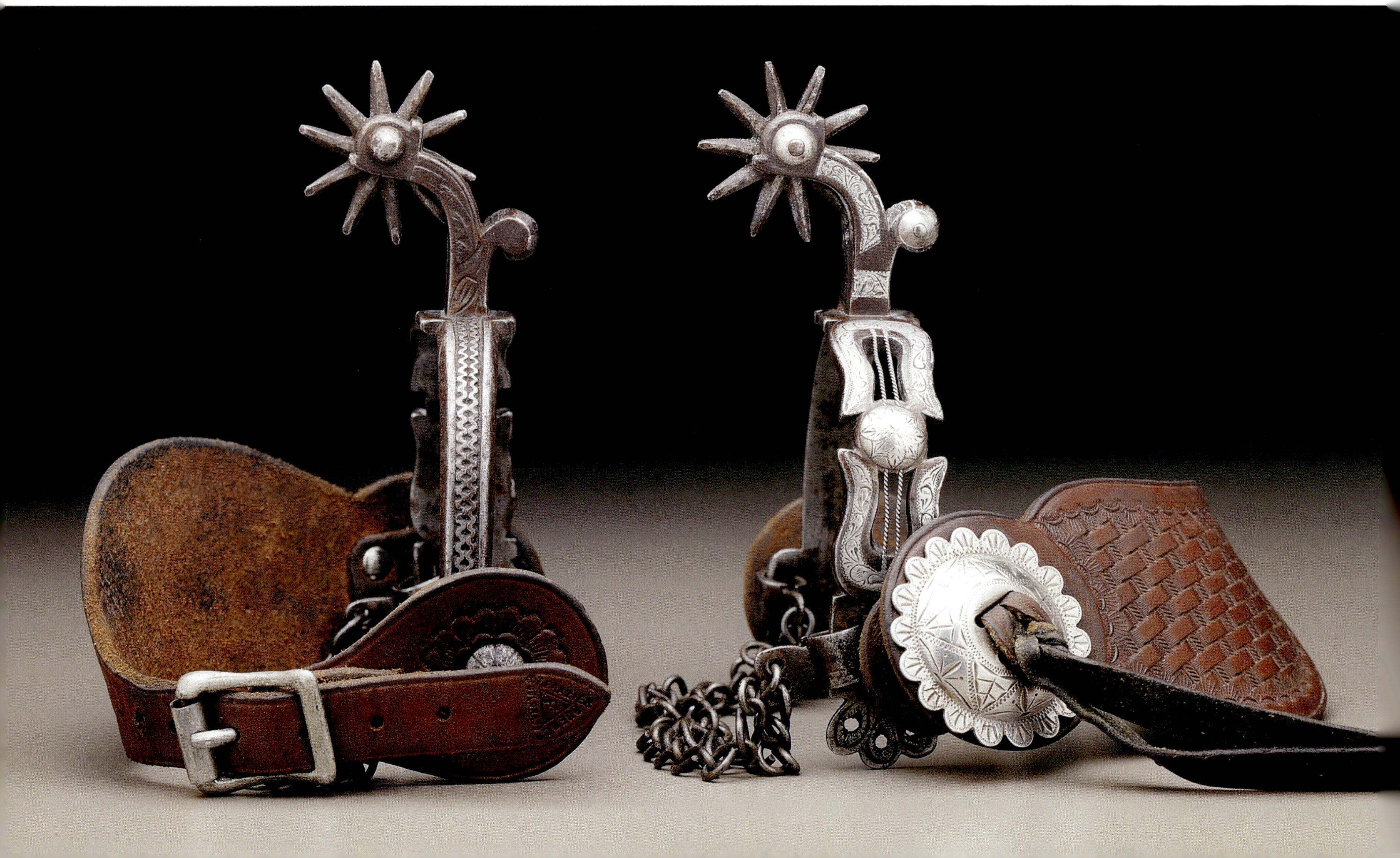

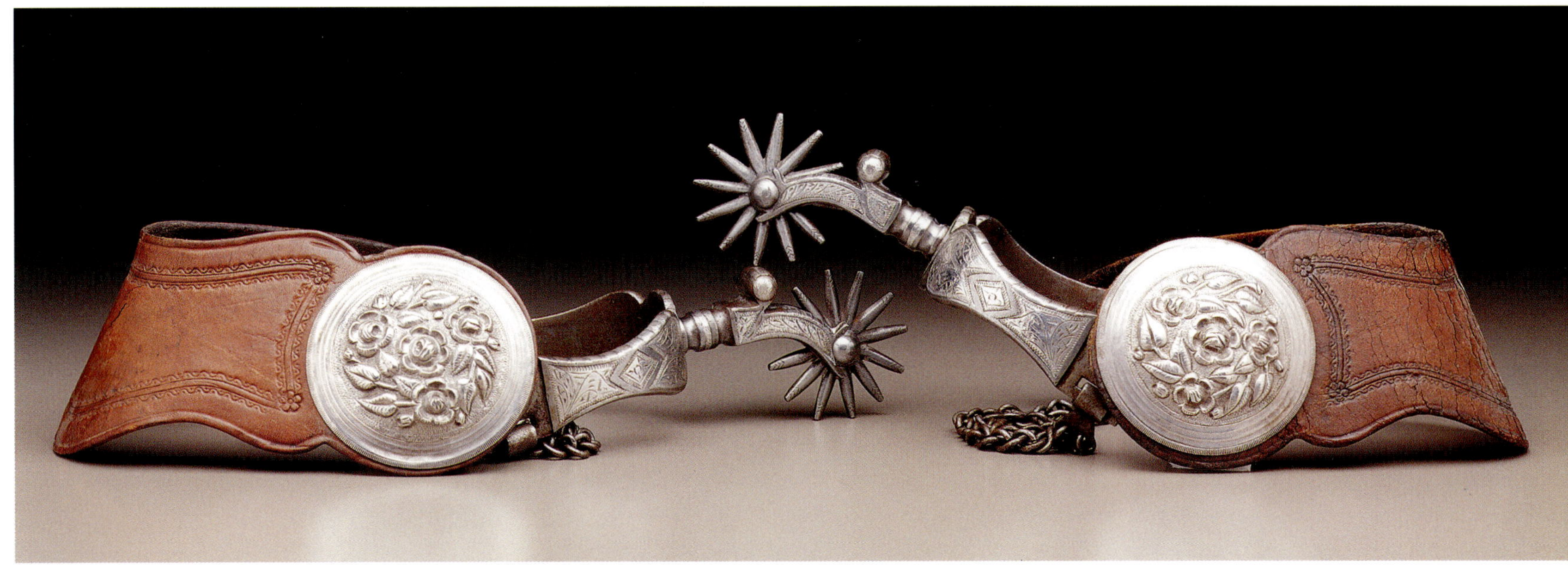

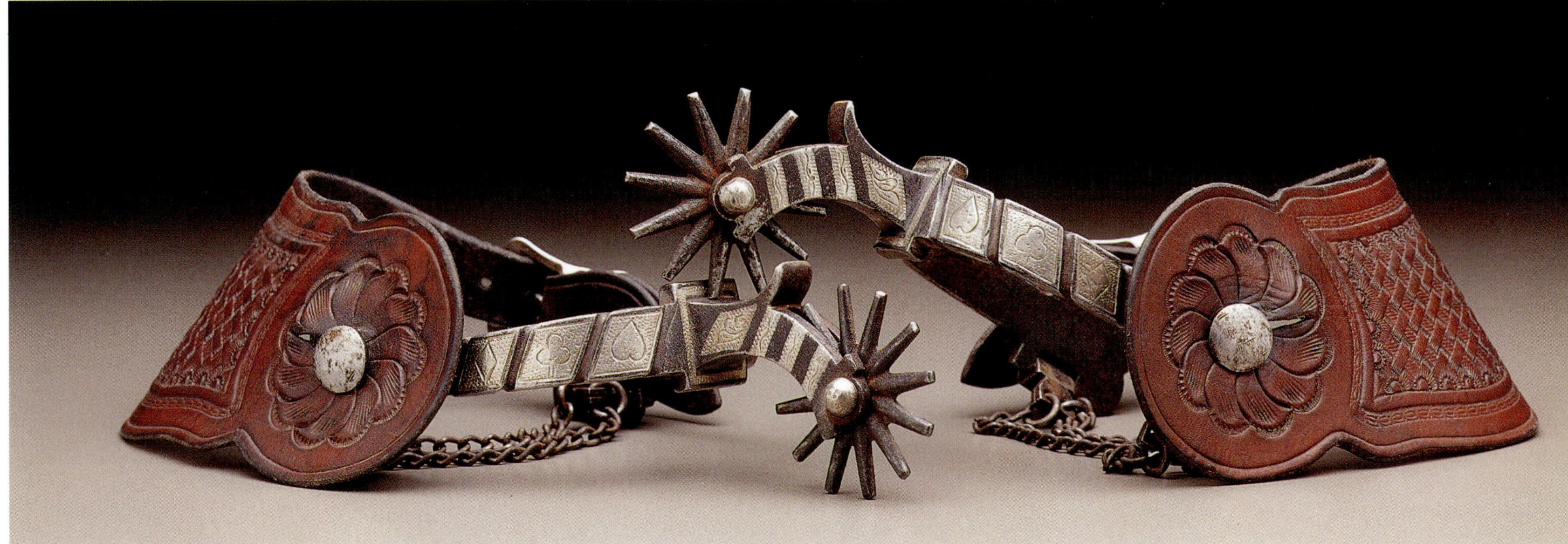

Usually of two-piece (heel band and shank) construction, California spurs of the mid-nineteenth century were generally smaller and sleeker than most of their Mexican counterparts. Fixed buttons placed at the ends of a flat heel band accommodated leather straps while slots beneath the buttons mounted double heel chains to help hold the spur in place on the boot. The drooping shanks characteristic of most West Coast–forged spurs typically sported a small upward-curving or ball-shaped appendage called a chap guard, which helped keep a vaquero's *chaparreras* (leggings) from interfering with the rowels. Some California spur rowels also sported a "buck" or "cinch" hook that cowboys used to snare their saddle cinches to help them stay aboard bucking horses. Other riders locked their spur rowels with the heel chains, pieces of rawhide or wire, or bent a

Goldberg-Staunton, Winnemucca, Nevada
Above: two-piece drop-shank spurs with chap guards, sculpted heel bands with engraved silver inlay, heel chains, and spur leathers with raised floral design on conchas; below: drop-shank spurs with chap guards, playing card symbols engraved on panels of inlaid silver, and leathers with pinwheel and basket-weave stamping
FLEISCHER COLLECTION, SCOTTSDALE

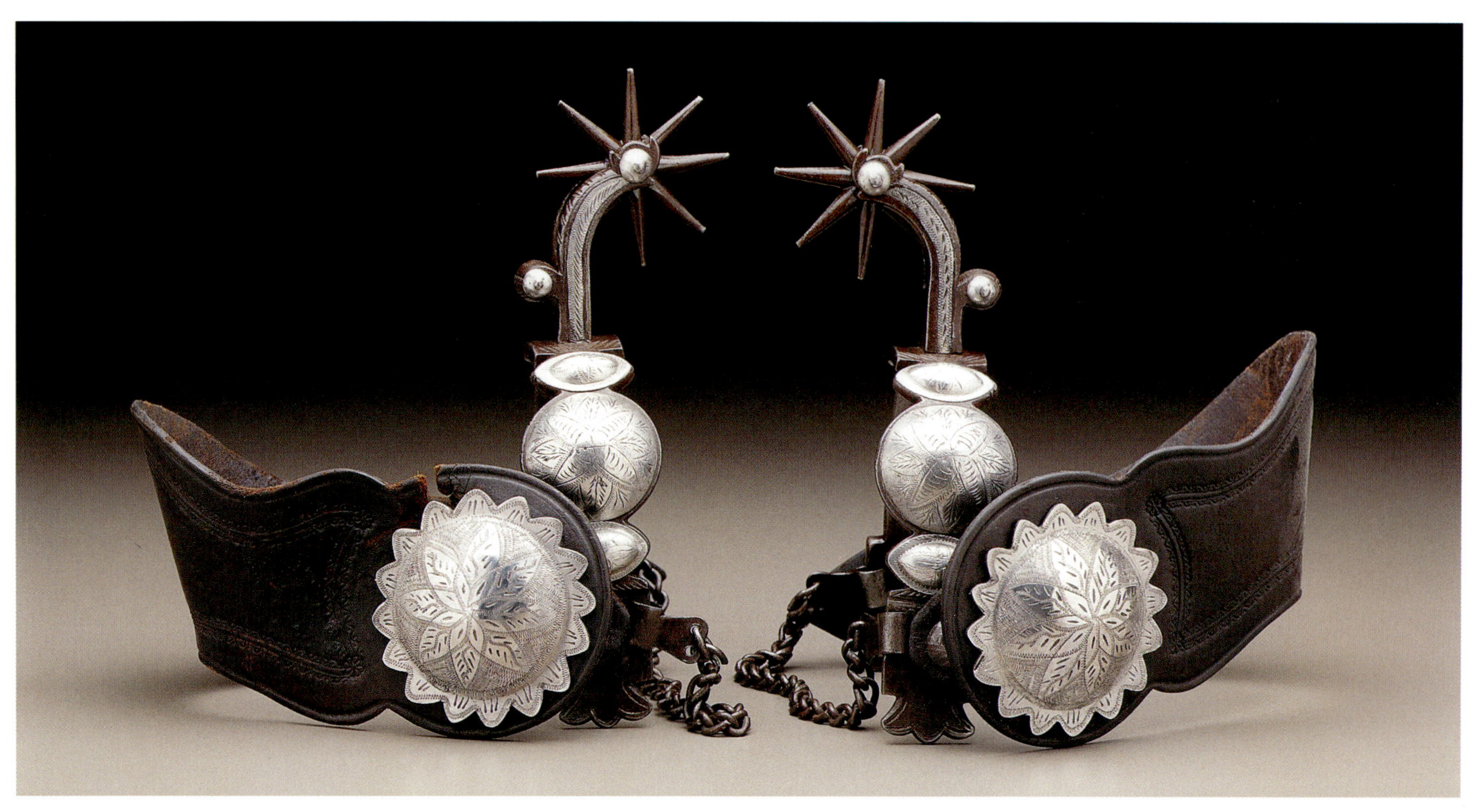

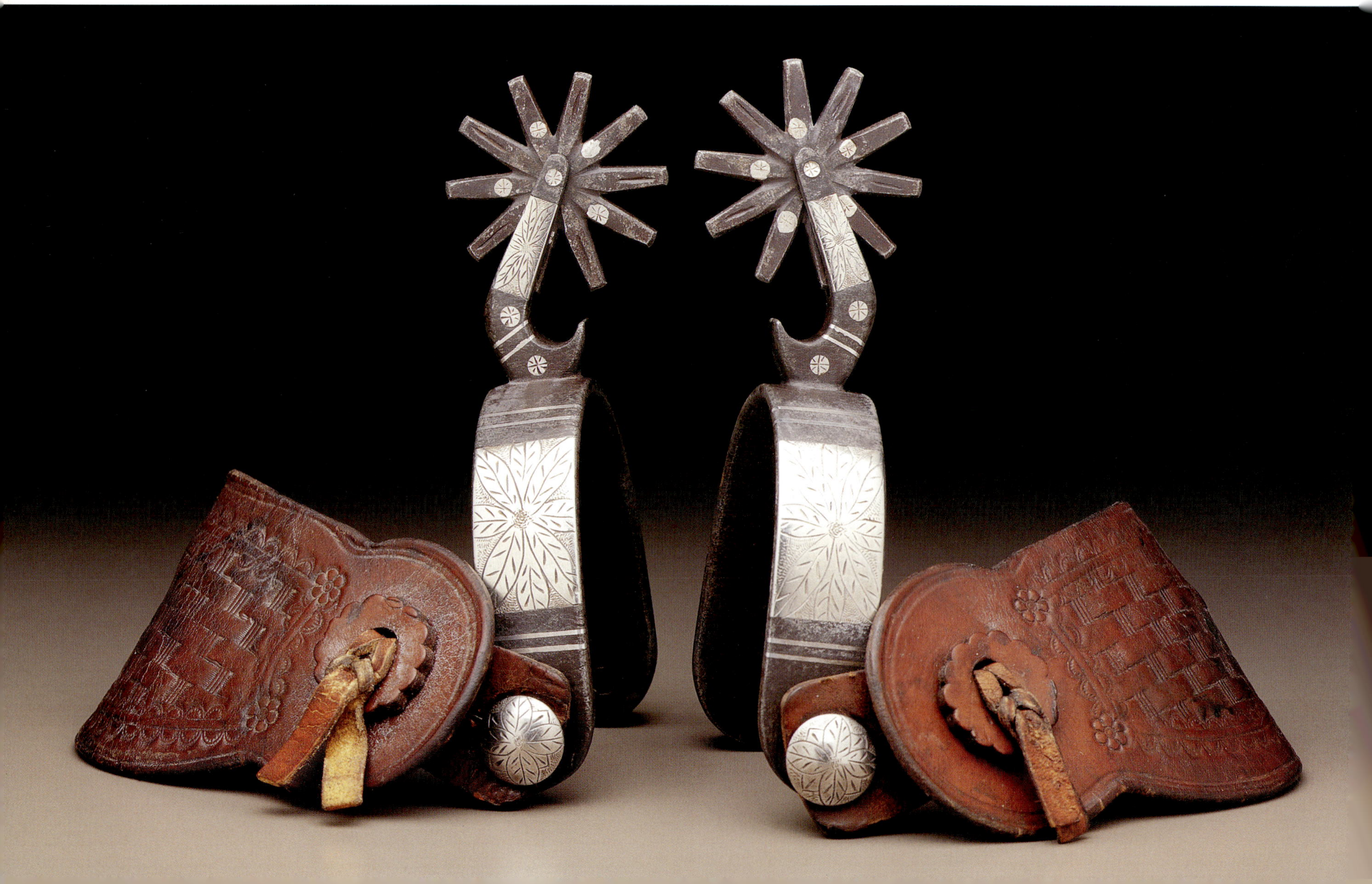

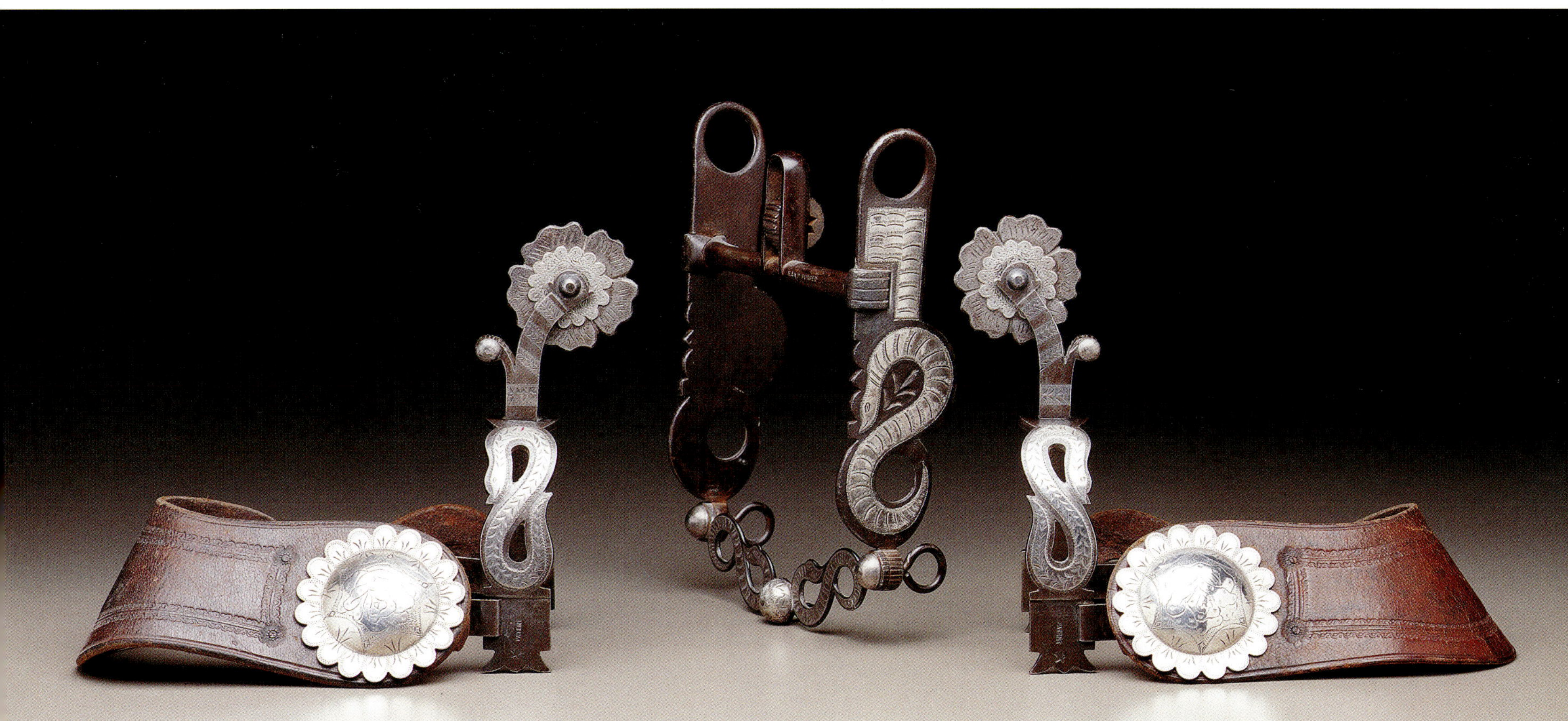

spoke on the rowels so they would not revolve freely. If the animal fell and the rider became hung up, however, the result could be catastrophic.

Using inlay, chasing, and engraving techniques perfected by Mexican craftsmen, California bit and spur makers in the late nineteenth century endowed their goods with a variety of fresh floral, figurative, and geometric motifs. Master artisans often accentuated their silver work by bluing the rest of the spur body.

A few prominent California saddle houses of the period established their own bit and spur shops and employed craftsmen to turn out such goods. Most contracted for the work of independent makers, many of whom supplied more than one company. To augment their product lines, some saddleries purchased plain, California-style bits and spurs, cast or drop forged at eastern foundries, and hired local silversmiths to embellish them. These mostly anonymous artisans also created conchas, rosettes, and other ornaments widely used in the decoration of saddles, bridles, and other riding gear.

As occurred with saddlery, California-style bits and spurs, made on both coasts, spread throughout the western range during the 1870s. Prominent Cheyenne saddle makers G. H. and J. S. Collins, for example, advertised California, Mexican, and Texas bits and spurs as early as 1876. More than 80 percent of the spurs illustrated in the trade literature of their local competitor F. A. Meanea during the period were of California styling. According to a contemporary,

Opposite, top
Drop-shank spurs with engraved silver inlay and overlay, heel bands marked CLC inside, heel chains, and spur leathers with floral engraved conchas
Fleischer Collection, Scottsdale

Opposite, bottom
Silver-inlaid and engraved spurs with "bottle opener" style shanks, made by an inmate at the Colorado State Penitentiary, Cañon City, Colorado
Fleischer Collection, Scottsdale

Above
August Buermann Mfg. Co., Newark, New Jersey
Cowboy spurs with snake-shaped heel bands and matching bridle bit, c. 1890s
Fleischer Collection, Scottsdale

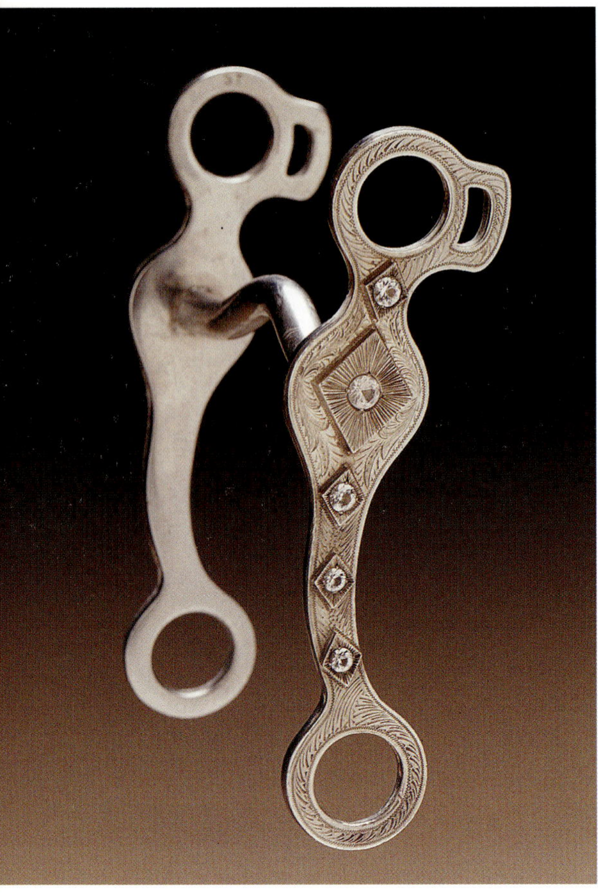

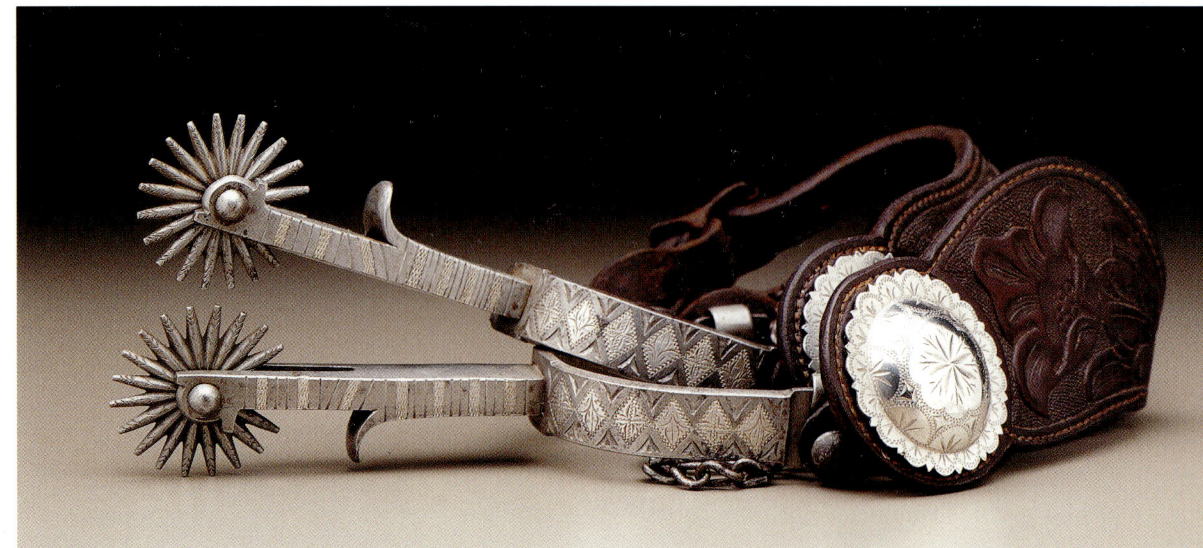

Meanea's shop boasted "a fine long show case containing bits, spurs and ornamental martingales, all gay with silver conchas or brass letters."[68] The Cheyenne saddler not only bought heavily from the bit and spur lines produced by August Buermann's New Jersey foundry, but also contracted for the ironwork of Holden Peterson, a Fort Fetterman, Wyoming, blacksmith.

By the 1880s cowhands throughout the Great Plains had embraced expensive West Coast–forged spurs costing as much as $25 a pair. According to a Nebraska rancher, eastern-bred cowboys, "decked out à la California vaquero, with fancy expensive silver spurs and bridle bits,"[69] were a common sight on the Nebraska range during the period. Further south, William Moore, a former California vaquero and range boss of the LX ranch in the Texas Panhandle, exposed his cowhands to the beauty of California gear, and several of them subsequently ordered silver-inlaid bits and spurs from the West Coast. Cowboys on the nearby T Anchor Ranch obtained spurs crafted in San Jose and Santa Clara, California, or cheaper versions costing as little as $1.75 from eastern foundries. At least one cowboy of the period thought the latter kind "just as good as if they had cost twenty dollars."[70]

Eastern foundries also turned out serviceable wrought iron ring bits, at less than half of the cost of the cheapest patterns produced on the West Coast. Of the three grades of hand-forged bits offered by D. E. Walker's Visalia saddlery in 1881, for example, plain types fetched $4 to $7; those ornamented with a single silver button on each cheek piece, $12; and models festooned with elaborate silver inlay, $20.

By this time California smiths also were producing sophisticated bridle bits with spade-shaped mouthpieces favored by expert California horsemen but rejected by most other riders as too severe. The cheek pieces of these bits exhibited much variety in style and ornament, and more than a dozen different models,

Above
Left: modern curb bit with imitation diamonds set in engraved mounts; right: spurs, straight shanks with chap guards, silver inlay in diamond and stripe motif, and engraved silver conchas
FLEISCHER COLLECTION, SCOTTSDALE

Opposite, above
L. D. Stone Co., San Francisco Spurs with drop shanks and chap guards; inlaid, engraved, and sculpted heel bands; and leathers with sombrero conchas, c. 1890s
FLEISCHER COLLECTION, SCOTTSDALE

Opposite, below
Pistol shaped bridle bits; left: North and Judd Mfg., Co., New Britain Connecticut, c. 1920s–1940s; right: Robert M. Hall, engraved cylinder and barrel, colored grip with incised star and border pattern, c. 1930s
FLEISCHER COLLECTION, SCOTTSDALE

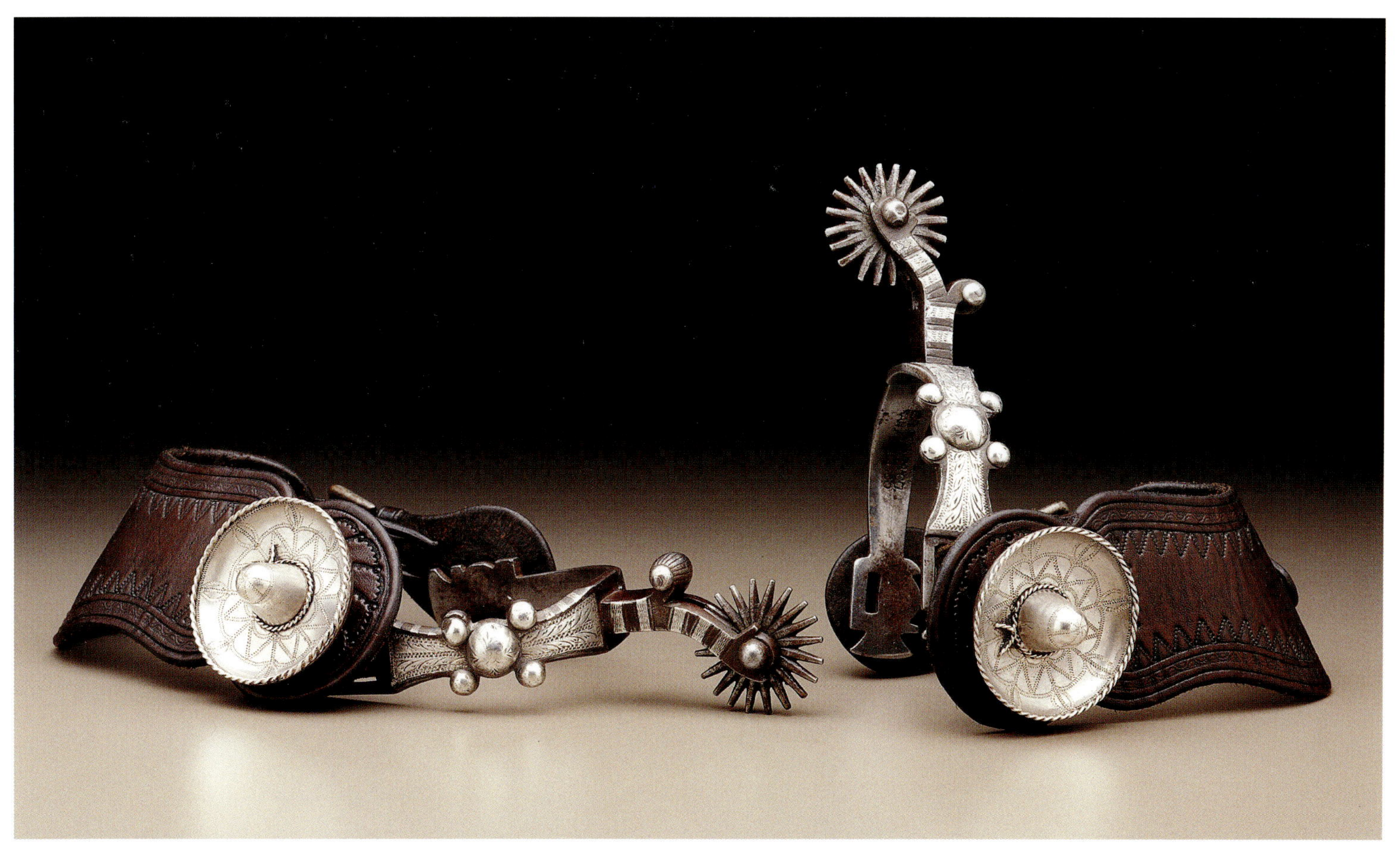

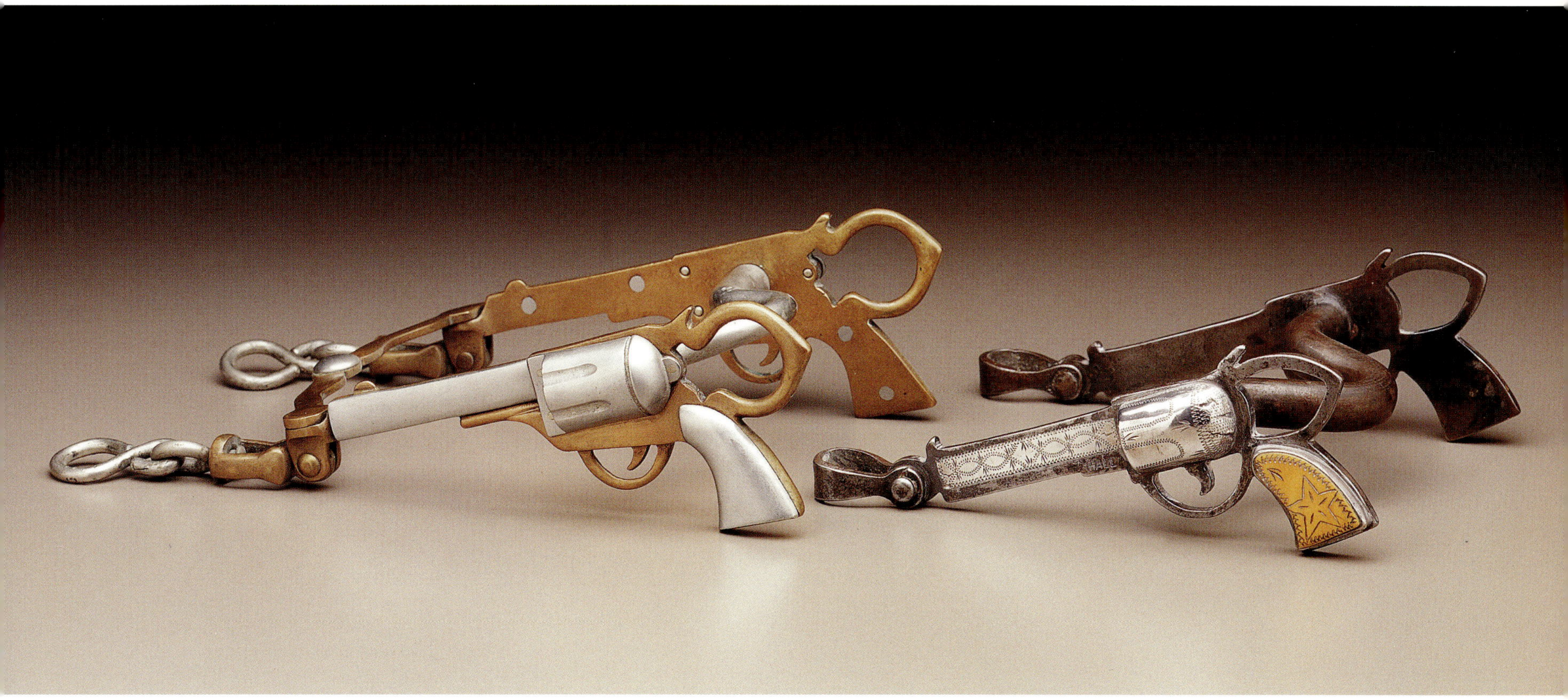

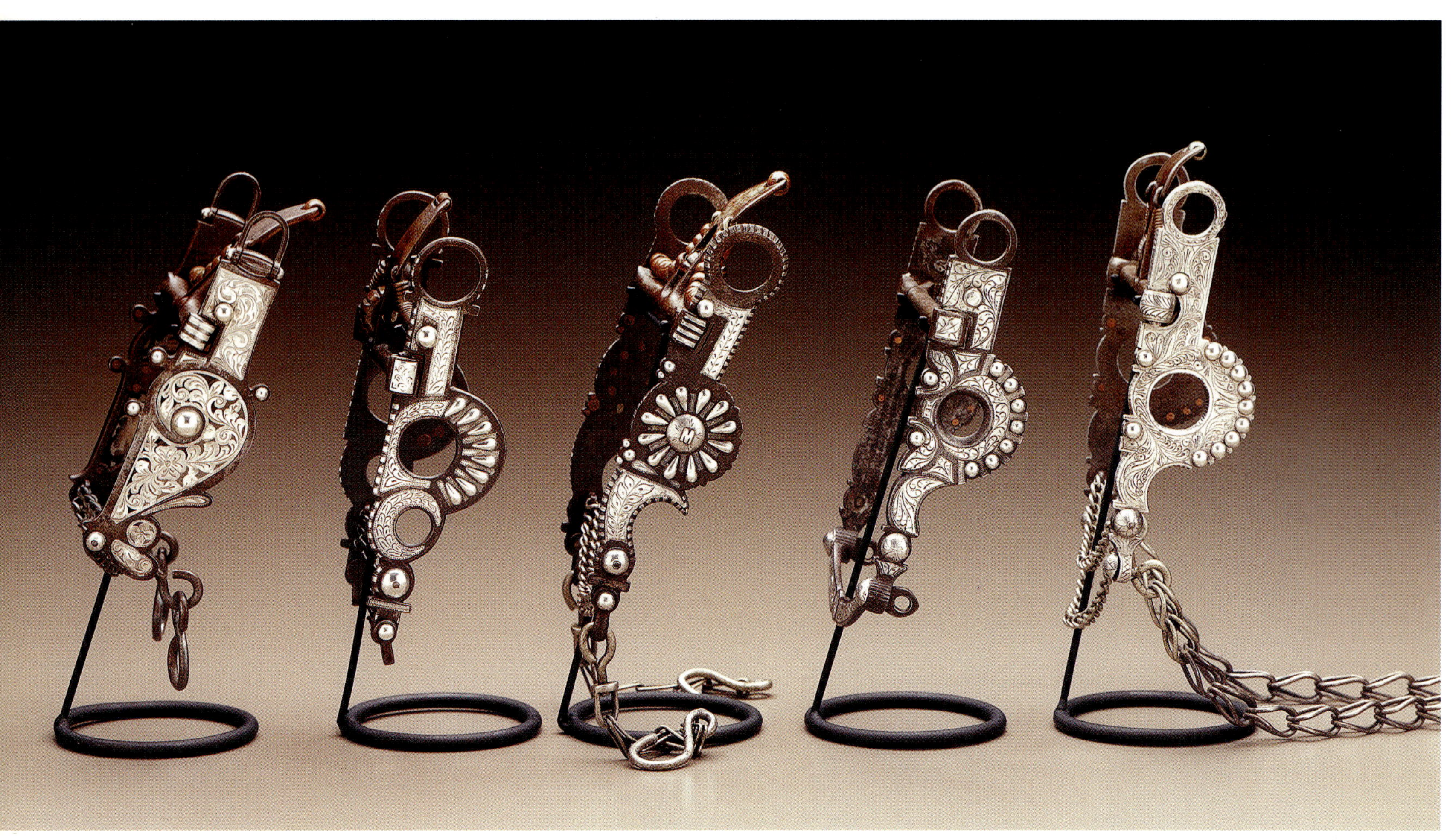

Ornate California-style bridle bits; third from left made by Abbe Hunt, other four examples made in Amazoc, Mexico, for Richard Fleming, with spade mouthpieces and silver-inlaid cheek pieces
FLEISCHER COLLECTION, SCOTTSDALE

nearly all of them named for their region or place of creation, eventually emerged. Among the most popular were the Santa Barbara pattern attributed to Carpinteria, California, craftsman Jose de Jesus Mardueño, and the Las Cruces style created by ranch blacksmith Juan Flores.

Like spurs, most California-style bits were made in pieces and riveted together. Certain "loose jaw" patterns featured hinged cheeks. Although stylistically distinctive, early California bits often were crudely forged. The cheek pieces of some did not match and silver inlay was scarce at first. The intricate pierced work and deep chasing of master smiths, however, sometimes simulated silver inlay.

While California bit and spur patterns claimed much of the cowboy market during the 1870s and early 1880s, heavier Mexican styles continued to attract adherents throughout the Southwest, particularly in southern Texas. Although similar in form to the often ornately embellished spurs created in the silver producing states of Puebla, Jalisco, Sonora, and Zacatecas, most of the Mexican patterns used north of the Rio Grande during the late nineteenth century were either plain or only modestly inlaid with silver, brass, and copper. Almost all possessed figure eight or question mark–shaped shanks that rarely exceeded two inches in length and dull rowels seldom more than 1 1/2 inches in diameter. Texas cowboys of the period called Mexican-style spurs "Chihuahuas," regardless of origin or design.

Although many local blacksmiths turned out serviceable tack as part of a general metalworking trade, specialized bit and spur makers remained scarce in Texas before 1890, notwithstanding a steady demand for such items. The only artisan with a significant reputation in the field was J. C. Petmecky, a German-born, Austin, Texas, gunsmith and engraver whose lightweight spurs had much in common with military patterns of the era. Petmecky's cowboy customers nicknamed his hooks "petmakers" and with good reason. One recalled that rowels on Petmecky spurs "were like a knife, and if you'd stick a horse, you'd cut him."[71]

North and Judd Mfg. Co.,
New Britain, Connecticut
Bridle bit matching spurs made of "Hercules Bronze" with nickel silver buffalo head ornaments, c. 1920s
FLEISCHER COLLECTION, SCOTTSDALE

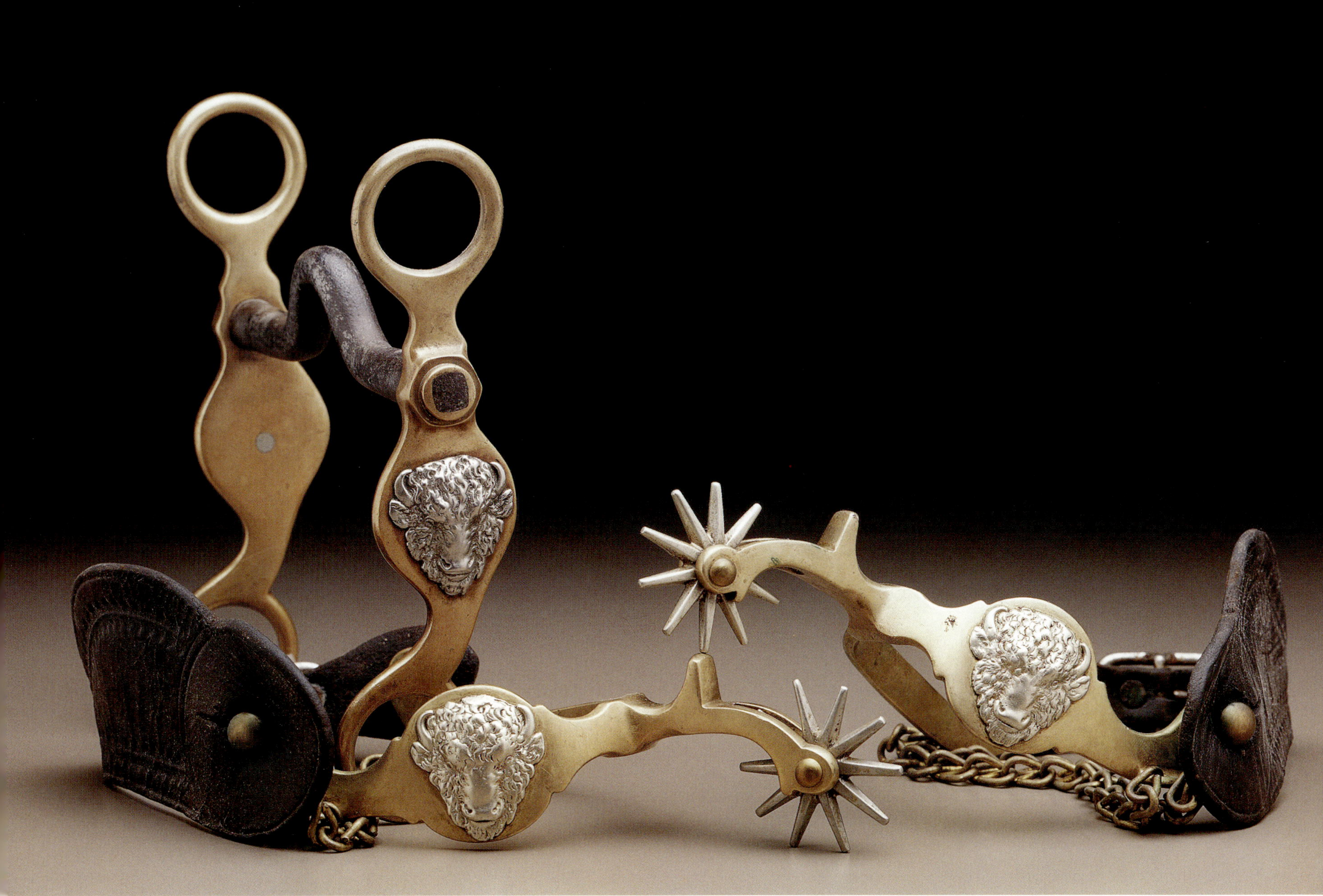

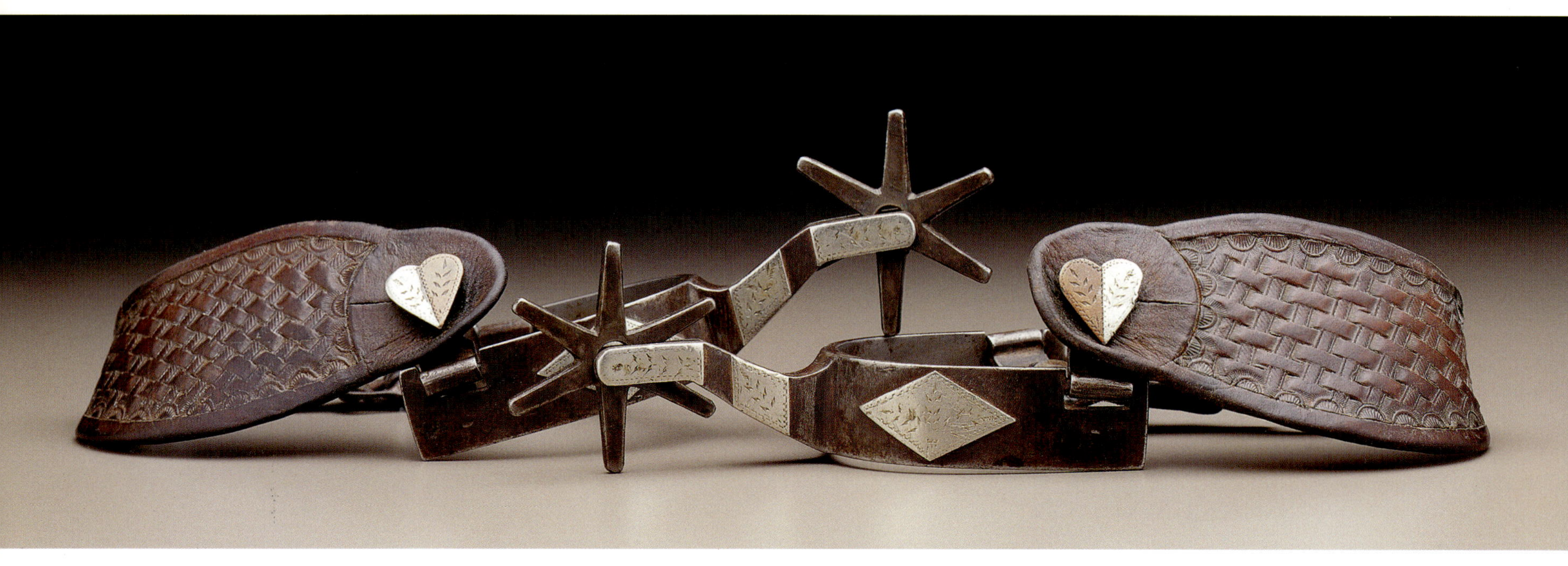

J. O. Bass, Tulia, Texas
Texas-style, one-piece, raised-shank spurs with silver-mounted heel bands and shanks and a silver and copper heart-shaped button, c. 1910
Fleischer Collection, Scottsdale

In the late 1880s a small cadre of Texas and Oklahoma blacksmiths introduced a style of spurs that differed from its predecessors in both design and construction. Hand-forged from a single piece of iron or steel, this new model possessed a narrow, often sculpted heel band, a short shank, and a small rowel. Makers dispensed with heel chains and rarely added the chap guards and bluing seen on California spurs. Less ornate than fine inlaid Mexican and California varieties, Texas-style spurs, and bits as well, often sported thin, hand-cut and engraved overlays of silver, German silver, copper, and brass mounted with solder.

Although a few Texas craftsmen fashioned bits and spurs from foundry-produced flatiron bars, many converted scrap metal into serviceable and often beautiful riding gear. Accomplished blacksmiths, for example, could transform a three-tine pitchfork into a spur by removing the middle prong, flattening the outer tines to form the heel band, and using the shaft as the shank. Similarly, makers altered the blades and wheel spokes of hay mowers, the teeth of harrows and threshing machines, and the axles and springs of buggies, and, eventually, automobiles into bits and spurs.

Smiths in remote regions were equally resourceful in locating the brass, bronze, copper, and silver used to mount and inlay their products. Many, for example, found Mexican and American coins a versatile and relatively plentiful source of silver. Others scavenged copper from discarded double boilers and pirated scarce metals and gemstones from jewelry, serving dishes, and tableware, some of the latter purloined from Harvey House restaurants that lined the route of the Santa Fe Railroad in the Southwest.

By the turn of the twentieth century, several Texas blacksmiths, including a few ex-cowboys, had become noted bit and spur makers. Some worked at the task only part time, combining metalwork with farming, well drilling, and other occupations. Through close observation, trial and error, and "how-to" books, at least a few of these craftsmen also taught themselves the rudiments of engraving and silversmithing, skills which were divided among several individuals in larger shops.

Typical of these talented artisans, J. O. Bass fashioned quality riding gear in the Texas Panhandle for nearly three decades, beginning in 1897 in the town of Quitaque and continuing in 1905 in the nearby community of Tulia. Before Bass abandoned metalworking in the mid-1920s to become a farmer, he had produced an estimated 2,000 pairs of spurs and 500 bridle bits. Many were special orders, embellished with heart-shaped buttons and overlaid with engraved silver, copper, and brass mounts in simple geometric shapes or card suits: hearts, spades, clubs, and diamonds. Bass sold his top-of-the-line spurs, embellished with forty-eight pieces of silver, twenty of them inlaid, and six brass overlays, for only $16 in 1912. His best bridle bits, modestly mounted by comparison with only four pieces of silver, retailed for $5.

Bass spent hours with a hand file imparting crisp lines and a smooth finish to his perfectly proportioned products. Over the course of his career, he filled a barrel in his shop with work that did not measure up to his rigorous standards.

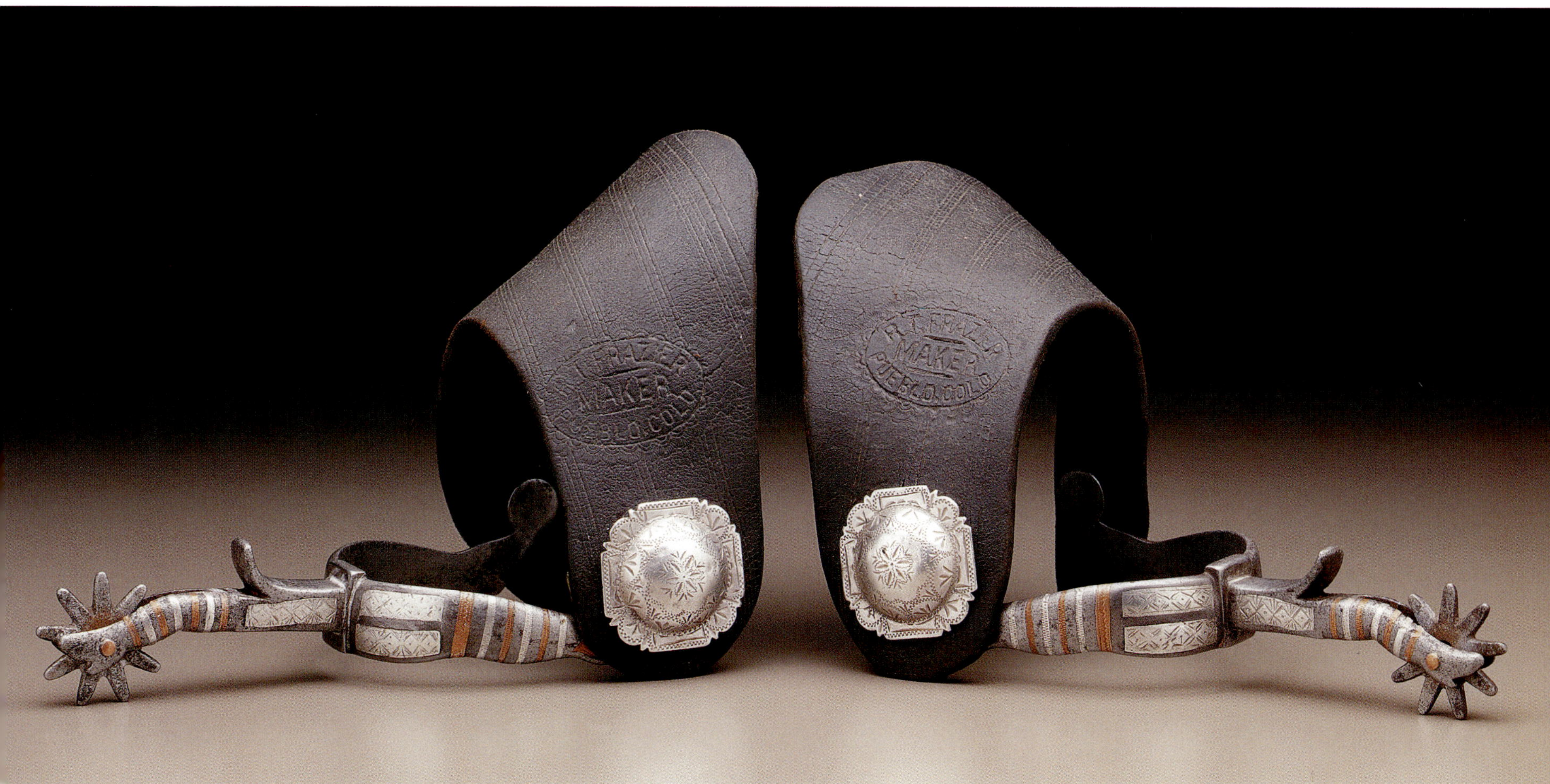

G. S. Garcia, Elko Nevada (metalwork) and R. T. Frazier, Pueblo, Colorado (leatherwork) Two-piece spurs with "gal-leg"—pattern shanks, chap guards, raised stationary buttons, and silver and copper inlays, c. 1900
FLEISCHER COLLECTION, SCOTTSDALE

Unlike many western craftsmen, who did not bother to mark their products, Bass carefully stamped his goods with his name, location, and order number. The reference notes and sketches that filled his order book served as a convenient guide if customers ever required replacement or duplicate items.

At the same time J. O. Bass was enjoying success in northwestern Texas, an Italian immigrant named Joseph Bianchi was forging stellar bits and spurs with a different look at the town of Victoria near the Gulf Coast. Trained as a blacksmith in Italy, Bianchi had joined his brother in the trade before launching his own career sometime between 1906 and 1909.

South Texas horsemen, including vaqueros from the fabled King Ranch, found Bianchi-made bits and spurs appealing and kept the smith busy at his forge into the 1940s. The thriving saddle shop operated by the King Ranch at Kingsville, Texas, stocked Bianchi spurs and advertised them in its trade catalogs.

The maker's signature spur pattern included a sleek, narrow heel band, turned up at the ends to better fit the boot, and a shank shaped like a bottle opener. Sometimes called a "Victoria shank," the basic design had appeared much earlier on Mexican spurs and was used by a few other American makers as well. Bianchi offered men's spurs in four weights ranging from light to extra heavy as well as a special lightweight ladies' spur. He customized the width and decoration of heel bands, buttons, shanks, and rowels according to the customer's taste and pocketbook. Simple, unengraved silver mounts, cut and shaped by hand, adorned most Bianchi spurs. The maker also used whole coins, especially Mexican *pesos*, in his decorative schemes, usually to cover spur buttons, rowel pins, and the heel bands of spurs or to decorate the cheek pieces on bridle bits. Customers could have their name, initials, or cattle brand hand-stamped on their goods at no extra charge.

In the realm of cowboy bits and spurs, however, creativity was not merely the province of craftsmen in Texas and California. By 1900 several innovative blacksmiths on the northern Great Plains had perfected a spur that blended the best qualities of the Texas and California styles. Usually equipped with chap guards and relatively large rowels, this single-piece hybrid exhibited both inlay and overlay ornamentation and sometimes-strange decorative motifs that included mice and wooden shoes.

A number of prison inmates also produced this type of spur as part of work programs inaugurated at several western penitentiaries in the late nineteenth and early twentieth centuries. Between the 1890s and the 1940s, for example, convicts at Colorado State Prison at Cañon City gained special renown for their fine quality spurs and bits. These inmate-artisans, at least one of whom was an experienced loriner before his incarceration, not only had access to a fully outfitted blacksmith shop, but also were allowed to purchase their own engraving tools and supplies. Prisoners typically received from 10 to 25 cents a day for their labor; most of the money paid in a lump sum upon their release.

Opposite
J. R. McChesney, Gainesville, Texas, and Pauls Valley, Oklahoma
"Gal-leg" spurs with brass slipper, and spade and panel overlays on heel band; bridle with bit and brass slipper and wheat pattern engraving on corset
Fleischer Collection, Scottsdale

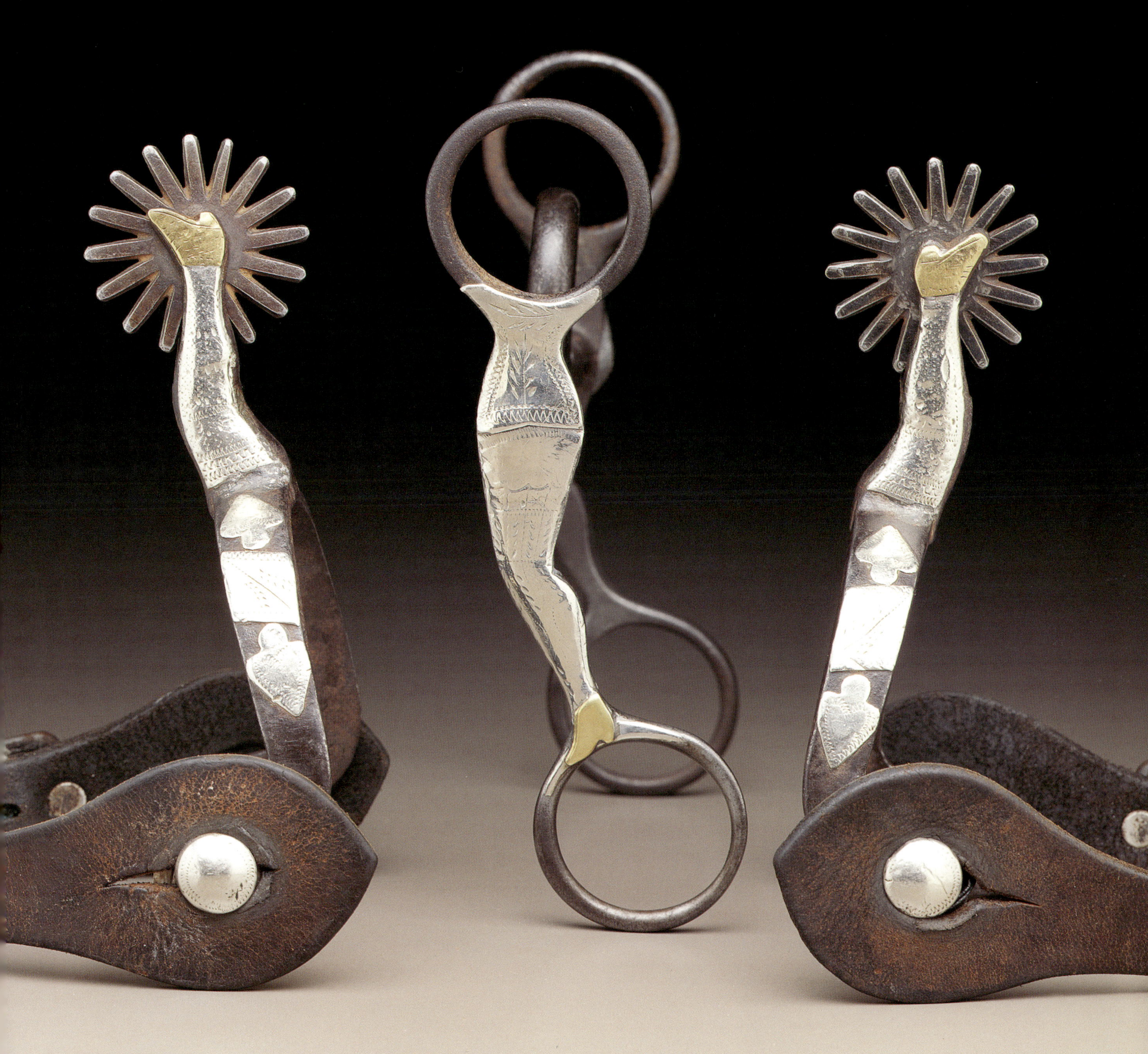

The bits and spurs made at Cañon City and other western prisons exhibited considerable variety and were often the products of several craftsmen working as specialists in forging metal and various forms of embellishment. In addition to their own ideas, prison artisans interpreted decorative motifs gleaned from the trade catalogs of prominent western saddle makers. German silver inlays and overlays, stamped and engraved with variations of vine and leaf, floral, diamond, sunburst, and Vallejo Star patterns, characterized the Cañon City style.

While sold primarily through prison curio shops and by mail, inmate-made bits, spurs, conchas, and saddle trimmings also were retailed by a few western saddleries. Such goods were rarely marked and even then only with the convict's number or perhaps the initials of the incarcerating institution.

Despite superior workmanship and avid local or regional patrons, one-man bit and spur shops were too ill-equipped and under-capitalized to serve a large-scale market. Tedious production methods severely limited their output, and only a few makers were able to issue catalogs or advertise much beyond the occasional raffling off of their work to cowboys and ranchers at local saloons. Thanks to ambition, acumen, innovation, and good luck, however, three country blacksmiths from Texas and Oklahoma managed to compete for the national bit and spur market in the early twentieth century.

The first and most artistic of these craftsmen was John Robert McChesney. A native of South Bend, Indiana, J. R. McChesney began building bits and spurs as part of a general blacksmithing business in Broken Bow, Oklahoma, in 1887. By

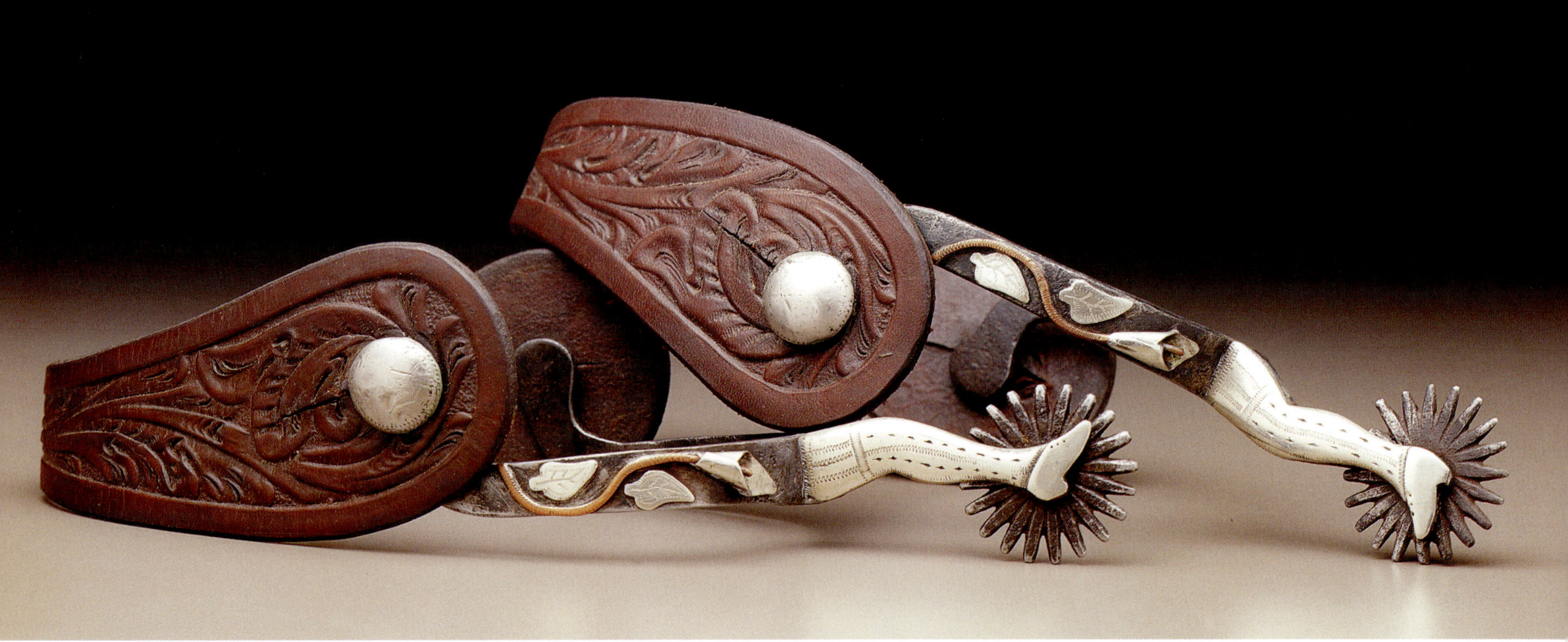

J. R. McChesney, Gainesville, Texas "Gal-leg shank" spurs with flower-vine and leaf design on heelband
FLEISCHER COLLECTION, SCOTTSDALE

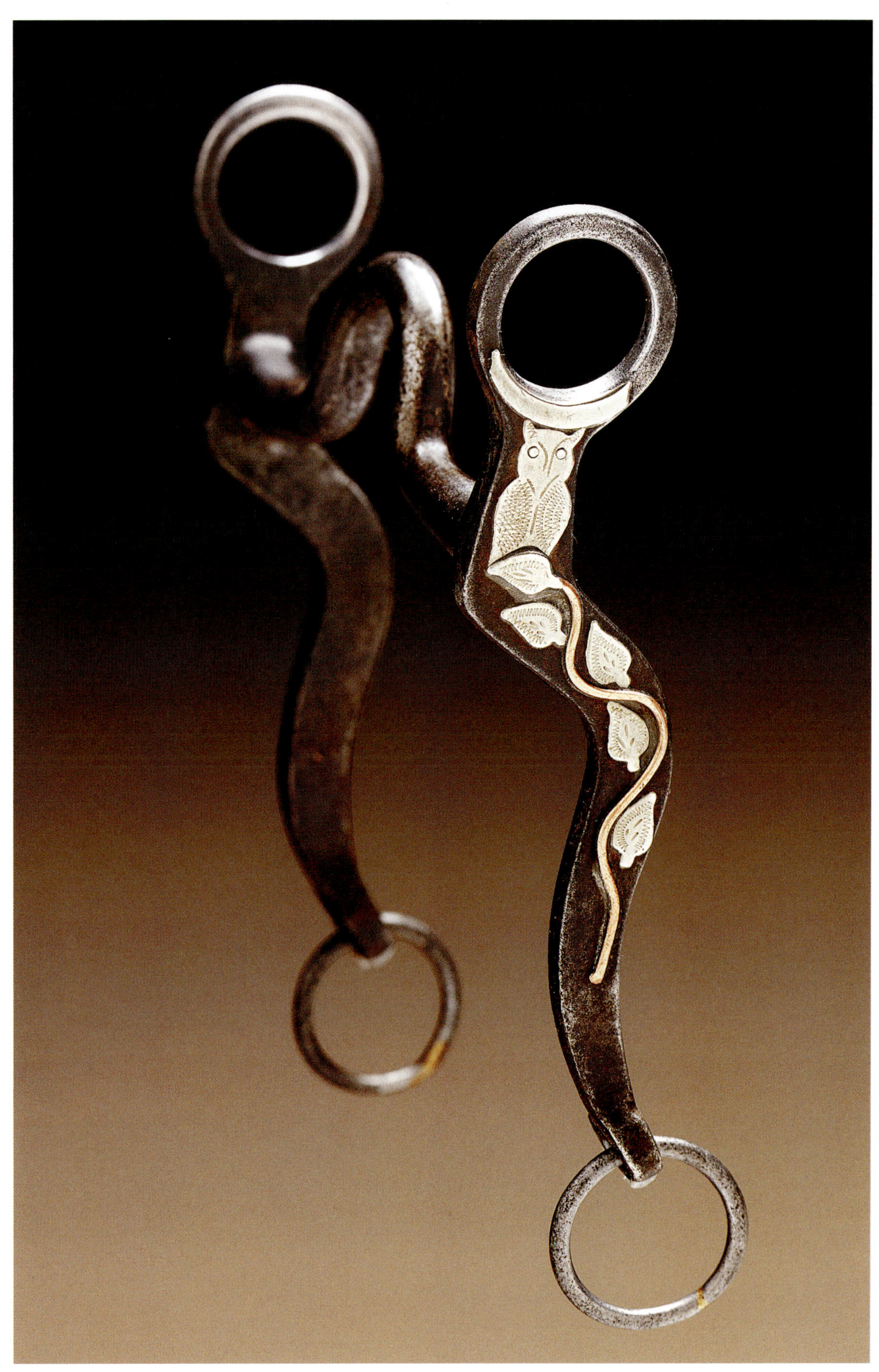

J. R. McChesney,
Gainesville, Texas, and
Pauls Valley, Oklahoma
Curb bit with owl, flower,
and leaf-and-vine motifs
mounted on cheek pieces
Fleischer Collection,
Scottsdale

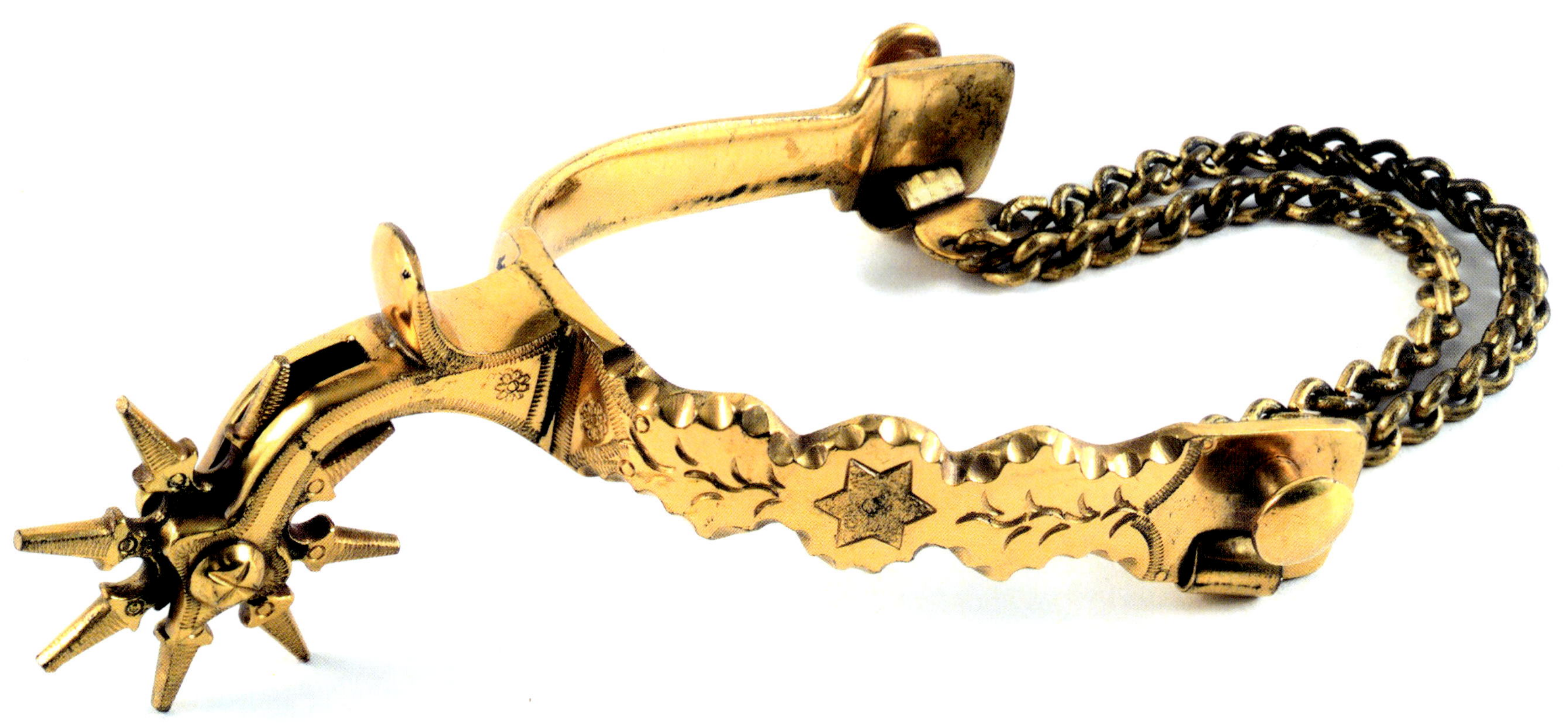

August Buermann Mfg. Co., Newark, New Jersey
Drop-shank spurs of "Hercules Bronze" alloy with chap guards, heel chains, stationary buttons, and sculpted heel bands incised with vine and Star of David motifs
BUFFALO BILL HISTORICAL CENTER, CODY, WYOMING

the mid-1890s, he had moved his shop to Gainesville, Texas, and was specializing in such goods. In order to expand and speed production to meet a growing demand for his products, McChesney employed additional mechanics, developed ornamental dies, and installed drill presses and other laborsaving machinery.

Design, however, was McChesney's forte, and it was largely this ability that enabled the craftsman to make the successful transition from lone blacksmith to large-scale operator. An amateur oil painter attuned to nature, McChesney adorned his best bits and spurs with flowing vines, elongated flamingos, proud peacocks, and other unusual motifs. The shanks of his spurs sometimes took on the outlines of shapely "gal-legs" and graceful goosenecks, although who originated these popular patterns is still the subject of debate. Whatever the case, McChesney often enhanced the visual impact of his designs by combining different metals and incorporating colored stones. He endowed the tail fan of his famous peacock pattern, for example, with synthetic gems resembling rubies and emeralds.

"I design every one of my spurs myself and copy nobody," McChesney crowed in an early trade catalog. "I always lead and let the imitator follow." [72] Many did and the Texas smith's unique patterns were soon widely copied by competitors. At least one of McChesney's customers, Kansas City saddle maker C. S. Shipley, marked the Texas maker's distinctive but unidentified products as his own.

Thanks to abundant talent and a single-minded approach to his craft, J. R. McChesney became the most influential bit and spur maker in the West between 1900 and 1920. Only the August Buermann Mfg. Co. of Newark, which copied McChesney's designs with abandon, surpassed his production figures. "I try to be nothing but a bit and spur maker," McChesney once confessed. "I think about nothing else, dream of nothing else and do nothing else." [73]

To expose his product line to the widest possible market McChesney issued his first trade catalog in 1906. That year an earthquake and fire destroyed much of San Francisco, including several major West Coast suppliers of bits and spurs. McChesney briefly flirted with the idea of adding California-style equipment to his inventory and even visited the state to observe the production process. He concluded, however, that the complexities involved in producing such ornate goods did not justify the expense nor fit his increasingly mechanized production scheme.

G. S. Garcia. Elko, Nevada
Two-piece silver-inlaid drop-shank spurs with chap guards, sculpted heel bands with heart motif, and jinglebobs hanging from rowel pins, c. 1920
FLEISCHER COLLECTION, SCOTTSDALE

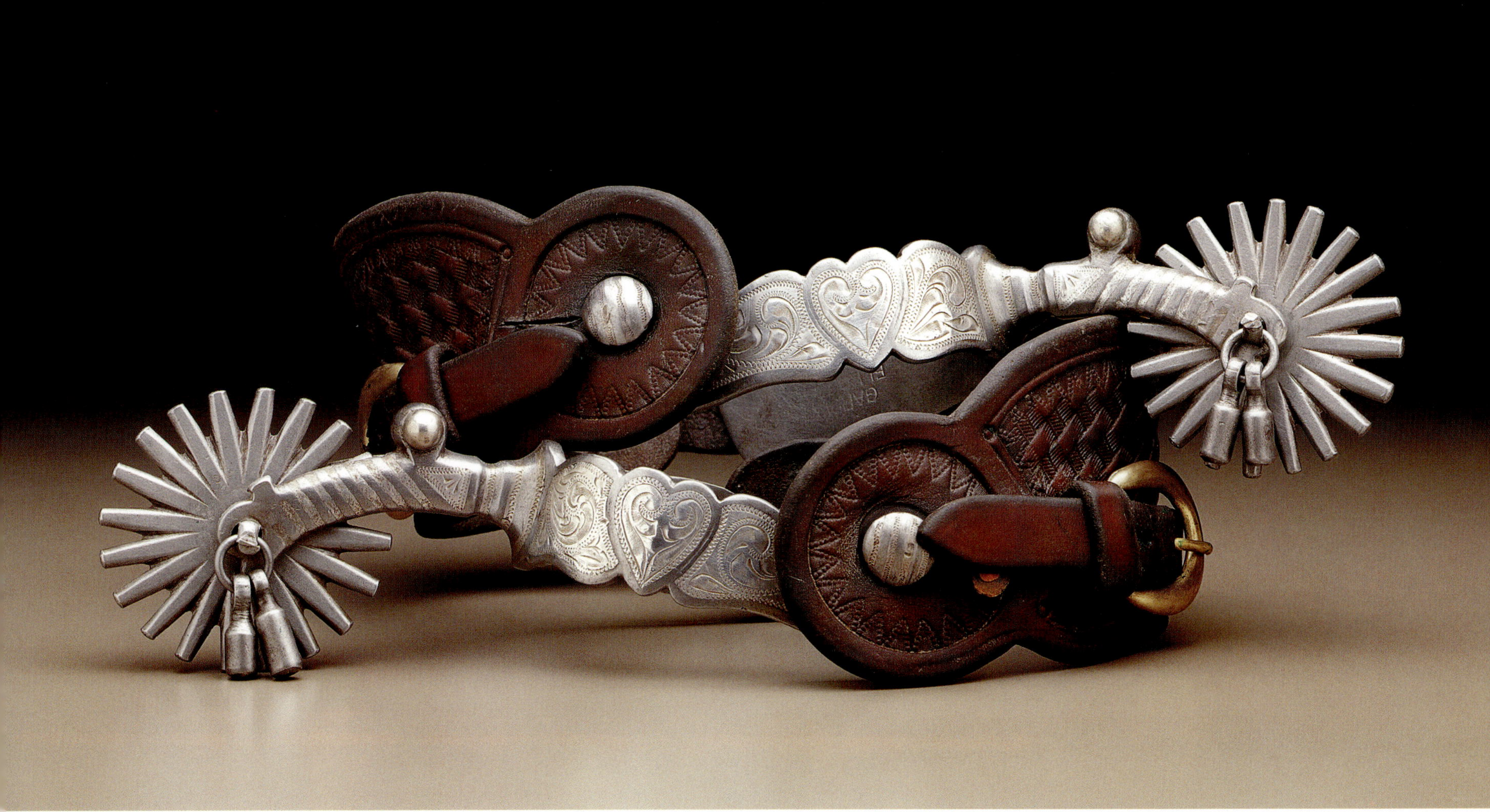

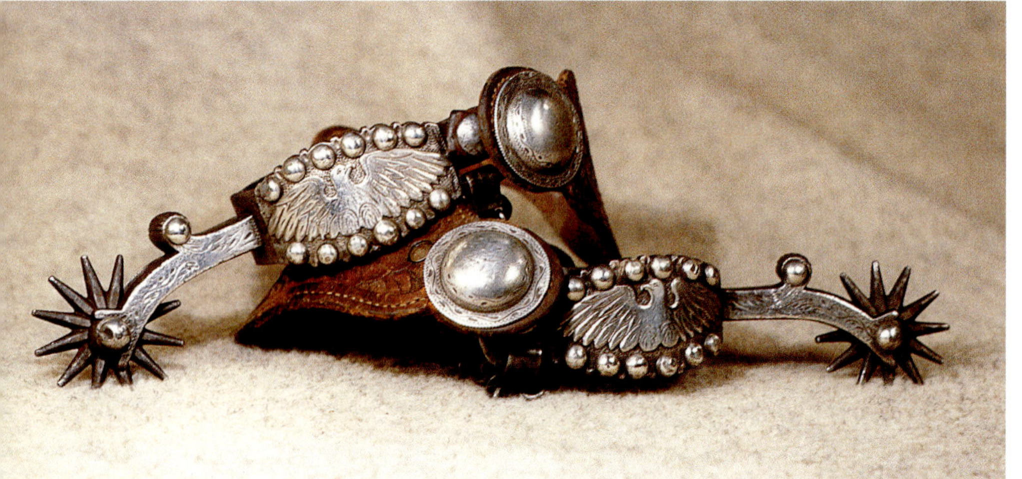

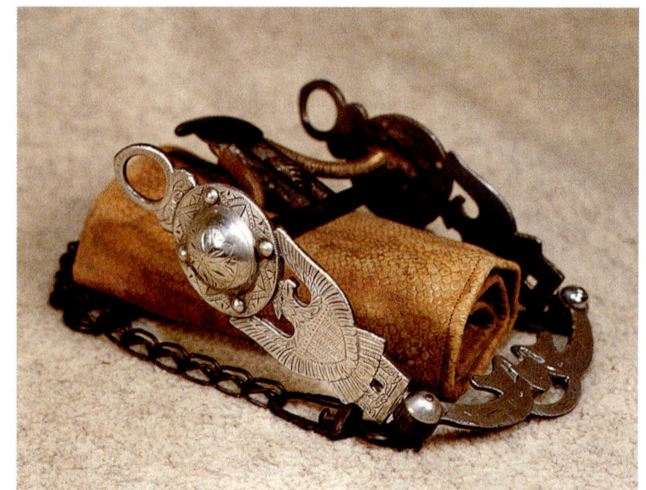

G. S. Garcia, Elko, Nevada
Above left: silver-inlaid drop-shank spurs with eagle motif on heel bands; above right: spade bit with eagle motif on cheeks; right: silver-inlaid drop-shank spurs with sculpted heel bands, with engraved rabbit motif, all c. 1915–25
WYLIE BUCHANAN COLLECTION, WASHINGTON, D.C.

Opposite
Top left: Jesus M. Tapia, Los Angeles
California-pattern drop-shank spurs, silver-inlaid with sculpted and filigreed heel bands, c. 1920
Other items: Jose or Jesus M. Tapia, Los Angeles
Top right: California-style spurs, silver-inlaid with sculpted heel band and fish motif on one side and straight heel band with silver-inlaid panels on other side; silver rowel covers; and Tapia-made conchas on spur leathers, c. 1890s; below left: ring bit, coin-silver–inlaid with gold accents on floral ornaments, c. 1900; below right: bridle bit with engraved silver concha and eagle and shield motif on cheeks
WYLIE BUCHANAN COLLECTION, WASHINGTON, D.C.

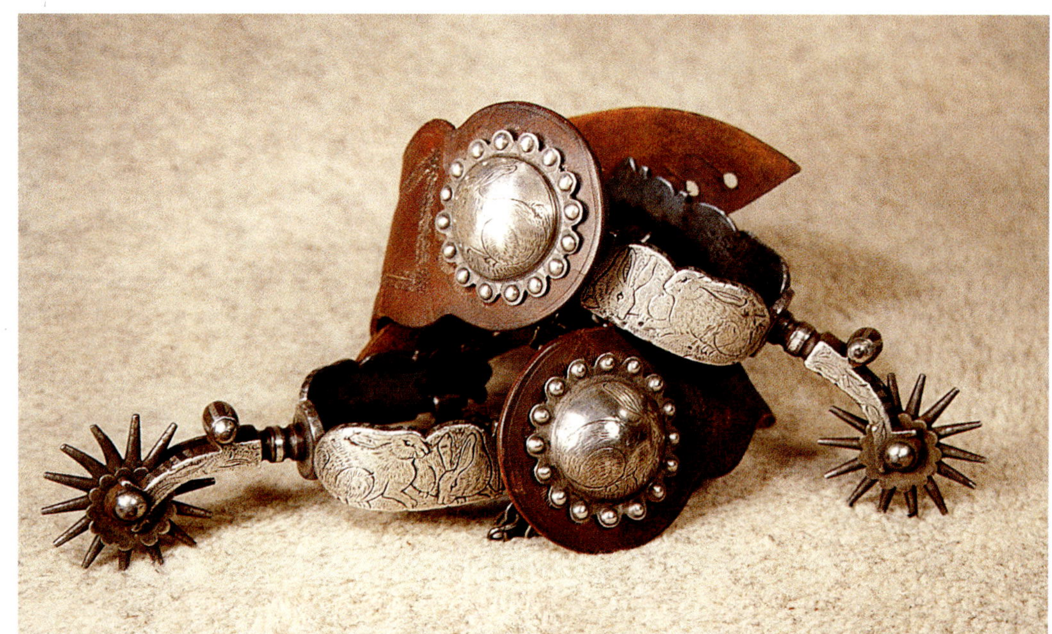

After two decades in Texas, a dispute with the town of Gainesville caused McChesney to relocate his operation to Pauls Valley, Oklahoma, in 1910. The move cost him the services of several key foundry men, including G. A. Bischoff, who launched his own bit and spur operation in Gainesville and began to produce his own versions of many of his former employer's familiar patterns. In 1915 C. S. Shipley bought Bischoff's shop and moved it to Kansas City.

At Pauls Valley, meanwhile, McChesney hired Pascal M. Kelly as shop foreman. The young Texas blacksmith had been forging one-piece spurs in his own shop since 1903, most recently in the town of Hansford, in the Texas Panhandle. Kelly had long admired his new boss's artistry, had visited his Gainesville operation, and had even filled some of his own back orders with McChesney-made products.

Talented and ambitious, Kelly stayed with McChesney less than a year but long enough to gain an understanding of how a large-scale bit and spur plant

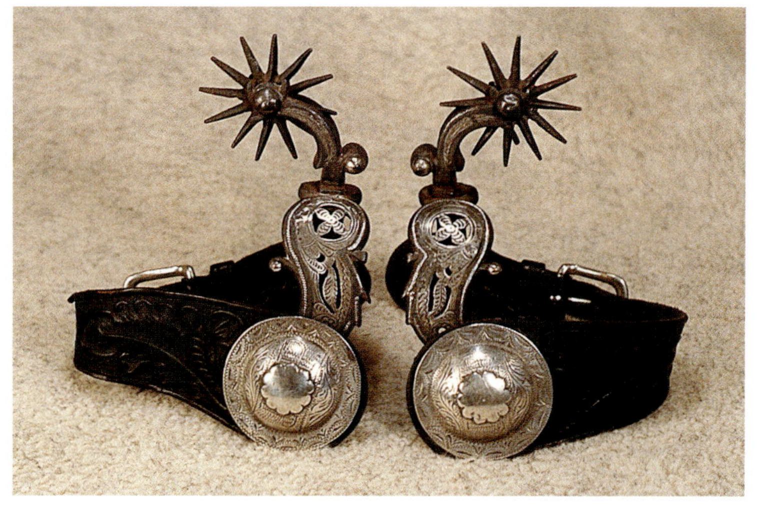

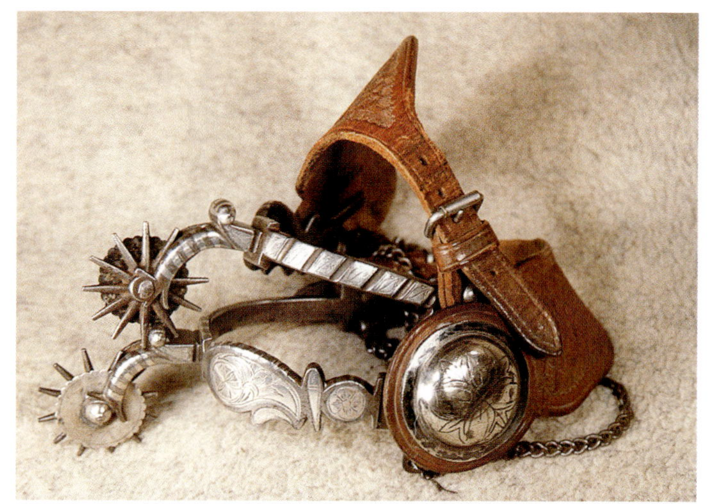

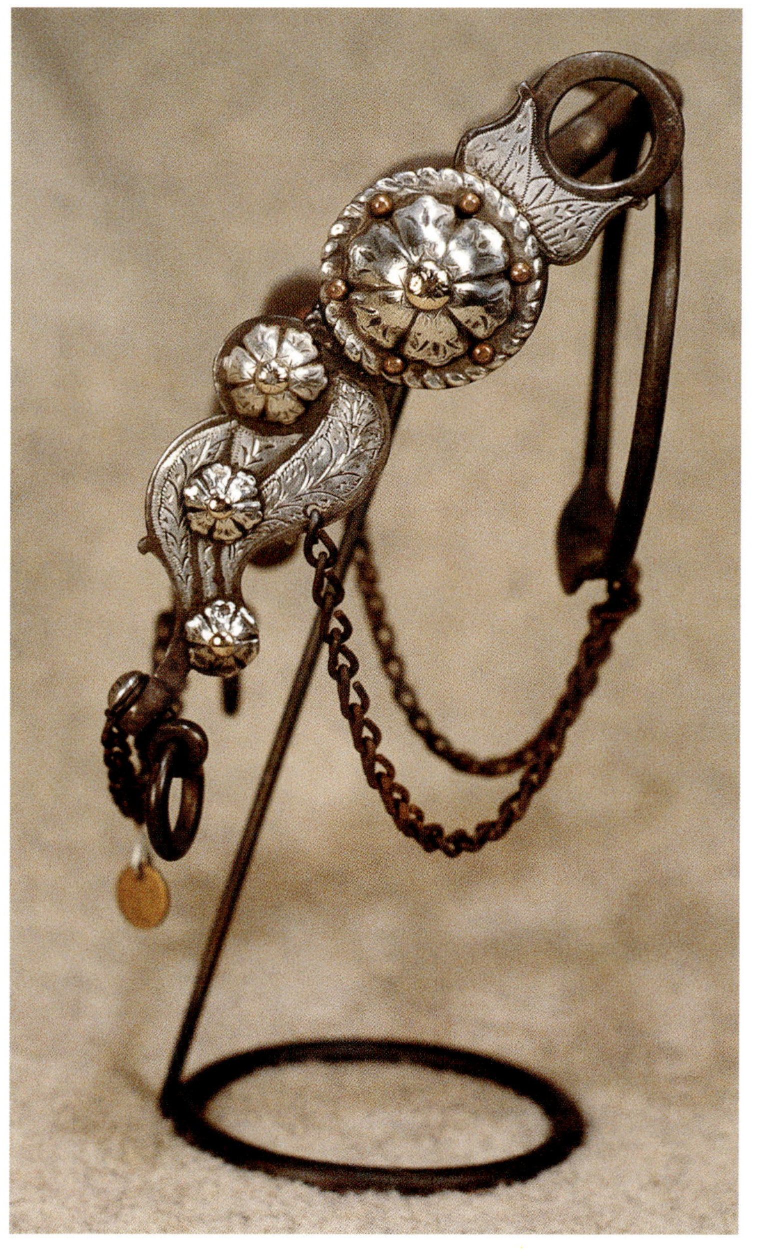

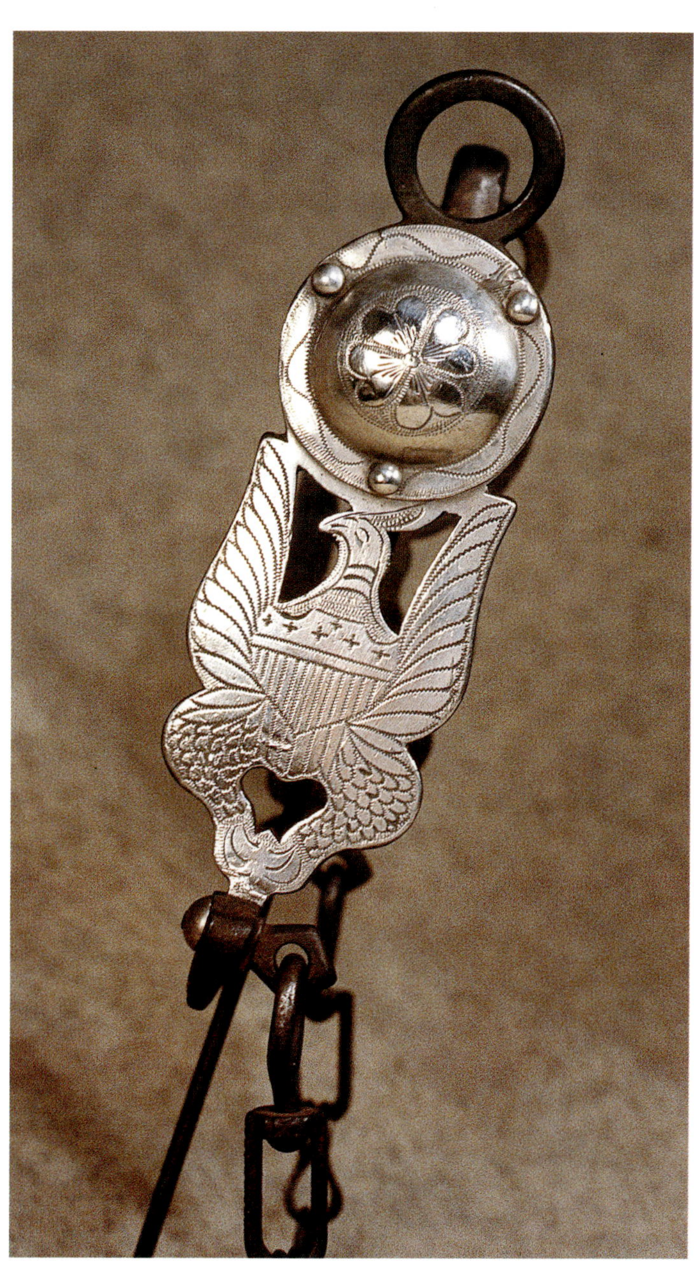

Qualey Brothers, Joseph, Idaho Below: single-mounted drop-shank woman's spurs with rodetes and sculpted and engraved Cheyenne-style heel bands with shield motif, made for Alma Qualey, c. 1930; opposite: cowboy spurs with silver overlay and inlay, domed spots, and card suit pattern engraving, c. 1920s
WYLIE BUCHANAN COLLECTION, WASHINGTON, D.C.

operated. Armed with this knowledge, Kelly opened his own shop at Dalhart, Texas, in 1911, in partnership with two brothers and another former McChesney hand, Clyde Parker. The firm Kelly Brothers and Parker employed several other ex-McChesney craftsmen including P. M. Kelly's brother-in-law Tom Johnson Jr., the son of a Texas spur maker.

Following McChesney's lead, Kelly turned his inventive genius toward developing new tools to mechanize the spur-making process. Soon a relentless punch press replaced muscle-powered hacksaws in the production of spur rowels, and a roller mill reduced the time and effort required to hammer out heel bands by

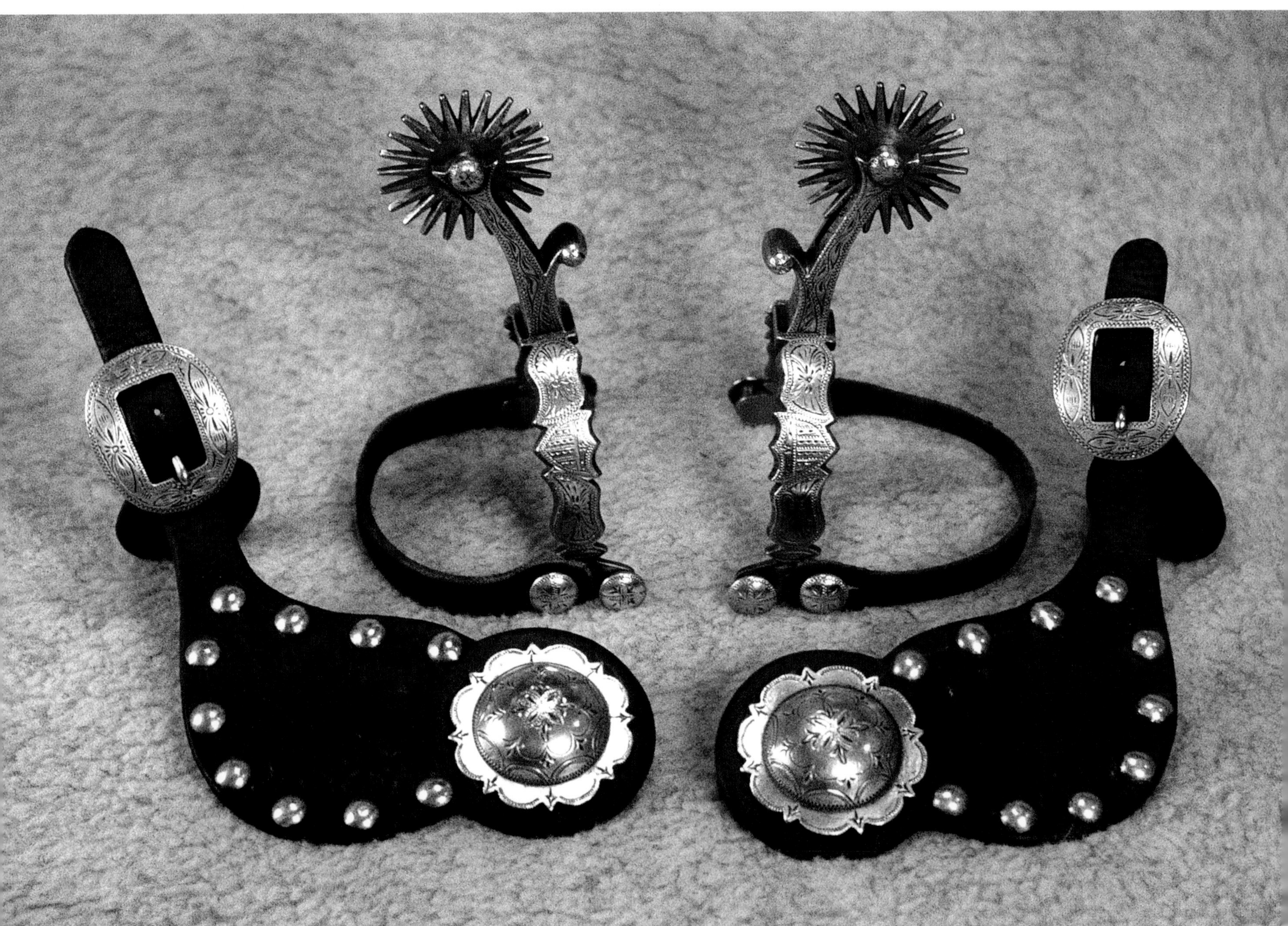

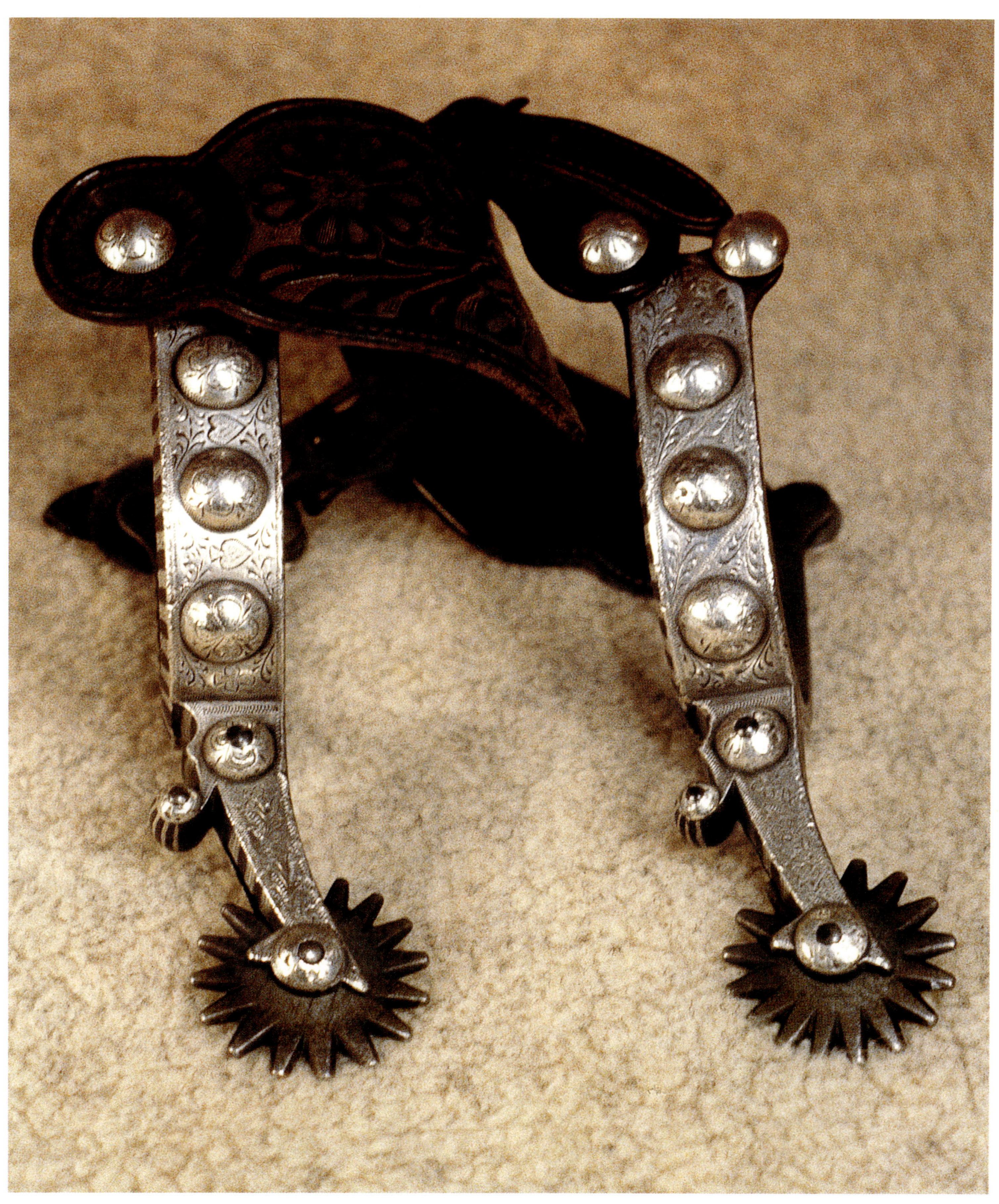

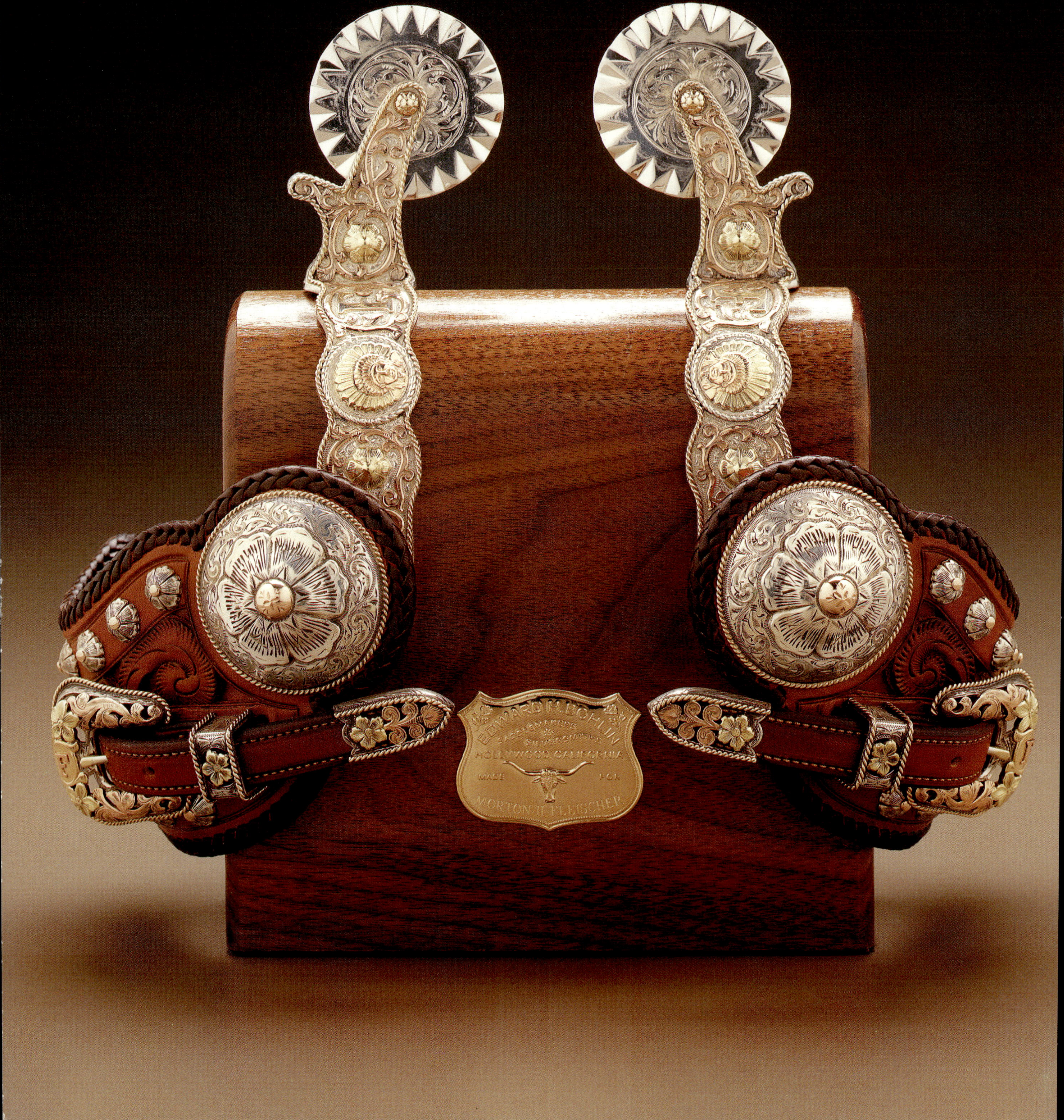
EDWARD H. BOHLIN
SADDLEMAKERS
&
SILVERSMITHS
HOLLYWOOD, CALIFORNIA
MADE FOR
MORTON H. FLEISCHER

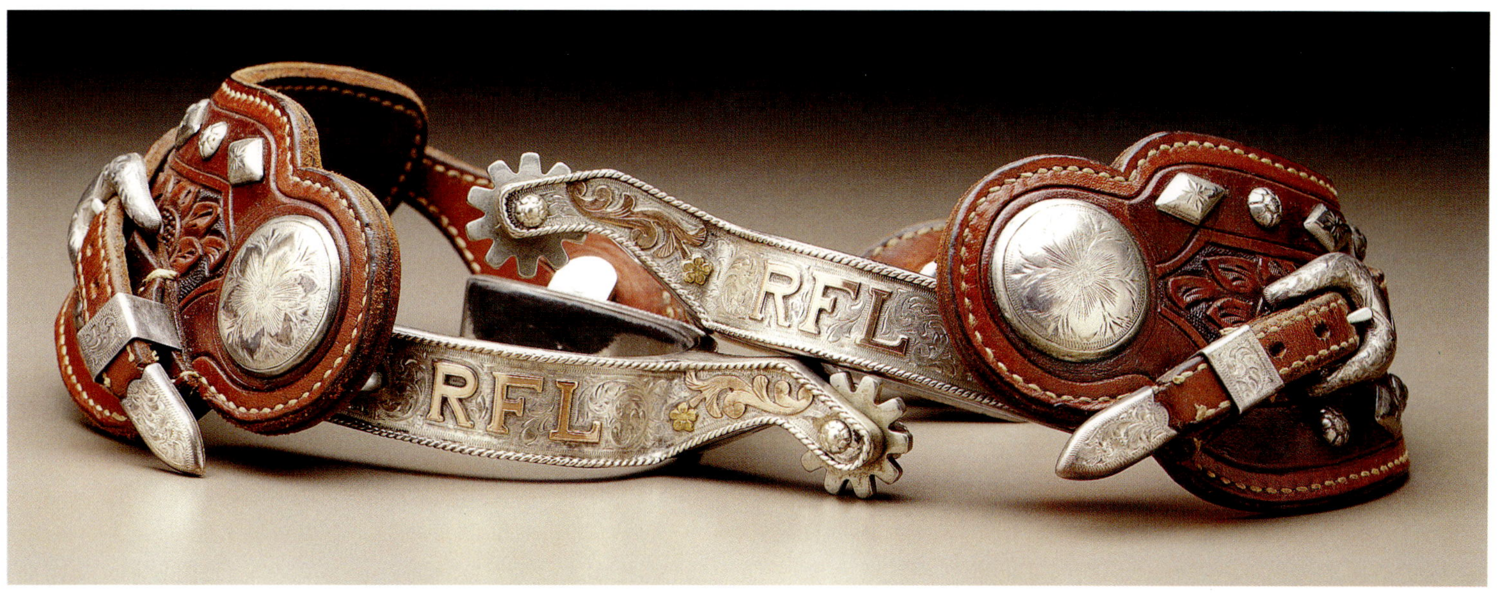

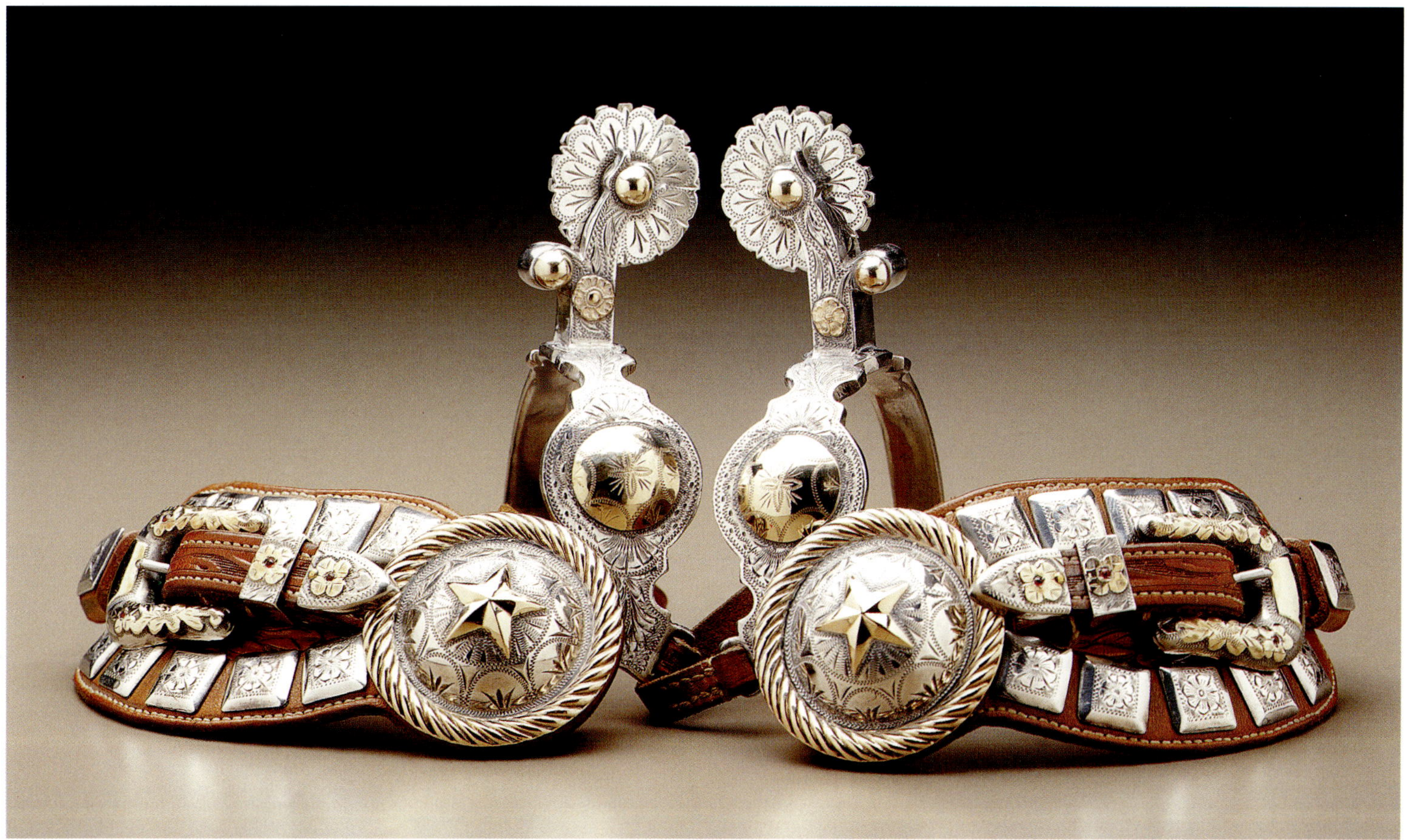

Opposite
Modern Bohlin Co. spurs, sterling silver and multicolored gold overlay, sculpted heel bands with chap guards, owner's initials and Indian head concha, rope style edge trim throughout, spur leathers with floral engraved conchas and spots, and three-piece silver and gold buckles
FLEISCHER COLLECTION, SCOTTSDALE

Above
Top: Edward H. Bohlin, Hollywood Spurs with raised shanks, silver-overlaid and engraved heel bands with owner initials and wire edge trim, and stamped leathers with three-piece silver buckles and engraved silver spots and conchas

Bottom: Olson-Nolte, San Francisco Drop-shank parade spurs with chap guards, engraved rowels, and sculpted heel bands with silver overlay with gold accents; silver mounted spur leathers with engraved panels, three-piece silver buckles, and conchas with gold rope edges and center star motif, c. 1940s
FLEISCHER COLLECTION, SCOTTSDALE

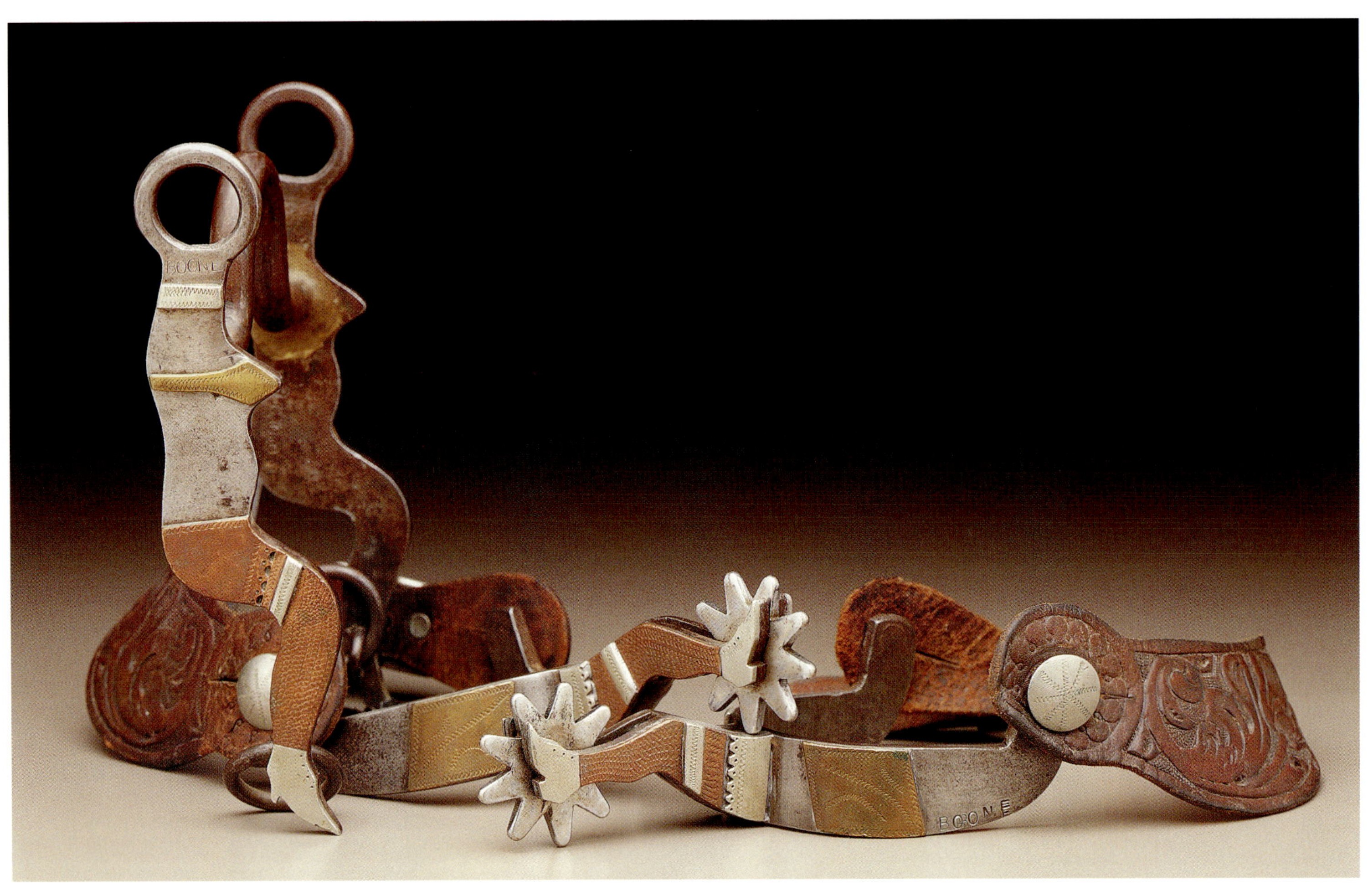
BOONE
BOONE

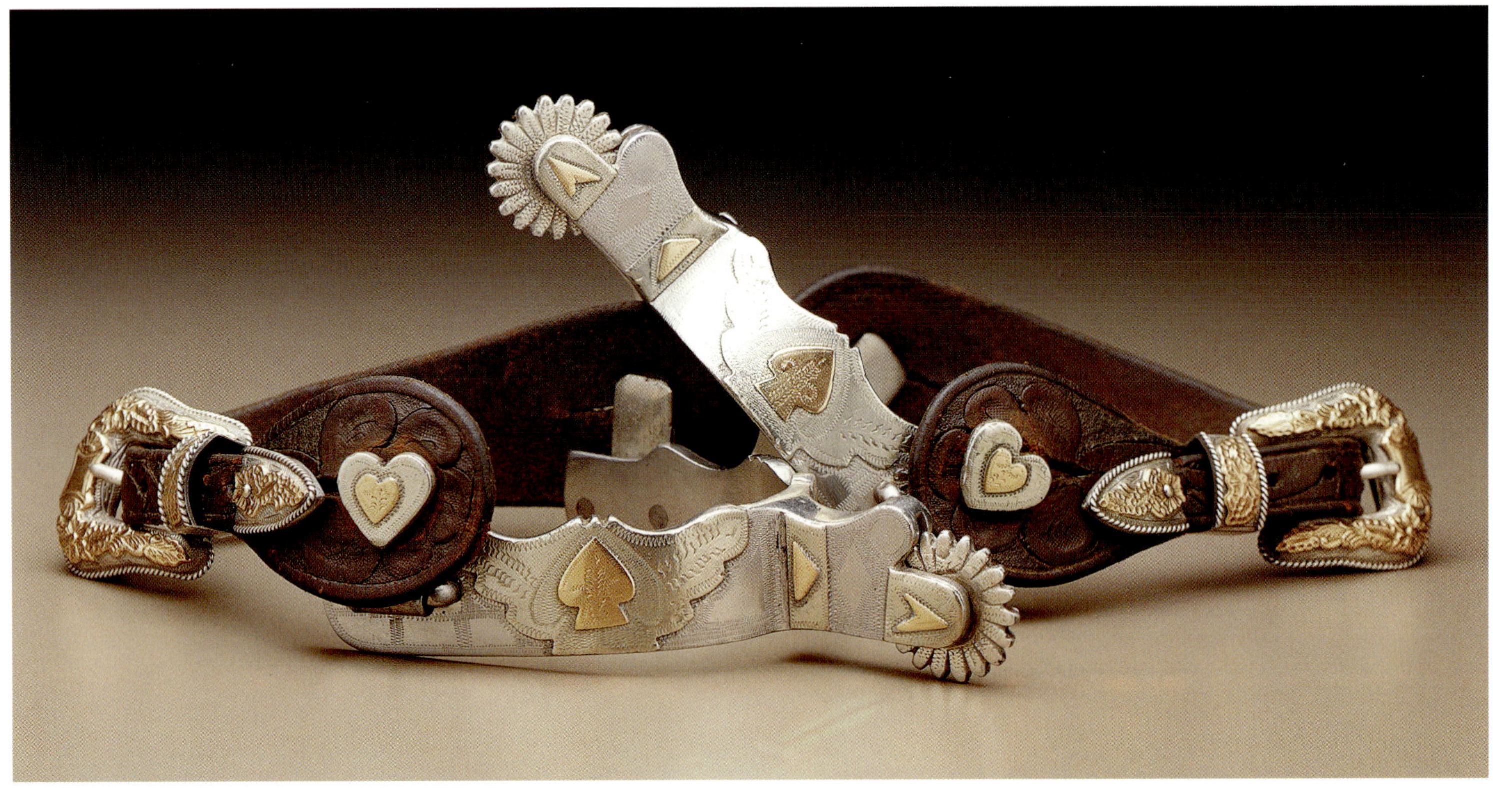

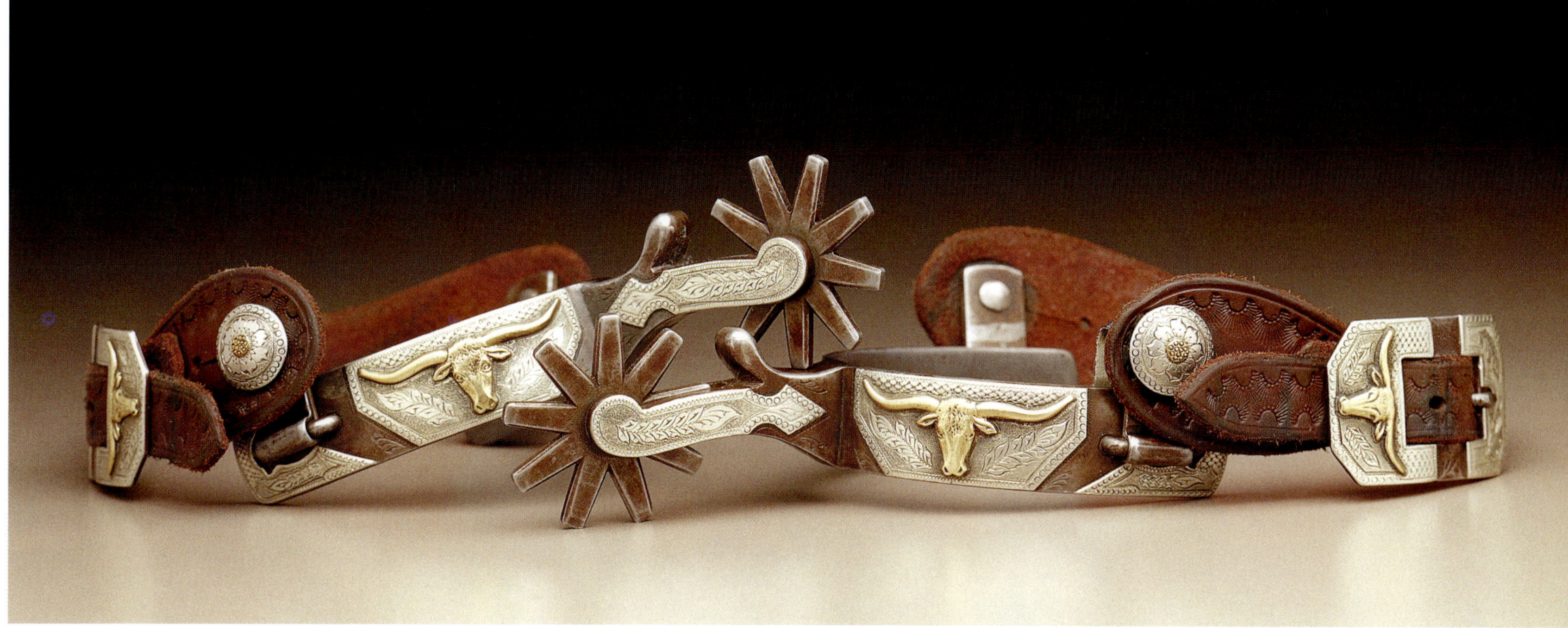

hand. Machines die cut decorative overlays and covered spur buttons in a fraction of the time and with greater accuracy than handwork. And while craftsmen still soldered the ornaments in place, Kelly invented a machine to adorn them with rudimentary engraving.

P. M. Kelly's penchant for innovation made him a formidable competitor. On the eve of World War I, the Dalhart maker showed some design prowess as well by introducing a larger, heavier style of spurs reminiscent of popular Mexican patterns of the period. His new models sold well for more than a decade and forced his rivals to respond in kind.

To meet the mounting challenge posed by their competitors on the Great Plains, California makers began producing one-piece Texas-style bits and spurs of their own. The Visalia Saddle Co., among others, offered more than a dozen such patterns at prices from $1.50 to $2.50 higher than two-piece West Coast varieties.

There was fresh cause for concern when the August Buermann Mfg. Co., introduced new rustproof metal alloys trademarked "Hercules Bronze" and "Star Steel Silver" and a hand-forged bit and spur line that imitated many popular California patterns. "This western country," the Visalia company grumbled,

> is flooded with imitation California Bits and Spurs made in Eastern factories by men who probably have never seen a cowboy except in moving pictures, and have not the least idea of how these goods are used. In California these goods were originated and developed, and all our work is made right here by experienced native California bit and spur makers, who know what is wanted and how to make it.[74]

Opposite, above
W. R. "Wallie" Boone, San Angelo, Texas
Bridle bit with "gal-leg"–pattern cheeks and matching spurs, c. 1930s
Fleischer Collection, Scottsdale

Opposite, below
W. R. "Wallie" Boone, San Angelo, Texas
Gold and silver–mounted spurs with short shanks, sculpted heel bands, and raised, heart-shaped buttons, c. 1940s
Fleischer Collection, Scottsdale

Above
R. F. Ford, San Angelo, Texas
Contemporary one-piece, Texas-style spurs with raised shanks with chap guards, swinging buttons, engraved silver overlays, Longhorn motif on heel band and spur buckle, c. 1990s
Fleischer Collection, Scottsdale

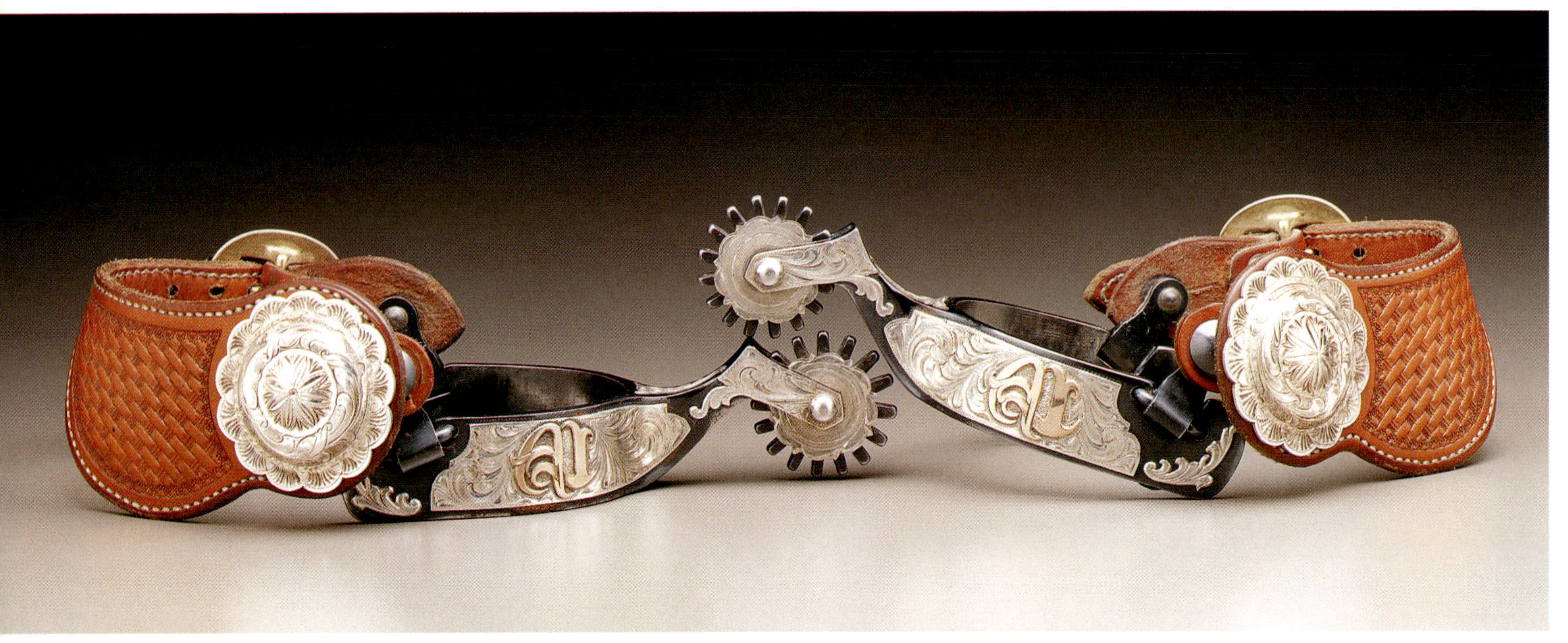

Jeremiah Watt, Coalinga, California (leatherwork only)
Contemporary spurs with large floral conchas and spur leathers with basket stamp

Similar issues faced Elko saddle maker G. S. Garcia, another large-scale producer of exceptional California-style bits and spurs. During the first two decades of the twentieth century, Garcia probably employed more talented bit and spur makers and silversmiths than any other shop in America. The roster of craftsmen included, among others, Asalio Herrera, Juan Estrada, Manuel V. Hernandez, and Miguel M. Morales, all born in Mexico; Louis Jackson, who hailed from Illinois; Martin Silverio and J. J. Bernal from California; and Thomas Jayo, from Spain. Jayo's son Julian also worked for Garcia as did engraver Susie McDonald, one of the few women working in the bit and spur trade.

Some of these individuals began their careers as apprentices of the incomparable Asalio Herrera, who joined Garcia in 1898 after a long stint with D. E. Walker in Visalia. The son of an ironworker, Herrera headed Garcia's bit and spur shop for two decades. Many of the master's protégés and colleagues later staffed other West Coast and Great Basin shops or established their own operations in such cities as San Francisco, Los Angeles, Portland, and Cheyenne. Both together and individually they further enriched the already illustrious California bit and spur tradition.

With the U.S. entry into World War I in 1917, money, supplies, and credit became scarce. Bits and spurs were subject to a 5 percent war tax, and the rapidly escalating price of labor, steel, and other raw materials caused makers to cease catalog pricing and to begin quoting the cost of finished goods at the time they were ordered. When describing their products, patriotic bit and spur makers ceased referring to German silver, calling it nickel silver or white brass instead.

Several bit and spur makers lent their metalworking talents to the war effort. J. R. McChesney, for example, secured a government contract to supply spurs for the U.S. Cavalry. P. M. Kelly found work in a West Coast shipyard, as did a young Pawhuska, Oklahoma, bit and spur maker named Oscar Crockett, who would become one of the largest spur makers in the West in the 1930s and 1940s. A native of Pecos City, Texas, and a former cowboy, Crockett had come to Oklahoma from Kansas City where he had spent six years as a wagon maker and loriner.

The postwar era proved tumultuous for Crockett and his contemporaries as automobiles increasingly replaced horses as the principal mode of transportation and a depression in the cattle business in the early 1920s cut into the cowboy market for bits and spurs. In 1926 aging foundryman August Buermann, by then the largest manufacturer of cowboy bits and spurs in the world, sold out to his longtime competitor North and Judd of New Britain. Two years later J. R. McChesney, who had never recovered financially from the debts he incurred in fulfilling his short-lived wartime government contract, suffered a fatal heart attack. The Nocona Boot Company acquired McChesney's business the following year and moved it back to Texas.

P. M. Kelly was on the move as well. After buying out his business partner Clyde Parker in 1919, Kelly had relocated his shop from Dalhart to El Paso in 1925 in search of cheaper and more plentiful labor and materials. Oscar Crockett, meanwhile, had returned to Kansas City after World War I and, with the help of his

Wayne Dollar, Hereford, Texas
Silver-mounted spurs with swinging buttons, gooseneck shank, emerald rowel pin covers, pierced, cloverleaf rowels, and heel band and buckle overlays pierced on one side with card symbols, c. 1995
TROY L. PRICE COLLECTION, LUBBOCK, TEXAS

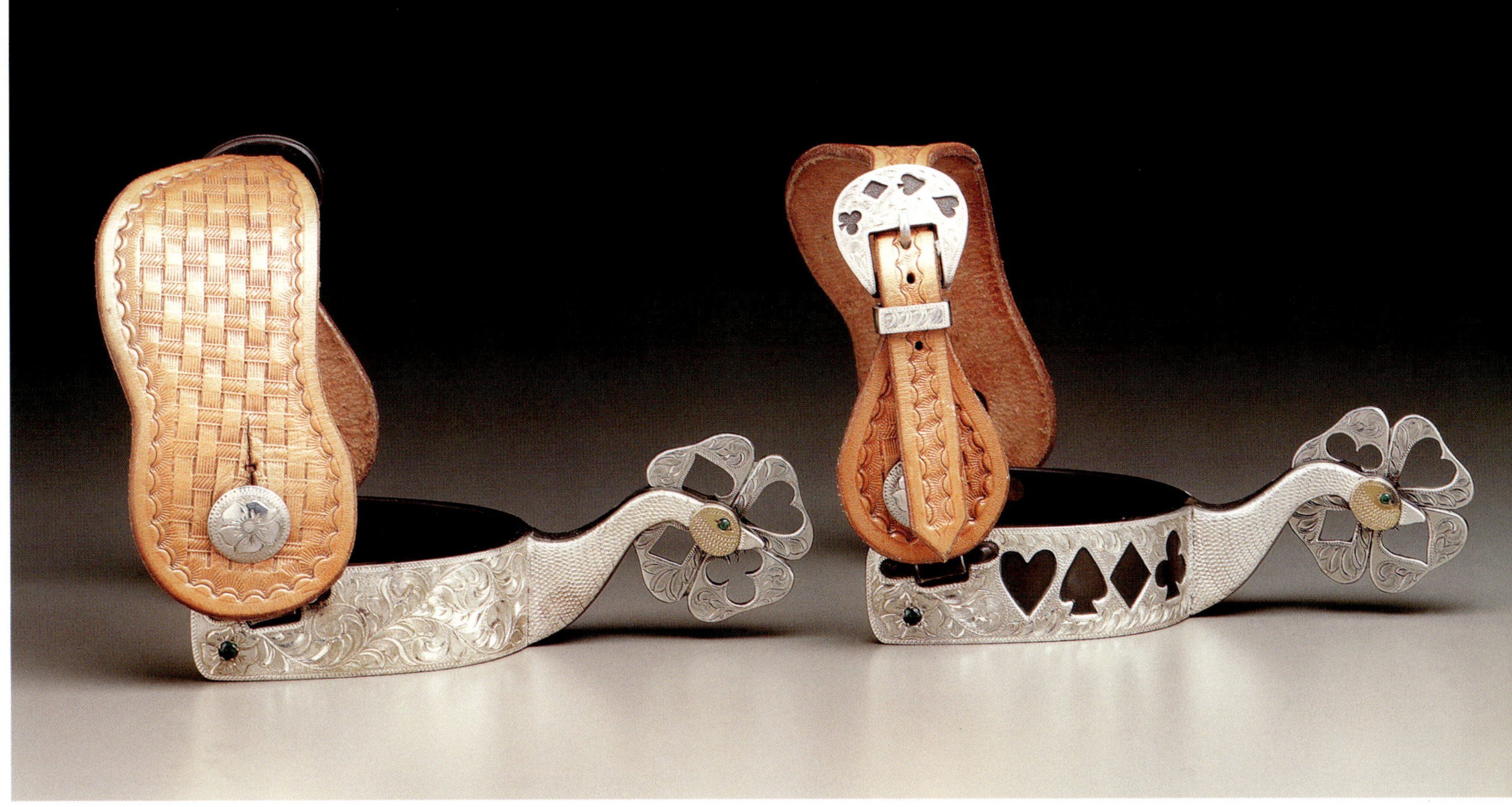

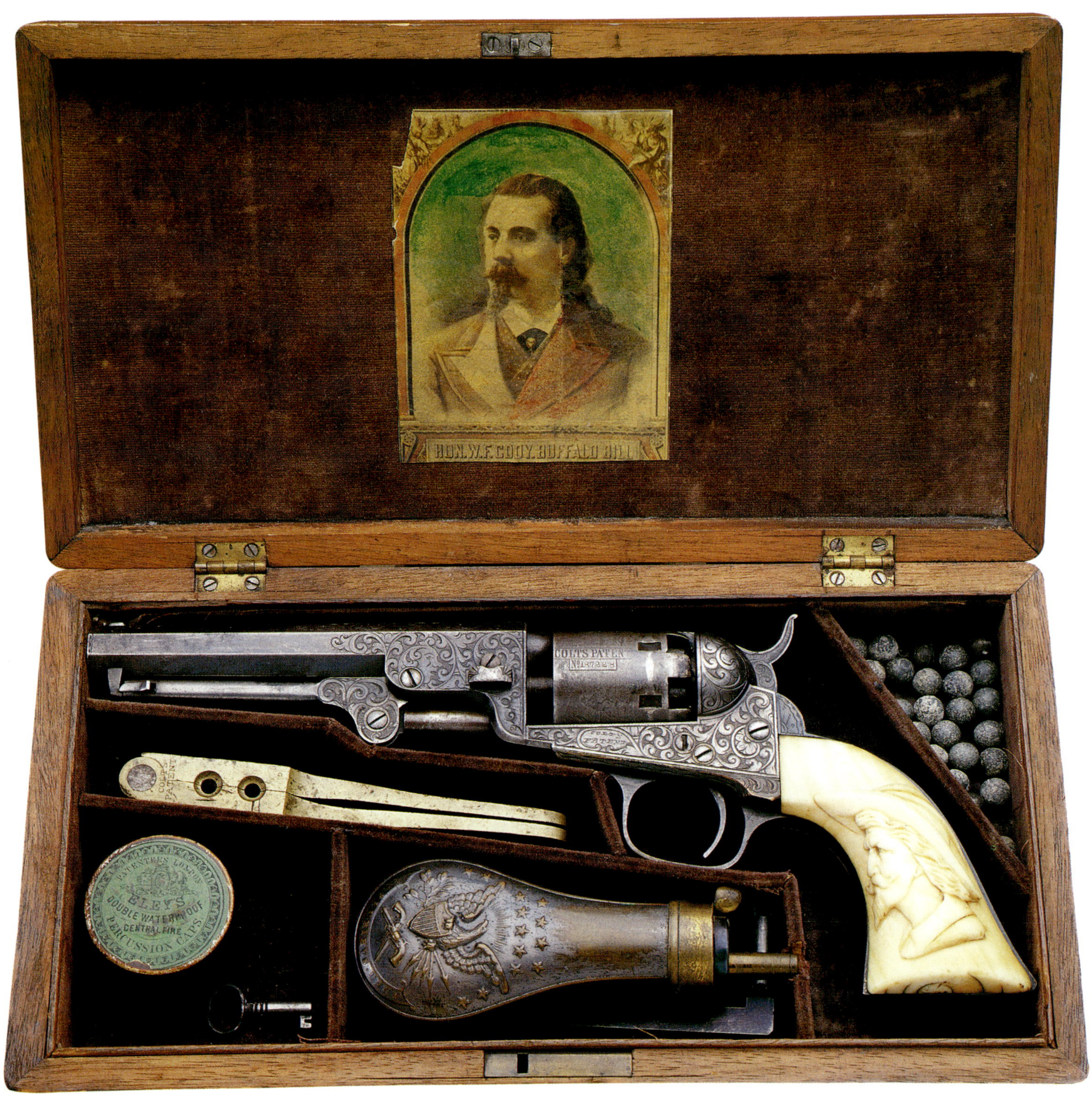

Colt's Patent Fire Arms Manufacturing Company, Hartford
Model 1849 Pocket Revolver produced c. 1861, with profile of William F.
"Buffalo Bill" Cody carved into grips; given to Cody by army scout Frank North
Buffalo Bill Historical Center, Cody, Wyoming

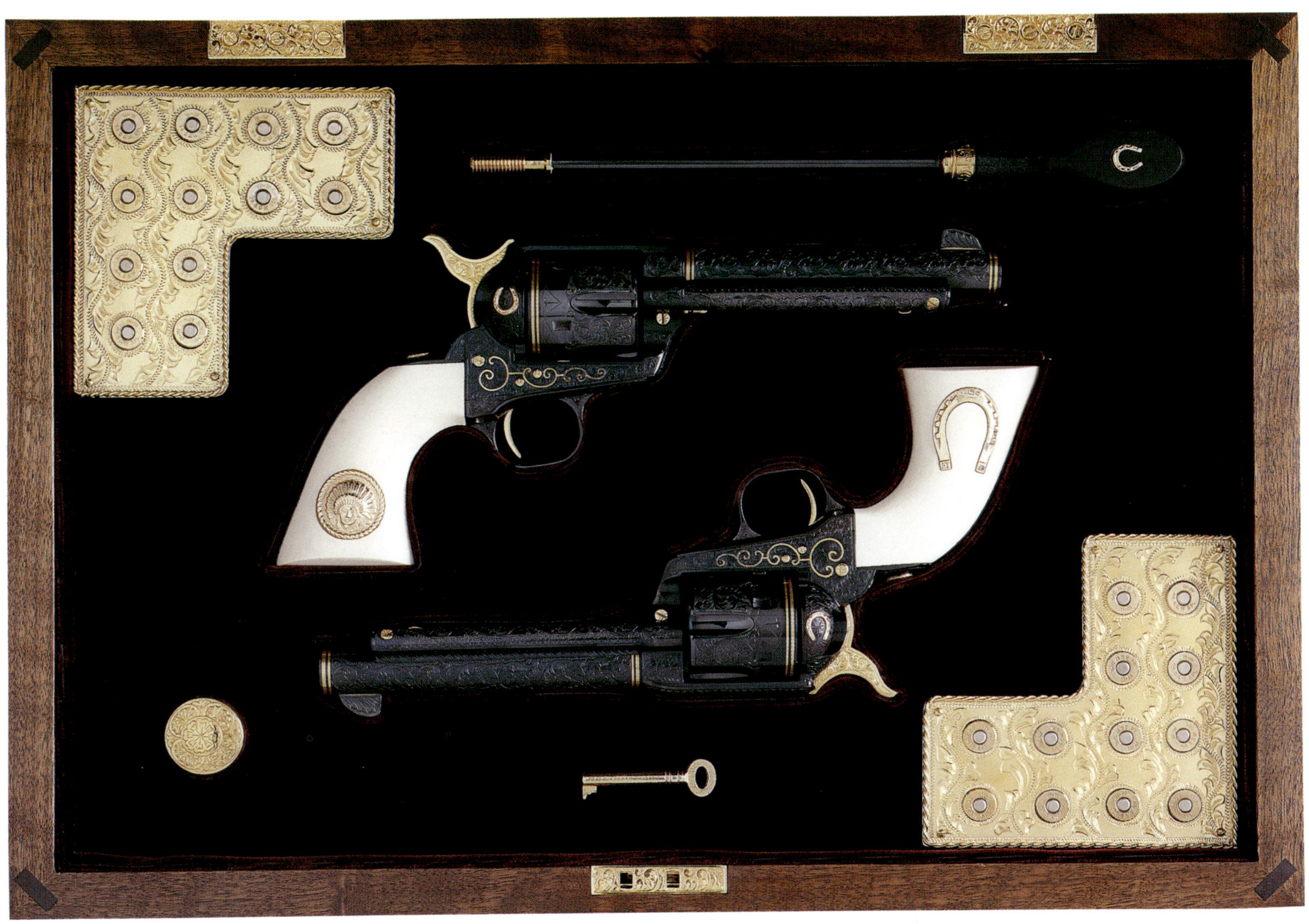

Colt's Patent Fire Arms Manufacturing Company, Hartford
Cased set of Colt Model 1873 second-generation single-action .44-caliber special army revolvers engraved by Philip Quigley, Phoenix, c. 1990s; ivory grips with gold Indian head and horseshoe inlay by the modern Bohlin Co.
Fleischer Collection, Scottsdale

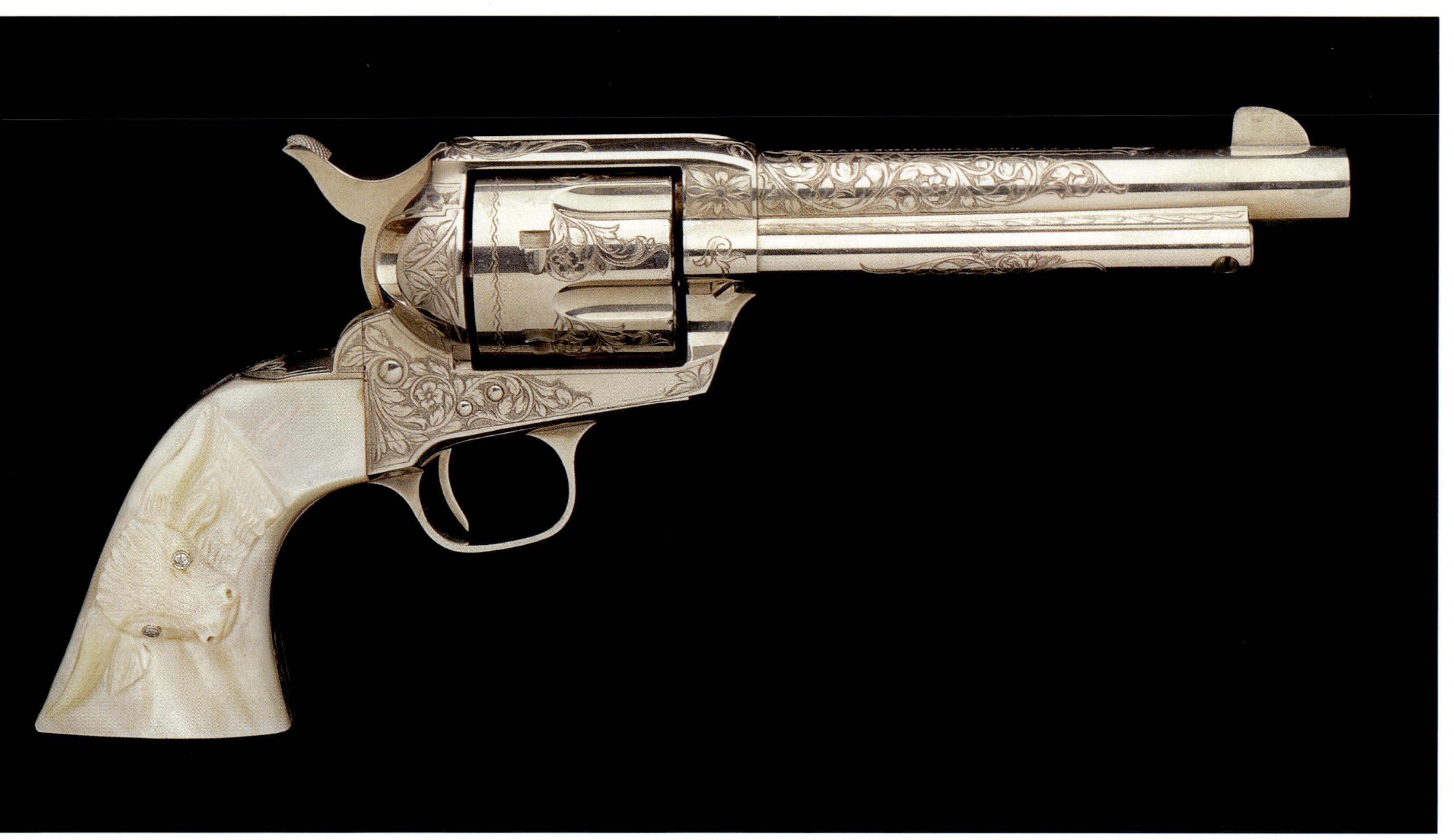

Colt's Patent Fire Arms Manufacturing Company, Hartford
Model 1873 single-action .45-caliber army revolver with steer head grips, presented to "21" Club owner Jack Kriendler by Amon Carter, c. 1950
BUFFALO BILL HISTORICAL CENTER, CODY, WYOMING

uncle, had bought saddle maker C. S. Shipley's Kansas City bit and spur shop. By 1927, Crockett was operating on his own and finding a niche in the marketplace.

Although large-scale makers with mechanized production lines and well-established sources of distribution continued to dominate the western bit and spur market, the finely forged goods of small custom shops still appealed to choosy cowboys and eager dudes. Eddy Hulbert, a self-taught Hillsboro, Montana, blacksmith and silversmith, for example, peddled fancy spurs, buckles, and jewelry to guests on about thirty dude ranches throughout Montana and Wyoming in the 1920s. During the same period he filled orders for such prominent saddleries as Hamley's of Pendleton, Otto Ernst of Sheridan, and Fred Mueller of Denver. Like most independents, however, Hulbert was seldom identified by name in his clients' trade catalogs.

Custom bit and spur makers and silversmiths throughout the West benefited from the bull market for ornate tack fueled during the 1920s and 1930s by Hollywood cowboys, rodeo performers, and recreational riders. None, however, profited more from this phenomenon than Hollywood saddle maker Edward H. Bohlin, who offered an elegant line of bits and spurs to complement his matchless silver-mounted rigs. Motifs that inhabited Bohlin saddle silver frequently appeared on his bits and spurs as well, and were often incorporated as part of matching outfits that included chaps, vests, and gun belts. Applying the full-fitted, cased overlays that embellished Bohlin's finest bits and spurs required a higher degree of skill than soldering on run-of-the-mill metal ornaments. In the early 1930s the Bohlin shop ceased producing bits and spurs from scratch when the fire marshal prohibited the use of a forge on the premises. Thereafter, Bohlin silversmiths mounted and engraved stainless steel spur blanks forged in Oscar Crockett's Kansas shop. When the demand required it, Bohlin also contracted for the work of independent makers including the able Carlos and Jose Figueroa of Los Angeles.

In 1931 Bohlin offered spurs priced from a modest $13.50 to a whopping $650. His most expensive pair, designed for cowboy movie star and fashion plate Tom Mix, was encrusted with sterling silver and three-color gold overlays rendered in high relief in a flower and scroll design. A delicate rope edge surrounded the heel band and each chap guard was fitted with a delicate one-inch

Colt's Patent Fire Arms Manufacturing Company, Hartford
Model 1911 .45-caliber semi-automatic pistol with custom gold and silver grips made and engraved by Clint Orms, Ingram, Texas, with raised and engraved floral and bucking horse motifs and owner's initials
FLEISCHER COLLECTION, SCOTTSDALE

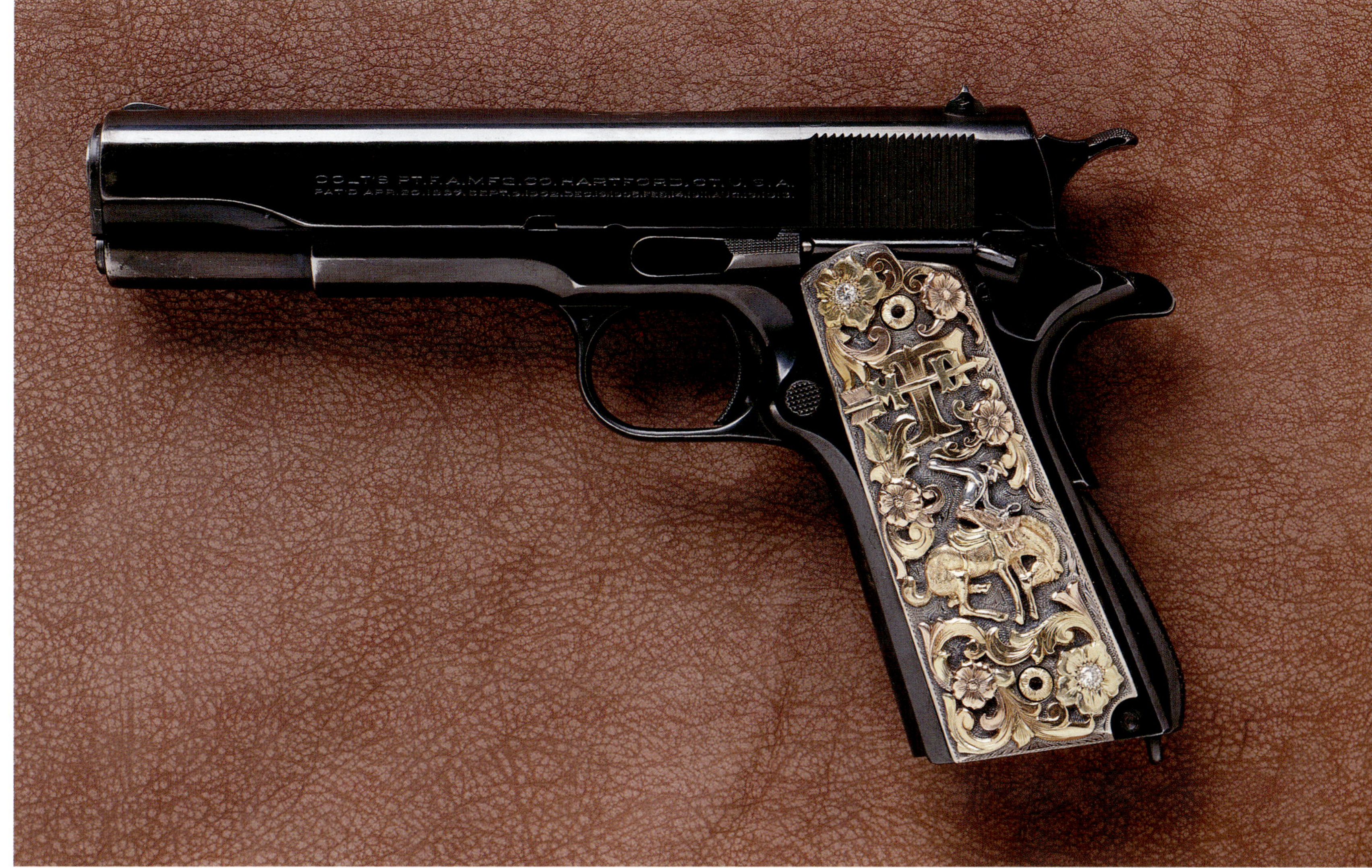

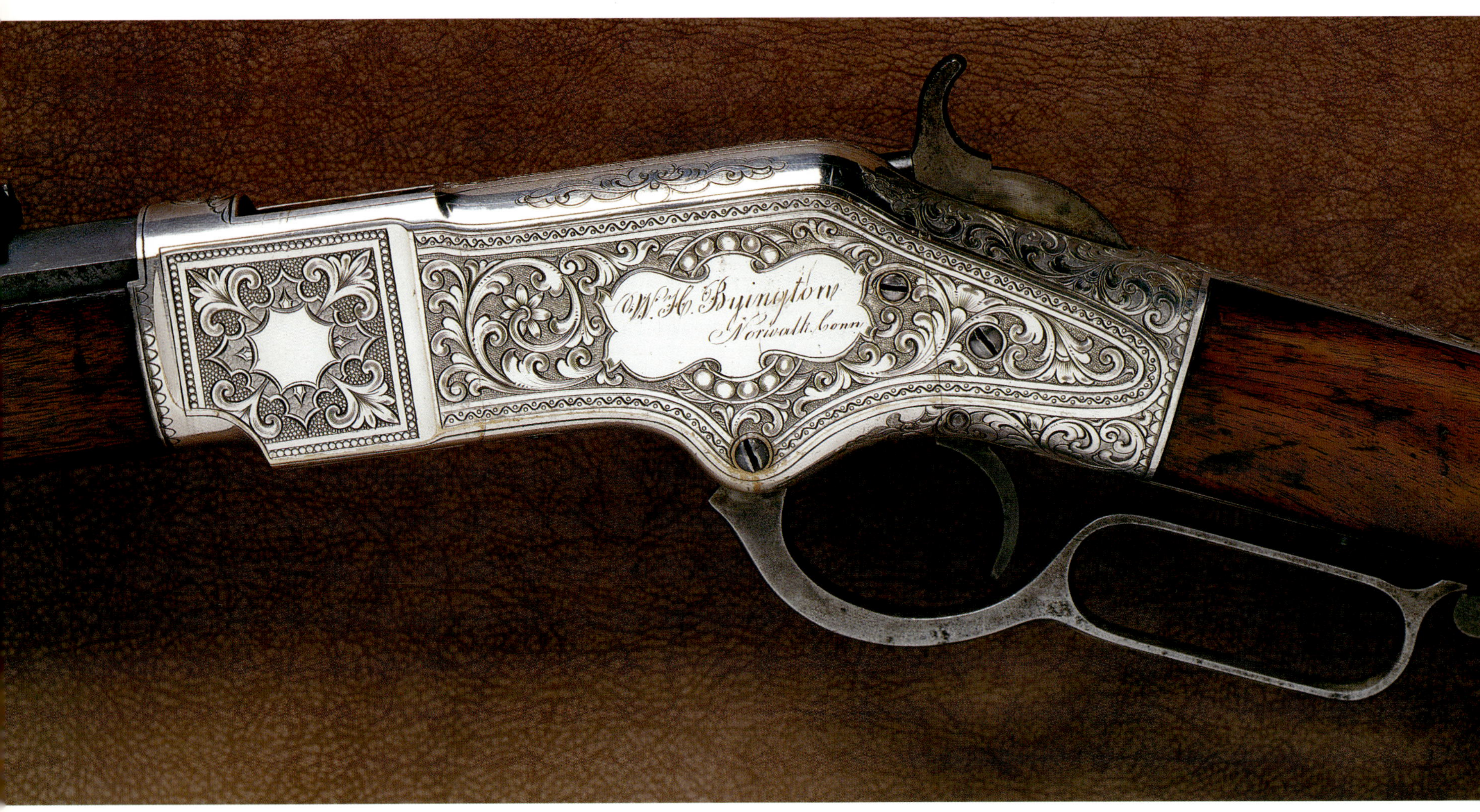

Winchester Repeating Arms Company, New Haven
Model 1866 lever action repeating rifle, detail of engraving by L. D. Nimschke
Fleischer Collection, Scottsdale

rowel. The spur maker added Mix's cattle brand to the heel bands. Matching spurs leathers costing an extra $245 a pair completed the outfit.

From the mid-1920s onward Bohlin artisans applied the same techniques used on bits and spurs to inlay and engrave firearms for actors, parade riders, and gun enthusiasts. Trade catalogs touted the company's silver inlay, almost always juxtaposed against chemically blued steel, as "the finest type . . . executed on any gun in America or any other country."[75]

The Bohlin Shop also offered several variations of heavy-gauge, floral-engraved, sterling silver grips for Colt single-action revolvers. Some types featured gold-mounted eagles, bison, steer heads, brands, and initials. Company craftsmen were equally adept at carving floral and figurative designs into wooden stocks or into ivory or mother of pearl grips, sometimes enhancing such work with ruby accents, colored enamel inlays, decorative screw plates, and gold lozenges housing the owner's initials.

Occasionally such embellishments evoked floral, scroll, and figurative motifs developed in Europe and the eastern U.S. in the nineteenth century by such talented engravers as Gustave Young, L. D. Nimschke, and the Ulrich brothers. The

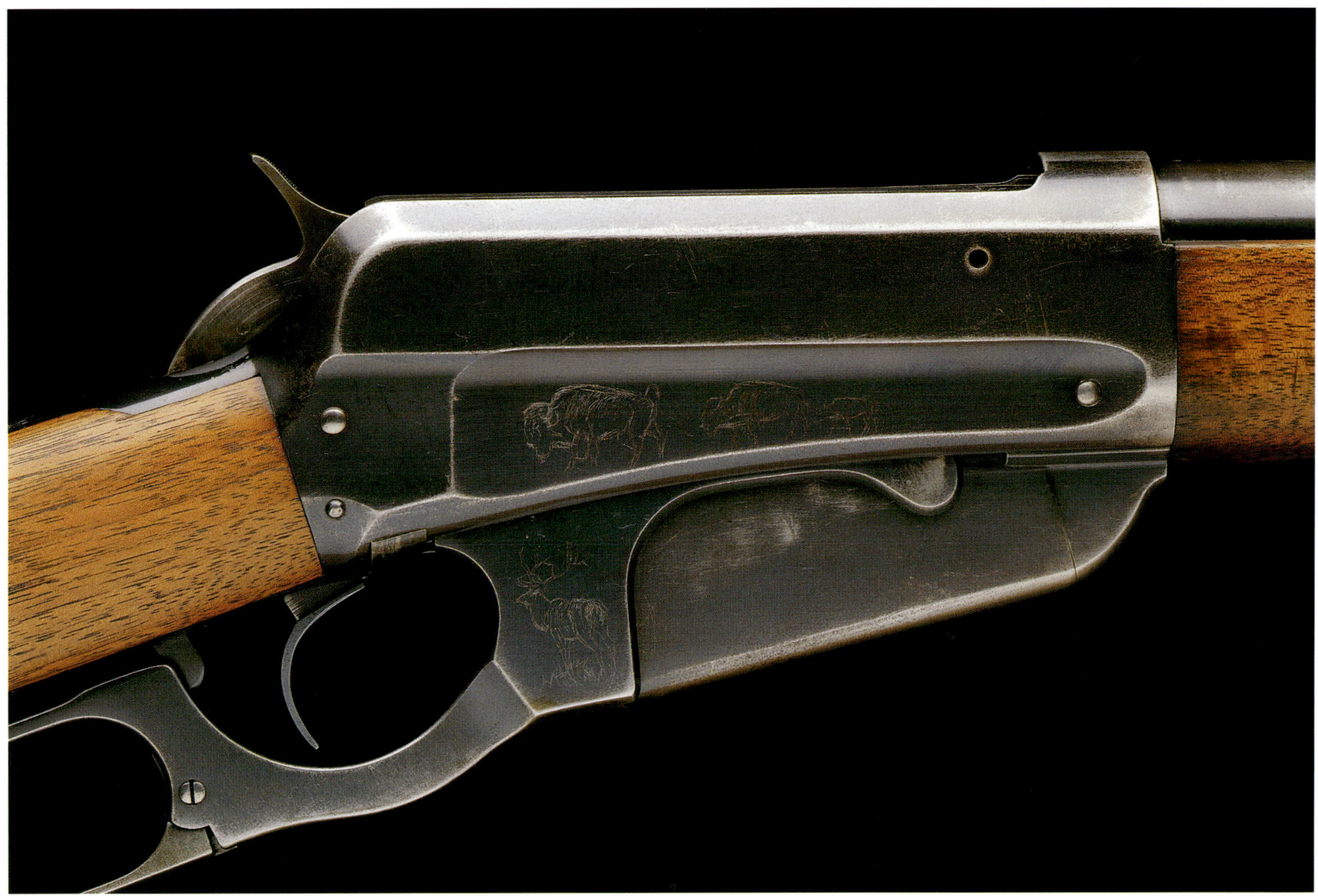

Winchester Repeating Arms Company, New Haven
Model 1895 sporting rifle, .35-caliber WCF, detail of wildlife engraving by Charles M. Russell
NATIONAL COWBOY AND WESTERN HERITAGE MUSEUM, OKLAHOMA CITY

longhorn steer head motif, for example, had been popular on carved ivory pistol grips since the open range days of the early 1880s, especially among western ranchers and lawmen. Bohlin claimed to have based his rendition on a photograph he took on the famous King Ranch in Texas.

Hunting scenes and wildlife motifs applied either at the arms factories or farmed out to independent engravers also were ubiquitous. In the nineteenth century, for example, iconic bison decorated the guns of such luminaries as Theodore Roosevelt and Buffalo Bill Cody. One of Cody's rifles bore a tableau of the frontier scout hunting the shaggy beast from horseback. Artist Charles M. Russell, a lover of western wildlife, accomplished one of the most unusual feats of firearms engraving while on a hunting trip in the mountains of Montana in 1913. Working by campfire light and using only a pocketknife, the cowboy artist deftly etched bison, bear, and other animal figures on the frame of his companion's hunting rifle, then passed the weapon back to his friend with the comment that henceforth fresh meat would always be " 'in sight.' "[76]

Most full-time firearms engravers were highly skilled specialists, however, and for most western bit and spur makers, gun engraving was rarely more than an

Winchester Repeating Arms Company, New Haven Model 1895 .30-06–caliber sporting rifle, factory engraved by Phillip Kundtz, presented to western writer Zane Gray by Winchester, February 28, 1924 (above), with detail of gold initials and engraving (below)
BUFFALO BILL HISTORICAL CENTER, CODY, WYOMING
DONATED IN LOVING MEMORY OF ROBERT JESSE MOORE BY HIS FAMILY

Opposite, above
Marlin Fire Arms Company, New Haven, Connecticut Engraved presentation Model 1893 rifle presented to Annie Oakley, c. 1917, detail of floral and animal engraving and checkered stock
BUFFALO BILL HISTORICAL CENTER, CODY, WYOMING

Opposite, below
H. Krieghoff, Ulm, Germany Cased Krieghoff Model 32 over and under shotgun, detail of cowboy scenes rendered in gold, engraving by Walter Kolouch
BUFFALO BILL HISTORICAL CENTER, CODY, WYOMING

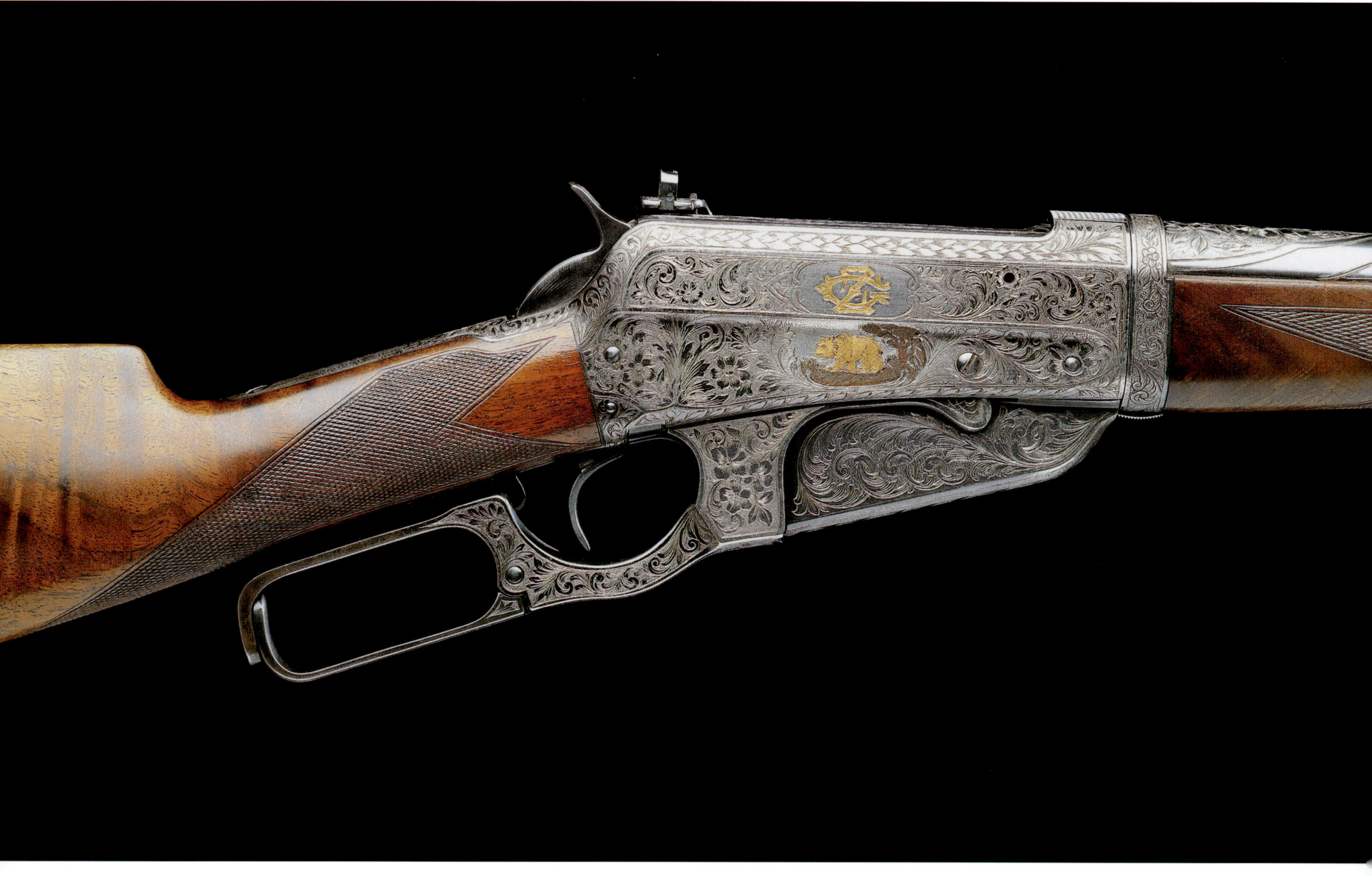

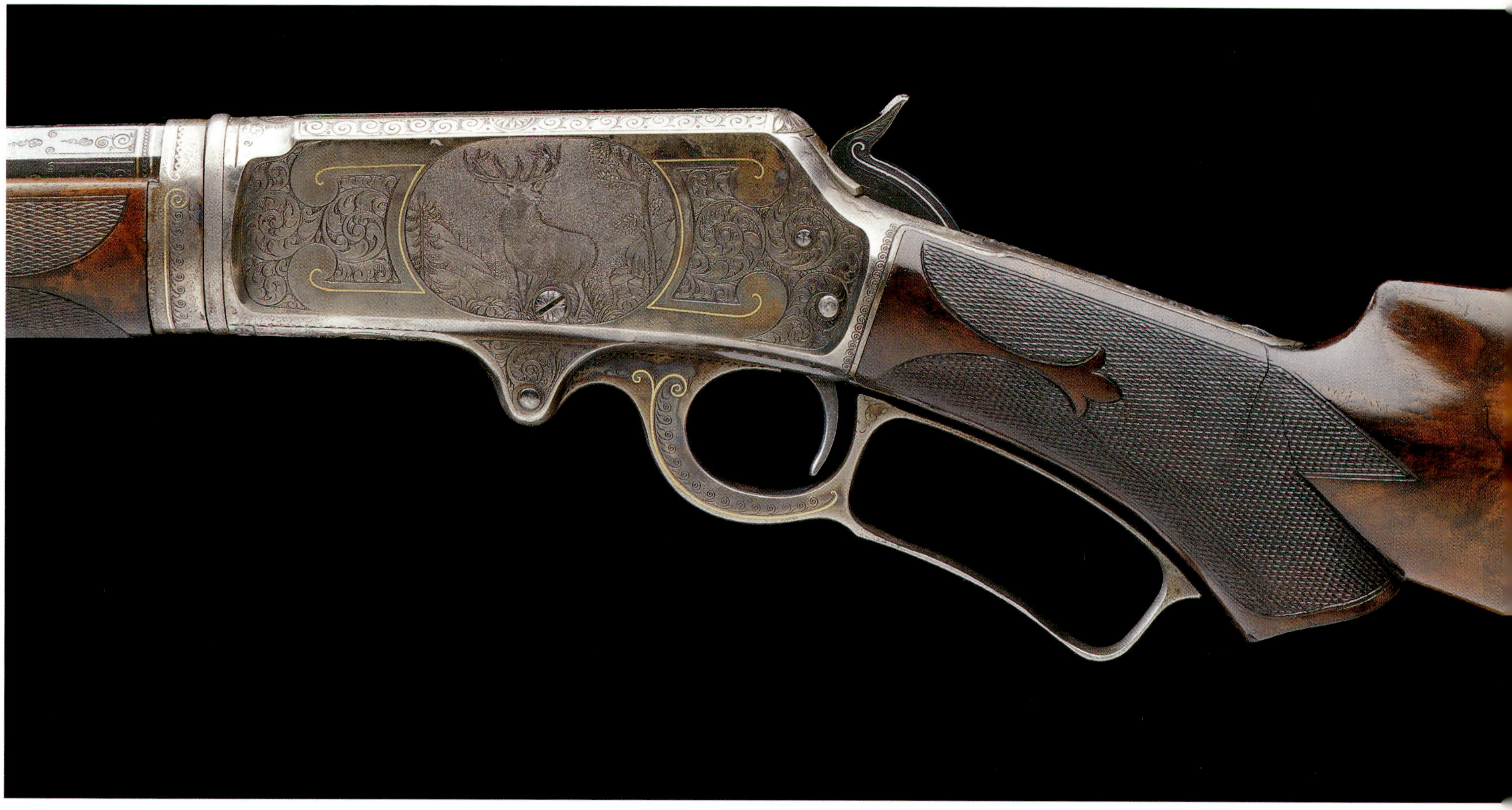

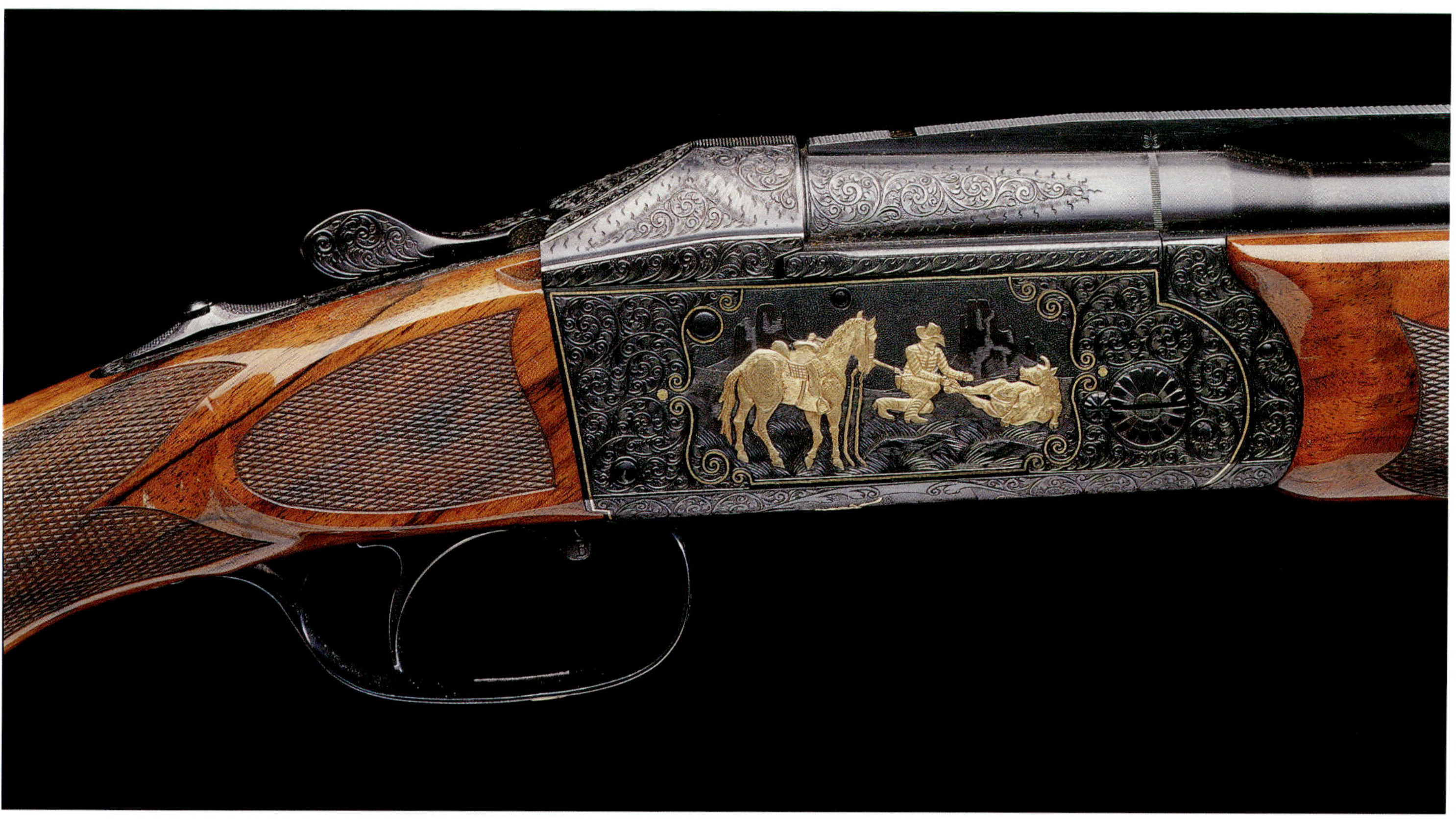

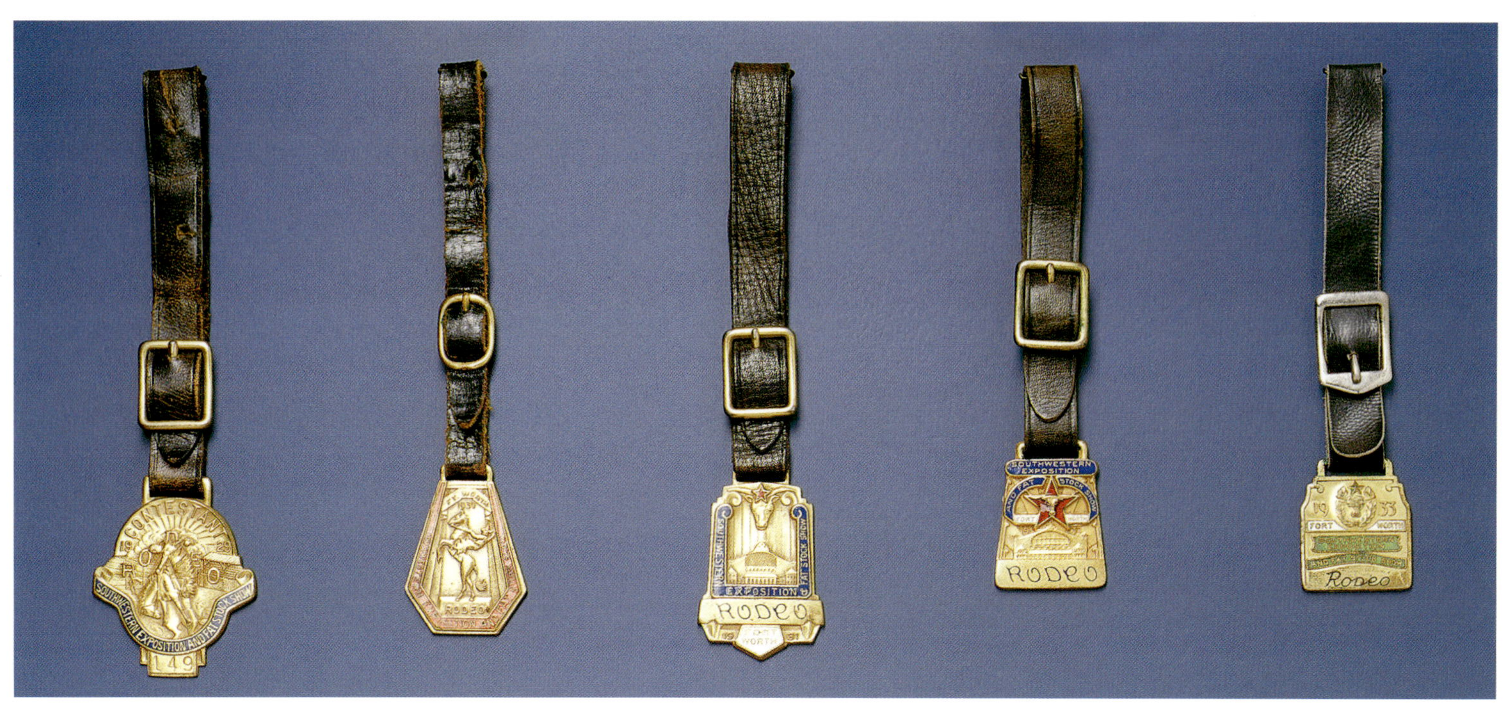
CONTESTANT
1929
SOUTHWESTERN EXPOSITION AND FAT STOCK SHOW
149
FT. WORTH
1930
RODEO
SOUTHWESTERN
EXPOSITION
FAT STOCK SHOW
RODEO
1931
FORT WORTH
SOUTHWESTERN
EXPOSITION
AND FAT STOCK SHOW
FORT WORTH
RODEO
1933
FORT WORTH
Rodeo

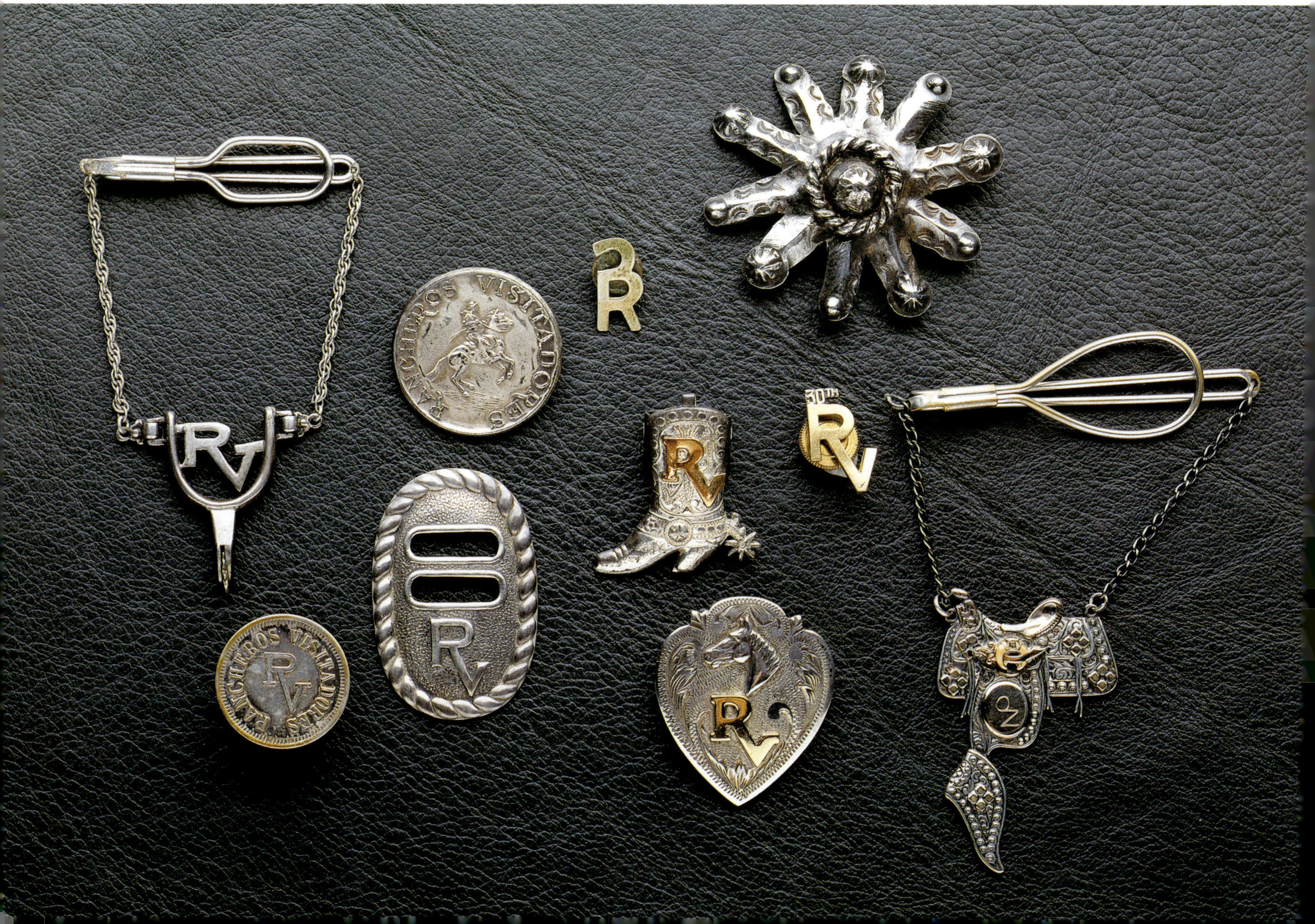

interesting sidelight or diversion from the routine. Such craftsmen usually lacked the advantages of location and clientele that enabled outfitters such as Ed Bohlin to take full advantage of the fantasies peddled by western movies and well-heeled cowboy stars. Nevertheless, at least a few shops outside of southern California attempted to capitalize on the magic of Hollywood. Kelly Brothers of El Paso and W. R. Boone of San Angelo, for example, each brought out an ornate design dubbed "Hollywood Special." Boone, who claimed that his staff produced more than 20,000 pair of Texas-style spurs between 1930 and 1935, is also credited with introducing the first nickel-plated types. The bright, polished surfaces of nickel, chrome, and stainless steel bits and spurs attracted droves of riders, many of whom could not afford the sterling silver types worn by wealthy horsemen.

In addition to flashy silver saddles, bits, and spurs, many saddleries also began to stock and/or produce western-style belt buckles and jewelry. Most such goods, however, were acquired from independent silversmiths and specialty companies, the most important of which were located in California. Among the most active players in the trade were R. Schaezlein and Son, founded in San Francisco in 1909, and two Los Angeles firms: the Srour Company and McCabe Silversmiths, both established in the early 1920s and later bought out by Sunset Trails. The jewelry lines of these companies typically included decorative pins, slides for bolo ties and neckerchiefs, and collar and boot tips, among other items. Typical motifs were as varied as cowboy boots; horseshoes; steer, horse, bison, and Indian heads; and representations of various rodeo events. The Srour Company also reproduced designs popular in nineteenth century Mexican California.

Distinctive western buckles and jewelry were also the stock and trade of several companies and individuals operating outside the West Coast. On the eve of World War I, for example, Cheyenne bit and spur makers Phillips and Gutierrez made and sold silver-mounted buckles, belts, hat bands, finger rings, and shirt sets consisting of concha-shaped cuff links and an engraved stick pin. The pair also fashioned oval and heart-shaped handkerchief holders from coin silver.

One of the most unlikely success stories in the field belonged to Chase Holland, who purchased an all-purpose jewelry store in San Angelo in 1918. After flourishing during the

Opposite, above
Watch fobs
National Cowboy and Western Heritage Museum, Oklahoma City

Opposite, below
Lapel pins and tie tacks and slides, some bearing the "RV" monogram of the California riding club, Rancheros Visitadores
National Cowboy and Western Heritage Museum, Oklahoma City

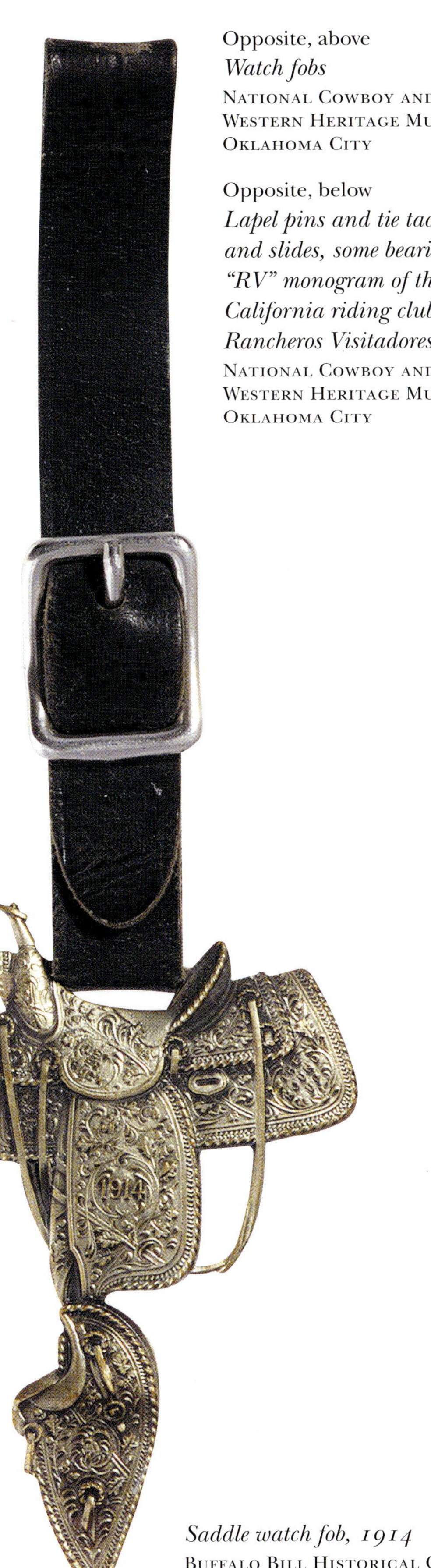

Saddle watch fob, 1914
Buffalo Bill Historical Center, Cody, Wyoming

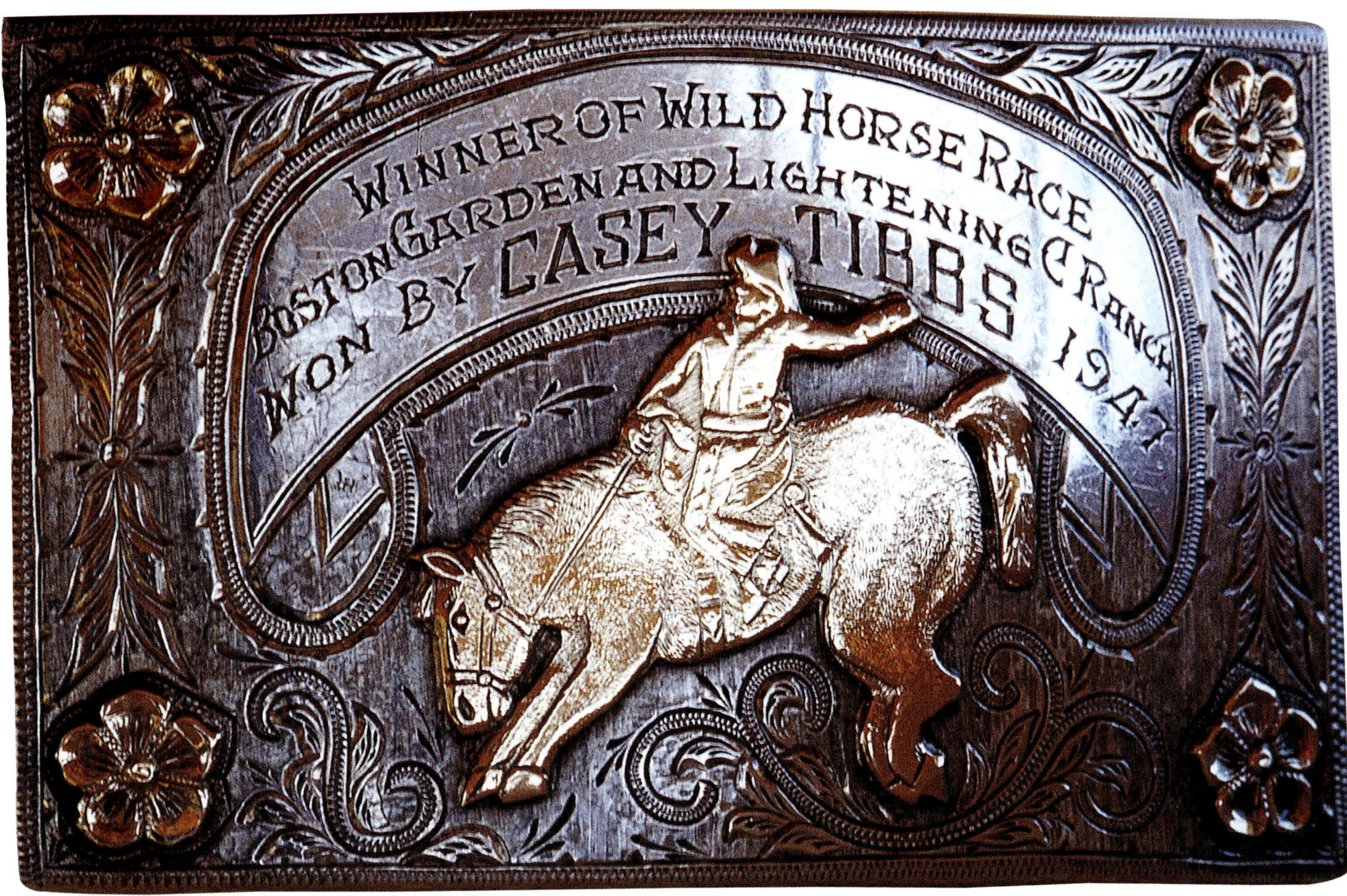

Engraved silver trophy buckle won by bronc rider Casey Tibbs, 1947
ROBERT BRANDES COLLECTION, FREDERICKSBURG, TEXAS

West Texas oil boom of the 1920s, Holland fell on hard times during the Great Depression. He survived thanks to loyal customers and suppliers, and to express his appreciation the jeweler created a sterling silver tie clip in the shape of a cowboy spur, which he gave away to some of his friends. The idea was such a hit that Holland launched an entire line of patented spur jewelry for which the company became known nationwide.

Typical of the wide-ranging custom work of individual craftsmen, were the sterling silver conchas, buckles, hatbands, earrings, and other jewelry, which Montanan Eddy Hulbert made and sold at nearby dude ranches and through a Billings, Montana, western wear store. Hulbert tailored his silver buckles to individual taste with hand engraving, rope edges made of hand twisted silver wire, and such elements as initials, horseshoes, and hearts rendered in gold. In addition to making traditional rectangular buckles and popular three-piece sets, consisting of a fastener, keeper, and tip, Hulbert and some of his contemporaries in the trade also made types shaped like snaffle bits and horseshoes. They also produced trophy buckles and fancy spurs awarded to winning contestants at area rodeos as well.

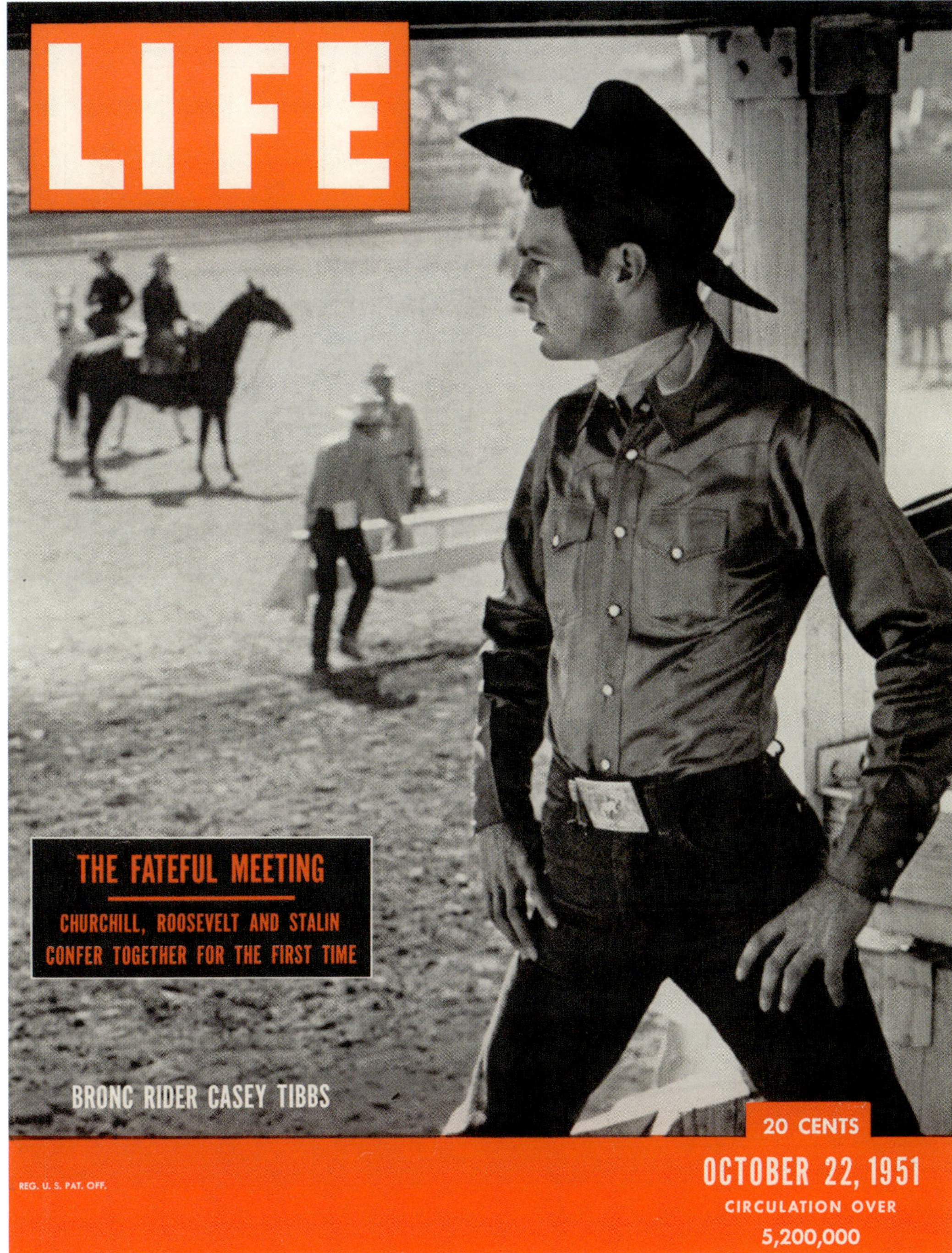

Casey Tibbs on the cover of Life *magazine, October 22, 1951.*

The sport of rodeo with its attendant parades and fiestas had bolstered a sagging bit and spur market in the 1920s and 1930s and had brought about changes in the prevailing spur styles. Rodeo riders, for example, tended to embrace spurs with shorter shanks and smaller rowels. Range riders soon followed suit and the heavy, Mexican-style spurs of the 1920s virtually disappeared from the scene the following decade.

To take advantage of rodeo's immense popularity, enterprising bit and spur makers began to name spur styles in honor of such emerging heroes of the sport

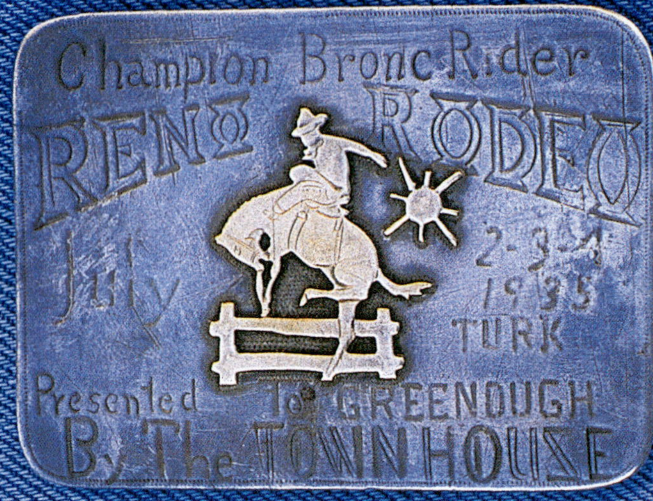

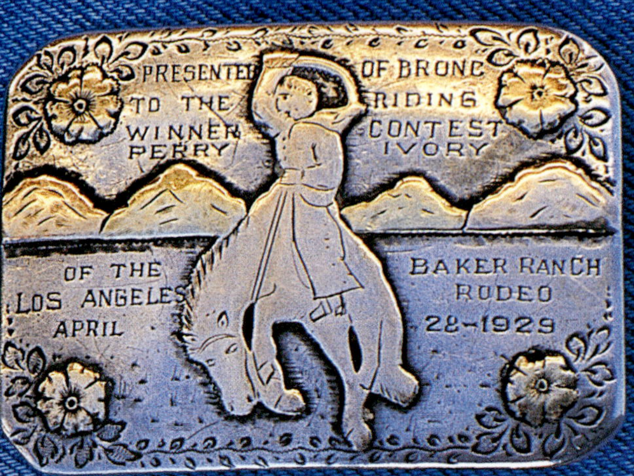

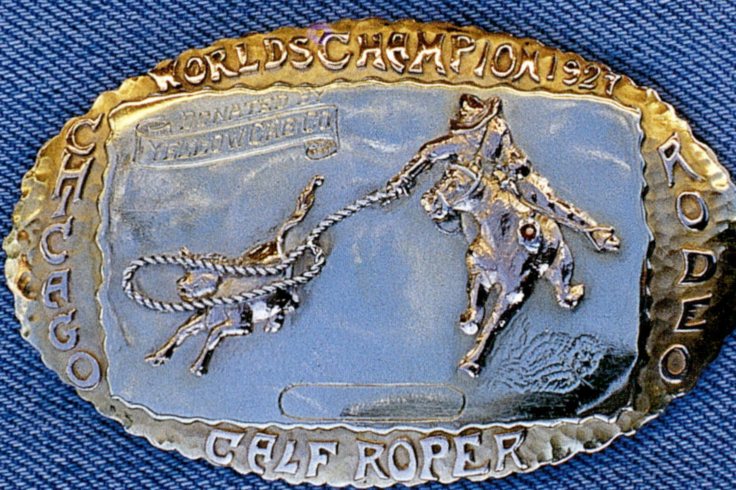

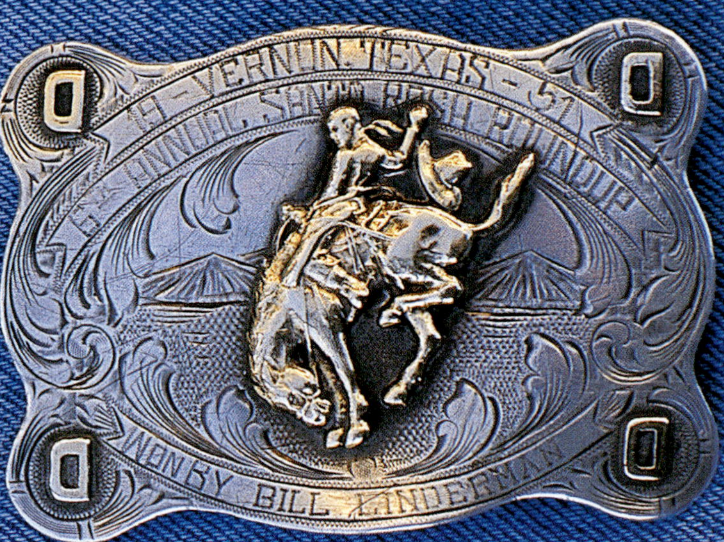

Trophy buckles (clockwise from upper left): champion bronc rider, presented to Turk Greenough, Reno Rodeo, 1935; winner, bronc riding contest, presented to Perry Ivory, Baker Ranch Rodeo, Los Angeles, 1929; bronc riding trophy, won by Bill Linderman, Santa Rosa Roundup, Vernon, Texas, 1951; world's champion calf roper, Chicago Rodeo
Robert Brandes Collection, Fredericksburg, Texas

as Johnny Mullins and Paddy Ryan. W. R. Boone's "Madison Square Spur," costing $360 and set with three diamonds, paid homage to rodeo's famous New York City venue. Aimed at the dude market and mass-produced from "Hercules Bronze," the "Frontier Day" and "Stampede" matching bit and spur sets of the August Buermann Mfg. Co. alluded to famous rodeos at Cheyenne and Calgary, Canada. A cheap nickel silver ornament cast in the shape of either an Indian head or a Lone Star decorated each item in the set.

Like other Americans, the West's bit and spur makers experienced hard times during the 1930s. When Kelly Brothers in El Paso began to flounder, P. M. Kelly left the business in the hands of his siblings and moved to Mexico at the invitation of the government to begin manufacturing gas engines and well pumps of his own design. He made enough in the venture to keep the bit and spur company afloat and returned to the U.S. in 1939.

As the Great Depression deepened, Oscar Crockett moved his Kansas City operation, by now producing 10,000 pairs of bits and spurs annually, to a farm near Lenexa, Kansas. In 1938 Crockett introduced a bit and spur line made in extruded forms of lightweight aluminum. "Airplane metal," as the new material was sometimes called, was not adapted to either inlay or overlay decoration and, if embellished at all, was only shallowly engraved.

With the onset of World War II, bit and spur foundries experienced shortages of manpower and silver that impacted large-scale makers more than smaller operators. Although quality steel was relatively plentiful, lucrative contracts for cavalry bits and spurs were canceled in the early 1940s as tanks replaced horses on the battlefield.

Trophy buckle won by Fritz Truan, Elko Rodeo, 1938
NATIONAL COWBOY AND WESTERN HERITAGE MUSEUM, OKLAHOMA CITY

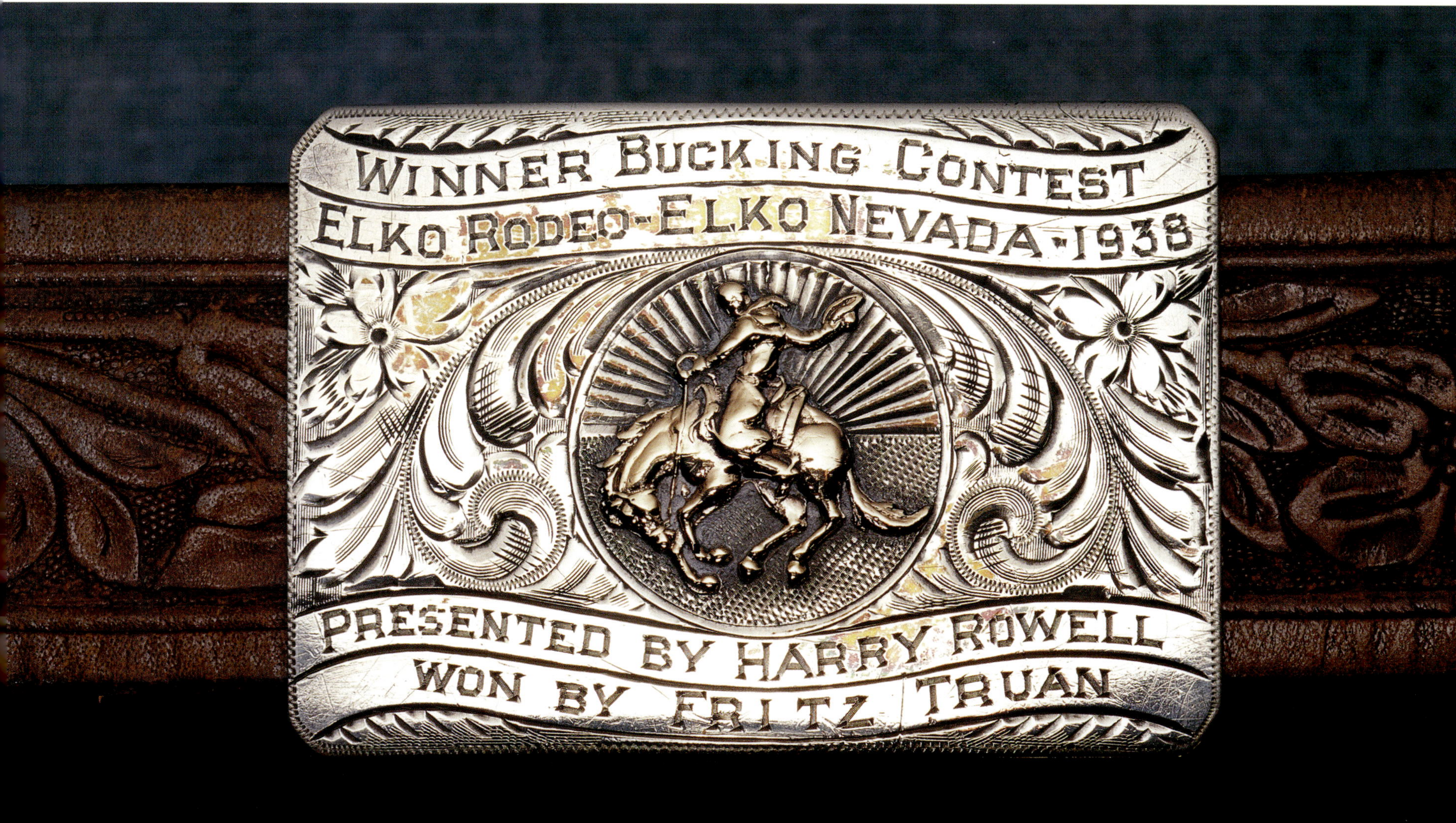

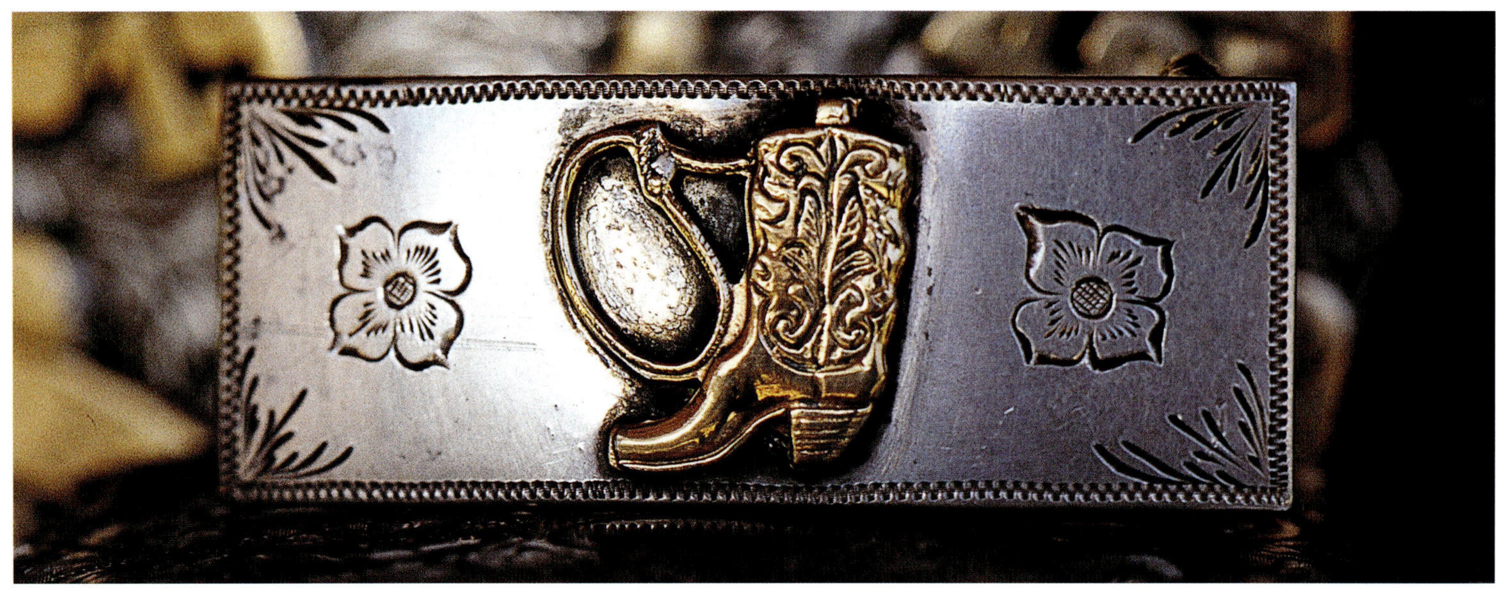

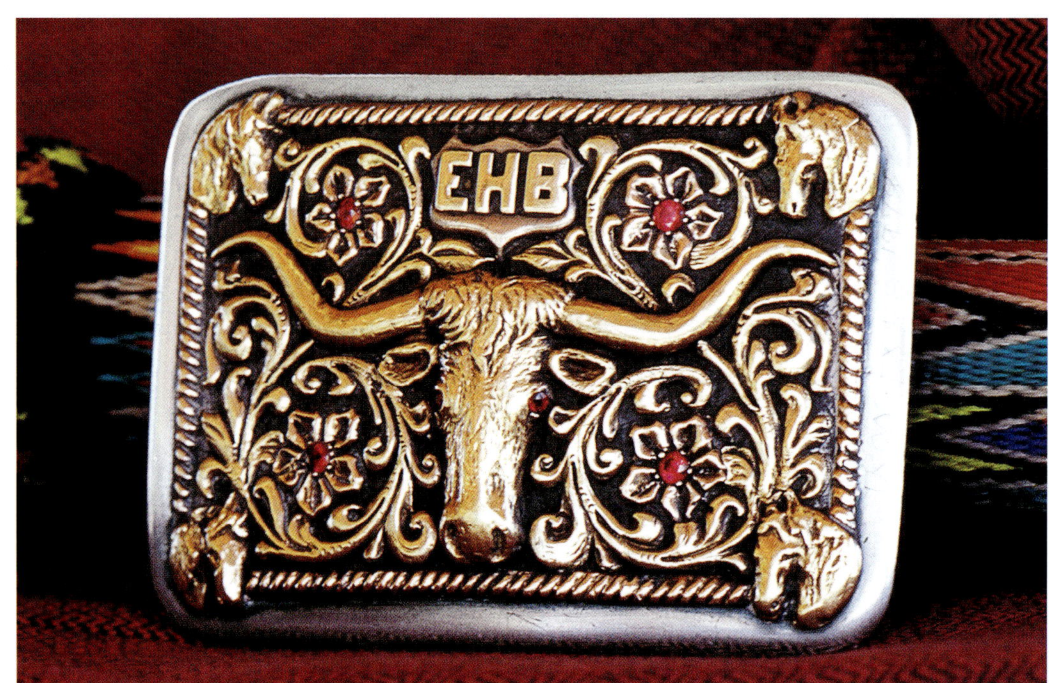

Above
Holland's Jewelry, San Angelo, Texas
Western-style belt buckle
ROBERT BRANDES COLLECTION, FREDERICKSBURG, TEXAS

Right
Edward H. Bohlin, Hollywood
Trophy-style gold buckle, floral, longhorn, and horse head motifs
ROBERT BRANDES COLLECTION, FREDERICKSBURG, TEXAS

The post–World War II era brought better economic times for the nation's bit and spur makers, thanks to a renewed interest in pleasure riding and the revival of dude ranching. Ornate bits and spurs made by Edward H. Bohlin and a few others enjoyed a few more years of popularity with recreational horsemen before the silver saddle phenomenon finally ran its course in the mid-1950s. During this period a host of Mexican-made bits and spurs, designed by Californians Les Garcia and Richard Fleming, but forged in government-supported shops at Amazoc, also were entering the U.S. Fleming established a similar arrangement with craftsmen in Guadalajara for the production of western-style buckles and jewelry.

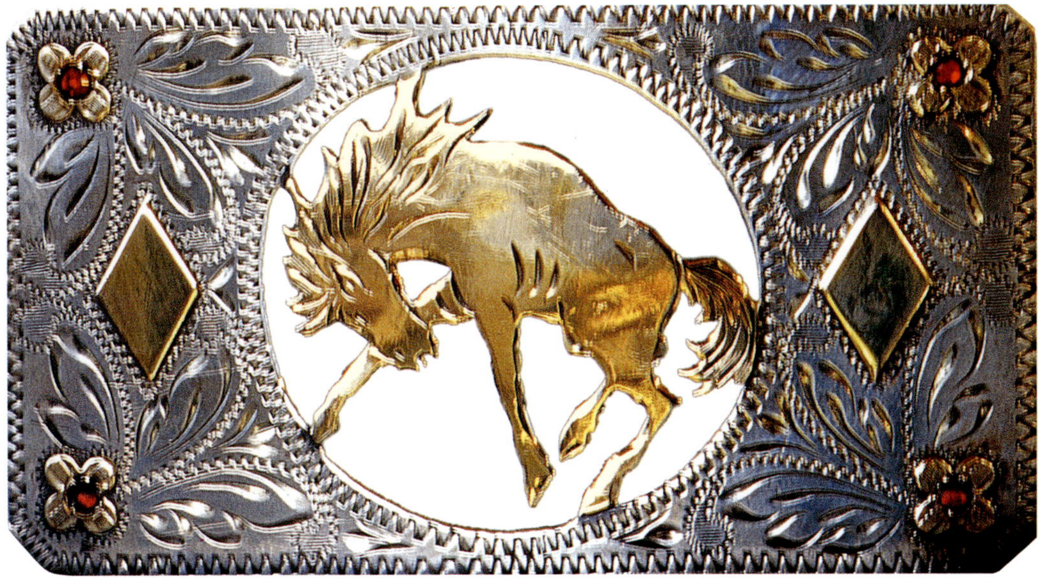

Ricardo, Denver
Western-style pierced and engraved silver buckle with mustang motif, c. 1950
Robert Brandes Collection, Fredericksburg, Texas

P. M. Kelly and Oscar Crockett, meanwhile, shared most of the mass market for western style bits and spurs. Crockett, who had relocated his plant to Boulder, Colorado, during World War II, died in 1949. His widow sold the company in the early 1950s to James Renalde, owner of the Denver Metals Foundry, who moved the operation to the Mile High City and continued mass-producing more than fifty styles of spurs and 125 different bits under the Crockett name. By now the

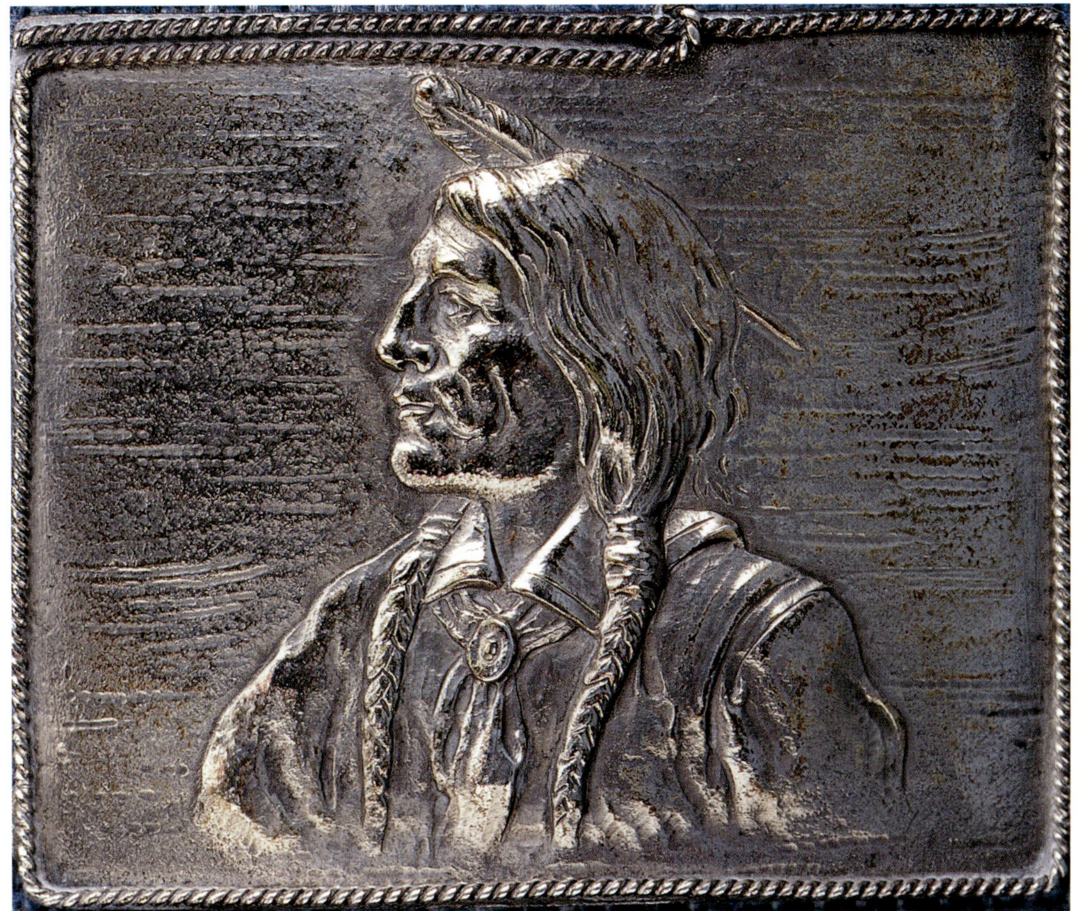

Deitsch Brothers Jewelers, Denver
Sterling silver rodeo trophy belt won by bronc rider Harry Brennan, 1902; detail showing one of nine segmented panels with chased imagery and rope trim
National Cowboy and Western Heritage Museum, Oklahoma City

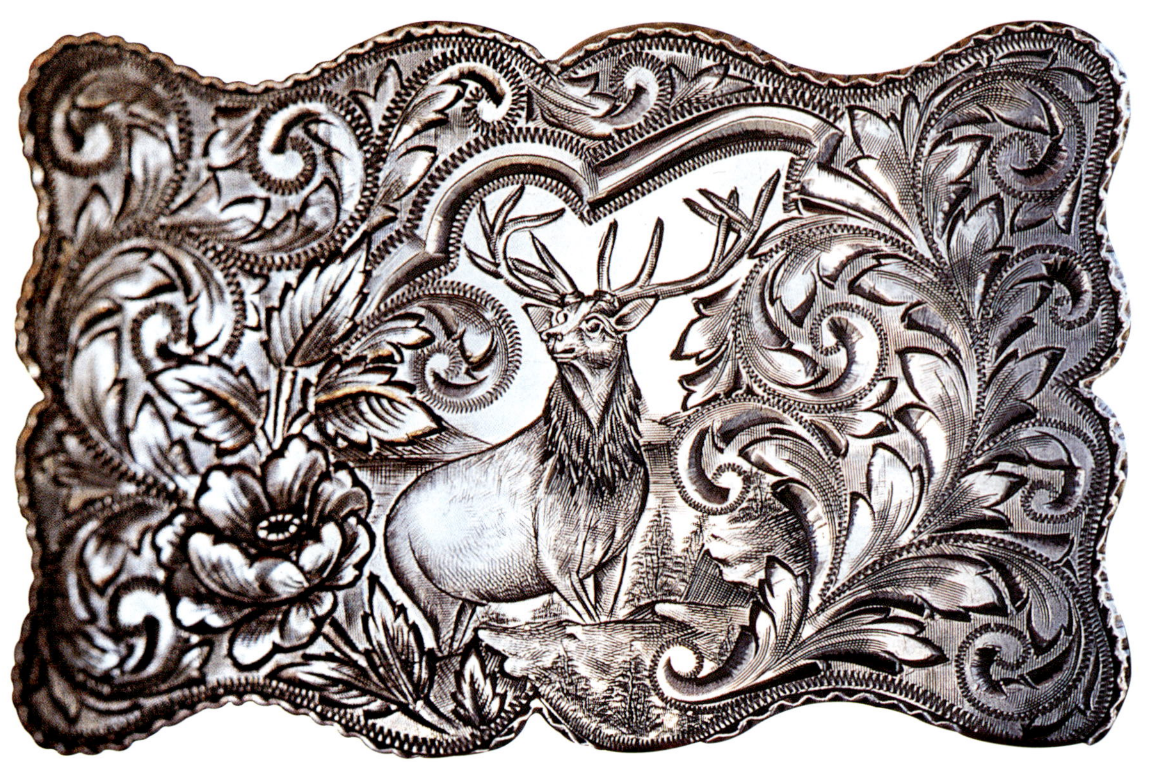

This page
Above: Don Ellis Co., Seattle
Sterling silver western-style buckle, salesman's sample engraved with floral and elk motifs
Below: Sunset Trails (attributed), Hollywood
Rodeo trophy buckle, Post, Texas, 1954
ROBERT BRANDES COLLECTION, FREDERICKSBURG, TEXAS

Opposite
Western belts with buckles
Makers left to right: McCabe Silversmiths, Hollywood, buckle, c. 1950s, and Hamley and Co., Pendleton, Oregon, belt; makers unknown, Cheyenne-pattern buckle, c. 1960s, and belt; The Nelson Co., Houston, buckle, and Don Butler, Sheridan, Wyoming, belt; Clint Orms, Ingram, Texas, buckle, and unknown maker, belt; R. W. Driskell, Rosenberg, Texas (Clint Orms, shield), buckle, and Capitol Saddlery, Austin, Texas, belt; Srour Company, Los Angeles, buckle, and unknown maker, Mexican, belt; Holland's Jewelry, San Angelo, Texas, buckle, and unknown maker, belt; McCabe Silversmiths, buckle, and Bob Anderson, New Mexico, belt
ROBERT BRANDES COLLECTION, FREDERICKSBURG, TEXAS

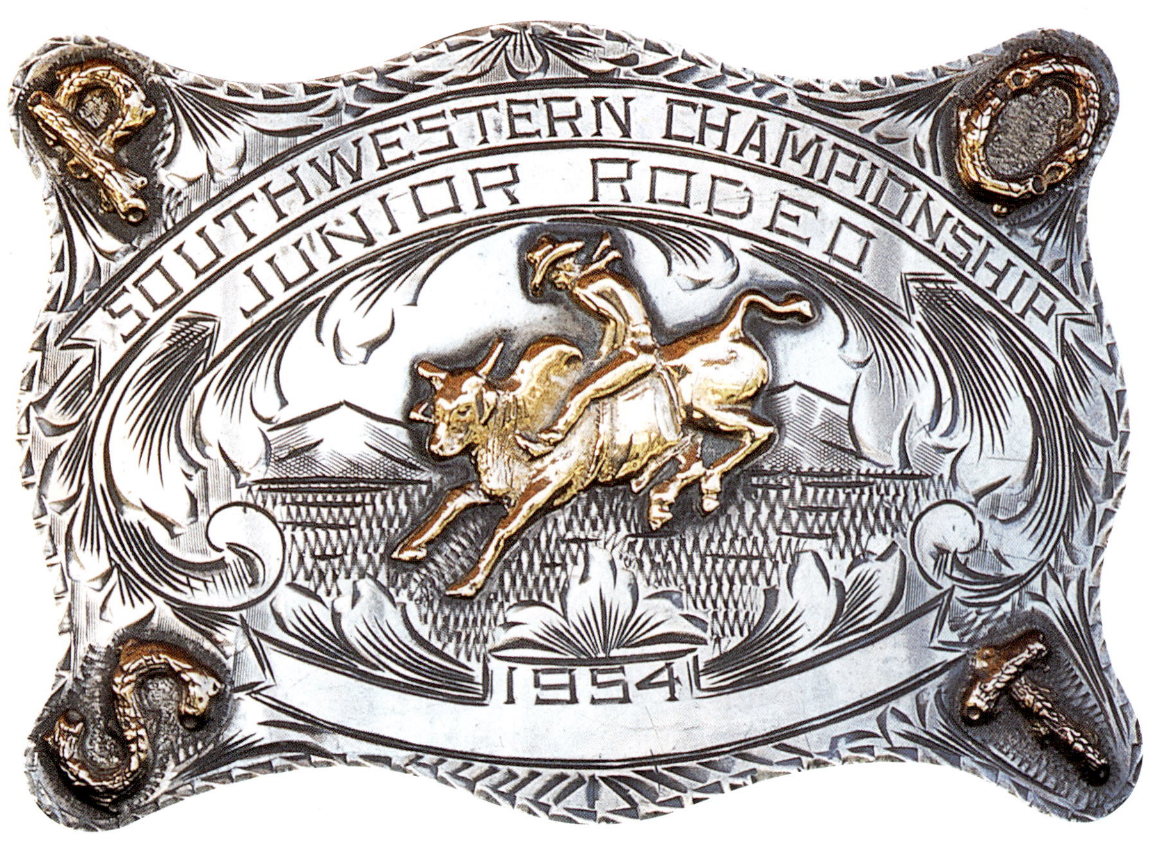

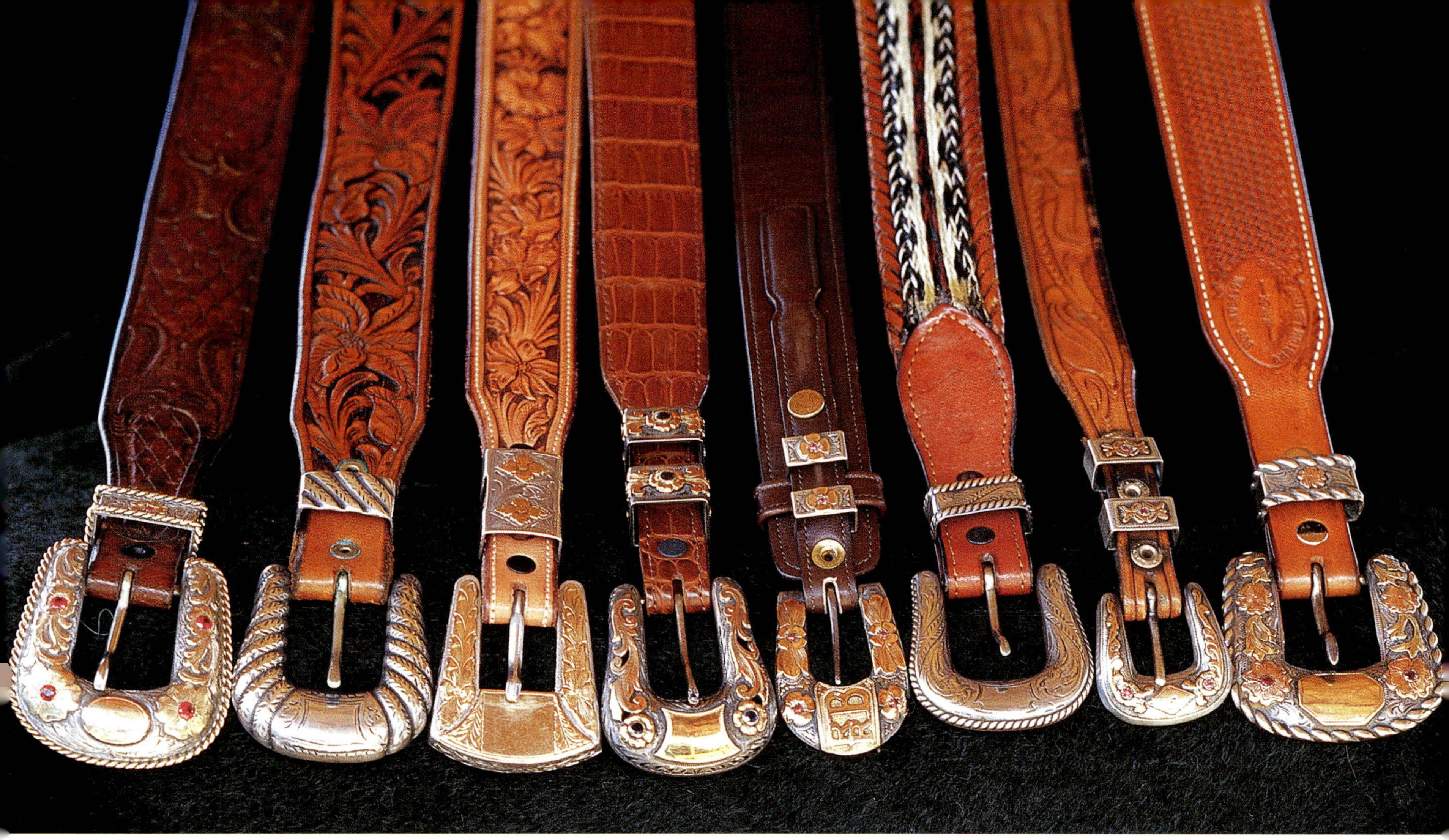

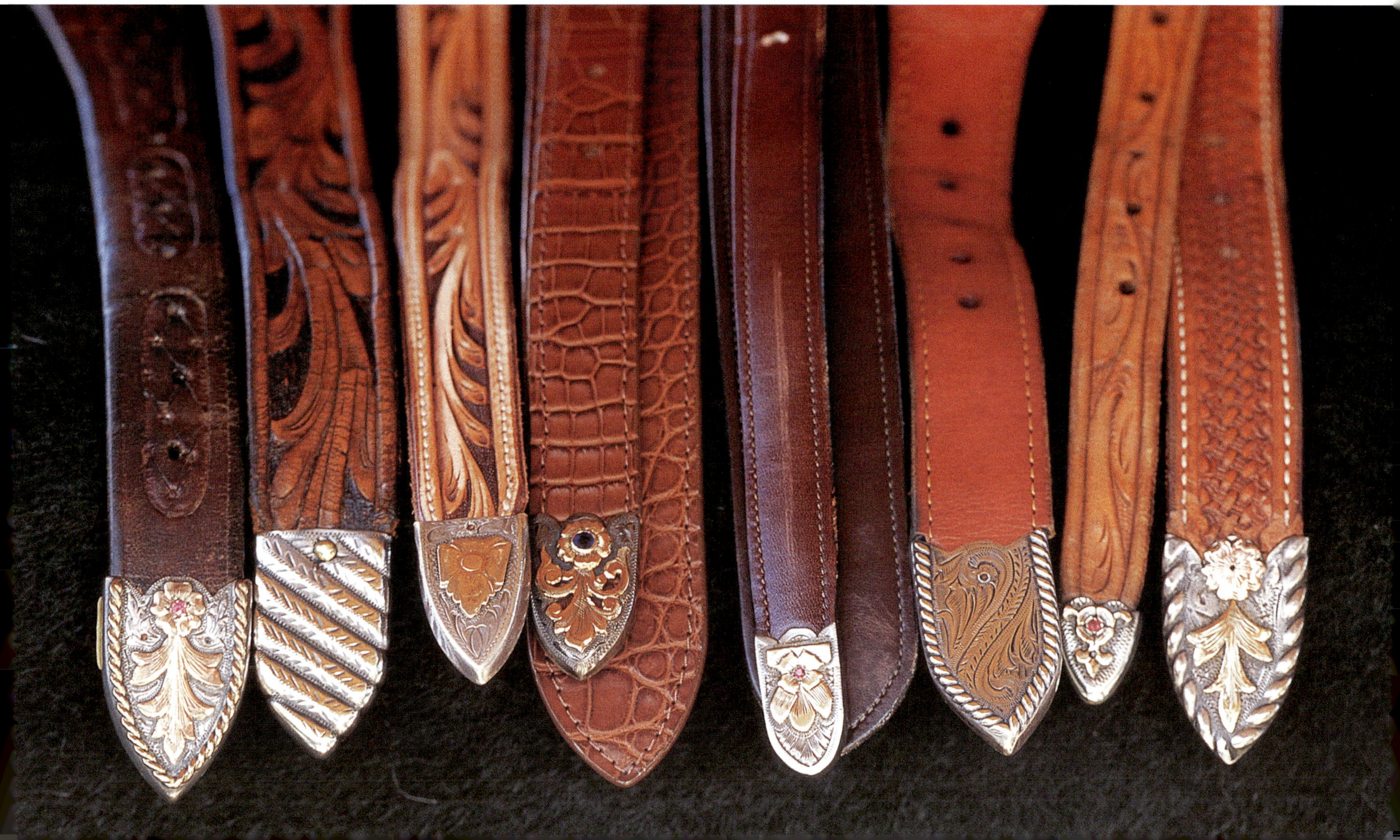

Right
Modern Bohlin Company
Three-piece buckle sets; left: filigree pattern, made and engraved by Ahmed Kahn; center: Saguaro cactus pattern
FLEISCHER COLLECTION, SCOTTSDALE

Below
Modern Bohlin Company
Trophy-style bronc belt buckle, bucking horse motif
FLEISCHER COLLECTION, SCOTTSDALE

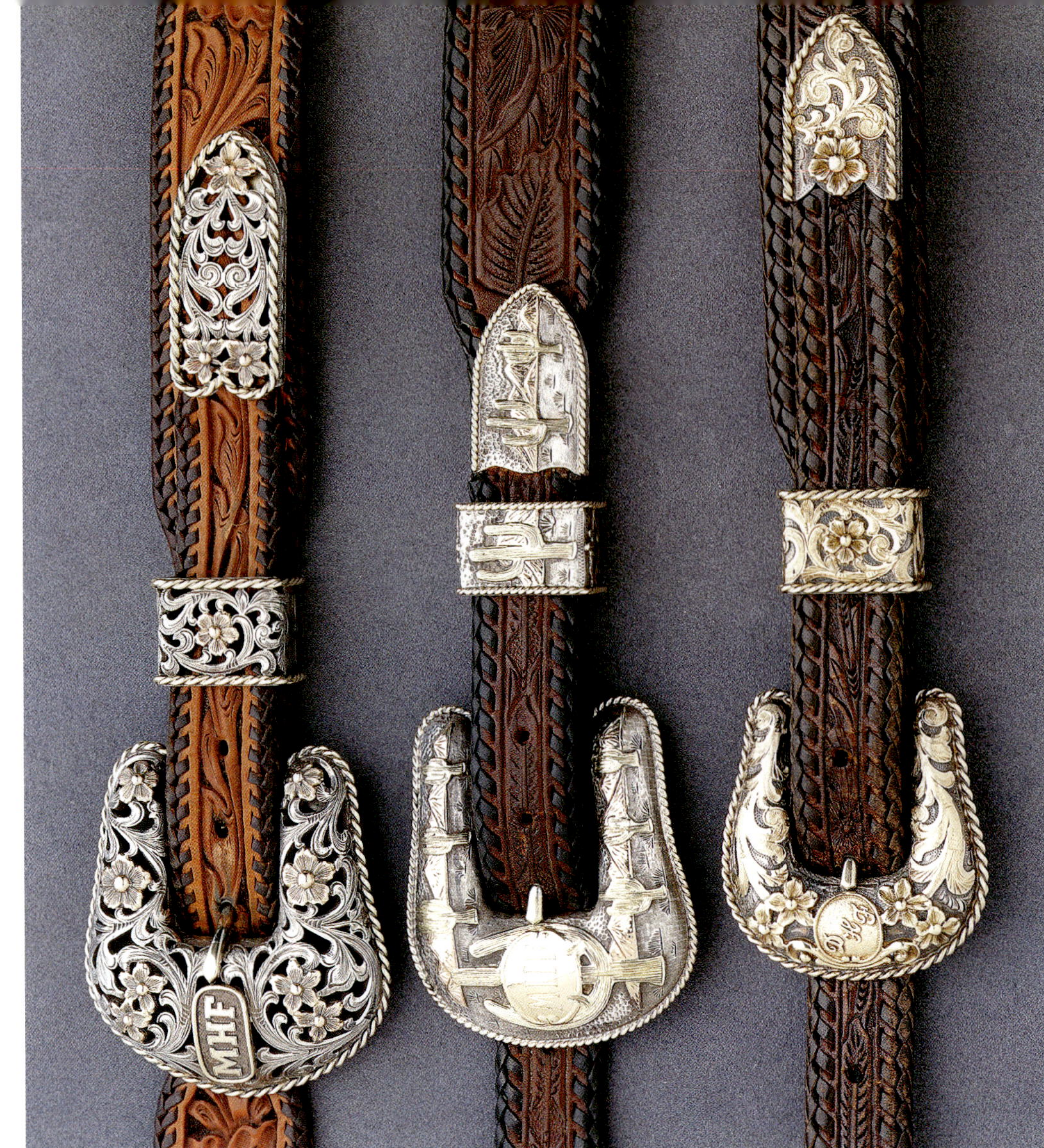

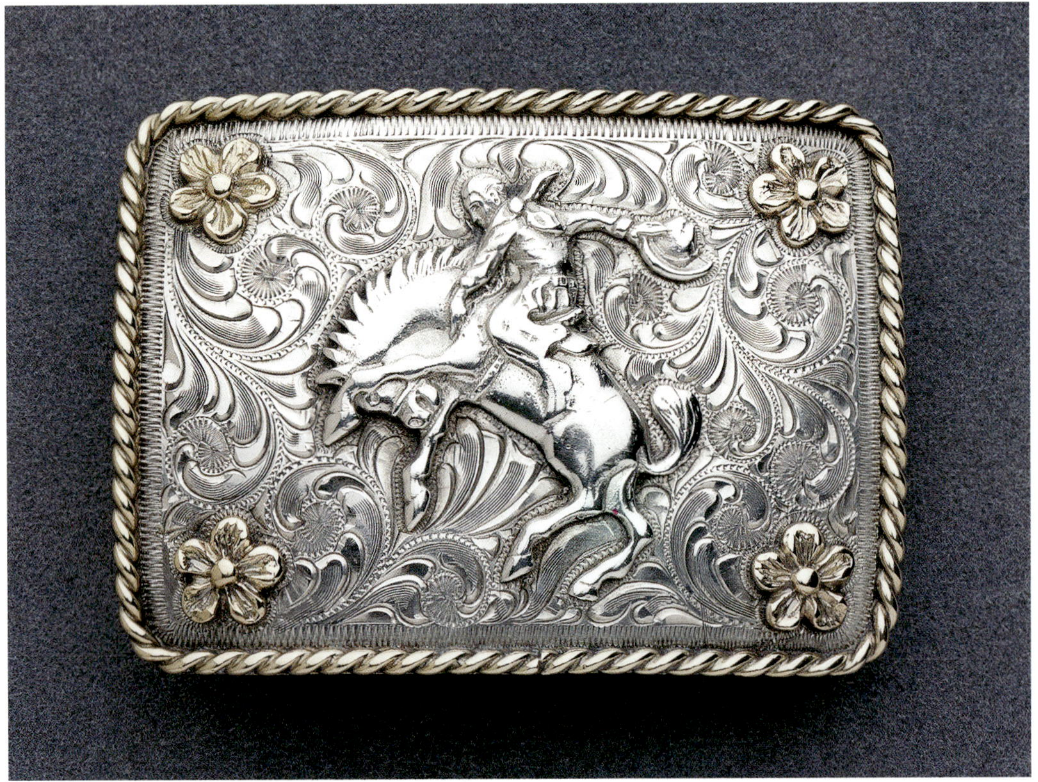

Opposite
Clint Orms, Ingram, Texas
Top: trophy-style buckle, hand engraved sterling silver with sterling overlay and concha, laced border; center: four-piece ranger-style buckle, 10 karat rose gold, hand-engraved with 14 karat yellow and green gold and 10 karat rose gold overlays, and five 10 karat rose gold flowers set with quarter carat diamonds; bottom: trophy buckle, filigreed and hand engraved sterling silver with 14 karat yellow gold overlays and longhorn, limited edition: 2/10
FLEISCHER COLLECTION, SCOTTSDALE

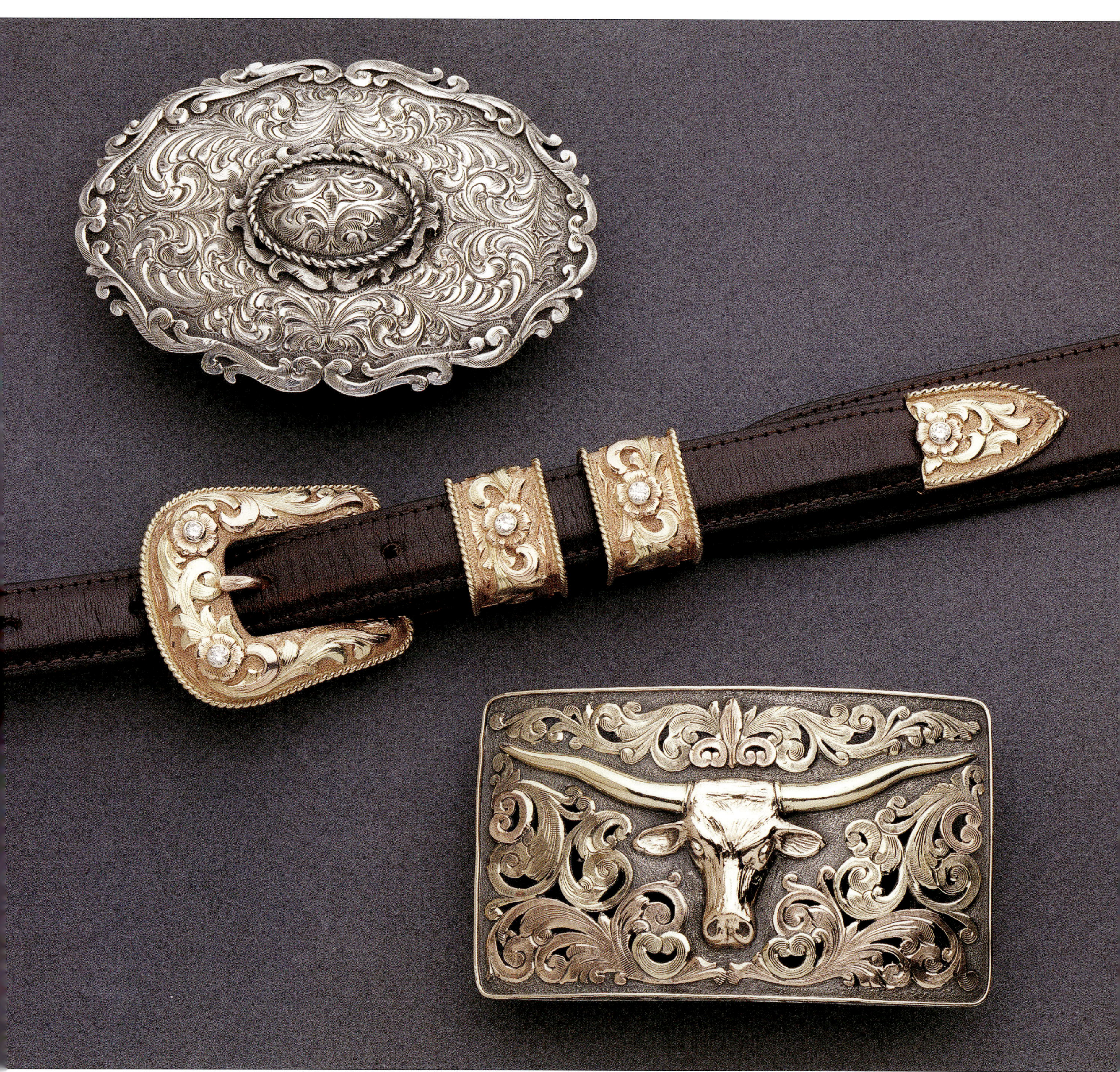

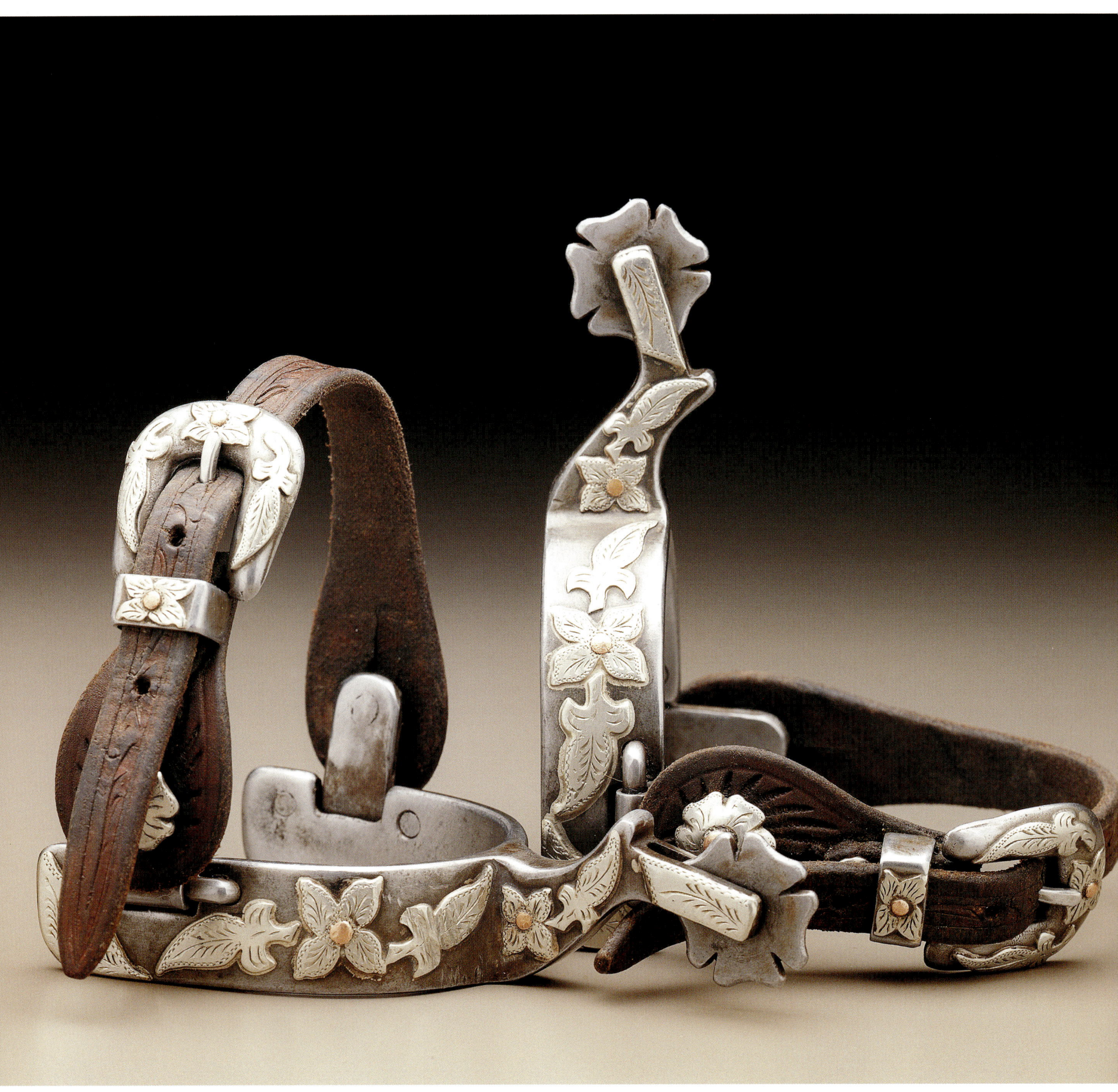

manufacturing process was fully mechanized and consisted of nearly one hundred separate operations. Although die cut ornaments of sterling or nickel silver were still soldered on and engraved by hand in the traditional manner, the polished chrome finish of most bits and spurs obscured the visual impact of the mounts.

The last major bit and spur maker of his generation, P. M. Kelly continued in business until 1965, after 1940 under the name P. M. Kelly and Sons. By 1960 his company supplied some eight hundred U.S. and Canadian retailers. That year, facing intense competition from Japanese and Korean imports and soaring labor costs, Kelly finally quit filling custom orders.

Kelly had come a long way since his days as a lone blacksmith, forging bits and spurs one at a time in the Texas Panhandle. Yet throughout the twentieth century, a few solitary makers still produced custom bits and spurs for fussy western horsemen. Most lived in out-of-the-way places—Channing, Texas; Danville, California; Prairie Creek, Oregon; Grangeville, Idaho; and Winnemucca, Nevada, to name a few. Few worked at the craft full time until they retired from other jobs. Although most of these artisans mechanized their operations to some degree, imagination and individuality still characterized the design and embellishment of their work. Thanks to improved communication and a willingness to experiment with new ideas and techniques, the gulf that once separated strong regional traditions narrowed considerably.

Typical of these latter-day metal wizards, Adolph Bayers hammered out one-piece bits, spurs, cinch rings, belt buckles, and a few knives for more than three decades while farming cotton in Texas after World War II. Like some of his predecessors, Bayers scrounged steel for his products, favoring early Ford car axles. He used dies and equipment once owned by the legendary J. R. McChesney and salvaged from the Nocona Boot Company, but also constructed his own hand-operated silver rolling press and cut out and engraved many of his silver overlays by hand. Before his death in 1978 Bayers passed some of his knowledge and skills along to a young cowboy named Billy Klapper who, along with more than 120 other craftsmen scattered throughout the West, still fashions quality bits and spurs in the twenty-first century.

Opposite
Billy Klapper, Pampa, Texas
Texas-style single-piece spurs with raised shanks, flower and leaf overlay, wheat pattern engraving, swinging buckles, and cloverleaf rowels, c. 1980s
FLEISCHER COLLECTION, SCOTTSDALE

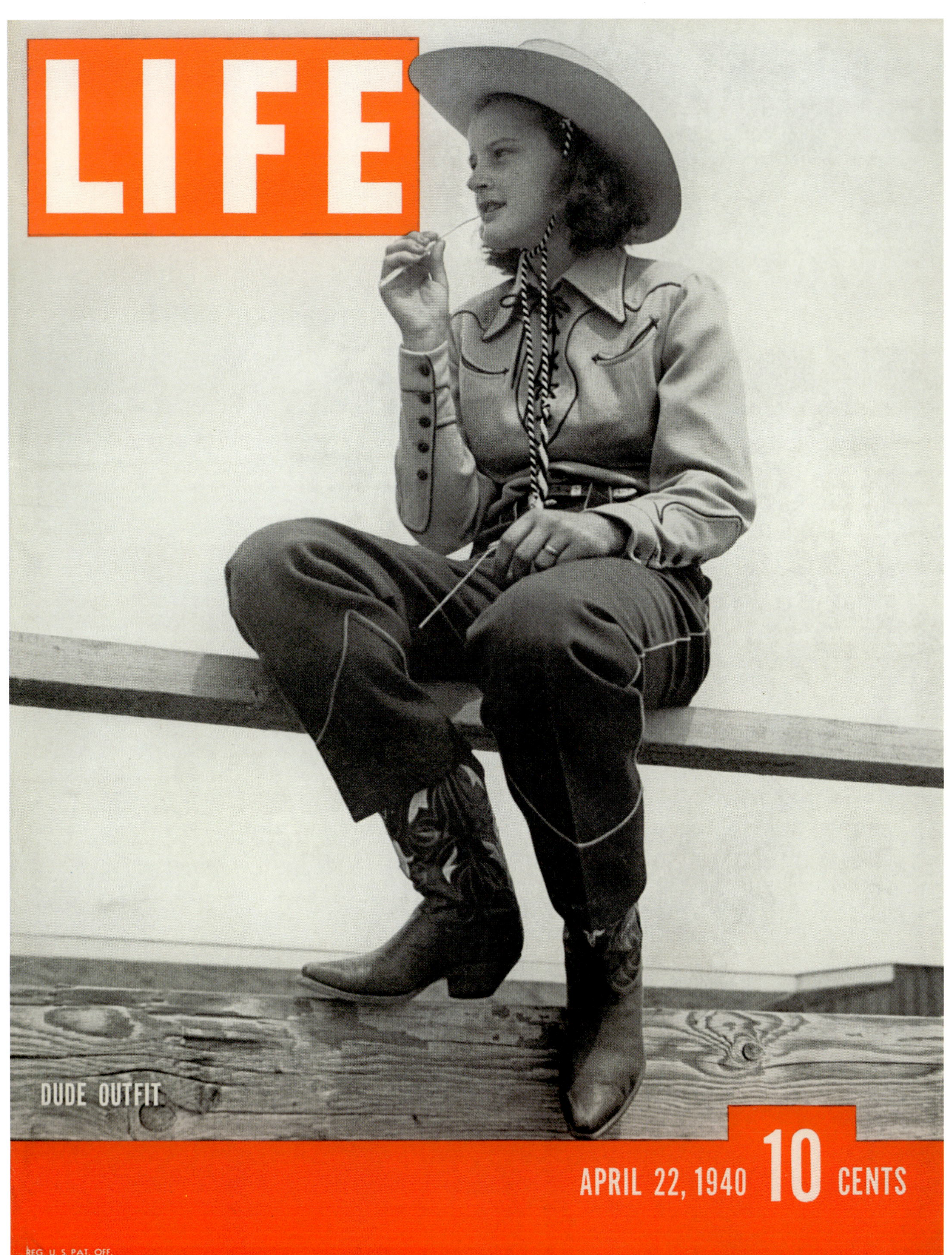
LIFE
DUDE OUTFIT
APRIL 22, 1940 10 CENTS
REG. U. S. PAT. OFF.

· 5 ·

Boots and Hats

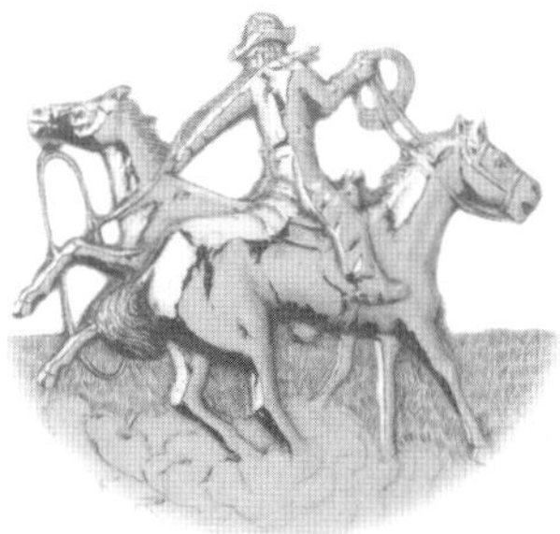

Of all the elements of a cowboy's wardrobe, none distinguished his occupation more clearly than his wide-brimmed hat and high-heeled boots. Always the best that he could afford, both headgear and footwear reflected the character as well as the calling of the wearer and frequently were decorative as well as practical.

Writing in *Scribner's Magazine* in 1887, Louis Swinburne called the distinctive boots worn by American cowboys of the era, "emphatically the most wonderful" part of their attire. "It is in boots," the author continued, "that the instinctive dandyism lying at the bottom of a savage's nature crops out unmistakably."[77] Only a dozen years earlier, however, boot styles specifically identified with western cattle herders were virtually unknown.

Before the first appearance of "cowboy boots" in the mid-1870s, most hired men on horseback depended upon the same kind of heavy-duty leather footwear worn by other common laborers. Often crude and ill-fitting, these flat-heeled, round-toed boots and shoes usually were the products of eastern factories, and the cheapest sorts could be readily obtained from local stores for a few dollars. Many were military surplus, part of the thousands of pairs that flooded the market in the years following the Civil War.

Opposite. *"Dude Outfit"*
Life *magazine cover, April 22, 1940*

The boots that cowboys came to favor were themselves the descendants of heavy-duty European and U.S. military footwear, modified with tall, underslung heels and metal-reinforced arches to meet the peculiar occupational and social requirements of the horsemen who wore them. Prominent heels, some of which reached a height of three inches and tapered to a point only an inch or two in diameter, not only helped cowpunchers secure their feet in saddle stirrups and avoid the risk of slipping through, but also added to their physical stature and to the feeling of superiority they sometimes expressed over those who labored on foot. "The heels...," claimed one florid observer, "are the chief points of pride. No Athenian buskin could have stood so majestically high; they lift a man several inches into the air of this poor world and lend him a sort of moral loftiness."[78] Cowboys also appreciated elevated heels because they contributed to trimmer looking feet.

The origin of cowboy-style boots is still disputed. Most authorities place their genesis in Kansas, either in the Olathe shop of Charles H. Hyer, who claimed to have produced a work boot with tall heels as early as 1875, or from the bench of John W. Cubine, who began making footwear in the town of Coffeyville a year later. While the cattle business boomed in the 1870s and early 1880s, custom boot makers in the cowtowns of Abilene, Dodge City, and Ellsworth, Kansas, also enjoyed a brisk trade with Texas drovers fresh off the trail. At Thomas C. McInerney's Abilene shop alone, between ten and twenty makers struggled to meet the demand for boots that sold for a princely $10 to 20 a pair, twice the cost of the store-bought variety. At least a few pair were fitted with stylish brass toes.

John Cubine's distinctive made-to-order Coffeyville pattern boots, a modified cavalry type with a rounded toe and a one-piece front that rose to the knee but was cut lower behind to insure free leg movement, gained special renown. Although the Kansas artisan fashioned most of his boots from plain, unlined black cowhide, by 1879 he began to cut at least a few pair out of tanned alligator hide.

To the tops of their most expensive creations, Cubine and other Kansas makers often added a panel of red or brown leather, a decorative touch reminiscent of the popular Wellington style of English riding boots. This surface often bore an embroidered or inlaid horseshoe, crescent, or star design, sometimes rendered in red morocco. Texas cowboys displayed a special affinity for the "Lone Star" motif, which not only adorned their state flag, but often their hats, clothing, and tack as well.

Demand for Kansas-style cowboy boots spread quickly throughout the Great Plains, thanks to word-of-mouth advertising, the footloose ways of cowpunchers, and wide-ranging drovers who pushed cattle herds from Texas to Montana. Yet in remote regions of the cattle kingdom it was not always easy to find craftsmen to execute new designs. In Texas, for example, fewer than one hundred boot

Opposite
Cowboy boots, with stitched stovepipe-style tops and narrow underslung heel, c. 1900
Buffalo Bill Historical Center, Cody, Wyoming

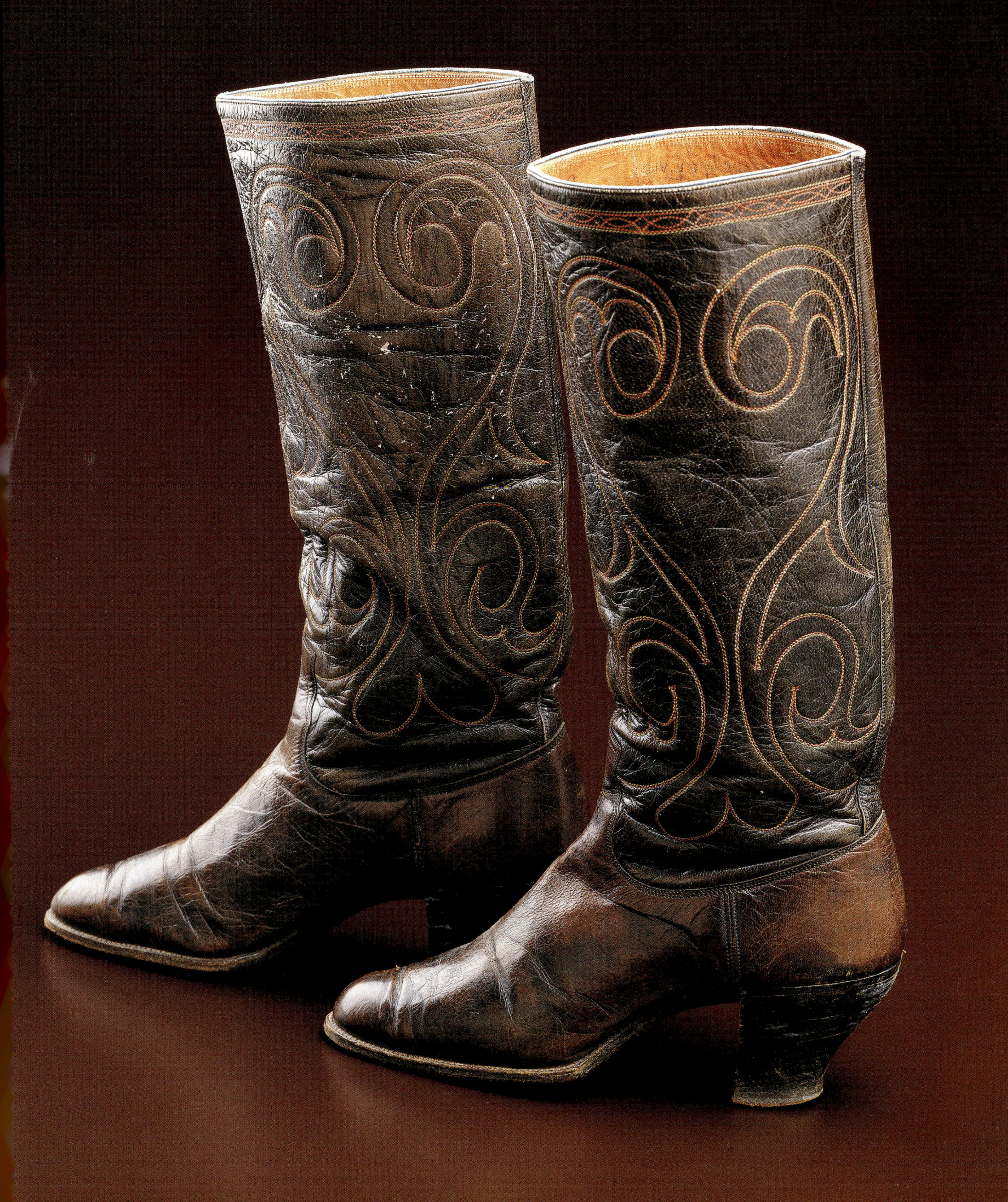

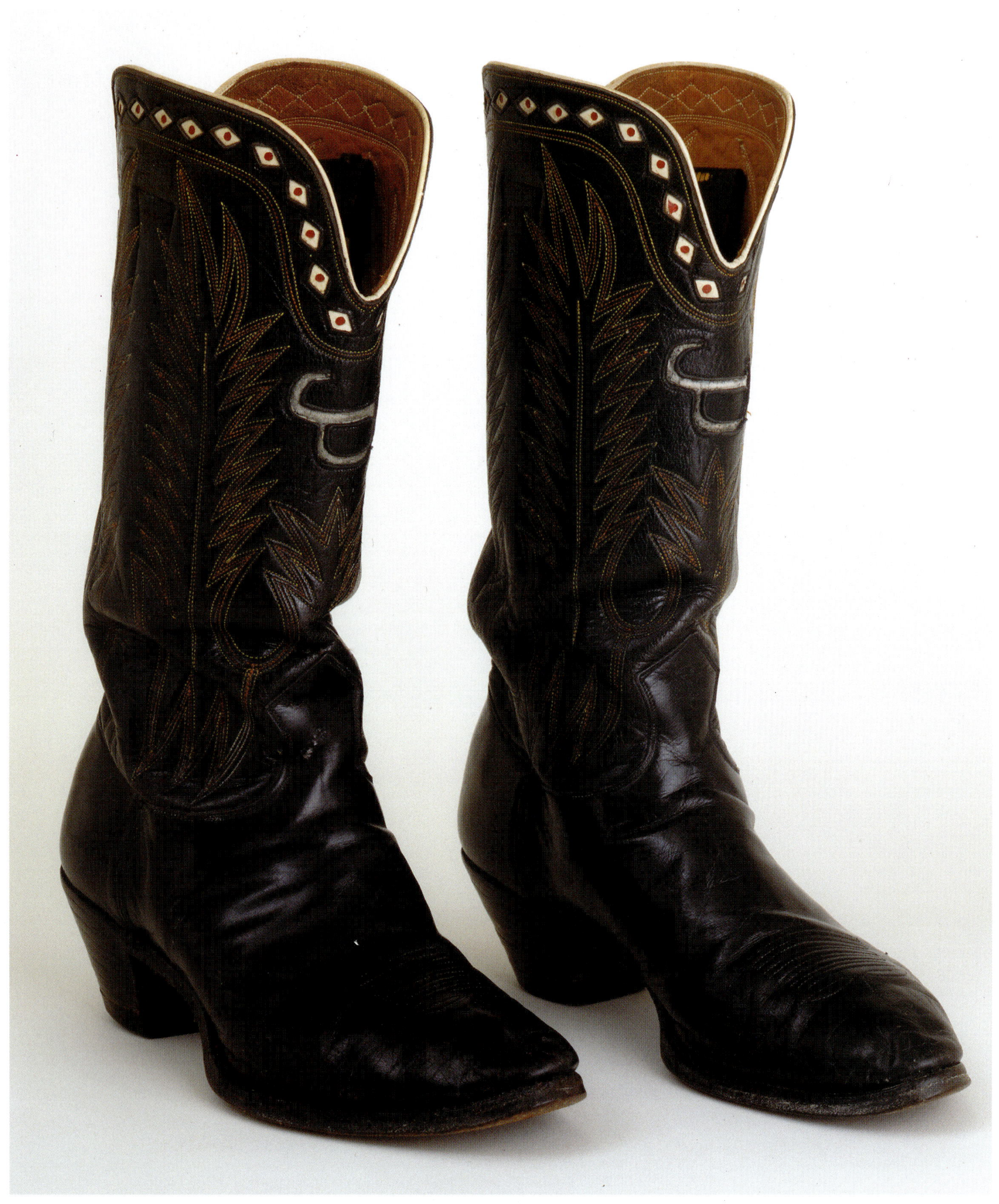

makers plied their trade in 1870, most of them in the more settled regions of the state. As Frank Collinson, a cowhand and drover in South Texas during the period, recalled,

> If there was a boot maker in Texas then, I never saw or heard of him. The cowboys wore custom-made boots, pegged soles, or government-made boots. They were big and clumsy. Sometimes a cowhand who had been up the trail returned home with a pair of "cowboy boots," as they were later known, but he looked out of place and foreign in them. My first pair of shop-made boots were [sic] made in Cheyenne.[79]

With made-to-order boots in short supply in many regions of the West, most cowpunchers either continued to acquire clumsy store-bought goods or purchased custom-made footwear from often-distant shops. The latter course required the customer to estimate the shape and size of his feet, a process that sometimes involved considerable guesswork. Faced with the dilemma of fitting cowboys on the Montana division of the XIT Ranch in 1894, Annie Justin, wife of Nocona, Texas, boot maker J. H. "Joe" Justin, developed a self-measurement kit that enabled her husband to supply remote customers with more confidence. Widely copied by other custom makers, Justin's measuring system proved a boon to the mail-order boot business. Most cobblers maintained an archive of tracings and foot measurements along with the various wooden lasts on which their customers' boots were fitted.

Early on, cowboys gained a reputation for wearing boots that fit so snugly that they often squeaked with the wearer's walk. "A cowboy's garments may be sometimes rather dilapidated," wrote one eyewitness, "but he would go without a coat or deny himself luxuries rather than wear a boot that had not a fine upper to its sole, or that did not fit like a glove."[80] To insure a close fit, experienced cowboys sometimes wet their new boots in oats and water and wore them until they were dry.

Tight boots, however, invariably were difficult to pull on and take off, and punchers were known to grease the inside of the heels with soap and apply flour to the insteps to loosen them up. To make their footwear easier to pull on, boot makers sewed finger grips of canvas or leather to the side seams inside the tops. Later, they fitted some styles with pointed, foot-long pull straps that hung outside the boot tops. These so-called "mule ears," allowed the wearer to grasp and tug with the entire hand. Pulling off a pair of obstinate boots, however, often required the efforts of two people.

Mary Jaques, a British visitor to central Texas in 1889 and 1890, noticed that, although cowboy boots hindered walking, they did not seem to impede dancing:

Opposite
Cowboy boots, scallop tops with diamond-shaped inlay, owner's brand and decorative stitch pattern, worn by Wyoming dude rancher I. H. "Larry" Larom, c. 1930
Buffalo Bill Historical Center, Cody, Wyoming

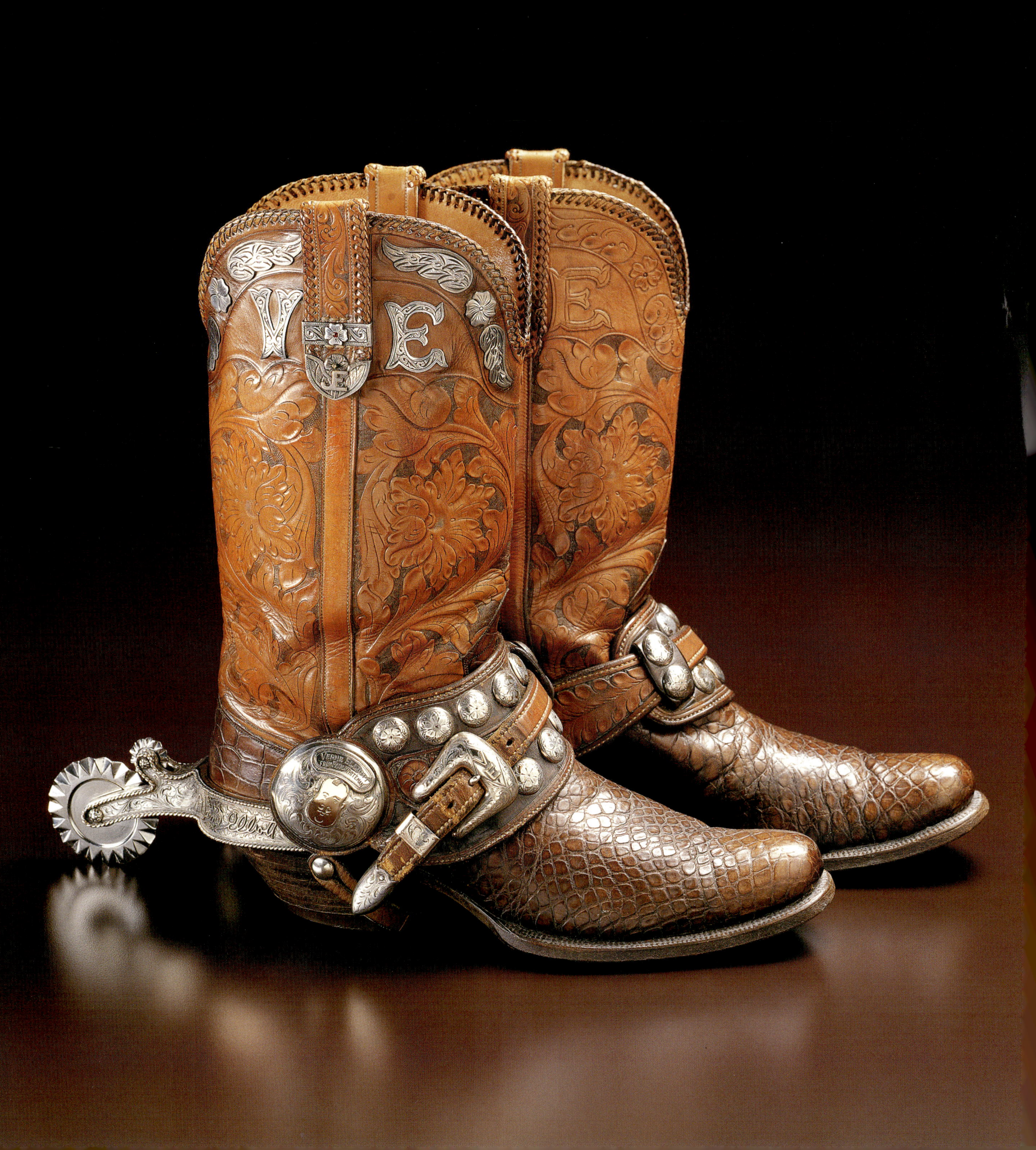
V E

> Cowboys are not exactly light-footed, but they are very springy, and make fun with their high action, while they pirouette on their high-heeled shoes. They are extremely particular about their shoes, which are always of the best make and fitting to perfection, whilst most of them possess the distinguishing mark of small, shapely feet.[81]

Another informed, late nineteenth-century observer, suggested that the "discriminating and fastidious" cowboys of Texas saved their best and tightest fitting footwear for visits to town and other social occasions:

> There the cow-boy sets himself out like the jay in the fable, with as small and narrow and high-heeled a boot as ever the cavaliers who followed Rupert could boast, so small and so tightly pinching that it is only donned and endured on certain solemn occasions.... The solemn occasion is commonly when he enters town after a long absence on "the trail." Nothing then can be allowed to dispense with the ceremony of boots; they must be worn, displayed, exulted in mightily and unctuously, as a monk exults in hair-cloth girdle. They are delectable things to the eyes of the nascent cow-boys, the novices of the trail. See how high they are! Look at the parti-colored laces in front!... But once out of town, and far from admiring eyes, off come these tormentors, and a few miles out of San Antonio you will meet your hero or martyr, as the case may be, with the beautiful boots hanging to his saddle and his eye surveying them with a defiant satisfaction.[82]

Cowboys proud of their footwear sometimes called attention to them by stuffing their pants legs inside the boot tops. This style came and went, however, and, if vintage photographs of late nineteenth-century cowhands may be believed, was a matter of personal preference and probably more in evidence in town than on the range.

Meanwhile, cowboy-style boots underwent a number of structural refinements. Unsupported leather and wooden shanks, for example, often broke down after prolonged use, as did pliant boot tops, which, with time, tended to sag and wrinkle at the ankle. Following a period of experimentation with various types of shank reinforcement, including flattened 20-penny nails, boot makers eventually settled on a thin steel truss. By the 1880s they also began to support drooping boot tops with lightweight calfskin lining, further strengthened with silk stitching, sometimes applied in a decorative geometric or floral pattern.

Opposite
Edward H. Bohlin, Hollywood Cowboy boots, hand carved and stamped tops with laced edges, silver initials, and appliqués; stainless-steel spurs with engraved sterling silver overlay, rope edge, rowel on chap guard, owned by rodeo stock contractor Verne Elliot, c. 1935
National Cowboy Hall of Fame and Western Heritage Center, Oklahoma City

Above
John B. Stetson Co., Philadelphia Cowboy hat with "Montana Peak"–style crease and floral stamped band with buckle
Buffalo Bill Historical Center, Cody, Wyoming

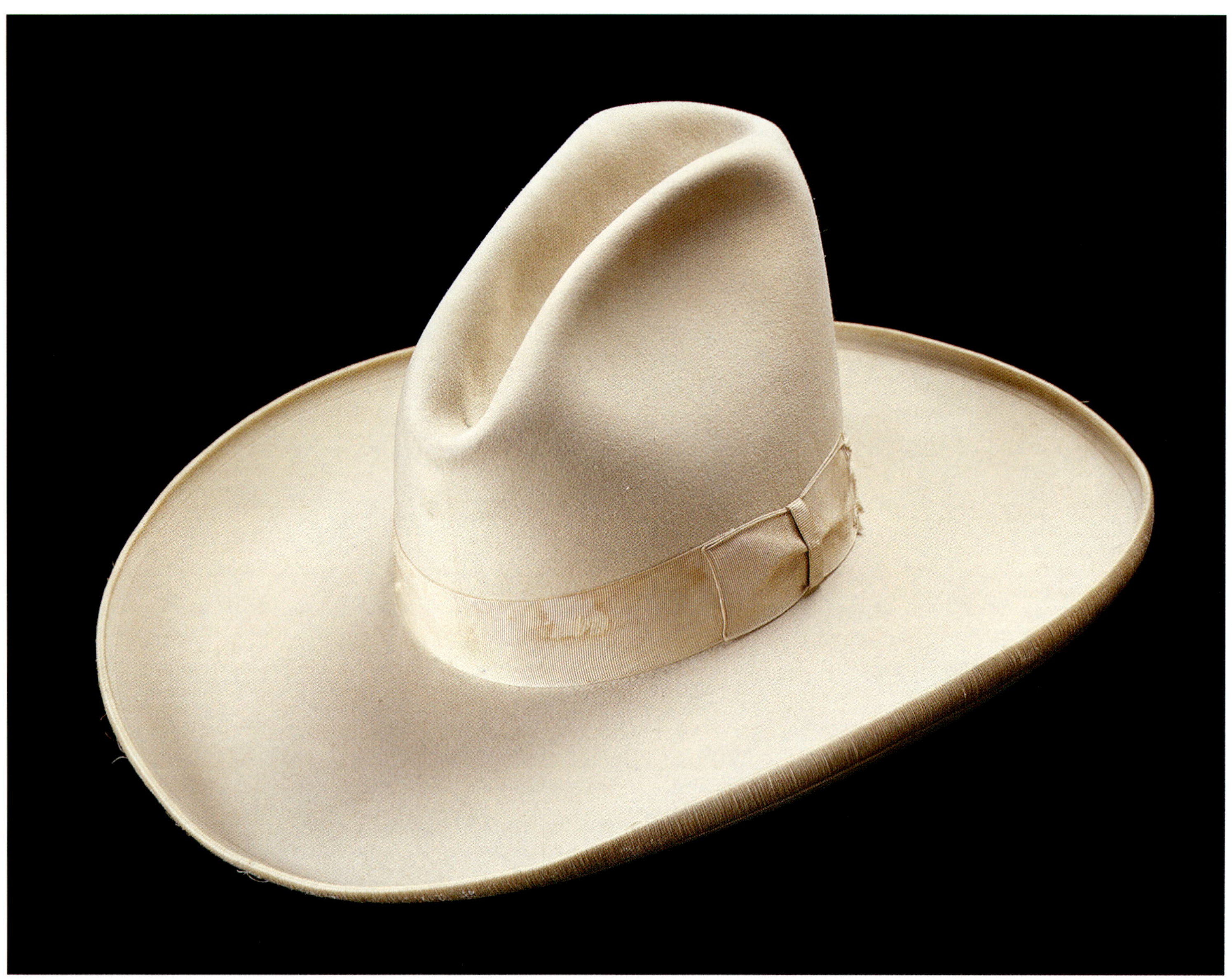

John B. Stetson Co., Philadelphia
Cowboy hat, white felt, cloth band and curled brim, worn by rodeo trick rider Tad Lucas
National Cowboy and Western Heritage Museum, Oklahoma City

Opposite
Stallion Boot Co., El Paso
Woman's cowboy boots with horseshoe and padded horse head and metal stars on tops, and stars and horseshoes inlaid in wingtips, c. 2000
Fleischer Collection, Scottsdale

The practice of cutting boot tops higher in front than in the rear soon gave way to square-cut tops. For variation, craftsmen eventually added V-shaped notches front and rear, in part to help relieve the pressure on a rider's shins and calves. At the same time, the boot makers' desire to save weight and conserve materials, coupled with cowboys' propensity to wear protective leather leggings in rough country, prompted a gradual reduction in the height of boot tops.

By the 1890s many western towns had one or more resident boot makers, some of them European-trained craftsmen. As custom boot makers became more plentiful and their products more accessible, made-to-order footwear became another mark of top hands. In 1919 Frank Hastings, manager of the vast SMS ranch, observed that cowboys had a passion for Stetson hats and $25 shop-made boots. Veteran cowhands often teased neophytes who wore brogan shoes or heavy flat-heeled boots, called "grangers," until they were properly "shod."

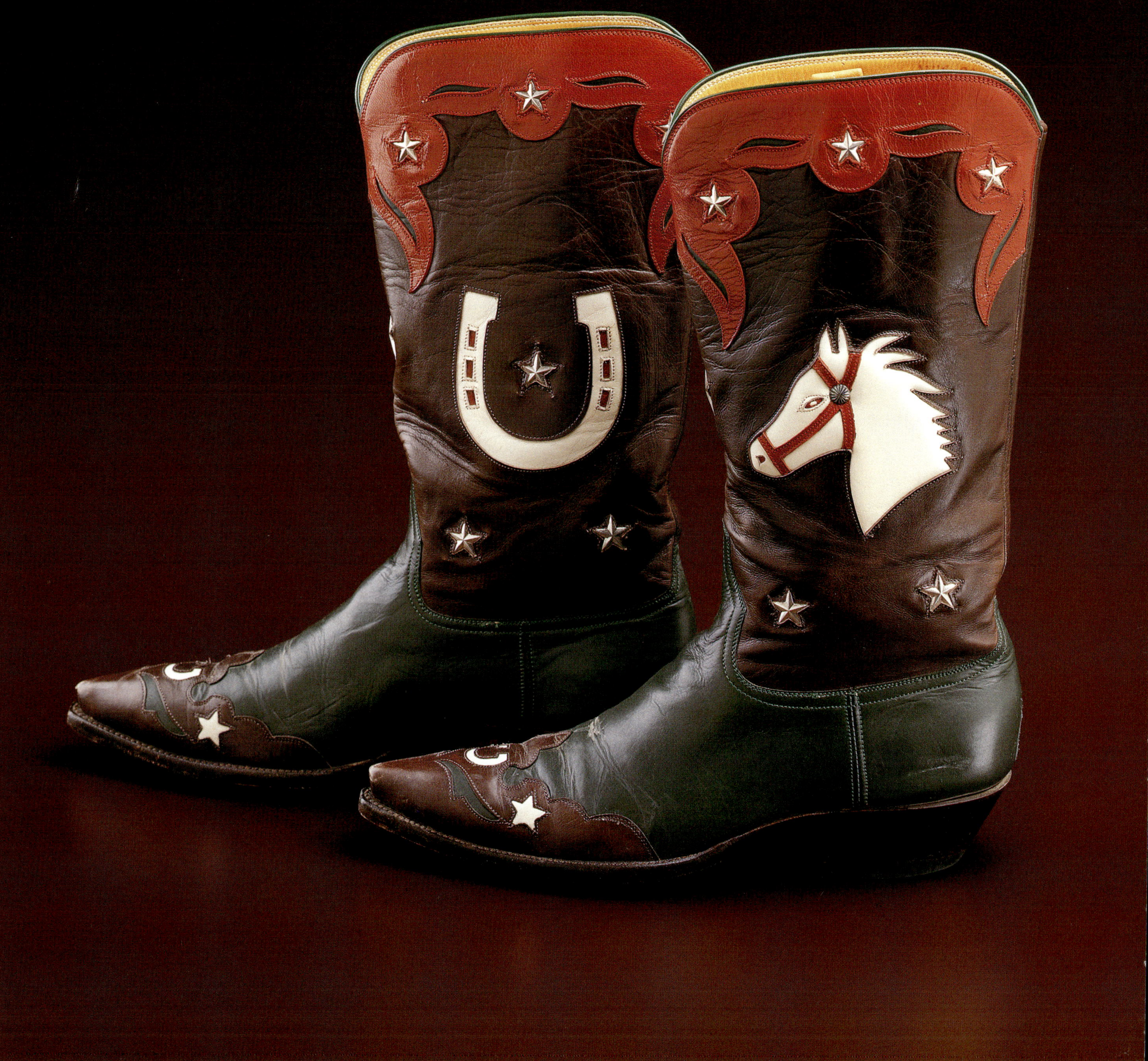

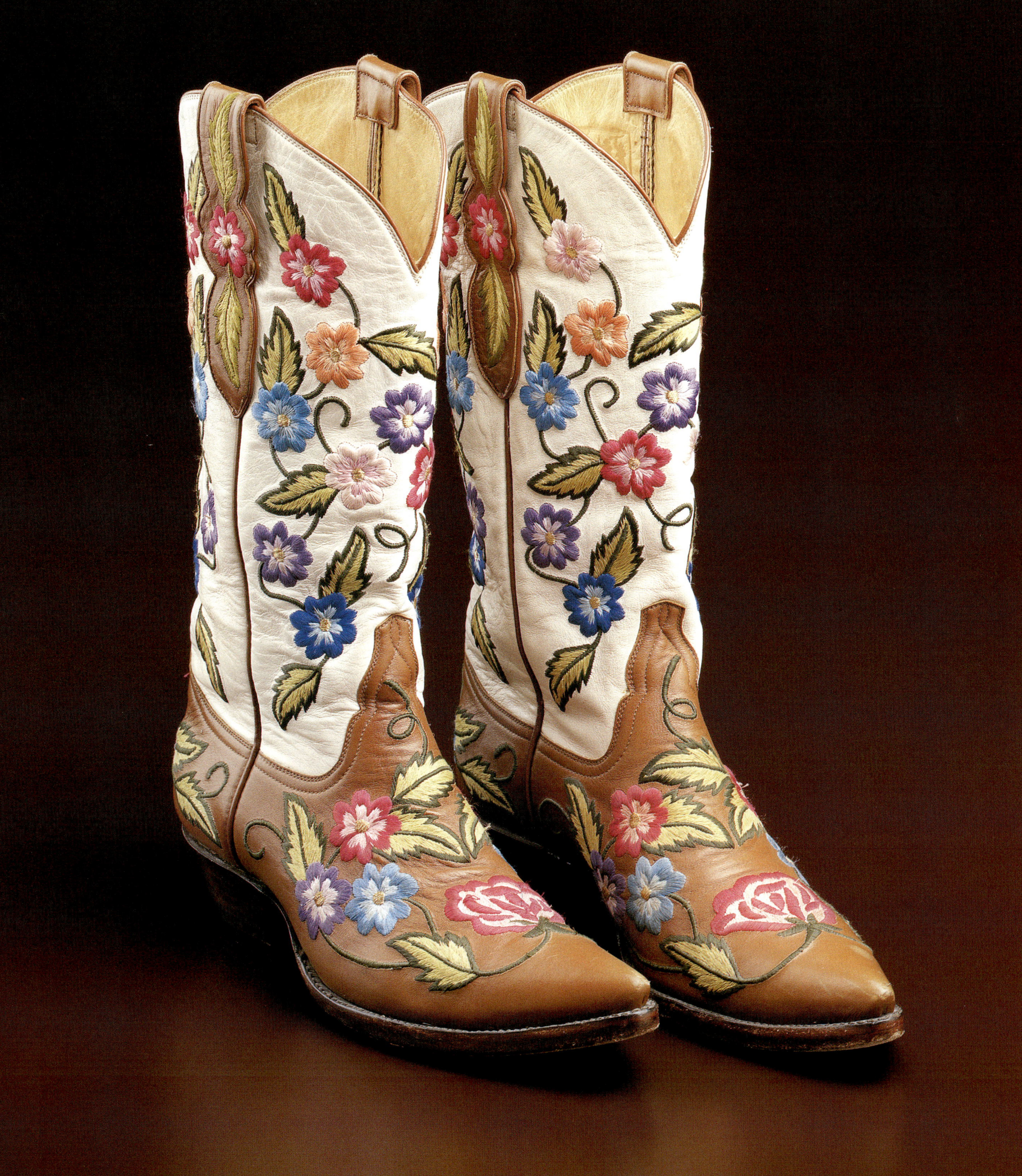

By the early twentieth-century, many custom boot makers had turned to technology to expand their operations. The advent of mechanization enabled larger companies and custom shops to divide the boot-making process, once the province of a single craftsman, among several specialists. One veteran cobbler called the mingling of old-time craftsmanship with the selective use of equipment, a "handcraft-production line."[83]

Machinery enabled companies to cope with a diminishing number of experienced, all-around craftsmen and talented apprentices while capitalizing on the individual skills of employees. Power tools impacted some aspects of boot making more than others. Sewing machines undoubtedly wielded the greatest initial influence. When operated with dexterity, mechanical stitchers not only produced footwear faster and more economically, but also with greater strength and uniformity. With the widespread adoption of sewing machines, many women found work in the boot trade stitching boot tops.

Although some blamed mechanization for the disappearance of many custom boot shops in the first two decades of the twentieth century, other factors also were at work. The coming of barbed wire fences and the close of the open range during the last quarter of the nineteenth century dramatically reduced the cowboy population and diminished the demand for high-heeled work boots. Increasingly, ranchers required their hands to engage in haying, fencing, and other groundwork. With the demise of full-time horseback work, some hands abandoned their distinctive footwear for something more comfortable in which to walk.

Between the 1880s and the mid-1910s, cowboy boot styles changed little. Cobblers fashioned most from black or dark brown domestic or French calfskin. Expensive kangaroo, alligator, and morocco kid leather was usually reserved for dress boots. The era's only important design innovations, Charles Hyer's 1903 introduction of decorative stitching on the boot toe, known as "toe wrinkles," and Gus Blucher's improved shank designs, which helped riders hold their stirrups better, were widely imitated. By the turn of the century a modest row or two of black, brown, green, or white silk stitching had replaced the colorful, if crude, decorative devices that had adorned early cowboy boot tops.

With the decline of the ranch trade, many boot companies diversified their product lines to include shoes, military and lace-up work boots, and such leather accessories as belts and purses. During the first three decades of the twentieth century, however, the development of dude ranching, the rising popularity of rodeo, and the impact of western motion pictures reinvigorated the cowboy boot market and led to colorful and dramatic changes in style.

Each summer, western outfitters introduced large numbers of eastern tourists, both male and female, to cowboy boots for the first time. At first, women simply slipped into smaller sizes of men's boots. During the 1920s and 1930s, however, many western boot makers introduced colorful and lightweight cowboy

Opposite
Tres Outlaws Boot Company, El Paso
Woman's cowboy boots with floral embroidered tops, vamps, and pulls, c. 2000
FLEISCHER COLLECTION, SCOTTSDALE

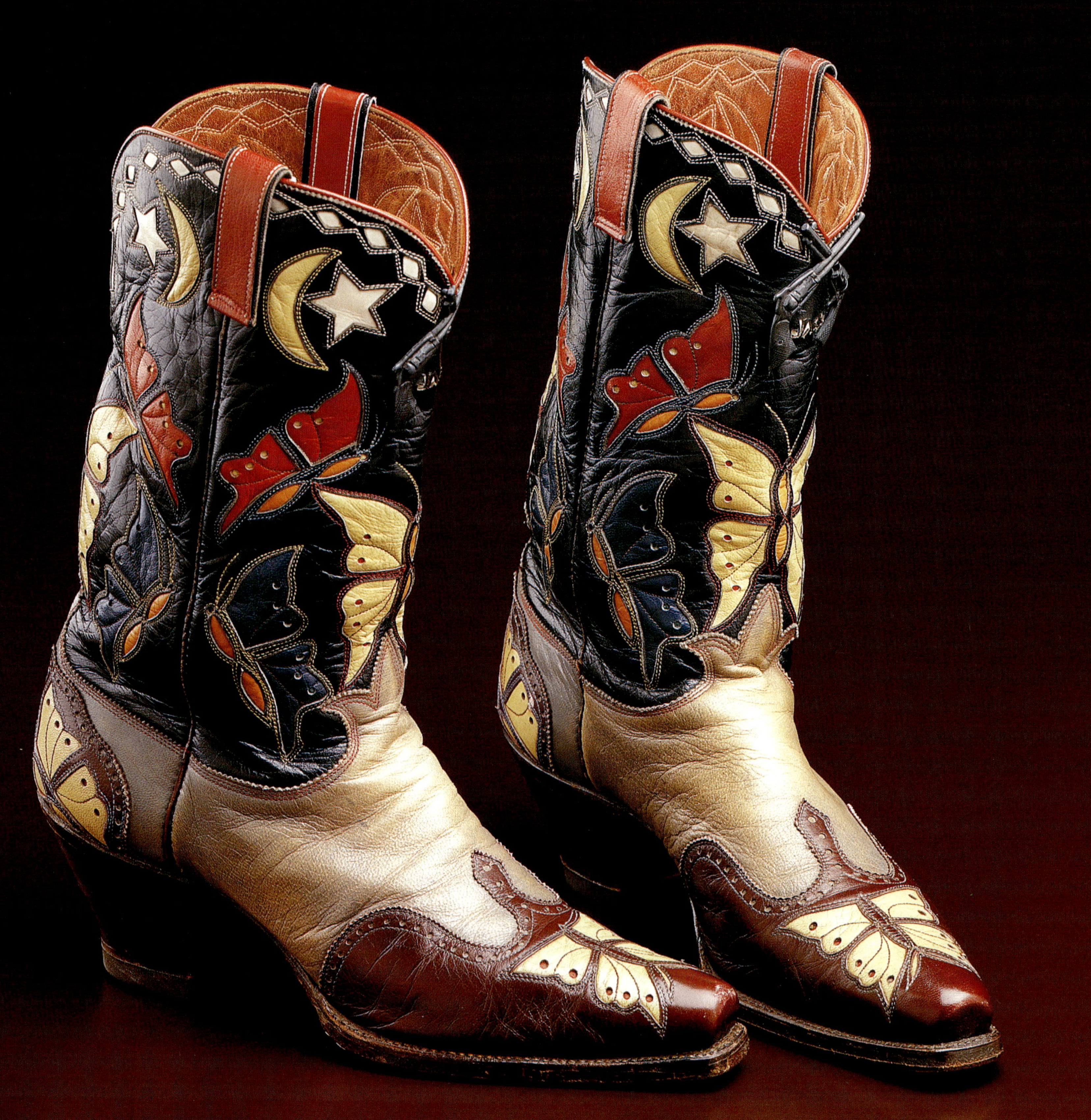

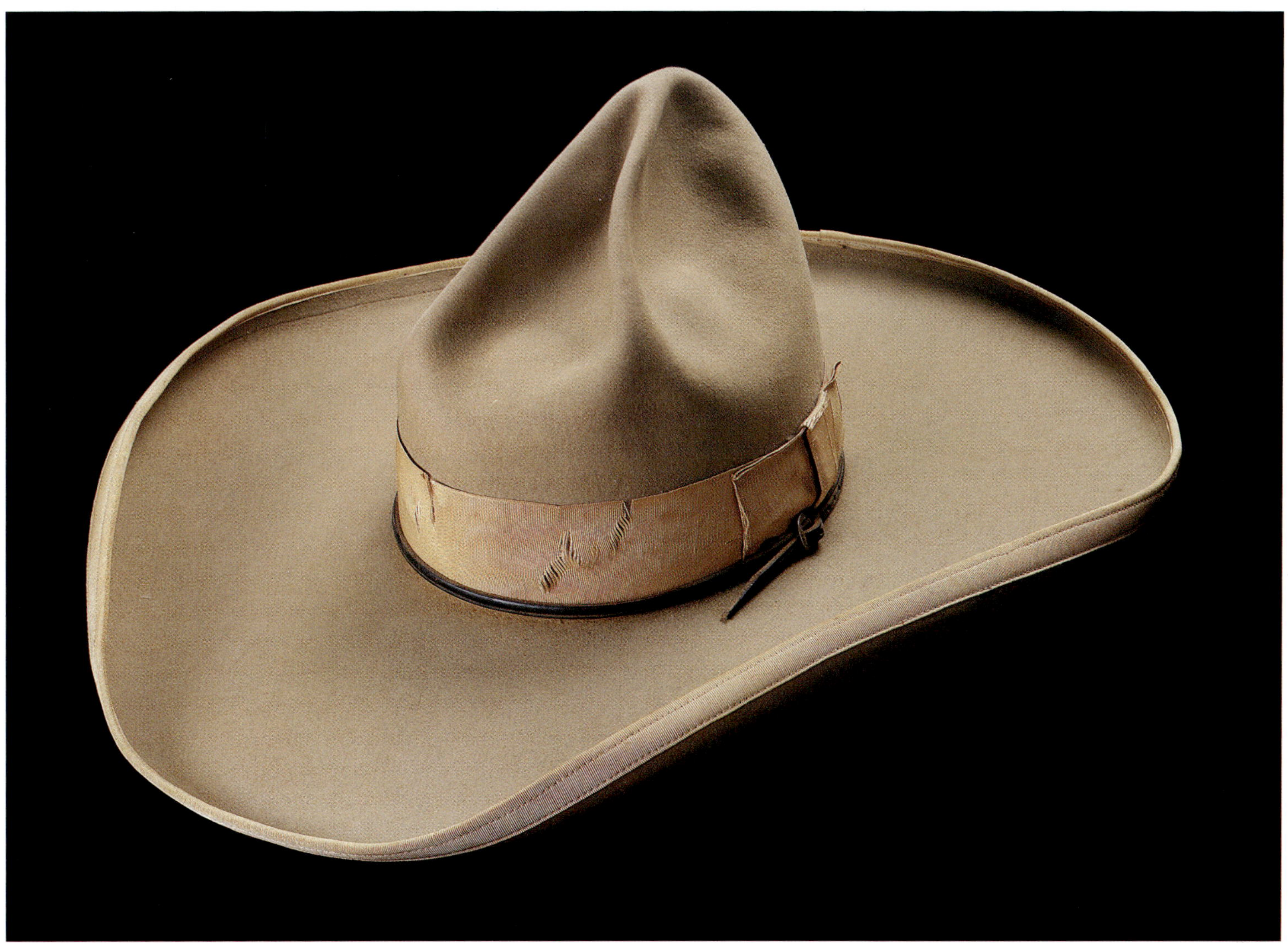

footwear designed especially for women. Justin, for example, offered a line of thin-soled women's cowboy boots under the trade name "Western Gypsy."

By this time movie cowboys and rodeo performers, too, had begun to demand flashier footwear. Boot makers responded with imaginative designs created from multicolored leathers, elaborate stitch and stamp patterns, complex leather inlays and overlays, and embossed or engraved silverwork applied to heels, tops, and toes. Shark- and sealskin joined kangaroo and alligator on the list of exotic leathers utilized by western boot makers of the period.

Many companies flaunted their lists of celebrity clients and often sought their endorsements in boot advertising and promotion. Rodeo champions not only promoted various boot makers, but also proposed modifications in boot design, especially the size and shape of heels. Ropers and bulldoggers, who prized ground mobility during timed events, called for lower, flatter types, while rough stock riders prized higher heels and shanks that allowed them to maintain a more secure seat in the saddle.

Opposite
Cowboy boots with butterfly and celestial motifs, c. 1940s
Buffalo Bill Historical Center, Cody, Wyoming

Above
John B. Stetson Co., Philadelphia Cowboy hat with "Carlsbad"–style crease, cloth band, bound brim with kettle roll, worn by western actor and rodeo star Jack Hoxie, c. 1920s
National Cowboy and Western Heritage Museum, Oklahoma City

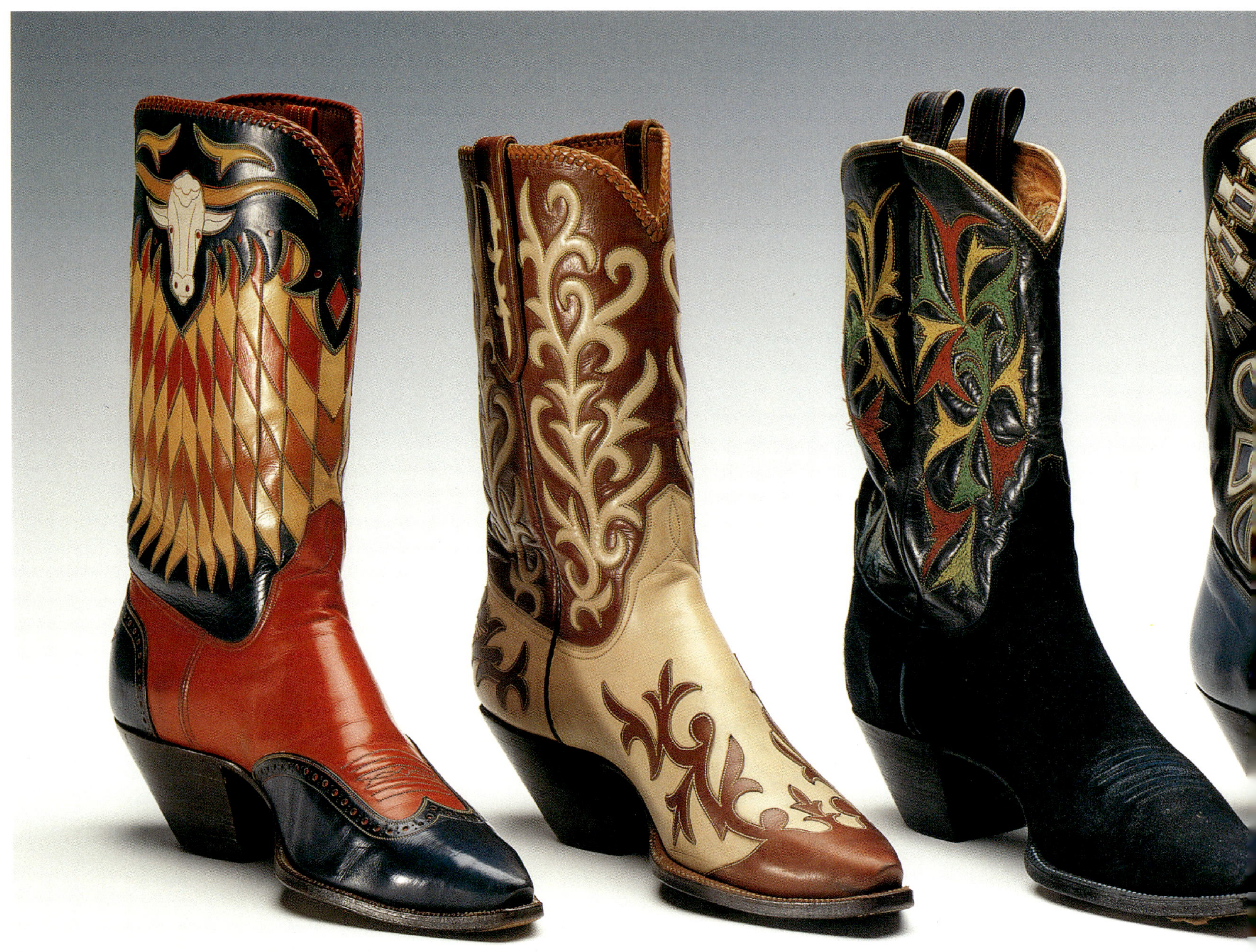

Lucchese Boot Co., San Antonio, Texas
Boots made for Gene Autry
MUSEUM OF THE AMERICAN WEST, LOS ANGELES

Tom Mix, who epitomized the Hollywood cowboy of the 1920s and 1930s, wore some of the most colorful boots of the era. Like many stars, he purchased distinctive footwear from several different makers. Using gold thread, Gus Blucher stitched the uppers of one pair of Mix's boots in a beautiful tulip pattern, which was accented with a row of inlaid white leather diamonds around the rim of the boot top. Another of Blucher's creations for the cowboy star incorporated a decorative, hand-stamped leather collar laced along the top edge of the upper. Fashion plates such as Mix invariably wore their tailored pants legs inside their boot tops so that their boot maker's creativity could be more fully appreciated.

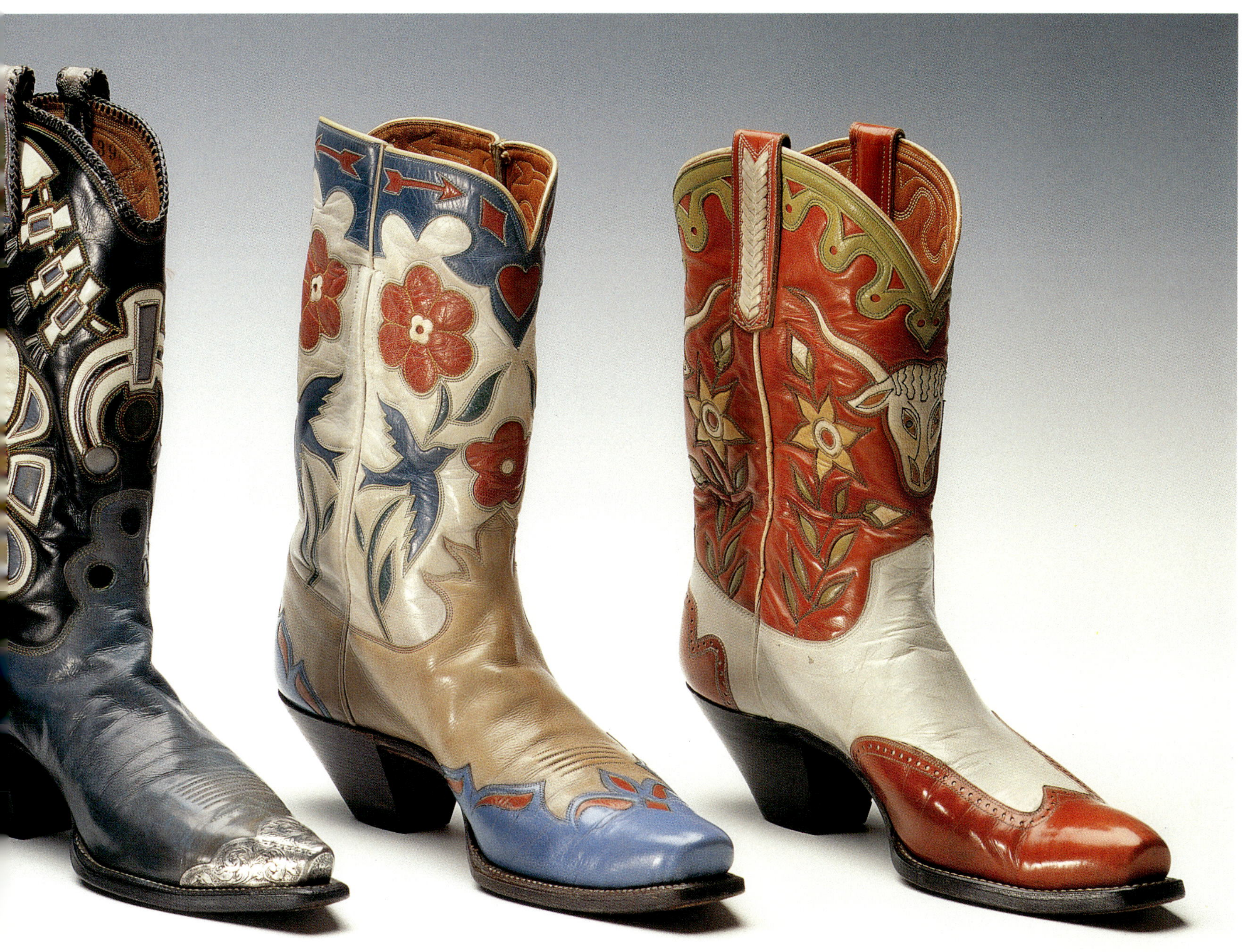

Several companies capitalized on Mix's popularity by introducing a line of stock boots named for the cowboy hero. In 1923, for example, Justin's catalog described its Tom Mix–style boot as having "black kangaroo vamps with a wrinkled and stitched toe, kidskin uppers inlaid with white tulips and long cloth pulls."[84] Legend tells that in the early 1920s engineers held a passenger train while Mix prowled Joe Justin's Nocona shop for a new pair of boots.

Several craftsmen fitted their creations with carved or stamped leather tops, some of which matched their owner's tack. In 1938 Justin offered two such styles. Priced at $55, one featured elaborate flower stamping on a black background.

The other, a $60 pattern, boasted a hand-stamped upper that included a longhorn head in front, the image of a bronc rider taken from the work of famous Montana cowboy artist Charles M. Russell on one side, and a cowboy riding a longhorn steer on the other, all surrounded by floral accents. The customer chose the background color. The trade catalog description called attention to the boot's "simple elegance that stands out at any gathering of cattle men like a prairie grassfire on a dark night. . . ."[85]

In the early 1940s leather shortages and rationing brought on by World War II temporarily sidetracked the boot market and necessitated structural adjustments to the boots themselves. In a 1944 article in *Hoofs and Horns* magazine, W. M. Shelton noted that: "Many of the boots in this great Southwest are at present filled, and kept in shape with 'trees,' while their owners ride strange steeds of steel, or wing through the flaming skies"[86] Yet at least a few diehard GIs were observed wearing their cowboy boots into battle instead of regulation combat boots.

In order to conserve leather, makers lowered the height of boot tops from the average fifteen inches to between eight and twelve inches. The lightweight "pee wee" style, as it became known, did not please everyone. Wearers often found it difficult to tuck their pants legs into the short flaring tops, which also tended to collect dirt and other trash. At least a few cowboys compensated by sewing the tops from a worn out pair of boots onto the "pee wee" upper to achieve the desired height.

The end of World War II brought another watershed in cowboy boot design and embellishment and the strongest market yet. To help meet the pent-up demand, the Justin Boot Company, which had moved to Fort Worth from Nocona in 1925, abandoned its other boot and shoe lines in 1948 to concentrate on producing cowboy-style footwear. An innovator in boot design, Justin had pioneered narrow square toes in the early 1940s and pointed, needle-nose styles a few years later. By 1949 several boot makers also had begun to add a shock-absorbing, ground cork cushion to the sole for increased comfort.

Boot companies, meanwhile, continued to push the style envelope, at times to the point of tastelessness. As John Justin told writer Jane Pattie, ". . . I bought some glove leather in yellow and a chartreuse green and a bilious red and a terrible blue, and I made boots in every combination you can think of. I made solids and I made them with different tops, and I made some with kind of a half wingtip on them."[87] Images of birds, butterflies, flowers, oil derricks, steer heads, and even human faces also found their way onto boot tops and vamps, as did college pennants and nicknames rendered in school colors. Amid the hum of sewing machines, talented artisans patiently applied decorative stitch patterns that, on some of the most ornate styles, consisted of as many as twenty rows of colored silk thread. Longtime San Antonio boot maker Cosimo Lucchese believed, however,

Opposite
Cowboy boots with inlaid designs, worn by singing cowboy Gene Autry, c. 1945
National Cowboy and Western Heritage Museum, Oklahoma City

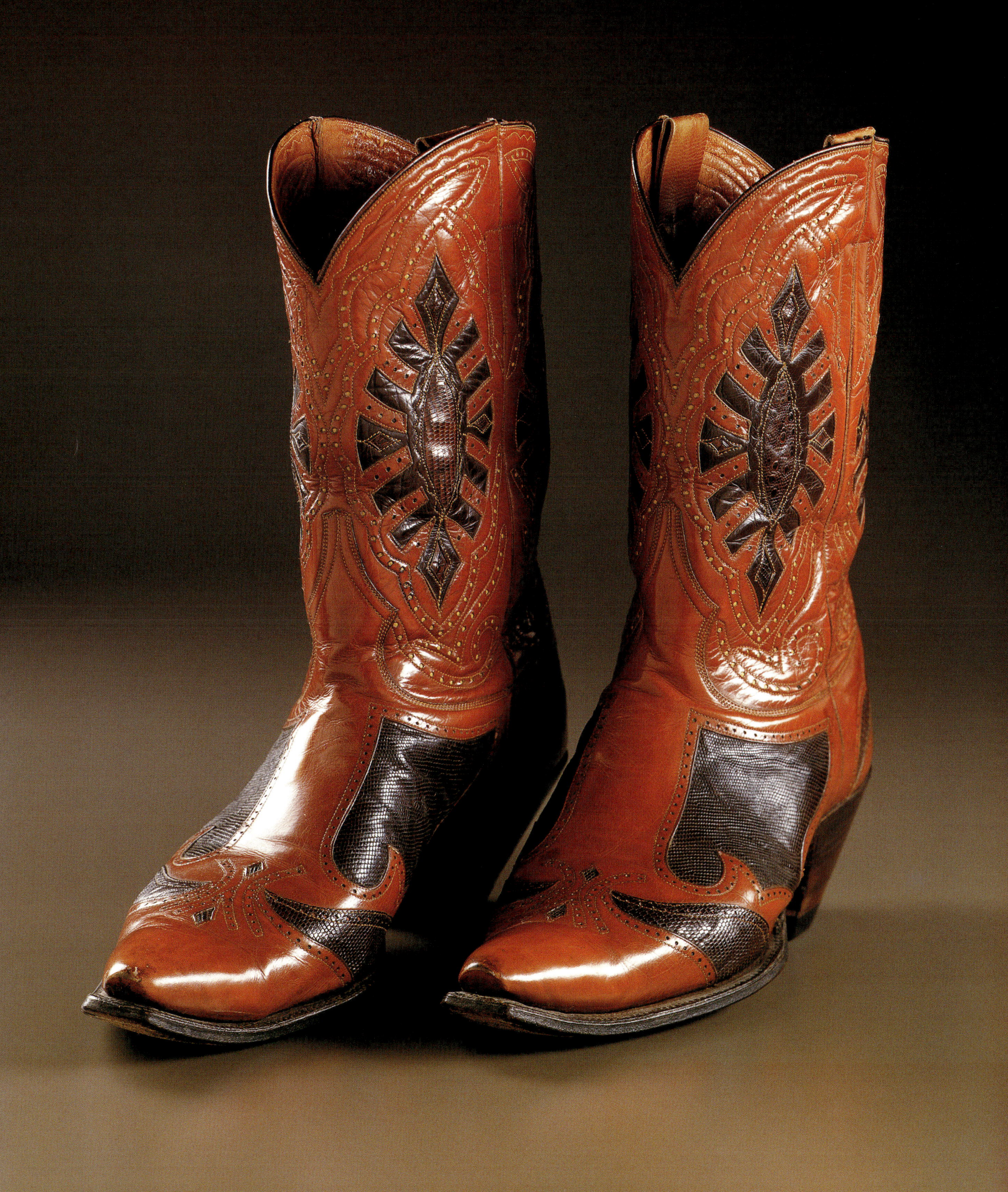

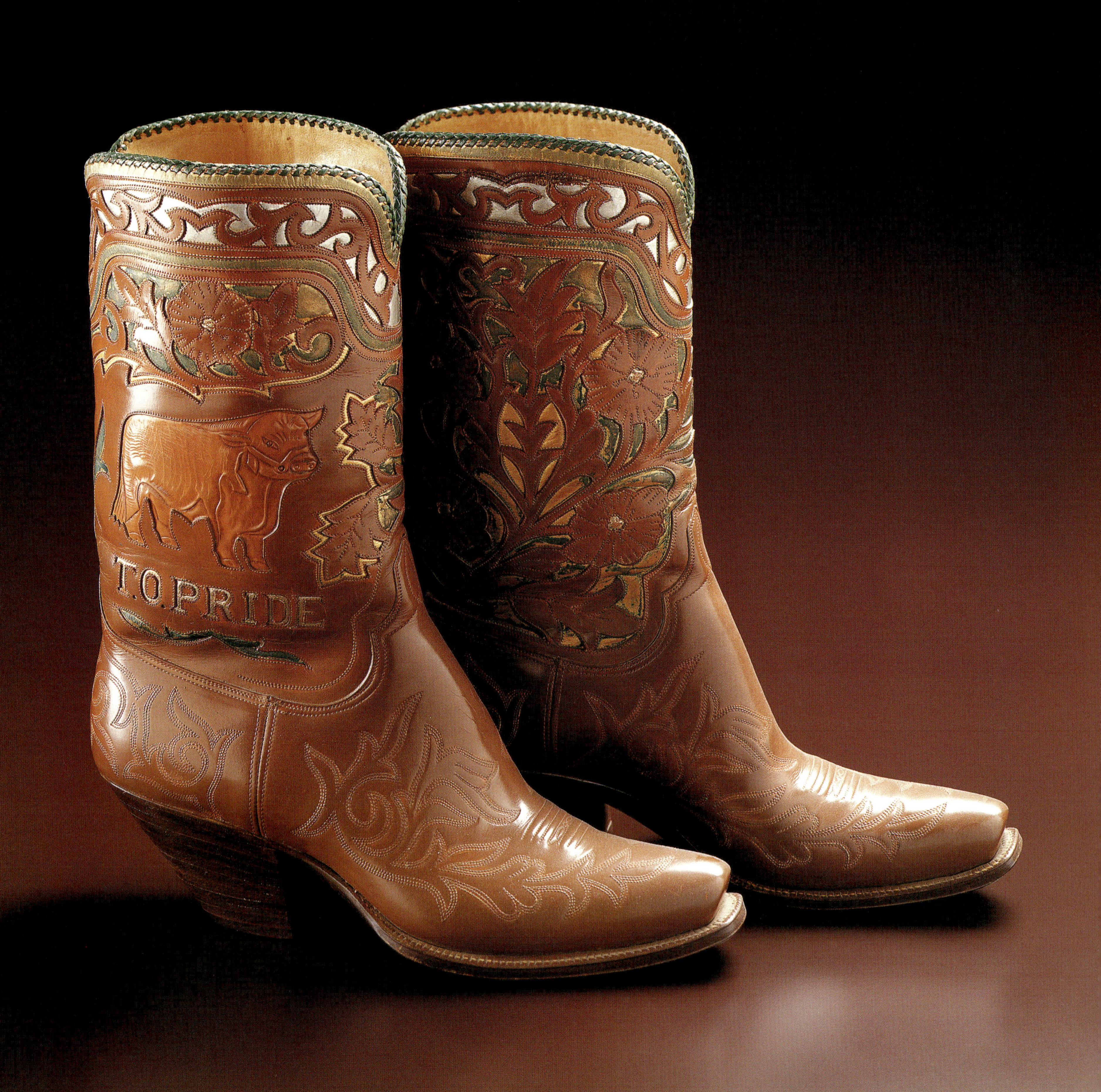
T.O.PRIDE

that six rows of stitching endowed a boot top with sufficient body and class and that more than eight was too extravagant.

According to one 1956 estimate, even among those companies that had invested most heavily in machinery, handwork still comprised over 50 percent of the boot-making process. Boot makers large and small spent more time embellishing their products than on any other procedure. Fully half of all Justin boot company workers in the mid-1950s were employed in this task.

Whatever their sources of inspiration, popular designs created by one maker were soon replicated or adapted by others. In the late 1940s Enid Justin, a gifted woman who had founded the Nocona Boot Company more than twenty years before, offered cowboy boots in some 400 different patterns and combinations. Most of the seventy-five major western boot makers of the period maintained

Opposite
Cowboy boots made of the hide of a Grand Champion steer, Denver Stock Show, with filigree, gold leaf, and laced tops and stitched vamps, worn by television personality Arthur Godfrey, c. 1965
National Cowboy and Western Heritage Museum, Oklahoma City

Below
John B. Stetson Co., Philadelphia Cowboy hat with "Montana Peak" crease, cloth band, and raw edge, made for movie star Tom Mix, c. 1930
National Cowboy and Western Heritage Museum, Oklahoma City

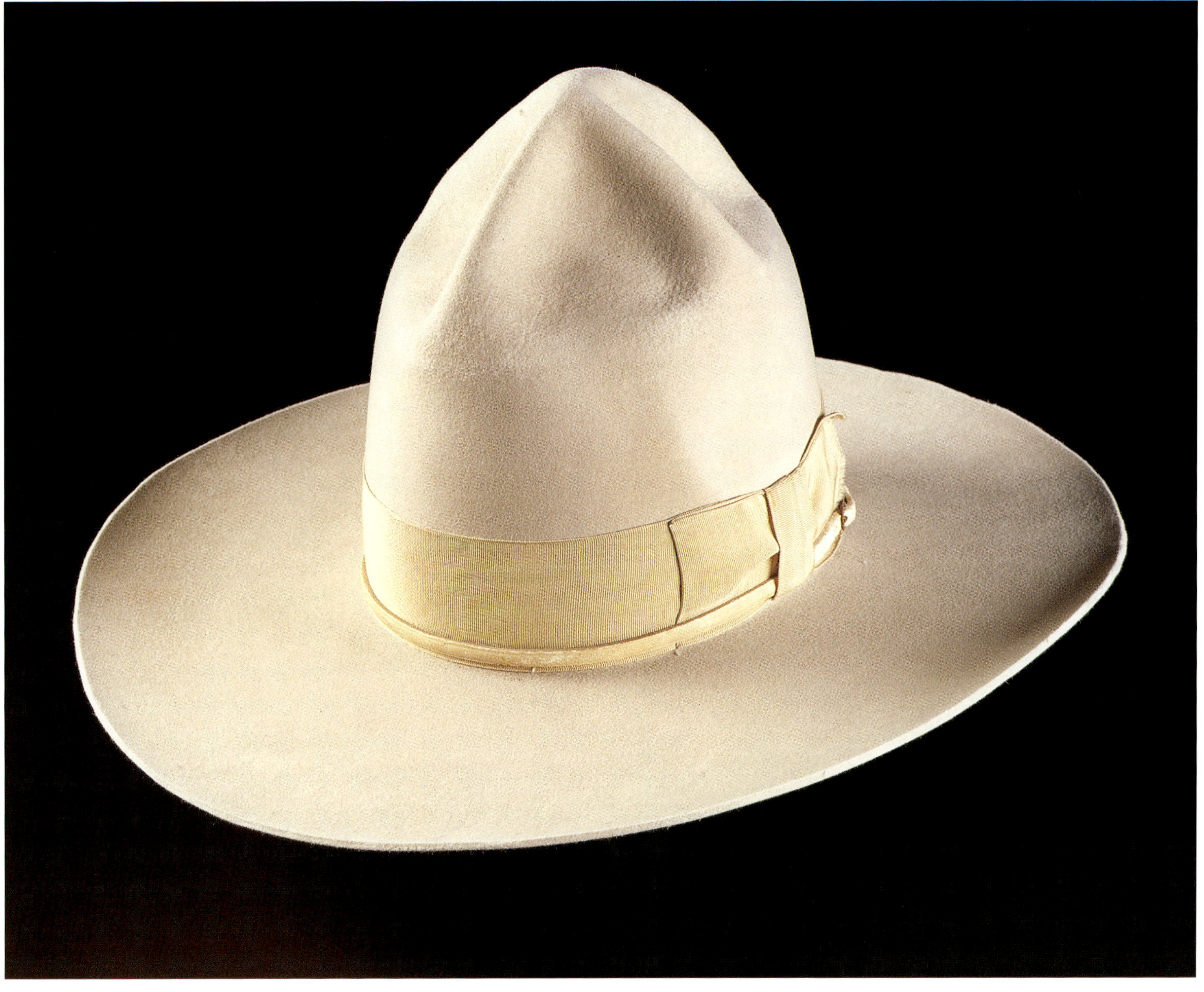

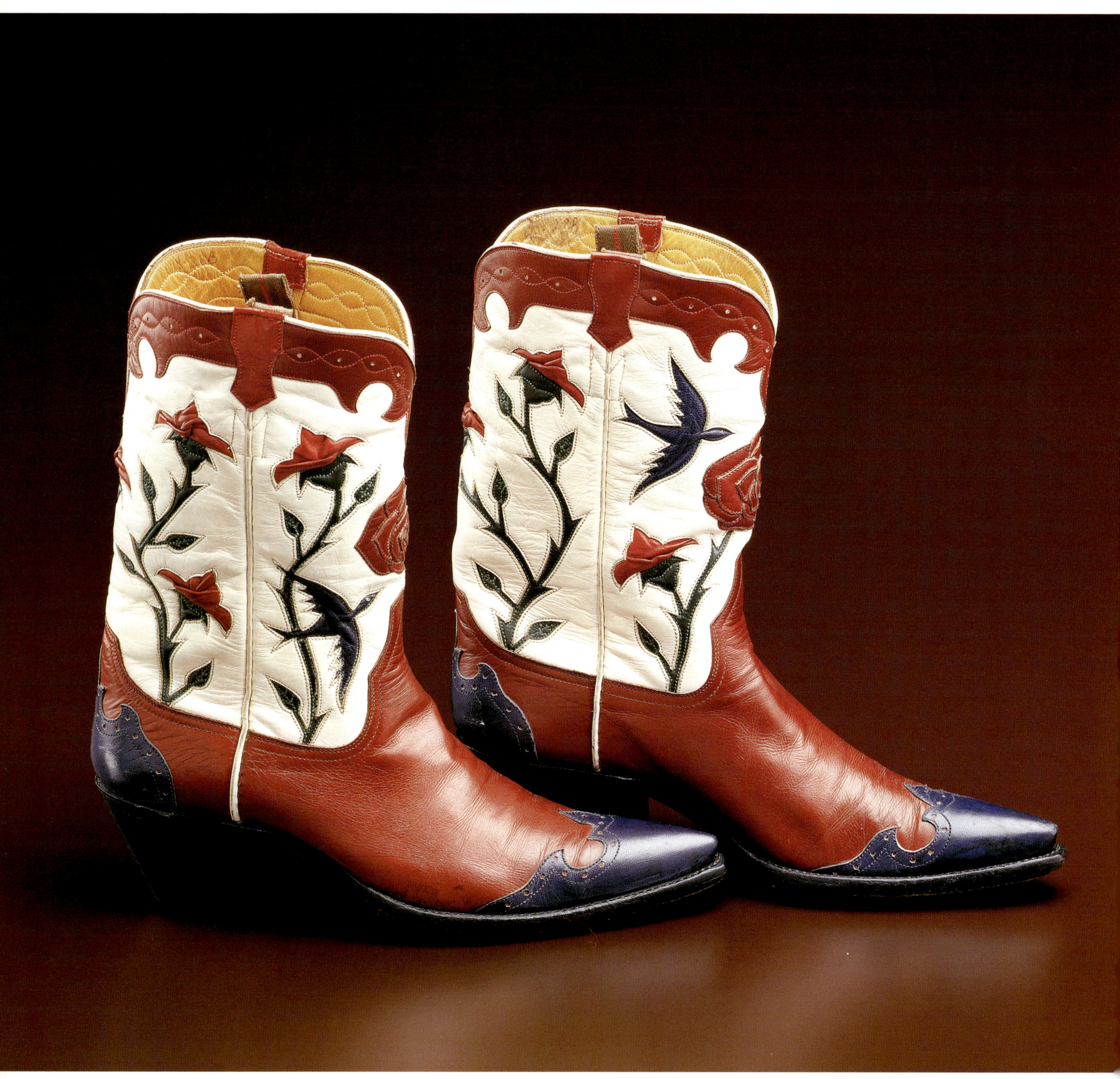

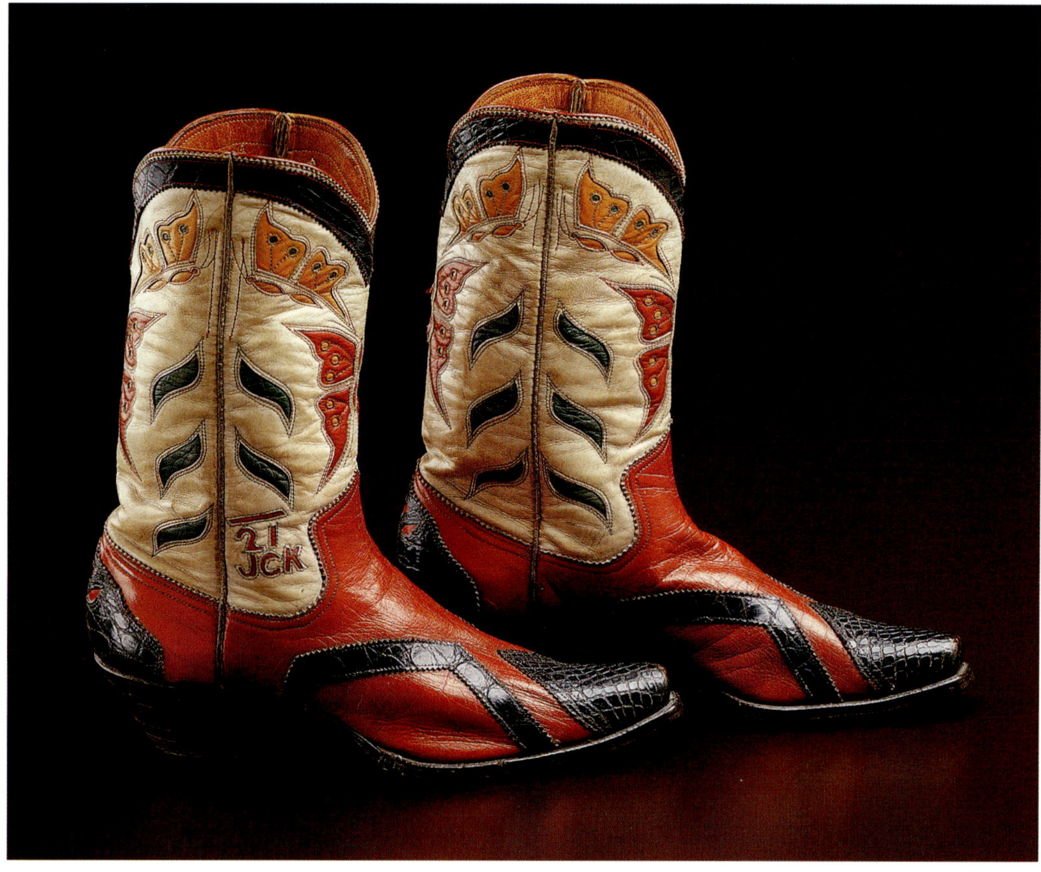

Opposite
Stallion Boot Co., El Paso
Woman's cowboy boots with padded red roses and blue bird motif, c. 2000
FLEISCHER COLLECTION, SCOTTSDALE

Left
Cowboy boots, butterfly pattern, worn by Jack Kriendler, owner of the "21" Club, New York, c. 1940s
BUFFALO BILL HISTORICAL CENTER, CODY, WYOMING

comprehensive design libraries so that old styles could be retrieved for special orders at a moment's notice. Cattle brands or other special orders typically added 50 cents to $1.50 to the price of a pair of boots and unusual color combinations $2 or $3.

In addition to traditional materials and motifs, some makers began to mount diamonds and other precious stones into boot tops. In 1955, for example, the Tony Lama Boot Co. of El Paso configured its $5,000 "El Rey" (The King) pattern, with thirty-two diamonds, rubies, and emeralds in platinum, gold, and silver settings. One rancher reportedly paid $1,500 for a pair of boots with his cattle brand outlined in diamonds.

The explosion of new boot designs prompted one writer's 1951 comment that: "Cowboy boots have always been practical, durable and a bit arty but today they are a genteel riot of color. . . ."[88] Bright hues, fantastic trimmings, sharp-pointed toes, and escalating prices, however, left some old-time boot makers shaking their heads in disbelief. Many conservative cowboys and cattlemen also recoiled at such stylistic excess and continued to favor more somber colors and traditional styling.

By the mid-1950s the era of "pee wee" boots had about run its course, and boot tops had returned to heights ranging from ten to fourteen inches. Rubber heels, which offered a firmer grip on smooth surfaces, had largely replaced leather

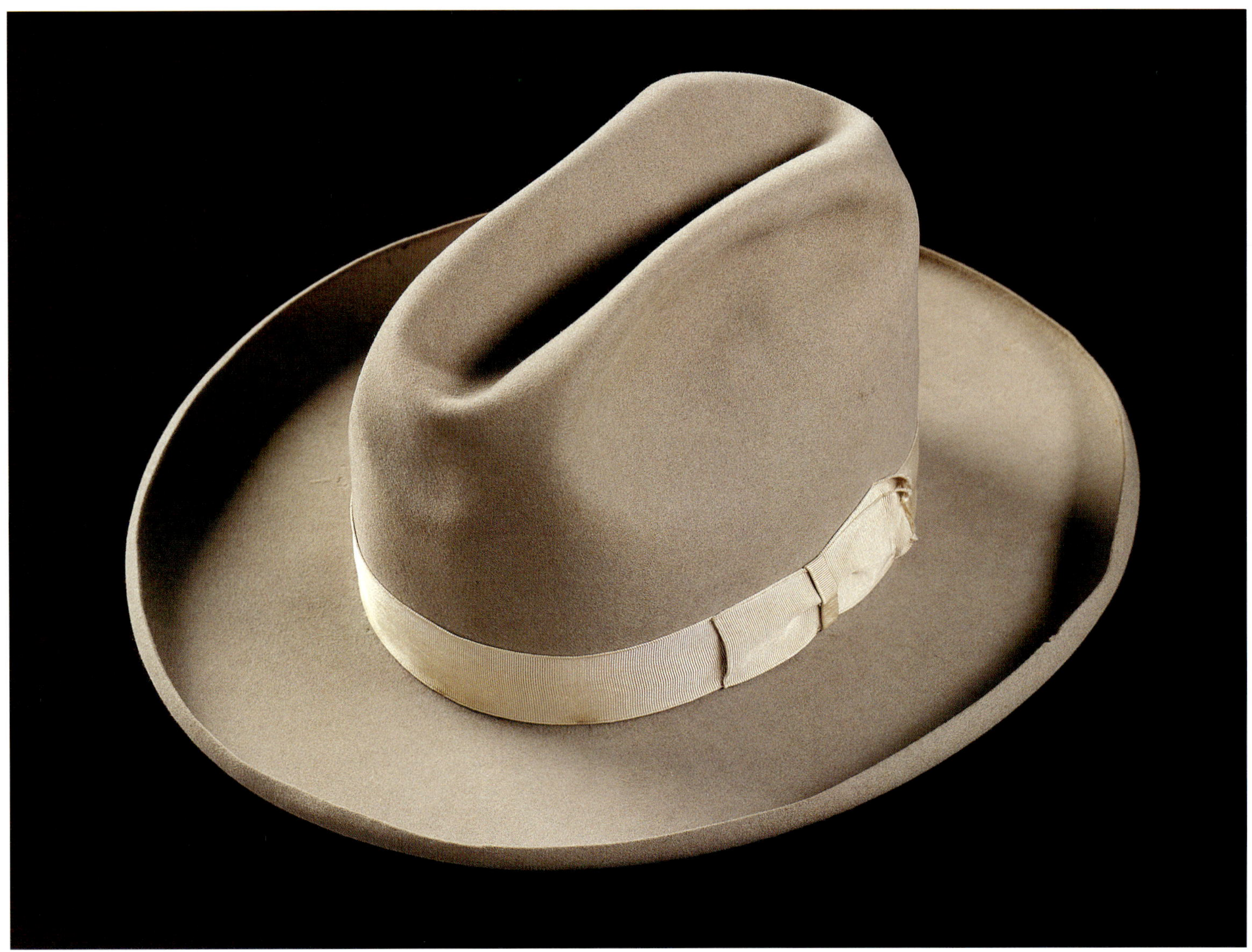

John B. Stetson Co., Philadelphia
Felt cowboy hat with cloth band and curled brim
National Cowboy and Western Heritage Museum, Oklahoma City

Opposite
Stallion Boot Co., El Paso
"The Texas Cowboy," limited edition boots, no. 13 of 100, with laced tops and pulls; Longhorn steerhead motif on tops and toes, c. 2000
Fleischer Collection, Scottsdale

types. Those worn by working cowboys rarely reached two inches in height while recreational riders favored types that seldom exceeded an inch. A Texas lawman of the period claimed to be able to be able to separate "drug store cowboys" from the real thing by the wobble in their walk.

With the onset of the Vietnam era and the decline in the popularity of western movies and television, the "golden age" of cowboy boots finally came to an end in the late 1960s. More conservative styles aimed primarily at the regional western market emerged. This hiatus was short-lived, however, as the mid-1970s and the early 1980s ushered in a fresh and unprecedented spurt of growth and creativity among cowboy boot makers. National fashion trends that again embraced western wear as emblematic of American culture contributed to the rapid rise of this phenomenon, as did the mass-market strategies of large-scale boot makers. The growing popularity of progressive country music with its redneck, outlaw image and the 1980 movie *Urban Cowboy* starring John Travolta also

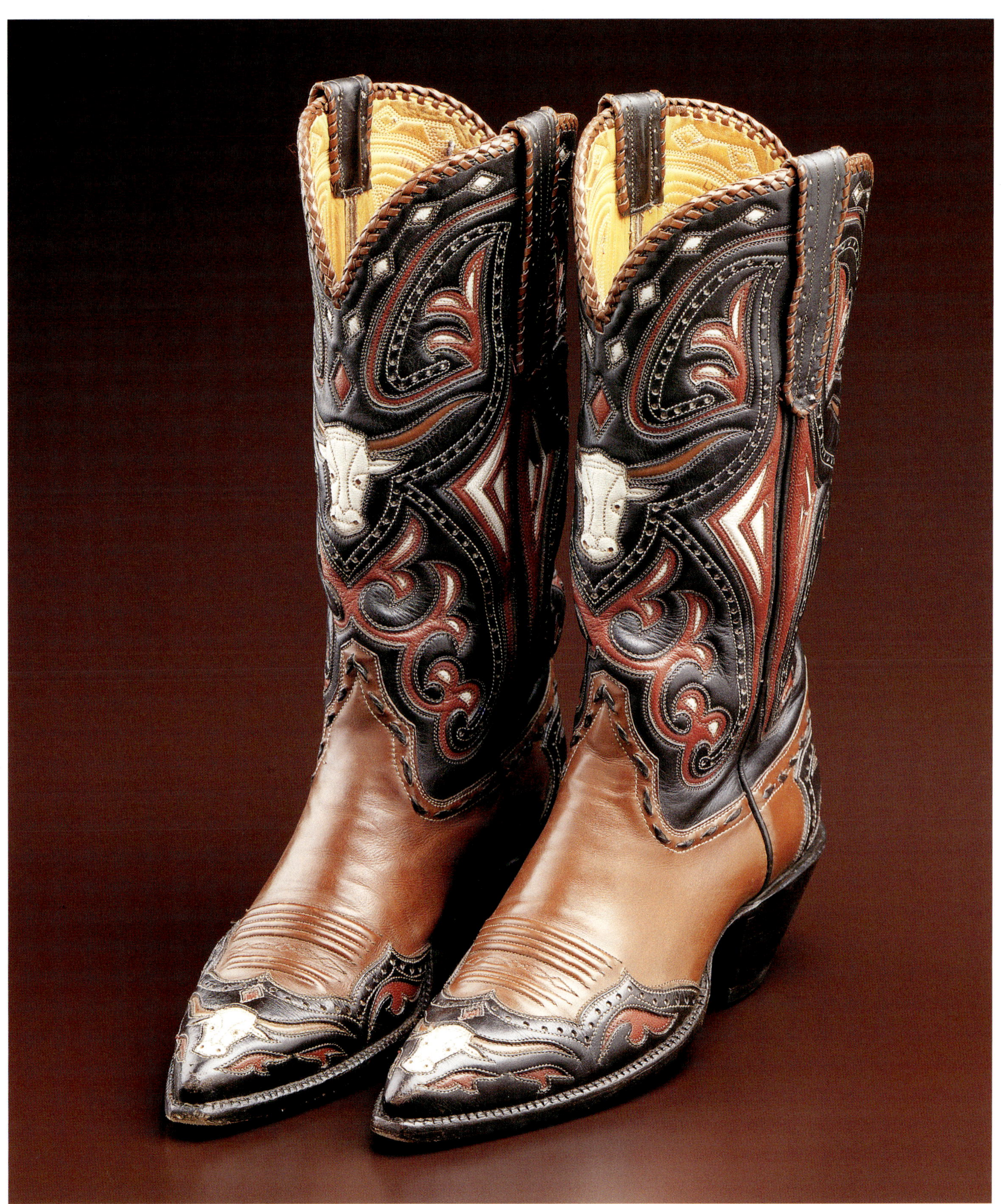

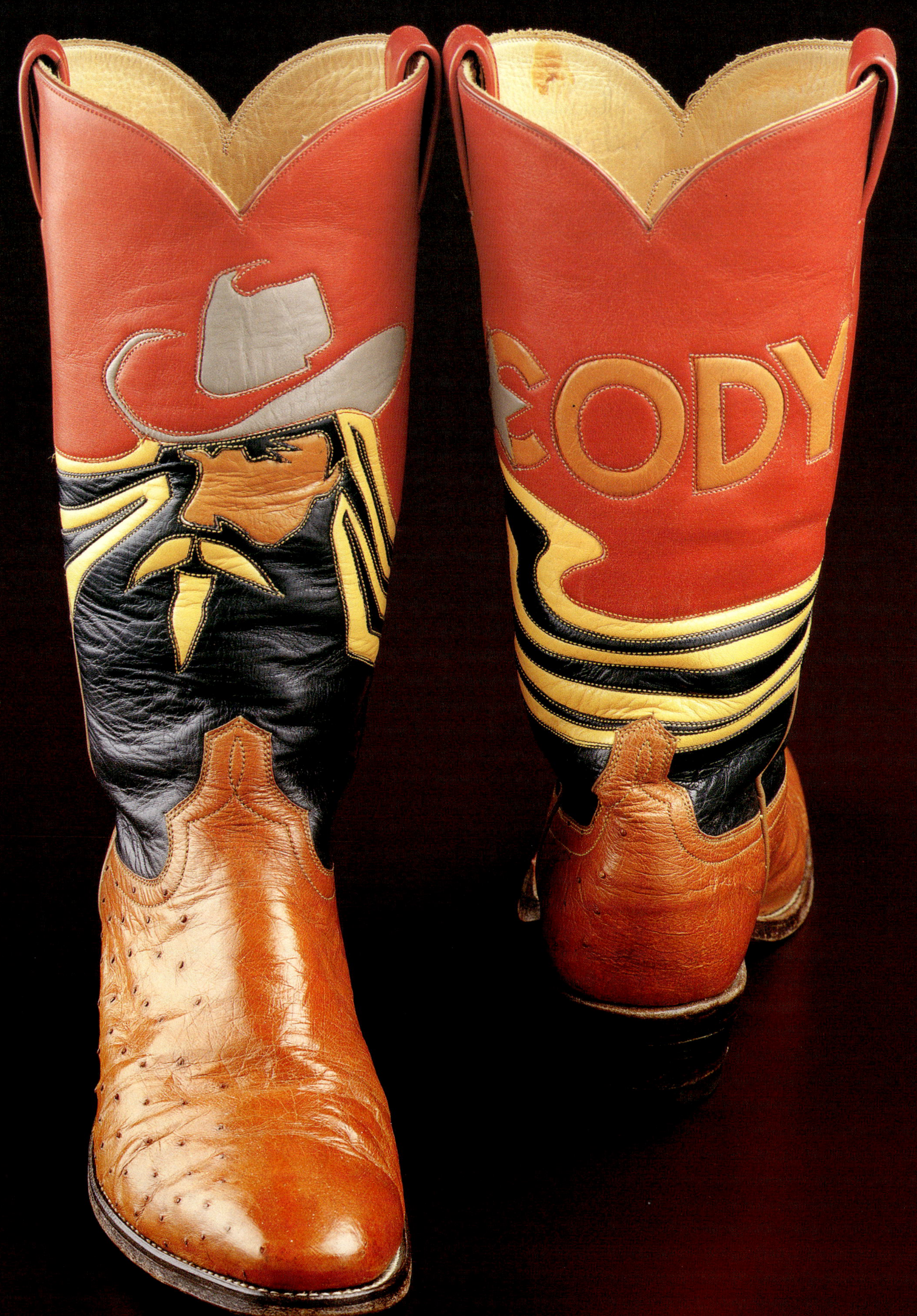
CODY

played important roles in popularizing western dress among Americans and influenced such mainstream fashion designers as Ralph Lauren to incorporate casual western styling into their clothing lines.

In design terms, boots fashioned from exotic leather dominated the upscale boot business during the last quarter of the twentieth century. Expensive western footwear derived from the hides of a wide variety of lizards, snakes, fish, turtles, and mammals, gathered from nearly every corner of the globe, became an unmistakable symbol of affluence and the western spirit. "If it walks, crawls, swims, or gallops," wrote one pundit, "you'll probably find its hide tanned and on somebody's foot."[89]

Exotic skins varied widely in durability, texture, and appearance. Hides such as alligator, elephant, and shark were both durable and stylish; others, like eel,

Opposite
Tom Farnworth, Cody, Wyoming
Cowboy boots designed by Wally Reber, with ostrich hide, uppers and tops depicting William F. "Buffalo Bill" Cody, c. 1995
WALLY WEBER COLLECTION, CODY, WYOMING

Below
John B. Stetson Co., Philadelphia
Felt cowboy hat with cloth band and curled brim worn by rodeo star Mike Hastings, c. 1920
NATIONAL COWBOY AND WESTERN HERITAGE MUSEUM, OKLAHOMA CITY

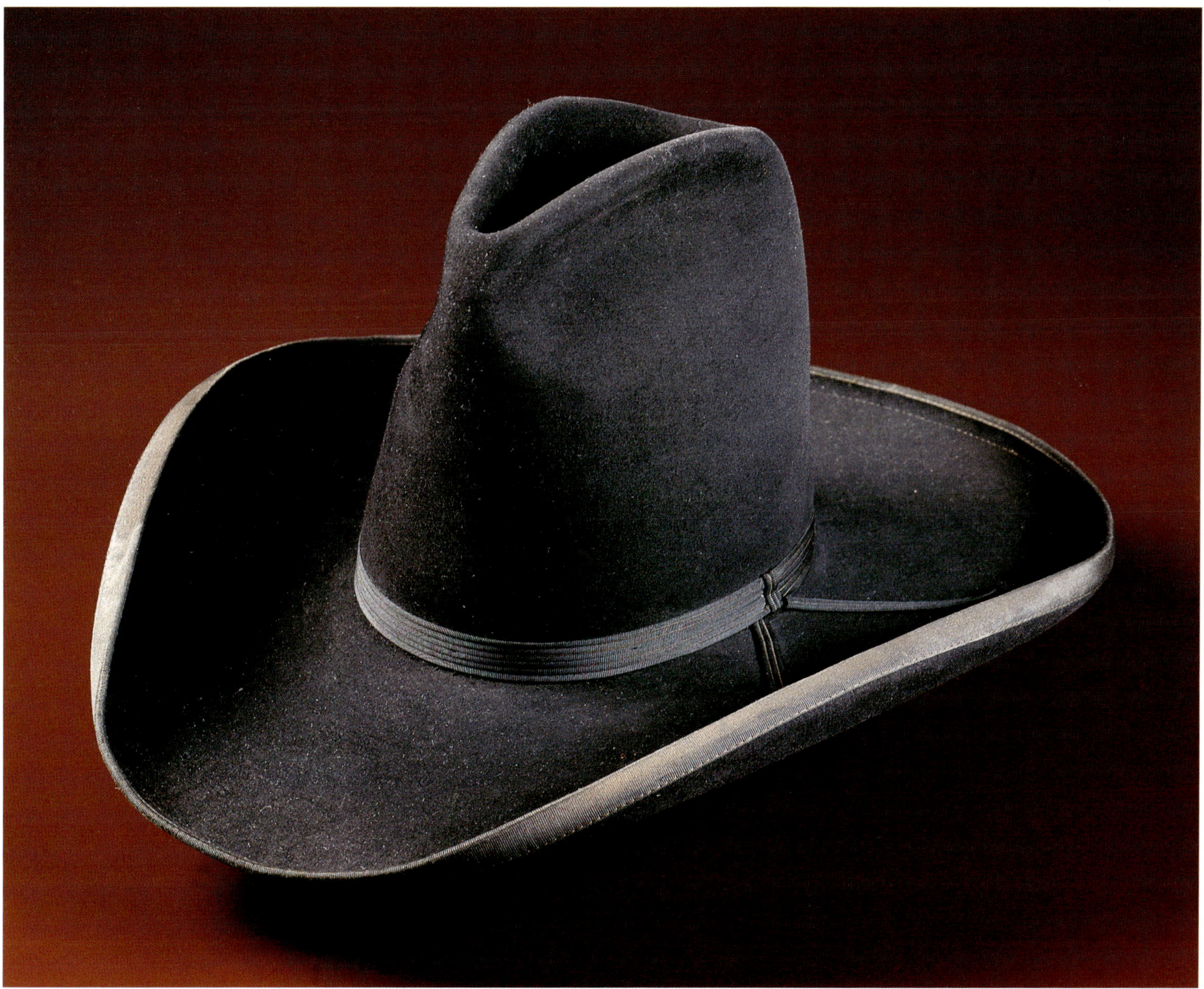

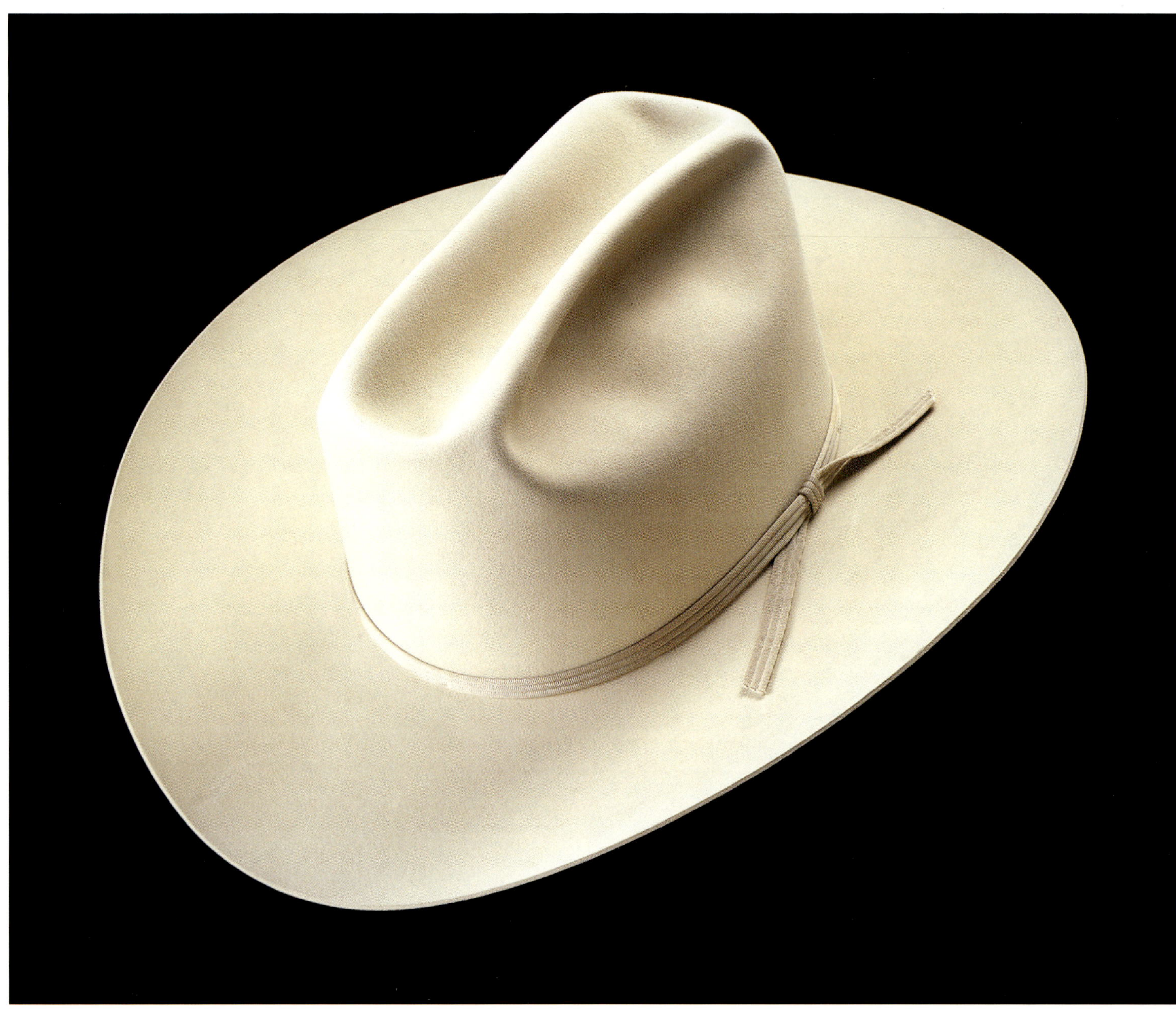

Felt cowboy hat worn c. 1960 by Bill Linderman, All-Around World Champion Cowboy, 1950 and 1953
National Cowboy and Western Heritage Museum, Oklahoma City

Opposite
Tony Lama Boots, El Paso
Cowboy boots with silver wing tips and inlaid presidential seal, made for President Ronald Reagan, 1980
National Cowboy and Western Heritage Museum, Oklahoma City

more fragile. Ostrich and kangaroo skins were in greatest demand for dress boots; water buffalo and horsehide, for work footwear. Lizard was the cheapest and therefore the most popular exotic skin.

Thanks to western movies and the mythical cowboy image, western-style boots enjoyed worldwide popularity at the turn of the millennium. While traditional boot makers struggled with the age-old problems of labor, capital, and market, newly minted companies bearing such names as Stallion and RocketBuster began to introduce retro styles from the 1940s and 1950s to a new generation of eager customers. Savvy collectors, meanwhile, were paying top dollar for vintage cowboy boots at such outlets as the Blues Suede Shoe in Dallas. Although the world and the West are far different places than they were in the days of Coffeyville boots, Joe

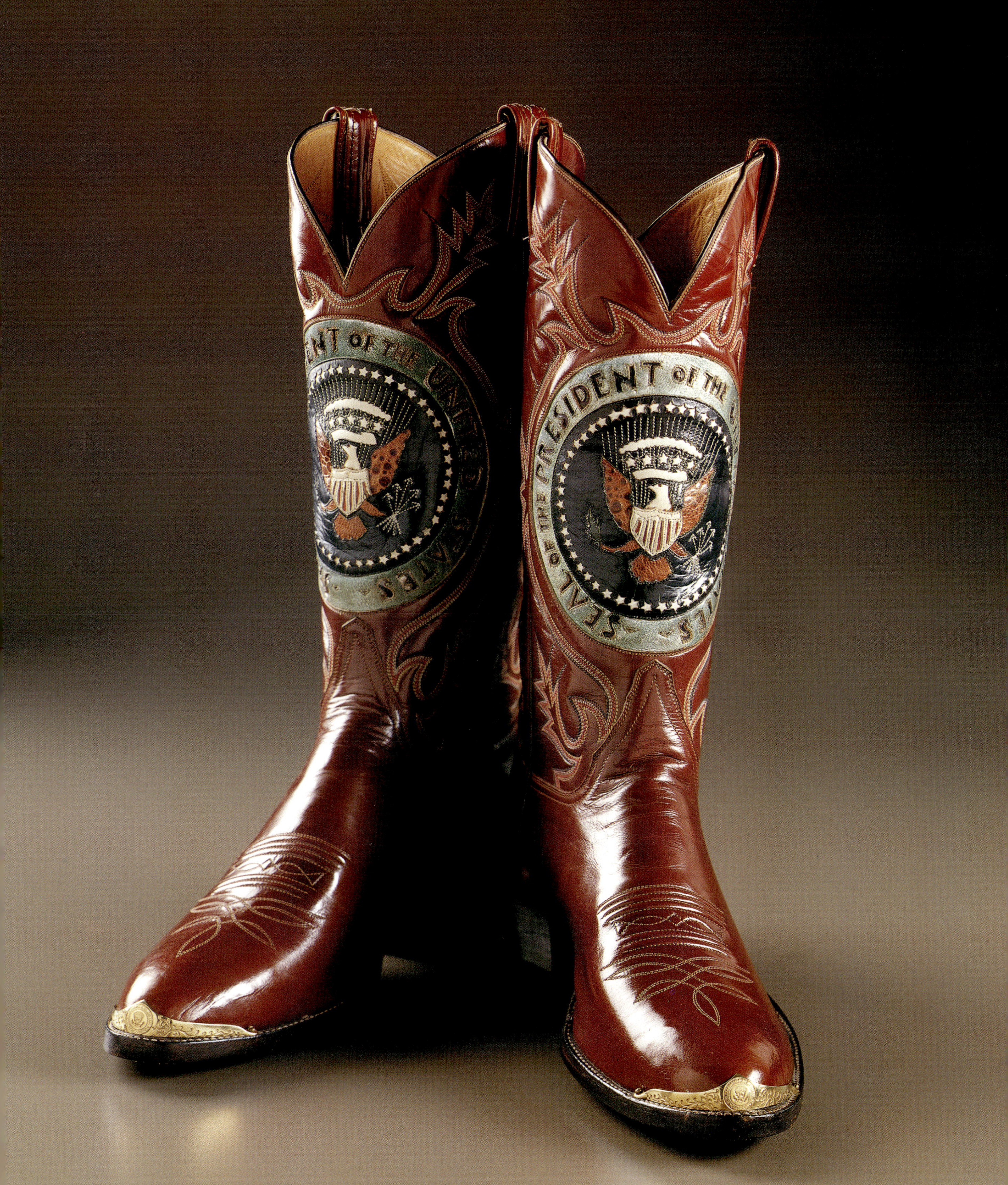
OF THE UNITED STATES
SEAL OF THE PRESIDENT OF THE

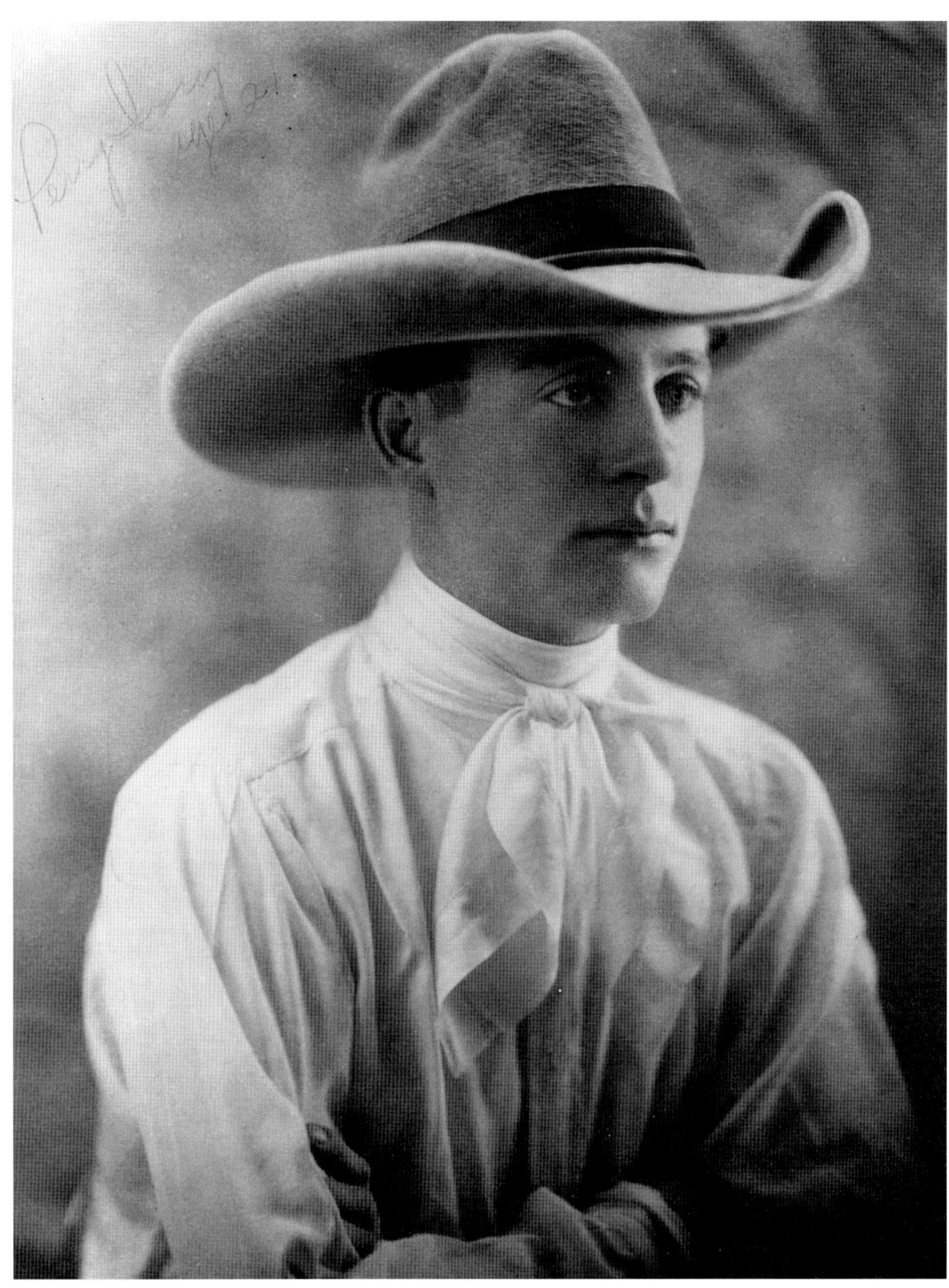

Ralph R. Doubleday (1881–1958)
Rodeo champion Perry Ivory, age 21, wearing a classic Stetson hat with kettle-curl brim and broad cloth band, 1926
NATIONAL COWBOY AND WESTERN HERITAGE MUSEUM, OKLAHOMA CITY

Justin, Tom Mix, and Gene Autry, Americans' fondness for cowboy boots and that for which they stand has never diminished. Alice Puckett's observation in *The Cattleman* magazine seems as apt today as it was when it first appeared in 1956:

> A man stands tall in boots. Boots are as satisfying as "son of a gun" stew; colorful as Buffalo Bill; romantic as a western ballad. The sky's the limit as to how far an individual can pamper his vanity if he teams up with a skilled craftsman, the boot maker.[91]

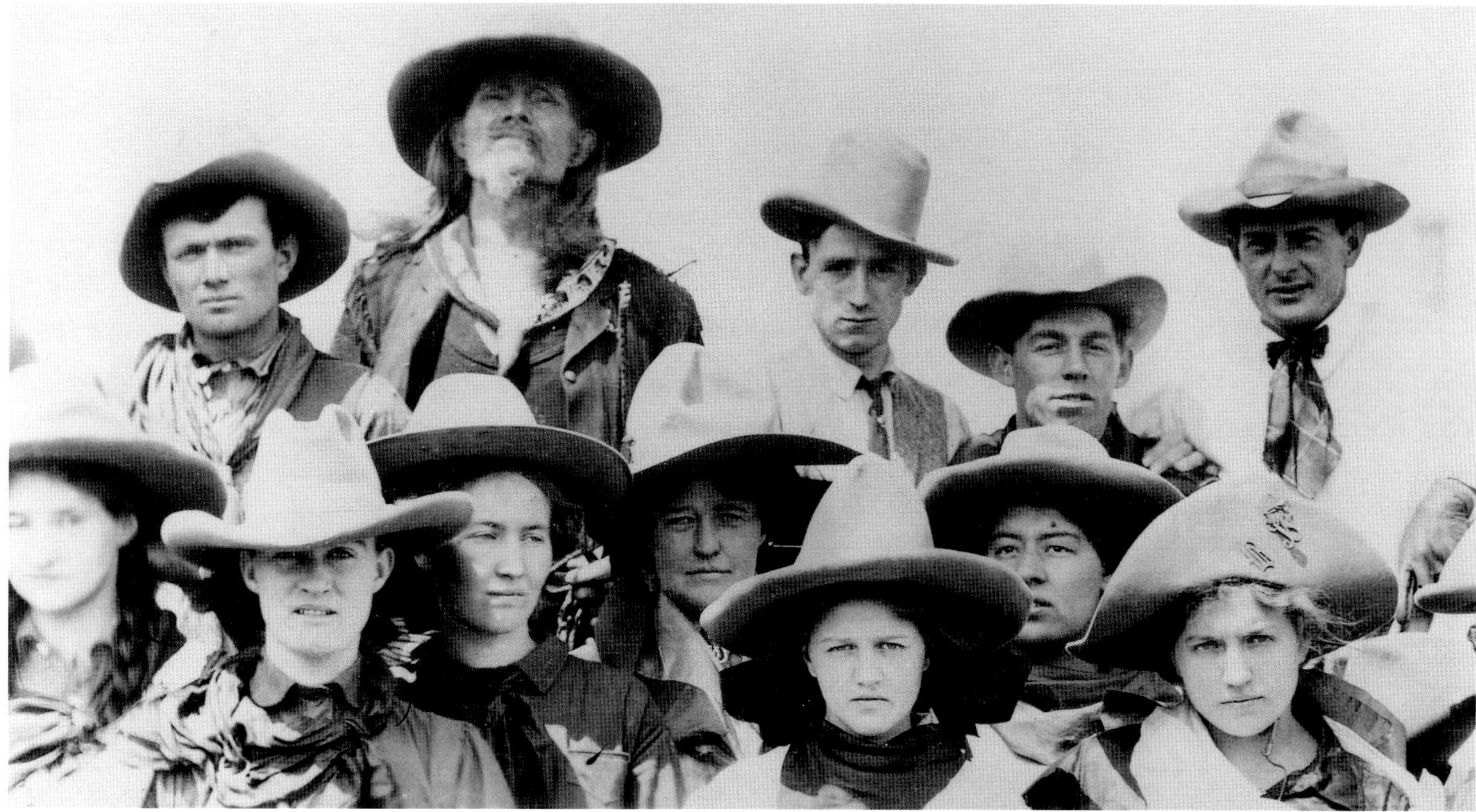

Wild West show performers wearing hats showing a variety of styles and creases
Buffalo Bill Historical Center, Cody, Wyoming

If cowboys clad in high-heeled boots stood a bit taller than did other mortals, the tall-crowned, wide-brimmed hats that they wore to block the sun, added physically and symbolically to their stature as well. Born in the late nineteenth century, the hats adopted by the cowboys of the frontier West were the lineal descendants of Mexican sombreros. Rural Americans began exchanging their shapeless wool felt slouch hats for exotic Mexican-style headgear in Texas as early as the 1820s. The process accelerated two decades later during the war with Mexico. American troops arriving on the Rio Grande encountered fantastic Mexican hats with uncreased, conical-shaped crowns covered, according to one observer, "with glazed cloth, and ornamented on the sides of the crown with silver balls, that resemble stop-cocks on the head of a steam boiler."[92] Many veterans returned home sporting such handsome headgear.

When Americans poured into California in the wake of the Gold Rush of 1849, many of the new arrivals adopted the style favored by Mexican rancheros, a black, low crowned affair with a flat, stiff brim of medium width and tie strings that could be knotted under the chin. Cords and tassels of gilt and tinsel often adorned the more expensive beaver felt types imported from Mexico or Peru. Bayard Taylor, a *New York Tribune* reporter, took note of the impact of Mexican-style hats among recent arrivals in the teaming berg of San Francisco in 1850.

> The effect of a growing prosperity and some little taste of luxury was readily seen in the appearance of the business community of San Francisco.

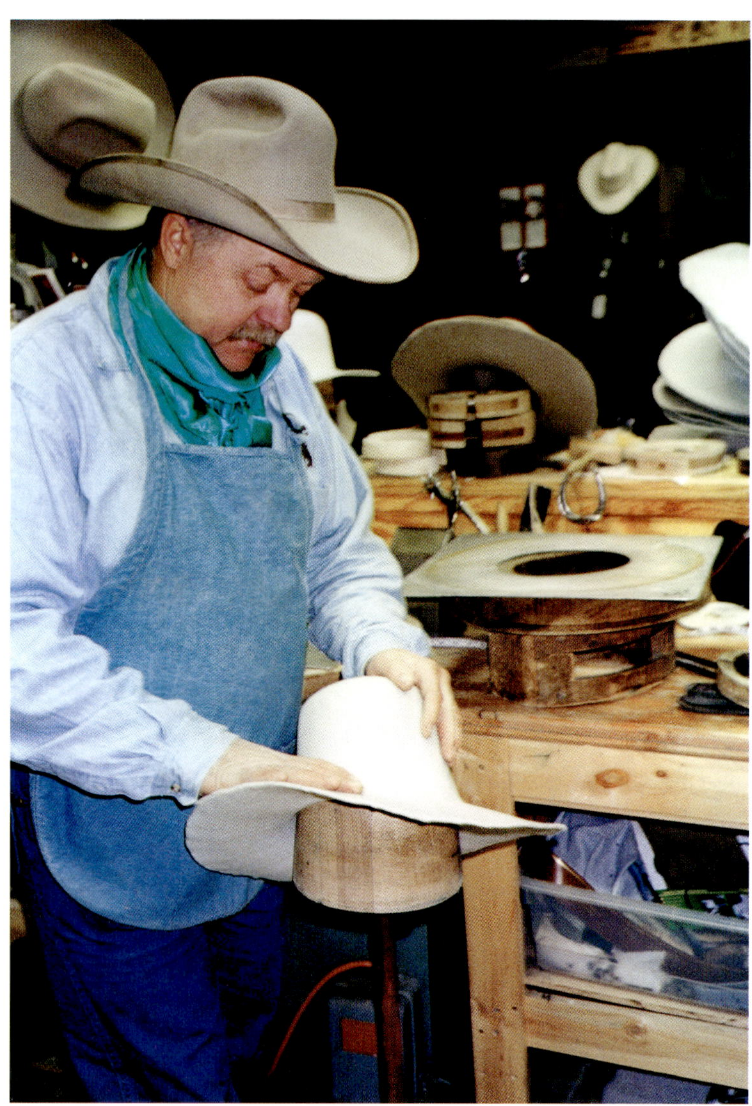

Hatmaker Gary Anderson, Wind River Hat Company, Cody, Wyoming

The slouched felt hats gave way to the narrow-brimmed black beavers.... and a variation of the Mexican sombrero—a very convenient and becoming headpiece—came into fashion among the younger class.[93]

Although at least a few eastern hatters joined the great migration westward, for many years the number was relatively small. In 1841, for example, only nine hat makers, compared to fifty-eight cobblers, made their homes in St. Louis, then the jumping-off point on the Santa Fe and Oregon Trails. Although most of the hats worn in the American West were imported from Mexico and the East Coast, in warmer climes settlers often wove homemade head coverings from bear grass, palmetto, or wheat straw. With eastern imports blockaded and suitable fur difficult to obtain in Civil War East Texas, at least one professional hatter created a few lightweight yet durable hats from the long and silky mohair of Angora goats. Not many, however, followed his example.

John B. Stetson, the tubercular son of a New Jersey hatter, headed West in the late 1850s in hopes of recovering his health and making his fortune. After spending two years in St. Joseph, Missouri, where he failed as a brick maker, Stetson joined the Colorado Gold Rush. His heath improved on the journey westward and during the trip he used his hat-making prowess to fashion felt cloth sleeping shelters for his companions, and when his own hat played out, fashioned a sombrero-like substitute from rabbit hair. A bullwhacker later bought it for $5.

Although his health continued to prosper, financial fortune eluded Stetson in the gold fields. He returned to Philadelphia in 1865 and resumed the hat trade. Stetson produced urban styles of the era with modest success and organized John B. Stetson & Company in 1867. Hoping to tap the western market, Stetson reprised the hat shape he had created on the way to Colorado years before and shipped samples to the region's retailers. The hat maker's timing could not have been more favorable. The introduction of his new product coincided with the rapid expansion of the western cattle industry and the emergence of cowboys as colorful and compelling folk figures. Orders poured in for Stetson's "Boss of the Plains" style, in numbers that soon forced the maker to erect a three-story factory to meet the demand.

Wearers found Stetson's new creations the epitome of durability. According to novelist and former trail driver, Andy Adams, Stetson hat brims were "as stiff as sheet-iron,"[94] and a welcome relief from the days when a rider had to lace the brim of his wool felt hat with rawhide or pin it to the crown with a thorn, to keep it from flapping in his face. If a brim exceeded three or four inches in width, Stetson typically bound the edge with silk or curled it upward to increase its stability.

Thanks to the consummate skill of the hatters in his employ, Stetson's western styles were not only sturdy but also attractive, lightweight, and smooth to the touch. Most were a blend of beaver, the finest hair available for hats, and other fur-bearing creatures, mainly muskrat, rabbit, hare, or nutria. The percentage of beaver fur determined the quality of the hat and was designated on the sweatband by an "X." A 10X hat, for example, was made of 100 percent beaver fur. Hats made of less than 50 percent beaver were considered inferior. Other makers later interpreted this scheme in different ways, until its original meaning was lost.

By 1885 Stetson employees were turning out 150 hats per day, many of them bound for the cattle ranges of the West, where cowboys called them "John B's" in the maker's honor. Within six years the number had zoomed to 2,000 daily, and in 1899 sales topped 50,000 dozen. By this time Stetson products were popular worldwide, thanks in part to the iconic stature of the American cowboy. "No man," wrote a Wyoming traveler in 1886,

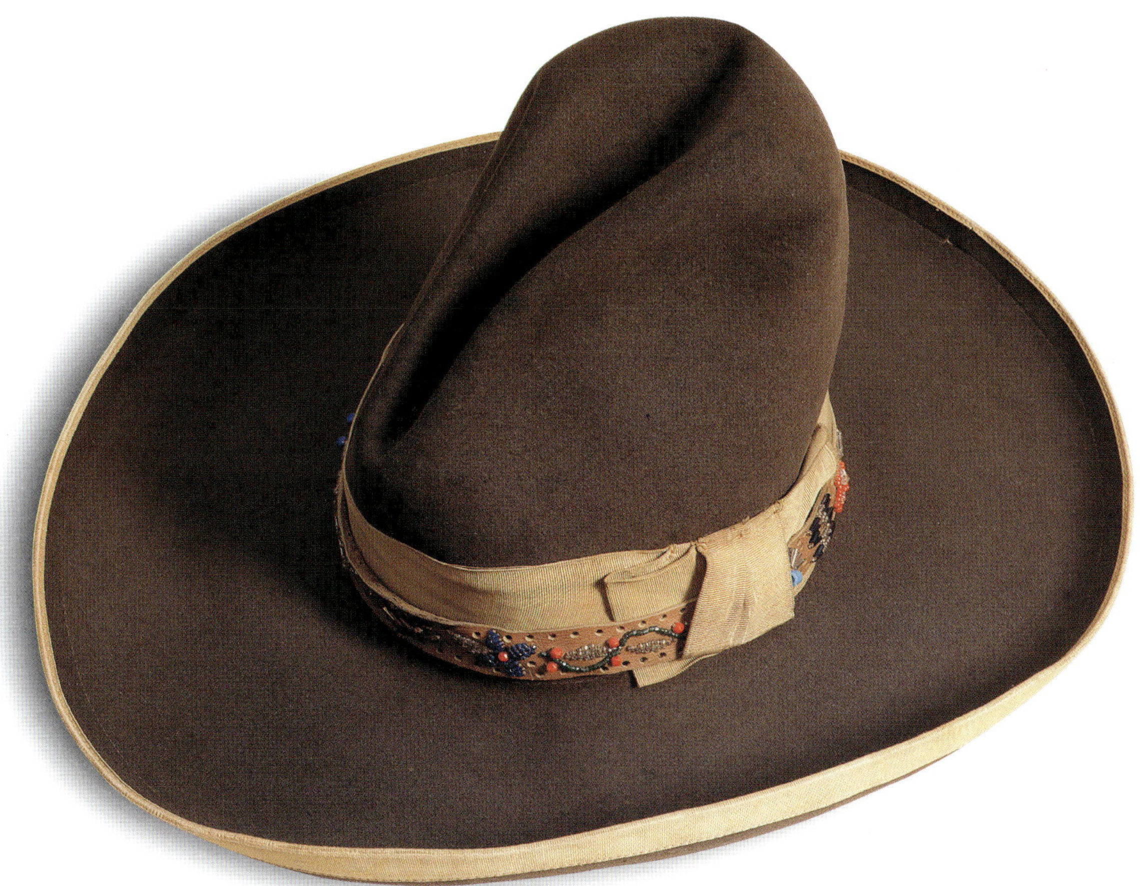

Felt cowboy hat with cloth and beaded bands, "Carlsbad style" crease, and curled, bound edge, c. 1925
Buffalo Bill Historical Center, Cody, Wyoming

> who can by any possibility avoid it, engages in any part of the business of cattle raising, however subordinate, without first procuring a white felt hat with an immensely broad brim, and a band consisting either of a leather strap and buckle, or a silk twist like a whip lash. These are expensive, like a fine Panama, frequently costing from fifty to seventy-five dollars.[95]

Nearly a decade later, writer Hamlin Garland noted a similar, but hardly surprising uniformity, among the cowboy hats he observed at a roundup near Cripple Creek, Colorado. The same year, Charles Whitman, owner of the LS Ranch in the Texas Panhandle, gave each of his forty employees a new Stetson hat. The recipients responded to the gesture by calling them "Whitmans."

Stetson's "Boss of the Plains" usually left the factory with an open crown and embellished only with a wide Japanese silk band tied in a flat bow on one side. As soon as a cowboy acquired a new hat, he individualized it with a distinctive crease, often of regional styling, and added a hatband of braided horsehair, tooled or concha-studded leather, or gold and silver thread. An early historian of the Texas range cattle industry wrote in 1894 that despite their meager wages many cowboys spent "as much as twenty-five dollars for silver medals on their hats . . ." [96] A few also added a leather chin strap or what some later called a "stampede string."

Beginning in 1883, Buffalo Bill's flamboyant Wild West troupe helped popularize Stetson hats throughout the U.S. and Europe. Stetson advertised regularly in the show's program. "Out-door life is hard on hats," the company's 1900 ad concluded, "and the continued patronage of these men is a strong endorsement of the satisfaction and wonderful wear that go with every 'Stetson.' "[97]

At the turn of the twentieth century, another colorful showman began offering his customers Stetson hats with oversize brims and crowns. Known as the "Big Hat King," Cheyenne vendor Max J. Meyer ordered the first of the behemoths for C. B. Irwin, impresario of the annual Cheyenne Frontier Days rodeo and celebration. A large and imposing figure, Irwin demanded a hat with a seven-inch crown and a five-inch brim, larger than any worn by his rodeo contestants. Meyer said later that he found the idea "slightly fantastic" but ordered a few extras "just in case."[98] The hat maker's instincts proved sound, and after Irwin's first appearance, patrons snapped up the new style.

In 1903 while attending the Cheyenne Frontier Days rodeo, President Theodore Roosevelt visited the Max Meyer Co. where the host committee planned to buy him a hat. Admiring one of the immense felts in Meyer's inventory, the president is said to have exclaimed with amazement, "That's a five-gallon fella', isn't it?"[99] Yet some were even bigger. After Wild West show and film performer Tim McCoy paid Meyer $125 each for two Stetsons with incredible 9 1/2 inch brims, Tom Mix kidded that they looked as if they could hold fifty gallons! Relatively modest by comparison, Stetson's Big Four style, with its seven-inch crown and four-inch curled brim, was sometimes called a "four quart" hat. Thanks largely to western movies, however, the term "ten-gallon hat" eventually stuck in the public imagination. More recently, writer Glen Vernam has suggested that the term "gallon" associated with hats actually may have emanated from the Mexican vaquero's practice of trimming his sombrero with "*gallones*," fancy decorations of braid, tassels, and the like.[100]

Life imitated art as many working cowboys embraced the same hat styles that the movie stars wore. Stetson, meanwhile, made the most of celebrity endorsements from emerging film and rodeo heroes, especially the incredibly popular Mix, who, during personal appearances, routinely dispensed autographed Stetsons bearing his trademark crease, to dignitaries and admirers around the world. Mix

John B. Stetson Co., Philadelphia "Montana Special"–style cowboy hat, with kettle-curl brim and cloth band, c. 1920s
BUFFALO BILL HISTORICAL CENTER, CODY, WYOMING

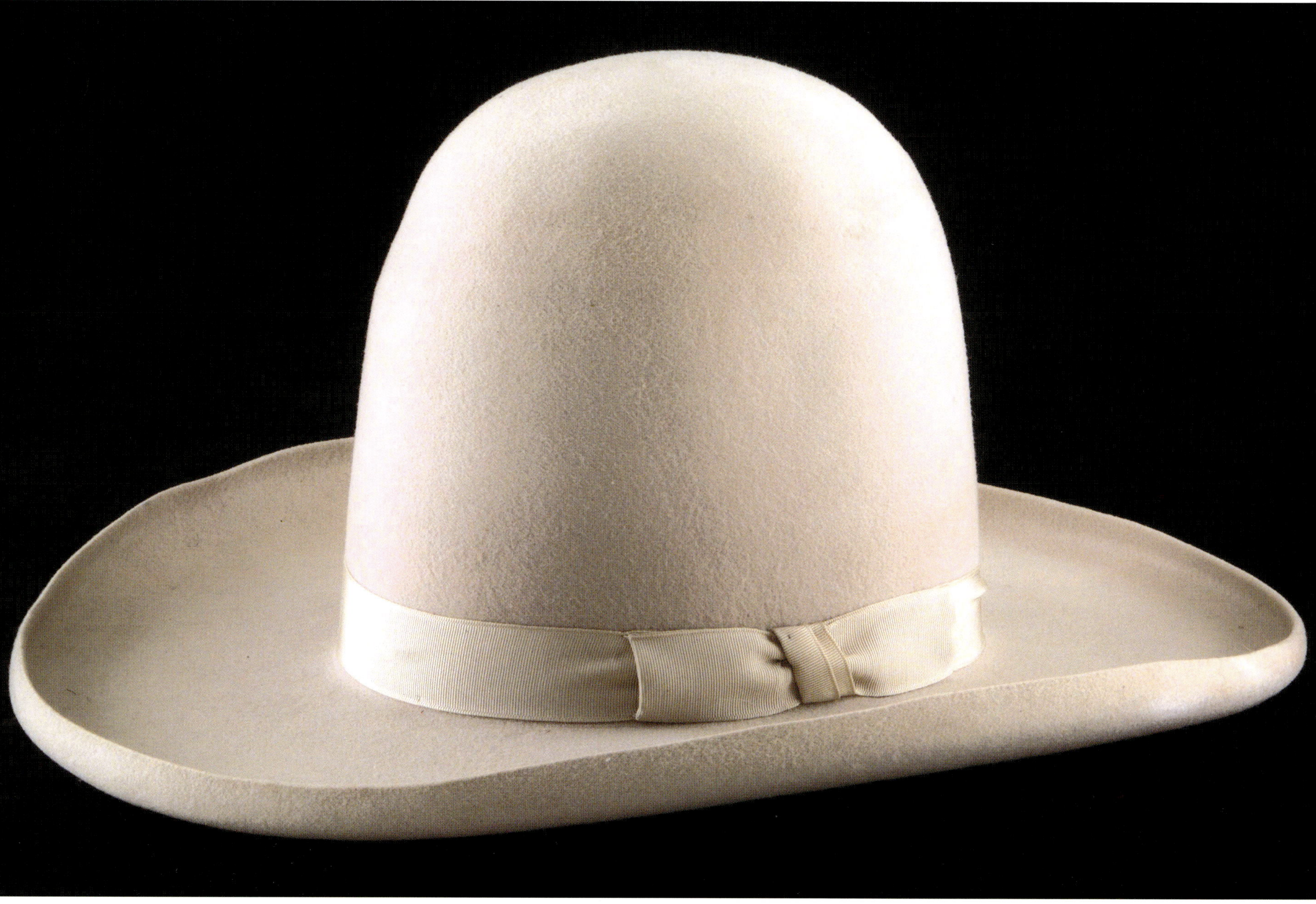

Below
John B. Stetson Co., Philadelphia
Felt cowboy hat with curled brim and bound edge worn by rodeo star Tommy Kirnan
National Cowboy and Western Heritage Museum, Oklahoma City

Opposite
John B. Stetson Co., Philadelphia
"Montana Special"—style cowboy hat, with cloth band and kettle-curl brim with bound edge, c. 1920s
Buffalo Bill Historical Center, Cody, Wyoming

and other notable clients rated their own hat blocks and brim flanges at the Stetson factory.

After John B. Stetson died in 1906 at the age of seventy-six, the company he founded lived on, and by 1915 employed more than 5,000 workers. By this time annual production had reached 3.36 million hats, which were sold through some 10,000 retailers, up significantly from the 2,800 dealers at the turn of the century.

Although cowboy hats comprised only a fraction of its market, Stetson relied heavily upon the power of its western image to help sell its entire men's line. During the early 1920s, for example, the company released *The Last Drop from his Stetson*, a compelling advertising poster created by Lon Megargee, a New

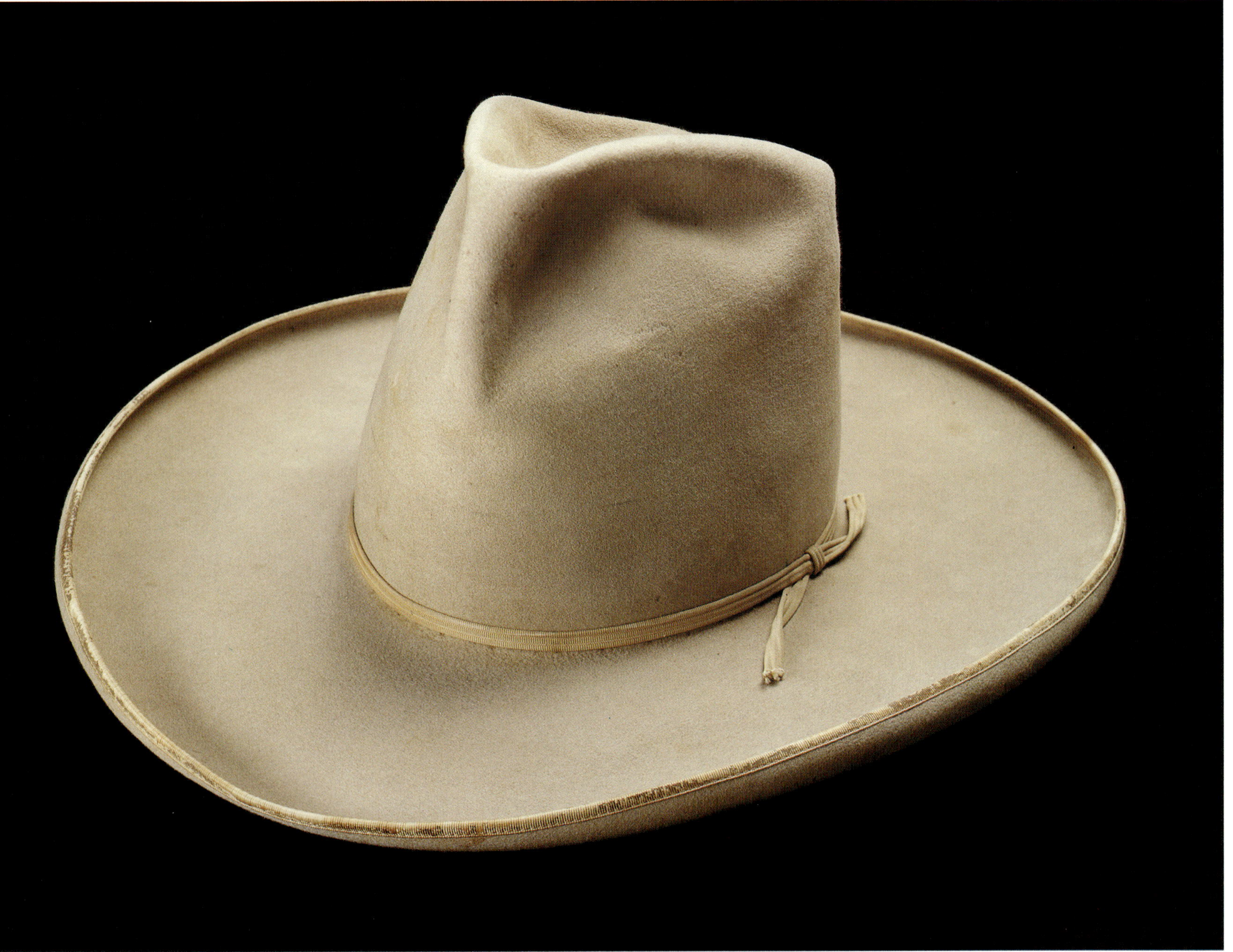

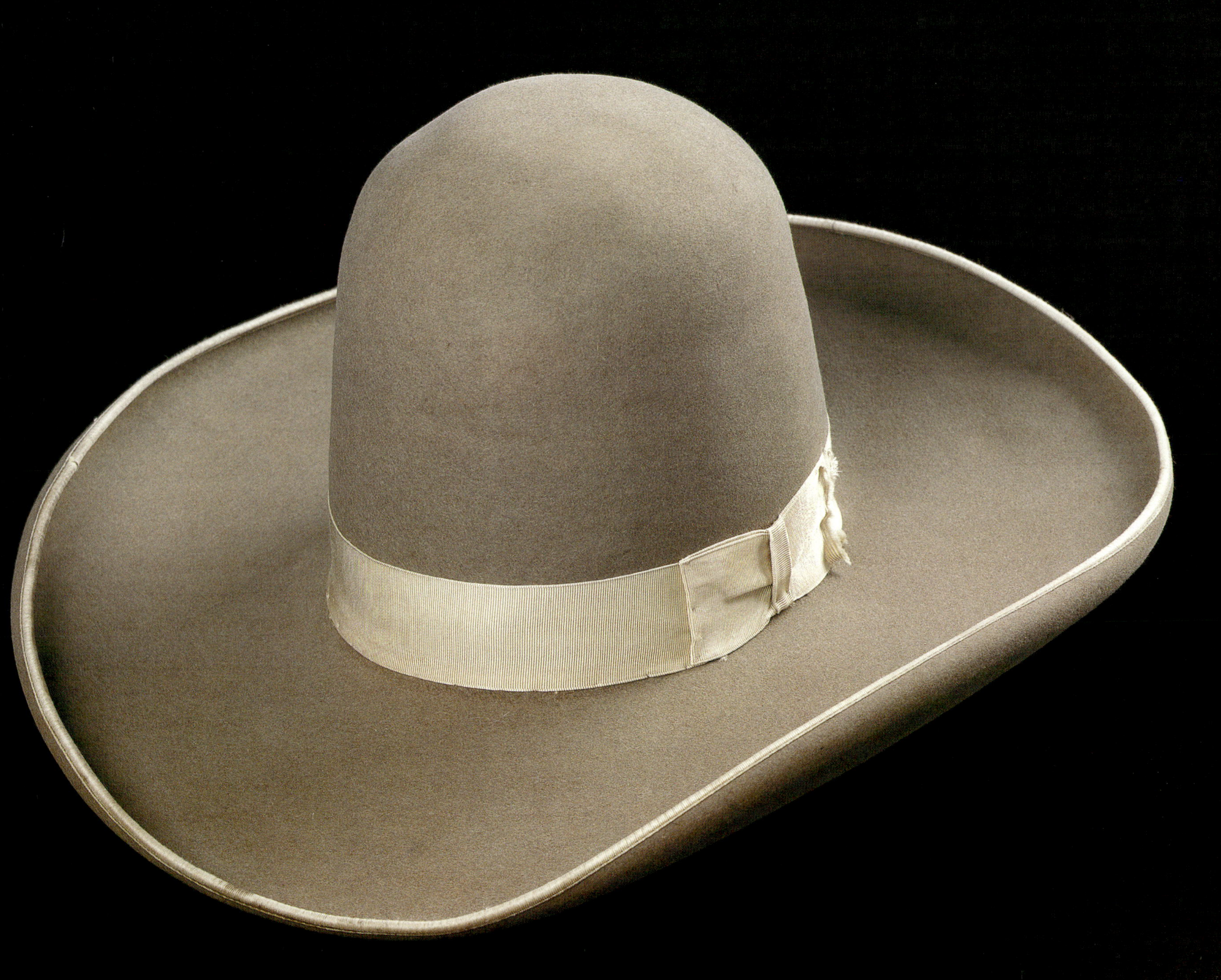

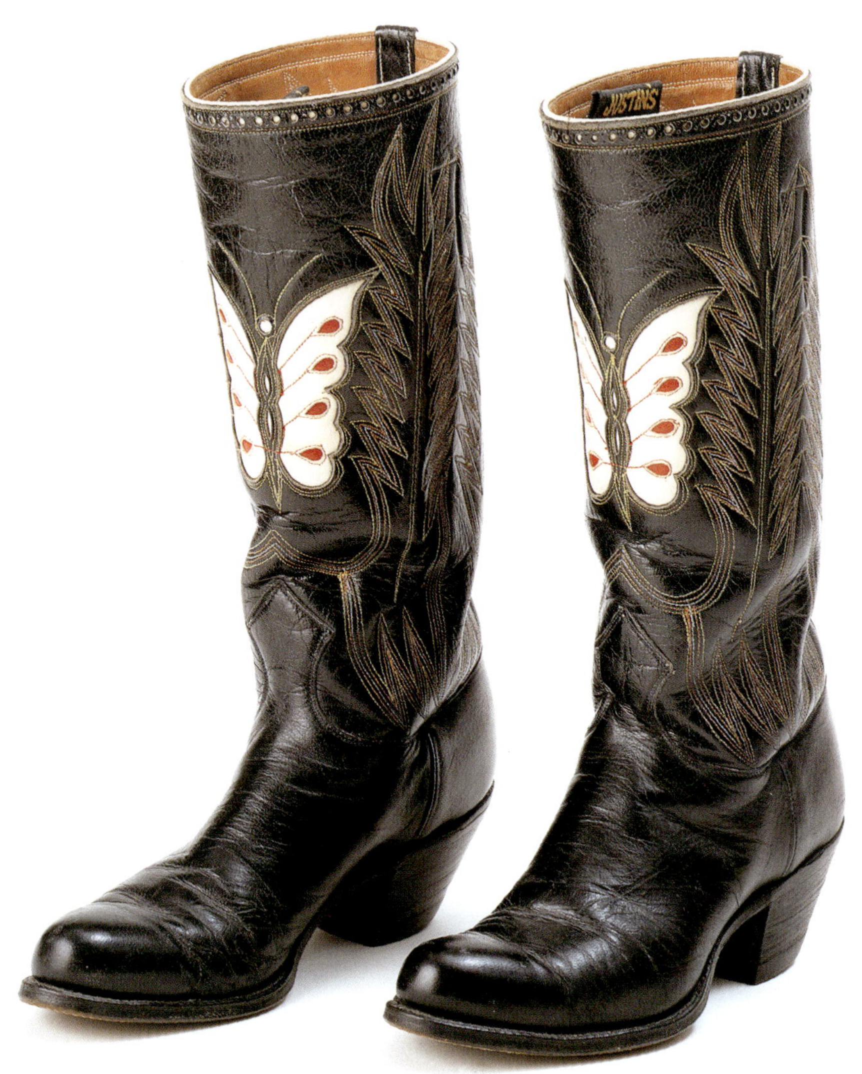

Justin Boots, Fort Worth
Woman's cowboy boots with flat stovetop tops and butterfly and fern design, c. 1930s
BUFFALO BILL HISTORICAL CENTER, CODY, WYOMING

York–based commercial artist and former Arizona cowpuncher. The touching image of a kneeling cowboy watering his horse from his hat resonated so powerfully and positively with the public that the Philadelphia hat maker continued to use it as a logo.

Early in the twentieth century, national and regional competitors began to challenge Stetson's dominance of the western hat market. The Knox Hat Co. of New York, for example, introduced nearly a dozen different western styles in the 1920s and 1930s, all of them designed by Arizona artist and rodeo champion Jack Van Ryder. Miller Bros., founded in 1902; Bailey Hat Co., two decades later; and Byer-Rolnick Hat Corporation, five years after that, began to erode Stetson's important Texas market.

On the eve of the 1936 Texas Centennial celebration, Byer-Rolnick added the first western styles to its already successful Resitol line of dress hats. In order to expand its share of western market, the Dallas-based upstart began to court cowboy movie stars and invoke the romance of the West in its advertising and promotion. In so doing they competed head to head with Stetson and reinforced the already powerful linkage between myth and reality in hat design.

Through the influence of literature, film, and rodeo, large numbers of noncowboys, including many women, began wearing western hats, more for their symbolism than their practical and protective functions. William S. Hart, Bronco Billy Anderson, Tom Mix, and other silver screen heroes helped transform cowboy hats into expressions of independence, self-reliance, and rugged individualism.

Beset by labor unrest and a shortage of skilled workers during the early twentieth century, American hat makers mechanized their complex operations as much as possible. Despite this development, hats continued to retain their handmade character.

Not all of the challenges confronting the hat-making industry, however, were internal. By 1930 such nations as Australia, Canada, Germany, Russia, England, and Belgium were providing most of the fur used in American hats. The increasing scarcity of such fur-bearing species as beaver and nutria, however, contributed to rising fur prices throughout the twentieth century and diminished the overall quality of felt hats.

The hat industry weathered the economic distress of the Great Depression but could not cope when many Americans abandoned the custom of wearing of hats after World War II. Overall, hat sales dropped more than 30 percent between 1947 and 1958, thanks in part to the nation's declining rural population. Although the downward spiral continued, the demand for western hats, fueled by recreational horsemen, working cowboys, rodeo contestants and fans, tourists, and dude ranches remained relatively steady. By the late 1960s no less than six hat companies (Stetson, Bailey, Bandera, Eddy Bros., Texas, and Miller Bros.) vied for the western market. All except Stetson were located either in Texas or California.

In 1971 the announcement that Stetson, after more than a century in the hat business, had ceased operation and licensed its name to the Stevens Hat Manufacturing Co. of St. Joseph marked the passing of an era. "No other commercial article," author Lewis Nordyke had written of Stetsons a few years before, "has had such a lasting effect on the habits and taste of the Westerner, and no other brand except possibly the Colt six-shooter has received so much notoriety in the literature of the West."[101]

The 1970s also marked the demise of movie and television cowboys as a staple of American entertainment and a promotional cornerstone of the western hat trade. Hatters continued to market the romance of the Old West but developed new advertising strategies featuring rebellious rodeo athletes and "outlaw" country music entertainers to reach a more youthful and diverse market. Bailey Hat Co., for example, not only secured the endorsements of such mainstream

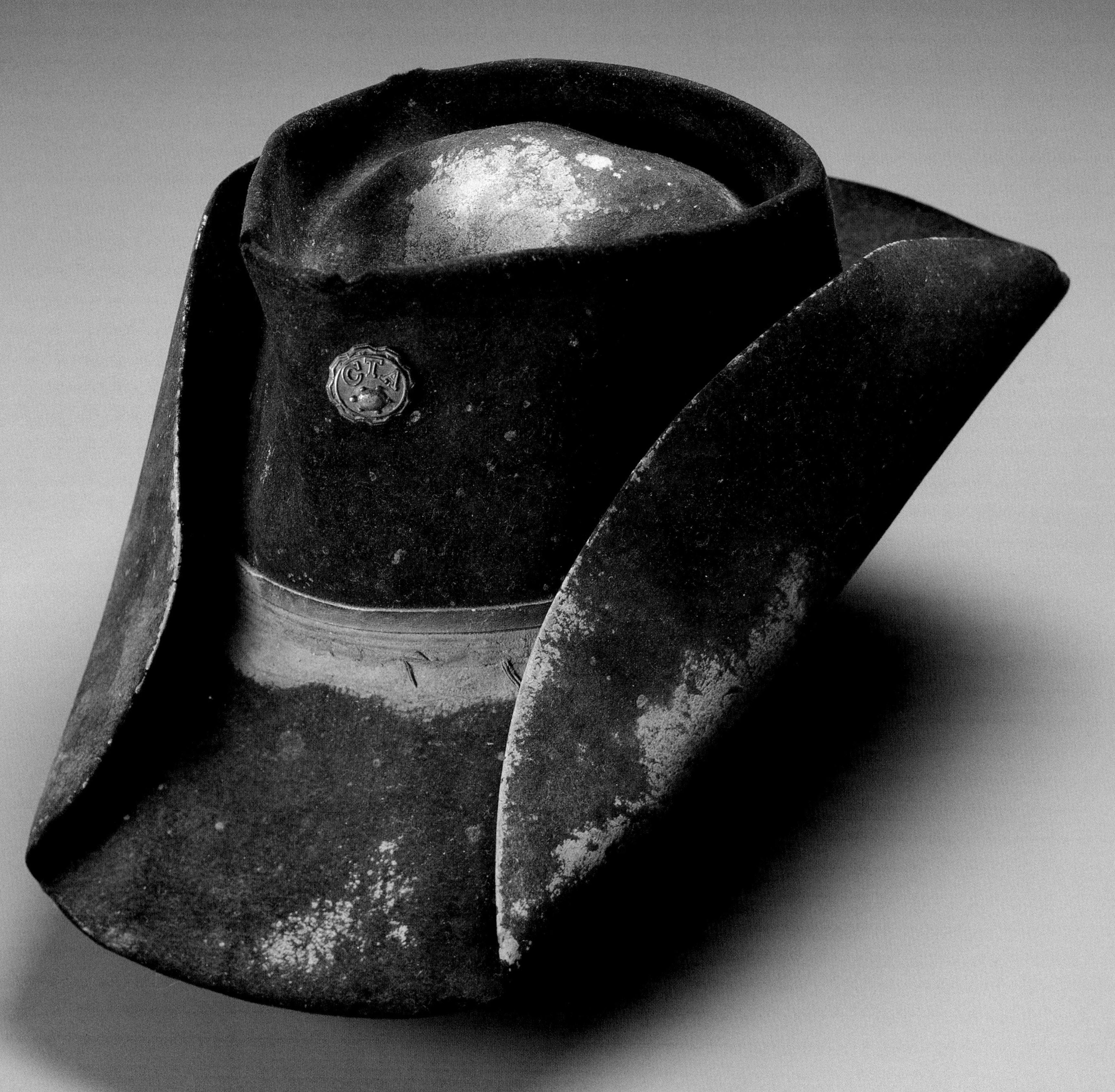
CTA

rodeo stars as Shawn Davis and Bobby Berger, but also that of champion Indian cowboy Felix Gilbert, described in a 1972 article as a "pacesetter for the Navajo Indian trade." [102]

The film *Urban Cowboy* briefly popularized hat wearing among the general population and fostered an unprecedented demand for colored cowboy hats and outlandish feathered hatbands. During a three-year period in the early 1980s, Byer-Rolnick's western hat business, already the largest in the nation, doubled, only to return to previous levels after the boom subsided. Writing about the phenomenon in *Texas Monthly* magazine in 1984, Peter Applebone, described the appeal of cowboy hats as

> more emotional than practical, but even that has its limits. Pushed beyond its natural borders and stuck on the heads of New Yorkers who frequent Second Avenue singles bars, the cowboy hat took on the forlorn look of parody. But at West Texas cafes, on the heads of burly truckers and rodeo kids and ranchers and oilmen, it will always have the irresistible aura of myth.[103]

That year the industry produced 2.8 million western-style hats, most of them bought by non-cowboys, at prices ranging from a $15 straw to an elegant $3,000 masterpiece of beaver and ermine. Although a few large companies continued to dominate the market, an increasing number of small custom hatters purchased raw hat bodies from wholesalers and turned out fresh designs for a limited clientele. The 1990s marked the comeback of the tall-crowned, large-brimmed styles popular in the 1910s and 1920s.

In the twenty-first century such custom makers as Michael Malone, Ritch Rand, Kevin O'Farrell, Tom Hirt, Jimmy and Jackie Harrison, and a few others honor the tradition of workmanship and artistry that once distinguished the products of John B. Stetson. Their own interpretations have included beaded brims with matching hatbands, contrasting leather lacing, and colored inlays in iconic shapes. Such exercises in creativity, of course, have little to do with protecting the head, fanning a fire into flame, signaling a distant companion, or any of the other practical ways that cowboy hats have been used for over a century. But as writer Karen Evans once observed, "form doesn't follow function these days; form follows fantasy and just about everybody feels better in a cowboy hat." [104]

Opposite
John B. Stetson Co., Philadelphia
Felt cowboy hat with C.T.A. (Cowboy Turtle Assn.) pin and distinctive crease worn by rodeo star "Wild Horse" Bob Crosby, c. 1940
NATIONAL COWBOY AND WESTERN HERITAGE MUSEUM, OKLAHOMA CITY

Page 256
Hair chaps, details of three pairs
FLEISCHER COLLECTION, SCOTTSDALE

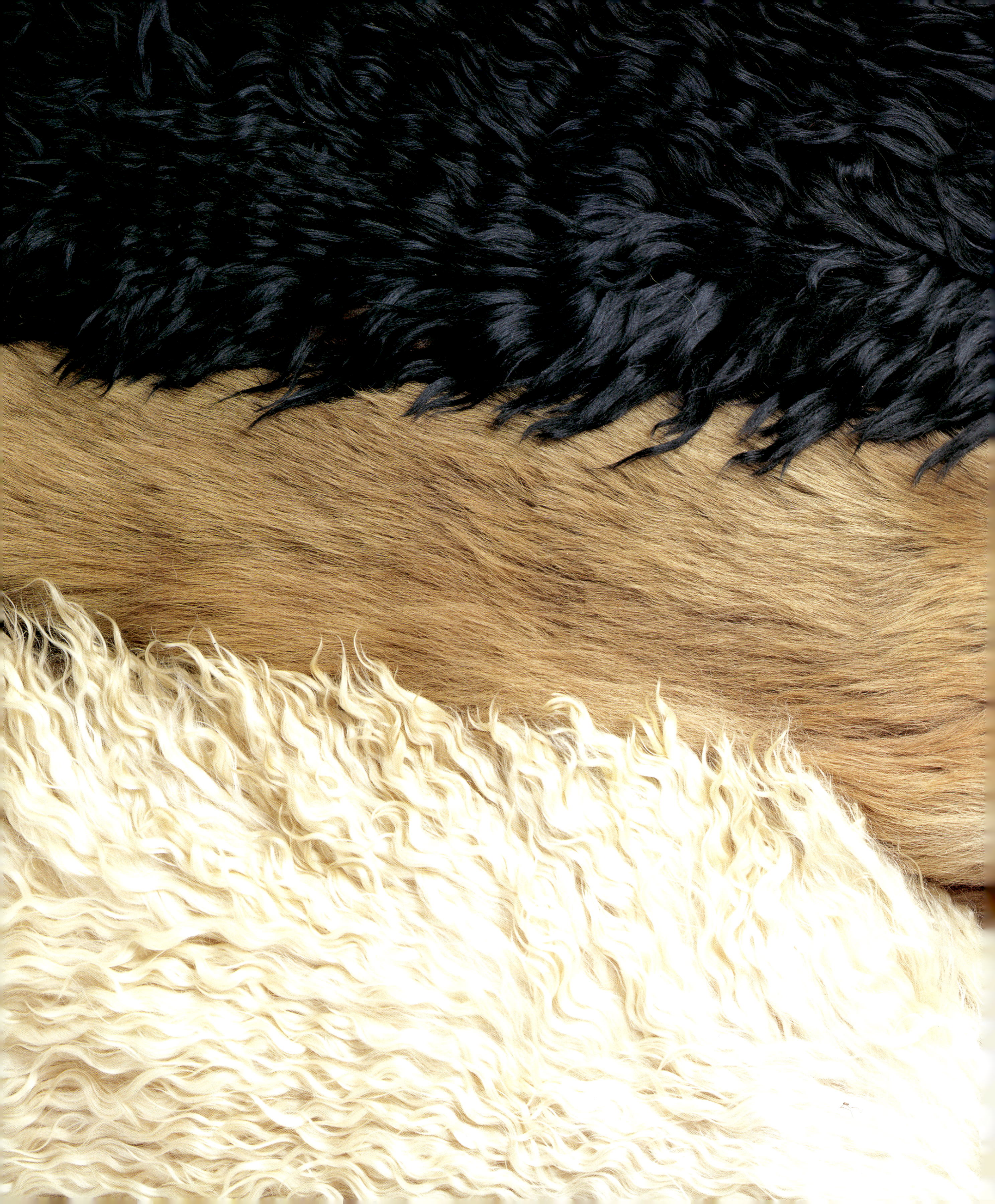

NOTES

STOCK SADDLES AND GUN LEATHER

1. *Matador Tribune* (Matador, Tex.), August 25, 1966.

2. Bruce Grant, *The Encyclopedia of Rawhide and Leather Braiding* (Centreville, Md.: Cornell Maritime Press, 1994), xxi.

3. Quoted in Jack Jackson, *Los Mesteños: Spanish Ranching in Texas, 1721–1821* (College Station: Texas A&M University Press, 1986), 84.

4. M. C. Frederick, "The Californian Montadura," *The Californian Illustrated Magazine* 4 (July, 1893): 182.

5. "Tourist in Santa Fe, 1840: Sketches by Matthew C. Field," *El Palacio* 66 (February 1959): 30.

6. Slang term for saddle.

7. Orville Howard, "More than 6,000 Saddles Hand Crafted in 58 Years," *Amarillo News-Globe* (Amarillo, Tex.), July 31, 1960.

8. "Riding Saddles," *Harness* 2 (January 1889), 277.

9. "Ornamenting Saddles," *Harness and Carriage Journal* 25 (April 1881), 278–79.

10. *Ibid.*

11. "Ornamenting Saddles," *Harness and Carriage Journal* 22 (February 1878), 148.

12. "Designing," *Harness and Carriage Journal* 27 (May 1882): 4.

13. *Ibid.*

TROPHY, PARADE, AND PRESENTATION SADDLES

1. William Heath Davis, *Sixty Years in California* (San Francisco: A. J. Leary, 1889), 86.

2. *The Texas State Gazette* (Austin, Tex.), September 23, 1854.

3. "Buffalo Bill's Riding Equipment," *Jeweler's Circular and Horological Review*, May 24, 1893, quoted in R. L. Wilson with Greg Martin, *Buffalo Bill's Wild West: An American Legend* (New York: Random House, 1998), 39.

4. "Jewel Mounted $10,000 Saddle," *Santa Clara Journal* (Santa Clara, Calif.), May 2, 1914: 1.

5. *Elko Daily Independent* (Elko, Nev.), December 10, 1903.

6. *Elko Independent* (Elko, Nev.), August 28, 1923.

7. *Las Animas Leader* (Las Animas, Colorado), December 15, 1882.

8. Allen Branin telegram to S. D. Myres, October 8, 1929, S. D. Myres Saddle Company Records, 1898–1966, Southwest Collection, Texas Tech University, Lubbock.

9. "Work of Noted Local Craftsman to Be Shown," *Santa Barbara News-Press* (Santa Barbara, Calif.), May 30, 1948.

10. Quoted in Kate Sanborn, *A Truthful Woman in Southern California* (New York: D. Appleton & Co., 1894), 177–78.

11. "Saddle That Has Cost $3,000," *Harness Gazette* 16 (September 1897): 64.

12. Sanborn, *A Truthful Woman in Southern California*, 176–177.

13. James H. Nottage, *Saddlemaker to the Stars: The Leather and Silver Art of Edward H. Bohlin* (Los Angeles: Autry Museum of Western Heritage, 1996), 34.

14. Edward H. Bohlin, Hollywood: Calif., *The Bohlin Shop of Edward H. Bohlin. Catalog of "The World's Finest" Riding Equipment, Riding Accessories and Silver and Leather Goods* (Hollywood: the company, 1937), 220.

15. "A Saddle for 'Bull' Halsey," *Western Horseman* 10 (September–October 1945): 21.

16. Joe Mora, *Trail Dust and Saddle Leather* (New York: C. Scribner's Sons, 1946), 106–7.

17. *Ibid.*, 7.

18. George Pitman, "Sterling Silver Parade Saddles: A Collector's Point of View," *Silver Magazine* 32 (May/June 2000): 24.

ARTISTRY WITH HIDE AND HAIR

1. Larry Brown, "'Meanie' Made the Best of Everything," *Casper Star-Tribune* (Casper, Wyo.), April 14, 1996, B2.

2. John H. (Jack) Culley, *Cattle Horses and Men* (Los Angeles: Ward Ritchie Press, 1940), 176.

3. Theodore Roosevelt, *Ranch Life in the Far West.* (Flagstaff, Ariz.: Northland Press, 1968), 88.

4. Ella Bird Dumont, *Ella Elgar Bird Dumont: An Autobiography of a West Texas Pioneer*, ed. Tommy J. Boley (Austin: University of Texas Press, 1988), 46.

5. Don Bell, "Rodeo of Yesteryears," unpublished typescript, Rodeo Historical Society Files, Donald C. and Elizabeth M. Dickenson Research Center, National Cowboy and Western Heritage Museum, Oklahoma City.

6. Max Coleman, *From Mustanger to Lawyer* (San Antonio: the author, 1952), 78.

7. "The Cowboy as He Is," *Democratic Leader* (Cheyenne, Wyo.), January 11, 1885, quoted in Clifford Westermeier, *Trailing the Cowboy* (Caldwell, Ida.: Caxton Printers, Ltd., 1955), 31.

8. Don Rickey, *$10 Horse, $40 Saddle: Cowboy Clothing, Arms, Tools and Horse Gear of the 1880's* (Ft. Collins, Colo.: Old Army Press, 1976), 46.

9. General George Wingate, "My Trip to the Yellowstone," *American Agriculturist* 45 (April 1886): 152.

10. N. A. Jennings, *A Texas Ranger*, reprint ed. (Chicago: Lakeside Press, 1992), 237.

11. L. A. Huffman, "Last Busting at Bow-Gun," *Scribner's* 42 (July 1907): 77.

12. Roosevelt, *Ranch Life in the Far West*, 8.

13. George Brock interview with C. Boone McClure, December 2, 1959, George Brock Interview File, Historical Research Center, Panhandle Plains Historical Museum, Canyon, Texas.

14. Hamlin Garland, "Round-Up on the Range," *Rocky Mountain News* (Denver, Colo.), August 18, 1895, quoted in Westermeier, *Trailing the Cowboy*, 75.

15. Philip Ashton Rollins, *The Cowboy*, rev. ed. (Norman: University of Oklahoma Press, 1936), 117.

16. "A Company of Cowboys," *Texas Live Stock Journal*, May 5, 1883: 1.

17. Edward Bohlin, Hollywood, Calif., *Catalog of "The World's Finest" Riding Equipment Accessories and Silver & Leather Goods* (Hollywood: the company, 1941), 175.

18. Joanna Dendel, "Urban Cowgirls Buckle Up," *Los Angeles Times*, March 13, 1992, E-6.

19. "Roping With the Lariat," *Deming Headlight* (Deming, N. Mex.) January 11, 1890, quoted in Westermeier, *Trailing the Cowboy*, 353.

20. Roosevelt, *Ranch Life in the Far West,* 24,

21. L. E. Sims interview with Pollyanna B. Hughes, February 21, 1956, p. 2, L. E. Sims Interview File, Historical Research Center, Panhandle Plains Historical Museum, Canyon, Texas.

22. "Ropes and Roping," *Cattlemen's Advertiser* (Trinidad, Colo.), December 2, 1886, quoted in Westermeier, *Trailing the Cowboy,* 353.

23. Lucia Bosley, "From Vaquero to Rawhide Artist," *The Horse* 19 (January–February 1938): 8.

24. Ada M. Morgan, "Luis B. Ortega—Versatile Rawhide Artist," *Horse Lover Magazine* (April/May 1948): 10.

METALWORK: BITS AND SPURS TO GUN ENGRAVING

1. Philip Ashton Rollins, *The Cowboy,* rev. ed. (Norman: University of Oklahoma Press, 1997), 116.

2. Edgar Rye, "Frontier Reminiscence," Albany (Tex.) *News,* January 30, 1891.

3. Captain Flack, *The Texas Ranger, or Real Life in a Backwoods* (London: Darton and Co., 1866), 305.

4. David M. Galzay, comp., *Galzay's San Francisco Business Directory for 1863* (San Francisco: the compiler, 1863), 21.

5. John J. Fox, "The Far West in the 80's," *Annals of Wyoming* 21 (January 1948): 7.

6. James H. Cóok, *Fifty Years on the Old Frontier, as Cowboy, Hunter, Guide, Scout and Ranchman* (New Haven: Yale University Press, 1923), 114.

7. Harry Ingerton interview by J. Evetts Haley, Amarillo, Texas, June 19, 1937, p. 2, J. Evetts Haley Collection, Nita Stewart Haley Memorial Library, Midland, Texas.

8. C. W. (Charlie) Walker, W. W. (Walter) Walker, W. D. (Bill) Walker interview by J. Evetts Haley, Dunlap, N. Mex., August 5, 1937, p. 36, Walker Biographical File, Nita Stewart Haley Memorial Library, Midland, Tex.

9. Quoted in Lee C. Jacobs, *J. R. McChesney, A Lifetime, A Legacy* (Colorado Springs, Colo.: ColorTec Printing, 1994), 18.

10. *Ibid.*

11. Visalia Stock Saddle Company, San Francisco, *Catalogue No. 21-C[,] D. E. Walker's Genuine Visalia Stock Saddles[.] Visalia Stock Saddle Co.* (n.p.: the company, n.d.), 48.

12. Bohlin, *Catalog,* 1941, 300.

13. Quoted in Frank Bird Linderman, *Recollections of Charley Russell* (Norman: University of Oklahoma Press, 1963), 9.

BOOTS AND HATS

1. Louis Swinburne, "The Bucolic Dialect of the Plains," *Scribner's Magazine* 2 (October 1887): 512.

2. *Ibid.*

3. Frank Collinson, *Life in the Saddle,* ed. by Mary Whatley Clarke (Norman: University of Oklahoma Press, 1963), 12.

4. Mary J. Jaques, *Texan Ranch Life: With Three Months through Mexico in a "Prairie Schooner"* (1894), reprint ed. (College Station: Texas A&M University Press, 1989), 99.

5. *Ibid.*

6. Swinburne, "The Bucolic Dialect of the Plains," 512.

7. John Justin, "There's Something About a Cowhand," *The Cattleman* 33 (September 1946): 108.

8. Larry Marshall, "Function Becomes Fashion: The Well-Booted Westerner," *Cattleman* 71 (May 1984): 93.

9. Visalia Stock Saddle Co., San Francisco *Catalog No. 31, Visalia Stock Saddle Co. San Francisco, Cal. 2117–2123 Market St.* (San Francisco: the company, 1938), 75.

10. W. M. Sheldon, "Boots, Their Origin and Adaptation to Man's Vanity and Use," *Hoofs and Horns* 14 (November 1944): 8.

11. Quoted in Jane Pattie, "Justin Boot: Standard of the West," *The Quarter Horse Journal* 29 (September 1977): 131.

12. Ruth McMillion, "Shod in Respectability," *The Cattleman* 38 (November 1951).

13. Brad Cooper, "Texas On My Feet," *Texas Monthly* 4 (September 1976): 98.

14. *Ibid.*, 99.

15. Alice Puckett, "Everybody Wears Cowboy Boots," *The Cattleman* 42 (July 1955): 17.

16. T. B. Thorpe, *Our Army on the Rio Grande* (Philadelphia: Carey & Hart, 1846), 134.

17. Quoted in Warren S. Tryson, ed., *A Mirror for Americans, Life and Manners in the U.S. 1790–1870 as Recorded by American Travelers,* 3 vols. (Chicago: University of Chicago Press, 1952), vol. 3, 713.

18. Quoted in Wilson M. Hudson, *Andy Adams: His Life and Writings* (Dallas: Southern Methodist University Press, 1964), 156.

19. Wingate, "My Trip to the Yellowstone": 152.

20. James Cox, ed., *Historical and Biographical Record of the Cattle Industry and the Cattlemen of Texas and the Adjacent Territory,* 2 vols. (St. Louis: Woodward & Tiernan Printing Co., 1894): vol. 1, 179.

21. Quoted in Wilson and Martin, *Buffalo Bill's Wild West,* 224.

22. "Max Meyer of 'Big Hat' Fame Passes Away," *Hat Life,* undated clipping, author's files.

23. *Ibid.*

24. Glen R. Vernam, *Man on Horseback* (New York: Harper and Row, 1964), 345.

25. Lewis Nordyke, "Boss of the Plains: The Story Behind the 'Stetson,'" in Lon Tinkle and Allen Maxwell, eds., *The Cowboy Reader* (New York: Longmans, Green and Co., 1959), 120–21.

26. Clara Locker, "Western Ware in America," *The Quarter Horse Journal* 24 (September 1972): 66.

27. Pete Applebone, "Texas Primer: The Resistol Hat," *Texas Monthly* 12 (June 1984): 141.

28. Karen Evans, "Nice Hat! Just Don't Throw it on the Bed," *Smart* 1 (November–December 1989): 107.

ACKNOWLEDGMENTS

This book is the product of more than two decades of haunting archives, libraries, museums, private collections, and the shops of craftsmen in search of the material culture of the American cowboy. My late father, Bill B. Price, for almost a half century the owner and operator of a retail western wear and saddle shop in Lubbock, Texas, launched me on this course and was an unfailing fount of information and inspiration. At every turn since, I have encountered generous kindred spirits who have shared freely of their own knowledge and enthusiasm for the subject.

I owe my greatest debt of gratitude to Mort and Donna Fleischer, whose magnificent collection forms the cornerstone of this book. Their patience, good humor, unflagging support, and great taste have all made this a better book. I am also especially grateful to Christopher Lyon, my editor at Abbeville Press, for his kind and patient guidance throughout the project. The stunning artifact photography that graces this book is largely the work of Adam Jahiel of Story, Wyoming, and Tom Travis of Denver, Colorado. Another gifted photographer, David Stocklein, of Ketchum, Idaho, responded at a critical moment with some superb images that helped round out the illustrations.

Over the years many individuals have helped to shape the historical content of this work. The collectors, craftsmen, and independent scholars who contributed include the following: Gary Anderson, Cody, Wyoming; Casey Backus, Casper, Wyoming; Michael Beaver, Hayden Lake, Idaho; Robert Brandes, Fredericksburg, Texas; Wylie Buchanan, Washington, D.C.; Verlane Desgrange, Cody, Wyoming; Griff Durham, Reno, Nevada; Dale Harwood, Shelly, Idaho; Abe Hays, Scottsdale, Arizona; James S. Hutchins, Vienna, Virginia; Bill King, Sheridan, Wyoming; Billy Klapper, Pampa, Texas; Jeff Minor, Salmon, Idaho; Luis Ortega, Paradise, California; Jane Patti, Aledo, Texas; Linda Paiche and Jim Grimm, Los Olivos, California; Troy Price, Lubbock, Texas; Ron Soodalter, Chappaqua, New York; and Jeremiah Watt, Coalinga, California.

Current and former staff members of many institutions also responded generously to our requests. I especially wish to thank Dan Davis and Leslie Shores of the American Heritage Center, University of Wyoming, Laramie; Courtney DeAngelis, Barbara McCandless, and Rick Stewart of the Amon Carter Museum, Fort Worth; Michael Duschamin, Marva Felchlin, John L. Gray, and James Nottage of the Autry National Center of the American West, Los Angeles; Armand Labbe of the Bowers Museum of Cultural Art, Santa Ana, California; Nathan Bender, Francis Clymer, Ann Marie Donoghue, Liz Holmes, Lynn Houze, Bob Pickering, and Wally Reber of the Buffalo Bill Historical Center, Cody, Wyoming; Michael Duty and Patricia L. Keats of the California Historical Society, San Francisco; Linda Kohn, Audrey Roberts, and Joseph Sherwood of High Noon Western Americana, Los Angeles; Chuck Rand, Richard Rattenbury, Don Reeves, and Dr. Bobby D. Weaver of the National Cowboy and Western Heritage Museum, Oklahoma City; Jennifer Nielsen and Patricia W. Riley of the National Cowgirl Museum and Hall of Fame, Fort Worth; Marcia Barker of the Northeastern Nevada Museum, Elko; Betty Bustos, Walt Davis, Bill Green, and Claire Kuehn of the Panhandle Plains Historical Museum, Canyon, Texas; Peter Georgi, Scott Powers, and Michael Redman of the Santa Barbara Carriage and Western Art Museum; Tai Kriedler, Janet Neugebauer, and William Tydeman of the Southwest Collection, Texas Tech University, Lubbock; Sharon Silengo of the State Historical Society of North Dakota, Bismarck; Carol Barber and Paula West-Chavoya of the Wyoming State Museum, Cheyenne; and Linda Stone of the Woolaroc Ranch, Museum, and Wildlife Preserve, Oklahoma.

Finally, I want to thank my wife Jeannie, who shares my enthusiasm for fine craftsmanship and who was a constant source of encouragement during the preparation of this volume.

BIBLIOGRAPHY

BOOKS

Abbott, Edward Charles (Teddy Blue). *We Pointed Them North: Recollections of a Cowpuncher.* New York: Farrar & Rinehart, Inc., 1939.

Adams, Ramon F. *The Old-Time Cowhand.* New York: Macmillan Co., 1961.

———. *Western Words: A Dictionary of the American West.* Rev. and enlarged ed. Norman: University of Oklahoma Press, 1968.

Allmendinger, Blake. *The Cowboy: Representations of Labor in an American Work Culture.* New York: Oxford University Press, 1992.

Bailey, Don, comp. *Saddle Strings.* [Colorado]: Bailey Ranch Pub. Co., 1995.

Bard, Floyd C. *Horse Wrangler: Sixty Years in the Saddle in Wyoming and Montana.* Norman: University of Oklahoma Press, 1960.

Baird, Floyd Oliver. *Leather Art.* [Los Angeles]: the author, [1946].

Barnard, Evan G. *A Rider of the Cherokee Strip.* Boston: Houghton Mifflin Co., 1936.

Barrows, John R. *Ubet.* Caldwell, Idaho: Caxton Printers, Ltd., 1934.

Beard, Casey. *Tools of the Cowboy Trade: Today's Crafters of Saddles, Bits, Spurs, and Trappings.* Salt Lake City: Gibbs Smith Publisher, 1997.

Beard, Tyler. *Art of the Boot.* Salt Lake City: Gibbs Smith Publisher, 1999.

———. *The Cowboy Boot Book.* Salt Lake City: Peregrine Smith Books, 1992.

———. *100 Years of Western Wear.* Salt Lake City: Gibbs Smith Publisher, 1993.

Beckstead, James H. *Cowboying: A Tough Job in a Hard Land.* Salt Lake City: University of Utah Press, 1991.

Benedict, Carl Peters. *A Tenderfoot Kid on Gyp Water.* Austin: Texas Folklore Society; Dallas: The University Press, 1943.

Brownlow, Kevin. *The War, the West, and the Wilderness.* New York: Alfred A. Knopf, 1979.

Campbell, Harry H. *The Early History of Motley County.* 2nd ed. Wichita Falls, Tex.: Nortex Offset Publications Inc., 1971.

Christensen, Erwin Ottomar. *The Index of American Design.* New York: Macmillan Co., 1950.

Coburn, Walt. *Pioneer Cattleman in Montana: The Story of the Circle C Ranch.* Norman: University of Oklahoma Press, 1968.

Coconino Center for the Arts. *Trappings of the American West.* Flagstaff, Ariz.: Coconino Center for the Arts, 1988.

Coe, Charles H. *Juggling a Rope; Lariat Roping and Spinning, Knots and Splices; also the Truth about Tom Horn, King of the Cowboys.* Pendleton, Ore.: Hamley & Co., 1927.

Coleman, Max. *From Mustanger to Lawyer.* Lubbock, Tex.: the author, 1952.

Collins, John S. *My Experiences in the West.* Edited by Colton Storm. Chicago: Lakeside Press, 1970.

Collinson, Frank. *Life in the Saddle.* Edited by Mary Whatley Clarke. Norman: University of Oklahoma Press, 1963.

Cook, James H. *Fifty Years on the Old Frontier, as Cowboy, Hunter, Guide, Scout, and Ranchman.* New Haven, Conn.: Yale University Press, 1923.

Cox, James, ed. *Historical and Biographical Record of the Cattle Industry and Cattlemen of Texas and Adjacent Territory.* 2 vols. St. Louis: Woodward & Tiernan Printing Co., 1895.

Culley, John H. (Jack). *Cattle, Horses, and Men of the Western Range.* Los Angeles: Ward Ritchie Press, 1940.

Davis, Richard Harding. *The West from a Car-Window.* New York: Harper & Brothers Publishers, 1892.

Davis, William Heath. *Sixty Years in California.* San Francisco: A. J. Leary, 1889.

Dobie, J. Frank. *A Vaquero of the Brush Country.* Dallas: Southwest Press, 1929.

Dumont, Ella Bird. *Ella Elgar Bird Dumont: An Autobiography of a West Texas Pioneer.* Edited by Tommy J. Boley. Austin: University of Texas Press, 1988.

Durham, Griff. *Everything for the Vaquero: The Legacy of G. S. Garcia.* Elko, Nev.: Western Folklife Center, 2003.

Dykstra, Robert R. *The Cattle Towns.* New York: Alfred A. Knopf, 1968.

Edwards, J. B. *Early Days in Abilene.* Edited by C. W. Wheeler. Abilene, Kans.: C. W. Wheeler, 1938.

Edwards, Richard. *Edward's Great West and Her Commercial Metropolis....* St. Louis: Edwards's Monthly, [1860].

Eggen, John E. *The West that Was.* West Chester, Pa.: Schiffer Publishing, Ltd., 1991.

Evans, Tim, Barbara Allen, Terry Kreuzer, and Richard Collier. *Saddles, Bits and Spurs: Cowboy Crafters at Work.* Cheyenne: Wyoming State Museum, 1993.

Evans, Timothy H. *King of the Western Saddle: The Sheridan Saddle and Art of Don King.* Jackson: University of Mississippi Press, 1998.

Farman, Irvin. *Standard of the West: The Justin Story.* Fort Worth: Texas Christian University Press, 1996.

Faulk, Odie B. *The Leather Jacket Soldier: Spanish Military Equipment and Institutions of the Late 18th Century.* Pasadena, Calif.: Socio-Technical Publications, 1971.

Flack, Captain. *The Texas Ranger, or, Real Life in the Backwoods.* London: Darton & Co., 1866.

Freeman, G. D. *Midnight and Noonday, or, The Incidental History of Southern Kansas and the Indian Territory, 1871–1890.* Norman: University of Oklahoma Press, 1984.

Furber, George C. *The Twelve Months Volunteer, or, Journal of A Private in the Tennessee Regiment of Cavalry, in the Campaign in Mexico, 1846–7.* Cincinnati: J. P. & U. P. James, 1848.

Galzay, David M., comp. *Galzay's San Francisco Business Directory for 1863.* San Francisco: David M. Galzay, 1863.

Gann, Walter. *Tread of the Longhorns.* San Antonio: Naylor Company, 1949.

Goodwyn, Frank. *Life on the King Ranch.* New York: Thomas Y. Crowell Company, 1951.

Graham, Joe S., ed. *Hecho en Tejas: Texas-Mexican Folk Arts and Crafts.* Denton: University of North Texas Press, 1991.

Grancsay, Stephen V. *A Loan Exhibition of Equestrian Equipment from the Metropolitan Museum of Art.* Louisville, Ky.: J. B. Speed Art Museum, 1955.

Grant, Bruce. *The Encyclopedia of Rawhide and Leather Braiding.* 5th printing. Centreville, Md.: Cornell Maritime Press, Inc., 1994.

Gray, S. A. *Mercantile and General City Directory of Austin, Texas, 1872–73.* Austin: S. A. Gray, 1872.

Hadley, C. J. *Trappings of the Great Basin Buckaroo.* Reno: University of Nevada Press, 1993.

Henderson, Debbie. *Cowboys & Hatters: Bond Street, Sagebrush & the Silver Screen.* Yellow Springs, Ohio: Wild Goose Press, 1996.

Hendrix, John. *If I Can Do It Horseback: A Cow-Country Sketchbook.* Austin: University of Texas Press, 1964.

Hoyt, Henry F. *A Frontier Doctor.* Boston: Houghton Mifflin Co., 1929.

Hudson, Wilson M. *Andy Adams: His Life and Writings.* Dallas, Southern Methodist University Press, 1964.

Hunter, J. Marvin. comp. & ed. *The Trail Drivers of Texas.* 2 vols. San Antonio: Jackson Printing Company, 1920, 1923.

Jackson, Jack. *Los Mesteños: Spanish Ranching in Texas, 1721–1821.* College Station: Texas A&M University Press, 1986.

Jacobs, Lee C. *J. R. McChesney, a Lifetime, a Legacy.* Colorado Springs, Colo.: ColorTek Printing, 1994.

James, Will S. *Cow-boy Life in Texas or 27 Years a Mavrick.* Chicago: M.A. Donohue, Henneberry, 1893.

Jaques, Mary J. *Texan Ranch Life: With Three Months Through Mexico in a "Prairie Schooner."* Reprint ed. College Station: Texas A&M University Press, 1989.

Jeffrey, John Mason. *Adobe and Iron: The Story of the Arizona Territorial Prison.* La Jolla Calif.: Prospect Avenue Press, 1969.

Jennings, N. A. *A Texas Ranger.* Reprint ed. Chicago: Lakeside Press, 1992.

Jordan, Terry G. *North American Cattle-Ranching Frontiers: Origins, Diffusion, and Differentiation.* Albuquerque: University of New Mexico Press, 1993.

Kane, Gale Morgan. *Frank's Fancy[:] Frank Phillips' Woolaroc.* Oklahoma City: Oklahoma Heritage Association, 2001.

Kennon, Bob. *From the Pecos to the Powder: A Cowboy's Autobiography.* Edited by Ramon Adams. Norman: University of Oklahoma Press, 1965.

Lacey, Charles de Lacy. *The History of the Spur.* London: Connoisseur Press, 1911.

Lanning, Jim, and Judy Lanning, eds. *Texas Cowboys: Memories of the Early Days.* College Station: Texas A&M University Press, 1984.

Lea, Tom. *The King Ranch.* 2 vols. Boston: Little Brown and Co., 1957.

Likewise, Bob. *Sheridan Style Carving with Bill Gardner and Clinton Fay.* Sheridan, Wyo.: BBC & W, 2000.

Linderman, Frank Bird. *Recollections of Charley Russell.* Norman: University of Oklahoma Press, 1963.

Lindmier, Tom, and Steve Mount. *I See By Your Outfit: Historic Cowboy Gear of the Northern Plains.* Glendo, Wyo.: High Plains Press, 1996.

Lurie, Alison. *The Language of Clothes.* New York: Vintage Books, 1983.

MacConnell, C. E. *XIT Buck.* Tucson: University of Arizona Press, 1968.

Mackey, Margaret, and Louise Sooy. *Early California Costumes 1769–1850.* Stamford, Calif.: Stamford University Press, 1932.

Markus, Kurt. *Buckaroo: Images from the Sagebrush Basin.* Boston: Little Brown and Co., 1987.

Marshall, Howard W., and Richard E. Ahlborn. *Buckaroos in Paradise: Cowboy Life in Northern Nevada.* Lincoln, Neb.: University of Nebraska Press, 1981.

Martin, Ned, and Jody Martin. *Bit and Spur Makers in the Vaquero Tradition: A Historical Perspective.* Nicasio, Calif.: Hawk Hill Press, 1997.

———. *Bits and Spurs: Motifs, Techniques and Modern Makers.* Nicasio, Calif.: Hawk Hill Press, 2003.

Martin, Ned, Jody Martin, and Kurt House. *Bit and Spur Makers in the Texas Tradition.* Nicasio, Calif.: Hawk Hill Press, 2000.

Maul, Patrice, and Jack Ferguson et. al. *Cañon City Spur[:] Colorado Prison Spurs and The Men Who Made Them.* Akron, Colo.: Canon City Spur Company & Old West Trading Company, 1994.

McCoy, Joseph G. *Historic Sketches of the Cattle Trade of the West and Southwest.* Kansas City, Mo.: Ramsey, Millett & Hudson, 1874.

Mitchell, Annie R. *The Way It Was[:] The Colorful History of Tulare County.* Fresno, Calif.: Panorama West Publishing, 1976.

Mora, Joe. *Trail Dust and Saddle Leather.* New York: Charles Scribner's Sons, 1946.

Morison, Samuel Eliot. *The Ropemakers of Plymouth.* Boston: Houghton Mifflin Co., 1950.

Myres, Sandra L. *S. D. Myres: Saddlemaker.* Kerrville, Tex.: the author, 1961.

Nathan, Maude. *The Decoration of Leather.* From the French of Georges de Récy. London: Archibald Constable & Co., 1905.

Newmark, Harris. *Sixty Years in Southern California 1853–1913.* 3rd ed. Boston: Houghton Mifflin Co., 1930.

Nottage, James H. *Saddlemaker to the Stars: The Leather and Silver Art of*

Edward H. Bohlin. Los Angeles: Autry Museum of Western Heritage, 1996.

Ortega, Luis Birabent. *California Hackamore: An Authentic Story of the Use of the Hackamore.* Walnut Creek, Calif., 1948.

de Pagès, [Pierre Marie Francois]. *Travels Round the World, in the Years 1767, 1768, 1769, 1770, 1771.* 3 vols. London: Printed for J. Murray, 1791–92.

Pattie, Jane. *Cowboy Spurs and Their Makers.* College Station: Texas A&M University Press, 1991.

Pattie, Jane, and Tom Kelly. *Cowboy Spur Maker: The Story of Ed Blanchard.* College Station: Texas A&M University Press, 2002.

Perissinotto, Giorgio, ed. *Documenting Everyday Life in Early Spanish California[:] Requisitions for the Santa Barbara Presidio 1779–1810*[,] *Memorias and Facturas.* Santa Barbara, Calif.: Santa Barbara Trust for Historic Preservation, 1998.

Raine, William MacLeod, and Will C. Barnes. *Cattle.* New York: Doubleday, Doran & Co., 1930.

Rattenbury, Richard. *Packing Iron: Gunleather of the Frontier West.* Millwood, New York: Zon International Publishing Co., 1993.

Reid, Shell. *Eddy Hulbert, Montana Silversmith.* Bozeman, Mont.: the author, 1998.

Rice, Lee M., and Glen R. Vernam. *They Saddled the West.* Cambridge, Md.: Cornell Maritime Press, 1975.

Rickey, Don. *$10 Horse, $40 Saddle: Cowboy Clothing, Arms, Tools, and Horse Gear of the 1880's.* Ft. Collins, Colo.: Old Army Press, 1976.

Roach, Joyce Gibson. *The Cowgirls.* 2nd rev. and enlarged ed. Denton: University of North Texas Press, 1990.

Roenigk, Adolph, ed. *Pioneer History of Kansas.* Lincoln, Kans.: A. Roenigk, [c.1933].

Rollins, Philip Ashton. *The Cowboy: His Characteristics, His Equipment and His Part in the Development of the West.* Rev. and enlarged ed. Norman: University of Oklahoma Press, 1997.

Rollinson, John K. *Wyoming Cattle Trails.* Caldwell, Idaho: Caxton Printers, Ltd., 1948.

Roosevelt, Theodore. *Ranch Life in the Far West.* Flagstaff, Ariz.: Northland Press, 1968.

Russell, J. H. *Cattle on the Conejo.* Pasadena, Calif.: Ward Ritchie Press, 1957.

Salaman, R. A. *Dictionary of Leather-Working Tools, c. 1700–1950.* Winchester, Mass.: Allen & Unwin, 1986.

Sanborn, Kate. *A Truthful Woman in Southern California.* New York: D. Appleton & Co., 1894.

Sands, Kathleen M. *Charrería Mexicana: An Equestrian Folk Tradition.* Tucson: University of Arizona Press, 1993.

Sartorius, Carl Christian. *Mexico about 1850.* Stuttgart, Germany: F. A. Brockhaus, 1961.

Scharf, John Thomas. *History of Saint Louis City and County.* 2 vols. Philadelphia: L. H. Everts & Co., 1883.

Schreier, Konrad F., Jr. "The Firm of Main & Winchester, Saddle Makers." *Brand Book No. 16 of the Westerners Los Angeles Corral.* Los Angeles: Los Angeles Corral of Westerners, 1982.

Severn, Bill. *Rope Roundup.* New York: David McKay Company, Inc., 1960.

Simmons, Marc, and Frank Turley. *Southwestern Colonial Ironwork: The Spanish Blacksmithing Tradition from Texas to California.* Santa Fe: Museum of New Mexico Press, 1980.

Sims, Orland L. *Cowpokes, Nesters, and So Forth.* Austin, Tex.: Encino Press, 1970.

Siringo, Charles A. *A Lone Star Cowboy: Being Fifty Years in the Saddle as Cowboy, Detective, and New Mexico Ranger.* Santa Fe., N. Mex.: Charles A. Siringo, 1919.

SMS Ranch [F. S. Hastings], *The Story of the S.M.S. Ranch.* Stamford, Tex.: n.p., n.d. [1919].

Snyder, Jeffery B. *Stetson Hats and the John B. Stetson Company 1865–1970.* Atglen, Pa.: Schiffer Publishing Ltd., 1997.

Sonnichsen, C. L. *Cowboys and Cattle Kings, Life on the Range Today.* Norman: University of Oklahoma Press, 1950.

Storke, Carol. *Bits and Spurs[:] Two Centuries of Fine Metal Craftsmanship from the Central Coast.* Santa Barbara, Calif.: Santa Barbara Trust for Historic Preservation, 2002.

Sullivan, Dulcie. *The LS Brand.* Austin: University of Texas Press, 1968.

Thorpe, Thomas Bangs. *Our Army on the Rio Grande.* Philadelphia: Carey & Hart, 1846.

Tinkle, Lon, and Allen Maxwell, eds. *The Cowboy Reader.* New York: Longmans, Green and Company, 1959.

Tryson, Warren S., ed. *A Mirror for Americans, Life and Manners in the U.S., 1790–1870, as Recorded by American Travelers.* 3 vols. Chicago: University of Chicago Press, 1952.

Van Meter, David L. *G. S. Garcia, Elko, Nev.: A History of the World Famous Saddlemaker.* Reno, Nev.: Avail Publishing Co., 1984.

Vernam, Glenn R. *Man on Horseback.* New York: Harper and Row, 1964.

Westermier, Clifford P. *Man, Beast, Dust: The Story of Rodeo.* Denver: the author, 1947.

———. *Trailing the Cowboy.* Caldwell, Idaho: Caxton Printers, Ltd., 1955.

White, Benton R. *The Forgotten Cattle King.* College Station: Texas A&M University Press, 1986.

Whitlock, Vivian H. (Ol' Waddy), *Cowboy Life on the Llano Estacado.* Norman: University of Oklahoma Press, 1970.

Wilson, Laurel. "The American Cowboy: Development of the Mythic Image," in *Dress in American Culture.* Edited by Patricia A. Cunningham and Susan Voso Lab. Bowling Green, Ky.: Bowling Green State University Popular Press, 1993.

Wilson, R. L., with Greg Martin, *Buffalo Bill's Wild West: An American Legend.* New York: Random House, 1998.

TRADE LITERATURE

Ahlstrom & Gunther. Lakeview, Ore. *Ahlstrom & Gunther (Incorporated)[,]*

Lakeview, Oregon[.] Saddles[.] Catalog Number Fourteen. Lakeview, Ore.: Examiner Press, n.d.

E. T. Amonett. Roswell, N. Mex. and El Paso, Tex. *E. T. Amonett Illustrated and Descriptive Catalogue and Price List 27.* El Paso: Ellis Bros Printing Co., n.d.

J. O. Bass. Tulia, Tex. *Catalog of Hand-Made Bridle Bits and Spurs Made by J. O. Bass, Tulia, Texas.* N.p.: the author, n.d.

Joseph Bianchi. Victoria, Tex. *Joe Bianchi[,] Manufacturer of Hand-Forged Spurs and Bits, Plain and Silver Mounted, Victoria, Texas, Catalogue "G."* n.p.: the author, n.d.

Edward H. Bohlin. Hollywood, Calif. *The Bohlin Shop of Edward H. Bohlin. Catalog of "The World's Finest"Riding Equipment, Riding Accessories and Silver and Leather Goods.* Hollywood: the company, 1937.

———. *Catalog of "The World's Finest" Riding Equipment Accessories and Silver & Leather Goods.* Hollywood: the company, 1941.

W. R. (Wallie) Boone. San Angelo, Tex. *W. R. (Wallie) Boone Catalogue No.3.* San Angelo, Tex.: the author, n.d.

Chicago Art Metal Works. Chicago Ill. *Chicago Art Metal Works, Chicago Ill. Catalogue No. 20.* N.p.: the company, n.d.

J. S. Collins & Co. Cheyenne, Wyo. *J. S. Collins & Co.[,] Wholesale and Retail Saddlers[,] Commercial Block, Cheyenne, WY.* N. p.: the company, n.d.

Crockett Bit and Spur Co.. Kansas City, Mo. *Catalog No. 11[,] Crockett's Most Complete Line of Bits and Spurs on the Market.* Kansas City, Mo.: the company, n.d.

Denver Manufacturing Co.. Denver, Colo. *Illustrated Catalogue of the Denver Manufacturing Company, Tanners, Manufacturers and Wholesale Dealers in Leather, Leather Goods, Whips, Lashes and Saddlery Hardware.* Denver: Daily Times, Spring Printing House, 1883.

Otto Ernst. Sheridan, Wyo. *Otto F. Ernst, Inc. Sheridan, Wyoming[,] Makers of Fine Saddles[,] Catalog No. 13.* Sheridan, Wyo.: Mills Company, n.d.

A. L. Furstnow. Miles City, Mont. *A.L. Furstnow The Originator and Sole Manufacturer of the Saddle That Made Miles City Famous.* Miles City, Mont.: the company, n.d.

Garcia Saddlery Co. Elko, Nev. *Garcia Saddlery Co. Catalog No.27—1929[,] Elko, Nevada.* Elko, Nev.: the company, 1929.

Hamley & Company. Pendleton, Ore. *Hamley's Cowboy Catalog No. 39.* Pendleton, Ore.: the company, n.d.

Hermann H. Heiser. Denver, Colo. *The Hermann H. Heiser Saddlery Co., Denver, Colo. U.S.A. [Catalog Number 15].* Denver: Press of Smith-Brooks, n.d.

———. *Illustrated Catalogue No. 13 of The Hermann H. Heiser Saddlery Co.* .... N.p.: the company, n.d.

———. *Illustrated Catalogue No. 21[.] Harness, Riding Saddles, Bridles, Harness Parts ... Manufactured and Sold by Hermann H. Heiser Manufacturing & Selling Company* .... N.p.: the company, n.d.

Holland Jewelry Company. San Angelo, Tex. *Holland's Touch o' the West.* San Angelo, Tex.: the company, n.d.

Kelly Brothers Manufacturers. El Paso, Tex. *No.22 Illustrated Catalog[,] Kelly's Bits and Spurs.* El Paso: the author, n.d.

Los Angeles Saddlery & Findings Co. Los Angeles, Calif. *Catalog No. 14 of the Los Angeles Saddlery and Finding Co.* .... *Issued August 1912.* Los Angeles: A. H. Gaarder, 1912.

Main and Winchester. San Francisco, Calif. *Illustrated Catalog No. 11[.] Main & Winchester 214, 216, 218 and 220 Battery St. San Francisco, California, U.S.A.* San Francisco: Murdock Press, n.d.

———. *Illustrated Catalogue No. 8 of Main & Winchester Manufacturers and Importers of Harness, Saddles, Bridles, Whips, Collars, Leather, Saddlery Hardware, Etc., Etc. 214, 216, 218 and 220 Battery Street, San Francisco, Cal.* San Francisco: Geo. Spaulding & Co., 1889.

Phillips and Gutierrez. Cheyenne, Wyo. *Catalog and Price List[,] Phillips & Gutierrez, 423 West Nineteenth Street.* Cheyenne, Wyo.: the company, n.d.

N. Porter Saddle and Harness Co. Phoenix, Ariz. *Catalog No. 6.* Los Angeles: A. H. Gaarder, 1912.

———. *N. Porter Saddle & Harness Co. Catalog No.17 for the Summer–Fall 1929 and Spring 1930.* N.p.: the company, n.d.

Stanton's Sunset Trails. Santa Monica, Calif. *Stanton's Sunset Trails.* N.p.: the company, 1990.

L. D. Stone & Co. San Francisco, Calif. *L. D. Stone & Co. Wholesale and Retail Manufacturers and Importers of Harness, Saddles, Saddlery Hardware, Etc. 422 & 424 Battery St. Catalog No. 6, January 1st, 1890.* San Francisco: the company, 1889.

Visalia Stock Saddle Co. San Francisco, Calif. *Saddle Section of Catalogue No. 20 showing part of our line of D.E. Walker's Genuine Visalia Stock Saddles.* ... San Francisco: the company, n.d.

———. *Catalogue No. 21-C[,] D. E. Walker's Genuine Visalia Stock Saddles[.] Visalia Stock Saddle Co.* N.p.: the company, n.d.

———. *Catalog No. 31 Visalia Stock Saddle Co. San Francisco, Cal. 2117–2123 Market St.* San Francisco: the company, 1938.

———. *Temporary Catalog No. 19[.] D. E. Walker's Genuine Visalia Stock Saddles[.] All previous Catalogs and Prices Cancelled[.] All Prices subject to change without Notice[.] Made and Sold Only by Visalia Stock Saddle Co. 2117 Market St. San Francisco, Cal.* San Francisco: the company, n.d.

D. E. Walker. Visalia, Calif. *D. E. Walker's Price List of Saddles, Spurs, Reins & Riatas.* N.p.: the company, n.d.

Walker and Wade [saddlers]. San Francisco, Calif. *Walker & Wade Genuine Visalia Stock Saddles.* ... San Francisco: William C. Brown, Printer, n.d.

ARTICLES

Abbott, Sigrid. "Miss Enid Justin: Lady Bootmaker." *Persimmon Hill* 7, no.4: 54–61.

Ahlborn, Richard. "European Dress in Texas, 1830: As Rendered by Lino Sánchez y Tapia." *American Scene* 13, no.4 (1972): 1–20.

Amarillo Globe-News. "Demand for Exotic Boots Boosts Smuggling." March 29, 1983.

Amarillo Globe-Times. "Man Makes Hobby of Exotic Boots." April 25, 1983.

Amarillo Globe-Times. "Western Craze Boots Rodeo Stars to Success." December 11, 1981, p.19.

"Angora Wool Hats." *Texas Live Stock Journal* 8 (November 12, 1887): 14.

Applebone, Peter. "Texas Primer: The Resistol Hat." *Texas Monthly* 12 (June 1984): 141.

"The Art of Hitching Horsehair." *Whitehawk August in Santa Fe Antique Show Guide 1998.* n.p.

Bailey, Alvin. "Carvajals: The Saddle Makers, a Vanishing Old West Craft." *San Antonio Express and News,* August 5, 1973, pt.1, p.1-C.

Barnes, Will C. "The New Cowboy of the New Century." *The Breeder's Gazette* 27 (August 5, 1920): 212.

Bergen, Yvonne. "Saddle Saga." *Western Horseman* 5 (March–April 1940): 34, 43–44; 5 (May–June 1940): 22, 34; 5 (July–August 1940): 19, 37.

Biasatti, Helena. "A Rawhide Legend." *The Quarter Horse Journal* 34 (December 1981): 260–67, 326, 330, 332, 334, 336, 339, 347, 348.

"Bits and Spurs." *Western Horseman* 23 (May 1956): 26–27, 80–83.

Bosley, Lucia. "From Vaquero to Rawhide Artist." *The Horse* 19 (January–February 1938): 7–9.

Bossay, Lyssa, "Putting Out The Clothes Lines." *Western Horseman,* 49 (August 1984): 44–46.

Bourque, Joseph. "Edward L. Gallatin: Maker of Saddles." *Persimmon Hill* 19 (Winter 1991): 36–40.

Boyd, E. "Colonial Horse Gear." *El Palacio* 81 (Fall 1975): 22–26.

Brewer, Steve. "Boot Boom Business Boon for El Paso." *Amarillo Globe-News,* April 26, 1981.

Brown, Larry K. " 'Meanie' Made the Best." *Cowboy Magazine* 9 (Summer 1998): 28.

Butte Miner (Butte, Mont.). "Passing of the Picturesque Swash-Buckling Cowboy Has Not Affected Manufacture of That Masterpiece of Leather Carver's Handicraft, the Stock Saddle," December 14, 1913, p. 6.

"California Saddles." *Harness and Carriage Journal* 24 (May 1879): 5.

Chace, Sue. "Silverwork Embodies Romance of Vaquero Days." *Star Free Press* (Ventura, Calif.), July 29, 1990, p. A-3.

Chriss, Nicholas C. "Behind the Boom in Cowboy Boots." *San Francisco Examiner & Chronicle,* December 26, 1976.

Cody Enterprise. "Custom Cowboy Owner Wins 'Saddle Maker of Year' Honor." August 4, 1999, p. B-4.

Collins, Dabney Otis. "How to Make a Horsehair Girt." *Western Horseman* 15 (January 1950): 22–23, 38.

"A Company of Cowboys." *Texas Live Stock Journal* (May 5, 1883): 1.

Cook, Alison. "The Western Boot." *Town & Country* 133 (September 1979): 94, 96, 98, 100, 104, 110, 112, 116.

Cooper, Brad. "Texas On My Feet." *Texas Monthly* 4 (September 1976): 97–101.

Curley, Cal. "Pages of the Past." *Western Horseman* 17 (March 1952): 24–25.

Dedera, Don. "The Boots That Won The West." *Arizona Highways* 56 (February 1980): 32–41.

Dendel, Joanna. "Urban Cowgirls Buckle Up." *Los Angeles Times,* March 13, 1992, p. E-6.

Denhardt, Robert. "The Mexican Saddle." *Western Horseman* 3 (July–August 1938): 7, 33.

"Designing." *Harness and Carriage Journal* 27 (May 1882): 4.

Dey, Mary. "Horsehair Braiding—A Lost Art?" *Western Horseman* 35 (August 1970): 118, 182–83.

Dobie, J. Frank. "Ab Blocker: Trail Boss." *Arizona and the West* 6 (Summer 1964): 97–103.

"Enid Justin, Boot Maker." *The Quarter Horse Journal* 6 (April 1954): 70–71.

Ensign, Arthur. "The Western Saddle." *Arizona Highways* 17 (February 1941): 26–29.

Erickson, Kenneth C. "Hats and Boots: Some Regional and Temporal Aspects of the Cowboy Complex as Seen in the Photographic Record." *Wyoming Contributions to Anthropology* 1 (Spring 1978): 1-10.

Evans, Karen. "Nice Hat! Just Don't Throw it on the Bed." *Smart* 1 (November–December 1989): 104–11.

Ewald, Chase Reynolds. "Heisman's Trophies." *American Cowboy* 8 (September–October 2001): 60–61.

———. "Never to Fade Away." *American Cowboy* 9, no. 4 (November–December 2002): 64–65.

Fox, John J. "The Far West in the 80's." *Annals of Wyoming* 21 (January 1948): 3–88.

Foy, Nichole. "The Heeling Power of Recycled Boots." *Dallas Morning News,* August 5, 1992, p. 5E.

Frederick, M. C. "The Californian Montadura." *The Californian Illustrated Magazine* IV 2 (July 1893): 179–86.

Fuqua, Carl. "Ideas on Saddlemaking," *Western Horseman* 15 (December 1950): 14–15, 36–37.

Gilmore, Gypsy H. "Master of Lost Art, Luis Ortega Relives Past at Western Center." *Daily Oklahoman/Times,* August 20, 1984, p. 9.

Gray, Sally M. "Cowboy Fashions from Days Gone By." *The Quarter Horse Journal* 24 (September 1972): 30–32, 50, 52–56, 92, 98.

Griffin, Bert. "F. O. Baird: Adios Amigo. Vaya con Dios." *The Craftsman* 15, no. 5 (1971): 10–11.

Haley, Katherine, H. "Edward Borien—Artist of the West." *Western Horseman* 37 no. 8 (August 1972): 46–48.

Halliday, Dick. "The Cowboy's Throne." *The Cattleman* 16 (August 1929): 37–38.

———. "Roofing the Rangeland Rider." *The Cattleman* 16 (March 1930): 59–62, 107.

———. "The Silver Saddle Business." *Western Horseman* 2 (May–June 1937): 6–7, 29.

———. "The Tale of the Reata." *The Horse* 28 (March–April 1947): 16–18.

Hendrix, John. "Boots." *The Cattleman* 23 (April 1937): 5.

———. "Bronk Busters Paid Top Wages." *The Cattleman* 22 (March 1936): 12, 14–16.

———. "A $10 Horse and a $40 Saddle." *The Cattleman* 25 (October 1938): 5.

Hewitt, Bob. "Chaps for the Cowboy." *Western Horseman* 48 (November 1983): 118–20.

Howard, Orville. "More than 6,000 Saddles Hand Crafted in 58 Years." *Amarillo News-Globe*, July 31, 1960.

———. "Tulia Spur Maker." *The Cattleman* 57 (November 1970): 36.

Hoy, Jim. "The Coffeyville Boot." *Persimmon Hill* 19 (Spring 1991): 15–19.

Huber, Dwight W. "Adolph Bayers, Texas Spur Maker." *Spur Collectors' Quarterly*. Pt.1 (Summer 1984): 4–8; pt.2 (Fall 1984): 4–8.

———. "Misconceptions and Facts: Some Observations on the Mexican Spur." *The Tack Room Journal* 1 (July 1978): 5.

———. "Selected Pairs of Spurs from the Panhandle-Plains Collection." *The Tack Room Journal* 2 (November 1978): 8–10.

———. "Spurs, An Illustrated History." *Western Horseman*. Pt.1, 44 (January 1979): 14–20; pt. 2, 44 (February 1979): 14–17.

———. "The Western Spur: An American Original." *The Tack Room Journal* 1 (May 1978): 2, 4–5.

Huffman, L. A. "Last Busting at Bow-Gun." *Scribner's* 42 (July 1907): 75–86.

Hughes, Pollyanna B. "The Crockett Spurs." *The Cattleman* 43 (September 1956): 100, 102, 104.

———. "Knight or Cowboy, Spurs Made the Man." *Western Horseman* 20 (October 1955): 21, 55–58.

"Japanning." *Harness and Carriage Journal* 19 (May 15, 1875): 21–22.

Jennings, Jim. "The Cowboy Boot." *The Quarter Horse Journal* 26 (September 1974): 66–70, 250.

Justin, John. "There's Something About a Cowhand." *The Cattleman* 33 (September 1946): 104, 106, 108.

Kniffen, Fred. "The Western Cattle Complex: Notes on Differentiation and Diffusion." *Western Folklore* 12 (1953): 179–85.

Kohn, Linda. "Luis B. Ortega 1897–1995." *Persimmon Hill* 23 (Summer 1995): 7.

Kuehlthau, Margaret. "Plaited Horsehair Bridles." *Western Horseman* 32 (August 1967): 65, 114–15.

Leslie, Mike "101 Saddle Among Gifts To Museum." *Persimmon Hill* 31 (Spring 2003): 6–7.

Lierle, Doug. "The Fashion Conscious Stockman." *Livestock* (October 1978): 45.

Lloyd, Bob. "The Pueblo Saddlemaker." *Frontier Times* 32, no. 2 (Spring 1958): 46–47.

Locker, Clara. "Western Wear in America." *The Quarter Horse Journal* 24 (September 1972): 64–77, 88, 114, 122.

"Luis Ortega Pays Visit to the Hall." *Persimmon Hill* 20 (Winter 1992): 62.

Lubbock Avalanche-Journal. "Cowboy Boot Craze Causing Foot Problems." June 27, 1982, p. 5-F.

Maher, Raymond E. "Forty Years at the Forge." *The Cattleman* 36 (August 1949): 24.

Manns, William, and Elizabeth Clair Flood. "A Cachet of Chaps." *American Cowboy* (July/August 2000): 40–42.

Markus, Kurt. "Frank Hansen: RAWHIDER." *Western Horseman* 46 (August 1981): 44–45, 47, 127–29.

Marlow, Del. "The Evolution of the Cowboy Boot." *Western Horseman*. Pt.1, 46 (June 1981): 13–16, 18–20, 22–23; pt. 2, 46 (July 1981): 13–16, 18–20.

Marshall, Larry. "Function Becomes Fashion: The Well-Booted Westerner." *The Cattleman* 71 (May 1984): 91–98.

"Max Meyer of 'Big Hat' Fame Passes Away." *Hat Life*, undated clipping, author's files.

McKern, Craig E. "Red Oyster—Rawhide Craftsman." *Western Horseman* 38 (April 1973): 45, 172–74.

McMechen, Edgar C. "The Gallatin Saddle." *The Colorado Magazine* 21 (1944): 56–58.

McMillan, Don. "Human Hair Rope." *Western Horseman* 39 (July 1974): 51–52.

MacMillion, Ruth. "Shod in Respectability." The Cattleman 38 (November 1951): 190.

McNichols, Charles Longstreth. "Horse Town." *The Horse* 19 (1938): 17–19.

Minutaglo, Bill. "A Well-Worn Friend." *Dallas Life Magazine* 6 (June 14, 1987): 14–16, 26–28, 30.

Morgan, Ada M. "Luis B. Ortega—Versatile Rawhide Artist." *Horse Lover's Magazine* 12 (April/May 1948): 10–11, 36.

National Cowboy and Western Heritage Museum, "National Cowboy Museum to Honor Hollywood's Cowboy Image Artist," press release, February 5, 2001.

Negri, Brenda M. "Horsehair Mecates Schutte Style." *Western Horseman* 51 (May 1986): 58, 61–62.

"Newark, N. J." *Coach Harness & Saddlery Weekly* 3 (January 26, 1884): 287–88.

Nottage, James N. "A Saddle Fit for a King." Leaflet accompanying *12th Annual Wild West High Noon Auction Catalog, January 19, 2002[,] Mesa[,] Arizona*. N.p.: High Noon, 2002.

"Ornamenting Saddles." *Harness and Carriage Journal* 22 (January 1878): 132.

"Ornamenting Saddles." *Harness and Carriage Journal* 22 (February 1878): 148.

"Ornamenting Saddles." *Harness and Carriage Journal* 22 (March 1878): 163.

"Ornamenting Saddles." *Harness and Carriage Journal* 25 (April 1881): 278–79.

Ortega, Luis B. "A Buckaroo's Craft." *Persimmon Hill* 4, no. 4: 29.

———. "Las Manellas[:] The Hobbles." *Western Horseman* pt. 1, 58 (July 1993): 16–17, 19, 22; pt. 2, 58 (August 1993): 40–43.

Pattie, Jane. "Justin Boot: Standard of the West." *The Quarter Horse Journal* 29 (September 1977): 124–32.

Pitman, George. "Sterling Silver Parade Saddles: A Collector's Point of View." *Silver Magazine* 32 (May/June 2000): 24—34.

———. "Visalia Stock Saddle Company—Since 1870." *Leather Crafters and Saddlers Journal* (September–October 1994): 36–37, 39–40.

Probert, Alan. "Cruciform Stirrups." *Western Horseman* 41 (December 1976): 130–32.

Puckett, Alice. "Everybody Wears Cowboy Boots." *The Cattleman* 42 (July 1955): 17–18, 30–32.

Ralph, Julian. "Wyoming—Another Pennsylvania." *Harper's New Monthly Magazine* 87 (June 1893): 63–77.

Rattenbury, Richard. "J. C. Petmecky: Texas Gun and Spurmaker." *Man at Arms* 11 (September/October 1989): 10–15.

Rice, Lee M. "Fresno County's Centennial Saddle." *Western Horseman* 22 (January 1957): 12.

"Riding Saddles." *Coach Harness & Saddlery Weekly* 1 (November 25, 1882): 152.

"Riding Saddles." *Harness* 2 (January 1889): 276–79.

"Riding Saddles." *Harness and Carriage Journal* 20 (November 6, 1875): 135.

"Riding Saddles." *Harness and Carriage Journal* 23 (October 1878): 83–84.

Roberts, C. M. "P. M. Kelly & Sons." *Western Horseman* 25 (May 1960): 78–79, 160–61.

Rodriguez, June N. "Urban Cowboys: These Boots Are Made for Gawking." *Edmond Evening Sun,* December 18, 1994, p. C-2.

Rye, Edgar. "Frontier Reminiscence." *Albany News* (Albany, Tex), January 30, 1891.

"A Saddle for 'Bull' Halsey." *Western Horseman* 10 (September–October 1945): 21.

"Saddle That Has Cost $3,000." *Harness Gazette* 16 (September 1897): 64.

"Saddlers' and Harness Tools." *Harness and Carriage Journal* 20 (February 15, 1876): 358.

"Saddlers' Tools." *Harness and Carriage Journal* 21 (September 1876): 65–66.

San Antonio Light (San Antonio, Tex.). "Auto Springs Used in Making Spurs." August 8, 1956.

Santa Barbara News-Press (Santa Barbara, Calif.). "Work of Noted Local Craftsman to Be Shown." May 30, 1948.

Santa Clara Journal (Santa Clara, Calif.). "Jewel Mounted $10,000 Saddle," May 2, 1914, p.1.

Searcy, Mildred, in collaboration with David Hamley. "Hamley & Co. Makers of Saddles Since 1883." *Persimmon Hill* 10 (Winter 1981), no. 4:20–31.

Sheldon, W. M. "Boots, Their Origin and Adaptation to Man's Vanity and Use." *Hoofs and Horns* 14 (November 1944): 3, 8.

Simison, Robert L. "At Tony Lama, You Get What You Want and More to Boot." *Wall Street Journal* (March 18, 1977), pp. 1, 15.

Sinisi, J. Sebastian. "Putting a Kick in Western Boots." *Sunday Denver Post* (January 11, 1987): Contemporary sec., pp. 16–17.

Spivey, W. C. "Rodeo Fads and Fancies." *Horse Lover's Magazine* 5 (September 1940): 5–6, 8.

Steffen, Randy. "The Cowboy's Boot." *Horse Lover's Magazine* 29 (August–September 1965): 14–16.

"Stetson: Hat of the West." *Persimmon Hill* 8 (Winter 1979): 42–51.

Stout, Wesley. "The Boot that Made Coffeyville Famous." *Coffeyville Weekly Journal,* October 3, 1914, p. 4.

Streeter, Benjamin. "The Millett Cattle Ranch in Baylor County, Texas." *Panhandle-Plains Historical Review* 22 (1949): 65–83.

"Styles of the 80's." *The Cattleman* 25 (June 1938): 6—7.

Swinburne, Louis. "The Bucolic Dialect of the Plains." *Scribner's* 2 (October 1887): 505–14.

Thomas, Jack. "A History of the Texas Spur." *Western Horseman.* Pt.1, 38 (August 1973): 86–88, 166, 168–70; pt. 2, 38 (September 1973): 4–6, 60–61.

Thomas, Loydean. "Saddle Shop Offers Ride Through History." *San Antonio Express-News,* January 11, 1981, p. 6E.

"Tourist in Santa Fe, 1840: Sketches by Matthew C. Field." *El Palacio* 66 (February 1959): 30.

Turner, Timothy G. "Aged Craftsman Spurs Tales of Prairie Life." *Los Angeles Daily Times,* June 10, 1923.

Valentry, Duane. "Horse Gear Brings History to Life." *Western Horseman* 32 (November 1967): 20, 32–33.

[Whitlock, V. H.] (Ol' Waddy). "Buttermilk and Trigger." *Western Horseman* 25 (September 1960): 16–17, 91, 94.

Walters, Keith "Chinks and Woolies." *Western Horseman* 51 (May 1986): 102–4.

———. "Cowboy Wrist Cuffs." *Western Horseman* 51 (November 1986): 30, 32.

Wenham, Edward. "Spanish American Saddlery in California." *International Studio* 97 (September 1930): 52–55.

———. "Spanish Saddlery in America." *Apollo* 17 (May 1933): 192–95.

Williams, J. W. "Old Cowhands of Fact and Fiction." *The Cattleman* 38 (October 1951): 32–33, 76, 78–80, 82, 84, 86–87.

Wilson, Laurel. " 'I Was a Pretty Proud Kid': An Interpretation of Differences in Posed and Unposed Photographs of Montana Cowboys." *Clothing and Textile Research Journal* 9 (Spring 1991): 49–58.

———. "The Cowboy: Real and Imagined." *Dress* 23 (1996): 3–15.

Wingate, George. "My Trip to the Yellowstone." *American Agriculturist* 45 (April 1886): 152.

Wister, Owen. "The Evolution of the Cow Puncher." *Harper's New Monthly Magazine* 41 (1895): 602–17.

Woodward, Arthur. "La Mochila: A Saddle Trapping of the Old West." *Los Angeles County Museum Quarterly* 7 (Autumn 1949): 4–10.

INTERVIEWS

Brock, George. Interview by C. Boone McClure, December 2, 1959.

George Brock Biographical File, Historical Research Center, Panhandle-Plains Historical Museum, Canyon, Tex.

Burns, R. C. Interview by J. Evetts Haley, Lubbock, Tex., July 28, 1937. R. C. Burns Biographical File, Nita Stewart Haley Memorial Library, Midland, Tex.

Combs, G. B. Interview by Lois Allen, Canyon, Tex., June 5, 23, 1937. Lois Allen Biographical File, Historical Research Center, Panhandle-Plains Historical Museum, Canyon, Tex.

Cottrell, M. G. Interview by J. Evetts Haley, June 22, 1937. M. G. Cottrell Biographical File, Nita Stewart Haley Memorial Library, Midland, Tex.

Crosby, R. H. Interview by J. Evetts Haley, Kenna, N. Mex., August 4, 1937. R. H. Crosby Biographical File, Nita Stewart Haley Memorial Library, Midland, Tex.

Ingerton, Harry. Interview by J. Evetts Haley, Amarillo, Tex., June 19, 1937. J. Evetts Haley Collection, Nita Stewart Haley Memorial Library, Midland, Tex.

Sims, L. E. Interview by Pollyanna B. Hughes, February 21, 1956. L. E. Sims Biographical File, Historical Research Center, Panhandle-Plains Historical Museum, Canyon, Tex.

Walker, C. W. (Charlie), W. W. (Walter) Walker, W. D. (Bill) Walker. Interview by J. Evetts Haley, Dunlap, N. Mex., August 5, 1937. Walker Biographical File, Nita Stewart Haley Memorial Library, Midland, Tex.

MANUSCRIPT MATERIAL

Bell, Don. "Rodeo of Yesteryears." Unpublished typescript, Rodeo Historical Society Files, Donald C. and Elizabeth M. Dickinson Research Center, National Cowboy and Western Heritage Museum, Oklahoma City.

"In Memory of Mr. Joe (Joseph) Bianchi." April 15, 1974, typescript, Bianchi File, Victoria College Library, Victoria, Tex.

Blucher Custom Boot Company Collection 1915–1999. Donald C. and Elizabeth M. Dickinson Research Center, National Cowboy and Western Heritage Museum.

Brown, Bob. Correspondence. High Noon Western Americana Collection, Los Angeles.

"Bob Brown the Master of Carved Leather and Design" (biographical sketch). High Noon Collection, Los Angeles.

Cator, James H. Papers. Historical Research Center, Panhandle-Plains Historical Museum, Canyon, Tex.

Field, John C. File. Biographical Collection, California Historical Society, San Francisco.

Grinnell, George Bird. Correspondence. High Noon Western Americana Collection, Los Angeles.

Koerner, W.H.D. Studio Collection. Buffalo Bill Historical Center, Cody, Wyo.

"Leather Industry." Vertical files. El Paso Public Library, El Paso

S. D. Myres Saddle Company Records, 1898–1966. Southwest Collection, Texas Tech University, Lubbock.

Parks-Janeway Carriage House Collection. Santa Ynez Valley Historical Society, Santa Ynez, Calif.

Saddles File. Nita Stewart Haley Memorial Library, Midland, Tex.

Smith, Erwin E., Collection. Nita Stewart Haley Memorial Library, Midland, Tex.

INDEX

C

D

I

J

K

L

S

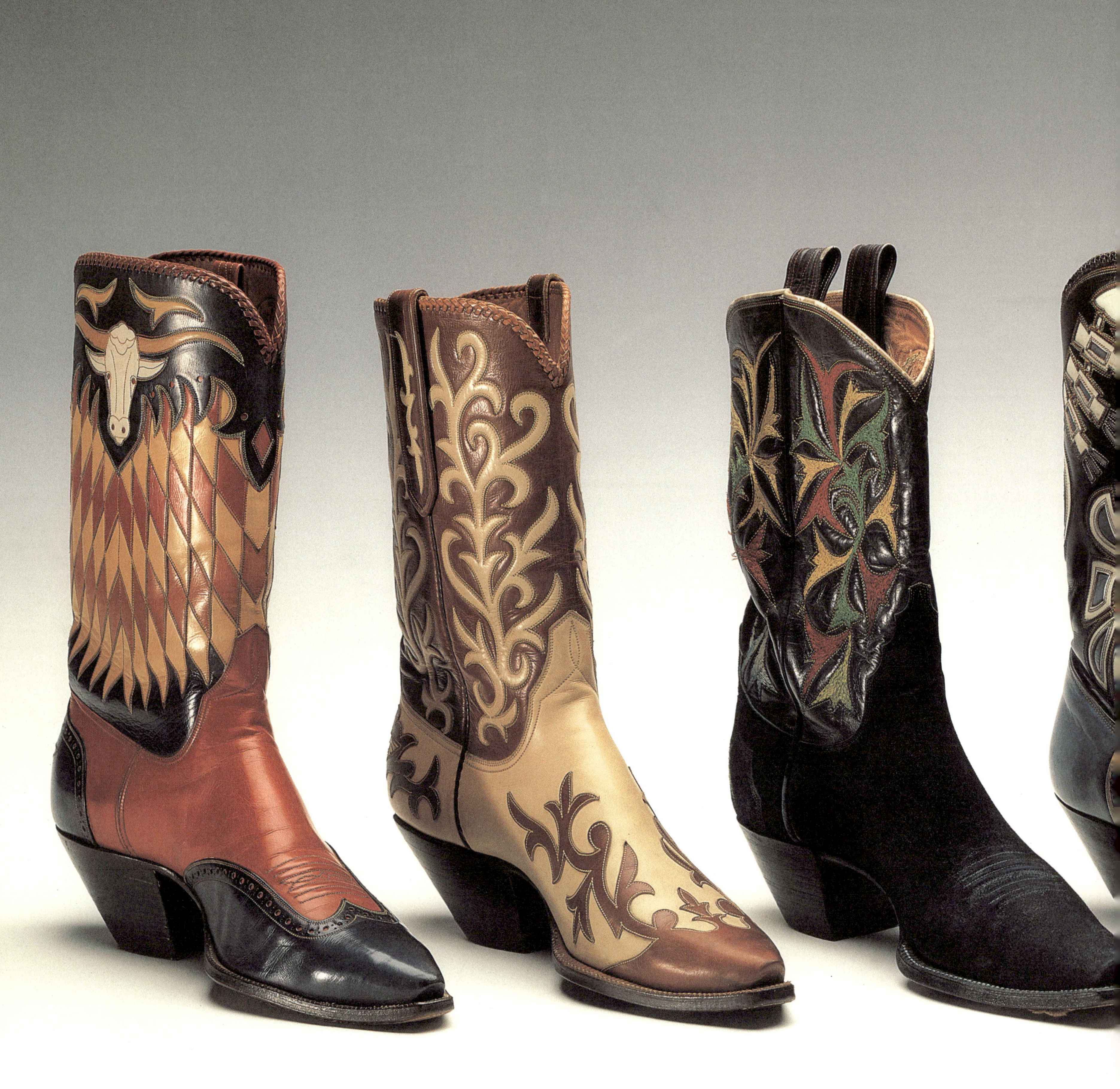